E2282510

7/78

Y0-CRP-187

WITHDRAWN

Index to
BOOK REVIEWS
IN
HISTORICAL PERIODICALS
1976

by
John W. Brewster
and
Joseph A. McLeod

The Scarecrow Press, Inc.
Metuchen, N.J. & London
1977

Ref.
Index/
Abstr.
D
|
B73
1976

ISBN: 0-8108-1078-6
LC: 75-18992

Copyright © 1977 by John W. Brewster
and Joseph A. McLeod
Manufactured in the United States of America

INTRODUCTION

The Index to Book Reviews in Historical Periodicals has developed out of a recognized need among the students at North Texas State University for aid in locating reviews of books assigned for class readings. The present volume includes 113 of the better known scholarly journals and historical society organs. Although the reviews concentrate more heavily upon U.S. history, an effort has been made to include materials relating to other countries as well. The index includes only English-language periodicals. Books written in foreign languages are included if the review is in English. The original title is indicated except where a translation is given, in which case the English version is used. In some periodicals, works are included which stress other disciplines as well as history. These are included for the sake of completeness; such entries comprise a very small minority of the total index.

In most cases, the complete title of the work is indicated although in the case of an exceptionally long title, an abridged form may appear. In all cases, the policy has been to include enough of the title to enable the researcher to identify the work. In regard to imprint, the editors have endeavored to provide enough information to identify the work clearly. Well-known publishers whose works appear frequently are cited by abbreviations (a key to academic press abbreviations appears before the beginning of the Index proper). States are included only when needed to identify a city.

Although designed primarily as a tool for locating book reviews, because the index includes some 5000 titles, most of which are current publications, it may also serve as a bibliographic guide in history. As nearly as possible, the editors have used the format of the University of Chicago Style Manual. Standardized abbreviations for months and seasons are used. In cases where reviewers' entries conflict, Books in Print has been followed.

The editors present this work with the belief that it will be a useful tool for the scholar, the student, and the general reader with an interest in history.

John W. Brewster
Joseph A. McLeod

Denton, Texas
June 1977

ACKNOWLEDGMENTS

The authors of the index recognize that their efforts have been made much easier by the indulgence and cooperation of others. Not least among those who have made the task easier were the families of the authors who bore with good grace and a minimum of complaint the cluttering of their homes with file cards, trays, and volumes of periodicals. In addition they have rendered valuable assistance in the compilation, typing, and proof-reading and in offering timely suggestions.

Besides members of their immediate families, the authors express appreciation to members of the library staffs of the North Texas State University Library and of the Howard Payne University Library.

PERIODICALS INDEXED (1976)

A & W	Arizona and the West
AfAf	African Affairs
Africa	Africa
AgH	Agricultural History
AHI	American History Illustrated
AHR	American Historical Review
AI	Annals of Iowa
AIQ	American Indian Quarterly
AJA	American Journal of Archaeology
AlaR	Alabama Review
Am Ant	American Antiquity
Am Arc	American Archivist
Americas	Americas
Antiquity	Antiquity
Archaeology	Archaeology
Archives	Archives
ArkHQ	The Arkansas Historical Quarterly
AS	American Studies
BH	Business History
BHH	Baptist History and Heritage
BHR	Business History Review
CaHR	The Catholic Historical Review
CH	Church History
CHIQ	Concordia Historical Institute Quarterly
ChOk	Chronicles of Oklahoma
CHQ	California Historical Quarterly
CHR	The Canadian Historical Review
Commentary	Commentary
CQ	China Quarterly
Crisis	Crisis

CSSH	Comparative Studies in Society and History
CurH	Current History
CWH	Civil War History
CWTI	Civil War Times Illustrated
EE	East Europe
EEQ	East European Quarterly
EHR	English Historical Review
E-I	Eire-Ireland
ESR	European Studies Review
ETHJ	East Texas Historical Journal
FCHQ	Filson Club History Quarterly
FHQ	Florida Historical Quarterly
GHQ	Georgia Historical Quarterly
GR	The Georgia Review
HAHR	The Hispanic American Historical Review
Historian	Historian
History	History
HJ	Historical Journal
HMPEC	Historical Magazine of the Protestant Episcopal Church
HRNB	History: Review of New Books
HT	The History Teacher
HTo	History Today
IESHR	Indian Economic and Social History Review
IJMES	International Journal of Middle East Studies
IMH	Indiana Magazine of History
IQ	India Quarterly
JAAS	Journal of Asian and African Studies
JAfH	The Journal of African History
JAH	The Journal of American History
JAmS	The Journal of American Studies
JAriH	The Journal of Arizona History
JAS	The Journal of Asian Studies
JCS	Journal of Church and State
JEccH	The Journal of Ecclesiastical History
JEH	The Journal of Economic History

JHP	The Journal of the History of Philosophy
JIH	The Journal of Interdisciplinary History
JISHS	The Journal of the Illinois State Historical Society
JJS	The Journal of Japanese Studies
JMAS	The Journal of Modern African Studies
JMH	Journal of Modern History
JMiH	Journal of Mississippi History
JNES	Journal of Near Eastern Studies
JNH	Journal of Negro History
JOW	Journal of the West
JSH	The Journal of Southern History
JSoH	Journal of Social History
JTH	Journal of Transport History
Judaism	Judaism
Mankind	Mankind
MAS	Modern Asian Studies
MHM	Maryland Historical Magazine
MHR	Missouri Historical Review
MiA	Mid America
MichH	Michigan History
MinnH	Minnesota History
MQR	Mennonite Quarterly Review
NCHR	North Carolina Historical Review
NDH	North Dakota History
NEQ	New England Quarterly
NMHR	New Mexico Historical Review
NYHSQ	New York Historical Society Quarterly
OH	Ohio History
OHQ	Ohio Historical Quarterly
OrHQ	Oregon Historical Quarterly
PH	Pennsylvania History
PHR	Pacific Historical Review
PNQ	Pacific Northwest Quarterly
RAH	Reviews in American History

SCHM	South Carolina Historical Magazine
SCQ	Southern California Quarterly
SWHQ	Southwestern Historical Quarterly
T & C	Technology and Culture
TAm	The Americas
Texana	Tenana
THQ	Tennessee Historical Quarterly
UHQ	Utah Historical Quarterly
VH	Vermont History
VMHB	Virginia Magazine of History and Biography
WHQ	Western Historical Quarterly
WMH	Wisconsin Magazine of History
WMQ	William and Mary Quarterly
WVH	West Virginia History

ABBREVIATIONS OF PUBLISHERS

Standard abbreviations are used for commercial publishers. The following abbreviations are used for university presses and educational presses:

Cam U Press	Cambridge University Press, Cambridge, England
Cath U Amer Press	Catholic University of America Press, Washington, D. C.
Coll and U Press	College and University Press, New Haven, Conn.
Cor U Press	Cornell University Press, Ithaca, N. Y.
CWRU Press	Case Western Reserve University Press, Cleveland, Ohio
Edin U Press	Edinburgh Univ. Press, Edinburgh, Scotland
Fla St U Press	Florida State Univ. Press, Tallahassee, Fla.
Har U Press	Harvard University Press, Cambridge, Mass.
Heb Union Coll Press	Hebrew Union College Press, Cincinnati, Ohio
Huntington	Huntington Library, San Marino, California
Ia St U Press	Iowa State University Press, Ames, Ia.
Ind U Press	Indiana University Press, Bloomington, Indiana
JHU Press	Johns Hopkins University Press, Baltimore, Md.
LSU Press	Louisiana State University Press, Baton Rouge, La.
MHS	Maryland Historical Society, Baltimore, Maryland
MIT Press	Massachusetts Institute of Technology Press, Cambridge, Mass.
N Ill U Press	Northern Illinois University Press, DeKalb, Ill.
NW St U La Press	Northwest State University of Louisiana, Natchitoches, La.
NWU Press	Northwestern University Press, Evanston, Ill.
NYU Press	New York University Press, New York, N. Y.

x

PHMC	Pennsylvania Historical and Museum Commission
Prin U Press	Princeton University Press, Princeton, N. J.
S Ill U Press	Southern Illinois University Press, Carbondale, Ill.
Stan U Press	Stanford University Press, Stanford, California
Syr U Press	Syracuse University Press, Syracuse, N. Y.
TCU Press	Texas Christian University Press, Ft. Worth, Texas
U and Coll Press Miss	University and College Press of Mississippi, Hattiesburg, Mississippi
UBC Press	University of British Columbia Press, Vancouver, B. C.
U Cal Press	University of California Press, Berkeley and Los Angeles
U Chi Press	University of Chicago Press, Chicago, Illinois
U Ga Press	University of Georgia Press, Athens, Georgia
U Ia Press	University of Iowa Press, Iowa City, Iowa
U Ill Press	University of Illinois Press, Urbana, Ill.
U Kan Press	University of Kansas Press, Lawrence, Kansas
U Mich Press	University of Michigan Press, Ann Arbor, Michigan
U Minn Press	University of Minnesota Press, Minneapolis, Minn.
U Mo Press	University of Missouri Press, Columbia, Mo.
U Mont Press	University of Montana Press, Missoula, Mont.
UNC Press	University of North Carolina Press, Chapel Hill, N. C.
U NMex Press	University of New Mexico Press, Albuquerque, N. M.
U Okla Press	University of Oklahoma Press, Norman, Oklahoma
U Press Ky	University Press of Kentucky, Lexington, Ky.
U Press NE	University Press of New England, Hanover, Vt.
U Press Va	University Press of Virginia, Charlottesville, Va.
USC Press	University of South Carolina Press, Columbia, S. C.
USNI	United States Naval Institute, Annapolis, Md.
U Tenn Press	University of Tennessee Press, Knoxville, Tenn.

U Tx Press	University of Texas Press, Austin, Texas
U Tor Press	University of Toronto Press, Toronto
U Utah Press	University of Utah Press, Salt Lake City, Utah
U Wash Press	University of Washington Press, Seattle, Washington
U Wis Press	University of Wisconsin Press, Madison, Wisconsin
Van U Press	Vanderbilt University Press, Nashville, Tenn.
W St U Press	Wayne State University Press, Detroit, Mich.
Wes U Press	Wesleyan University Press, Middletown, Conn.

THE INDEX: 1976

Abbondanza, Roberto, ed. Il Notariato a Perugia. Rome: Consiglio Nazionale del Notariato, 1973. Rev. by D. Waley, EHR, 91(Jl 1976):630-1.

Abbot, W. W. The Colonial Origins of the United States, 1607-1763. New York: Wiley, 1975. Rev. by P. R. Lucas, JAH, 62(Mar 1976):959-60.

Abbott, Carl. Colorado: A History of the Centennial State. Boulder: Colorado Assoc U Press, 1976. Rev. by M. F. Taylor, A&W, 18(Win 1976):375-6.

Abdallah, Yohanna B. and Meredith Sanderson, comp. and ed. The Yaos: Chiikala Cha Wayao. London: Frank Cass, 1973. Rev. by A. D. R., JAfH, 17(Num 3, 1976):474.

Abel, Elie see Harriman, W. Averell

Abella, Irving Martin. Nationalism, Communism, and Canadian Labour: The CIO, the Communist Party, and the Canadian Congress of Labour, 1936-1956. Toronto: U Tor Press, 1973. Rev. by R. Wilbur, AHR, 81(Je 1976):697.

Abendroth, Hans-Henning. Hitler in der spanischen Arena. Paderborn: Ferdinand Schöningh, 1973. Rev. by G. Jackson, JMH, 48(Mar 1976):135-8.

Abernethy, Francis E. Some Still Do: Essays on Texas Customs. Austin: Encino, 1975. Rev. by R. G. Dean, ETHJ, 14 (Fall 1976):72-3.

Aberson, G. Twenty-five Years of Arnhem Trolleybuses. Berkshire: Trolleybooks, n.d. Rev. by T. C. Barker, JTH, 3 (Sep 1976):301.

Abraham, Henry J. Justices and Presidents: A Political History of Appointments to the Supreme Court. New York: Oxford U Press, 1974. Rev. by R. T. Miller, JCS, 17(Aut 1975): 530-2.

Abramowski, Günter, ed. Die Kabinette Marx I und II: 30. November 1923 bis 3. Juni 1924; 3. Juni 1924 bis 15. Januar

1

1925. Vols. I and II. Boppard am Rhein: Harald Boldt Verlag, 1973. Rev. by H. A. Turner, Jr., AHR, 81(Feb 1976): 168-9.

Abrams, William S., ed. Oregon Regional Union List of Serials. Portland: Portland St U, 1976. Rev. by A. Moody, OrHQ, 77(Dec 1976):382.

Abramsky, Chimen and Beryl J. Williams, eds. Essays in Honour of E. H. Carr. Hamden: Archon, 1974. Rev. by N. V. Riasanovsky, AHR, 81(Je 1976):568; R. Pethybridge, EHR, 91 (Jan 1976):231-2; A. J. P. Taylor, History, 61(Feb 1976):69; J. Keep, HJ, 19(Mar 1976):275-7.

Abu-Lughod, Janet L. Cairo: 1001 Years of the City Victorious. Princeton, N.J.: Prin U Press, 1971. Rev. by W. Madelung, JNES, 35(Jl 1976):203-4.

Acomb, Frances. Mallet Du Pan (1749-1800). A Career in Political Journalism. Durham, N.C.: Duke U Press, 1973. Rev. by J. Q. C. Mackrell, ESR, 6(Jan 1976):149-50.

Acton, Janice, et al., eds. Women at Work: Ontario, 1850-1930. Toronto: Canadian Women's Educational Press, 1974. Rev. by L. Holcombe, AHR, 81(Apr 1976):471; K. Peterson, CHR, 57(Je 1976):206-7.

Adamec, Ludwig W. Afghanistan's Foreign Affairs to the Mid-Twentieth Century. Tucson: U Ariz Press, 1974. Rev. by A Guha, IQ, 32(Jan-Mar 1976):82-3.

Adams, Eleanor B. and Angélico Chávez, trans. The Missions of New Mexico, 1776: A Description by Francisco Antanasio Domínguez with Other Contemporary Documents by Francisco A. Dominquez. Albuquerque: UNM Press, 1975. Rev. by O. L. Jones, NMHR, 51(Jl 1976):252-3.

Adams, Robert. The Architecture and Art of Early Hispanic Colorado. Boulder: Colorado Associated U Press, 1974. Rev. by B. Bunting, CaHR, 62(Jl 1976):519.

Adams, Robert M. The Roman Stamp: Frame and Facade in Some Forms of Neo-Classicism. Berkeley: U Cal Press, 1974. Rev. by J. P. Russo, JMH, 48(Je 1976):320-2.

Adams, Willi Paul. Republikanische Verfassung und bürgerliche Freiheit: Die Verfassungen und politischen Ideen der amerikanischen Revolution. Neuwied: Luchterhand, 1973. Rev. by A. C. Land, AHR, 81(Oct 1976):965-6.

Adamson, David. The Ruins of Time. London: George Allen and Unwin, 1975, Rev. by N. Hammond, Antiquity, 50(Mar 1976): 83.

Adamson, J. H. and H. F. Folland. Sir Harry Vane: His Life and Times, 1613-1662. London: Bodley Head, 1974. Rev. by I. Roots, EHR, 91(Jan 1976):200-1.

Adas, Michael. The Burma Delta: Economic Development and Social Change on an Asian Rice Frontier, 1852-1941. Madison: U Wis Press, 1974. Rev. by B. J. Terwiel, AgH, 50 (Jl 1976):538; A. D. Moscotti, JAAS, 11(Jl-Oct 1976):235-6.

Adcock, Frank and D. J. Mosley. Diplomacy in Ancient Greece. New York: St. Martin's Press, 1975. Rev. by C. Roebuck, AHR, 81(Oct 1976):828; T. Kelly, HRNB, 4(Jan 1976):63.

Addo-Fening, R., et al. Akyem Abuakwa and the Politics of the Inter-War Period in Ghana. Basel: Afrika Verlag der kreis, 1975. Rev. by B. Crook, JAfH, 17(Num 1, 1976):158-9.

Adedeji, A. and C. Baker, eds. Education and Research in Public Administration in Africa. n. p.: Hutchinson, 1974. Rev. by G. Glentworth, AfAf, 75(Apr 1976):265-6.

Adler, Jack. Exploring Historic California. Pasadena: Ward Ritchie, 1974. Rev. by K. M. Johnson, JOW, 15(Jan 1976): 138.

Adolph, Walter. Kardinal Preysing und zwei Diktaturen: Sein Widerstand gegen die totalitäre Macht. Berlin: Morus-Verlag, 1971. Rev. by D. J. Diephouse, JCS, 17(Aut 1975):524-6.

Agaev, S. L. Iran: Foreign Policy and Problems of Independence, 1925-1941. Moscow: Izdatel'stvo "Nauka," 1971. Rev. by F. Kazemzadeh, AHR, 81(Apr 1976):430.

Agarwal, Vinod K. Initiative, Enterprise, and Economic Choices in India: A Study of the Patterns of Entrepreneurship. Columbia, Mo.: South Asia Books, 1975. Rev. by D. Tripathi, BHR, 50(Sum 1976):248-50.

Agassi, Joseph. Faraday as a Natural Philosopher. Chicago: U Press, 1971. Rev. by M. A. Finocchiaro, JHP, 14(Oct 1976): 488-9.

Agee, Rucker. Twenty Alabama Books. Miami, Fla.: E. A. Seeman, 1975. Rev. by M. B. Howard, Jr., AlaR, 29(Oct 1976):813-4.

Agnew, Theodore L. The South Central Jurisdiction, 1939-1972. A Brief History and an Interpretation. Oklahoma City: United Methodist Church, 1973. Rev. by P. F. Erwin, JAH, 63(Je 1976):181-2.

Ahern, Emily M. The Cult of the Dead in a Chinese Village. Stanford, Cal.: Stanford U Press, 1973. Rev. by A. V. Dessaint, JAAS, 11(Jan & Apr 1976):123-4.

Ahmad, Aziz. A History of Islamic Study. Edinburgh: Edinburgh U Press, 1973. Rev. by K. Stowasser, AHR, 81(Je 1976): 570.

Aiken, George D. Aiken: Senate Diary, January 1972-January 1975. Brattleboro, Vt.: Stephen Green Press, 1976. Rev. by T. S. Conlon, VH, 44(Fall 1976):246-8.

Ainsztein, Reuben. Jewish Resistance in Nazi-Occupied Eastern Europe: With a Historical Survey of the Jew as a Fighter and Soldier in the Diaspora. New York: Barnes and Noble, 1975. Rev. by Y. Bauer, AHR, 81(Oct 1976):896-7; N. Lucas, History, 61(Feb 1976):147.

Aitken, M. J. Physics and Archaeology. Oxford: Clarendon Press, 1974. Rev. by A. Aspinall, Antiquity, 50(Je 1976): 159-60.

Aizcorbe, Roberto. Argentina: The Peronist Myth. An Essay on the Cultural Decay in Argentina After the Second World War. New York: Exposition, 1975. Rev. by L. C. Fennell, HAHR, 56(Aug 1976):492.

Ajayi, J. F. Ade and Tekena N. Tamuno, eds. The University of Ibadan 1948-73. Ibadan: Ibadan U Press, 1973. Rev. by A. H. M. Kirk-Greene, Africa, 46(Num 1, 1976):103-4.

Akenson, Donald Harris. Education and Enmity. New York: Barnes and Noble, 1973. Rev. by D. W. Miller, CaHR, 62 (Oct 1976):653-4.

Akerström-Hougen, Gunilla. The Calendar and Hunting Mosaics of the Villa of the Falconer in Argos. A Study in Early Byzantine Iconography. Stockholm: Paul Astroms, 1974. Rev. by A. Cutler, AJA, 80(Win 1976):109-10.

Akinari, Uyeda. Ugetsu Monogatori: Tales of Moonlight and Rain. Vancouver, B.C.: U British Columbia Press, 1975. Rev. by K. Brazell, JJS, 2(Sum 1976):452-5; D. E. Mills, MAS, 10 (Apr 1976):311-15.

Akintoye, S. A. Ten Years of the University of Ife. Ile-Ife: U Ife Press, 1973. Rev. by A. H. M. Kirk-Greene, Africa, 46(Num 1, 1976):103-4.

Akinyemi, A. B. Foreign Policy and Federalism: The Nigerian Experience. Ibadan: Ibadan U Press, 1974. Rev. by T. M. Shaw, JAAS, 11(Jl-Oct 1976):241-3.

Akten zur Deutschen Auswärtigen Politik, 1918-1945. Göttingen:

5 ALBERTI

Vandenhoeck & Ruprecht, 1974. Rev. by F. E. Hirsch, AHR, 81(Feb 1976):169-70; K. Robbins, EHR, 91(Apr 1976):460; K. Robbins, EHR, 91(Oct 1976):937-8; J. Gimbel, JAH, 13(Je 1976):171-2.

Alberti, Giorgio and Rodrigo Sanchez. Poder y conflicto social en el valle del Mantaro (1900-1974). Lima: Instituto de Estudios Peruanos, 1974. Rev. by B. Orlove, AgH, 50(Jl 1976):528-32.

Aldcroft, Derek H. British Transport Since 1914: An Economic History. Newton Abbot: David and Charles, 1975. Rev. by P. S. Bagwell, History, 61(Je 1976):314-15.

_____. Studies in British Transport History, 1870-1970. Newton Abbot: David and Charles, 1974. Rev. by W. Ashworth, JTH, 3(Sep 1976):294-5.

Alder, Douglas D., ed. Cache Valley: Essays on Her Past and People. Logan: Logan City Bicentennial Committee, 1976. Rev. by L. Thatcher, UHQ, 44(Fall 1976):406-7.

Aldred, Cyril. Akhenaten and Nefertiti. New York: Viking, 1973. Rev. by C. F. Nims, JNES, 35(Oct 1976):279-80.

Alexander, Charles C. Holding the Line: The Eisenhower Era, 1952-1961. Bloomington: Ind U Press, 1975. Rev. by H. S. Parmet, AHR, 81(Je 1976):692-3; R. Polenberg, JAH, 63 (Je 1976):196-7; R. E. Darilek, JSH, 42(Feb 1976):145-6.

Alexander, G. and O. B. Williams, eds. The Pastoral Industries of Australia: Practice and Technology of Sheep and Cattle Production. Sydney: Sydney U Press, 1973. Rev. by G. Harman, AgH, 50(Jan 1976):319.

Alexander, J. J. G. and M. T. Gibson, eds. Medieval Learning and Literature: Essays Presented to Richard William Hunt. New York: Oxford U Press, 1975. Rev. by J. C. Moore, HRNB, 4(Sep 1976):229.

Alexander, Margaret A. and Mongi Ennaïfer, eds. Corpus des Mosaiques de Tunisie. Vol. I. Washington: Dumbarton Oaks, 1973. Rev. by K. M. D. Dunbabin, AJA, 80(Win 1976):105-6.

Alexander, Michael Van Cleave. Charles I's Lord Treasurer: Sir Richard Weston. Chapel Hill: UNC Press, 1975. Rev. by R. Ashton, EHR, 91(Oct 1976):907-8; W. J. Hoffman, Historian, 39(Nov 1976):119-20; M. Hawkins, History, 61(Je 1976):286-7; J. H. Gleason, HRNB, 4(Feb 1976):92.

Alexander, Robert L. The Architecture of Maximilian Godefroy. Baltimore: JHU Press, 1974. Rev. by P. R. Baker, AHR, 81(Je 1976):658; L. B. Miller, JAH, 62(Mar 1976):985-6.

Alexander, Sidney. Lions and Foxes: Men and Ideas of the Italian Renaissance. New York: Macmillan, 1974. Rev. by D. Herlihy, Historian, 38(Feb 1976):324-5.

Alexander, Thomas G. Essays on the American West, 1973-1974. Provo: BYU Press, 1975. Rev. by T. A. Larson, PNQ, 67(Jl 1976):130-1; B. D. Madsen, UHQ, 44(Spr 1976):182-3.

_____, ed. Charles Redd Monographs in Western History 1973-1974. Provo, Utah: BYU Press, 1975. Rev. by L. I. Perrigo, JAH, 62(Mar 1976):1007.

_____, ed. see Allen, James B., ed.

_____ see Arrington, Leonard J.

Alföldy, Géza. Noricum. Boston: Routledge and Kegan Paul, 1974. Rev. by H. C. Boren, AHR, 81(Feb 1976):107; C. M. Wells, EHR, 91(Jan 1976):168.

Alford, B. W. E. W. D. and H. O. Wills and the Development of the U. K. Tobacco Industry, 1786-1965. New York: Barnes and Noble, 1973. Rev. by E. J. Perkins, JEH, 36(Je 1976): 450-1.

Algar, Hamid. Religion and State in Iran, 1785-1906: The Role of the Ulama in the Qajar Period. Berkeley: U Cal Press, 1969. Rev. by R. E. Frykenberg, JCS, 18(Spr 1976):330-1.

Aliano, Richard A. American Defense Policy from Eisenhower to Kennedy: The Politics of Changing Military Requirements, 1957-1961. Athens, Ohio: Ohio U Press, 1975. Rev. by R. A. Divine, HRNB, 4(Jan 1976):50-1.

All Africa Conference of Churches. Africa's Refugees. Nairobi: All Africa Conference of Churches, 1975. Rev. by W. Weinstein, JMAS, 14(Mar 1976):161-2.

Alladi, Mary. Canadian Watercolours and Drawings in the Royal Ontario Museum. Toronto: The Royal Ontario Museum, 1974. Rev. by A. Davis, CHR, 57(Mar 1976):40-7.

Allain, Mathé and Glenn R. Conrads, eds. France and North America: The Revolutionary Experience. Lafayette, La.: USL Press, 1974. Rev. by E. J. Gum, ETHJ, 14(Fall 1976): 75.

Allan, Ted and Sydney Gordon. The Scalpel, the Sword: The Story of Doctor Norman Bethune. New York: Monthly Review Press, 1952, 1973. Rev. by J. N. Hawkins, JAAS, 11(Jl-Oct 1976): 215-19.

Allard, Sven. Stalin and Hitler: Die Sowjetrussische Aussenpolitik

1930-1941. Bern: Francke Verlag, 1974. Rev. by A. J. P. Taylor, History, 61(Feb 1976):145.

Allen, E. John B. Post and Courier Service in the Diplomacy of Early Modern Europe. The Hague: Martinus Nijhoff, 1972. Rev. by H. Robinson, AHR, 81(Apr 1976):374; R. B. Wernham, EHR, 91(Jan 1976):199-200.

Allen, James B. and Thomas G. Alexander, eds. Manchester Mormons: The Journal of William Clayton, 1840 to 1842. Santa Barbara: Peregrine Smith, 1974. Rev. by J. Shipps, JAH, 62(Mar 1976):993-4; S. G. Ellsworth, PHR, 45(Aug 1976):446-7; W. D. Russell, UHQ, 44(Win 1976):99-100.

Allen, John L. Passage Through the Garden. Urbana: U Ill Press, 1975. Rev. by W. R. Jacobs, A & W, 18(Spr 1976): 87-8; A. M. Gibson, HRNB, 4(Jan 1976):52-3; T. C. Hinckley, IMH, 72(Je 1976):265-7; J. E. Sunder, JAH, 63(Je 1976): 113-14; J. H. Nottage, JOW, 15(Apr 1976):129; J. P. Ronda, OH, 85 (Spr 1976):162-3; R. E. Lange, OrHQ, 77(Je 1976): 191-2; H. N. Smith, RAH, 4(Mar 1976):64-7; B. W. Marley, UHQ, 44(Win 1976):103-4; D. Jackson, WHQ, 7(Jl 1976):309-10; R. Nash, WMH, 60(Aut 1976):60.

Allen, Kevin and Andrew Stevenson. An Introduction to the Italian Economy. New York: Barnes and Noble, 1975. Rev. by S. B. Clough, AHR, 81(Apr 1976):415-16.

Allen, Richard. The Social Passion: Religion and Social Reform in Canada, 1914-1928. Toronto: U Tor Press, 1971. Rev. by J. S. Moir, JCS, 17(Spr 1975):322-3.

Allinson, Gary D. Japanese Urbanism: Industry and Politics in Kariya, 1872-1972. Berkeley: U Cal Press, 1975. Rev. by P. Duus, JJS, 2(Sum 1976):455-9.

Allison, Henry E. The Kant-Eberhard Controversy. Baltimore: JHU Press, 1973. Rev. by T. B. Humphrey, JHP, 14(Jan 1976):112-15.

Allison, K. J., ed. A History of the County of York. Vol. II. London: Oxford U Press, 1974. Rev. by D. Read, EHR, 91(Jan 1975):169-70.

Allmendinger, David F., Jr. Paupers and Scholars: The Transformation of Student Life in Nineteenth-Century New England. New York: St. Martin's, 1975. Rev. by H. K. Macauley, Jr., JAH, 63(Sep 1976):409; J. D. Hoeveler, Jr., NEQ, 49 (Je 1976):302-5.

Allum, P. A. Italy--Republic Without Government? New York: Norton, 1974. Rev. by R. A. H. Robinson, History, 61(Je 1976):331-2.

Alpers, Edward A. Ivory and Slaves: Changing Patterns of International Trade in East Central Africa to the Later Nineteenth Century. Berkeley: U Cal Press, 1975. Rev. by A. Roberts, AfAf, 75(Jl 1976):403-4; J. E. G. Sutton, AHR, 81(Oct 1976): 926-7; M. Newitt, JAfH, 17(Num 3, 1976):450-2; D. M. P. McCarthy, JEH, 36(Je 1976):451-2.

Al Roy, Gil Carl. The Kissinger Experience: American Policy in the Middle East. n.p.: Horizon, n.d. Rev. by V. Baras, Commentary, 61(Mar 1976):74-6.

Alter, Robert. Partial Magic: The Novel as a Self-Conscious Genre. Berkeley: U Cal Press, 1975. Rev. by R. Schleifer, GR, 30(Sum 1976):479-81.

Altholz, Josef L., Damian McElrath, and James C. Holland, eds. The Correspondence of Lord Acton and Richard Simpson, Vol. III. Cambridge: Cam U Press, 1975. Rev. by H. A. MacDougall, CaHR, 62(Oct 1976):628-9; B. Aspinwall, History, 61(Oct 1976):491; R. J. Schiefen, JEccH, 27(Jl 1976): 321-2.

Altick, Richard D. Victorian People and Ideas. London: Dent, 1974. Rev. by O. Anderson, History, 61(Feb 1976):124.

Alvarez, Eugene. Travel on Southern Antebellum Railroads, 1828-1860. University, Ala.: U Ala Press, 1974. Rev. by J. H. Broussard, AekHQ, 35(Spr 1976):106-8; M. C. Clark, SCHM, 77(Jan 1976):56-7.

Amann, Peter H. Revolution and Mass Democracy: The Paris Club Movement in 1848. Princeton, N.J.: Prin U Press, 1975. Rev. by G. Allardyce, CHR, 57(Je 1976):231-2; J. P. T. Bury, EHR, 91(Jan 1976):149-52; R. Price, History, 61 (Je 1976):298.

Amato, Joseph. Mounier and Maritain: A French Catholic Understanding of the Modern World. University: U Ala Press, 1975. Rev. by J.-J. D'Aoust, CH, 45(Sep 1975):395-6; J. W. Hellman, CaHR, 62(Oct 1976):659-60.

Ambrose, Stephen E. Crazy Horse and Custer: The Parallel Lives of Two American Warriors. Garden City, N.Y.: Doubleday, 1975. Rev. by R. A. Van Orman, A & W, 19 (Spr 1976):103-4; R. M. Utley, AHI, 11(Je 1976):50; R. A. Trennert, Jr., JAH, 63(Sep 1976):428-9; J. W. Bailey, JOW, 15(Apr 1976):132; M. Young, RAH, 4(Je 1976):218-21.

American Anthropological Association. Anthropology and the American Indian: A Symposium. San Francisco: Indian Historian Press, 1973. Rev. by L. R. Stucki, AA, 78(Je 1976): 404.

American Enterprise Institute. America's Continuing Revolution.
Garden City, N.Y.: Anchor/Doubleday, 1976. Rev. by J. J.
Crow, NCHR, 53(Aut 1976):413-14.

Ames, Charles Edgar. Pioneering the Union Pacific: A Reappraisal of the Builders of the Railroad. New York: Appleton-Century-Crofts, 1969. Rev. by J. A. Ward, JAH, 62(Mar
1976):1014-15.

Amin, Samir. Neo-Colonialism in West Africa. New York: Penguin, 1973. Rev. by R. C. O'Brien, AfAf, 75(Jan 1976):111-
12.

_____, ed. Modern Migrations in Western Africa. Oxford:
Oxford U Press, 1975. Rev. by D. Rimmer, JAfH, 17(Num
3, 1976):471-3.

Amis, Kingsley. Rudyard Kipling and His World. New York:
Scribner's, 1976. Rev. by R. N. Soffer, Mankind, 5(Dec
1976):58, 60.

Ammerman, David. In the Common Cause: American Response to
the Coercive Acts of 1774. Charlottesville: U Press Va,
1974. Rev. by P. D. Nelson, AHR, (Oct 1976):961-2; L. E.
Olm, NYHSQ, 60(Jan/Apr 1976):75-6.

Amos, Preston E. Above and Beyond in the West: Black Medal
of Honor Winners, 1870-1890. Washington, D.C.: The
Westerners, 1974. Rev. by B. Procter, PNQ, 67(Jan 1976):
38-9.

Anati, Emmanuel. Rock Art in Central Arabia. Vol. 3. Corpus ⸙
of the Rock Engravings. Louvain-la-Neuve: Institut Oriental-
iste, 1972. Rev. by F. V. Winnelt, JNES, 35(Apr 1976):135-
7.

Anders, Leslie. The Twenty-First Missouri: From Home Guard
to Union Regiment. Westport, Conn.: Greenwood, 1975.
Rev. by H. Hattaway, CWH, 22(June 1976):180; J. F. Mars-
zalek, HRNB, 4(Jan 1976):57; A. Castel, JAH, 63(Sep 1976):
423-4; L. C. Rampp, JOW, 15(Jl 1976):103; G. T. Edwards,
JSH, 42(Aug 1976):434-5; J. W. Goodrich, MHR, 71(Apr 1976):
350-2; C. L. Christman, MiA, 58(Oct 1976):197.

Andersen, Arlow W. The Norwegian-Americans. Boston: Twayne,
1975. Rev. by O. S. Lovoll, JAH, 63(Mar 1976):1023-4.

Anderson, B. L. and P. L. Cottrell. Money and Banking in England:
The Development of the Banking System, 1694-1914. Newton
Abbot: David and Charles, 1974. Rev. by A. J. Robertson,
BH, 75(Jl 1975):203-5.

Anderson, Irvine H. The Standard-Vacuum Oil Company and United

States East Asian Policy 1933-1941. Princeton, N.J.: Prin
U Press, 1975. Rev. by R. Dingman, BHR, 50(Spr 1976):
121-2; K. E. Shewmaker, PHR, 45(Nov 1976):628-9; S. E.
Pelz, RAH, 4(Mar 1976):115-9.

Anderson, James Lavern see Kennett, Lee

Anderson, Marjorie O. Kings and Kingship in Early Scotland.
Edinburgh: Scottish Academic Press, 1973. Rev. by A. A.
M. Duncan, History, 61(Feb 1976):94-5.

Anderson, Mary see Ashby, Eric

Anderson, Perry. Lineages of the Absolutist State. Atlantic Highlands, N.J.: Humanities Press, 1974. Rev. by L. Rothkrug,
AHR, 81(Apr 1976):373-4.

_____. Passages from Antiquity to Feudalism. London: NLB,
1974. Rev. by B. Behrens, HJ, 19(Mar 1976):245-50.

Anderson, R. D. Education in France, 1848-1870. New York:
Oxford U Press, 1975. Rev. by S. J. Idzerda, AHR, 81(Je
1976):604-5; J. P. T. Bury, EHR, 91(Jl 1976):675; M. S.
Archer, History, 61(Je 1976):298-9; J. K. Burton, JMH, 48
(Sep 1976):555-7.

Anderson, William. The Wild Man from Sugar Creek: The Political Career of Eugene Talmadge. Baton Rouge: LSU Press,
1975. Rev. by G. Osborn, AHR, 81(Oct 1976):995; N. V.
Bartley, FHQ, 55(Jl 1976):99-100; B. P. Spaulding, GR, 30
(Spr 1976):215-17.

Andreae, Bernard see Conticello, Baldassare

André-Félix, Annette. Les Débuts de l'industrie chimique dans
les Pays-Bas autrichiens. Brussels: Université Libre de
Bruxelles, 1971. Rev. by L. F. Haber, AHR, 81(Apr 1976):
402.

Andrews, E. Wyllys IV and Anthony P. Andrews. A Preliminary
Study of the Ruins of Xcaret, Quintana Roo, Mexico. New
Orleans: Tulane U, 1975. Rev. by D. Phillips, HAHR, 56
(Feb 1976):182.

Andrews, Edward Deming and Faith Andrews. Fruits of the Shaker
Tree of Life: Memoirs of Fifty Years of Collecting and Research. Stockbridge, Mass.: Berkshire Traveller Press,
1975. Rev. by P. Littlefield, NEQ, 49(Sep 1976):480-2.

Andrews, George F. Maya Cities: Placemaking and Urbanization.
Norman: U Okla Press, 1975. Rev. by M. J. McLeod, AIQ
2(Sum 1975):142-5; E. W. Andrews, V, AmAnt, 41(Apr 1976):
241-3; T. P. Culbert, HAHR, 56(Aug 1976):471.

11   ANGELL

Angell, Charles and Charles La Fontaine. Prophet of Reunion.
New York: Seaburg, 1975. Rev. by J. F. Woolverton, CH,
45(Je 1976):266-7.

Angermeier, Heinz. Geschichte oder Gegenwart: Reflexionen über
das Verhältnis von zeit und Geist. Munich: Verlag C. H.
Beck, 1974. Rev. by G. G. Iggers, AHR, 81(Feb 1976):102-
3.

Angle, Paul M. On a Variety of Subjects. Chicago: Chicago Historical Society, 1974. Rev. by S. Lilly, JISHS, 69(Feb 1976):
76.

Angold, Michael. A Byzantine Government in Exile: Government
and Society Under the Laskarids of Nicaea, 1204-1261. London: Oxford U Press, 1975. Rev. by R. Browning, EHR, 91
(Apr 1976):356-8; C. Foss, History, 61(Je 1976):256.

Ansel, Walter. Hitler and the Middle Sea. Durham, N.C.: Duke
U Press, 1972. Rev. by W. A. Fletcher, AHR, 81(Oct 1976):
884-7.

Anstey, Roger. The Atlantic Slave Trade and British Abolition,
1760-1810. London: Macmillan, 1975. Rev. by F. W.
Knight, AHR, 81(Je 1976):585-6; C. Fyfe, JAfH, 17(Num 1,
1976):139-41; J. White, JAmS, 10(Apr 1976):113-17; C. Taylor, WMQ, 33(Apr 1976):337-9.

Anthony, J. Garner. Hawaii Under Army Rule: The Real Story
of Three Years of Martial Law in a Loyal American Territory. Honolulu: U Press Hawaii, 1975. Rev. by F. C. L.
Ng, HRNB, 4(Jan 1976):60-1; L. Kaufman, JOW, 15(Apr
1976):138.

Anton, Thomas J. Governing Greater Stockholm: A Study of
Policy Development and System Change. Berkeley: U Cal
Press, 1975. Rev. by S. Koblik, JMH, 48(Sep 1976):573-4.

Antonini, Gustavo A., et al. Population and Energy: A Systems
Analysis of Resource Utilization in the Dominican Republic.
Gainesville: U Fla Press, 1975. Rev. by J. P. Augelli,
HAHR, 56(Nov 1976):687-9.

Anweiler, Oskar. The Soviets: The Russian Workers, Peasants,
and Soldiers Councils, 1905-1921. New York: Pantheon,
1975. Rev. by S. Harcave, AHR, 81(Apr 1976):427.

Appadorai, A. and V. K. Arora. India in World Affairs, 1957-58.
New Delhi: Sterling, 1975. Rev. by J. Bandhyopadhyaya,
IQ, 32(Jan-Mar 1976):95-6.

Appleman, Roy E. Lewis and Clark: Historic Places Associated
with Their Transcontinental Exploration. Washington, D.C.:

U.S. Dept Interior, 1975. Rev. by T. C. Hinkley, IMH, 72 (Je 1976):265-7; E. G. Chuinard, OrHQ, 77(Mar 1976):82-3; B. W. Marley, UHQ, 44(Win 1976):103-4; G. M. Franzwa, WHQ, 7(Jl 1976):326-7; R. Nash, WMH, 60(Aut 1976):66.

Appleton, Thomas E. Ravenscrag: The Allan Royal Mail Line. Toronto: McClelland and Stewart, 1974. Rev. by E. C. Wright, CHR, 57(Je 1976):207-8.

Aptheker, Herbert, ed. The Correspondence of W. E. B. DuBois. Vols. I and II. Amherst: U Mass Press, 1976. Rev. by E. Rudwick, JNH, 61(Oct 1976):401-4.

Aquarone, Alberto. Le origini dell'imperialismo americano: Da McKinley a Taft (1897-1913). Bologna: Società editrice il Mulino, 1973. Rev. by A. DeConde, AHR, 81(Apr 1976):459.

Arbuckle, Robert D. Pennsylvania Speculator and Patriot: The Entrepreneurial John Nicholson, 1757-1800. University Park: Pa St U Press, 1975. Rev. by G. S. Rowe, JAH, 62(Mar 1976):976-7; R. F. Oaks, WMQ, 33(Jan 1976):174-5.

Archdeacon, Thomas F. New York City, 1664-1710: Conquest and Change. Ithaca, N.Y.: Cornell U Press, 1976. Rev. by T. H. Breen, HRNB, 4(Apr 1976):121.

Archer, Jules. They Made a Revolution: 1765-1776. New York: St. Martin's Press, 1975. Rev. by D. Lindsey, Mankind, 5 (Dec 1976):6.

Archer, Margaret Scotford see Vaughan, Michalina

Ardant, Gabriel. Histoire de l'impôt. Book 2. Paris: Fayard, 1972. Rev. by C. P. Kindelberger, AHR, 81(Oct 1976):868.

Are, Giuseppe. Alle origini dell'Italia industriale. Naples: Guida Editori, 1974. Rev. by S. B. Clough, AHR, 81(Apr 1976): 415-16.

Argersinger, Peter H. Populism and Politics: William Alfred Peffer and the People's Party. Lexington: U Press Ky, 1974. Rev. by F. H. Heller, AS, 16(Fall 1975):98; J. A. Thompson, HJ, 19(Mar 1976):257-74; W. T. K. Nugent, JAH, 63(Je 1976):147-8; R. Ridgley, WHQ, 7(Apr 1977):213-14.

Arhin, Kwame, ed. see Ferguson, George Ekem

Armah, Ayi Kwei. Two Thousand Seasons. Nairobi: East Africa Publishing House, 1973. Rev. by M. M. Mahood, AfAf, 75 (Apr 1976):262-4.

Armah, Kwesi. Ghana: Nkrumah's Legacy. London: Rex Collings, 1974. Rev. by D. Cohen, JMAS, 14(Sep 1976):533-6.

13   ARMSTRONG

Armstrong, Alan. Stability and Change in an English County Town.
Cambridge: Cam U Press, 1974. Rev. by T. J. Nossiter,
AHR, 81(Je 1976):588; N. McCord, EHR, 91(Jan 1976):212; R.
Smith, History, 61(Je 1976):304; D. Roberts, JIH, 7(Aut 1976):
332-3.

Armstrong, Christopher J. R. Evelyn Underhill (1875-1941): An
Introduction to Her Wife and Writings. Oxford: Mowbray,
1975. Rev. by C. James, JEccH, 27(Jl 1976):324-5.

Armstrong, Edward A. Saint Francis: Nature Mystic. Berkeley:
U Cal Press, 1973. Rev. by D. C. West, Jr., CaHR, 62
(Jan 1976):89-90.

Armstrong, William W., ed. The Gilded Age Letters of E. L.
Godkin. Albany: SUNY Press, 1974. Rev. by O. A. Pease,
AHR, 81(Oct 1976):988-9; D. Klebanow, NYHSQ, 60(Jan/Apr
1976):79-80.

Arndt, Karl J. R., comp. and ed. A Documentary History of the
Indiana Decade of the Harmony Society, 1814-1824. Vol. I.
Indianapolis: Ind Historical Society, 1975. Rev. by D. E.
Pitzer, IMH, 72(Mar 1976):65-6; D. F. Carmony, JAH, 62
(Mar 1976):948-9; R. Francis, JAmS, 10(Dec 1976):390-3;
L. Filler, OH, 85(Win 1976):87-8.

Arnold, Eberhard and Emmy Arnold. Seeking for the Kingdom of
God: Origins of the Bruderhof Community. Rifton, N.Y.:
Plough, 1974. Rev. by J. W. Kuykendall, MQR, 50(Jan 1976):
78-80.

_____, _____, and Heini Arnold. The Heavens Are Opened.
Rifton, N.Y.: Plough Publ., 1974. Rev. by J. W. Kuykendall, MQR, 50(Jan 1976):78-80.

Arnold, Klaus, ed. Johannes Trithemius: In Praise of Scribes.
Lawrence, Kan.: Coronado Press, 1974. Rev. by T. J.
Brown, JEccH, 27(Jan 1976):82-3.

Aron, Jean-Paul, et al. Anthropologie du Conscrit français,
d'après les comptes numériques et sommaires du recrutement de l'armée (1819-1826): Présentation Cartographique.
Paris: Mouton, 1972. Rev. by J. F. Traer, AHR, 81(Oct
1976):869.

Aron, Raymond. The Imperial Republic: The United States and
the World, 1945-1973. Englewood Cliffs, N.J.: Prentice-
Hall, 1974. Rev. by R. A. Esthus, AHR, 81(Feb 1976):221;
T. L. Kenedy, PHR, 45(May 1976):304-5.

Arora, V. K. see Appadorai, A.

Arrighi, G. and J. S. Saul. Essays on the Political Economy of

Africa. New York: Monthly Review, 1973. Rev. by F. Stewart, AfAf, 75(Apr 1976):253-4.

Arrington, Leonard J. Charles C. Rich: Morman General and Western Frontiersman. Provo, Utah: BYU Press, 1974. Rev. by J. Shipps, AHR, 81(Oct 1976):980-1; E. E. Campbell, WHQ, 7(Apr 1976):201-2.

_____. David Eccles: Pioneer Western Industrialist. Logan: Utah St U Press, 1975. Rev. by A. C. Spencer, III, OrHQ, 77(Sep 1976):296; M. Wells, PHR, 45(Aug 1976):445-6; A. Egbert, UHQ, 44(Win 1976):97-8; E. E. Campbell, WHQ, 7 (Apr 1976):201-2.

_____ and Thomas G. Alexander. A Dependent Commonwealth: Utah's Economy from Statehood to the Great Depression. Provo: Utah: BYU Press, 1974. Rev. by N. G. Bringhurst, AgH, 50(Apr 1976):434-5; E. Nelson, PHR, 45(Feb 1976):132-3.

Arschinow, Peter. Anarchisten im Freiheitskampf: Die Geschichte der Machno-Bewegung 1918-1921. Zurich: Flamberg, 1971. Rev. by J. Joll, ESR, 6(Apr 1976):271-2.

Arshinov, Peter. History of the Makhnovist Movement (1918-1921). Chicago: Solidarity, 1974. Rev. by J. R. Braun, MQR, 50(Jan 1976):71-2.

Arzáns de Orsúa y Vela, Bartolomé. Tales of Potosí. Providence, R.I.: Brown U Press, 1975. Rev. by I. A. Leonard, HAHR, 56(Aug 1976):483-4.

Ashbee, Paul. Ancient Scilly from the First Farmers to the Early Christians. Vancouver: David and Charles, 1974. Rev. by B. Wailes, Antiquity, 50(Sep-Dec 1976):242-3.

Ashby, Eric and Mary Anderson. Portrait of Haldane at Work on Education. London: Macmillan, 1974. Rev. by K. O. Morgan, EHR, 91(Apr 1976):454-5; J. S. Hurt, History, 61(Je 1976):314.

Ashtor, E. A Social and Economic History of the Near East in the Middle Ages. Berkeley: U Cal Press, 1976. Rev. by W. B. Bishai, HRNB, 4(Aug 1976):195-6.

Assante, Franca. Città e campagne nella Puglia del secolo XIX: L'evoluzione demografica. Geneva: Librairie Droz, 1974. Rev. by L. Saville, JEH, 36(Je 1976):452-3.

Athearn, Robert G. Union Pacific Country. Lincoln: U Neb Press, 1976. Rev. by B. Luckingham, JOW, 15(Jl 1976): 107.

Atherton, Herbert M. Political Prints in the Age of Hogarth. Oxford: Clarendon Press, 1974. Rev. by H. H. Schless, AHR, 81(Feb 1976):133; S. Meacham, JIH, 7(Sum 1976):146-8.

Auerbach, Jerold S. Unequal Justice: Lawyers and Social Change in Modern America. New York: Oxford U Press, 1976. Rev. by J. W. Bishop, Jr., Commentary, 62(Aug 1976):65-8; O. E. S., CurH, 71(Jl-Aug 1976):29; H. M. Hyman, JSH, 42 (Aug 1976):444-5; J. P. O'Keefe, WMH, 60(Aut 1976):75-6.

Auguet, Roland. Cruelty and Civilization: The Roman Games. New York: Humanities, 1972. Rev. by N. Harris, JIH, 7 (sum 1976):71-7.

August, Eugene. John Stuart Mill: A Mind at Large. New York: Scribner's, 1975. Rev. by W. T. Deininger, HRNB, 4(Feb 1976):94-5.

Austin, Mary. The Land of Little Rain. Albuquerque: U NM Press, 1974. Rev. by R. W. Etulain, JOW, 15(Apr 1976): 143.

Auty, Phyllis and Richard Clogg, eds. British Policy Towards Wartime Resistance in Yugoslavia and Greece. London: Macmillan, 1975. Rev. by A. J. P. Taylor, EHR, 91(Oct 1976):939; D. Wilson, HJ, 19(Mar 1976):313-15.

Avakian, Anne M., comp. Armenia and the Armenians in Academic Dissertations. Berkeley: Professional Press, 1974. Rev. by R. G. Hovannisian, IJMES, 7(Apr 1976):309-10.

Avakumovic, Ivan. The Communist Party in Canada: A History. Toronto: McClelland and Stewart, 1975. Rev. by H. P. Quinn, AHR, 81(Oct 1976):1007; P. Wigley, EHR, 91(Oct 1976):936-7; H. S. Ferns, History, 61(Oct 1976):396-7; R. H. Babcock, JAH, 62(Mar 1976):1053-4.

Avant, David A., Jr. Florida Pioneers and Their Alabama, Georgia Carolina, Maryland and Virginia Ancestors. Tallahassee, Fla.: Privately printed, 1974. Rev. by W. M. Billings, VMHB, 84(Apr 1976):206-7.

Avery, David. Not on Queen Victoria's Birthday: The Story of the Rio Tinto Mines. London: Collins, 1974. Rev. by R. A. H. Robinson, History, 61(Feb 1976):150-1.

Avnery, Uri. Israel Without Zionism: A Plan for Peace in the Middle East. New York: Collier, 1971. Rev. by D. L. Baker, JCS, 17(Win 1975):145-50.

Avtorkhanov, A. The Origin of Partocracy: The Central Committee and Lenin and Stalin. 2 vols. Frankfurt/Main: Possev-Verlag, 1973. Rev. by R. V. Daniels, AHR, 81(Je 1976): 633-4.

Axtell, James. The School Upon a Hill: Education and Society in Colonial New England. New Haven, Conn.: Yale U Press, 1974. Rev. by M. McGiffert, AHR, 81(Apr 1976):440-1; D. Cressy, HJ, 19(Mar 1976):277-8.

Axton, William F. Tobacco and Kentucky. Lexington: U Press Ky, 1975. Rev. by J. C. Ellen, Jr., AgH, 50(Jl 1976):552-4; R. F. Durden, BHR, 50(Sum 1976):231-2.

Aydelotte, W. O., A. G. Bogue, and R. W. Fogel, eds. The Dimensions of Quantitative Research in History. Princeton, N.J.: Prin U Press, 1973. Rev. by R. Schofield, History, 61(Feb 1976):75-6.

Aylmer, G. E., ed. The Levellers in the English Revolution. London: Thames and Hudson, 1975. Rev. by W. Lamont, JEccH, 27(Apr 1976):206.

Ayoob, Mohammad. India, Pakistan and Bangladesh. New Delhi: Indian Council of World Affairs, 1975. Rev. by B. G. Verghese, IQ, 32(Jl-Sep 1976):348-50.

Babcock, Robert H. Gompers in Canada. Buffalo: U Tor Press, 1974. Rev. by J. A. Boudreau, JAH, 63(Je 1976):204; G. S. Kealey, JEH, 36(Sep 1976):735-6.

Bachmann, Peter R. Roberto Nobili, 1577-1656. Rome: Institutum Historicum Societatis Iesu, 1972. Rev. by A. de Silvo Rego, CaHR, 62(Apr 1976):273-5.

Bachstein, Martin K. Wenzel Jaksch und die Sudetendeutsche Sozialdemokratie. Munich: R. Oldenbourg, 1974. Rev. by J. W. Bruegel, EEQ, 10(Mar 1976):127-8.

Backer, Dorothy Anne Liot. Precious Women. New York: Basic Books, 1974. Rev. by E. I. Perry, AHR, 81(Feb 1976):154-5.

Backhaus, Wilhelm. Marx, Engels und die Sklaverei: zur ökonomischen Problematik der Unfreiheit. Düsseldorf: Padagogischer Verlag Schwann, 1975. Rev. by O. J. Hammen, AHR, 81(Je 1976):561.

Backman, Milton V., Jr. Christian Churches of America: Origins and Beliefs. Provo, Utah: BYU Press, 1976. Rev. by E. J. Hill, HRNB, 4(Sep 1976):211.

Backstrom, Philip N. Christian Socialism and Cooperation in Victorian England. London: Croom Helm, 1974. Rev. by H. Weisser, AHR, 81(Apr 1976):389; G. Rowell, EHR, 91(Apr 1976):444-5; D. M. Thompson, History, 61(Je 1976):309.

Baczko, Bronisław. Rousseau: Solitude et communauté. Paris:

17   BADE

Mouton, 1974.   Rev. by G. J. Cavanaugh, AHR, 81(Feb
1976):137-8.

Bade, Klaus J.   Friedrich Fabri und der Imperialismus in der
Bismarckzeit: Revolution--Depression--Expansion. Freiburg:
Atlantis, 1975. Rev. by T. S. Hamerow, AHR, 81(Oct 1976):
880-1.

Bagwell, Philip S.   The Transport Revolution from 1770.   New
York: Barnes and Noble, 1974. Rev. by J. R. Hepple, AHR,
81(Je 1976):559.

Baig, M. R. A.   The Muslim Dilemma in India.   Portland, Ore.:
International Scholarly Book Services, 1974. Rev. by J.
Breckenridge, JCS, 18(Aut 1976):565-7.

Baigell, Matthew.   The American Scene: American Painting of the
1930's. New York: Praeger, 1974. Rev. by L. B. Miller,
AHR, 81(Feb 1976):202-3.

Bailey, David C.   Viva Cristo Rey! The Cristero Rebellion and
the Church-State Conflict in Mexico. Austin: U Texas Press,
1974. Rev. by R. L. Millett, JCS, 17(Aut 1976):520-1; V.
Hennessey, TAm, 32(Jan 1976):490-2.

Bailey, Derrick Sherwin.   Homosexuality and the Western Christian
Tradition. Hamden, Conn.: Archon, 1975. Rev. by V. L.
Bullough, AHR, 81(Apr 1976):352-3.

_____, ed. Wells Cathedral Chapter Act Book, 1666-83. Lon-
don: Her Majesty's Stationery Office, 1973. Rev. by R. A.
Beddard, JEccH, 27(Apr 1976):207.

Bailey, Kenneth.   Christopher Gist: Colonial Frontiersman, Explorer, and Indian Agent. Hamden, Conn.: Shoe String,
1976. Rev. by V. G. Spence, HRNB, 4(Aug 1976):189; J.
Sosin, JAH, 63(Dec 1976):690-1; D. B. Trimble, VMHB,
84(Oct 1976):489-90.

Bailey, Robert, Jr.   Radicals in Urban Politics: The Alinsky
Approach. Chicago: U Chicago Press, 1974. Rev. by T.
J. Ticknor, JISHS, 69(May 1976):147-8.

Bailey, Thomas Andrew and Paul B. Ryan.   The Lusitania Disaster:
An Episode in Modern Warfare and Diplomacy. New York:
Free Press, 1975. Rev. by R. Maddox, AHI, 11(Aug 1976):
49; G. E. Silberstein, HRNB, 4(Mar 1976):100; C. Enders,
JAH, 63(Sep 1976):445-6.

Baillie, Alexander F.   Kurrachee: Past, Present and Future.
New York: Oxford U Press, 1975. Rev. by G. Minault,
AHR, 81(Je 1976):645-7.

Bailyn, Bernard. The Ordeal of Thomas Hutchinson. London:
Allen Lane, 1975. Rev. by D. K. Fieldhouse, EHR, 91(Oct
1976):918-19; E. Wright, History, 61(Oct 1976):402-3; W.
Rundell, Jr., Mankind 5(Dec 1976):6-7; P. J. Schwarz,
NYHSQ, 60(Jan/Apr 1976):70-1.

Bainer, Roy. The Engineering of Abundance: An Oral History
Memoir. Davis: U Cal, Davis, Library, 1975. Rev. by
R. M. Wik, CHQ, 55(Spr 1976):85-6.

Baird, Jay W. The Mythical World of Nazi War Propaganda, 1939-
1945. Minneapolis: U Minn Press, 1975. Rev. by R. E.
Herzstein, AHR, 81(Apr 1976):410-11; J. D. Noakes, EHR,
91(Jl 1976):691; A. J. P. Taylor, History, 61(Je 1976):323.

Bairoch, Paul. The Economic Development of the Third World
Since 1900. Berkeley: U Cal, 1975. Rev. by T. R. de
Gregori, JEH, 36(Je 1976):453-4.

Baker, A. R. H. and R. A. Butlin, eds. Studies of Field Systems in the British Isles. Cambridge: Cam U Press, 1973.
Rev. by M. W. Beresford, History, 61(Feb 1976):80-1.

Baker, C., ed. see Adedeji, A., ed.

Baker, Derek, ed. The Bibliography of the Reform 1450-1648.
Oxford: Blackwell, 1975. Rev. by C. Cross, History, 61
(Oct 1976):445-6; W. D. J. Cargill Thompson, JEccH, 27(Oct
1976):444-6.

_____, ed. Church, Society and Politics. Oxford: Blackwell,
1975. Rev. by O. Chadwick, JEccH, 27(Jl 1976):303-7.

_____, ed. The Materials, Sources and Methods of Ecclesiastical
History. Oxford: Blackwell, 1975. Rev. by O. Chadwick,
JEccH, 27(Jl 1976):303-7.

_____. Partnership in Excellence: A Late-Victorian Educational
Venture: The Leys School, Cambridge, 1875-1975. Cambridge: W. Heffer, 1975. Rev. by J. Roach, JEccH, 27(Jl
1976):323.

Baker, Elliot S. The Great Southwest. Kansas City, Mo.: Lowell,
1975. Rev. by H. E. Chrisman, A & W, 18(Spr 1976):88-9.

Baker, Keith Michael. Condorcet: From Natural Philosophy to
Social Mathematics. Chicago: U Chicago Press, 1975. Rev.
by R. Birn, AHR, 81(Je 1976):602-3; N. Hampson, EHR, 91
(Oct 1976):864-5; J. Lough, History, 61(Je 1976):294-5.

Baker, Leonard. John Marshall: A Life in Law. New York:
Macmillan, 1974. Rev. by C. T. Cullen, VMHB, 84(Jan
1976):108-10.

19   BAKER

Baker, Pearl. Robbers Roost Recollections. Logan: Utah St U
     Press, 1976. Rev. by K. R. Boren, UHQ, 44(Fall 1976):
     400-1.

Baker, Robert A. The Southern Baptist Convention and Its People
     1607-1972. Nashville: Broadman, 1974. Rev. by J. M.
     Self, ETHJ, 14(Spr 1976):73-4.

Baker, Ronald L. and Marvin Carmony. Indiana Place Names.
     Bloomington: Ind. U Press, 1975. Rev. by D. Zimmer,
     IMH, 72(Je 1976):360-1.

Balasubrahmanyam, S. R. Early Chola Temples: Parantaka I to
     Rajaraja I (A. D. 907-985). New Delhi: Orient Longmans,
     1971. Rev. by M. W. Meister, JAS, 36(Nov 1976):167-8.

Balázs, E. H., ed. see Kopecki, Béla, ed.

Balderston, Marion and David Syrett, eds. The Lost War: Letters
     from British Officers During the American Revolution. New
     York: Horizon, 1975. Rev. by P. D. Nelson, JAH, 63(Sep
     1976):396-7; R. Beeston, Smithsonian, 7(Je 1976):116-17.

Baldwin, Alice Blackwood. An Army Wife on the Frontier: the
     Memoirs of Alice Blackwood Baldwin, 1867-1877. (Robert C.
     and Eleanor R. Carriker, eds.) Salt Lake City: U Utah Li-
     brary, 1975. Rev. by M. Benson, NMHR, 51(Apr 1976):165-
     6; D. R. Mathis, UHQ, 44(Fall 1976):401-2.

Baldwin, Frank, ed. Without Parallel: The American-Korean Re-
     lationship Since 1945. New York: Pantheon, 1974. Rev. by
     W. G. Hermes, AHR, 81(Apr 1976):434.

Baldwin, Hanson W. The Crucial Years, 1939-1941: The World
     at War. New York: Harper & Row, 1976. Rev. by R. W.
     Love, Jr., HRNB, 4(May/Je 1976):156.

Baldwin, James. If Beale Street Could Talk. New York: Dial,
     1974. Rev. in Crisis, 83(Mar 1976):102.

Baldwin, John W. and Richard A. Goldthwaite, eds. Universities
     in Politics: Case Studies from the Late Middle Ages. Balti-
     more: JHU Press, 1972. Rev. by G. F. Lytle, CaHR, 62
     (Jan 1976):83-4.

Baldwin, Marshall W., ed. Christianity Through the Thirteenth
     Century. London: Macmillan, 1971. Rev. by D. Baker,
     JEccH, 27(Oct 1976):428-30.

Ball, Berenice. Barns of Chester County, Pennsylvania. West
     Chester, Pa.: Chester County Day Committee, 1974. Rev.
     by C. J. Hopf, PH, 43(Apr 1976):190-1.

Ball, Bryan W. A Great Expectation: Eschatological Thought in English Protestantism to 1660. Leiden: Brill, 1975. Rev. by W. Lamont, JEccH, 27(Jl 1976):319-20.

Ball, George W. Diplomacy for a Crowded World. Boston: Atlantic-Little, Brown, n.d. Rev. by J. Shattan, Commentary, 62(Oct 1976):80, 82-3.

Ballard, Allen B. The Education of Black Folk: The Afro-American Struggle for Knowledge in White America. New York: Harper and Row, 1974. Rev. by W. N. Ikemma, JMAS, 14 (Je 1976):364-6.

Balmas, Enea and Vittorio Diena, eds. Histoire memorable de la guerre faite par le Duc de Savoye, Emanuel Philebert, contre ses subjectz des Vallées d'Angrogne, Perosse, S. Martin, et autres vallées circonvoisines, pour compte de la Religion. Turin: Libreria Editrice Claudiana, 1972. Rev. by J. S. Valone, CaHR, 62(Apr 1976):266-7.

Balzer, Richard J. see Hsü-Balzer, Eileen

Bamford, Paul W. Fighting Ships and Prisons. The Mediterranean Galleys of France in the Age of Louis XIV. Minneapolis: U Minn press, 1973. Rev. by L. S. Greenbaum, CaHR, 62(Apr 1976):283-4.

Banham, Reyner. Age of Masters: A Personal View of Modern Architecture. New York: Harper and Row, 1975. Rev. by M. Hollander, Commentary, 61(Jl 1976):70, 72-3.

_____. Los Angeles: The Architecture of Four Ecologies. Harmondsworth, Eng.: Allan Lane, 1971. Rev. by S. G. L., AS, 16(Spr 1975):73-4.

Banks, Arthur. A Military Atlas of the First World War. London: Heinemann, 1975. Rev. by B. Bond, History, 61(Je 1976):317.

Banner, János and István Bóna. Mittelbronzezeitliche Tell-Siedlung bei Békés. Budapest: Akadémiai Kiadó, 1974. Rev. by H. L. Thomas, AJA, 80(Win 1976):88-9.

Bannerman, J. Studies in the History of Dalriada. London: Scottish Academic Press, 1974. Rev. by A. P. Smyth, EHR, 91(Jan 1976):173; A. A. M. Duncan, History, 61(Feb 1976): 94-5.

Bansal, Prem Lata. Administrative Development in India. New Delhi: Sterling, 1974. Rev. by H. K. Paranijape, IQ, 32 (Jl-Sep 1976):362-5.

Banta, R. E. Hoosier Caravan: A Treasury of Indiana Life and

21   BANTON

Lore. Bloomington: Ind. U Press, 1975. Rev. by J. G.
Williams, IMH, 72(Dec 1976):361-3.

Banton, Michael and Jonathan Harwood. The Race Concept. London: David and Charles, 1975. Rev. by T. O. Odetola,
JMAS, 14(Sep 1976):548-50.

Bar, Carl Ludwig von see von Bar, Carl Ludwig

Barba, Enrique M. Quiroga y Rosas. Buenos Aires: Editorial
Pleamar, 1974. Rev. by J. R. Barager, HAHR, 56(May
1976):343-4.

Barber, Benjamin R. The Death of Communal Liberty: a History
of Freedom in a Swiss Mountain Canton. Princeton, N.J.:
Prin U Press, 1974. Rev. by P. J. Katzenstein, JIH, 7(Sum
1976):161-4.

Barber, James. South Africa's Foreign Policy, 1945-70. London:
Oxford U Press, 1973. Rev. by D. Schreuder, CHR, 57(Mar
1976):79-81.

Barber, Melanie, ed. Index to the Letters and Papers of Frederick
Temple, Archbishop of Canterbury, 1896-1902 in Lambeth
Palace Library. London: Mansell, 1975. Rev. by D. M.
Owen, Archives, 12(Spr 1976):149.

Barber, William J. British Economic Thought and India, 1600-
1858: A Study in the History of Development Economics.
New York: Clarendon Press, 1975. Rev. by L. G. Sandberg, AHR, 81(Je 1976):581-2; E. Stokes, EHR, 91(Jl 1976):
649.

Barié, Ottavio. Luigi Albertini. Turin: Unione Tipografico-
Editrice Torinese, 1972. Rev. by P. J. Devendittis, AHR,
81(Je 1976):625-6.

Barkas, Janet. The Vegetable Passion: A History of the Vegetarian State of Mind. New York: Scribner's, 1975. Rev.
by M. Prewitt, Smithsonian, 6(Je 1975):101-3.

Barker, Dudley. G. K. Chesterton. New York: Stein and Day,
1973. Rev. by J. R. McCarthy, CaHR, 62(Oct 1976):655-6.

Barker, John. Strange Contrarieties: Pascal in England During
the Age of Reason. Montreal: McGill-Queen's U Press,
1976. Rev. by Schlatter, AHR, 81(Oct 1976):858.

Barker, Michael. Gladstone and Radicalism: The Reconstruction
of Liberal Policy in Britain, 1885-94. New York: Barnes and
Noble, 1975. Rev. by D. Brooks, HJ, 19(Mar 1976):295-6;
M. V. Hazel, JMH, 48(Mar 1976):143-5.

Barker, T. C. see Hatcher, John

Barker, Thomas Mack. The Military Intellectual and Battle:
Raimondo Montecuccoli and the Thirty Years' War. Albany:
SUNY Press, 1973. Rev. by B. Nischan, CH, 45(Sep 1976):
388-9; K. A. Roider, Jr., Historian, 39(Nov 1976):116-17;
A. R. Sunseri, HRNB, 4(Mar 1976):109.

Bar-Kochva, Bezalel. The Seleucid Army: Organization and Tactics in the Great Campaigns. New York: Cam U Press,
1976. Rev. by B. F. Cooling, HRNB, 5(Oct 1976):16.

Barkun, Michael. Disaster and the Millennium. New Haven,
Conn.: Yale U Press, 1974. Rev. by A. F. C. Wallace,
AHR, 81(Feb 1976):98; J. F. H. New, CHR, 57(Je 1976):
173-4.

Barnard, Francis Pierrepont, ed. Edward IV's French Expedition
of 1475: The Leaders and Their Badges. Totowa, N. J.:
Rowman and Littlefield, 1975. Rev. by D. E. Queller, AHR,
81(Oct 1976):852.

Barnard, T. C. Cromwellian Ireland: English Government and
Reform in Ireland, 1649-1600. New York: Oxford U Press,
1975. Rev. by D. F. Cregan, AHR, 81(Je 1976):597-8;
G. E. Aylmer, EHR, 91(Oct 1976):909-10; K. T. Hoppen,
JMH, 48(Sep 1976):538-9.

Barnard, William D. Dixiecrats and Democrats: Alabama Politics,
1942-1950. University: Ala U Press, 1974. Rev. by R. F.
de Bedts, AHR, 81(Apr 1976):466-7; E. C. Williamson, AlaR,
29(Jan 1976):72-4; W. C. Havard, FHQ, 55(Jl 1976):100-2;
A. Yarnell, PNQ, 67(Jan 1976):44-5.

Barnes, James J. Authors, Publishers and Politicians. London:
Routledge and Kegan Paul, 1974. Rev. by A. H. Hudson,
BH, 17(Jl 1975):202.

Barnes, Thomas G., ed. and comp. List and Index to the Proceedings in Star Chamber for the Reign of James I. 3 vols.
n. p.: American Bar Foundation, 1975. Rev. by J. A. Guy,
Archives, 12(Aut 1976):195-7.

Barnett, A. Doak. Uncertain Passage: China's Transition to the
Post-Mao Era. Washington, D. C.: Brookings Institution,
1974. Rev. by E. A. Shea, JAAS, 11(Jl-Oct 1976):247-8.

Barnett, Becky, ed. see Grove, Pearce, ed.

Barnett, Corelli. The Swordbearers: Supreme Command in the
First World War. Bloomington: Ind U Press, 1975. Rev.
by L. L. Farrar, Jr., AHR, 81(Oct 1976):847.

23   BARON

Baron, Salo W., et al. Economic History of the Jews. New
York: Schocken, 1975. Rev. by P. P. Abrahams, HRNB,
4(Jan 1976):62-3.

Barr, John J. The Dynasty: The Rise and Fall of Social Credit
in Alberta. Toronto: McClelland and Stewart, 1974. Rev.
by J. R. Mallory, CHR, 57(Je 1976):216-17.

Barraclough, Geoffrey. The Crucible of Europe: The Ninth and
Tenth Centuries in European History. Los Angeles: U Cal
Press, 1976. Rev. by J. F. Kelly, CH, 45(Sep 1976):378-9;
R. E. Sullivan, HRNB, 4(May/Je 1976):157; C. W. Hollister,
HT, 10(Nov 1976):159-61.

Barratt, Glyn. The Rebel on the Bridge: A Life of the Decem-
brist Baron Andrew Rozen (1800-84). Athens: Ohio U Press,
1976. Rev. by R. F. Leslie, History, 61(Oct 1976):464; E.
Anderson, HRNB, 4(May/Je 1976):155.

Barrett, Leonard E. Soul Force: African Heritage in Afro-American Religion. New York: Doubelday, Anchor, 1974. Rev.
by C. Winters, JMAS, 14(Mar 1976):175-7.

Barron, Caroline M. The Medieval Guildhall of London. London:
Corporation of London, 1974. Rev. by H. M. Colvin, History, 61(Je 1976):251.

Barrow, G. W. S. The Kingdom of the Scots: Government, Church
and Society from the Eleventh to the Fourteenth Century. New
York: St. Martin's, 1973. Rev. by J. Collins, Historian, 38
(Feb 1976):327-9.

_____, ed. The Scottish Tradition: Essays in Honour of Ronald
Gordon Cant. Totowa, N.J.: Rowman and Littlefield, 1974.
Rev. by R. Nicholson, AHR, 81(Feb 1976):148; I. B. Cowan,
History, 61(Feb 1976):82-3.

Barry, John G., ed. Historical Studies. Vol. IX. Belfast:
Blackstaff, 1974. Rev. by T. C. Beckett, History, 61(Feb
1976):83-4.

Barth, Gunther. Instant Cities: Urbanization and the Rise of San
Francisco and Denver. New York: Oxford U Press, 1975.
Rev. by L. W. Dorsett, JAH, 62(Mar 1976):1015; R. W.
Lotchin, PHR, 45(May 1976):287-8; D. W. Meinig, PNQ, 67
(Jl 1976):128.

Bartke, Wolfgang. China's Economic Aid. n.p.: Hurst, 1975.
Rev. by M. Bailey, AfAf, 75(Apr 1976):251-2.

Bartlett, C. J. The Rise and Fall of Pax Americana: United
States Foreign Policy in the Twentieth Century. London:
Paul Elek, 1974. Rev. by J. A. Thompson, EHR, 91(Jan

1976):229-30; P. Boyle, JAmS, 10(Apr 1976):121; W. Lafeber, PHR, 45(Nov 1976):635-6.

Bartlett, Richard A.   Nature's Yellowstone.   Albuquerque: U NMex Press, 1974.   Rev. by R. Nash, AHR, 81(Oct 1976): 980; H. D. Hampton, PHR, 45(Feb 1976):123-4.

_____. The New Country: A Social History of the American Frontier, 1776-1890. New York: Oxford U Press, 1974. Rev. by D. Brown, AHI, 10(Feb 1976):49; R. V. Hine, AHR, 81(Feb 1976):206; R. A. Burchell, EHR, 91(Apr 1976):436; T. D. Clarke, FHQ, 54(Jan 1976):393-6; M. Walsh, History, 61(Oct 1976):411.

Bartley, Numan V. and Hugh D. Graham. Southern Politics and the Second Reconstruction. Baltimore: JHU Press, 1975. Rev. by R. V. Haynes, ETHJ, 14(Spr 1976):71-3; R. C. Mc-Math, Jr., GHQ, 60(Spr 1976):69-71; D. K. Adams, History, 61(Oct 1976):419-20; J. A. Rawley, HRNB, 4(Jan 1976):51; K. I. Polakoff, HT, 10(Nov 1976):155-8; H. W. Allen, JAH, 63(Je 1976):194-5; D. P. Jordan, JMiH, 38(May 1976):225-6; N. R. McMillen, JSH, 42(Feb 1976):146-7; A. R. Stoesen, NCHR, 53(Win 1976):99-100.

Barton, H. Arnold, ed.   Letters from the Promised Land: Swedes in America, 1840-1914. Minneapolis: U Minn Press, 1975. Rev. by J. R. Christianson, AI, 43(Spr 1976):311-13; K. O. Bjork, AHR, 81(Je 1976):670-2; G. E. Arden, CH, 45(Mar 1976):120; P. A. M. Taylor, History, 61(Oct 1976):411-12; J. I. Dowie, JAH, 63(Sep 1976):416; R. A. Burchell, JAmS, 10(Apr 1976):118; R. Nelson, NDH, 43(Sum 1976):42; D. E. Weinberg, OH, 85(Sum 1976):273; W. Mulder, WHQ, 7(Oct 1976):427-8.

Barton, Josef J.   Peasants and Strangers: Italians, Rumanians and Slovaks in an American City, 1890-1950. Cambridge: Mass.: Harvard U Press, 1975. Rev. by V. Greene, AHR, 81(Je 1976):674-5; H. B. Leonard, CaHR, 62(Oct 1976):675-6; J. M. Allswang, JAH, 62(Mar 1976):1017-18; V. Yans-McLaughlin, JIH, 7(Aut 1976):343-5; H. P. Chudacoff, RAH, 4(Mar 1976):99-104.

Bartra, Roger.   Caciquismo y Poder Político en el Mexico Rural. Mexico: Siglo Veintiuno Editores, 1975. Rev. by R. A. Camp, HAHR, 56(Nov 1976):682-3.

Barzun, Jacques.   Clio and the Doctors: Psycho-History, Quanto-History and History. Chicago: U Chicago Press, 1974. Rev. by R. J. Parks, AHR, 81(Je 1976):557; P. Burke, History, 61(Feb 1976):73-4; F. Weinstein, JMH, 48(Mar 1976):117-18; L. O. Saum, PNQ, 67(Oct 1976):177-8.

Bascom, William R.   African Dilemma Tales.   Chicago: Aldine,

25 BASHARIN

1975. Rev. by T. M. Samkange, JNH, 61(Oct 1976):412-14.

Basharin, G. P. Some Questions on the Historiography of Siberia's
Entry into the Russian State. Iakutsk: Iakutskoe Knizhnoe
Izdatel'stvo, 1971. Rev. by S. Watrous, AHR, 81(Oct 1976):
905-6.

Basin'skii, Z., et al., eds. Dokumenty i materialy po istorii
sovetski-pol'skikh otnoshenii. Voo. 7, 1939-1943 gg. Moscow: Izdatel'stvo "Nauka," 1973. Rev. by R. V. Burks,
AHR, 81(Oct 1976):913.

Basler, Roy P., ed. The Collected Works of Abraham Lincoln:
Supplement, 1832-1865. Westport, Conn.: Greenwood, 1974.
Rev. by R. D. Hoffsommer, AHI, 11(May 1976):49.

Basu, Aparna. The Growth of Education and Political Development
in India, 1898-1920. Bombay: Oxford U Press, 1974. Rev.
by S. Mathai, IQ, 32(Jl-Sep 1976):365-7.

Bate, W. N. General Sidney Sherman: Texas Soldier, Statesman,
and Builder. Waco, Tx.: Texian, 1974. Rev. by J. Os-
burn, ETHJ, 14(Spr 1976):60-1.

Battiscombe, Georgina. Shaftesbury: A Biography of the Seventh
Earl, 1801-1885. London: Constable, 1974. Rev. by G. B.
A. Finlayson, History, 61(Feb 1976):126-7.

Bauer, Arnold J. Chilean Rural Society from the Spanish Conquest
to 1930. New York: Cam U Press, 1975. Rev. by F. B.
Pike, HAHR, 56(Aug 1976):462-3; A. Angell, History, 61(Oct
1976):429; F. Safford, HRNB, 4(Feb 1976):81.

Bauer, K. Jack. The Mexican War, 1846-1848. New York: Macmillan, 1974. Rev. by A. P. McDonald, CWH, 22(Mar
1976):81-3; G. Connell-Smith, History, 61(Oct 1976):406;
W. H. Marti, PHR, 45(May 1976):286-7; O. B. Faulk, PNQ,
67(Jan 1976):34-5.

Baugh, Daniel A., ed. Aristocratic Government and Society in
Eighteenth-Century England: The Foundations of Stability.
New York: New Viewpoints, 1975. Rev. by S. Hartt, HRNB,
4(Sep 1976):227.

Baum, Charlotte, Paula Hyman and Sonya Michel. The Jewish
Woman in America. New York: Dial, 1976. Rev. by R. R.
Wisse, Commentary, 61(Jl 1976):68-70; L. Nilson, Mankind,
5(Oct 1976):6, 55.

Baum, Richard. Prelude to Revolution: Mao, the Party, and the
Peasant Question, 1962-66. New York: Columbia U Press,
1975. Rev. by R. Kraus, CQ, Jan 1976, pp. 138-40.

Baum, Willa K. Oral History for the Local Historical Society.
Nashville, Tenn.: American Assn for State and Local History, 1975. Rev. by L. J. Hackman, AmArc, 39(Apr 1976): 208-9.

Baxter, Douglas Clark. Servants of the Sword: French Intendants of the Army 1630-1690. Urbana: U Ill Press, 1976. Rev. by P. F. Riley, HRNB, 5(Oct 1976):18-19.

Bazant, Jan. Cinco Haciendas Mexicanas. Tres siglos de vida rural en San Luis Potosí (1600-1910). México: El Colegio de Mexico, 1975. Rev. by T. G. Powell, TAm, 33(Jl 1976): 178-9.

Beaglehole, John. The Life of Captain James Cook. London: A & C Black, 1974. Rev. by B. Greenhill, EHR, 91(Jan 1976):207-8.

Beals, Ralph L. The Peasant Marketing System of Oaxaca, Mexico. Berkeley: U Cal Press, 1975. Rev. by R. Symanski, HAHR, 56(Feb 1976):183.

Beasley, W. G., ed. Modern Japan: Aspects of History, Literature, and Society. Berkeley: U Cal Press, 1975. Rev. by T. R. H. Havens, HRNB, 4(Mar 1976):104.

Beck, Curt W., ed. Archaeological Chemistry. Dallas, Tx.: Fifth Symposium on Archaeological Chemistry, 1973. Rev. by R. E. M. Hedges, Antiquity, 50(Mar 1976):82-3.

Beck, Thomas D. French Legislators, 1800-1834: A Study in Quantitative History. Berkeley: U Cal Press, 1974. Rev. by A. B. Spitzer, AHR, 81(Je 1976):606-7.

Beck, Warren A. and Ynez D. Haase. Historical Atlas of California. Norman: U Ok Press, 1974. Rev. by D. C. Cutter, JOW, 15(Apr 1976):126-7; W. Bean, PHR, 45(Feb 1976):134-5.

Becker, Josef. Liberaler Staat und Kirche in der Ära von Reichsgründung und Kulturkampf. Mainz: Matthias-Grünewald Verlag, 1973. Rev. by J. Zeender, CaHR, 52(Oct 1976):619-22.

Beckman, Björn. Organizing the Farmers. Uppsala: Scandinavian Institute of African Studies, 1976. Rev. by R. Southall, JMAS, 14(Dec 1976):722-5.

Beckwith, Frank A. Indian Joe in Person and in Background: Historical Perspective into Piute Life. Delta, Utah: DuWil Pub. Co., 1975. Rev. by M. B. Murphy, UHQ, 44(Sum 1976):306-7.

Bédarida, François. L'Angleterre Triomphante, 1832-1914. Paris: Hatier, 1974. Rev. by H. Perkin, History, 61(Feb 1976):133.

27 BEDINI

Bedini, Silvio A. Thinkers and Tinkers: Early American Men of
Science. New York: Scribner's, 1975. Rev. by N. Reingold,
AHR, 81(Oct 1976):952-3; J. L. Heilbron, HRNB, 4(Feb 1976):
76; J. H. Cassedy, JAH, 63(Sep 1976):385; M. A. Calvert,
JSH, 42(Aug 1976):422-3; M. Olmert, Smithsonian, 6(Nov
1975):157-60.

Bedouelle, Guy. L'Eglise d'Angleterre et la société politique con-
temporaine. Paris: Librairie Générale de Droit et de Juris-
prudence, 1968. Rev. by H. L. Robinson, JCS, 17(Aug 1976):
352.

Beeman, Richard R. Patrick Henry. New York: McGraw-Hill,
1974. Rev. by R. Hoffman, AHR, 81(Apr 1976):442-3; J. B.,
AS, 16(Fall 1975):94; F. Cassell, PH, 43(Jan 1976):80-1.

Beer, Adolf. Die Finanzen Österreichs im XIX. Jahrhundert, nach
archivalischen Quellen. Vienna: H. Geyer, 1973. Rev. by
H. Freudenberger, AHR, 81(Feb 1976):173.

Beer, Barrett L. Northunberland: The Political Career of John
Dudley, Earl of Warwick and Duke of Northumberland. Kent,
Ohio: Kent St U Press, 1973. Rev. by G. R. Elton, EHR,
91(Jan 1976):193; E. W. Ives, History, 61(Feb 1976):109-10.

Beer, William R., trans. Slavery and Serfdom in the Middle Ages.
Selected Essays by Marc Bloch. Berkeley: U Cal Press,
1975. Rev. by B. D. Hill, AHR, 81(Oct 1976):832-3.

Beeson, Trevor. Discretion and Valour: Religious Conditions in
Russia and Eastern Europe. Glasgow: Collins, Fontana, 1974.
Rev. by P. B. Anderson, JCS, 18(Spr 1976):321-7.

Beevers, John. A Man for Now: The Life of Damien de Veuster,
Friend of Lepers. Garden City, N.Y.: Doubleday, 1973.
Rev. by J. T. Ellis, CaHR, 62(Jl 1976):502-5.

Beghin, P. Guided Change in an African Community: Bushi in the
Colonial Period. Brussels: Academie royale, 1974. Rev.
by J. Vansina, Africa, 46(Num 1, 1976):109-10.

Behrens, Christine. Les Kroumen de la côte occidentale d'Afrique.
Talence, France: Domaine Universitaire de Bordeaux, 1974.
Rev. by E. Tonkin, JAfH, 17(Num 3, 1976):470-1.

Beisner, Robert L. From the Old Diplomacy to the New, 1865-
1900. New York: Crowell, 1975. Rev. by S. J. Kneeshaw,
MiA, 58(Oct 1976):196-7; P. S. Holbo, PHR, 45(Feb 1976):
145-6.

Beitzell, Edwin W. St. Mary's County, Maryland in the American
Revolution. Leonardtown, Md.: Md Bicentennial Commission,
1975. Rev. by B. E. Marks, MHM, 71(Sum 1976):277-8.

BELANGER   28

Bélanger, André-J. L'Apolitisme des idéologies québécoises: Le
    grand tournant de 1934-1936. Portland, Ore.: International
    Scholarly Book Services, 1974. Rev. by J. A. Boudreau,
    AHR, 81(Feb 1976):225.

Bell, Daniel. The Cultural Contradiction of Capitalism. New York:
    Basic Books, 1976. Rev. by P. L. Berger, Commentary,
    61(Apr 1976):82-3.

Bell, E. J., Jr. Homesteading in Montana: Life in the Blue
    Mountain Country, 1911-1923. Bozeman: Big Sky Books,
    1975. Rev. by B. Luckingham, NDH, 43(Fall 1976):38-9.

Bell, J. Bowyer. The Myth of the Guerrilla: Revolutionary Theory
    and Malpractice. New York: Knopf, 1971. Rev. by J. J.
    Roth, AHR, 81(Je 1976):567-8.

Bell, P. M. H. A Certain Eventuality. London: Saxon House,
    1974. Rev. by M. R. D. Foot, EHR, 91(Jl 1976):691-2.

Bell, R. C., ed. Diaries from the Age of Saul. n. p.: Barrie
    and Jenkins, 1974. Rev. by R. Davis, JTH, 3(Sep 1976):
    300-1.

Bell, Rudolph M. Party and Faction in American Politics. Lon-
    don: Greenwood, 1974. Rev. by C. C. Bonwick, History,
    61(Oct 1976):403-4.

Bell, S. Peter. Dissertations on British History, 1815-1914: An
    Index to British and American Theses. Metuchen, N. J.:
    Scarecrow, 1974. Rev. by B. Harrison, History, 61(Feb
    1976):122-3.

Bell, Trevor. Industrial Decentralization in South Africa. London:
    Oxford U Press, 1973. Rev. by P. Mosley, JMAS, 14(Sep
    1976):543-6.

Bell, Whitfield J., Jr. The Colonial Physican and Other Essays.
    New York: N. Watson Academic Publ., 1975. Rev. by M.
    H. Saffron, HRNB, 4(May/Je 1976):143; B. Hindle, WMQ,
    33(Apr 1976):343-5.

Bellah, Robert N. The Broken Covenant: American Civil Religion
    in Time of Trial. New York: Seabury Press, 1975. Rev.
    by E. S. Gaustad, CH, 45(Sep 1976):399; B. E. Steiner, JAH,
    62(Mar 1976):964-5.

Bellamy, John. Crime and Public Order in the Later Middle Ages.
    London: Routledge and Kegan Paul, 1973. Rev. by P. R.
    Hyams, EHR, 91(Jl 1976):632.

Bellanger, Claude, et al. Histoire générale de la presse française.
    Vol. 4: De 1940 a 1958. Paris: Presses U France, 1975.

Rev. by P. C. F. Bankwitz, AHR, 81(Oct 1976):873-4.

Bellard, Alfred see Donald, David Herbert, ed.

Bellow, Saul. To Jerusalem and Back. New York: Viking, 1976.
Rev. by E. Grossman, Commentary, 62(Nov 1976):80, 82-4.

Bellush, Bernard. The Failure of the NRA. New York: Norton,
1975. Rev. by E. W. Hawley, AHR, 81(Oct 1976):995-6; R.
J. Tosiello, BHR, 50(Sum 1976):238-9; R. J. Plowman,
HRNB, 4(Jl 1976):162-3; I. F. Gellman, JAH, 63(Dec 1976):
771-3; A. F. McClure, JSH, 42(Nov 1976):602-3; J. R. Conlin, WMH, 60(Aut 1976):74.

Belmont, Nicole. Arnold Van Gennup: le créateur de l'ethnographie
française. Paris: Payot, 1974. Rev. by M. R. Marrus,
JSoH, 8(Spr 1975):142-9.

_____. Mythes et croyances dans l'ancienne France. Paris:
Flammarion, 1973. Rev. by M. R. Marrus, JSoH, 8(Spr
1975):142-9.

Belt, Thomas. El Naturalista en Nicaragua. Managua: Banco
Central de Nicaragua, 1976. Rev. by F. Meissner, Américas,
28(Aug 1976):23.

Bence-Jones, Mark. Clive of India. London: Constable, 1974.
Rev. by K. Balihatchet, History, 61(Feb 1976):163-4.

Bender, Barbara. Farming in Prehistory. London: John Baker,
1975. Rev. by E. S. Higgs, Antiquity, 50(Je 1976):164-5.

Bender, Lynn Darrell. The Politics of Hostility: Castro's Revolution and United States Policy. Hato Rey, P.R.: American U
Press, 1975. Rev. by L. D. Langley, HAHR, 56(Feb 1976):
147-8.

Bender, Thomas. Toward an Urban Vision: Ideas and Institutions
in Nineteenth-Century America. Lexington: U Ky Press,
1975. Rev. by S. Persons, AHR, 81(Je 1976):664-5; A. F.
Davis, JAH, 62(Mar 1976):984-5; L. P. Cain, JEH, 36(Sep
1976):736-7; N. Harris, JIH, 7(Aut 1976):364-6.

Bendiner, Elmer. A Time for Angels: The Tragicomic History of
The League of Nations. New York: Knopf, 1975. Rev. by
G. Ginsburgs, CurH, 70(Mar 1976):124-5; B. I. Kaufman,
JAH, 62(Mar 1976):1036-7.

Benecke, G. Society and Politics in Germany 1500-1750. London:
Routledge and Kegan Paul, 1974. Rev. by H. J. Cohn, History, 61(Je 1976):277.

Benedict, Michael Les. A Compromise of Principle: Congressional

Republicans and Reconstruction, 1863-1869. New York: Norton, 1974. Rev. by W. L. Williams, OH, 85(Sum 1976):270-1.

Benedict, Peter, et al., eds. Turkey: Geographic and Social Perspectives. Leiden: E. J. Brill, 1974. Rev. by W. F. Weiker, IJMES, 7(Apr 1976):302-5.

Benitez, Fernando. In the Magic Land of Peyote. Austin: U Texas Press, 1975. Rev. by J. L. Zentner, TAm, 32(Jan 1976):492-4.

Benjamin, Gilbert Giddings. The Germans in Texas: A Study in Immigration. Austin, Tx.: Jenkins, 1974. Rev. by W. S. Shepperson, AHR, 81(Oct 1976):972.

Benjamin, Philip S. The Philadelphia Quakers in the Industrial Age, 1865-1920. Philadelphia: Temple U Press, 1976. Rev. by W. Smith, HRNB, 5(Oct 1976):3.

Bennett, Edward M., ed. see Burns, Robert Dean, ed.

Bennett, Evan. The Maya Epic. River Falls: U Wis, River Falls Press, 1974. Rev. by W. Madsen, HAHR, 56(Feb 1976):162-3; A. J. Mann, TAm, 32(Apr 1976):640-1.

Bennett, G. V. The Tory Crisis in Church and State, 1688-1730; The Career of Francis Atterbury, Bishop of Rochester. New York: Oxford U Press, 1976. Rev. by A. McInnes, History, 61(Oct 1976):451; L. Colley, HJ, 19(Dec 1976):1030-3; H. T. Blethen, HRNB, 4(May/Je 1976):151.

Bennett, James D. Frederick Jackson Turner. Boston: Twayne, 1975. Rev. by W. Rundell, Jr., JAH, 63(Je 1976):161-2.

Bennett, Norman R. Africa and Europe: From Roman Times to the Present. New York: Africana, 1975. Rev. by J. J. Cooke, AHR, 81(Je 1976):640; W. Schmokel, HRNB, 4(Jan 1976):64.

Bentinck-Smith, William. Building a Great Library: The Coolidge Years at Harvard. Cambridge: Cam U Press, 1976. Rev. by R. F. Byrnes, JAH, 63(Dec 1976):752-3.

Benzoni, Gino, ed. Il Mediterraneo nella seconda metà del 1500 alla luce di Lepanto. Florence: Leo S. Olschki, 1974. Rev. by H. C. Butters, EHR, 91(Oct 1976):905-6.

Bérard, Claude. Anodoi, essai sur L'imagerie des Passages Chthoniens. Rome: Institut Suisse, 1974. Rev. by H. Hoffman, AJA, 80(Win 1976):95-6.

Bercé, Yves-Marie. Histoire des Croquants: Etude des soulève-

31   BERCOVITCH

ments populaires au XVIIᵉ siècle dans le sud-ouest de la
France. 2 vols. Geneva: Librairie Droz, 1974. Rev. by
S. Kettering, AHR, 81(Apr 1976):396.

Bercovitch, Sacvan. The Puritan Origins of the American Self.
New Haven, Conn.: Yale U Press, 1975. Rev. by G. J.
Goodwin, AHR, 81(Oct 1976):954-5; R. A. Burchell, History,
61(Oct 1976):397; J. P. Greene, HRNB, 4(Feb 1976):74; R.
W. Beales, Jr., JAH, 63(Sep 1976):382-3; J. W. Raime,
JAmS, 10(Dec 1976):387-8; H. P. Segal, NEQ, 49(Je 1976):
299-301; Y. Kawashima, RAH, 4(Je 1976):164-70.

Bercuson, David Jay. Confrontation at Winnipeg: Labour, Industrial Relations, and the General Strike. Montreal: Mc-
Gill-Queen's U Press, 1975. Rev. by B. L. Blakeley, AHR,
81(Oct 1976):1007-8; H. S. Ferns, EHR, 91(Apr 1976):458;
J. R. Conlin, PNQ, 67(Jl 1976):134.

_____ see McNaught, Kenneth

Berend, Ivan T. and Gregori Ranki. Hungary: A Century of
Economic Development. New York: Barnes and Noble, 1974.
Rev. by O. E. S., CurH, 70(Mar 1976):123.

Berenson, Bernard. Looking at Pictures with Bernard Berenson.
New York: Harry N. Abrams, n.d. Rev. by R. L. Lowe,
Mankind, 5(Apr 1976):51, 69.

Berger, Elena L. Labour, Race and Colonial Rule: The Copperbelt from 1924 to Independence. Oxford: Clarendon, 1974.
Rev. by E. Ehrlich, AfAf, 75(Jan 1976):115; M. Peil, Africa,
46(Num 1, 1976):108; I. Henderson, EHR, 91(Apr 1976):458-
9; S. E. Katzenellenbogen, History, 61(Feb 1976):156; C. van
Onselen, JAfH, 17(Num 1, 1976):146-7.

Bergier, Jean-Françoise. Naissance et croissance de la Suisse
industrielle. Bern: Francke Editions, 1974. Rev. by H. K.
Meier, AHR, 81(Feb 1976):175.

Berkeley, Edmund and Dorothy Smith Berkeley. Dr. John Mitchell:
The Man Who Made the Map of North America. Chapel Hill:
U NC Press, 1974. Rev. by S. Hilliard, AHR, 81(Feb 1976):
204-5.

Berkin, Carol. Jonathan Sewall: Odyssey of an American Loyalist.
New York: Columbia U Press, 1974. Rev. by P. D. Nelson,
AHR, 81(Oct 1976):961-2.

Berlanstein, Lenard R. The Barristers of Toulouse in the
Eighteenth Century (1740-1793). Baltimore: JHU Press,
1975. Rev. by M. H. Schneider, HRNB, 4(Jan 1976):66-7.

Berlin, Brent, Dennis E. Breedlove, and Peter H. Raven. Princi-

ples of Tzeltal Plant Classification: An Introduction to the
Botanical Ethnology of a Mayan-Speaking People of Highland
Chiapas. New York: Academic, 1974. Rev. by T. E. Hays,
AA, 78(Mar 1976):143-4.

Berlin, Ira. Slaves Without Masters: The Free Negro in the Ante-
bellum South. New York: Pantheon, 1974. Rev. by E. Rudwick, AHR, 81(Je 1976):665; D. C. Rankin, JSH, 42(May
1976):280-1; E. Cox, MHM, 71(Spr 1976):105-7; A. Makechnie,
WMH, 60(Aut 1976):60-2.

Berlin, Isaiah. Vico and Herder: Two Studies in the History of
Ideas. New York: Viking, 1976. Rev. by J. Beatty, Com-
mentary, 62(Nov 1976):86-8; 90-1; L. B. Zimmer, HRNB, 4
(Sep 1976):224-5.

Berman, Edward H., ed. African Reactions to Missionary Education. New York: Teachers College Press, 1975. Rev. by
J. D. Y. Peel, JAfH, 17(Num 3, 1976):467-9.

Bernand, J. F. Talleyrand: a Biography. New York: Putnam's,
1973. Rev. by M. E. Goldstein, JMH, 48(Mar 1976):132-5.

Bernardo, Flavio di. Un vescovo umanista alla Corte Pontificia:
Giannantonio Campano (1429-1477). Rome: Gregorian U
Press, 1975. Rev. by J. R. L. Highfield, JEccH, 27(Jl
1976):315-16.

Bernstein, Burton. Thurber. New York: Dodd, Mead, 1975.
Rev. by P. G. Miller, Jr., OH, 85(Spr 1976):178-9.

Bernstein, Harry. Dom Pedro II. New York: Twayne, 1973.
Rev. by P. L. Eisenberg, HAHR, 56(Feb 1976):135-8.

Berselli, Aldo. L'opinione pubblica inglese e l'avvento del fascismo
(1919-1925). Milan: Franco Angeli Editore, 1971. Rev. by
A. W. Gendebien, AHR, 81(Apr 1976):391.

Bershady, Harold J. Ideology and Social Knowledge. Oxford Blackwell, 1973. Rev. by W. E. de Villiers-Westfall, CHR, 57
(Je 1976):174-6.

Berza, M., et al., eds. Romanian-Bulgarian Relations in the
Course of the Centuries (12th-19th Centuries). Bucharest:
Editura Academiei Republicii Socialiste România, 1971. Rev.
by S. Fischer-Galaţi, AHR, 81(Feb 1976):181-2.

Best, Gary Dean. The Politics of American Individualism: Herbert
Hoover in Transition, 1918-1921. Westport, Conn.: Greenwood, 1975. Rev. by R. H. Zieger, 81(Oct 1976):800-10;
D. M. Shockley, AI, 43(Fall 1976):478-80; J. T. Gay, HRNB,
4(May/Je 1976):140; A. S. Link, JAH, 63(Dec 1976):757-8.

Betenson, Lula Parker. Butch Cassidy, My Brother. Provo:
BYU Press, 1975. Rev. by J. Springer, UHQ, 44(Win 1976):
94-5.

Bethell, Nicholas. The Last Secret: Forcible Repatriation to Russia 1944-7. London: André Deutsch, 1974. Rev. by A.
Polonsky, History, 61(Je 1976):330-1.

Bethge, Eberhard and Ronald C. D. Jasper, eds. An der Schwelle
zum Gespaltenen Europa. Stuttgart: Kreug Verlag, 1974.
Rev. by K. von Klemperer, JMH, 48(Mar 1976):138-40.

Bettelheim, Charles. Cultural Revolution and Industrial Organization in China. New York: Monthly Review Press, 1974. Rev.
by S. Uhalley, Jr., JAAS, 11(Jl-Oct 1976):229-31.

Betts, John Rickards. America's Sporting Heritage: 1850-1950.
Reading, Mass.: Addison-Wesley, 1974. Rev. by R. D.
Mandell, AHR, 81(Apr 1976):448-9.

Betts, Raymond F. The False Dawn: European Imperialism in the
Nineteenth Century. Minneapolis: U Minn Press, 1975.
Rev. by R. V. Pierard, HRNB, 4(Aug 1976):199.

Betzler, Paul. Die Fibeln in Süddeutschland, Österreich und der
Schweiz I. München: Beck'sche Verlagsbuchhandlung, 1974.
Rev. by H. L. Thomas, AJA, 80(Win 1976):88-9.

Beukel, Erik. The Social Democrats and the Problem of the Sta-
tioning of Foreign Troops: 1952-53; A Political Decision of
Security. Odense: Odense U Press, 1974. Rev. by F. J.
Bowman, AHR, 81(Feb 1976):163-4.

Beyrau, Dietrich. Russische Orientpolitik und die Entstehung des
deutschen Kaiserreiches 1866-1870/71. Wiesbaden: Otto
Harrassowitz, 1974. Rev. by F. R. Bridge, EHR, 91(Jl
1976):609-11.

Bezou, Henry C. Metairie, a Tongue of Land to Pasture. Gretna,
La.: Pelican, 1973. Rev. by C. E. Nolan, CaHR, 62(Jl
1976):480-1.

Bezucha, Robert J. The Lyon Uprising of 1834: Social and Politi-
cal Conflict in the Early July Monarchy. Cambridge, Mass.:
Harvard U Press, 1974. Rev. by D. P. Resnick, AHR, 81
(Je 1976):608-9; D. J. Walkowitz, JIH, 7(Aut 1976):335-8.

Bhana, Surendra. The United States and the Development of the
Puerto Rican Status Question, 1936-1968. Lawrence: U Kan
Press, 1975. Rev. by E. J. Berbusse, HAHR, 56(Feb 1976):
163-5; J. A. Gaudet, JAH, 63(Sep 1976):460; T. R. Clark,
PHR, 45(Nov 1976):629-30.

Bhargava, P. K. Taxation of Agriculture in India. Bombay:
Vora, 1976. Rev. by T. Shingh, IQ, 32(Jl-Sep 1976):371-2.

Bhatia, Krishna. Indira: A Biography of Prime Minister Gandhi.
New York: Praeger, 1974. Rev. by L. A. Gordon, AHR,
81(Apr 1976):436-7; A. Z. Rubenstein, CurH, 70(Apr 1976):
179, 184.

Bianco, Carla. The Two Rosetos. Bloomington: Ind U Press,
1974. Rev. by J. Gowaski, PH, 43(Apr 1976):189-90.

Bickley, R. Bruce, Jr. The Method of Melville's Short Fiction.
Durham, N.C.: Duke U Press, 1975. Rev. by C. Al-
banese, NEQ, 49(Sep 1976):492-4.

Biddle, Sheila. Bolingbroke and Harley. London: Allen and
Unwin, 1975. Rev. by H. T. Dickinson, History, 61(Je
1976):293.

Bidwell, Robin. Morocco Under Colonial Rule: French Administration of Tribal Areas, 1912-1956. London: Frank Cass,
1973. Rev. by K. Perkins, IJMES, 7(Apr 1976):310-12.

Biedrzycki, Emil. History of the Poles in Bukovina. Cracow:
Universytetu Jagiellonskiego, 1973. Rev. by L. J. Haczyn-
ski, AHR, 81(Je 1976):628-9.

Bieler, Ludwig, ed. see O'Meara, John J., ed.

Biezais, Haralds, ed. New Religions. Stockholm: Almqvist and
Wiksell, 1975. Rev. by S. S. Sizer, CH, 45(Sep 1976):401-2.

Bigler, Robert M. The Politics of German Protestantism: The
Rise of the Protestant Church Elite in Prussia, 1815-1848.
Berkeley: U Cal Press, 1972. Rev. by W. O. Shanahan,
CaHR, 62(Apr 1976):314-15.

Bigsby, C. W. E. Superculture: American Popular Culture and
Europe. London: Paul Elek, 1975. Rev. by P. Messent,
JAmS, 10(Dec 1976):396-7.

Bilbao, Jon see Douglass, William A.

Billig, Joseph. Les Camps de concentration dans l'economie du
Reich hitlérien. Paris: Presses Universitaires de France,
1973. Rev. by A. S. Milward, JMH, 48(Sep 1976):567-8.

Billings, Warren M., ed. The Old Dominion in the Seventeenth
Century: A Documentary History of Virginia, 1606-1689.
Chapel Hill: UNC Press, 1975. Rev. by W. S. Price, Jr.,
AmArc, 39(Jan 1976):57-8; J. D. Leonard, WMQ, 33(Jan
1976):170-1.

35   BILLINGTON

Billington, Monroe Lee. The Political South in the Twentieth Century. New York: Scribner's, 1975. Rev. by H. D. Graham,
AHR, 81(Apr 1976):460; J. W. Silver, FHQ, 54(Jan 1975):
410-11; J. S. Ezell, JAH, 62(Mar 1976):1029-30.

Billington, Ray Allen, comp. Allen Nevins on History. New York:
Scribner's, 1975. Rev. by M. I. Elzy, AmArc, 39(Apr 1976):
213; C. V. Woodward, RAH, 4(Mar 1976):25-6; S. G. Ellsworth, WHQ, 7(Oct 1976):425-6; O. K. Rice, WVH, 38(Oct
1976):66-8.

_____, comp. see Nevins, Allan

Binder, Frederick M. The Age of the Common School, 1830-1865.
New York: Wiley, 1974. Rev. by J. Messerli, AHR, 81(Je
1976):666-7.

_____. Coal Age Empire: Pennsylvania Coal and Its Utilization
to 1860. Harrisburg: Pennsylvania Historical and Museum
Commission, 1974. Rev. by J. H. Madison, AHR, 81(Oct
1976):983-4.

Binder, Hans-Otto. Reich und Einzelstaaten Wahrend der Kanzel-
schaft Bismarcks 1871-1890. Tubingen: J. C. B. Mohr,
1971. Rev. by W. Carr, ESR, 6(Jl 1976):389-92.

Binfield, Clyde. George Williams and the YMCA: A Study in Victorian Social Attitudes. London: Heinemann, 1973. Rev. by
J. H. Y. Briggs, History, 61(Je 1976):308.

Biobaku, S. O., ed. Sources of Yoruba History. New York: Oxford U Press, 1973. Rev. by A. H. M. Kirk-Greene, Africa,
46(Num 1, 1976):102; M. Crowder, AHR, 81(Oct 1976):923-4.

Biondi, Albano. L'Autorità della storia profana. Turin: Giappichelli, 1973. Rev. by P. Burke, EHR, 91(Jan 1976):192.

Birchall, Ann, ed. see Crossland, R. A., ed.

Bird, Caroline. Enterprising Women. New York: Norton, 1976.
Rev. by W. E. Brownlee, BHR, 50(Sum 1976):227-9; D. C.
Brown, JSH, 42(Nov 1976):607-8.

Birley, Anthony. Septimius Severus: The African Emperor. Garden City, N.Y.: Doubleday, 1972. Rev. by J. Linderski,
AHR, 81(Oct 1976):830-1.

Bisson, T. A. Yenan in June 1937: Talks with the Communist
Leaders. Berkeley: U Cal, 1973. Rev. by J. P. Harrison,
AHR, 81(Oct 1976):938-9.

Bjork, Kenneth O., ed. Norwegian-American Studies. Northfield,
Minn.: Norwegian American Historical Assn., 1974. Rev. by

J. Dahlie, PNQ, 67(Jan 1976):41-2.

Black, Cyril E., et al. The Modernization of Japan and Russia: A Comparative Study. New York: Free Press, 1975. Rev. by W. W. Rostow, AHR, 81(Oct 1976):940; M. Patoski, HRÑB, 4(Apr 1976):129.

Black, Esther B. Rancho Cucamonga and Dona Merced. Redlands, Cal.: San Bernardino County Museum Associates, 1975. Rev. by S. Jackson, SCQ, 58(Fall 1976):432-4.

Black, Hugo, Jr. My Father: A Remembrance. New York: Random House, 1975. Rev. by D. Roper, Historian, 39(Nov 1976):164-6.

Black, J. L. Nicholas Karamzin and Russian Society in the Nineteenth Century: A Study in Russian Political and Historical Thought. Toronto: U Tor Press, 1975. Rev. by C. W. Reddel, AHR, 81(Oct 1976):908.

Black, Jeannette, ed. The Blathwayt Atlas. Vols. 1 and 2. Providence, R.I.: Brown U Press, 1970, 1975. Rev. by W. E. Washburn, AHR, 81(Apr 1976):385-6.

Blackburn, Joyce. George Wythe of Williamsburg. New York: Harper & Row, 1975. Rev. by W. E. Hemphill, VMHB, 84 (Jan 1976):110-111.

Blacker, Carmen. The Catalpa Bow. A Study of Shamanistic Practices in Japan. London: George Allen and Unwin, 1975. Rev. by R. J. Smith, JJS, 2(Sum 1976):474-8; M. Pye, MAS, 10(Oct 1976):621-2.

Blackmore, John T. Ernst Mach: His Work, Life, and Influence. Berkeley: U Cal Press, 1972. Rev. by S. Goldberg, AHR, 81(Je 1976):563.

Bladen, V. W. From Adam Smith to Maynard Keynes: The Heritage of Political Economy. Toronto: U Tor Press, 1974. Rev. by R. C. McIvor, CHR, 57(Je 1976):176-7.

Blainey, Geoffrey. Triumph of the Nomads: A History of Aboriginal Australia. Woodstock, N.Y.: Overlook, 1976. Rev. by A. S. Trickett, HRNB, 4(Sep 1976):222-3.

Blair, Robert. Tales of the Superstitions: The Origins of the Lost Dutchman Legend. Tempe: Ariz Historical Foundation, 1975. Rev. by W. H. Lyon, A & W, 18(Aut 1976):293-4; B. H. Granger, JAriH, 17(Spr 1976):108-9; R. W. Paul, NMHR, 51(Jl 1976):256.

Blake, Lord. The Office of Prime Minister. Oxford: Oxford U Press, 1975. Rev. by D. Southgate, History, 61(Oct 1976): 490.

Blakemore, Harold. British Nitrates and Chilean Politics, 1886-
  1896: Balmaçeda and North. Highlands, N.J.: Humanities
  Press, 1974. Rev. by F. B. Pike, AHR, 81(Oct 1976):1014-
  15.

Blanc, Cécile, ed. Origène: Commentaire sur s. Jean, Tome 3
  (Livré 13). Paris: Editions du Cerf, 1975. Rev. by P.
  Henry, CH, 45(Sep 1976):374-5.

Blanchard-Lemée, Michèle. Maisons à Mosaiques du quartier central de Djemila. Aiz-en-Provence: Editions Ophrys, 1975.
  Rev. by D. J. Smith, AJA, 80(Fall 1976):444.

Blanco, Hugo. Land or Death: The Peasant Struggle in Peru.
  New York: Pathfinder, 1972. Rev. by H. Dietz, HAHR, 56
  (Feb 1976):184.

Blancpain, Jean-Pierre. Les Allemands au Chili, 1816-1945.
  Cologne: Böhlau Verlag Köln Wien, 1974. Rev. by P.
  Vayssiere, HAHR, 56(May 1976):346-8; E. H. Korth, TAm,
  33(Jl 1976):171-3.

Blanning, T. C. W. Reform and Revolution in Mainz, 1743-1803.
  New York: Cam U Press, 1974. Rev. by J. F. Flynn, AHR,
  81(Feb 1976):165-6; W. O. Henderson, BH, 17(Jan 1975):85-
  6; R. Schulmann, JMH, 48(Je 1976):343-5.

Blassingame, John W. The Slave Community: Plantation Life in
  the Antebellum South. New York: Oxford U Press, 1972.
  Rev. by J. G. Taylor, CWTI, 15(May 1976):46.

Blau, Joseph L. Judaism in America from Curiosity to Third
  Faith. Chicago: U Chicago Press, 1976. Rev. by M. I.
  Urofsky, HRNB, 4(Aug 1976):186-7; R. J. Wachman, JAH,
  63(Dec 1976):747.

Blet, Pierre, et al., eds. Actes et documents du Saint Siège
  relatifs à la seconde guerre mondiale. Vol. 9. Rome:
  Libreria Editrice Vaticana, 1975. Rev. by J. J. Hughes,
  CH, 45(Sep 1975):396-7.

_____, et al., eds. Le Saint Siège et les victimes de la guerre,
  Janvier 1941-Décember 1942. Vatican City: Libreria Editrice Vaticana, 1974. Rev. by J. Lukacs, CaHR, 62(Oct
  1976):667-8.

Blevins, Leon W. The Young Voter's Manual: A Topical Dictionary of American Government and Politics. Totowa, N.J.:
  Littlefield, Adams, 1973. Rev. by M. W. Mansfield, JCS,
  17(Spr 1975):348-9.

Bley, Helmut. Bebel und die Strategie der Kriegsverhütung 1904-
  1913. Göttingen: Vandenhoeck und Rupprecht, 1975. Rev. by

G. Eley, HJ, 19(Mar 1976):299-302.

Blickle, P. Die Revolution von 1525. Munich: R. Oldenbourg Verlag, 1975. Rev. by G. D. Ramsay, EHR, 91(Oct 1976): 904.

Blinkhorn, Martin. Carlism and Crisis in Spain, 1931-1939. New York: Cam U Press, 1975. Rev. by G. Jackson, AHR, 81 (Oct 1976):875; A. J. Ryder, History, 61(Oct 1976):472-3.

Bliss, Michael. A Living Profit: Studies in the Social History of Canadian Business, 1883-1911. Toronto: McClelland and Stewart, 1974. Rev. by D. Cole, AHR, 81(Apr 1976):472.

Bloch, Marc. Slavery and Serfdom in the Middle Ages: Selected Essays. Berkeley: U Cal Press, 1975. Rev. by R. E. Sullivan, HRNB, 4(Mar 1976):108.

Block, Seymour Stanton. Benjamin Franklin: His Wit, Wisdom, and Women. New York: Hastings House, 1975. Rev. by W. J. Bell, Jr., NEQ, 49(Mar 1976):134-6.

Bloom, John Porter, ed. and comp. The Territorial Papers of the United States. Vol. XXVIII. Washington: National Archives and Records Service, 1975. Rev. by F. P. Prucha, JAH, 63(Dec 1976):671-2; R. C. Nesbit, WHQ, 7(Oct 1976):429-30; H. D. Moser, WMH, 60(Aut 1976):55-6.

Bloomer, D. C. Life and Writings of Amelia Bloomer. New York: Schocken, 1975. Rev. by K. K. Sklar, AHR, 81(Je 1976):672-3; E. Stansfield, Mankind, 5(Apr 1976):69-70.

Bluche, Frederic. Le plébiscite des Cent-jours (Avril-mai 1815). Geneva: Librairie Droz, 1974. Rev. by P. Dawson, AHR, 81(Je 1976):608.

Blum, Carol. Diderot: The Virtue of a Philosopher. New York: Viking, 1974. Rev. by V. W. Topazio, JHP, 14(Oct 1976): 481-3.

Blume, Friedrich, et al. Protestant Church Music: A History. New York: Norton, 1974. Rev. by K. C. Sessions, CH, 45 (Sep 1976):400-1.

Blumenson, Martin. The Patton Papers: 1940-1945. Boston: Houghton Mifflin, 1974. Rev. by J. K. Mahon, AHR, 81 (Feb 1976):218.

Blumenthal, Henry. American and French Culture, 1800-1900: Interchanges in Art, Science, Literature and Society. Baton Rouge: LSU Press, 1976. Rev. by L. E. Ambrosius, HRNB, 4(Sep 1976):214; H. W. Morgan, JAH, 63(Dec 1976):707-8; M. L. Brown, Jr., JSH, 42(Nov 1976):587-8.

Blumstein, James F. and Benjamin Walter, eds. Growing Metrop-
    olis: Aspects of Development in Nashville. Nashville, Tenn. :
    Vanderbilt U Press, 1975. Rev. by R. Flowerdew, JAmS,
    10(Aug 1976):277-8.

Boardman, John. Attic Red Figure Vases, the Archaic Period.
    London: Thames and Hudson, 1975. Rev. by R. M. Cook,
    Antiquity, 50(Je 1976):166-7.

_____. Corpus Vasorum Antiquorum, Great Britain fasc. 14.
    Oxford: Oxford U Press, 1975. Rev. by D. von Bothmer,
    AJA, 80(Sum 1976):316-17.

Boarman, Patrick M. , ed. Trade with China: Assessments by
    Leading Businessmen and Scholars. New York: Praeger,
    1974. Rev. by S. B. Lubman, CQ, May 1976, pp. 379-82.

Bodde, Derk. Festivals in Classical China: New Year and Other
    Annual Observances During the Han Dynasty 206 B. C. -A. D.
    220. Princeton, N. J. : Prin U Press, 1975. Rev. by J. L.
    Dull, JAS, 36(Nov 1976):124-6.

Bode, Frederick A. Protestantism in the New South: North Caro-
    lina Baptists and Methodists in Political Crisis 1894-1903.
    Charlottesville: U Press Va, 1975. Rev. by S. C. Pearson,
    Jr. , CH, 45(Sep 1976):393-4.

Bodenheimer, Edgar. Power, Law, and Society: A Study of the
    Will to Power and the Will to Law. New York: Crane, Rus-
    sak, 1973. Rev. by L. Pospisil, AA, 78(Je 1976):402-3.

Boese, Donald L. John C. Greenway and the Opening of the West-
    ern Mesabi. Grand Rapids, Mich. : Greenway, 1975. Rev.
    by D. A. Walker, MinnH, 45(Spr 1976):37-8.

Bog, Ingomar, et al. Wirtschaftliche und soziale Strukturen im
    säkularen Wandel: Festschrift für Wilhelm Abel zum 70.
    Geburtstag. Hanover: Verlag M. and H. Schaper, 1974.
    Rev. by M. P. Fleischer, AgH, 50(Apr 1976):427-9.

Bogart, Leo. Premises for Propaganda: The United States In-
    formation Agency's Operating Assumptions in the Cold War.
    New York: Free Press, 1976. Rev. by P. M. Buzanski,
    HRNB, 4(Aug 1976):192-3.

Bogue, Allan G. and Robert Taylor, eds. The University of Wis-
    consin: One Hundred and Twenty-Five Years. Madison: U
    Wis Press, 1975. Rev. by W. U. Solberg, JAH, 63(Sep
    1976):470-1.

_____, ed. see Aydelotte, W. O. , ed.

Bogumil, Karlotto. Das Bistum Halberstadt im 12. Jahrhundert.

Cologne: Böhlau Verlag, 1972. Rev. by J. B. Freed, CaHR, 62(Jan 1976):77-8.

Bohm, Ekkehard. Überseehandel und Flottenbau. Hanseatische Kaufmannschaft und deutsche Seerüstung, 1879-1902. Düsseldorf: Bertelsmann Universtätsverlag, 1972. Rev. by G. D. Feldman, JMH, 48(Mar 1976):168-9.

Boia, Lucian. Eugen Brote (1850-1912). Bucharest: Editura litera, 1974. Rev. by P. Eidelberg, AHR, 81(Apr 1976):420.

Bojarska, Barbara. Extermination of the Polish Intelligentsia in the Gdańsk-Pomerania Region (September-December 1939). Poznań: Instytut zachodni, 1972. Rev. by J. Karski, AHR, 81(Je 1976):630.

Boles, John B., ed. Maryland Heritage: Five Baltimore Institutions Celebrate the American Bicentennial. Baltimore: Maryland Historical Society, 1976. Rev. by Sister M. V. Geiger, VMHB, 84(Oct 1976):499-501.

Bolitho, Harold. Treasures Among Men: The Fudai Daimyo in Tokugawa Japan. New Haven, Conn.: Yale U Press, 1974. Rev. by J. B. Cornell, AHR, 81(Apr 1976):433-4.

Bolkhovitinov, N. N. Russko-amerikanskie otonoshenii, 1815-1832. Moscow: "Nauka," 1975. Rev. by B. Dmytryshyn, JAH, 63(Sep 1975):403-5.

_____. Stanovlenie russko-amerikanskikh otonoshenii, 1775-1815. Moscow: "Nauka," 1966. Rev. by B. Dmytryshyn, JAH, 63 (Sep 1976):403-5.

Bolkosky, Sidney M. The Distorted Image: German Jewish Perceptions of Germans and Germany, 1918-1935. New York: Elsevier, 1975. Rev. by W. Braatz, HRNB, 4(Jan 1976): 68; J. Remak, HRNB, 4(Feb 1976):90.

Bollen, J. D. Australian Baptists: A Religious Minority. London: Baptist Historical Society, 1975. Rev. by F. H. Thomas, Jr., BHH, 11(Apr 1976):125.

Boller, Paul F., Jr. American Transcendentalism, 1830-1860: An Intellectual Inquiry. New York: Putnam's, 1974. Rev. by P. K. Conkin, JAH, 62(Mar 1976):988-9.

Bóna, István see Banner, János

Bonamici, Marisa. I Buccheri con Figurazioni Graffite. Florence: L. Olschki, 1974. Rev. by M. A. Del Chiaro, AJA, 80(Win 1976):97-8.

Bond, Brian. France and Belgium 1939-1940 (The Politics and

Strategy of the Second World War). London: Davis-Poynter, 1975. Rev. by P.-H. Laurent, AHR, 81(Apr 1976):381-2; A. J. P. Taylor, EHR, 91(Apr 1976):467-8; P. M. H. Bell, History, 61(Oct 1976):475.

_____, ed. Chief of Staff: The Diaries of Lieutenant General Sir Henry Pownall. Vol. 2. London: Leo Cooper, 1974. Rev. by M. Howard, EHR, 91(Apr 1976):464-5; J. Gooch, History, 61(Oct 1976):475-6.

Bone, Ann, trans. The Bolsheviks and the October Revolution: Minutes of the Central Committee of the Russian Social-Democratic Labour Party (Bolsheviks), August 1917-February 1918. London: Pluto, 1974. Rev. by R. Pethybridge, History, 61(Feb 1976):140.

Bonelli, Franco. La crisi del 1907: Una tappa dello sviluppo industriale in Italia. Turin: Fondazione Luigi Einaudi, 1971. Rev. by S. B. Clough, AHR, 81(Apr 1976):415-16.

Bonelli, M. L. Righini and William R. Shea, eds. Reason, Experiment, and Mysticism in the Scientific Revolution. New York: Science History Publications, 1975. Rev. by J. L. Heilbron, HRNB, 4(May/Je 1976):149-50.

Bones, Jim, Jr. see Graves, John

Bonfante, Larissa. Etruscan Dress. Baltimore: JHU Press, 1976. Rev. by R. H. Lytton, HRNB, 4(Aug 1976):198.

Bontinck, François and Koen Janssen, eds. and trans. L'Autobiographie de Hamed ben Mohammed el-Murjebi Tippu Tip (ca 1840-1905). Bruxelles: Académie Royale des Sciences d'outre-Mer, 1974. Rev. by A. Roberts, Africa, 46(Num 1, 1976):104-5; G. A. Akinola, EHR, 91(Jl 1976):666-7.

Bonwetsch, Bernd. Kriegsallianz und Wirtschaftsinteressen: Russland in den Wirtschaftsplänen Englands und Frankreichs, 1914-1917. Gütersloh: Bertelsmann Universitätsverlag, 1973. Rev. by S. R. Williamson, Jr., AHR, 81(Oct 1976):909.

Booker, J. Essex and the Industrial Revolution. Chelmsford: Essex County Council, 1974. Rev. by D. Read, EHR, 91(Jan 1976):213.

Boon, George C. Silchester: The Roman Town of Calleva. Newton Abbott: David and Charles, 1974. Rev. by A. L. F. Rivet, EHR, 91(Jan 1976):168-9; S. I. Oost, Historian, 38(Feb 1976):320.

Boon, James A. From Symbolism to Structuralism: Levi Strauss in a Literary Tradition. New York: Harper and Row, 1972. Rev. by I. Rossi, AA, 78(Mar 1976):145.

Boorstin, Daniel J.   The Exploring Spirit: America and the World
Then and Now.   New York: Random House, 1976.   Rev. by
C. E. Finn, Jr., Commentary, 62(Sep 1976):126-8; R. Wog-
gan, Smithsonian, 7(Je 1976):112, 114, 116.

Booty, John E., ed.   The Book of Common Prayer 1559, The
Elizabethan Prayer Book.   Charlottesville, Va.:   U Virginia
Press, 1976.   Rev. by R. C. Martin, HMPEC, 45(Dec 1976):
462-3.

Borah, Woodrow see Cook, Sherburne F.

Borg, Dorothy, Shumpei Okamoto, and Dale K. A. Finlayson, eds.
Pearl Harbor as History: Japanese-American Relations,
1931-1941.   New York: Columbia U Press, 1973.   Rev. by
G. M. Wilson, JAH, 63(Je 1976):185-7.

Borgiotti, Alberto and Cesare Gori.   La guerra aerea in Africa
Settentrionale: Assalto dal cielo 1940-41; 1942-43.   2 vols.
Modena: S. T. E. M.-Mucchi, 1972, 1973.   Rev. by D.
Koenig, AHR, 81(Apr 1976):364-5.

Borisov, O. B. and B. T. Koloskov.   Soviet-Chinese Relations,
1945-1970.   Bloomington: Ind U Press, 1975.   Rev. by G.
A. Lensen, AHR, 81(Oct 1976):913; F. H. Tucker, HRNB,
4(Feb 1976):88.

Bornet, Vaughn Davis see Robinson, Edgar Eugene

Bose, Arun Coomer.   Indian Revolutionaries Abroad, 1905-1922:
In the Background of International Developments.   Patna:
Bharati Bhawan, 1971.   Rev. by N. G. Barrier, AHR, 81
(Je 1976):647.

_____.   Marxian and Post-Marxian Political Economy.   Balti-
more: Penguin, 1975.   Rev. by M. Bronfenbrenner, JEH,
36(Sep 1976):761-3.

Bosl, Karl, ed.   Lebensbilder zur Geschichte der böhmischen
Länder.   Munchen/Wien: R. Oldenbourg Verlag, 1974.   Rev.
by R. V. Luza, EEQ, 10(Mar 1976):129-30.

_____, et al.   Biographisches Wörterbuch zur deutschen
Geschichte.   Munich: Francke Verlag, 1974.   Rev. by H.
P. Liebel, AHR, 81(Feb 1976):165; H. M. Scott, History,
61(Feb 1976):88.

Bossy, John.   The English Catholic Community, 1570-1850.   London: Darton, Longman and Todd, 1975.   Rev. by E. Duffy,
JEccH, 27(Oct 1976):447-50.

Botterall, Anthony F., ed. see Hunter, Guy, ed.

Bottomore, T. B. Sociology as a Social Criticism. New York:
Pantheon, 1974. Rev. A. Beteille, IQ, 32(Apr-Je 1976):
232-3.

Botz, Gerhard. Die Eingliederung Österreichs in das Deutsche
Reich: Planung und Verwirklichung des politisch-adminis-
trativen Anschlusses (1938-1940). Vienna: Europaverlag,
1972. Rev. by S. B. Winters, AHR, 81(Feb 1976):174-5.

Bouju, Paul M., ed. see Pacaut, Marcel, ed.

Bourcier, Elisabeth, ed. The Diary of Sir Simonds D'Ewes 1622-
24. Paris: Didier, 1974. Rev. by A. G. R. Smith, History, 61(Je 1976):285.

Bourdeaux, Michael, ed. Georgi Vins: Testament from Prison.
Elgin, Ill.: David C. Cook, 1975. Rev. by C. W. Deweese,
BHH, 11(Apr 1976):126.

Bourgeois, Albert. Lépreux et maladreries du Pas-de-Calaix
(Xe-XVIIIe siècles): Psychologie collective et institutions
charitables. Arras: Commission Departementale des Monuments Historiques du Pas-de-Calais, 1972. Rev. by R. C.
Howard, AHR, 81(Feb 1976):113.

Bourgeois, Daniel. Le Troisième Reich et la Suisse, 1933-1941.
Neuchâtel: Editions de la Baconniere, 1974. Rev. by G. R.
Kleinfeld, AHR, 81(Apr 1976):413.

Bourne, Eulalia. Ranch Schoolteacher. Tucson: U Ariz Press,
1974. Rev. by S. Hernandez, JOW, 15(Jan 1976):126; D.
Welsh, NDH, 43(Sum 1976):45.

Bouvard, Marguerite. The International Community Movement.
Port Washington, N.Y.: Kennikat, 1975. Rev. in AS, 16
(Fall 1975):99-100.

Bowen, Catherine Drinker. The Most Dangerous Man in America:
Scenes from the Life of Benjamin Franklin. Boston: Atlantic
Monthly, 1974. Rev. by M. Savelle, AHR, 81(Feb 1976):
205; H. Alexander, Smithsonian, 6(Mar 1975):108; L. Gerlach, PH, 43(Oct 1976):372-4.

Bowers, John Z. Western Medicine in a Chinese Palace, Peking
Union Medical College 1917-1951. New York: Josiah Macy,
Jr., Foundation, 1972. Rev. by J. N. Hawkins, JAAS, 11
(Jl-Oct 1976):215-19.

Bowers, William L. The Country Life Movement in America,
1900-1920. Port Washington, N.Y.: Kennikat, 1974. Rev.
in AS, 16(Fall 1975):100.

Bowker, Alan, ed. The Social Criticism of Stephen Leacock: The

Unsolved Riddle of Social Justice and Other Essays. Toronto:
U Tor Press, 1973. Rev. by I. R. Robertson, CHR, 57(Je
1976):208-10.

Bowle, John. The Imperial Achievement: The Rise and Transformation of the British Empire. London: Secker and Warburg, 1974. Rev. by D. K. Fieldhouse, History, 61(Feb
1976):85-6.

Bowler, R. Arthur. Logistics and the Failure of the British Army
in America, 1775-1783. Princeton, N.J.: Prin U Press,
1975. Rev. by H. H. Jackson, GHQ, 60(Spr 1976):80-1; P.
Mackesy, History, 61(Oct 1976):401-2; P. D. Nelson, JAH,
62(Mar 1976):975-6; W. R. Higgins, JSH, 42(Feb 1976):113-
14; F. C. Mevers, NCHR, 53(Win 1976):89-91; D. C. Twining,
OH, 85(Spr 1976):161-2; G. A. Billias, NEQ, 49(Mar 1976):
167-9; R. H. Kohn, RAH, 4(Je 1976):178-83.

Bowles, Samuel and Herbert Gintis. Schooling in Capitalist America.
New York: Basic Books, 1976. Rev. by C. E. Finn, Jr.,
Commentary, 61(Je 1976):72-5.

Bowman, Albert Hall. The Struggle for Neutrality: Franco-Ameri-
can Diplomacy During the Federalist Era. Knoxville: U Tenn
Press, 1974. Rev. by G. Seed, EHR, 91(Apr 1976):438;
R. E. Smith, FCHQ, 50(Apr 1976):94-5.

Bowman, Lynn. Los Angeles: Epic of a City. Berkeley: Howell-
North, 1974. Rev. by A. Rolle, PHR, 45(Feb 1976):135-6;
B. Luckingham, SCQ, 58(Fall 1976):431-2.

Bowron, Bernard R., Jr. Henry B. Fuller of Chicago: The Or-
deal of a Genteel Realist in Ungenteel America. Westport,
Conn.: Greenwood, 1974. Rev. by J. Tomsich, JAH, 63
(Sep 1976):434-5; D. F. Tingley, JISHS, 69(May 1976):149.

Bowser, Frederick P. The African Slave in Colonial Peru, 1524-
1650. Stanford, Cal.: Stanford U Press, 1974. B. Orlove,
AgH, 50(Jl 1976):528-32; J. Lockhart, AHR, 81(Feb 1976):
225-6.

Boxer, C. R. Anglo-Dutch Wars of the Seventeenth Century. London: H.M.S.O., 1975. Rev. by H. Dunthorne, History, 61
(Feb 1976):114-15.

_____. Women in Iberian Expansion Overseas, 1415-1815:
Some Facts, Fancies and Personalities. New York: Oxford
U Press, 1975. Rev. by C. Gibson, AHR, 81(Oct 1976):
1009; M. Newitt, History, 61(Je 1976):266-7.

Boyajian, Dickran H. Armenia: The Case for a Forgotten Genocide. Westwood, N.J.: Educational Book Crafters, 1972.
Rev. by R. H. Dekmejian, AHR, 81(Oct 1976):916-17.

Boyd, Doug. Rolling Thunder: A Personal Exploration into the
Secret Healing Powers of an American Indian Medicine Man.
New York: Random House, 1974. Rev. by A. Beidler, AIQ,
2(Sum 1976):145-6.

Boyd, James W. Satan and Māra: Christian and Buddhist Symbols
of Evil. Leiden: E. J. Brill, 1975. Rev. by F. E. Reynolds, JAS, 36(Nov 1976):119-20.

Boyd, Robin H. S. India and the Latin Captivity of the Church:
The Cultural Context of the Gospel. New York: Cam U
Press, 1975. Rev. by T. Bachmann, CH, 45(Mar 1976):125;
J. Breckenridge, JCS, 18(Aut 1976):588-9.

Boyer, Paul and Stephen Nissenbaum. Salem Possessed: The Social Origins of Witchcraft. Cambridge, Mass.: Harvard U
Press, 1974. Rev. by C. Brooks, EHR, 91(Jan 1976):202-3;
R. Thompson, JAmS, 10(Apr 1976):109-10; J. Butler, JSoH,
8(Spr 1975):151-3.

_____ see James, Edward T.

Boyer, Richard Everett. Le gran inundación: Vida y sociedad
en la ciudad de México, 1629-1638. México: SepSetentas,
1975. Rev. by W. M. Mathes, HAHR, 56(Aug 1976):506-7.

Bracher, Frederick, ed. Letters of Sir George Etherege. Berkeley:
U Cal Press, 1974. Rev. by J. P. Kenyon, EHR, 91(Jan
1976):202.

Brack, Gene M. Mexico Views Manifest Destiny, 1821-1846: An
Essay on the Origins of the Mexican War. Albuquerque:
U NM Press, 1976. Rev. by J. Z. Vasquez, HAHR, 56(Nov
1976):656-7; T. Schoonover, HRNB, 4(Apr 1976):126.

Brackman, Arnold C. The Last Emperor. New York: Scribner's,
1975. Rev. by S. Karnow, Smithsonian, 6(Jan 1976):106-8.

Bradfute, Richard Wells. The Court of Private Land Claims: The
Adjudication of Spanish and Mexican Land Grant Titles, 1891-
1904. Albuquerque: U NM Press, 1975. Rev. by F. J.
Yonce, A & W, 18(Sum 1976):205-7; M. F. Taylor, WHQ, 7
(Apr 1976):202-3.

Bradley, Glenn D. The Story of the Pony Express: An Account of
the Most Remarkable Mail Service Ever in Existence, and Its
Place in History. Detroit: Gale Research, 1974. Rev. by B.
D. Ledbetter, JOW, 15(Apr 1976):131.

Bradley, Ian, ed. see Simon, Brian, ed.

Bradley, John. Civil War in Russia 1917-1920. London: Batsford,
1975. Rev. by R. Pethybridge, History, 61(Je 1976):318-19;
N. Saul, HRNB, 4(May/Je 1976):155.

Bradshaw, Barbara, ed. <u>see</u> Faderman, Lillian, ed.

Bradshaw, Brendan. <u>The Dissolution of Religious Orders in Ire-</u>
<u>land Under Henry VIII.</u> New York: Cam U Press, 1974.
Rev. by W. J. Jones, AHR, 81(Feb 1976):150; J. Bossy,
History, 61(Je 1976):272-3; W. R. Jones, JCS, 17(Spr 1975):
302-5.

Brady, David W. <u>Congressional Voting in a Partisan Era: A</u>
<u>Study of the McKinley Houses and a Comparison to the Modern</u>
<u>House of Representatives.</u> Lawrence: U Kan Press, 1973.
Rev. by J. L. McCarthy, JIH, 7(Sum 1976):181-4.

Braeman, John, et al., eds. <u>The New Deal.</u> Vols. 1 and 2.
Columbus: Ohio St U Press, 1975. Rev. by O. L.
Graham, Jr., AHR, 81(Oct 1976):996-7; R. W. Larson,
Historian, 39(Nov 1976):162-3; F. Annunciata, IMH, 72(Je
1976):283-5; F. Freidel, JAH, 63(Dec 1976):766-8; P. K.
Conkin, JSH, 42(Feb 1976):132-3.

Brailsford, John. <u>Early Celtic Masterpieces from Britain in the</u>
<u>British Museum.</u> London: British Museum, 1975. Rev. by
S. Piggott, Antiquity, 50(Je 1976):151-2.

Brain, Robert <u>see</u> Eyongetah, Tambi

Branca, Patricia. <u>Silent Sisterhood: Middle Class Women in the</u>
<u>Victorian Home.</u> Pittsburgh: Carnegie-Mellon U Press, 1975.
Rev. by C. M. Prelinger, HRNB, 4(Aug 1976):199-200; C. N.
Degler, JSoH, 10(Fall 1976):103-5.

Brandeis, Louis. <u>Letters of Louis D. Brandeis.</u> Vol. IV. (Melvin I. Urofsky and David W. Levy, eds.) Albany, N.Y.:
SUNY Press, 1975. Rev. by P. L. Murphy and M. L. Ost-
ling, JAH, 63(Dec 1976):673-5.

Brandmüller, Walter. <u>Das Konzil von Pavia-Siena, 1423-1424.</u>
2 vols. Münster: Verlag Aschendorff, 1968, 1974. Rev. by
B. Tierney, AHR, 81(Feb 1976):118.

Brandon, William. <u>The Last Americans: The Indian in American</u>
<u>Culture.</u> New York: McGraw-Hill, 1974. Rev. by R. E.
Powless, AIQ, 2(Sum 1975):141-2; A. H. De Rosier, Jr.,
FHQ, 54(Jan 1975):405-6.

Brandt, Patricia and Nancy Guilford. <u>Oregon Biography Index.</u>
Corvallis: Ore St U Press, 1976. Rev. by G. Manning,
OrHQ, 77(Sep 1976):297.

Branigan, Keith and P. J. Fowler, eds. <u>The Roman West Coun-</u>
<u>try: Classical Culture and Celtic Society.</u> North Pomfret,
Vt.: David and Charles, 1976. Rev. by E. J. Polak, HRNB,
5(Oct 1976):16-17.

47   BRANSON

Branson, Noreen. Britain in the Nineteen Twenties. Minneapolis:
U Minn Press, 1976. Rev. by T. J. Spinner, HRNB, 4(Jl
1976):178.

Braudel, Fernand, et al., eds. Conjoncture économique, Structures sociales. Hommage à Ernest Labrousse. Paris: Mouton, 1974. Rev. by T. F. Glick, HAHR, 56(May 1976):307-
9; P. Dawson, JIH, 7(Sum 1976):150-4.

_____. The Mediterranean and the Mediterranean World in the
Age of Philip II. Vol. II. New York: Harper and Row,
1973. Rev. by T. F. Glick, HAHR, 56(May 1976):307-9.

Braun, Hans-Joachim. Technologische Beziehungen zwischen
Deutschland und England von der Mitte des 17. bis zum
Ausgang des 18. Jahrhunderts. Dusseldorf: Verlag Schwann,
1974. Rev. by S. Pollard, EHR, 91(Jl 1976):648-9; H.
Kisch, JEH, 36(Jl 1976):455-6.

Bravmann, René A. Islam and Tribal Art in West Africa. New
York: Cam U Press, 1974. Rev. by J. R. Willis, AHR, 81
(Apr 1976):431-2.

Bravo, Gian Mario. Il socialismo: Da Moses Hess alla Prima
Internazionale nella recente storiografia. Turin: Edizioni
Giappichelli, 1971. Rev. by P. Piccone, AHR, 81(Oct 1976):
845.

Brawley, James S. Rowan County. Raleigh: NC Div Archives
and History, 1974. Rev. by J. W. Linn, NCHR, 53(Spr
1976):218-19.

Brecher, Michael. Israel, the Korean War and China: Images,
Decisions, and Consequences. Jerusalem: Jerusalem Academic Press, 1974. Rev. by V. Shicor, CQ, May 1976, pp.
388-90.

Brecht, Arnold. The Political Education of Arnold Brecht: An
Autobiography, 1884-1970. Princeton, N.J.: Prin U Press,
1970. Rev. by J. C. Fout, JCS, 17(Spr 1975):318-20.

Bredsdorff, Elias. Hans Christian Andersen: The Story of His
Life and Work, 1805-75. New York: Scribners, 1975. Rev.
by W. D. Andersen, HRNB, 4(May/Je 1976):157.

Breeden, James O. Joseph Jones, M.D.: Scientist of the Old
South. Lexington: U Press Ky, 1975. Rev. by J. Erlen,
FCHQ, 50(Jan 1976):75-6; J. H. Young, FHQ, 55(Jl 1976):
93-4; L. P. Curry, JAH, 63(Je 1976):117-18; J. L. Roark,
JSH, 42(May 1976):285-6; T. C. Parramore, NCHR, 53(Win
1976):88-9.

Breedlove, Dennis E. see Berlin, Brent

Breman, Jan. Patronage and Exploitation: Changing Agrarian Relations in South Gujarat India. Berkeley: U Cal Press, 1974.
Rev. by M. L. Dantwala, IESHR, 13(Jan-Mar 1976):111-13.

Brendon, Piers. Hawker of Morwenstow: Portrait of a Victorian
Eccentric. London: Jonathan Cape, 1975. Rev. by A. T.
Hart, JEccH, 27(Apr 1976):208-9.

————————. Hurrell Froude and the Oxford Movement. London:
Elek, 1974. Rev. by V. H. H. Green, EHR, 91(Jl 1976):
672; B. Coleman, History, 61(Je 1976):305-6.

Brentano, Robert. Rome Before Avignon: A Social History of
Thirteenth-Century Rome. London: Longman, 1974. Rev.
by D. Waley, History, 61(Feb 1976):100-1.

Bresc, Henri, ed. La correspondance de Pierre Ameilh archevêque
de Naples, puis d'Embrun (1363-1369). Paris: Editions du
Centre National de la Recherche Scientifique, 1972. Rev. by
J. E. Weaklund, CaHR, 62(Jan 1976):104-6.

Brett, Martin. The English Church Under Henry I. London: Oxford U Press, 1975. Rev. by R. W. Pfaff, CH, 45(Sep
1976):379; M. Chibnall, EHR, 91(Oct 1976):889-90; H. E. J.
Cowdrey, History, 61(Je 1976):257-8.

Breuer, Isaac. Concepts of Judaism. Jerusalem: Israel U Press,
1974. Rev. by L. Jacobs, Judaism, 25(Fall 1976):501-5.

Brewster, John W. and Joseph A. McLeod. Index to Book Re-
views in Historical Periodicals, 1973, 1974. Metuchen, N. J.:
Scarecrow, 1976, 1975. Rev. by C. R. Schultz, SWHQ, 80
(Jl 1976):124-6.

Bridenbaugh, Carl. Fat Mutton and Liberty of Conscience: Society
in Rhode Island, 1636-1690. Providence, R.I.: Brown U
Press, 1974. Rev. by R. C. Simmons, AgH, 50(Jan 1976):
320; P. J. Coleman, AHR, 81(Je 1976):650-1; G. L. Main,
JEH, 36(Je 1976):456-7; P. T. Conley, NEQ, 49(Mar 1976):
136-8.

————————. Silas Downer: Forgotten Patriot: His Life and Writings. Providence: R.I. Bicentennial Foundation, 1974. Rev.
by W. M. Fowler, Jr., JAH, 62(Mar 1976):973.

————————. The Spirit of '76: The Growth of American Patriotism
Before Independence, 1607-1776. New York: Oxford U
Press, 1975. Rev. by J. P. Cullen, AHI, 11(Aug 1976):49;
R. C. Ritchie, JAH, 63(Sep 1976):394; C. R. Ferguson, JSH,
42(May 1976):274-5; R. J. Chaffin, NEQ, 49(Je 1976):293-5.

Bridges, R. C., ed. Senegambia: Proceedings of a Colloquium
at the University of Aberdeen, April 1974. Aberdeen: Aber-

U African Studies Group, 1974.   Rev. by G. Innes, Africa,
46(Num 2, 1976):212.

Bridges, William.   Gathering of Animals; an Unconventional History
of the New York Zoological Society.   New York: Harper and
Row, 1974.   Rev. by F. Sartwell, Smithsonian, 6(Jan 1975):
102-4.

Bridle, Paul A., ed.   Documents on Relations Between Canada and
Newfoundland. I: 1935-1949.   Ottawa: Information Canada,
1974.   Rev. by G. E. Panting, CHR, 57(Je 1976):217-18.

Briggs, Walter.   Without Noise of Arms.   Flagstaff, Ariz.:
Northland, 1976.   Rev. by B. L. Fontana, JAriH, 17(Aut
1976):347-8.

Bright, John.   A History of Israel.   Philadelphia: Westminster
Press, 1972.   Rev. by S. H. Horn, JNES, 35(Jl 1976):218-19.

Brilliant, Richard.   Arts of the Ancient Greeks.   New York:
McGraw-Hill, 1973.   Rev. by B. S. Ridgway, Archaeology,
29(Apr 1976):138-9.

_____. Roman Art: From the Republic to Constantine.   New
York: Praeger, 1974.   Rev. by M. Hammond, AHR, 81(Apr
1976):367-8.

Brinckerhoff, Sydney B., ed.   see   Crowe, Rosalie, ed.

Brisbane, Robert H.   Black Activism: Racial Revolution in the
United States, 1954-1970.   Valley Forge, Pa.: Judson, 1974.
Rev. by E. Rudwick, AHR, 81(Apr 1976):469; H. M. Davis,
JCS, 18(Spr 1976):346-7.

Brissaud, André.   The Nazi Secret Service.   New York: Norton,
1974.   Rev. by W. Carr, History, 61(Je 1976):322-3.

Brock, Michael.   The Great Reform Act.   London: Hutchinson U
Library, 1973.   Rev. by G. A. Cahill, CHR, 57(Mar 1976):
71-3.

Brock, William R.   Conflict and Transformation.   Harmondsworth:
Penguin, 1973.   Rev. by S. G. J. Spackman, History, 61(Oct
1976):408-9.

_____. The United States, 1789-1890.   Ithaca, N.Y.: Cornell
U Press, 1975.   Rev. by T. L. Haskell, JAH, 62(Mar 1976):
983-4; R. E. Smith, JOW, 15(Jan 1976):123.

Broder, Patricia Janis.   Bronzes of the American West.   New
York: Abrams, 1974.   Rev. by V. A. Paladin, WHQ, 7(Apr
1976):193-4.

Brodie, Bernard. War and Politics. New York: Macmillan, 1973.
Rev. by K. L. Nelson, PHR, 45(Feb 1976):152-3.

Broesamle, John J. William Gibbs McAdoo: A Passion for Change,
1863-1917. Port Washington, N. Y.: Kennikat, 1973. Rev.
by R. Jeffreys-Jones, History, 61(Oct 1976):415; R. M.
Abrams, JAH, 62(Mar 1976):1032-4.

Brogan, Denis, et al. Burke's Presidential Families of the United
States of America. London: Burke's Peerage, 1975. Rev.
by M. Rubincam, AmArc, 39(Apr 1976):214-15.

Broneer, Oscar. Isthmia. Vol. II, Topography and Architecture.
Princeton, N. J.: American School of Classical Studies at
Athens, 1973. Rev. by H. S. Robinson, AJA, 80(Win 1976):
89-90.

Brooke, Christopher. The Monastic World, 1000-1300. New
York: Random House, 1974. Rev. by J. Dahmus, AHR, 81
(Feb 1976):110-11; C. Morris, History, 61(Feb 1976):96-7.

Brooke, Christopher N. L. and Gillian Keir. London 800-1216:
The Shaping of a City. Berkeley: U Cal Press, 1975. Rev.
by J. T. Rosenthal, AHR, 81(Oct 1976):835-6; D. Kenne,
Archives, 12(Spr 1976):141-2; F. Barlow, JEccH, 27(Jan
1976):76-8.

Brooke, Rosalind B., ed. The Coming of the Friars. New York:
Barnes and Noble, 1975. Rev. by K. Edwards, EHR, 91(Oct
1976):891-2; A. W. Godfrey, HT, 10(Nov 1976):161-2; C.
Morris, History, 61(Oct 1976):442-3.

Brookfield, Harold. Independent Development. London: Methuen,
1975. Rev. by P. O'Brien, JMAS, 14(Sep 1976):539-40.

Brooks, H. Allen. Prairie School Architecture. Toronto: U Tor
Press, 1975. Rev. by B. Cavin, MinnH, 45(Spr 1976):35-6.

Brooks, John. Telephone. New York: Harper and Row, n. d.
Rev. by B. Atwater, Mankind, 5(Dec 1976):64, 66.

Brooks, Juanita. Emma Lee. Logan: Utah St U Press, 1975.
Rev. by R. J. Roske, UHQ, 44(Spr 1976):185-6.

_____. The History of Jews in Utah and Idaho. Salt Lake City:
Western Epics, 1973. Rev. by D. L. Crowder, PNQ, 67(Jan
1976):40.

Brook-Shepherd, Gordon. Uncle of Europe: The Social and Diplomatic Life of Edward VII. London: Collins, 1975. Rev. by
P. M. Hayes, EHR, 91(Oct 1976):930; R. N. Soffer, Mankind,
5(Dec 1976):58, 60.

Broome, Harvey. Out Under the Sky of the Great Smokies. n. p. :
    Greenbrier, n. d. Rev. by M. Frome, Smithsonian, 6(Feb
    1976):129-31; C. Brewer, THQ, 35(Win 1976):425-6.

Brower, Daniel R. Training the Nihilists: Education and Radical-
    ism in Tsarist Russia. London: Cornell U Press, 1975.
    Rev. by E. D. J. Acton, History, 61(Oct 1976):464-5.

Brown, Benjamin F. , ed. Opera Omnia di Sidney Sonnino. 5 vols.
    Lawrence: U Press Kans, 1975. Rev. by C. Seton-Wallace,
    History, 61(Oct 1976):468-70.

Brown, Curtis F. Star-Spangled Kitsch. New York: Universe,
    1975. Rev. by B. Groseclose, OH, 85(Aut 1976):340-1.

Brown, Douglas Summers. Chase City and Its Environs, 1765-
    1975: The Southside Virginia Experience. Chase City, Va. :
    Publication Committee for Chase City and Its Environs, 1975.
    Rev. by A. J. Mapp, Jr. , VMHB, 84(Oct 1976):506-7.

Brown, Emily C. Har Dayal: Hindu Revolutionary and Rationalist.
    Tucson: U Ariz Press, 1975. Rev. by N. G. Barrier, AHR,
    81(Je 1976):647.

Brown, Gilbert T. Korean Pricing Policies and Economic Develop-
    ment in the 1960's. Baltimore: JHU Press, 1974. Rev. by
    J. R. Behrman, AgH, 50(Jl 1976):536-7.

Brown, John A. see Ruby, Robert H.

Brown, Kenneth D. , ed. Essays in Anti-Labour History: Re-
    sponses to the Rise of Labour in Britain. Hamden, Conn. :
    Archon, 1974. Rev. by B. Malament, AHR, 81(Feb 1976):
    144-5; H. C. G. Matthew, EHR, 91(Apr 1976):451-2; P.
    Thompson, History, 61(Feb 1976):135-6.

Brown, Michael Barratt. The Economics of Imperialism. Har-
    mondsworth: Penguin, 1974. Rev. by P. J. Cain, History,
    61(Oct 1976):466-8.

Brown, Norman D. Edward Stanly: Whiggery's Tarheel "Con-
    queror. " University: U Ala Press, 1975. Rev. by E. A.
    Miles, AHR, 81(Oct 1976):973-4; W. S. Hoffman, Historian,
    39(Nov 1976):152-3.

Brown, R. Allen. Origins of English Feudalism. London: Allen
    and Unwin, 1973. Rev. by J. C. Holt, EHR, 91(Apr 1976):
    408-9.

Brown, Ralph Adams. The Presidency of John Adams. Lawrence:
    U Press Kan, 1975. Rev. by W. B. Fowler, HRNB, 5(Oct
    1976):10; J. Howe, IMH, 72(Dec 1976):367-8; M. Borden,
    JAH, 63(Sep 1976):401; R. R. Beeman, JSH, 42(Aug 1976):
    425-6.

Brown, Richard Maxwell. Strain of Violence: Historical Studies
of American Violence and Vigilantism. New York: Oxford U
Press, 1975. Rev. by S. E Ambrose, AHR, 81(Oct 1976):
1006-7; R. B. Toplin, JAH, 63(Sep 1976):441-2; H. R. Grant,
JOW, 15(Jl 1976):107; C. N. Degler, JSH, 42(Aug 1976):413-
15; D. A. Walker, NDH, 43(Fall 1976):37-8; T. Walch, WMH,
60(Aut 1976):64; R. Slotkin, WHQ, 7(Jl 1976):321-2; M. Wallace, WMQ, 33(Apr 1976):339-41.

Brown, Robert Craig. Robert Laird Borden. Vol. I. Toronto:
Macmillan, 1975. Rev. by G. Smith, JAH, 63(Dec 1976):
787-8.

_____ and Ramsay Cook. Canada, 1896-1921: A Nation Trans-
formed. Toronto: McClelland and Stewart, 1974. Rev. by
C. W. Humphries, CHR, 57(Je 1976):212-14; A. F. McC.
Madden, EHR, 91(Apr 1976):453.

Brown, Robert McAfee. Religion and Violence: A Primer for
White Americans. Philadelphia: Westminster Press, 1973.
Rev. by C. J. Dyck, JCS, 17(Win 1975):136-8.

Brown, Sanborn C. and Leonard M. Rieser. Natural Philosophy at
Dartmouth: From Surveyors' Chains to the Pressure of Light.
Hanover, N.H.: U Press New England, 1974. Rev. by S. A.
Bedini, AHR, 81(Oct 1976):959-60.

_____ , ed. see Oleson, Alexandra, ed.

Brown, Virginia Pounds. The Gold Disc of Coosa. Huntsville,
Ala.: Strode, 1975. Rev. by L. R. Atkins, AlaR, 29(Apr
1976):156.

Brown, Weldon A. Prelude to Disaster: The American Role in
Vietnam 1940-1963. Port Washington, N.Y.: Kennikat, 1975.
Rev. by R. F. de Bedts, HRNB, 5(Oct 1976):7: G. R. Hess,
JAH, 63(Dec 1976):775-6.

Brown, William see Kahn, Herman

Browne, D. Principles and Practice in Modern Archaeology. London: Hodder and Stoughton, 1975. Rev. by B. Hobby, Antiquity, 50(Mar 1976):83-4.

Browne, J. Ross. Adventures in the Apache Country: A Tour
Through Arizona and Sonora, 1864. Tucson: U Ariz Press,
1974. Rev. by L. D. Ball, ChOk, 54(Spr 1976):166; A. T.
Row, NDH, 43(Win 1976):38-9; A. Wallace, NMHR, 51(Apr
1976):161-2.

Browne, R. A., trans. and ed. The Holy Jerusalem Voyage of
Ogier VIII, Seigneur d'Anglure. Gainesville: U Presses Fla,
1975. Rev. by J. H. Denton, JEccH, 27(Jl 1976):329.

Brownell, Blaine A. The Urban Ethos in the South, 1920-1930.
    Baton Rouge: LSU Press, 1976. Rev. by J. C. Klotter,
    ChOk, 54(Win 1976):537-8; P. L. Simon, HRNB, 4(Sep 1976):
    210-11; G. E. Holt, JAH, 63(Dec 1976):758-9; R. E. Perdue,
    JNH, 61(Jl 1976):320-2; A. T. Brown, JSH, 42(Aug 1976):442-
    3.

Browning, Reed. The Duke of Newcastle. New Haven, Conn.:
    Yale U Press, 1975. Rev. by R. Middleton, WHQ, 33(Apr
    1976):342-3.

Browning, Robert. Byzantium and Bulgaria: A Comparative Study
    Across the Early Medieval Frontier. Berkeley: U Cal Press,
    1975. Rev. by C. N. Tsirpanlis, CH, 45(Mar 1976):100-1;
    S. Runciman, EHR, 91(Jl 1976):621-2; D. M. Nicol, History,
    61(Je 1976):254-5.

_____. The Emperor Julian. London: Weidenfeld & Nicholson,
    1975. Rev. by W. H. C. Frend, JEccH, 27(Oct 1976):414-5.

Brownlee, W. Elliot, Jr. Progressivism and Economic Growth:
    The Wisconsin Income Tax, 1911-1929. Port Washington,
    N. Y.: Kennikat, 1974. Rev. by R. C. Haney, AHR, 81(Oct
    1976):991-2.

Brownmiller, Susan. Against Our Will: Men, Women and Rape.
    New York: Simon and Schuster, 1975. Rev. by M. Novak,
    Commentary, 61(Feb 1976):90; D. Simon, Mankind, 5(Apr
    1976):8-9.

Bruce, Dickson D., Jr. And They All Sang Hallelujah: Plain-Folk
    Camp-Meeting Religion, 1800-1845. Knoxville: U Tenn Press,
    1974. Rev. by J. M. Mulder, AHR, 81(Feb 1976):207-8; R.
    L. Bushman, JIH, 7(Sum 1976):170-2; E. Dick, PHR, 45(Aug
    1976):439-40.

Bruce-Mitford, Rupert. Aspects of Anglo-Saxon Archaeology: Sut-
    ton Hoo and Other Discoveries. London: Gollancz, 1974.
    Rev. by P. H. Blair, EHR, 91(Jan 1976):172-3.

_____, ed. Recent Archaeological Excavations in Europe. Lon-
    don: Routledge and Kegan Paul, 1975. Rev. by J. V. S.
    Megaw, Antiquity, 50(Je 1976):158-9.

Bruchey, Stuart. Growth of the Modern American Economy. New
    York: Dodd, Mead, 1975. Rev. by S. J. DeCanio, JAH,
    62(Mar 1976):956-7.

Bruckner, A. and Brigitte Degler-Spangler, eds. Helvetia Sacra.
    Pt. 5 and 6. 2 vols. Bern: Francke Verlag, 1974. Rev.
    by R. Daniel, CH, 45(Mar 1976):110-11; E. D. Stoye, JEccH,
    27(Apr 1976):201-3.

Bruford, W. H.   The German Tradition of Self-Cultivation.   London: Cam U Press, 1975. Rev. by R. H. Thomas, History, 61(Oct 1976):460-1.

Brugger, William.   Democracy and Organization in the Chinese Industrial Enterprise, 1948-1953. New York: Cam U Press, 1976. Rev. by J. Israel, HRNB, 4(Jl, 1976):171; S. Andors, JEH, 36(Sep 1976):738-9.

Brumfield, Kirby.   The Wheat Album. Seattle: Superior, 1974. Rev. by E. Bern, NDH, 43(Win 1976):39-40.

Brundage, Burr Cartwright.   Two Earths, Two Heavens.   Albuquerque: UNM Press, 1975. Rev. by J. Lockhart, HAHR, 56 (Nov 1976):642-3.

Bruneau, Thomas C.   The Political Transformation of the Brazilian Catholic Church. New York: Cam U Press, 1974. Rev. by A. Q. Tiller, JCS, 17(Win 1975):129-31.

Brunhouse, Robert L.   Pursuit of the Ancient Maya: Some Archaeologists of Yesterday. Albuquerque: U NM Press, 1975. Rev. by J. A. Sabloff, AmAn, 41(Jl 1976):408-9; R. E. W. Adams, HAHR, 56(Feb 1976):161-2; M. J. Becker, TAm, 32(Apr 1976):241-3.

Brüning, Heinrich.   Briefe und Gespräche, 1934-1945.   Stuttgart: Deutsche Verlags-Anstalt, 1974. Rev. by F. E. Hirsch, AHR, 81(Apr 1976):410.

Brunschwig, Henri.   Enlightenment and Romanticism in Eighteenth-Century Prussia. Chicago: U Chicago Press, 1974. Rev. by W. J. Greenwald, Jr., Historian, 38(Feb 1976):332; T. C. W. Blanning, History, 61(Je 1976):295.

Brus, Wlodzimierz.   Socialist Ownership and Political Systems. Boston: Routledge and Kegan Paul, 1975. Rev. by D. Granick, JEH, 36(Sep 1976):739-40.

Brusher, Joseph S.   Consecrated Thunderbolt: Father York of San Francisco. Hawthorne, N. J.: Wagner, 1973. Rev. by J. P. Walsh, CaHR, 62(Jl 1976):515-16.

Brushwood, John S.   The Spanish American Novel: A Twentieth-Century Survey. Austin: U Texas Press, 1975. Rev. by G. Evans, HAHR, 56(Aug 1976):499-500.

Bryant, Keith L., Jr.   History of the Atchison, Topeka and Santa Fe Railway. New York: Macmillan, 1974. Rev. by H. R. Grant, ChOk, 54(Spr 1976):157-8; A. M. Johnson, NMHR, 51 (Apr 1976):159-60; W. S. Greever, WHQ, 7(Jan 1976):65-6.

Bryden, Kenneth.   Old Age Pensions and Policy Making in Canada.

Montreal: McGill-Queens U Press, 1974. Rev. by Laycock,
CHR, 57(Je 1976):214-16.

Buarque de Holanda, Sérgio. História geral de civilização
brasileira. Tomo II. São Paulo: Difusão Europa do Livro,
1972. Rev. by P. L. Eisenberg, HAHR, 56(Feb 1976):135-8.

Buchanan, Robert W., ed. see Wax, Murray L., ed.

Buchholz, Hans-Günter and Vassos Karageorghis. Prehistoric
Greece and Cyprus. An Archaeological Handbook. London:
Phaidon, 1973. Rev. by S. A. Immerwahr, AJA, 80(Win
1976):86-7.

Buck, Lawrence P. and Jonathan W. Zophy, eds. The Social History of the Reformation. Columbus: Ohio U Press, 1972.
Rev. by P. Peachey, CaHR, 62(Jan 1976):118-19.

Buczek, Daniel S. Immigrant Pastor: The Life of the Right
Reverend Monsignor Lucyan Bojnowski of New Britain, Connecticut. Waterbury, Conn.: Assn of Polish Priests in Connecticut, 1974. Rev. by A. J. Kuzniewski, CaHR, 61(Jl
1976):510-12.

Budge, Ian and Cornelius O'Leary. Belfast. Approach to Crisis.
New York: St. Martin's, 1973. Rev. by D. W. Miller,
CaHR, 62(Oct 1976):653-4.

Buell, Thomas B. The Quiet Warrior: A Biography of Admiral
Raymond A. Spruance. Boston: Little, Brown, 1974. Rev.
by P. A. Crowl, AHR, 81(Feb 1976):217-18.

Bueno, Patricia, ed. see Maciel, David, ed.

Buisseret, David see Pawson, Michael

Buist, Marten G. At Spes Non Fracta, Hope & Co., 1770-1815.
The Hague: Martinus Nijhoff, 1974. Rev. by W. Kirchner,
AHR, 81(Apr 1976):402: W. O. Henderson, BH, 17(Jan 1975):
85.

Bullen, Roger. Palmerston, Guizot and the Collapse of the Entente
Cordiale. Atlantic Highlands, N.J.: Humanities, 1974. Rev.
by L. C. Jennings, AHR, 81(Feb 1976):123-4; R. T. Shan-
non, EHR, 91(Apr 1976):441-2; Donald Southgate, History, 61
(Feb 1976):130-1.

Bulloch, James see Drummond, Andrew L.

Bullough, Vern L. see Naroll, Raoul and Frada

Bullough, William A. Cities and Schools in the Gilded Age: The
Evolution of an Urban Institution. Port Washington, N.Y.:

Kennikat, 1974. Rev. by M. Lazerson, AHR, 81(Apr 1976): 456-7.

Bulst, Neithard. Untersuchungen zu den Klosterreformen Wilhelms von Dijon (962-1031). Bonn: Ludwig Röhrscheid Verlag, 1973. Rev. by G. Constable, EHR, 91(Jl 1976):627-8.

Bulst-Thiele, M. L. Sacrae Domus Militiae Templi Hierosolymitani Magistri. Göttingen: Vandenhoeck and Ruprecht, 1974. Rev. by A. J. Forey, EHR, 91(Jan 1976):176-7.

Buni, Andrew. Robert L. Vann of the Pittsburgh Courier: Politics and Black Journalism. Pittsburgh: U Pittsburgh Press, 1974. Rev. by S. Fox, AS, 16(Spr 1975):78: R. M. Smith, PH, 43(Jl 1976):281-2.

Bunselmeyer, Robert E. The Cost of the War 1914-1919: British Economic War Aims and the Origins of Reparation. Hamden, Conn.: Shoe String, 1975. Rev. by W. Ashworth, History, 61(Oct 1976):496-7; R. L. Blanco, HRNB, 4(Jan 1976):70.

Burdick, Charles B. Unternehmen Sonenblume: Der Entschluss zum Afrika-Feldzug. Neckargemünd: Kurt Vowinckel Verlag, 1972. Rev. by W. A. Fletcher, AHR, 81(Oct 1976):884-7.

Burg, David F. Chicago's White City of 1893. Lexington: U Press Ky, 1976. Rev. by D. R. Jamison, HRNB, 5(Oct 1976):9.

Burgess, Keith. The Origins of British Industrial Relations: The Nineteenth-Century Experience. Totowa, N.J.: Rowman and Littlefield, 1975. Rev. by T. M. Kemnitz, AHR, 81(Je 1976):587-8; R. Harrison, History, 61(Je 1976):310-11; S. Pollard, JEH, 36(Sep 1976):740-2.

Burgess, Robert F. Ships Beneath the Sea. New York: McGraw-Hill, 1975. Rev. by R. V. Jenkins, OH, 85(Aut 1976):329-30.

Burke, Peter. Venice and Amsterdam: A Study of Seventeenth-Century Elites. London: Temple Smith, 1974. Rev. by R. Grassby, EHR, 91(Apr 1976):425; A. C. Carter, History, 61 (Feb 1976):113.

Burma, John H. Spanish-Speaking Groups in the United States. Detroit: Blaine Ethridge, 1974. Rev. by M. T. García, HAHR, 56(Feb 1976):158-61.

Burnes, Alexander. A Voyage on the Indus. London: Oxford U Press, 1973. Rev. by G. L. Possehl, JAAS, 11(Jan-Apr 1976):132-4.

Burnette, Robert and John Koster. The Road to Wounded Knee.

New York: Bantam, 1974. Rev. by M. E. F. Mathur, AIQ,
2(Spr 1975):32-3.

Burney, Eugenia see Christensen, Gardell Dano

Burns, Helen M. The American Banking Community and New Deal
Banking Reforms, 1933-1935. Westport, Conn.: Greenwood,
1974. Rev. by J. Nichols, AHR, 81(Apr 1976):464.

Burns, Richard Dean and Edward Bennett, eds. Diplomats in
Crisis: United States-Chinese-Japanese Relations, 1919-1941.
Santa Barbara, Cal.: ABC-Clio, 1974. Rev. by J. H. Boyle,
AHR, 81(Apr 1976):363-4; I. J. B. Singh, IQ, 32(Jl-Sep 1976):
345-8.

Burns, Robert Ignatius. Medieval Colonialism: Postcrusade Exploitation of Islamic Valencia. Princeton, N.J.: Prin U
Press, 1976. Rev. by G. Jackson, AHR, 81(Oct 1976):837-8;
M. C. Hilferty, CH, 45(Sep 1976):380; C. J. Bishko, HAHR,
56(Nov 1976):644-5; L. C. Rose, HRNB, 4(May/Je 1976):158;
P. A. Linehan, JEccH, 27(Oct 1976):427-8; J. Boswell, JEH,
36(Sep 1976):742-4.

Burton, Jimalee. Indian Heritage, Indian Pride: Stories That
Touched My Life. Norman: U Ok Press, 1974. Rev. by
M. R. Blaine, AIQ, 2(Sum 1975):157-8.

Burts, Robert Milton. Richard Irvine Manning and the Progressive
Movement in South Carolina. Columbia: U SCar Press, 1974.
Rev. by T. H. Coode, AHR, 81(Je 1976):679; S. Kerber, FHQ,
54(Jan 1976):401-2.

Bury, J. P. T. Gambetta and the Making of the Third Republic.
London: Longmans, 1973. Rev. by S. Elwitt, JMH, 48(Mar
1976):152-4.

Busch, Noel F. Winter Quarters: George Washington and the Con-
tinental Army at Valley Forge. New York: Liveright, 1974.
Rev. by S. S. Smith, NYHSQ, 60(Jan/Apr 1976):74-5; R. F.
Oaks, PH, 43(Jan 1976):83-4.

Bush, M. L. The Government Policy of Protector Somerset. London: Edward Arnold, 1975. Rev. by H. Miller, History, 61
(Je 1976):273.

Bushell, Gerard, ed. see Kelly, Celsus, ed.

Buss, Claude A. China: The People's Republic of China and
Richard Nixon. San Francisco: W. H. Freeman, 1974. Rev.
by C. MacDougall, CQ, May 1976, p. 405; R. K. Nehru, IQ,
32(Jan-Mar 1976):86-8.

Bustin, Edouard. Lunda Under Belgian Rule: The Politics of

Ethnicity. Cambridge, Mass.: Har U Press, 1975. Rev.
by D. L. Wheeler, AHR, 81(Oct 1976):925-6.

Butel, Paul. Les Négociants Bordelais: L'Europe et les îles au
XVIIIe Siècle. Paris: Aubier-Montaigne, 1974. Rev. by
R. Davis, EHR, 91(Jl 1976):650-1; J. S. Bromley, History,
61(Feb 1976):116.

Butler, Jeffrey, ed. see Thompson, Leonard, ed.

Butler, William J. and George Obiozor. The Burundi Affair.
Geneva: International Commission of Jurists, 1972. Rev. by
W. Weinstein, JMAS, 14(Mar 1976):161-3.

Butlin, R. A., ed. see Baker, A. R. H., ed.

Butow, R. J. C. The John Doe Associates: Backdoor Diplomacy
for Peace, 1941. Stanford, Cal.: Stanford U Press, 1974.
Rev. by B. L. Villa, AHR, 81(Je 1976):687; H. J. Kerner,
CaHR, 62(Oct 1976):685-7; J. A. Thompson, History, 61(Oct
1976):418; A. Iriye, JJS, 2(Aut 1975):127-31.

Butterfield, L. H., et al., eds. The Book of Abigail and John:
Selected Letters of the Adams Family, 1762-1784. Cambridge,
Mass.: Harvard U Press, 1975. Rev. by J. H. Hutson,
AHR, 81(Oct 1976):960-1; C. W. Akers, NEQ, 49(Mar 1976):
151-3.

Buxbaum, Melvin H. Benjamin Franklin and the Zealous Presby-
terians. University Park: Pa St U Press, 1975. Rev. by
R. Middlekauff, JAH, 63(Je 1976):104-5; B. H. Newcomb,
WMQ, 33(Apr 1976):350-1.

Buyken, Thea. Die Constitutionen von Melfi und das Jus Fran-
corum. Opladen: Westdeutscher Verlag, 1973. Rev. by
D. J. A. Matthew, EHR, 91(Jl 1976):628-9.

Byington, Margaret. Homestead: The Households of a Mill Town.
Pittsburgh: U Pittsburgh, 1974. Rev. by J. B. Frantz, PH,
43(Jl 1976):276-8.

Byrne, Frank L. and Andrew T. Weaver, eds. Haskell of Gettysburg: His Life and Civil War Papers. Madison: St. Historical Society of Wis, 1970. Rev. by F. E. Vandiver, JAH,
63(Sep 1976):422-3.

Caballero, Romeo Flores. Counterrevolution. The Role of the
Spaniards in the Independence of Mexico, 1804-1838. Lincoln:
U Neb Press, 1974. Rev. by P. J. Vanderwood, SCQ, 58
(Win 1976):539-42.

Cable, Mary. The Little Darlings: A History of Child Rearing
in America. New York: Scribner's, 1975. Rev. by J. R.

59 · CABRAL

Jeffrey, JSH, 42(Feb 1976):151-2.

Cabral de Mello, Evaldo. Olinda restaurada: Guerra e açúcar no nordeste, 1630-1654. São Paulo: Editora da Universidade de São Paulo, 1975. Rev. by S. Schwartz, AHR, 81(Oct 1976): 1011-12; C. R. Boxer, HAHR, 56(Aug 1976):484-5.

Cadenhead, Ivie E., Jr. Benito Juárez. New York: Twayne, 1973. Rev. by R. C. Overfelt, JCS, 17(Win 1975):119-21.

Cadieux, Lorenzo. Frédéric Romanet du Caillaud, "Comte" de Sudbury (1847-1919). Montreal: Les Editions Bellarmin, 1971. Rev. by G. C. Brandt, CHR, 57(Je 1976):210-11.

Cail, Robert E. Land, Man, and the Law: The Disposal of Crown Lands in British Columbia, 1871-1913. Vancouver: U BC Press, 1974. Rev. by D. Cole, AHR, 81(Je 1976):697; L. H. Thomas, CHR, 57(Je 1976):195-6; L. B. Lee, PNQ, 67(Jl 1976):132-3.

Calder, Kenneth J. Britain and the Origins of the New Europe, 1914-1918. New York: Cam U Press, 1976. Rev. by J. P. Zaccano, Jr., HRNB, 4(Jl 1976):174-5.

Caldwell, John C. Population Growth and Socioeconomic Change in West Africa. New York: Columbia U Press, 1975. Rev. by J. Gregory and V. Piché, JMAS, 14(Je 1976):370-5.

Calhoon, Robert McCleur. The Loyalists in Revolutionary America, 1760-1781. New York: Harcourt Brace Jovanovich, 1973. Rev. by S. B. Kim, NYHSQ, 60(Jan/Apr 1976):65-6.

Calhoun, Frances Boyd. Miss Minerva and William Green Hill. Knoxville: U Tenn Press, 1976. Rev. by L. V. Bauch, THQ, 35(Sum 1976):228.

Calhoun, John C. The Papers of John C. Calhoun. Vol. VIII. 1823-1824. (W. Edwin Hemphill, ed.) Columbia: U SCar Press, 1975. Rev. by T. P. Govan, FHQ, 55(Jl 1976):89-90.

Callahan, Raymond. The East India Company and Army Reform, 1783-1798. Cambridge, Mass.: Harvard U Press, 1972. Rev. by R. D. Miles, AHR, 81(Oct 1976):859-60.

Callahan, Nelson J. A Case for Due Process in the Church: Father Eugene O'Callaghan, American Pioneer of Dissent. Staten Island, N.Y.: Alba House, 1971. Rev. by G. T. Miller, JCS, 17(Spr 1975):345-6.

Callipolitis-Feytmans, Denise. Les plats attiques a figures noires. Paris: Diffusion de Boccard, 1974. Rev. by M. B. Moore, AJA, 80(Sum 1976):313-14.

Calmeyer, Peter. Reliefbronzen in Babylonischem Stil. Eine
Westiranische Werkstatt des 10. Jahrhunderts v. Chr.
München: Verlag der Bayerischen Akademie der Wissenschaften, 1973. Rev. by E. Porada, AJA, 80(Spr 1976):
200-1.

Cámara, Dom Hélder. Race Against Time. Denville, N.J.:
Dimension, 1971. Rev. by J. C. Anderson, JCS, 17(Spr
1975):350-1.

Camariano-Cioran, Ariadna. Les Académies Princières de Bu-
carest et de Jassy et leur Professeurs. Thessaloniki: Institute for Balkan Studies, 1974. Rev. by J. C. Counelis,
CH, 45(Mar 1976):115-16.

Camarillo, Albert, ed. see Castillo, Pedro, ed.

Cameron, David. The Social Thought of Rousseau and Burke.
Toronto: U Tor Press, 1973. Rev. by J. P. Burke, JHP,
14(Jl 1976):370-1.

Camp, Walter. Custer in '76: Walter Camp's Notes on Custer
Fight. (Kenneth Hammer, ed.) Provo, Utah: BYU Press,
1976. Rev. by B. Procter, HRNB, 4(Jl 1976):165; M. Kernan, Smithsonian, 7(Je 1976):106-8.

Campbell, Charles S. From Revolution to Rapprochement: The
United States and Great Britain, 1783-1900. New York:
Wiley, 1974. Rev. by F. Merli, JAH, 62(Mar 1976):977-9.

Campbell, D. and R. A. MacLean. Beyond the Atlantic Roar:
A Study of the Nova Scotia Scots. Toronto: McClelland and
Stewart, 1974. Rev. by D. M. Schurman, CHR, 57(Je 1976):
204-5.

Campbell, Eugene E. see Gowans, Fred R.

Campbell, F. Gregory. Confrontation in Central Europe: Weimar
Germany and Czechoslovakia. Chicago: U Chicago Press,
1975. Rev. by S. D. Spector, Historian, 39(Nov 1976):131-
2; B. K. Kiraly, HRNB, 4(Mar 1976):114.

Campbell, John C., ed. Successful Negotiation: Trieste 1954.
Princeton, N.J.: Prin U Press, 1976. Rev. by W. D.
Briggs, HRNB, 4(Aug 1976):201-2.

Campbell, Leslie Caine. Two Hundred Years of Pharmacy in Mississippi. Jackson: U Press Miss, 1974. Rev. by R. J.
Bennett, JMiH, 38(May 1976):228-30.

Campbell, Richard L. Historical Sketches of Colonial Florida.
Gainesville: U Presses Fla, 1975. Rev. by F. L. Owsley,
Jr., AlaR, 29(Jl 1976):239-40; J. L. Holmes, JMiH, 38(Nov
1976):375-6.

61   CAMPBELL

Campbell, Thomas M. and George C. Herring, eds. The Diaries
of Edward R. Stettinius, Jr., 1943-1946. New York: New
Viewpoints, 1975. Rev. by B. J. Bernstein, AHR, 81(Oct
1976):1000-1.

Canary, Robert H. George Bancroft. New York: Twayne, 1974.
Rev. by H. Brogan, History, 61(Oct 1976):423-4.

Cancian, Frank. Another Place: Photographs of a Mayan Community. San Francisco: Scrimshaw, 1974. Rev. by K.
Noble, AA, 78(Mar 1976):153-4.

Canfield, Cass. Samuel Adam's Revolution 1765-1776. New York:
Harper and Row, 1976. Rev. by R. J. Cooke, HRNB, 4(May/
Je 1976):145; R. Ketcham, HRNB, 4(Sep 1976):215; D. Lind-
sey, Mankind, 5(Dec 1976):6.

Cannistraro, Philip V., Edward D. Wynot, Jr., and Theodore P.
Kovaleff, eds. Poland and the Coming of the Second World
War: The Diplomatic Papers of A. J. Drexel Biddle, Jr.,
United States Ambassador to Poland, 1937-1939. Columbus,
Ohio: Ohio St U Press, 1976. Rev. by W. J. Woolley, HRNB,
5(Oct 1976):6.

Cannon, John. Parliamentary Reform 1640-1832. Toronto: Macmillan, 1973. Rev. by S. W. Jackman, CHR, 57(Mar 1976):
69-71.

Cantin, Eileen. Mounier: A Personalist View of History. New
York: Paulist Press, 1973. Rev. by J. Amato, CaHR, 62(Oct
1976):658-9.

Cantlie, Sir Neil. A History of the Army Medical Department. 2
vols. New York: Longman, 1974. Rev. by J. O. Baylen,
AHR, 81(Feb 1976):132.

Cantor, Milton, ed. see Fink, Gary, ed.

Cappon, Lester J., et al., eds. Atlas of Early American History:
The Revolutionary Era, 1760-1790. Princeton, N.J.: Prin U
Press, 1976. Rev. by D. E. Leach, JSH, 42(Nov 1976):582-
4; W. P. Cumming, VMHB, 84(Oct 1976):486-8.

Capps, Benjamin. The Great Chiefs. New York: Time-Life
Books, 1975. Rev. by J. Cambell, ChOk, 54(Fall 1976):407-
8.

_____. The Indians. New York: Time-Life, 1973. Rev. by
G. L. Walke, ChOk, 54(Sum 1976):293.

Caracciolo, Francesco. Uffici, difesa e corps rappresentativi nel
Mezzogiorno in età spagnola. Reggio Calabria: Editori
Meridionali Riunita, 1974. Rev. by E. P. Noether, AHR, 81
(Je 1976):620-1.

Cardiff, Sara. The Severing Line. New York: Random House, 1974. Rev. by M. Howard, VH, 44(Spr 1976):119-20.

Cardona, Nicolás de. Geographic and Hydrographic Descriptions of Many Northern and Southern Lands and Seas in the Indies. Los Angeles: Dawson's, 1974. Rev. by J. Sánchez, HAHR, 56(Fall 1976):175.

Carlisle, Rodney. The Roots of Black Nationalism. Port Washington, N.Y.: Kennikat, 1975. Rev. by R. M. Johnson, HRNB, 4(Apr 1976):125; B. Quarles, WVH, 38(Oct 1976):64-5.

Carlson, Ellsworth C. The Foochow Missionaries, 1847-1880. Cambridge, Mass.: Harvard U Press, 1974. Rev. by P. A. Varg, AHR, 81(Feb 1976):193-4; J. M. Downs, PHR, 45(Feb 1976):142-4.

Carlson, Norman, ed. Iowa Trolleys. Chicago: Central Electric Railfans' Association, 1975. Rev. by D. L. Hofsommer, AI, 43(Win 1976):235-6.

Carlsson, Anni and Wolker Michels, eds. The Hesse/Mann Letters. New York: Harper and Row, 1975. Rev. by A. Cardona-Hine, Mankind, 5(Apr 1976):51.

Carlton, C. The Court of Orphans. Leicester: Leicester U Press, 1974. Rev. by E. W. Ives, History, 61(Je 1960): 283-4.

Carmagnani, Marcello. Les Mecanisme de la vie economique dans une société coloniale: le Chili, 1680-1830. Paris: S.E.V.P.E.N., 1973. Rev. by J. A. Barbier, TAm, 33 (Oct 1976):383-4.

Carmi, Ozer. La Grande-Bretagne et la petite entente. Genèva: Droz, 1972. Rev. by W. V. Wallace, EHR, 91(Jl 1976): 686-7.

Carmichael, Joel. Trotsky: An Appreciation of His Life. New York: St. Martin's, 1975. Rev. by C. Gershman, Commentary, 62(Jl 1976):73-5; J. L. Wieczynski, HRNB, 4(Feb 1976):88-9.

Carmony, Marvin see Baker, Ronald L.

Caro, Robert A. The Power Broker: Robert Moses and the Fall of New York. New York: Knopf, 1974. Rev. by S. Buder, AHR, 81(Apr 1976):463.

Carpenter, L. P. G. D. H. Cole. Cambridge: Cam U Press, 1974. Rev. by T. Lloyd, EHR, 91(Jan 1976):232-3.

Carranco, Lynwood and John T. Labbe. Logging the Redwoods.

Caldwell, Idaho: Caxton, 1975. Rev. by L. L. Morrison,
JOW, 15(Jan 1976):137; H. Lundy, OrHQ, 77(Je 1976):190-1.

Carré, J.-J., P. Dubois, and E. Malinvaud. French Economic
Growth. Stanford, Cal.: Stanford U Press, 1975. Rev. by
L. G. Franko, BHR, 50(Sum 1976):251-5.

Carreras de Velasco, Mercedes. Los Mexicanos que devolvió la
crisis, 1929-1932. Mexico: Secretaría de Relaciones Ex-
teriores, 1974. Rev. by J. Gómez-Quiñones, HAHR, 56(May
1976):325-7.

Carriker, R. C. and E. R. Carriker. An Army Wife on the Frontier. Salt Lake City: U Utah Press, 1975. Rev. by S. L.
Myres, A & W, 18(Sum 1976):188-9.

Carrington, Evelyn M., ed. Women in Early Texas. Austin,
Tex.: Jenkins, 1975. Rev. by S. L. Myres, A & W, 18
(Sum 1976):188-9; A. E. Taylor, JSH, 42(Aug 1976):448-9.

Carroll, Berenice A. Liberating Women's History. Urbana: U
Ill Press, 1975. Rev. by L. Nilson, Mankind, 5(Dec 1976):
63.

Carroll, John M., comp. and ed. Custer in Texas: An Interrupted Narrative. New York: Sol Lewis and Liveright, 1975.
Rev. by R. M. Utley, AHR, 81(Oct 1976):981; Rev. by B.
Procter, HRNB, 4(Jan 1976):56; R. G. Athearn, JSH, 42(May
1976):290-1.

_____, ed. The Papers of the Order of Indian Wars. Fort
Collins, Colo.: Old Army Press, 1975. Rev. by H. D.
Langley, A & W, 18(Sum 1976):198-9.

Carroll, Joseph T. Ireland in the War Years, 1939-1945. Newton
Abbot: David and Charles, 1975. Rev. by J. C. Beckett,
EHR, 91(Jl 1976):689; P. Buckland, History, 61(Je 1976):
328-9.

Carte, Gene E. and Elaine H. Carte. Police Reform in the United
States: The Era of August Vollmer, 1905-1932. Berkeley:
U Cal Press, 1976. Rev. by S. T. McSeveney, HRNB, 4
(Sep 1976):219; R. Lane, JAH, 63(Dec 1976):751-2.

Carter, Alice Clare. Neutrality or Commitment. New York:
Norton, 1976. Rev. by J. R. Jones, EHR, 91(Oct 1976):
910-11; H. Dunthorne, History, 61(Je 1976):292; D. C. Baxter, HRNB, 4(Sep 1976):230.

Carter, Harry. A History of the Oxford University Press. Vol. 1.
Oxford: Clarendon Press, 1975. Rev. by J. Y. Cole,
AmArc, 39(Apr 1976):212-13; C. F. Mullett, AHR, 81(Je
1976):584-5; W. R. Ward, EHR, 91(Oct 1976):912-13.

Carter, Luther J. The Florida Experience: Land and Water Policy
    in a Growth State. Baltimore: JHU Press, 1974. Rev. by
    J. K. Mahon, FHQ, 54(Jan 1976):380-2.

Cary, Diana Serra. The Hollywood Posse: The Story of a Gallant
    Band of Horsemen Who Made Movie History. Boston: Hough-
    ton Mifflin, 1975. Rev. by P. J. Vanderwood, A & W, 18
    (Sum 1976):181-3; R. D. Batman, JOW, 17(Apr 1976):137.

Cary, Otis, ed. War-Wasted Asia: Letters 1945-46. New York:
    Kodansha International, 1975. Rev. by L. Olson, JAS, 36
    (Nov 1976):150-2; S. K. Johnson, JSS, 2(Sum 1976):437-48.

Case, J. Hogue. Salt Lake Sketchbook: Historic Buildings from an
    Artist's View. Salt Lake City: Clyde E. Harvey, 1975. Rev.
    by P. L. Goss, UHQ, 44(Spr 1976):188.

Case, Lynn M., ed. see Thomas, Daniel H., ed.

Casebier, Dennis G. The Mojave Road. Norco, Cal.: Tales of
    the Mohave Road, 1975. Rev. by H. P. Walker, JAriH, 17
    (Aut 1976):350-2.

_____, comp. The Mojave Road in Newspapers. Noroc, Cal.:
    Tales of the Mohave Road, 1976. Rev. by H. P. Walker,
    JAriH, 17(Aut 1976):350-2.

Cash, Kevin. Who The Hell Is William Loeb? Hookset, N.H.:
    Amoskeag Press, 1975. Rev. by E. May, VH, 44(Sum 1976):
    168-73.

Cashin, Edward J., Jr., and Heard Robertson. Augusta and the
    American Revolution: Events in the Georgia Back Country,
    1773-1783. Darien, Ga.: Ashantilly Press/Richmond County
    Historical Society, 1975. Rev. by H. H. Jackson, GHQ, 60
    (Spr 1976):88-90.

Cassara, Ernest. The Enlightenment in America. Boston: Twayne,
    1975. Rev. by M. L. Bradbury, CH, 45(Sep 1976):389-90;
    F. V. Mills, Sr., JAH, 63(Dec 1976):693-4.

_____, ed. Universalism in America: A Documentary History.
    Boston: Beacon, 1971. Rev. by C. C. Wright, JCS, 17(Spr
    1976):343-4.

Castellio, Sebastian. Advice to a Desolate France. Shepherdstown,
    W. Va.: Patmos, 1975. Rev. by C. F. Johnston, CH, 45
    (Sep 1976):386; N. M. Sutherland, JEccH, 27(Apr 1976):216-
    17.

Castillo, Petro and Albert Camarillo, eds. Furia y muerte: Los
    bandidos chicanos. Los Angeles: U Cal, 1973. Rev. by V.
    C. Dahl, JOW, 15(Apr 1976):133-4.

Catalano, Gaetano. Studi sulla Legazia Apostolica di Sicilia. Reggio Calabria: Edizioni Parallelo, 1973. Rev. by H. G.
Koenigsberger, JMH, 48(Mar 1976):159-60.

Catlin, Sir George. For God's Sake, Go! An Autobiography. Montreal: Palm, 1972. Rev. by N. Wood, AHR, 81(Feb 1976):
147.

_____. Letters and Notes on the Manners, Customs, and Con-
ditions of North American Indians. 2 vols. New York: Dover,
1973. Rev. by R. W. Richmond, AIQ, 2(Sum 1975):146-8.

Catton, Bruce. Michigan: A Bicentennial History. New York:
Norton, 1976. Rev. by T. A. Hartig, HRNB, 5(Oct 1976):4.

Cawelti, John G. Adventure, Mystery, and Romance. Chicago:
U Chicago Press, 1976. Rev. by G. S. Jowett, JAH, 63(Dec
1976):786-7.

Ceccuti, Cosimo. Un Editore del Risorgimento. Florence: Le
Monnier, 1974. Rev. by A. Ramm, EHR, 91(Jl 1976):675.

Center for Immigration Studies. Guide to the Manuscript Holdings
of the Immigrant Archives. St. Paul: U Minn, 1974. Rev.
by H. L. Applegate, AmArc, 39(Jan 1976):50.

Centre d'Histoire de l'Afrique. Enquêtes et documents d'histoire
africaine. Vol. I. Leuven: Université Catholique de Louvain, 1975. Rev. by C. Perrings, JAfH, 17(Num 3, 1976):
475-6.

Centro Studi per la Storia del Modernismo. Fonti e Documenti I.
Urbino: Armando Argalia Editore, 1972. Rev. by J. Hennesey, CaHR, 62(Oct 1976):645.

Cerutti, Toni. Antonio Gallenga: An Italian Writer in Victorian
England. New York: Oxford U Press, 1974. Rev. by D.
Beales, AHR, 81(Feb 1976):179-80.

Chadwick, John. The Mycenaean World. New York: Cam U
Press, 1976. Rev. by T. Kelly, HRNB, 4(Jl 1976):174.

Chadwick, Owen. The Secularization of the European Mind in the
Nineteenth Century. New York: Cam U Press, 1976. Rev.
by G. Himmelfarb, Commentary, 62(Oct 1976):87-92; A. Ryan,
HJ, 19(Sep 1976):801-2; V. L. Lidtke, HRNB, 4(Sep 1976):
230-1.

Chafe, William H. The American Woman: Her Changing Social,
Economic and Political Role 1920-1970. New York: Oxford
U Press, 1972. Rev. by W. L. O'Neill, JSoH, 8(Spr 1975):
154-5.

Chalklin, C. W.   The Provincial Towns of Georgian England: A
    Study of the Building Process, 1740-1820.   London: Edward
    Arnold, 1974.   Rev. by J. N. Tarn, BH, 17(Jl 1975):206-8;
    G. C. F. Forster, History, 61(Feb 1976):118-19; D. N.
    Cannadine, HJ, 19(Mar 1976):280-3.

_____ and M. A. Havinden, eds.   Rural Change and Urban
    Growth 1500-1800.   London: Longman, 1974.   Rev. by L.
    A. Clarkson, EHR, 91(Apr 1976):381-3; S. J. Watts, His-
    torian, 39(Nov 1976):117-18; P. Slack, History, 61(Feb 1976):
    70-1.

Challener, Richard D.   Admirals, Generals, and American Foreign
    Policy 1898-1914.   Princeton, N.J.:   Prin U Press, 1973.
    Rev. by E. Ions, EHR, 91(Apr 1976):453-4.

Chamberlin, E. R.   The Fall of the House of Borgia.   New York:
    Dial, 1974.   Rev. by E. Cochrane, AHR, 81(Feb 1976):175-
    7.

Chamberlin, J. E.   The Harrowing of Eden.   New York: Seabury,
    1975.   Rev. by P. Iverson, A & W, 18(Sum 1976):202-3;
    T. P. Wilson, JAH, 63(Sep 1976):379-80; R. K. Munkres,
    JOW, 15(Apr 1976):144; J. W. Bailey, NDH, 43(Spe 1976):
    106-7.

Chambers, G. W. and C. L. Sonnichsen.   San Augustin.   Tucson:
    Ariz Historical Society, 1974.   Rev. by C. C. Colley, A & W,
    18(Spr 1976):91-2.

Chambers, Robert.   Managing Rural Development: Ideas and Ex-
    periences from East Africa.   Uppsala: Scandinavian Institute
    of African Studies, 1974.   Rev. by L. Mair, Africa, 46(Num
    2, 1976):213; E. J. Keller, JMAS, 14(Sep 1976):536-9.

Champagne, Roger J.   Alexander McDougall and the American
    Revolution in New York.   Schenectady, N.Y.:   Union College
    Press, 1975.   Rev. by R. A. Becker, JAH, 63(Je 1976):111;
    J. K. Martin, PH, 43(Oct 1976):375-7; C. Collier, RAH, 4
    (Mar 1976):53-8; E. Countryman, WMQ, 33(Jan 1976):163-5.

Chan, Leslie W.   The Taching Oilfield: A Maoist Model for Eco-
    nomic Development.   Canberra: Australian National U Press,
    1974.   Rev. by C. MacDougall, CQ, Jan 1976, p. 155.

Chandaman, C. D.   The English Public Revenue, 1660-1688.   Ox-
    ford: Clarendon, 1975.   Rev. by G. O. Nichols, AHR, 81
    (Je 1976):583-4; K. H. D. Haley, EHR, 91(Apr 1976):387-9;
    J. P. Kenyon, History, 61(Je 1976):288-9; D. C. Coleman,
    HJ, 19(Mar 1976):278-9; L. Neal, JEH, 36(Je 1976):457-8.

Chandler, David.   The Art of Warfare in the Age of Marlborough.
    n.p.:   Bedford, n.d.   Rev. by C. C. Trench, HTo, 26(Jl
    1976):482-3.

Chaney, Charles L. The Birth of Missions in America. South
    Pasadena, Cal.: William Carey Library, 1976. Rev. by
    J. A. Andrew, III, JAH, 63(Dec 1976):691-2.

Chang, Chun-shu, ed. The Making of China: Main Themes in
    Premodern Chinese History. Englewood Cliffs, N.J.: Pren-
    tice-Hall, 1975. Rev. by J. H. Bailey, HRNB, 4(Apr 1976):
    129-30.

Chang, Ming-Kai, comp. see Long-Hsuen, Hsu, comp.

Chapman, Carl H. The Archaeology of Missouri, I. Columbia,
    Mo.: U MO Press, 1975. Rev. by R. S. Brownlee, MHR, 71
    (Apr 1976):348-50.

Chaput, Donald. Francois X. Aubry: Leader, Trailmaker and
    Voyageur in the Southwest, 1846-1854. Glendale, Cal.:
    Arthur H. Clark, 1975. Rev. by H. G. Jordan, ChOk, 54
    (Sum 1976):282-3; D. L. Beene, JAriH, 17(Sum 1976):242-3;
    L. McFarlane, WHQ, 7(Apr 1976):197-9.

Charles, B. G. George Owen of Henllys: A Welsh Elizabethan.
    Aberystwyth: National Library of Wales Press, 1973. Rev.
    by A. L. Rowse, EHR, 91(Jan 1976):196; P. Williams, His-
    tory, 61(Je 1976):275.

Charlton, D. G., J. Gaudon and A. R. Pugh, eds. Balzac and the
    Nineteenth Century. Leicester: Leicester U Press, 1972.
    Rev. by A. J. Mount, ESR, 6(Jan 1976):153-5.

Charvet, John. The Social Problem in the Philosophy of Rousseau.
    New York: Cam U Press, 1974. Rev. by G. J. Cavanaugh,
    AHR, 81(Feb 1976):157-8.

Chary, Frederick B. The Bulgarian Jews and the Final Solution,
    1940-1944. Pittsburgh: U Pittsburgh Press, 1972. Rev. by
    J. F. Clarke, AHR, 81(Apr 1976):419-20.

Chassaing, J. F. see Morange, J.

Chau, Phan Thien. Vietnamese Communism: A Research Bibli-
    ography. Westport, Conn.: Greenwood, 1975. Rev. by
    W. S. Turley, JAS, 36(Nov 1976):186.

Chavez, Angelico. My Penitente Land: Reflections on Spanish New
    Mexico. Albuquerque: U NM Press, 1974. Rev. by L. R.
    Murphy, A & W, 18(Win 1976):385-6; R. E. Isais, CaHR, 62
    (Jl 1976):500-1.

————, trans. see Adams, Eleanor B., trans.

Chávez, Fermín. La Cultura en la época de Rosas: Aportes a la
    decolonización mental de la Argentina. Buenos Aires: Edi-

ciones Theoria, 1973. Rev. by F. L. Hoffmann, HAHR, 56 (Aug 1976):510-11.

Chayes, Abram. The Cuban Missile Crisis: International Crises and the Role of Law. New York: Oxford U Press, 1974. Rev. by C. Quigley, AHR, 81(Je 1976):695.

Chazan, Robert. Mediaeval Jewry in Northern France: A Political and Social History. Baltimore: JHU Press, 1973. Rev. by P. R. Hyams, EHR, 91(Jl 1976):629-30.

Cheetham, Nicolas. New Spain: The Birth of Modern Mexico. London: V. Gollancz, 1974. Rev. by A. L. Michaels, AHR, 81(Je 1976):701; A. Lavrin, HAHR, 56(Feb 1976):124-5.

Cheetham, Russell J. see Kelley, Allen C.

Chejne, Anwar G. Muslim Spain: Its History and Culture. Oxford U Press, 1974. Rev. by D. W. Lomax, History, 61 (Feb 1976):95-6.

Chen, Lincoln C., ed. Disaster in Bangladesh: Health Crises in a Developing Nation. New York: Oxford U Press, 1973. Rev. by R. J. Barber, JAAS, 11(Jl-Oct 1976):225-7.

Chenery, Hollis, Moises Syrquin, and Hazel Elkington. Patterns of Development 1950-1970. London: Oxford U Press, 1975. Rev. by G. Rosen, JAS, 36(Nov 1976):117-19.

Cheney, Anne. Millay in Greenwich Village. University, Ala.: U Ala Press, 1975. Rev. by L. B. Miller, HRNB, 4(Mar 1976):101-2.

Cheney, C. R. Medieval Texts and Studies. Oxford: Oxford U Press, 1973. Rev. by A. Erskine, Archives, 12(Spr 1976): 143-4.

Cheney, John L., Jr., ed. North Carolina Government, 1585-1974. Raleigh: NC Dept Secretary of State, 1975. Rev. by W. S. Powell, NCHR, 53(Spr 1976):215-17.

Chenhall, Robert G. Museum Cataloging in the Computer Age. Nashville, Tenn.: American Association for State and Local History, 1975. Rev. by H. L. P. Stibbe, AmArc, 39(Apr 1976):199-200.

Cheshire, Neil M., ed. see Quinn, David B., ed.

Chesneaux, Jean. Peasant Revolts in China, 1840-1949. New York: Norton, 1973. Rev. by S. W. Barnett, JIH, 7(Sum 1976):136-40.

_____, ed. Popular Movements and Secret Societies in China,

69 CHESTER

1840-1950. Stanford, Cal.: Stanford U Press, 1972. Rev.
by S. W. Barnett, JIH, 7(Sum 1976):136-40.

Chester, Edward W. Clash of Titans: Africa and U.S. Foreign
Policy. Maryknoll, N.Y.: Orbis, 1974. Rev. by H. G.
Marcus, AHR, 81(Feb 1976):220; J. M. Lutz, JCS, 18(Aut
1976):579-81.

Chevallier, Raymond. Roman Roads. London: Batsford, 1976.
Rev. by C. W. Phillips, Antiquity, 50(Je 1976):156-7.

Ch'i, Hsi-sheng. Warlord Politics in China, 1916-1928. Stanford,
Cal.: Stanford U Press, 1976. Rev. by G. F. Botjer,
HRNB, 4(Jl 1976):171-2.

Chibnall, A. C. The Certificate of Musters for Buckinghamshire
in 1522. London: HMSO, 1974. Rev. by M. E. James,
EHR, 91(Jan 1976):191-2.

Chibnall, Marjorie, ed. and trans. The Ecclesiastical History of
Orderic Vitalis. Oxford: Clarendon Press, 1975. Rev. by
D. J. A. Matthew, History, 61(Oct 1976):441; J. Le Patourel,
JEccH, 27(Jan 1976):78-9.

Chickering, Roger. Imperial Germany and a World Without War:
The Peace Movement and German Society, 1892-1914. Prince-
ton, N.J.: Prin U Press, 1976. Rev. by H. H. Herwig,
AHR, 81(Oct 1976):882-3; J. Remak, HRNB, 4(Aug 1976):204.

Chilcote, Ronald H. and Joel C. Edelstein, eds. Latin America:
The Struggle with Dependency and Beyond. Cambridge, Mass.:
Schenckman, 1974. Rev. by H. F. Salamini, HAHR, 56(Feb
1976):151-3.

Childs, David. Marx and the Marxists: An Outline of Practice
and Theory. New York: Barnes and Noble, 1973. Rev. by
P. Avrich, AHR, 81(Feb 1976):124-5.

Childs, Marquis. Witness to Power. New York: McGraw-Hill,
1975. Rev. by G. R. Hess, OH, 85(Aut 1976):330-2.

Chirila, Eugen, Nicolae Gudea, and Ioan Stratan. Drei Münzhorte
des 4. Jahrhunderts aus dem Banat. Lugoj, Romania:
Muzeul de Istorii si Ethnographie, 1974. Rev. by D. W.
Wade, AJA, 80(Sum 1976):325.

Chittick, H. Neville and Robert I. Rotberg, eds. East Africa and
the Orient: Cultural Syntheses in Pre-Colonial Times. New
York: Africana, 1975. Rev. by R. W. Strayer, HRNB, 4(Apr
1976):128-9.

Choudhary, Sukhbir. Growth of Nationalism in India. 2 vols. New
Delhi: Trimurti Publications, 1973. Rev. by A. A. Yang,

AHR, 81(Apr 1976):435-6; J. Bandyopadhyaya, IQ, 32(Jan-Mar 1976):96-7.

Christensen, Gardell Dano and Eugenia Burney. Colonial Delaware. New York: Nelson, 1974. Rev. by J. Anderson, PH, 43(Jl 1976):271-2.

Christiansen, Paige. The Story of Mining in New Mexico. Socorro: New Mexico Bureau of Mines & Mineral Resources, 1974. Rev. by C. C. Spence, NMHR, 51(Oct 1976):343.

Christie, Agatha. Curtain. New York: Dodd, Mead, 1975. Rev. by E. Rothstein, Commentary, 61(Je 1976):80-4.

Christie, Ian R. and Benjamin W. Labaree. Empire or Independence 1760-1776: A British-American Dialogue on the Coming of the American Revolution. New York: Norton, 1976. Rev. by J. H. Flannagan, Jr., HRNB, 5(Oct 1976):11.

Christoff, Peter K. An Introduction to Nineteenth-Century Russian Slavophilism. Paris: Mouton, 1972. Rev. by M. C. Chapman, ESR, 6(Apr 1976):263-4.

Ch'ü, T'ung-Tsu. Han Social Structure. Seattle: U Wash Press, 1972. Rev. by S. F. Tobias, AA, 78(Je 1976):411-12.

Chubb, H. J. and C. L. D. Duckworth. The Irawaddy Flotilla Company. n.p.: National Maritime Museum, 1973. Rev. by R. Craig, JTH, 3(Sep 1976):298.

Chudacoff, Howard P. The Evolution of American Urban Society. Englewood Cliffs, N.J.: Prentice-Hall, 1975. Rev. by T. Bender, JAH, 62(Mar 1976):955-6.

Church, Benjamin. Diary of King Philip's War, 1675-76. Chester, Conn.: Pequot, 1975. Rev. by B. Graymont, AHR, 81(Oct 1976):856; D. E. Leach, JAH, 62(Mar 1976):962-3; A. T. Klyberg, NEQ, 49(Mar 1976):162-3.

Church, R. A. The Great Victorian Boom, 1850-1873. London: Macmillan, 1975. Rev. by W. Ashworth, History, 61(Oct 1976):485-6.

Church, Robert L. and Michael W. Sedlak. Education in the United States. New York: Free Press, 1976. Rev. by S. Cohen, JAH, 63(Dec 1976):706-7.

Church, William F. Louis XIV in Historical Thought: From Voltaire to the Annales School. New York: Norton, 1976. Rev. by R. M. Isherwood, HRNB, 3(May/Je 1976):154.

Chyet, Stanley F. Lopez of Newport: Colonial American Merchant Prince. Detroit: Wayne St U Press, 1970. Rev. by J. Gwyn, JEH, 36(Sep 1976):744.

_____, ed. see Gutman, Joseph, ed.

Ciasca, Raffaele. Aspetti economici e sociali dell'Italia preunitaria: Saggi. Rome: Istituto Storico Italiano, 1973. Rev. by E. P. Noether, AHR, 81(Feb 1976):177-8.

Ciccorello, Aubra Dair and Patricia Lee Ciccorello. Crossing the Crest. Boston: Branden, 1975. Rev. by H. Sitkoff, JAH, 63(Dec 1976):783-4.

Ciechanowski, Jan. The Warsaw Rising of 1944. Cambridge: U Press, 1974. Rev. by A. Polonsky, EHR, 91(Apr 1976):465-6.

Cipolla, Carlo M. Before the Industrial Revolution: European Society and Economy, 1000-1700. New York: Norton, 1976. Rev. by F. Frankfort, HRNB, 4(Aug 1976):198-9.

_____. Cristofano and the Plague: A Study in the History of Public Health in the Age of Galileo. Berkeley: U Cal Press, 1973. Rev. by D. B. Weiner, AHR, 81(Je 1976):621.

_____, ed. The Fontana Economic History of Europe: The Sixteenth and Seventeenth Centuries. London: Collins/Fontana, 1974. Rev. by G. D. Ramsay, History, 61(Je 1976):268-9.

_____. Public Health and the Medical Profession in the Renaissance. New York: Cam U Press, 1976. Rev. by K. H. Dannenfeldt, HRNB, 4(Aug 1976):199.

Ciria, Alberto. Parties and Power in Modern Argentina (1930-1946). Albany: SUNY, 1974. Rev. by S. L. Baily, AHR, 81(Oct 1976):1014.

Cirino, Linda see Edmiston, Susan

Clain-Stefanelli, Elvira and Vladimir Clain-Stefanelli. The Beauty and the Lore of Coins, Currency, and Medals. New York: Riverwood, n.d. Rev. by M. Russell, Smithsonian, 6(Jan 1975):104, 6.

Clark, Dennis, ed. Philadelphia: 1776-2076. Port Washington, N.Y.: Kennikat, 1975. Rev. by M. H. Ebner, JAH, 63(Dec 1976):697.

Clark, Ellery H. Boston Red Sox: 75th Anniversary History, 1901-1975. Hecksville, N.Y.: Exposition, 1975. Rev. by S. A. Riess, JAH, 63(Sep 1976):441.

Clark, Henry. Ministries of Dialogue: The Church Confronts the Power Structures. New York: Association Press, 1971. Rev. by J. W. Ousley, JCS, 18(Win 1976):149-50.

Clark, J. D. Kalambo Falls Prehistoric Site. 2 vols. New York: Cam U Press, 1969, 1974. Rev. by F. Willett, AHR, 81(Feb 1976):191-2.

Clark, Ronald W. The Life of Bertrand Russell. New York: Knopf, 1976. Rev. by W. D. Jones, HRNB, 4(Mar 1976): 112-13.

_____. The Scientific Breakthrough: The Impact of Modern Invention. New York: Putnam's, 1974. Rev. by P. C. Ritterbush, Smithsonian, 6(Jan 1975):101-2.

Clark, Walter Van Tilburg, ed. see Doten, Alfred

Clarke, Basil. Mental Disorder in Earlier Britain. Cardiff: U Wales Press, 1975. Rev. by A. Gransden, History, 61(Oct 1976):437-8.

Clarke, Charles G. Early Film Making in Los Angeles. Los Angeles: Dawson's Book Shop, 1976. Rev. by R. Knutson, SCQ, 58(Win 1976):534-5.

Clarke, M. L. Paley: Evidences for the Man. Toronto: U Tor Press, 1974. Rev. by D. L. Lemahieu, AHR, 81(Je 1976): 586-7.

Clarkson, Leslie. Death, Disease and Famine in Pre-Industrial England. New York: St. Martin's, 1975. Rev. by P. B. Cares, HRNB, 4(May/Je 1976):152.

Clason, A. T., ed. Archaeozoological Studies. Papers of the Archaeozoological Conference, Groningen, 1974. Amsterdam: North Holland Publishing Co., 1974. Rev. by R. Harcourt, Antiquity, 50(Mar 1976):80-1.

Claus, Robert, comp. Guide to Archives in the Connecticut State Library. Hartford, Conn.: Conn St Library, 1974. Rev. by W. N. Davis, Jr., AmArc, 39(Apr 1976):202-3.

Clavell, James. Shōgun: A Novel of Japan. New York: Atheneum, 1975. Rev. by S. K. Johnson, JJS, 2(Sum 1976):437-8.

Clay, James W., et al., eds. North Carolina Atlas. Chapel Hill: U NC Press, 1975. Rev. by J. F. Steelman, NCHR, 53(Aut 1976):399-400.

Clay, Lucius D. The Papers of General Lucius D. Clay. Vols. I and II. (Jean Edward Smith, ed.) Bloomington: Ind U Press, 1975. Rev. by E. L. Homze, AHR, 81(Je 1976):690; F. C. Pogue, JAH, 63(Je 1976):190-1.

Claybrook, Harry Dixon see Crouch, Arthur Weir

Clayton, Anthony and Donald C. Savage. Government and Labour
    in Kenya, 1895-1963. London: Frank Cass, 1974. Rev. by
    C. Ehrlich, AfAf, 75(Apr 1976):259-60; J. F. Munro, EHR,
    91(Oct 1976):931-3; T. Ranger, History, 61(Feb 1976):159;
    J. Spencer, JMAS, 14(Mar 1976):170-1.

Cleary, Karen A. see Levitan, Sar A.

Clem, Ralph S., ed. The Soviet West, Interplay Between Nation-
    ality and Social Organization. New York: Praeger, 1975.
    Rev. by A. Ezergailes, EEQ, 10(Mar 1976):135-6.

Clementi, Hebe. La abolición de la esclavitud en América Latina.
    Buenos Aires: Editorial La Pléyade, 1975. Rev. by A. F.
    Corwin, HAHR, 56(Feb 1976):114-16.

Clemoes, Peter, ed. Anglo-Saxon England III. Cambridge: Cam
    U Press, 1974. Rev. by J. L. Nelson, History, 61(Je 1976):
    250-1.

_____, et al., eds. Anglo-Saxon England, IV. Cambridge:
    Cam U Press, 1975. Rev. by B. D. Hill, AHR, 81(Oct
    1976):832-3; S. Keynes, JEccH, 27(Apr 1976):188-9.

Cleveland, William L. The Making of an Arab Nationalist: Otto-
    manism and Arabism in the Life and Thought of Sâti' al-Husri.
    Princeton, N.J.: Prin U Press, 1971. Rev. by R. N. Ver-
    dery, IJMES, 7(Jan 1976):137-8.

Clinch, George. English Costume: From Prehistoric Times to
    the Eighteenth Century. Totowa, N.J.: Rowman and Little-
    field, 1975. Rev. by J. T. Rosenthal, AHR, 81(Je 1976):
    580.

Cline, Gloria Griffen. Peter Skene Ogden and the Hudson's Bay
    Company. Norman: U Ok Press, 1975. Rev. by G. Wil-
    liams, History, 61(Oct 1976):395-6.

Cline, Howard F., ed. see Wauchope, Robert et al., eds.

Cline, Platt. They Came to the Mountain. Flagstaff, Ariz.:
    Northland, 1976. Rev. by W. H. Lyon, JAriH, 17(Aut
    1976):355-6.

Clogan, Paul Maurice, ed. Medievalia et Humanistica: Studies in
    Medieval and Renaissance Culture. New York: Cam U
    Press, 1976. Rev. by C. T. Marshall, HRNB, 4(May/Je
    1976):157-8.

Clogg, Richard, ed. see Auty, Phyllis, ed.

Clotfelter, James see Naylor, Thomas H.

Clutterbuck, Richard. Riot and Revolution in Singapore and Malaya, 1945-1963. London: Faber and Faber, 1973. Rev. by V. Suryanarayan, IQ, 32(Jan-Mar 1976):83-4.

Clymer, Kenton J. John Hay: The Gentleman as Diplomat. Ann Arbor: U Mich Press, 1975. Rev. by W. B. Fowler, HRNB, 4(Feb 1976):76; D. M. Pletcher, IMH, 72(Je 1976): 278-9; S. Prisco, III, JAH, 63(Je 1976):155-6; F. C. Jaher, JISHS, 69(Feb 1976):78-9; M. J. Devine, OH, 85(Aut 1976): 332-3; D. R. Gow, MiA, 58(Oct 1976):198-9; H. W. Morgan, PHR, 45(Nov 1976):623-4; P. S. Holbo, RAH, 4(Mar 1976): 92-8.

Coates, David. The Labour Party and the Struggle for Socialism. Cambridge: Cam U Press, 1975. Rev. by V. Bogdanor, History, 61(Je 1976):332.

Cobb, Richard. Paris and Its Provinces, 1792-1802. London: Oxford U Press, 1975. Rev. by C. H. Church, EHR, 91(Oct 1976):921-2; C. Lucas, History, 61(Oct 1976):458-9; J. P. T. Bury, HJ, 19(Sep 1976):793-7.

_____. The Police and the People: French Popular Protest, 1789-1820. Oxford: Oxford U, 1972. Rev. by J. P. T. Bury, HJ, 19(Sep 1976):793-7.

_____. Reactions to the French Revolution. Oxford: Oxford U Press, 1972. Rev. by J. P. T. Bury, HJ, 19(Sep 1976): 793-7.

_____. A Second Identity: Essays on France and French History. Oxford: Oxford U Press, 1969. Rev. by J. P. T. Bury, HJ, 19(Sep 1976):793-97.

Cobban, A. B. The Medieval Universities: Their Development and Organisation. London: Methuen, 1975. Rev. by G. Leff, History, 61(Je 1976):248; M. Wilks, JEccH, 27(Oct 1976):425-7.

Coe, David, ed. Mine Eyes Have Seen the Glory: Combat Diaries of Union Sergeant Hamlin Alexander Coe. Rutherford, N.J.: Fairleigh Dickinson U Press, 1975. Rev. by F. N. Boney, AHR, 81(Oct 1976):977-8; R. D. Hoffsommer, CWTI, 15(Jl 1976):49-50.

Coe, Michael D. Classic Maya Pottery at Dumbarton Oaks. Washington, D.C.: Dumbarton Oaks, n.d. Rev. by G. H. S. Bushnell, Antiquity, 50(Sep-Dec 1976):253-4.

Coen, Rena Neumann. Painting and Sculpture in Minnesota, 1820-1914. Minneapolis: U Minn Press, 1976. Rev. by J. F. Jensen, WMH, 60(Aut 1976):59-60.

Coffey, Thomas M. The Long Thirst: Prohibition in America, 1920-1933. New York: Norton, 1975. Rev. by J. M. Harrison, HRNB, 4(Feb 1976):79; L. Sponholtz, OH, 85(Sum 1976): 275-6.

Coffin, C. C. Dakota Wheat Fields 1880. Fargo, N. D.: Box Elder Bug Press, 1974. Rev. by Editor, NDH, 43(Sum 1976): 47.

Cogswell, Seddie, Jr. Tenure, Nativity, and Age as Factors in Iowa Agriculture, 1850-1880. Ames: Iowa St U Press, 1975. Rev. by R. P. Swierenga, AI, 43(Spr 1976):314-17; J. F. Stover, IMH, 72(Je 1976):272-3; D. R. Leet, JEH, 36(Sep 1976):744-5; E. L. Schapsmeier, JOW, 15(Apr 1976):143.

Cohen, David S. The Ramapo Mountain People. New Brunswick, N. J.: Rutgers U Press, 1974. Rev. by L. A. Glasco, JNH, 61(Apr 1976):219-21.

Cohen, Edward H. Ebenezer Cooke: The Sot-Weed Canon. Athens: U Ga Press, 1975. Rev. by G. J. Goodwin, JSH, 42(Feb 1976):101-2.

Cohen, H. F. Toward the Renewal of Socialism: The Political Orientation of the Dutch Social-Democratic Party 1919-1930. Leiden: Universitaire Pers, 1974. Rev. by F. G. Eyck, AHR, 81(Feb 1976):162-3.

Cohen, Kathleen. Metamorphosis of a Death Symbol. The Transi Tomb in the Late Middle Ages and the Renaissance. Berkeley: U Cal Press, 1973. Rev. by C. Olds, CaHR, 62(Jan 1976): 108-9.

Cohen, Naomi W. American Jews and the Zionist Idea. New York: KTAV, 1975. Rev. by D. W. Noble, HRNB, 4(Mar 1976):99; M. I. Urofsky, JAH, 63(Je 1976):193-4.

Cohen, Ralph, ed. New Directions in Literary History. Baltimore: JHU Press, 1974. Rev. by C. Molesworth, GR, 6(Spr 1976): 217-22.

Cohn, Norman. Europe's Inner Demons. London: Sussex U Press, 1975. Rev. by R. I. Moore, History, 61(Oct 1976):444-5.

Cole, C. Robert and Michael E. Moody, eds. The Dissenting Tradition: Essays for Leland H. Carlson. Athens: Ohio U Press, 1975. Rev. by L. F. Solt, CH, 45(Je 1976):258-9.

Cole, Patrick. Modern and Traditional Elites in the Politics of Lagos. New York: Cam U Press, 1975. Rev. by B. Weinstein, AHR, 81(Oct 1976):924-5; A. J. H. Latham, History, 61(Feb 1976):153.

Cole, Wayne S. Charles A. Lindbergh and the Battle Against Intervention in World War II. New York: Harcourt Brace Jovanovich, 1974. Rev. by R. H. Ferrell, JAH, 63(Je 1976): 183-4; E. M. Bennett, PNQ, 67(Jan 1976):42-3.

Coleman, D. C. Industry in Tudor and Stuart England. London: Macmillan, 1975. Rev. by G. Hammersley, History, 61(Je 1976):270-1.

Coleman, John F. The Disruption of the Pennsylvania Democracy, 1848-1860. Harrisburg: Pa Historical Museum Commission, 1975. Rev. by S. W. Higginbotham, AHR, 81(Je 1976):665; D. E. Meerse, CWH, 22(Je 1976):177-8; E. B. Smith, JAH, 63(Je 1976):123-4; J. K. Folmer, OH, 85(Win 1976):89.

Coleman, John M. Thomas McKean: Forgotten Leader of the Revolution. Rockaway, N.J.: American Faculty Press, 1975. Rev. by P. D. Nelson, AHR, 81(Oct 1976):961-2; W. S. Hanna, JAH, 62(Mar 1976):972; R. M. Baumann, WMQ, 33(Jan 1976):166-8.

Coleman, Peter J. Debtors and Creditors in America: Insolvency, Imprisonment for Debt, and Bankruptcy, 1607-1900. Madison: St Historical Society of Wis, 1974. Rev. by C. W. McCurdy, AHR, 81(Je 1976):649-50; D. B. Graddy, JEH, 36(Sep 1976): 746-7; G. G. Eggert, PH, 43(Jl 1976):274-5.

Coleridge, Samuel Taylor. On the Constitution of the Church and State According to the Idea of Each. London: Dent, 1973. Rev. by C. T. Goode, JCH, 18(Win 1976):124-5.

Coles, John. Archaeology by Experiment. New York: Scribner's, 1974. Rev. by J. A. Sabloff, JIH, 7(Sum 1976):125-6.

Coles, Robert. William Carlos Williams. New Brunswick, N.J.: Rutgers U Press, 1975. Rev. by R. E. Brown, Mankind, 5 (Feb 1976):67-8.

Coletta, Paolo E. The Presidency of William Howard Taft. Lawrence: U Press Kan, 1973. Rev. in AS, 16(Spr 1976):76.

Collaer, Paul. Music of the Americas: An Illustrated Music Ethnology of the Eskimo and American Indian Peoples. New York: Praeger, 1973. Rev. by C. J. Frisbie, AA, 78(Mar 1976):155.

Colletti, Lucio. Marxism and Hegel. Atlantic Highlands, N.J.: Humanities, 1973. Rev. by N. Levine, AHR, 81(Apr 1976): 359-60.

Collins, June McCormick. Valley of the Spirits: The Upper Skagit Indians of Western Washington. Seattle: U Press, 1974. Rev. by P. T. Amoss, PNQ, 67(Apr 1976):92-3; R. L. De-Lorme, WHQ, 7(Apr 1976):207-8.

Collins, Robert E. Theodore Parker: American Transcendentalist;
    A Critical Essay and a Collection of His Writings. Metuchen,
    N.J.: Scarecrow, 1973. Rev. by J. A. Tetlow, CaHR, 62
    (Jl 1976):520.

Colonial Society of Massachusetts. Boston Furniture of the Eight-
    eenth Century. Conference of Colonial Society of Mass. 11
    and 12 May 1972. Boston: Colonial Society of Massachusetts,
    1974. Rev. by J. F. Page, NEQ, 49(Mar 1976):146-8.

Comisión Económica Para América Latina. Estudio económica de
    América Latina. New York: United Nations, 1974. Rev. by
    E. N. Baklanoff, HAHR, 56(Feb 1976):155-7.

Comité d'Histoire de la Deuxiéme Guerre Mondiale. La guerre en
    Mediterranée 1939-1945: Actes du Colloque International tenu
    à Paris du 8 au 11 avil 1969. Paris: Editions du Centre Na-
    tional de la Recherche Scientifique, 1971. Rev. by G. F.
    Howe, AHR, 81(Je 1976):578-9.

Commager, Henry Steele and Richard B. Morris, eds. The Spirit
    of 'Seventy-Six: The Story of the American Revolution as Told
    by Participants. New York: Harper and Row, 1975. Rev.
    by J. F. Sefcik, HRNB, 4(Feb 1976):80-1.

Commoner, Barry. The Poverty of Power: Energy and the Eco-
    nomic Crisis. New York: Knopf, 1976. Rev. by B. Kovnor,
    Commentary, 62(Sep 1976):114, 116.

Confalonieri, Antonio. Banca e industria in Italia, 1894-1906.
    Vol. I. Milan: Banca Commerciale Italiana, 1974. Rev. by
    J. S. Cohen, JEH, 36(Je 1976):458-60.

Confessore, Ornella. Conservatorismo politico e riformismo
    religioso: La "Rassegna Nazionale" dal 1898 al 1908.
    Bologna: Il Mulino, 1971. Rev. by R. Grew, AHR, 81
    (Je 1976):624-5.

Confino, Michael, ed. Daughter of a Revolutionary: Natalie Herzen
    and the Bakunin-Nechayev Circle. London: Alcove, 1974.
    Rev. by E. Action, History, 61(Je 1976):299-300.

Conkin, Paul K. Self-Evident Truths: Being a Discourse on the
    Origins and Development of the First Principles of American
    Government--Popular Sovereignty, Natural Rights, and Balance
    and Separation of Powers. Bloomington: Ind U Press, 1974.
    Rev. by W. M. Dabney, AHR, 81(Feb 1976):205-6.

Conlin, Joseph R., ed. The American Radical Press, 1880-1960.
    Westport, Conn.: Greenwood, 1974. Rev. by G. S. Kealey,
    CHR, 57(Je 1976):225-6.

Conlin, Katherine E. Windsor Heritage: Birthplace of Vermont's
    Constitution and Industry. Taftsville, Vt.: Countrymen Press,

1975. Rev. by R. D. Nuquist, VH, 44(Win 1976):51-4.

Connah, Graham. The Archaeology of Benin. Oxford: Clarendon Press, 1975. Rev. by J. Alexander, Antiquity, 50(Je 1976): 172.

Connor, Seymour V. Texas in 1776. Austin, Tex.: Jenkins, 1975. Rev. by B. E. Pingenot, SWHQ, 80(Jl 1976):119-20.

Constable, G. and B. Smith, eds. Libellus de Diversis Ordinibus et Professionibus qui sunt Aecclesia. New York: Oxford U Press, 1972. Rev. by J. R. Sommerfeldt, CaHR, 62(Jan 1976):82-3.

Conticello, Baldassare and Bernard Andreae. Die Skulpturen von Sperlonga. Berlin: Gebr. Mann Verlag, 1974. Rev. by P. H. von Blanckenhagen, AJA, 80(Win 1976):99-104.

Conzemius, Victor. Propheten und Vorläufer, Wegbereiter des neuzeitlichen Katholizismus. Zürich: Benziger Verlag, 1972. Rev. by J. F. Broderick, CaHR, 62(Apr 1976):312-13.

Coogan, M. Jane. The Price of Our Heritage. Vol. I. Dubuque, Iowa: Mt Carmel Press, 1975. Rev. by J. Bland, CaHR, 62(Jl 1976):485-6.

Cook, Adrian. The Alabama Claims: American Politics and Anglo-American Relations, 1865-1872. Ithaca, N.Y.: Cornell U Press, 1975. Rev. by C. P. Cullop, JAH, 63(Je 1976):138; H. Brogan, JAmS, 10(Aug 1976):276-7.

_____. The Armies of the Streets: The New York City Draft Riots of 1863. Lexington: U Ky Press, 1974. Rev. by D. Lindsey, AHI, 10(Jan 1976):39.

Cook, Cecil. Marquette: The Biography of an Iowa Railroad Town. Des Moines: Waukon and Mississippi Press, 1975. Rev. by W. S. Greever, AI, 43(Sum 1976):398-9.

Cook, Chris. The Age of Alignment, Electoral Politics in Britain, 1922-29. London: Macmillan, 1975. Rev. by R. K. Middlemas, EHR, 91(Oct 1976):935-6.

_____. Sources in British Political History 1900-1951. Vols. I and II. Guide to the Archives of Selected Organizations and Societies. London: Macmillan, 1975. Rev. by R. Storey, Archives, 12(Spr 1976):149-50; A. E. B. Owen, Archives, 12 (Aut 1976):198-9; P. F. Clarke, History, 61(Je 1976):311-12.

_____. and Brendan Keith. British Historical Facts, 1830-1900. London: Macmillan, 1975. Rev. by J. R. Vincent, History, 61(Oct 1976):488.

Cook, M. A. Population Pressure in Rural Anatolia, 1450-1600.
London: Oxford U Press, 1972. Rev. by M. Çizakça, JEH,
(Je 1976):460-1.

Cook, Ramsay see Brown, Robert Craig

Cook, Reginald. Robert Frost: A Living Voice. Amherst: U
Mass Press, 1974. Rev. by C. E. Eaton, GR, 30(Sum 1976):
447-60.

Cook, Scott and Martin Diskin, eds. Markets in Oaxaca. Austin:
U Tex Press, 1976. Rev. by D. J. Thomas, HAHR, 56(Nov
1976):680-1.

Cook, Sherburne F. and Woodrow Borah. Essays in Population
History: Mexico and the Caribbean. Berkeley: U Cal Press,
1974. Rev. by U. M. Cowgill, AmAn, 41(Apr 1976):240-1.

Cooke, A. B. and John Vincent. The Governing Passion: Cabinet
Government and Party Politics in Britain 1885-6. Brighton:
Harvester, 1974. Rev. by A. Warren, EHR, 91(Jan 1976):
152-5; A. Jones, HJ, 19(Mar 1976):251-6.

Cookridge, E. H. Gehlen: Spy of the Century. New York: Random House, 1972. Rev. by W. A. Fletcher, AHR, 81(Oct
1976):884-7.

Cookson, J. E. Lord Liverpool's Administration: the Crucial
Years, 1815-1822. London: Scottish Academic Press, 1975.
Rev. by B. Hilton, EHR, 91(Apr 1976):395-7.

Coolhaas, W. Ph., ed. Generale Missiven van Gouverneurs-General
en Raden aan Heren XVII der Verenigde Oostlindische Com-
pagnie, v, 1686-1697. The Hague: Martinus Nijhoff, 1975.
Rev. by D. K. Bassett, EHR, 91(Jl 1976):606-8.

Cooling, Benjamin Franklin. Symbol, Sword, and Shield: Defend-
ing Washington During the Civil War. Hamden, Conn.:
Archon, 1975. Rev. by E. C. Murdock, AHR, 81(Je 1976):
668; E. B. Long, JAH, 62(Mar 1976):1001-2; H. M. Hattaway,
JSH, 42(Feb 1976):126-7.

Cooper, David D. The Lesson of the Scaffold: The Public Execu-
tion Controversy in Victorian England. London: Allen Lane,
1974. Rev. by O. Anderson, EHR, 91(Apr 1976):447-8.

Cooper, Michael. Rodrigues the Interpreter: An Early Jesuit in
Japan and China. New York: Weatherhill, 1974. Rev. by L.
La Davy, CQ, Jan 1976, pp. 146-7.

Copeland, Pamela C. and Richard K. MacMaster. The Five George
Masons: Patriots and Planters of Virginia and Maryland.
Charlottesville: U Press Va, 1975. Rev. by R. Lowe,

HRNB, 4(Aug 1976):187-8; W. C. Smith, JAH, 63(Dec 1976): 689-90; G. W. Pilcher, JSH, 42(Nov 1976):577-8; M. B. D. McCurdy, VMHB, 84(Jl 1976):371-2.

Copeland, William R. The Uneasy Alliance. Collaboration Between the Finnish Opposition and the Russian Underground 1899-1904. Helsinki: Suomalainen Tiedeakatemia, 1973. Rev. by L. Kochan, EHR, 91(Jl 1976):678-9.

Copp, Terry. The Anatomy of Poverty: The Condition of the Working Class in Montreal 1897-1929. Toronto: McClelland and Stewart, 1974. Rev. by G. S. French, AHR, 81(Feb 1976):224-5.

Coppa, Frank J. Camillo di Cavour. New York: Twayne, 1973. Rev. by R. S. Cunsolo, CaHR, 62(Oct 1976):624-5.

Coppock, Paul R. Memphis Sketches. Memphis: Friends of Memphis and Shelby County Libraries, 1976. Rev. by C. W. Crawford, THQ, 35(Win 1976):422-3.

Corbin, Alain. Archaïsme et modernité en Limousin au XIXe siècle, 1845-1880: La rigidité des structures économiques, sociales et mentales. Paris: Editions Marcel Rivière, 1975. Rev. by C. Tilly, AHR, 81(Oct 1976):870.

Corda, Salvatore. Veritas Sacramenti: A Study in Vermigli's Doctrine of the Lord's Supper. Zurich: Theologischer Verlag, 1975. Rev. by R. L. Harrison, Jr., CH, 45(Sep 1976): 385-6.

Corder, Jim W. More than a Century. Fort Worth: TCU Press, 1973. Rev. by D. Pitcaithley, JOW, 15(Jan 1976):125.

Cordier, Andrew W. and Wilder Foote, eds. Public Papers of the Secretaries-General of the United Nations. Vols. 4, 5 and 6. New York: Columbia U Press, 1975. Rev. by L. M. Goodrich, AHR, 81(Oct 1976):820-1; W. F. Kuehl, JAH, 63 (Dec 1976):675-7.

Córdova, Arnaldo. La formación del poder politico en México. México: Ediciones Era, 1972. Rev. by D. C. Bailey, TAm, 33(Jl 1976):173-5.

_____. La ideología de la Revolución Mexicana: La formación del nuevo régimen. México: Editiones Era, 1973. Rev. by D. C. Bailey, TAm, 33(Jl 1976):173-5.

Cornelius, Friedrich. Geschichte der Hethiter. Darmstadt: Wissenschaftliche Buchgesellschaft, 1973. Rev. by H. A. Hoffner, Jr., JNES, 35(Jl 1976):205-6.

Corner, Paul. Fascism in Ferrara, 1915-1925. New York: Ox-

ford U Press, 1975. Rev. by C. F. Delzell, AHR, 81(Oct
1976):893-4; H. Hearder, EHR, 91(Jl 1976):681-2; R. A. H.
Robinson, History, 61(Oct 1976):470-1.

Corpuz, Paula, ed. see Thornbrough, Gayle, ed.

Cortés, Carlos E. Gaúcho Politics in Brazil: The Politics of
Rio Grande do Sul, 1930-1964. Albuquerque: U NM Press,
1975. Rev. by S. Lauderdale, HAHR, 56(Feb 1976):134-5;
R. M. Levine, TAm, 32(Jan 1976):483-4.

Costello, F. B. The Political Philosophy of Luis De Molina, S.J.
(1535-1600). Rome: Institutum Historicum S.I., 1974. Rev.
by B. Hamilton, History, 61(Je 1976):281-2.

Costeloe, Michael P. La primera república federal de Mexico
(1824-1835). Mexico: Fondo de cultura Econòmica, 1975.
Rev. by C. R. Berry, HAHR, 56(Nov 1976):654-6.

Cotler, Julio and Richard Fagen, eds. Latin America and the
United States: The Changing Political Realities. Stanford:
Stanford U Press, 1974. Rev. by D. Dozer, PHR, 45(Aug
1976):455-7.

Cotterell, Arthur and David Morgan. China's Civilization: A Survey of Its History, Arts, and Technology. New York:
Praeger, 1975. Rev. by E. C. Lydon, HT, 10(Nov 1976):
127-8.

Cottrell, P. L. British Overseas Investment in the Nineteenth
Century. London: Macmillan, 1975. Rev. by P. J. Cain,
History, 61(Oct 1976):487-8.

_____ see Anderson, B. L.

Coughlan, Neil. Young John Dewey: An Essay in American Intel-
lectual History. Chicago: U Chicago Press, 1975. Rev. by
L. H. Cohen, HRNB, 4(Apr 1976):125; C. Strout, JAH, 63
(Sep 1976):440-1.

Couilloud, Marie-Thérèse. Les Monuments funéraires de Rhénée.
Paris: Diffusion de Boccard, 1974. Rev. by J. G. Pedley,
AJA, 80(Sum 1976):312.

Coulson, Noel J. Succession in the Muslim Family. Cambridge:
Cam U Press, 1971. Rev. by C. J. Adams, JAAS, 11(Jl-
Oct 1976):244-5.

Court, David and Dharam P. Ghai, eds. Education, Society and
Development: New Perspectives from Kenya. Nairobi: Oxford U Press, 1974. Rev. by B. Lindsay, JMAS, 14(Je 1976):
361-4.

Courteau, Guy. Le docteur J-Raoul Hurtubise, M. D. , M. P. : 40 ans de vie française à Sudbury. Montreal: Les Editions Bellarmin, 1971. Rev. by G. C. Brandt, CHR, 57(Je 1976):210-11.

Courtin, Jean. Le Néolithique de la Provence. Paris: Klincksieck, 1974. Rev. by P. Phillips, Antiquity, 50(Mar 1976):79-80.

Couse, G. S. , ed. see Mudroch, Vaclav, ed.

Cover, Robert M. Justice Accused: Antislavery and the Judicial Process. New Haven, Conn.: Yale U Press, 1975. Rev. by H. M. Hyman, AHR, 81(Je 1976):663-4; D. J. MacLeod, History, 61(Oct 1976):406-7.

Coverdale, John F. Italian Intervention in the Spanish Civil War. Princeton, N.J.: Prin U Press, 1976. Rev. by F. Rosengarten, AHR, 81(Oct 1976):876; C. Keserich, HRNB, 4(Apr 1976):134.

Cowan, Ian B. and David E. Easson, eds. Medieval Religious Houses: Scotland. New York: Longman, 1976. Rev. by D. Baker, JEccH, 27(Oct 1976):431-2.

Cowling, Maurice. The Impact of Hitler. London: Cam U Press, 1975. Rev. by J. P. D. Dunbabin, HJ, 19(Mar 1976):305-8.

Cox, Archibald. The Role of the Supreme Court in American Government. New York: Oxford U Press, 1976. Rev. by S. Levinson, NEQ, 49(Sep 1976):474-6.

Cox, Eugene L. The Eagles of Savoy: The House of Savoy in Thirteenth-Century Europe. Princeton, N.J.: Prin U Press, 1974. Rev. by W. M. Bowsky, AHR, 81(Feb 1976):117-18; D. M. Bueno de Mesquita, EHR, 91(Apr 1976):411-12; F. L. Cheyette, Historian, 38(Feb 1976):322.

Cox, Robert W. , et al. The Anatomy of Influence: Decision Making in International Organizations. New Haven, Conn.: Yale U Press, 1973. Rev. by A. F. Ewing, JMAS, 14(Je 1976):345-8.

Cox, Thomas R. Mills and Markets: A History of the Pacific Coast Lumber Industry to 1900. Seattle: U Wash Press, 1975. Rev. by R. L. Mathney, A & W, 18(Sum 1976):190-1; T. F. Gedosch, AHR, 81(Oct 1976):985; G. B. Engberg, Historian, 39(Nov 1976):158; T. C. Hinkley, PHR, 45(Aug 1976):449-50; J. H. Kemble, PNQ, 67(Apr 1976):94; R. J. Fahl, WHQ, 7(Jan 1976):63-4.

Crampton, C. Gregory, ed. The Mariposa Indian War, 1850-1851: Diaries of Robert Eccleston: The California Gold Rush, Yosemite, and the High Sierra. Salt Lake City: University

of Utah Press, 1975. Rev. by G. H. Phillips, PHR, 45(Aug
1976):442-3; R. H. Dillon, CHQ, 55(Spr 1976):92; J. H.
O'Donnell, III, OH, 85(Spr 1976):170.

_____, ed. see Hall, Sharlot M.

_____ see Rusho, W. L.

Crane, Sophie and Paul Crane. Tennessee Taproots. Old Hickory,
    Tenn.: Earle-Shields, 1976. Rev. by H. L. Harper, THQ,
    35(Win 1976):417-18.

Crapanzano, Vincent. The Hamadsha: A Study in Moroccan Ethno-
    psychiatry. Berkeley: U Cal Press, 1973. Rev. by N. S.
    Hopkins, IJMES, 7(Jan 1976):141-3.

Craven, Avery O. Rachel of Old Louisiana. Baton Rouge: LSU
    Press, 1975. Rev. by J. H. Broussard, AgH, 50(Apr 1976):
    441-2.

Crawford, Charles W. Yesterday's Memphis. Miami: E. A. See-
    mann, 1976. Rev. by J. E. Roper, THQ, 35(Win 1976):420-1.

Crawford, James, ed. Studies in Southeastern Indian Languages.
    Athens: U Ga Press, 1975. Rev. by J. Campbell, ChOk, 54
    (Spr 1976):160-1.

Crawford, Michael H. Roman Republican Coinage. Cambridge:
    Cam U Press, 1975. Rev. by H. C. Boren, AHR, 81(Apr
    1976):366-7; W. E. Metcalf, AJA, 80(Spr 1976):215-16.

Crawford, Richard see McKay, David P.

Crawley, Aiden. The Rise of Western Germany, 1945-1972. Lon-
    don: Collins, 1973. Rev. by R. Lenman, EHR, 91(Apr
    1976):471.

Creel, Herrlee G. Shen Pu-hai: A Chinese Political Philosopher
    of the Fourth Century B.C. Chicago: U Chicago Press,
    1974. Rev. by I. J. H. Ts'ao, JAS, 36(Nov 1976):123-4.

Creighton, James A. A Narrative History of Brazoria County,
    Texas. Brazoria County Historical Commission, 1975.
    Rev. by H. B. Simpson, Texana, 12(Num 4, 1976):384.

Crenson, Matthew A. The Federal Machine: Beginnings of
    Bureaucracy in Jacksonian America. Baltimore: JHU Press,
    1975. Rev. by F. H. Heller, AS, 16(Fall 1975):97; W. G.
    Shade, CWH, 22(Mar 1976):85-6; M. J. Heale, History, 61
    (Oct 1976):404; C. E. Prince, IMH, 72(Mar 1976):74-5;
    J. M. McFaul, JAH, 62(Mar 1976):989-90.

Crew, Harvey see True, C. W. Meighan

Crimson, Leo Taylor, ed. Baptists in Kentucky, 1776-1976. Middleton, Ky.: Kentucky Baptist Convention, 1975. Rev. by L. E. M. , BHH, 11(Jan 1976):63-4.

Crocker, Lester G. Diderot's Chaotic Order: Approach to Synthesis. Princeton, N. J.: Prin U Press, 1974. Rev. by V. G. Wexler, AHR, 81(Feb 1976):138-9.

Croll, Elisabeth. The Women's Movement in China: A Selection of Readings, 1949-1973. London: Anglo-Chinese Educational Institute, 1974. Rev. by R. Witke, CQ, May 1976, pp. 394-6.

Cromwell, Giles. The Virginia Manufactory of Arms. Charlottesville: U Press Va, 1975. Rev. by R. W. Donnelly, JSH, 42(Feb 1976):136-7.

Cromwell, Richard S. David Friedrich Strauss and His Place in Modern Thought. Fair Lawn, N. J.: R. E. Burdick, 1974. Rev. by G. D. Drummond, AHR, 81(Feb 1976):166.

Cronin, James E. , ed. see Smith, Elihu Hubbard

Cronin, Vincent. Louis and Antoinette. London: Collins, 1974. Rev. by J. M. J. Rogister, History, 61(Feb 1976):119.

Crook, D. P. Diplomacy During the American Civil War. New York: Wiley, 1975. Rev. by K. J. Brauer, HRNB, 4(Apr 1976):119.

_____. The North, the South, and the Powers, 1861-1865. New York: Wiley, 1974. Rev. by M. Klein, AHI, 11(Dec 1976):50; F. C. Drake, CWH, 22(Je 1976):178-80.

Crosby, Travis L. Sir Robert Peel's Administration: 1841-1846. Hamden, Conn.: Shoestring, 1976. Rev. by B. McGill, HRNB, 5(Oct 1976):22.

Cross, George L. Blacks in White Colleges: Oklahoma's Landmark Cases. Norman: U Ok Press, 1975. Rev. by J. T. Hubbell, A & W, 18(Win 1976):379-80.

Crossland, R. A. and Ann Birchall, eds. Bronze Age Migrations in the Aegean. Park Ridge, N. J.: Noyes, 1974. Rev. by M. H. Jameson, Historian, 39(Nov 1976):111-12.

Crossley, Alan, ed. Victoria County History of Oxford. Vol. X. Oxford: Oxford U Press, 1972. Rev. by R. H. C. Davis, History, 61(Feb 1976):77-8.

Crossley, Robert N. Luther and the Peasants' War: Luther's Actions and Reactions. New York: Exposition, 1974. Rev. by J. M. Stayer, CaHR, 62(Jan 1976):123-4; B. C. Weber, JCS, 17(Win 1975):152-3.

Crouch, Arthur Weir and Harry Dixon Claybrook. Our Ancestors
Were Engineers. Nashville: American Society of Civil
Engineers, 1976. Rev. by R. E. Dalton, THQ, 35(Win 1976):
423-4.

Crouch, Thomas W. A Yankee Guerrillero: Frederick Funston and
the Cuban Insurrection 1896-1897. Memphis: Memphis St U
Press, 1975. Rev. by N. Macaulay, HAHR, 56(Nov 1976):
648-50; J. A. Lewis, HRNB, 4(May/Je 1976):147-8; R. H.
Spector, JAH, 63(Dec 1976):744-5; H. W. Morgan, SWHQ, 80
(Oct 1976):244.

Crouzet, François. Le Conflit de Chypre, 1946-1959. 2 vols.
Brussels: Establissements Emile Bruylant, 1973. Rev. by
R. Albrecht-Carrié, AHR, 81(Feb 1976):126-7.

Crow, Jeffrey J. A Chronicle of North Carolina During the American
Revolution, 1763-1789. Raleigh: N.C. Dept. of Cultural Resources, 1975. Rev. by G. Troxler, NCHR, 53(Win 1976):81-2.

Crowder, Michael. Revolt in Bussa. London: Faber, 1973.
Rev. by P. E. H. Hair, EHR, 91(Jan 1976):236-7.

Crowe, Rosalie and Sydney B. Brinckerhoff, eds. Early Yuma:
A Graphic History of the American Nile. Flagstaff, Ariz.:
Northland, 1976. Rev. by H. P. Walker, JAriH, 17(Sum
1976):233-4.

Crowley, F. K., ed. A New History of Australia. New York:
Holmes and Meier, 1975. Rev. by A. S. Trickett, HRNB,
4(Mar 1976):104-5.

Crowley, J. E. This Sheba, Self: The Conceptualization of Economic Life in Eighteenth-Century America. Baltimore: JHU
Press, 1974. Rev. by T. Cochran, AHR, 81(Apr 1976):440;
T. Colbourn, JAH, 62(Mar 1976):965-6; H. N. Scheiber, JIH,
7(Aut 1976):358-9.

Crowther, J. G. The Cavendish Laboratory 1874-1974. n.p.:
Science History Publications, 1974. Rev. by R. C. Post,
Smithsonian, 6(Apr 1975):108-10.

Crozier, Brian. De Gaulle. I and II. London: Eyre Methuen,
1973. Rev. by D. N. Baker, CHR, 57(Mar 1976):106-8.

Cruickshank, Charles. The German Occupation of the Channel Islands. Oxford: Oxford U Press, 1975. Rev. by R. Callahan,
AHR, 81(Apr 1976):391-2; D. Read, History, 61(Je 1976):328.

Cruise O'Brien, Donal B. Saints and Politicians: Essays on the
Organisation of a Senegalese Peasant Society. New York:
Cam U Press, 1975. Rev. by N. S. Hopkins, JAAS, 11(Jl-
Oct 1976):250-1.

Crummey, Robert O. The Old Believers & the World of Antichrist. Madison: U Wis Press, 1970. Rev. by A. W. Wardin, Jr., JCS, 18(Aut 1976):586-7.

Crunican, Paul. Priests and Politicians: Manitoba Schools and the Election of 1896. Toronto: U Tor Press, 1974. Rev. by J. R. Miller, CHR, 57(Je 1976):200-2.

Crutchfield, James A. Early Times in the Cumberland Valley, from Its Beginnings Until 1800. Nashville: First American National Bank, 1976. Rev. in THQ, 35(Sum 1976):229-30.

Csatári, Dániel. Dans la Tourmente: Les Relations Hungaro-Roumaines de 1940 à 1945. Budapest: Akadémiai Kiadó, 1974. Rev. by N. Stone, History, 61(Je 1976):329.

Cudd, John Michael. The Chicopee Manufacturing Company, 1823-1915. Wilmington, Del.: Scholarly Resources, 1975. Rev. by D. J. Jeremy, AHR, 81(Je 1976):659.

Cuddihy, John Murray. The Ordeal of Civility. New York: Basic Books, 1974. Rev. by M. Wyschogrod, Judaism, 25(Fall 1976):505-9.

Cuff, R. D. and J. L. Granatstein. Canadian-American Relations in Wartime: From the Great War to the Cold War. Toronto: Hakkert, 1975. Rev. by G. F. G. Stanley, AHR, 81(Je 1976): 698-9.

Culbert, David Holbrook. News for Everyman: Radio and Foreign Affairs in Thirties America. Westport, Conn.: Greenwood, 1976. Rev. by J. M. Harrison, HRNB, 4(Aug 1976):192; E. W. Chester, HRNB, 4(Sep 1976):214-15.

Cullen, Michael J. The Statistical Movement in Early Victorian Britain. New York: Harper and Row, 1975. Rev. by N. A. Ferguson, Historian, 39(Nov 1976):120-1; A. E. Musson, History, 61(Oct 1976):483.

Culler, Jonathan. Structuralist Poetics. Ithaca, N.Y.: Cornell U Press, 1975. Rev. by P. R. Olson, GR, 30(Sum 1976): 467-79.

Cumming, W. P., et al. The Exploration of North America 1630-1776. London: Elek, 1974. Rev. by G. V. Scammell, History, 61(Oct 1976):447-8.

Cumming, William P. and Hugh F. Rankin. The Fate of a Nation: The American Revolution Through Contemporary Eyes. London: Phaidon, 1975. Rev. by G. R. Lamplugh, HT, 10(Nov 1976):151-3; A. K. Austin, JAH, 63(Je 1976):109; W. S. Price, Jr., NCHR, 53(Win 1976):93-4; T. W. Tate, VMHB, 84(Jan 1976):105-6.

87   CUMMINS

Cummins, Cedric. The University of South Dakota, 1862-1966.
Vermillion, S. D.: Dakota Press, 1975. Rev. by J. E.
Horner, IMH, 72(Je 1976):273-5; L. G. Geiger, JAH, 63
(Sep 1976):426-7; M. E. Jarchow, MinnH, 45(Spr 1976):38.

Cuninggim, Merrimon. Private Money in Public Service: The
Role of Foundations in American Society. New York: Mc-
Graw-Hill, 1972. Rev. by T. Z. Parrish, JCS, 17(Win
1975):131-3.

Cunliffe, Barry. Iron Age Communities in Britain: An Account of
England, Scotland, and Wales from the Seventh Century B. C.
Until the Roman Conquest. Boston: Routledge and Kegan
Paul, 1974. Rev. by B. S. Bachrach, AHR, 81(Feb 1976):
103; J. V. S. Megaw, History, 61(Oct 1976):432.

Cunningham, Hugh. The Volunteer Force: A Social and Political
History. London: Croom Helm, 1975. Rev. by J. A.
Sabine, History, 61(Oct 1976):491-2.

Curtin, Philip D. Economic Change in Precolonial Africa. 2
vols. Madison: U Wis Press, 1975. Rev. by D. H. Jones,
AfAf, 75(Jl 1976):392-4; B. M. Perinham, AHR, 81(Oct 1976):
922-3.

Curtis, James C. Andrew Jackson and the Search for Vindication.
Boston: Little, Brown, 1976. Rev. by J. D. Haeger, HT,
10(Nov 1976):144-5; W. J. Gilmore, JSH, 42(Nov 1976):589-91.

Cushing, Irene, ed. and Irene Stafford, ed. Bethel, The Early
Years: A Collection of Photographs with Text. Bethel, Vt.:
Bethel Historical Society, 1974. Rev. by R. D. Nuquist,
VH, 44(Win 1976):51-4.

Cuttino, G. P. Gascon Register A. 2 vols. London: Oxford U
Press, 1975. Rev. by P. S. Lewis, EHR, 91(Oct 1976):898.

Czaplicka, M. A. The Turks of Central Asia. New York: Barnes
and Noble, 1973. Rev. by M. Rossabi, JAAS, 11(Jl-Oct
1976):223-4.

d'Abbadie, J. Vandier. Les Objets de toilette egyptiens au Musée
du Louvre. Paris: Editions des Musées Nationaux, 1972.
Rev. by W. H. Peck, JNES, 35(Jl 1976):216-17.

Dabney, Virginius, ed. The Patriots. New York: Atheneum,
1975. Rev. by L. B. Miller, JAH, 63(Dec 1976):694-5.

Dachs, Anthony J., ed. Papers of John Mackenzie. Johannesburg: Witwatersrand U Press, 1975. Rev. by J. A. Casada,
AHR, 81(Oct 1976):931; Q. N. Parsons, JAfH, 17(Num 3,
1976):456-8.

D'AGOSTINO   88

d'Agostino, Bruno, ed. see Modesti, Gianni Bailo, ed.

Dagron, Gilbert. Naissance d'une capitale: Constantinople et ses
    institutions de 330 à 451. Paris: Presses Universitaires de
    France, 1974. Rev. by D. DeF. Abrahamse, AHR, 81(Apr
    1976):373.

Dahlerup, Merete, ed. Herlufsholm Frie Skoles Regnskab 1585-86.
    Copenhagen: Landbohistorisk Selskab, 1975. Rev. by S. P.
    Oakley, EHR, 91(Oct 1976):900.

Daiches, David. Moses: The Man and His Vision. New York:
    Praeger, n.d. Rev. by W. Kramer, Mankind, 5(Je 1976):12-
    13.

Dakin, Julian, Brian Tiffin and H. G. Widdowson. Language in
    Education. The Problem in Commonwealth Africa and the
    Indo-Pakistan Sub-Continent. London: Oxford U Press, 1968.
    Rev. by M. Kehoe, JAAS, 11(Jl-Oct 1976):243-4.

Daly, Anne, ed. Kingston upon Thames Register of Apprentices,
    1563-1713. n.p.: Surrey Record Society, 1974. Rev. by
    J. S. Morrill, Archives, 12(Aut 1976):194-5.

Daly, Dominic. The Young Douglas Hyde: The Dawn of the Irish
    Revolution and Renaissance, 1874-1893. Totowa, N.J.: Row-
    man and Littlefield, 1974. Rev. by G. Costigan, AHR, 81
    (Feb 1976):151.

Daniel, E. Randolph. The Franciscan Concept of Mission in the
    High Middle Ages. Lexington: U Press Ky, 1975. Rev. by
    T. Callahan, Jr., CH, 45(Mar 1976):105-6; J. Muldoon,
    HRNB, 5(Oct 1976):19-20.

Daniel, Norman. Arabs and Medieval Europe. London: Longman,
    1975. Rev. by J. Riley-Smith, EHR, 91(Oct 1976):887-8;
    D. W. Lomax, History, 61(Je 1976):255.

Daniels, Elizabeth Adams. Jessie White Mario: Risorgimento
    Revolutionary. Athens: Ohio U Press, 1972. Rev. by A.
    Natali, AHR, 81(Apr 1976):414-15.

Dank, Milton. The French Against the French: Collaboration and
    Resistance. Philadelphia: J. B. Lippincott, 1974. Rev. by
    R. O. Paxton, AHR, 81(Apr 1976):382-3.

Danziger, Edmund J., Jr. Indians and Bureaucrats: Administer-
    ing the Reservation Policy During the Civil War. Urbana:
    U Ill Press, 1974. Rev. by W. G. Robbins, AI, 43(Sum
    1976):390-4; H. T. Hoover, AIQ, 2(Spr 1975):35-7; H. E.
    Fritz, JAH, 62(Mar 1976):1002-3; P. R. Metcalf, NMHR, 51
    (Apr 1976):167-8; A. M. Gibson, PHR, 45(May 1976):282-3.

Darby, H. C. and G. R. Versey. Domesday Gazeteer. Cambridge:
Cam U Press, 1975. Rev. by H. R. Loyn, History, 61(Oct
1976):439-41.

_____, ed. A New Historical Geography of England. Cam-
bridge: Cam U Press, 1973. Rev. by A. Everitt, EHR, 91
(Jan 1976):121-3.

Dargo, George. Jefferson's Louisiana: Politics and the Clash of
Legal Traditions. Cambridge, Mass.: Harvard U Press,
1975. Rev. by J. G. Tregle, Jr., AHR, 81(Je 1976):657;
D. O. Dewey, JAH, 62(Mar 1976):986-7.

Darroch, Elizabeth and Barry Taylor, eds. A Bibliography of Norfolk History. n.p.: U East Anglia, 1975. Rev. by P. Rut-
ledge, Archives, 12(Spr 1976):151.

da Silva, A. Trent's Impact on the Portuguese Patronage Mission.
Lisboa: Centro de Estudos Históricos Ultramarinos, 1969.
Rev. by J. C. Anderson, JCS, 17(Aut 1975):539-41.

Dathorne, O. R. The Black Mind: A History of African Literature.
Minneapolis: U Minn Press, 1974. Rev. by T. O. Beidelman, Africa, 46(Num 1, 1976):106-7.

Daube, David. Civil Disobedience in Antiquity. Chicago: Aldine-
Atherton, 1972. Rev. by W. C. West, AHR, 81(Je 1976):
569.

Daumard, Adeline. Les Fortunes Françaises au XIXe Siècle.
Paris: Mouton, 1973. Rev. by C. Lucas, EHR, 91(Oct 1976):
866-8.

Davenport, John B., comp. Guide to the Orin G. Libby Manuscript
Collection ... at the University of North Dakota. Grand
Forks, N.D.: Libby Manuscript Collections, 1975. Rev. by
D. P. Swanson, NDH, 43(Spr 1976):104-5.

David, Paul A. Technical Choice: Innovation and Economic Growth:
Essays on American and British Experience in the Nineteenth
Century. New York: Cam U Press, 1975. Rev. by W. N.
Parker, AgH, 50(Jan 1976):310-14; R. Floud, JIH, 7(Sum
1976):199-23; H. D. Woodman, RAH, 4(Je 1976):230-6.

David, Pierre. Journal d'un voiage fait en Bambouc en 1744.
Paris: Société française d'histoire d'outremer, 1974. Rev.
by P. D. Curtin, JAfH, 17(Sum 1, 1976):157.

Davidowicz, Lucy. The War Against the Jews. New York: Holt,
Rinehart and Winston, 1975. Rev. by D. J. Schnall, JSoH,
10(Fall 1976):120-4.

Davidson, Homer K. Black Jack Davidson: A Cavalry Commander

DAVIDSON   90

on the Western Frontier. Glendale, Cal.: A. H. Clark,
1974. Rev. by R. C. Carriker, PHR, 45(Feb 1976):126-7.

Davidson, J. W.   Peter Dillon on Vanikoro: Chevalier of the South
     Seas. New York: Oxford U Press, 1975. Rev. by E. D.
     Fitchen, HRNB, 4(Feb 1976):85-6.

Davies, D. W.   Sir John Moore's Peninsular Campaign 1808-1809.
     The Hague: Martinus Nijhoff, 1974. Rev. by B. Bond, EHR,
     91(Jl 1976):659; R. Carr, History, 61(Je 1976):301.

Davies, David. The Last of the Tasmanians. New York: Barnes
     and Noble, 1974. Rev. by S. C. McCulloch, AHR, 81(Oct
     1976):948-9.

Davies, Horton. Worship and Theology in England: From Andrews
     to Baxter and Fox, 1603-1690. Princeton, N.J.: Prin U
     Press, 1975. Rev. by C. Cross, EHR, 91(Oct 1975):847-8;
     S. E. Lehmberg, HRNB, 4(Feb 1976):93.

Davies, K. G., ed. Documents of the American Revolution, 1770-
     1783. 5 vols. Shannon: Irish U Press, 1972. Rev. by P.
     S. Haffenden, EHR, 91(Jan 1976):139-41; G. C. Gibbs, His-
     tory, 61(Oct 1976):398-400; R. D. Higginbotham, JSH, 42(Aug
     1976):418-19.

_____. The North Atlantic World in the Seventeenth Century.
     Minneapolis: U Minn Press, 1974. Rev. by L. B. Wright,
     AHR, 81(Apr 1976):375; R. Davis, History, 61(Oct 1976):448.

Davies, Nigel. The Aztecs: A History. New York: Putnam's,
     1974. Rev. by S. A. Colston, TAm, 33(Jl 1976):164.

Davies, P. N. The Trade Makers: Elder Dempster in West
     Africa, 1852-1972. London: Allen and Unwin, 1973. Rev.
     by P. L. Payne, BH, 17(Jl 1975):201.

Davies, Thomas M., Jr. Indian Integration in Peru: A Half
     Century of Experience, 1900-1948. Lincoln: U Neb Press,
     1974. Rev. by J. H. Williams, TAm, 32(Jan 1976):498-9.

Davies, W. J. Frank. Teaching Reading in Early England. New
     York: Barnes and Noble, 1974. Rev. by J. D. A. Ogilvy,
     AHR, 81(Feb 1976):111.

Davis, Allen F. and Mark H. Haller, eds. The Peoples of Phila-
     delphia: A History of Ethnic Groups and Lower-Class Life,
     1790-1940. Philadelphia: Temple U Press, 1973. Rev. by
     D. M. Reimers, AHR, 81(Je 1976):677-8; J. A. Tarr, JIH,
     7(Sum 1976):172-8.

Davis, Calvin DeArmond. The United States and the Second Hague
     Peace Conference: American Diplomacy and International

Organization 1899-1914. Durham, N.C.: Duke U Press, 1976.
Rev. by L. E. Gelfand, HRNB, 5(Oct 1976):6-7.

Davis, Carl L. Arming the Union: Small Arms in the Civil War.
Folkestone: Bailey Bros., 1975. Rev. by S. G. F. Spackman, History, 61(Oct 1976):408-9.

Davis, David Brion. The Problem of Slavery in the Age of Revolution 1770-1823. Ithaca, N.Y.: Cornell U Press, 1975. Rev.
by R. McColley, AgH, 50(Apr 1976):439-40; B. I. Wiley, AHI,
10(Feb 1976):49-50; B. I. Wiley, AHI, 11(May 1976):48-9; A.
Meier, AHR, 81(Apr 1976):443-4; H. S. Smith, CH, 45(Je
1976):262-3; S. H. Strom, CWH, 22(Je 1976):175-7; R. Anstey,
EHR, 91(Jan 1976):141-8; H. Temperley, JAmS, 10(Apr 1976):
111-13; R. M. Brace, JMH, 48(Mar 1976):129-31; F. W.
Knight, JSoH, 10(Fall 1976):107-15; H. M. Ward, JOW, 15
(Jan 1976):123-4; M. Mullin, MHM, 71(Sum 1976):266-8; R.
B. Sheridan, NYHSQ, 60(Jan/Apr 1976):85-7; W. Toll, PNQ,
67(Jl 1976):129-30; K. Greenberg, WMH, 60(Aut 1976):62-3.

Davis, David L., et al. Medieval Japan: Essays in International
History. New Haven, Conn.: Yale U Press, 1974. Rev. by
P. Duus, AHR, 81(Feb 1976):194-5.

Davis, Dorothy. John George Jackson. Parsons, W.Va.: McClain
Printing, 1976. Rev. by S. W. Brown, WVH, 38(Oct 1976):
58-60.

Davis, Earl N. and Davis, Mary O. Rochester Remembers, 1781-
1981: A Collection of Photographs. Rochester, Vt.: n.p.,
1975. Rev. by R. D. Nuquist, VH, 44(Win 1976):51 [dates sic].

Davis, Harold Eugene and Larman C. Wilson, eds. Latin American
Foreign Policies: An Analysis. Baltimore: JHU Press,
1975. Rev. in CurH, 70(Feb 1976):77; by A. Lowenthal,
HAHR, 56(Aug 1976):461-2.

Davis, James C. A Venetian Family and Its Fortune, 1500-1900:
The Donà and the Conservation of Their Wealth. Philadelphia:
American Philosophical Society, 1975. Rev. by G. A.
Brucker, AHR, 81(Apr 1976):413-14; L. B. Robbert, JEH,
36(Je 1976):461-2.

Davis, Jefferson. The Papers of Jefferson Davis. Vol. 2 (James
T. McIntosh, ed.). Baton Rouge: LSU Press, 1974. Rev.
by B. I. Wiley, AmArc, 39(Apr 1976):210-11; J. F. Morgan,
ChOk, 54(Sum 1976):287-8; C. Eaton, FHQ, 54(Jan 1976):
397-9; G. C. Chalon, IMH, 72(Mar 1976):77-9; C. P. Roland,
JAH, 62(Mar 1976):950-2; L. H. Johnson, III, JSH, 42(Feb
1976):119-21.

Davis, John L. The Texas Rangers: Their First 150 Years.
San Antonio: Institute of Texan Cultures, 1975. Rev. by

DAVIS 92

W. Gard, SWHQ, 80(Oct 1976):244-5.

Davis, Joseph S. The World Between the Wars, 1919-39: An
Economist's View. Baltimore: JHU Press, 1975. Rev. by
W. R. Rock, AHR, 81(Apr 1976):362-3; S. A. Schuker, BHR,
50(Sum 1976):260-2; J. E. Wiltz, IMH, 72(Mar 1976):88-9.

Davis, Kenneth Ronald. Anabaptism and Asceticism: A Study in Intellectual Origins. Scottdale, Pa.: Herald Press, 1974. Rev.
by H. J. Hillerbrand, CaHR, 62(Jan 1976):124-5; P. C. Erb,
MQR, 50(Jl 1976):251-2.

Davis, Lawrence B. Immigrants, Baptists, and the Protestant
Mind in America. Urbana: U Ill Press, 1973. Rev. by L.
McBeth, JCS, 17(Aut 1975):513-15.

Davis, Lynn Etheridge. The Cold War Begins: Soviet-American
Conflict Over Eastern Europe. Princeton, N.J.: Prin U
Press, 1974. Rev. by G. F. Herken, AHR, 81(Je 1976):
694-5; P. G. Boyle, History, 61(Je 1976):329-30; J. L.
Gaddis, PHR, 45(Feb 1976):150-1.

Davis, Melton S. Who Defends Rome? The Forty-Five Days,
July 25-September 8, 1943. New York: Dial, 1972. Rev.
by C. F. Delzell, AHR, 81(Je 1976):626.

Davis, Natalie Zemon. Society and Culture in Early Modern
France. Stanford, Cal.: Stanford U Press, 1975. Rev. by
C. J. Blaisdell, AHR, 81(Je 1976):599-600; C. Garrett, Historian, 39(Nov 1976):123-4; R. J. Knecht, History, 61(Je
1976):278-9; P. Benedict, JMH, 48(Je 1976):330-1.

Davis, Norman and Colin M. Kraay. The Hellenistic Kingdoms:
Portrait Coins and History. London: Thames and Hudson,
1973. Rev. by M. Thompson, Archaeology, 29(Apr 1976):139.

Davis, William C. The Battle of New Market. Garden City,
N. Y.: Doubleday, 1975. Rev. by E. C. Murdock, AHR, 81
(Je 1976):668; H. H. Wubben, AI, 43(Spr 1976):306-9; R. J.
Sommers, CWH, 22(Mar 1976):88-9; S. Z. Starr, JAH, 62
(Mar 1976):1003-4; J. G. Barrett, JSH, 42(Feb 1976):127-8;
W. H. Hassler, NCHR, 53(Win 1976):98-9; G. M. Grooke,
Jr., VMHB, 84(Jan 1976):114-15.

_____. Breckinridge. Baton Rouge: LSU Press, 1974. Rev.
by R. R. Davis, Jr., PH, 43(Jan 1976):92-3.

_____. Duel Between the First Ironclads. Garden City, N.Y.:
Doubleday, 1975. Rev. by A. A. Fahrner, JSH, 42(Aug
1976):435-6.

Daws, Gavan. Holy Man. Father Damien of Molokai. New York:
Harper and Row, 1973. Rev. by J. T. Ellis, CaHR, 62(Jl
1976):502-5.

93   DAWSON

Dawson, Adele Godchaux. James Franklin Gilman: Nineteenth Century Painter. Canaan, N.H.: Phoenix Publishing, 1975. Rev. by R. Pfeiffer, VH, 44(Sum 1976):177-9.

Dawson, Carol Ruth (Anderson). Dawsons in the Revolutionary War (and Their Descendants), Volume I. Eau Claire, Wis.: Graphic Printing, 1974. Rev. by J. F. Dorman, VMHB, 84 (Jan 1976):104-5.

Dawson, Christopher. Religion and World History. Garden City, N.Y.: Image Books, 1975. Rev. by L. D. Rue, CH, 45(Mar 1976):126.

Dawson, Philip. Provincial Magistrates and Revolutionary Politics in France, 1789-1795. Cambridge, Mass.: Harvard U Press, 1973. Rev. by C. Lucas, History, 61(Feb 1976):119-20.

Dayananda, James Y. Manohar Malgonkar. Boston: Twayne, 1974. Rev. by L. Wood, JAS, 36(Nov 1976):162-3.

Deakin, F. W. D. The Embattled Mountain. New York: Oxford U Press, 1971. Rev. by J. C. Campbell, AHR, 81(Oct 1976): 897-9.

_____, H. Shickman and H. T. Willetts. A History of World Communism. London: Weidenfeld and Nicolson, 1975. Rev. by M. Perrie, History, 61(Feb 1976):94.

Dean, Robert W., ed. see King, Robert R., ed.

Dean, Warren. Rio Claro: A Brazilian Plantation System, 1820-1920. Stanford, Cal.: Stanford U Press, 1976. Rev. by F. Safford, HRNB, 4(Sep 1976):220-1.

De Bary, William Theodore, et al., eds. The Unfolding of Neo-Confucianism. New York: Columbia U Press, 1975. Rev. by J. P. Dennerline, AHR, 81(Oct 1976):931-2.

De Beer, C. see Jackson, M. H.

Debien, Gabriel. Les Esclaves aux Antilles françaises (XVIIe-XVIIIe Siècles). Basse Terre: Société d'Histoire de la Guadeloupe, 1974. Rev. by E. V. Goveia, AHR, 81(Je 1976): 700.

DeBoe, David C., Van Mitchell Smith, Elliot West, and Norman A. Graebner. Essays on American Foreign Policy. Austin: U Tex Press, 1974. Rev. by R. N. Current, PHR, 45(May 1976):302-3.

de Botlard, Michel. Manuel d'archéologie médiévale: de la fouille à l'histoire. Paris: Collection Regards sur l'Histoire, 1975. Rev. by B. K. Young, Antiquity, 50(Sep-Dec 1976):247-8.

Decanio, Stephen J. Agriculture in the Postbellum South: The Economics of Production and Supply. Cambridge, Mass.: MIT Press, 1974. Rev. by H. D. Woodman, JAH, 63(Je 1976):140-2.

de Cecco, Marcello. Money and Empire: The International Gold Standard, 1890-1914. Totowa, N.J.: Rowman and Littlefield, 1975. Rev. by F. W. Fetter, BHR, 50(Spr 1976):107-9.

DeChantal, M. Out of Nazareth: A Centenary of the Sisters of the Holy Family of Nazareth in the Service of the Church. New York: Exposition, 1974. Rev. by A. J. Kuzniewski, CaHR, 62(Jl 1976):510-12.

Dechêne, Louise. Habitants et marchands de Montreal au XVIIe siècle. Montreal: Plon, 1974. Rev. by C. Nish, AHR, 81 (Je 1976):696.

De Crespigny, Anthony and Kenneth Minogue, eds. Contemporary Political Philosophers. New York: Dodd, Mead, 1975. Rev. by N. Wood, AHR, 81(Je 1976):564-5.

Dee, John. The Mathematical Praeface to the Elements of Geometrie of Euclid of Megara (1570). New York: Science History Publications, 1975. Rev. by N. T. Gridgeman, AHR, 61(Oct 1976):840-1.

de Espalza, Miguel and Ramon Petit, eds. Recueil d'études sur les Moriscos Andalous en Tunisie. Madrid: Dirección General de Relaciones Culturales, 1973. Rev. by N. S. Hopkins, IJMES, 7(Jl 1976):461-2.

De Felice, Franco. L'agricoltura in terra di Bari dal 1880 al 1914. Milan: Banca Commerciale Italiana, 1971. Rev. by I. A. Glazier, AHR, 81(Oct 1976):892-3.

de Figueiredo, Antonio. Portugal: Fifty Years of Dictatorship. New York: Penguin, 1975. Rev. by D. Birmingham, AfAf, 75(Jan 1976):119-20.

Degler-Spangler, Briggite see Bruckner, A.

de Grauwe, Jan. Histoire de la chartreuse de Val-Royal à Grand et de la chartreuse du Bois-Saint-Martin à Lierde-Saint-Martin. Salzburg: Institut für Englische Sprache, 1974. Rev. by R. Kay, CH, 45(Je 1976):250-1.

Deiner, Edward. Reinterpreting American History. New York: Philosophical Library, 1975. Rev. by R. Lewis, History, 61 (Oct 1976):421-2; S. Kesselman, JAH, 63(Dec 1976):724-5; R. S. Taylor, NDH, 43(Sum 1976):45-6.

De Jong, Gerald F. The Dutch in America, 1609-1974. Boston:

Twayne, 1975. Rev. by W. Vander Hill, JAH, 62(Mar 1976):
960-1; A. C. Leiby, WMQ, 33(Apr 1976):352.

Dejung, Karl-Heinz. Die Okumenische Bewegung im Entwicklungskon-
flikt, 1910-1968. Stuttgart: Ernst Klett Verlag, 1973. Rev.
by J. J. Hughes, CaHR, 62(Oct 1976):646-7.

Delancey, Mark W. and Virginia H. Delancy. A Bibliography of
the Cameroon. New York: Africana, 1975. Rev. by H. O.
H. Vernon-Jackson, JMAS, 14(Sep 1976):553-5.

de la Peña, José Enrique. With Santa Anna in Texas: A Personal
Narrative of the Revolution. College Station: Texas A & M
U Press, 1975. Rev. by B. Procter, ETHJ, 14(Fall 1976):
70; O. L. Jones, HAHR, 56(Aug 1976):486-7; S. E. Siegel,
JSH, 42(May 1976):283-4.

de la Roncière, Charles M. Un changeur florentin du Trecento:
Lippo di Fede del Sega (1285 env-1363 env). Paris:
S. E. V. P. E. N. , 1973. Rev. by B. G. Kohl, JEH, 36(Sep
1976):768.

de Las Casas, Bartolome. In Defense of the Indians. (Stafford
Poole, ed.) DeKalb: N Ill U Press, 1974. Rev. by M. V.
Gannon, FHQ, 54(Jan 1976):387-90.

Delbrück, Hans. History of the Art of War Within the Framework
of Political History. Vol. I, Antiquity. Westport, Conn.:
Greenwood, 1975. Rev. by P. Paret, AHR, 81(Oct 1976):
826-7.

Del Chiaro, Mario A. Etruscan Red-Figured Vase-Painting at
Caere. Berkeley: U Cal Press, 1975. Rev. by U Cal
Press, 1975. Rev. by R. D. De Puma, AJA, 80(Sum 1976):
320-1.

D'Elia, Donald J. Benjamin Rush: Philosopher of the American
Revolution. Philadelphia: American Philosophical Society,
1974. Rev. by J. A. Schutz, AHR, 81(Oct 1976):963; J.
M. Coleman, JAH, 62(Mar 1976):974-5.

Delivorrias, Angelos. Attische Giebelskulpturen und Akrotere des
Fünften Jahrhunderts. Tübingen: Verlag Ernst Wasmuth,
1974. Rev. by E. B. Harrison, AJA, 80(Spr 1976):209-10.

Delivré, A. L'Histoire des rois d'Imerina: Interpretation d'une
tradition orale. Paris: Klincksieck, 1974. Rev. by J.
Vansina, JAfH, 17(Num 1, 1976):135-7.

Dell, Christopher. Lincoln and the War Democrats: The Grand
Erosion of Conservative Tradition. Rutherford, N. J.: Fair-
leigh Dickinson U Press, 1975. Rev. by L. H. Harrison,
AHI, 11(Je 1976):50; E. J. Cardinal, CWH, 22(Mar 1976):

87-8; G. R. Tredway, IMH, 72(Dec 1976):373-4; R. W.
Johannsen, JAH, 63(Dec 1976):721-2.

Delpar, Helen, ed. Encyclopedia of Latin America. New York:
McGraw-Hill, 1974. Rev. by F. P. Hebblethwaite, Américas,
28(Oct 1976):26; N. L. Benson, HAHR, 56(Feb 1976):119.

Delzell, Charles F., ed. The Papacy and Totalitarianism Between
Two World Wars. New York: Wiley, 1974. Rev. by J. J.
Hughes, JCS, 18(Spr 1976):333-6.

De Maddalena, Aldo. Prezzi e mercedi a Milano dal 1701 et 1860.
Vols. 1 and 2. Milan: Banca Commerciale Italiana, 1974.
Rev. by I. A. Glazier, AHR, 81(Oct 1976):892-3.

De Maio, Romeo. Riforme e miti nella Chiesa del Cinquecento.
Naples: Guida Editori, 1973. Rev. by J. W. O'Malley,
CaHR, 62(Jan 1976):113-15.

Demargne, Pierre. Fouilles de Xanthos V: Tombes-Maisons,
Tombes Rupestres et Sarcophages. Paris: Librairie C.
Klincksieck, 1974. Rev. by W. A. P. Childs, AJA, 80(Spr
1976):212-13.

De Mause, Lloyd, ed. The New Psychohistory. New York: Psychohistory Press, 1975. Rev. by W. J. Gilmore, HRNB, 4
(Mar 1976):106-7; N. L. Buckley, PHR, 45(Nov 1976):603-4.

Dempsey, Hugh A. Men in Scarlet. Calgary, Alta.: McClelland
and Stewart West, 1974. Rev. by P. F. Sharp, CHR, 57(Mar
1976):54-5.

de Nave, Francine, ed. De oudst Antwerpse lijsten van nieuwe
poorters (28 januari 1390-28 december 1414). Brussels:
Commission Royale d'Histoire, 1973. Rev. by R. Vaughan,
EHR, 91(Jl 1976):635-6.

Denhardt, Robert M. The Horse of the Americas. Norman: U
Ok Press, 1975. Rev. by D. R. Daniels, ChOk, 54(Fall
1976):406-7; S. P. B., HAHR, 56(Feb 1976):181; E. H. Elam,
JSH, 42(May 1976):300-1; D. E. Worcester, WHQ, 7(Apr
1976):194-5.

Dennis, Frank Allen, ed. Kemper County Rebel: The Civil War
Diary of Robert Masten Holmes, C. S. A. Jackson: U and
College Press, Miss., 1973. Rev. by R. D. Hoffsommer,
CWTI, 15(May 1976):46-7.

Dennison, George M. The Dorr War: Republicanism on Trial,
1831-1861. Lexington: U Press Ky, 1976. Rev. by J. E.
Sefton, HRNB, 4(Aug 1976):187; M. E. Gettleman, JAH, 63
(Dec 1976):715-16.

den Tex, Jan. Oldenbarnevelt. Cambridge: Cam U Press, 1973. Rev. by R. G. Collmer, JCS, 17(Aut 1975):508-11.

Department of State see United States Department of State

Derrick, Jonathan. Africa's Slaves Today. London: George Allen and Unwin, 1975. Rev. by L. Mair, AfAf, 75(Apr 1976):255.

Derricourt, Robin, ed. see Saunders, Christopher, ed.

Derry, John W. Castlereagh. New York: St. Martin's, 1976. Rev. by S. B. Baxter, HRNB, 4(Jl 1976):175.

Derry, T. K. A History of Modern Norway, 1814-1972. Oxford: Oxford U Press, 1973. Rev. by M. Drake, History, 61(Feb 1976):148-9.

Deschner, John, Leroy T. Howe and Klaus Penzel, eds. Our Common History as Christians. New York: Oxford U Press, 1975. Rev. by S. L. Greenslade, JEccH, 27(Oct 1976):451-2.

Desdunes, Rodolphe Lucien. Our People and Our History. Baton Rouge: LSU Press, 1973. Rev. by J. D. Winters, JAH, 63(Je 1976):99-100.

Des Gagniers, J. see Karageorghis, Vassos

Dessain, Charles Stephen and Thomas Gornall, eds. The Letters and Diaries of John Henry Newman. Vols. XXIII, XXIV and XXV. New York: Oxford U Press, 1973. Rev. by J. D. Holmes and F. J. Cwiekowski, CaHR, 62(Oct 1976):631-5.

_____ and _____, eds. The Letters and Diaries of John Henry Newman. Vols. 26, 27, 28. Oxford: Clarendon Press, 1975. Rev. by R. J. Schieffen, JEccH, 27(Jan 1976):86-87.

Dethloff, Henry C. A Centennial History of Texas A & W University, 1876-1976. 2 vols. College Station: Texas A & M U Press, 1975. Rev. by A. P. McDonald, ETHJ, 14(Fall 1976):77.

_____. A Pictorial History of Texas A & M University, 1876-1976. College Station: Texas A & M U Press, 1975. Rev. by A. P. McDonald, ETHJ, 14(Fall 1976):77.

Deutsch, Harold C. Hitler and His Generals: The Hidden Crisis, January-June 1938. Minneapolis: U Minn Press, 1974. Rev. by A. J. P. Taylor, EHR, 91(Apr 1976):463-4; N. Reynolds, History, 61(Feb 1976):144-5.

Devadoss, T. S. Sarvodaya and the Problem of Political Sovereignty. Madras: U Madras Press, 1974. Rev. by M. Venkatarangaiya, IQ, 32(Apr-Je 1976):255-7.

De Vaux, R. Archaeology and the Dead Sea Scrolls. London:
Oxford U Press, 1973. Rev. by J. C. Greenfield, JNES,
35(Oct 1976):287-90.

Dever, William G., et al. Gezer II: Report of the 1967-70 Seasons in Fields I and II. Jerusalem: Hebrew Union College,
1974. Rev. by W. E. Rast, AJA, 80(Sum 1976):307-8.

Devine, T. M. The Tobacco Lords: A Study of the Tobacco
Merchants of Glasgow and Their Trading Activities, c. 1740-
90. Edinburgh: John Donald, 1975. Rev. by P. G. E.
Clemens, AHR, 81(Je 1976):597; T. C. Barker, EHR, 91(Oct
1976):916; R. H. Campbell, History, 61(Oct 1976):478-80;
A. L. Jensen, JAH, 63(Je 1976):105-6; J. C. Robert, VMHB,
84(Jan 1976):100-2.

Devlin, Patrick. Too Proud to Fight: Woodrow Wilson's Neutrality.
London: Oxford U Press, 1974. Rev. by C. A. MacDonald,
EHR, 91(Jan 1976):234-5; A. E. Campbell, History, 61(Oct
1976):415-16.

De Vooght, Paul. Jacobellus de Střibro (1429), premier theologien
du hussitisme. Louvain: Publications Universities Louvain,
1972. Rev. by L. Nemec, CaHR, 62(Jan 1976):110-12.

de Vries, Jan. The Dutch Rural Economy in the Golden Age, 1500-
1700. New Haven, Conn.: Yale U Press, 1974. Rev. by
J. E. Kurland, AHR, 81(Apr 1976):401; G. D. Homan, Historian, 38(Feb 1976):330-2.

Dewdney, Selwyn. The Sacred Scrolls of the Southern Ojibway.
Toronto: U Tor Press, 1975. Rev. by C. Vecsey, AA, 78
(Mar 1976):162.

De Wit, C. H. E. The Revolution in the Netherlands in the
Eighteenth Century, 1780-1787: Oligarchy and Proletariat.
Oirsbeek: H. J. J. Lindelauf, 1974. Rev. by H. H. Rowen,
AHR, 81(Feb 1976):161-2.

DeWitt, Howard A. Images of Ethnic and Radical Violence in Cali-
fornia Politics, 1917-1930. San Francisco: R and E Research
Associates, 1975. Rev. by W. Bean, JAH, 63(Sep 1976):443-4;
B. Luckingham, JOW, 15(Jl 1976):106-7.

D'Harcourt, Raoul. Textiles of Ancient Peru and Their Techniques.
Seattle: U Wash Press, 1974. Rev. by A. R. Sawyer, HAHR,
56(Feb 1976):181.

Dial, Adolph L. and David K. Eliades. The Only Land I Know: A
History of the Lumbee Indians. San Francisco: Indian Historian, 1975. Rev. by W. S. Robinson, AHR, 81(Oct 1976):

951; S. J. Gluckman, NCHR, 53(Win 1976):83.

Díaz-Guerrero, R. Psychology of the Mexican: Culture and Per-
    sonality. Austin: U Texas Press, 1975. Rev. by M. Mac-
    coby, HAHR, 56(Feb 1976):154.

Dibble, Ernest F. Ante-Bellum Pensacola and the Military Presence.
    Pensacola: Pensacola-Escambia Development Commission,
    1974. Rev. by F. L. Owsley, Jr., JSH, 42(Feb 1976):117-18.

Dick, Everett. Conquering the Great American Desert. Lincoln:
    Neb St Historical Society, 1975. Rev. by M. L. Olsen,
    A & W, 18(Win 1976):384-5; A. B. Sageser, JOW, 15(Jl
    1976):98.

Dick, Robert C. Black Protest: Issues and Tactics. Westport,
    Conn.: Greenwood, 1974. Rev. by B. Quarles, AHR, 81(Feb
    1976):208-9; P. D. Klingman, FHQ, 55(Jl 1976):96-7; A. P.
    Cannon, WMH, 60(Aut 1976):66-7.

Dick, William M. Labor and Socialism in America. Port Washing-
    ton, N.Y.: Kennikat, 1972. Rev. by J. A. Thompson, HJ,
    19(Mar 1976):257-74.

Dickens, A. G. The German Nation and Martin Luther. London:
    Edward Arnold, 1974. Rev. by A. Duke, EHR, 91(Jan 1976):
    189-90; H. J. Cohn, History, 61(Je 1976):276-7.

Diena, Vittorio, ed. see Balmas, Enea, ed.

Diener, Edward. Reinterpreting American History. New York:
    Philosophical Library, 1975. Rev. by R. S. Taylor, NDH,
    43(Sum 1976):45-6.

Diggins, John P. Up from Communism: Conservative Odysseys
    in American Intellectual History. New York: Harper and
    Row, 1975. Rev. by N. W. Polsby, Commentary, 62(Aug
    1976):62-5; S. Persons, JAH, 63(Dec 1976):764-5.

Dillon, Francis. The Pilgrims. New York: Doubleday, 1975.
    Rev. by W. Rundell, Jr., Mankind, 5(Dec 1976):6-7.

Dillon, Merton L. The Abolitionists: The Growth of a Dissenting
    Minority. DeKalb: N Ill U Press, 1974. Rev. by B. Wyatt-
    Brown, AHR, 81(Je 1976):662.

Dillon, Richard. Siskiyou Trail: The Hudson's Bay Company Route
    to California. New York: McGraw-Hill, 1975. Rev. by T.
    O'Donnell, OrHQ, 77(Je 1976):194; R. W. Davenport, WHQ,
    7(Apr 1976):197.

Dilworth, Mark. The Scots in Franconia: A Century of Monastic
    Life. Totowa, N.J.: Rowman and Littlefield, 1974. Rev.

by M. Walker, AHR, 81(Feb 1976):148-9; J. Bosey, EHR, 91(Apr 1976):424-5.

Dinkins, Captain James. 1861-1865 by an Old Johnnie: Personal Recollections and Experiences in the Confederate Army. Dayton, Ohio: Morningside Bookshop, 1975. Rev. by J. I. Robertson, Jr., VMHB, 84(Jan 1976):112-14.

Dinnerstein, Leonard and David M. Reimers. Ethnic Americans: A History of Immigration and Assimilation. New York: Dodd, Mead, 1975. Rev. by A. W. Hoglund, JAH, 63(Je 1976):174-5.

Diószegi, István. Österreich-Ungarn und der französisch-preussische Krieg, 1870-1871. Budapest: Akadémiai Kiadó, 1974. Rev. by L. A. Gebhard, AHR, 81(Feb 1976):125.

Di Peso, Charles C. Casas Grandes: A Fallen Trade Center of the Gran Chichimeca. 3 vols. Flagstaff, Ariz.: Northland, 1974. Rev. by E. J. Burrus, A & W, 18(Spr 1976):83-7.

Dippie, Brian W. Custer's Last Stand: The Anatomy of an American Myth. Missoula: U Montana Press, 1976. Rev. by L. M. Hauptman, HRNB, 5(Oct 1976):5.

Director-General ILO. Employment Growth and Basic Needs: A One-World Problem. Geneva: ILO, 1976. Rev. by J. H. Cobbe, JMAS, 14(Dec 1976):713-15.

_____. World Employment Programme. Geneva: ILO, 1976. Rev. by J. H. Cobbe, JMAS, 14(Dec 1976):713-15.

Diskin, Martin, ed. see Cook, Scott, ed.

Dittmer, Lowell. Liu Shao-ch'i and the Chinese Cultural Revolution: The Politics of Mass Criticism. Berkeley: U Cal Press, 1974. Rev. by R. Weidenbaum, CQ, May 1976, pp. 375-7.

Divine, Robert A. Foreign Policy and U.S. Presidential Elections. 2 vols. New York: New Viewpoints, 1974. Rev. by R. Griffith, AHR, 81(Apr 1976):464-6; R. W. Leopold, PHR, 45 (May 1976):303-4.

_____. Since 1945: Politics and Diplomacy in Recent American History. New York: Wiley, 1975. Rev. by E. V. Toy, Jr., JAH, 62(Mar 1976):1046-7; R. J. Caridi, PHR, 45(Nov 1976): 632-4.

Dixon, Thomas, Jr. The Clansman. New York: Gordon Press, 1973. Rev. by R. Ashley, CWTI, 15(Apr 1976):45-6.

Dobie, J. Frank. The Flavor of Texas. Austin, Tex.: Jenkins,

1975. Rev. by F. E. Abernethy, ETHJ, 14(Spr 1976):62;
L. C. Rampp, JOW, 15(Jan 1976):136.

————. Prefaces. Boston: Little, Brown, 1975. Rev. by C.
M. Johnson, A & W, 18(Spr 1976):94-6; R. Wilson, JOW,
15(Jl 1976):101.

Dobkin de Rios, Marlene. Visionary Vine: Psychedelic Healing
in the Peruvian Amazon. San Francisco: Chandler, 1972.
Rev. by A. J. Rubel, AA, 78(Jan 1976):394-5.

Dobson, E. J. Moralities on the Gospels: A New Source of
"Ancrene Wisse." Oxford: Clarendon Press, 1975. Rev.
by P. I. Kaufman, CH, 45(Sep 1976):380-1.

Dobson, R. B. The Jews of Medieval York and the Massacre of
March 1190. York: St. Anthony's, 1974. Rev. by F. Barlow, JEccH, 27(Apr 1976):214-15.

Dobson, W. A. C. H. A Dictionary of the Chinese Particles.
Toronto: U Tor Press, 1974. Rev. by K. Chang, JAS, 36
(Nov 1976):137-8.

Dobyns, Henry F. Spanish Colonial Tucson: A Demographic
History. Tucson: U Ariz Press, 1976. Rev. by J. F. Bannon, HRNB, 4(Aug 1976):190.

Dodd, George. Days at the Factories: or, the Manufacturing Industry of Great Britain Described, and Illustrated by Numerous
Engravings of Machines and Processes. Totowa, N.J.: Rowman and Littlefield, 1975. Rev. by E. Batteson, AHR, 81(Je
1976):590.

Dodd, Kenneth Melton, ed. The Field Book of Walsham-le-Willows,
1577. Suffolk: Suffolk Record Society, 1974. Rev. by J.
Ravensdale, Archives, 12(Spr 1976):145-6.

Dodwell, Barbara, ed. The Charters of Norwich Cathedral Priory,
Part One. London: Pipe Roll Society, 1974. Rev. by K.
Edwards, History, 61(Je 1976):256.

Doerries, Reinhard R. Washington-Berlin 1908/1917: Die Tätigkeit
des Botschafters Johann Heinrich Graf von Bernstorff in Washington vor dem Eintritt der Vereinigten Staaten von Amerika
in den Ersten Weltkrieg. Düsseldorf: Pädagogischer Verlag
Schwann, 1975. Rev. by M. Jonas, JAH, 63(Je 1975):170-1.

Dogan, Mattei, ed. The Mandarins of Western Europe: The Political Role of Top Civil Servants. New York: Halstead, 1975.
Rev. by O. E. S., CurH, 70(Apr 1976):177.

Doherty, Terence. The Anatomical Works of George Stubbs. Boston: Godine, 1975. Rev. by R. Watson, Smithsonian, 6(Sep
1975):106, 108.

Doke, Clement M. <u>Trekking in South Central Africa.</u> Johannesburg: South African Baptist Historical Society, 1975. Rev. by LEM, BHH, 10(Oct 1975):253.

Dokstadter, Frederick J. <u>Indian Art of the Americas.</u> New York: Heye Foundation, 1974. Rev. by E. Hatcher, AA, 78(Mar 1976):155-6.

Dolan, Jay P. <u>The Immigrant Church: New York's Irish and German Catholics, 1815-1865.</u> Baltimore: JHU Press, 1975. Rev. by F. X. Curran, CaHR, 62(Jl 1976):484-5; J. Hennesey, CH, 45(Sep 1976):391; L. Billington, History, 61(Oct 1976): 408; A. M. Greeley, JAH, 63(Je 1976):121-2; F. C. Luebke, RAH, 4(Mar 1976):68-72.

Dolan, Winthrop W. <u>A Choice of Sundials.</u> Brattleboro, Vt.: Stephen Greene, 1975. Rev. by H. Christner, Smithsonian, 6(Apr 1975):106-8.

Dolkart, Ronald H., ed. <u>see</u> Falcoff, Mark, ed.

Domínguez Ortiz, Antonio. <u>Alteraciones Andaluzas.</u> Madrid: Ediciones Narcea, 1973. Rev. by M. D. Gordon, HAHR, 56 (May 1976):310-12.

_____. <u>Hechos y figuras del siglo XVIII español.</u> Madrid: Siglo XXI de España Editores, S.A., 1973. Rev. by M. D. Gordon, HAHR, 56(May 1976):310-12.

Dominquez, Francisco A. <u>see</u> Adams, Eleanor B., trans.

Donald, David Herbert, ed. <u>Gone for a Soldier: The Civil War Memoirs of Private Alfred Bellard.</u> Boston: Little, Brown, 1975. Rev. by B. I. Wiley, CWTI, 15(May 1976):49; L. A. Wallace, Jr., VMHB, 84(Apr 1976):211-12.

Donaldson, Frances. <u>Edward VIII.</u> London: Weidenfeld and Nicolson, 1974. Rev. by H. Pelling, History, 61(Feb 1976):146-7.

Donaldson, Gordon. <u>Mary, Queen of Scots.</u> London: English U Press, 1974. Rev. by I. B. Cowan, History, 61(Feb 1976): 110.

_____. <u>Scotland: The Shaping of a Nation.</u> North Pomfret, Vt.: David and Charles, 1975. Rev. by W. A. Moffett, HRNB, 4(Feb 1976):91.

Donaldson, Peter, ed. and trans. <u>A Machiavellian Treatise by Stephen Gardiner.</u> Cambridge: Cam U Press, 1975. Rev. by D. Fenlon, HJ, 19(Dec 1976):1019-23.

Donfried, Karl Paul. <u>The Setting of Second Clement in Early Christianity.</u> Leiden: E. J. Brill, 1974. Rev. by E. H. Pagels, CH, 45(Mar 1976):98-9.

Donnan, Christopher B. Moche Occupation of the Santa Valley,
    Peru. Berkeley: U Cal Press, 1973. Rev. by A. R. Saw-
    yer, HAHR, 56(Feb 1976):181.

Donnelly, James S., Jr. The Land and the People of Nineteenth-
    Century Cork: The Rural Economy and the Land Question.
    Boston: Routledge and Kegan Paul, 1975. Rev. by G. E.
    Mingay, EHR, 91(Jan 1976):148-9; C. O. Grada, History, 61
    (Je 1976):300-1; E. D. Steele, HJ, 19(Mar 1976):287-9; J.
    Vincent, JIH, 7(Aut 1976):334-5; R. Crothy, JMH, 48(Sep 1976):
    543-4.

Donovan, Timothy Paul. Historical Thought in America: Postwar
    Patterns. Norman: U Ok Press, 1973. Rev. by J. Higham,
    JAH, 62(Mar 1976):1049-50.

Dormer, Elinore M. The Sea Shell Islands: A History of Sanibel
    and Captiva. New York: Vantage, 1975. Rev. by E. A.
    Hammond, FHQ, 55(Jl 1976):81-3.

Dorough, C. Dwight. The Bible Belt Mystique. Philadelphia:
    Westminster Press, 1974. Rev. by D. E. Harrell, Jr.,
    JCS, 18(Win 1976):140-1.

Dorwart, Jeffery M. The Pigtail War: American Involvement in
    the Sino-Japanese War of 1894-1895. Amherst: U Mass
    Press, 1975. Rev. by G. E. Paulsen, PHR, 45(Nov 1976):
    624-5.

Doten, Alfred. The Journals of Alfred Doten, 1849-1903. (Walter
    Van Tilburg Clark, ed.). Reno: U Nev Press, 1973. Rev.
    by F. Egan, CHQ, 55(Spr 1976):90-1; W. T. Jackson, WHQ,
    7(Jan 1976):73-4.

Dougherty, James, ed. and comp. Writings on American History,
    1973-4: A Subject Bibliography of Articles. Washington,
    D.C.: American Historical Assn., 1974. Rev. by O. H.
    Orr, Jr., AmArc, 39(Apr 1976):215-16.

Doughty, Robin W. Feather Fashions and Bird Preservation: A
    Study in Nature Protection. Berkeley: U Cal Press, 1975.
    Rev. by L. B. Lee, PNQ, 67(Oct 1976):176; L. Regenstein,
    Smithsonian, 6(Jl 1975):108-9.

Douglas, David C. The Norman Fate, 1100-1154. Berkeley: U
    Cal Press, 1976. Rev. by C. W. Hollister, HT, 10(Nov
    1976):159-61.

Douglas, Roy. Land, People and Politics: A History of the Land
    Question in the United Kingdom, 1878-1952. New York: St.
    Martin's, 1976. Rev. by T. J. Spinner, Jr., HRNB, 5(Oct
    1976):22.

Douglass, William A. and Jon Bilbao. Amerikanuak: Basques in the New World. Reno: U Nev Press, 1975. Rev. by W. S. Shepperson, PHR, 45(Nov 1976):618-9; A. Rolle, SCQ, 58(Win 1976):533-4.

Doukas see Magoulias, Harry J., trans.

Dow, George F., ed. Records and Files of the Quarterly Courts of Essex County, Massachusetts. Vol. IX: 1683-1686. Salem: Essex Institute, 1975. Rev. by D. T. Konig, NEQ, 49 (Mar 1976):163-5.

Dower, John W., ed. Origins of the Modern Japanese State: Selected Writings of E. H. Norman. New York: Pantheon, 1975. Rev. by H. Webb, AHR, 81(Oct 1976):941-2.

Downery, Bill. Tom Bass, Black Horseman. St. Louis: Saddle and Bridle, 1975. Rev. by M. K. Dains, MHR, 71(Oct 1976): 120-30.

Downey, Fairfax and J. N. Jacobsen. The Red-Bluecoats: The Indian Scouts. Ft. Collins, Colo.: Old Army Press, 1973. Rev. by H. T. Hoover, AIQ, 2(Sum 1975):158-61.

Doxiadis, C. A. Architectural Space in Ancient Greece. Cambridge: MIT Press, 1972. Rev. by S. Howard, AJA, 80 (Win 1976):90-1.

Doyle, William. The Parliament of Bordeaux and the End of the Old Regime 1771-1790. New York: St. Martin's, 1974. Rev. by R. I. Boss, AHR, 81(Apr 1976):396-7; O. Hufton, EHR, 91 (Apr 1976):437-8.

Dragnich, Alex N. Serbia, Nikola Pašić and Yugoslavia. New Brunswick, N.J.: Rutgers U Press, 1974. Rev. by E. M. Despalatovic, EEQ, 10(Sum 1976):269-70.

Drago, Harry Sinclair. The Legend Makers: Tales of the Old-Time Peace Officers and Desperadoes of the Frontier. New York: Dodd, Mead, 1975. Rev. by H. J. Weiss, Jr., WHQ, 7(Apr 1976):210-11.

Dreifort, John E. Yvon Delbos at the Quai d'Orsay: French Foreign Policy During the Popular Front 1936-1938. Lawrence: U Press Kan, 1973. Rev. by J. C. Cairns, CHR, 57(Mar 1976):102-4.

Drekonja, Gerhard, ed. Conferencia Internacional: Modelos de desarrollo en América Latina. Berlin: Fundación Alemana para el Desarrollo Internacional, 1974. Rev. by J. L. Weaver, HAHR, 56(Feb 1976):180.

Drews, Robert. The Greek Accounts of Eastern History. Cam-

bridge, Mass: Harvard U Press, 1973. Rev. by J. J.
Keaney, AHR, 81(Feb 1976):104-5; J. D. Muhly, JNES, 35
(Jan 1976):41-3.

Dreyer, Peter. A Gardener Touched with Genius: The Life of
Luther Burbank. New York: Coward, 1975. Rev. by R.
Ornduff, CHQ, 55(Sum 1976):188-9.

Drinnon, Richard and Anna Maria Drinnon, eds. Nowhere at Home:
Letters from Exile of Emma Goldman and Alexander Berkman.
New York: Schocken, 1975. Rev. by W. G. Nowlin, Jr.,
AHR, 81(Apr 1976):362.

Droz, Jacques, ed. Histoire générale du Socialisme. Vol. 2.
Paris: Presses U France, 1974. Rev. by C. Landauer,
AHR, 81(Feb 1976):101-2.

Drummond, Andrew L. and James Bulloch. The Church in Victorian Scotland 1843-1874. Edinburgh: St. Andrew Press,
1975. Rev. by J. H. Glassman, CH, 45(Sep 1976):391-2;
E. R. Norman, EHR, 91(Apr 1976):445-6.

Drummond, Ian M. British Economic Policy and the Empire,
1919-1939. New York: Barnes and Noble, 1972. Rev. by
A. P. Thronton, AHR, 81(Feb 1976):140-1.

_____. Imperial Economic Policy 1917-1939: Studies in Expan-
sion and Protection. London: Allen and Unwin, 1974. Rev.
by S. Constantine, EHR, 91(Jan 1976):235-6; P. J. Cain, History, 61(Je 1976):315-16.

Dubay, Robert W. John Jones Pettus, Mississippi Fire-Eater:
His Life and Times, 1813-1867. Jackson: U Press Miss.,
1975. Rev. by W. F. Holmes, GHQ, 60(Sum 1976):193-4;
N. F. Magruder, HRNB, 4(Jan 1976):55; W. N. Still, Jr.,
JMiH, 38(Feb 1976):119-20; G. McWhiney, JSH, 42(Aug 1976):
429-30.

Du Bois, David Graham. ... And Bid Him Sing. Palo Alto, Cal.:
Ramparts, 1971. Rev. by G. E. Osborne, Crisis, 83(Jan
1976):33.

Dubois, P. see Carré, J.-J.

du Boulay, Juliet. Portrait of a Greek Mountain Village. Oxford:
Clarendon Press, 1974. Rev. by P. Warren, Antiquity, 50
(Je 1976):167-8.

Duckett, Kenneth W. Modern Manuscripts: A Practical Manual
for Their Management, Care, and Use. Nashville: American
Assn for State and Local History, 1974. Rev. by J. C.
Broderick, AmArc, 39(Jan 1976):45-6; R. Storey, Archives,
12(Aut 1976):203-4.

Duckworth, C. L. D. see Chubb, H. J.

DuClos, Katharine F. The History of Braintree, Vermont. Vol.
II, 1883-1975. Braintree, Vermont: History Book Committee,
1976. Rev. by R. Teagle, VH, 44(Fall 1976):239-42.

Dudley, Edward and Maximillian E. Novak, eds. The Wild Man
Within: An Image in Western Thought from the Renaissance
to Romanticism. Pittsburgh: U Pittsburgh Press, 1972.
Rev. by R. Birn, AHR, 81(Apr 1976):353-4.

Duff, Ernest A., et al. Violence and Repression in Latin America:
A Quantitative and Historical Analysis. New York: Free
Press, 1976. Rev. by T. Schoonover, HRNB, 4(Aug 1976):
193.

Duffus, R. L. The Santa Fe Trail. New York: David McKay,
1975. Rev. by H. R. Grant, JOW, 15(Jan 1976):122-3.

Duffy, Christopher. Borodino and the War of 1812. New York:
Scribner's, 1973. Rev. by D. D. Howard, AHR, 81(Je 1976):
607-8.

Duffy, John. A History of Public Health in New York City, 1625-
1866. 1866-1966. New York: Russell Sage Foundation, 1968,
1974. Rev. by J. W. Leavitt, RAH, 4(Je 1976):150-157.

_____. A History of Public Health in New York City, 1866-1966.
New York: Russell Sage, 1974. Rev. by G. H. Brieger,
AHR, 81(Apr 1976):453-4.

_____, ed. Early Vermont Broadsides. Hanover: U Press of
New England, 1975. Rev. by S. W. Jackman, NEQ, 49(Je
1976):307-8; M. A. McCorison, VH, 44(Sum 1976):185.

Duignan, Peter and L. H. Gann, eds. Colonialism in Africa,
1870-1960. New York: Cam U Press, 1975. Rev. by L.
E. Meyer, HRNB, 4(Jl 1976):168-9.

Duiker, William J. The Rise of Nationalism in Vietnam, 1900-
1941. Ithaca, N.Y.: Cornell U Press, 1976. Rev. by J.
K. Whitmore, HRNB, 4(Jl 1976):173.

Dukes, Paul. A History of Russia: Medieval, Modern, Contemporary. London: Macmillan, 1974. Rev. by I. De Madariaga,
History, 61(Feb 1976):89-91.

Dull, Jack L., ed. see T'ung-Tsu Ch'ü

Dull, Jonathan R. The French Navy and American Independence:
A Study of Arms and Diplomacy, 1774-1787. Princeton: Prin
U Press, 1976. Rev. by H. F. Rankin, HRNB, 3(May/Je
1976):154-5; W. Stinchcombe, JAH, 63(Dec 1976):699-700; O.

Connelly, NCHR, 53(Aut 1976):414-15; E. M. Eller, VMHB,
84(Oct 1976):492-4.

Dumbarton Oaks Center for Byzantine Studies. Dumbarton Oaks
Papers, Number 27. Locust Valley, N.Y.: J. J. Augustin,
1973. Rev. by R. Cormack, AHR, 81(Feb 1976):120-1.

Dumont, René. L'Utopie ou la Mort! Paris: Editions du Seuil,
1973. Rev. by P. O'Brien, JMAS, 14(Sep 1976):539-40.

Dunbabin, J. P. D. Rural Discontent in Nineteenth-Century Britain.
New York: Holmes and Meier, 1975. Rev. by D. Spring,
AgH, 50(Jl 1976):542-3; D. Baugh, AHR, 81(Je 1976):588-9;
J. T. Ward, History, 61(Feb 1976):128.

Duncan, Archibald A. M. Scotland: The Making of the Kingdom.
Edinburgh: Oliver and Boyd, 1975. Rev. by D. P. Kirby,
EHR, 91(Oct 1976):837-41; G. W. S. Barrow, History, 61(Je
1976):252-3.

Duncan, Bingham. Whitelaw Reid: Journalist, Politician, Diplomat.
Athens: U Ga Press, 1975. Rev. by V. P. De Santis, AHR,
81(Oct 1976):981-2; J. E. Sefton, GHQ, 60(Sum 1976):195-6;
B. Aspinwall, History, 61(Oct 1976):414-15; J. F. Wall,
HRNB, 4(May/Je 1976):140-1; C. D. Davis, IMH, 72(Dec
1976):379-80; H. L. Trefousse, JAH, 63(Sep 1976):429-30;
S. J. Kneeshaw, JSH, 42(Aug 1976):438-40.

Duncan, Francis see Hewlett, Richard G.

Duncan, Graeme. Marx and Mill: Two Views of Social Conflict and
Social Harmony. Cambridge: Cam U Press, 1973. Rev. by
W. Thomas, EHR, 91(Jl 1976):664-5.

Dungen, P. H. M. VanDen. The Punjab Tradition ... in Nineteenth-Century India. London: Allen and Unwin, 1972. Rev.
by C. Dewey, MAS, 10(Jl 1976):477-9.

Dunn, John. Modern Revolutions: An Introduction to the Analysis
of a Political Phenomenon. New York: Cam U Press, 1972.
Rev. by J. J. Roth, AHR, 81(Je 1976):567-8.

_____ and A. F. Robertson. Dependence and Opportunity:
Political Change in Ahafo. Cambridge: Cam U Press, 1973.
Rev. by J. Simensen, JAfH, 17(Num 2, 1976):317-18; D. M.
P. McCarthy, JEH, 36(Sep 1976):747-8.

Dunning, R. W., ed. A History of the County of Somerset. Vol.
3. New York: Oxford U Press, 1974. Rev. by T. G.
Barnes, AHR, 81(Je 1976):581; M. Havinden, EHR, 91(Apr
1976):474; J. Youings, History, 61(Feb 1976):79-80.

Duram, James C. Norman Thomas. New York: Twayne, 1974.

Rev. by J. P. Holsinger, Historian, 39(Nov 1976):163-4.

Durant, Will and Ariel Durant. The Age of Napoleon: A History of European Civilization from 1789 to 1815. New York: Simon and Schuster, 1975. Rev. by J. I. Shulim, HRNB, 4 (Mar 1976):108; B. Atwater, Mankind, 5(Oct 1976):57-8.

Durden, Robert F. The Dukes of Durham, 1865-1929. Durham, N.C.: Duke U Press, 1975. Rev. by J. E. Brittain, Historian, 39(Nov 1976):154-5; D. M. Chalmers, JSH, 42(Feb 1976):128-9.

Durham, Walter T. Daniel Smith, Frontier Statesman. Gallatin, Tenn.: Sumner County Library Board, 1976. Rev. by R. E. Corlew, THQ, 35(Fall 1976):336-7.

Durnbaugh, Donald F., ed. Every Need Supplied. Philadelphia: Temple U Press, 1974. Rev. by C. J. Dyck, JCS, 18(Aut 1976):583-4; P. J. Klassen, MQR, 50(Apr 1976):142-3.

Dusenberry, William Howard. The Waynesburg College Story: 1849-1974. Kent, Ohio: Kent St U Press, 1975. Rev. by G. W. Chessman, JAH, 62(Mar 1975):994.

Dush, Joseph F. History of Willard, Ohio. Willard, Ohio: Lakeside Press, 1974. Rev. by B. Sahers, OH, 85(Spr 1976): 175-6.

Dussell, Enrique. Historia de la Iglesia en America Latina. Barcelona: Editorial Nova Terra, 1972. Rev. by D. F. D'Amico, JCS, 18(Aut 1976):554-6.

_____. History and the Theology of Liberation: A Latin American Perspective. Maryknoll, N.Y.: Orbis, 1976. Rev. by W. J. Kilgore, HAHR, 56(Nov 1976):669-70.

Du Toit, Brian M. People of the Valley: Life in an Isolated Afrikaner Community of South Africa. Cape Town: Balkema, 1974. Rev. by M. Legassick, AfAf, 75(Apr 1976):264-5.

Dutton, Bertha P. Indians of the American Southwest. Englewood Cliffs, N.J.: Prentice-Hall, 1975. Rev. by R. W. Ellis, JAriH, 17(Spr 1976):112-13; W. A. Minge, WHQ, 7(Jan 1976): 71-2.

Duval, Paul. High Realism in Canada. Toronto: Clarke, Irwin, 1974. Rev. by A. Davis, CHR, 57(Mar 1976):40-7.

Dwyer, D. J., ed. China Now. Harlow: Longman, 1974. Rev. by D. S. G. Goodman, CQ, May 1976, pp. 403-5.

Dykeman, Wilma. Tennessee: A Bicentennial History. New York: Norton, 1975. Rev. by L. R. Gerlach, HRNB, 4(Aug 1976):

190-1; J. W. McKee, Jr., JSH, 42(Nov 1976):610-11.

Dykmans, Marc. Les Sermons de Jean XXII sur la Vision Béatifique. Rome: Presses de l'Université Gregorienné, 1973.
Rev. by A. C. Rush, CaHR, 62(Jan 1976):95-6.

Dyos, H. J. and M. Wolff, eds. The Victorian City: Images and
Realities. London: Routledge and Kegan Paul, 1973. Rev.
by P. J. Waller, EHR, 91(Apr 1976):446-7.

Eagleson, John, ed. Christians and Socialism: Documentation of
the Christians for Socialism Movement in Latin America.
Maryknoll, N.Y.: Orbis, 1975. Rev. by E. J. Williams,
HAHR, 56(May 1976):350-1.

Earle, Carville V. The Evolution of a Tidewater Settlement System.
Chicago: U Chicago Press, 1975. Rev. by M. B. Lapping,
JSH, 42(Nov 1976):578-9; G. E. Clemens, MHM, 71(Sum
1976):275-7.

Earle, John see Muir, John

_____. Italy in the 1970's. North Pomfret, Vt.: David and
Charles, 1975. Rev. by C. F. Delzell, JCS, 18(Aut 1976):
590-1.

Easson, David E., ed. see Cowan, Ian B., ed.

East, Robert A. and Jacob Judd, eds. The Loyalist Americans:
A Focus on Greater New York. Tarrytown, N.Y.: Sleepy
Hollow Restorations, 1975. Rev. by D. Greenberg, AHR, 81
(Oct 1976):962-3; J. T. Reilly, JAH, 63(Je 1976):112-13; R.
M. Jellison, OH, 85(Sum 1976):265-6.

Eaton, Clement. A History of the Old South: The Emergence of a
Reluctant Nation. New York: Macmillan, 1975. Rev. by
G. R. Bentley, FHQ, 55(Jl 1976):85-6.

Eayrs, James. In Defence of Canada: Peacemaking and Deterrence. Toronto: U Tor Press, 1972. Rev. by G. F. G.
Stanley, AHR, 81(Je 1976):698-9.

Ebert, John and Katherine Ebert. American Folk Painters. New
York: Scribner's, 1975. Rev. by D. Flower, NEQ, 49(Sep
1976):470-2.

Eckermann, Willigis see Mayer, Cornelius Petrus

Eckes, Alfred E., Jr. A Search for Solvency: Bretton Woods and
the International Monetary System, 1941-1971. Austin: U
Texas Press, 1975. Rev. by E. R. Wicker, BHR, 50(Sum
1976):262-3; F. J. Munch, HRNB, 4(Aug 1976):197; M. Wilkins, JAH, 63(Je 1976):188-9; L. C. Gardner, WMH, 60(Aut
1976):75.

Eckhart, George B. and James S. Griffith. Temples in the Wilderness. Tucson: Arizona Historical Society, 1975. Rev. by
R. L. Ives, A & W, 18(Aut 1976):298-9.

Edelstein, Joel C., ed. see Chilcote, Ronald H., ed.

Edmiston, Susan and Linda Cirino. Literary New York. New
York: Houghton Mifflin, n.d. Rev. by R. E. Brown, Mankind, 5(Dec 1976):64.

Edmondson, Munro S., ed. The Work of Sahagún. Albuquerque:
U NM Press, 1974. Rev. by J. D. Riley, TAm, 33(Oct
1976):365-6.

_____, ed. Sixteenth-Century Mexico: The Work of Sahagún.
Albuquerque: U NM Press, 1974. Rev. by T. H. Carlton,
AmAn, 41(Jl 1976):403-5; E. T. Baird, HAHR, 56(Feb 1976):
125-6.

Edwardes, Michael. Red Year: The Indian Rebellion of 1857.
London: Hamish Hamilton, 1973. Rev. by R. J. Bingle, History, 61(Feb 1976):164.

Edwards, I. E. S., N. G. L. Hammond and E. Sollberger, eds.
The Cambridge Ancient History. Vol. II, Part 2: History of
the Middle East and the Aegean Region, c. 1380-1000 B.C.
New York: Cam U Press, 1975. Rev. by R. Brilliant,
HRNB, 4(Jan 1976):63-4.

Edwards, Kathleen and Dorothy M. Owen. The Registers of Roger
Martival, Bishop of Salisbury, 1315-1330. Vol. 4. Canter-
bury: Canterbury and York Society, 1975. Rev. by F. D.
Logan, Archives, 12(Aut 1976):190-1.

Edwards, Mark U., Jr. Luther and the False Brethren. Stan-
ford, Cal.: Stanford U Press, 1975. Rev. by J. P. Ryan,
Jr., CH, 45(Je 1976):256-7; W. D. J. Cargill Thompson,
JEccH, 27(Oct 1976):436-8.

Edwards, Steward. The Paris Commune 1871. Chicago: Quadrangle 1973. Rev. by T. W. Margadant, JIH, 7(Sum 1976):
91-7.

Effross, Harris I. County Governing Bodies in New Jersey. New
Brunswick, N.J.: Rutgers U Press, 1975. Rev. by E. M.
Tobin, JAH, 63(Dec 1976):705-6.

Eger, Wolfgang, ed. Kirche und Staat im 19. und 20. Jahrhundert.
Neustadt an der Aisch: Verlag Degener, 1968. Rev. by W.
A. Mueller, JCS, 18(Win 1976):140.

Eggenberger, David I., ed. The McGraw-Hill Encyclopedia of
World Biography. New York: McGraw-Hill, 1973. Rev. by

R. E. Brown, Mankind, 5(Aug 1976):8.

Eggert, Gerald G. Richard Olney: Evolution of a Statesman.
University Park: Penn St U Press, 1974. Rev. by R. L.
Beisner, PHR, 45(Feb 1976):147-9.

Ehle, John. The Journey of August King. New York: Avon,
1973. Rev. by R. Ashley, CWTI, 15(Apr 1976):45-6.

Ehrenberg, Ralph E., ed. Pattern and Process: Research in Historical Geography. Washington, D.C.: Howard U Press,
1975. Rev. by L. C. Allin, HRNB, 4(May/Je 1976):148;
E. K. Muller, JNH, 61(Jl 1976):314-16.

Eichenbaum, V. M. The Unknown Revolution. New York: Free
Life, 1974. Rev. by J. R. Braun, MQR, 50(Jan 1976):71-2.

Eichler, Fritz and Wolfgang Oberleitner. Corpus Vasorum Antiquorum, Austria fasc. 3, Vienna, Kunsthistorisches Museum,
fasc. 3. Vienna: Verlag der Österreichischen Akademie der
Wissenschaften 1974. Rev. by D. von Bothmer, AJA, 80(Spr
1976):210-11.

Eidelberg, Philip G. The Great Rumanian Peasant Revolt of 1907:
Origins of a Modern Jacquerie. Leiden: E. J. Brill, 1974.
Rev. by W. Hagen, AgH, 50(Jl 1976):543-5; D. McKay, History, 61(Je 1976):316-17; J. W. Cole, JMH, 48(Je 1976):358-
60.

Eisenberg, Peter. The Sugar Industry in Pernambuco: Modernization Without Change, 1840-1910. Berkeley: U Cal Press,
1974. Rev. by J. Reis, HAHR, 56(May 1976):338-40.

Eisenhower, Milton S. The President Is Calling. Garden City,
N.Y.: Doubleday, 1974. Rev. by E. Richardson, PNQ, 67
(Jl 1976):134.

Ekelund, Robert B., Jr., and Robert F. Hebert. A History of
Economic Theory and Method. New York: McGraw-Hill,
1975. Rev. by R. V. Eagly, JEH, 36(Je 1976):463-4.

Ekirch, Arthur A., Jr. Progressivism in America: A Study of the
Era from Theodore Roosevelt to Woodrow Wilson. New York:
New Viewpoints, 1974. Rev. by O. A. Pease, AHR, 81(Oct
1976):988-9; B. F. Fisher, IV, AS, 16(Fall 1975):93-4; J. A.
Thompson, HJ, 19(Mar 1976):257-74.

Eksteins, Modris. The Limits of Reason: The German Democratic
Press and the Collapse of the Weimar Democracy. New York:
Oxford U Press, 1975. Rev. by A. Rudhart, AHR, 81(Je
1976):617-18; A. J. Ryder, History, 61(Je 1976):321.

El-Ayonty, Yassin, ed. The Organization of African Unity After

Ten Years: Comparative Perspectives. New York:
Praeger, 1975. Rev. by J. E. Okolo, JMAS, 14(Je
1976):348-50.

Eldredge, H. Wentworth, ed. World Capitals: Toward Guided Urbanization. n. p. : Anchor/Doubleday, 1975. Rev. by J. H.
Kay, Smithsonian, 6(Dec 1975):128-30.

Eldridge, C. C. England's Mission: The Imperial Idea in the Age
of Gladstone and Disraeli 1868-1880. Chapel Hill: UNC Press,
1973. Rev. by A. P. Thornton, AHR, 81(Feb 1976):140-1.

Eliades, David K. see Dial, Adolph L.

Elkana, Yehuda. The Discovery of the Conservation of Energy.
Cambridge, Mass.: Harvard U Press, 1974. Rev. by H. I.
Sharlin, AHR, 81(Feb 1976):101; J. R. R. Christie, EHR, 91
(Jan 1976):219-20; C. Smith, JMH, 48(Je 1976):323-4.

Elkington, Hazel see Chenery, Hollis

Elkins, Stanley and Eric McKitrick, eds. The Hofstadter Aegis:
A Memorial. New York: Knopf, 1974. Rev. by A. P. Dud-
den, AHR, 81(Apr 1976):468-9.

Elliger, Walter. Thomas Müntzer: Leben und Werk. Göttingen:
Vandenhoeck & Ruprecht, 1975. Rev. by E. W. Gritsch, CH,
45(Sep 1976):382-3.

Elliott, Clark A. , comp. A Descriptive Guide to the Harvard University Archives. Cambridge, Mass.: Harvard U Library,
1974. Rev. by J. R. K. Kantor, AmArc, 39(Jan 1976):49-50.

Elliott, Emory. Power and the Pulpit in Puritan New England.
Princeton, N.J.: Prin U Press, 1975. Rev. by R. Middlekauff, AHR, 81(Oct 1976):955-6; R. C. Pope, CaHR, 62(Oct
1976):673-4; S. Foster, JAH, 63(Sep 1976):383-4; G. Selement,
NEQ, 49(Je 1976):317-20.

Elliott, John B. Contest for Empire, 1500-1775. Indianapolis:
Indiana Historical Society, 1975. Rev. by R. W. Van Alstyne,
IMH, 72(Dec 1976):363-4.

Elliott, Lawrence. The Long Hunter: A New Life of Daniel Boone.
New York: Reader's Digest, 1976. Rev. by C. G. Talbert,
FCHQ, 50(Jl 1976):324-5.

Elliott, Ward E. Y. The Rise of Guardian Democracy: The Supreme Court's Role in Voting Rights Disputes, 1845-1969.
Cambridge, Mass.: Harvard U Press, 1974. Rev. by H. M.
Hyman, AHR, 81(Je 1976):663-4; A. A. Morris, PNQ, 67(Jl
1976):131-2.

Elliott-Bateman, Michael, et al. The Fourth Dimension of War-
     fare. Vol. II. Revolt to Revolution: Studies in the 19th-
     and 20th-Century European Experience. Totowa, N.J.: Row-
     man and Littlefield, 1975. Rev. by J. J. Roth, AHR, 81(Je
     1976):567-8; P. Calvert, History, 61(Feb 1976):93-4.

Ellis, Edward Robb. Echoes of Distant Thunder: Life in the United
     States, 1914-1918. New York: Coward, McCann and Geoghegan,
     Rev. by M. Olmert, Smithsonian, 6(Mar 1976):114-15.

Ellis, John. A Short History of Guerrilla Warfare. New York:
     St. Martin's, 1976. Rev. by D. Eggenberger, HRNB, 5(Oct
     1976):15.

_____. The Social History of the Machine Gun. New York:
     Pantheon, 1975. Rev. by P. D. Thomas, HRNB, 4(Apr 1976):
     131; B. Farwell, Smithsonian, 7(Apr 1976):128-9.

Ellis, Joseph. The New England Mind in Transition: Samuel John-
     son of Connecticut, 1696-1772. New Haven, Conn.: Yale U
     Press, 1973. Rev. by F. E. Sugeno, HMPEC, 45(Sep 1976):
     348-50.

Ellis, Peter Berresford. Hell or Connaught! The Cromwellian Col-
     onisation of Ireland, 1652-1660. New York: St. Martin's, 1975.
     Rev. by D. F. Cregan, AHR, 81(Je 1976):597-8.

Ellis, Richard N., ed. New Mexico Historic Documents. Albu-
     querque: U NM Press, 1975. Rev. by B. D. Ledbetter,
     JOW, 15(Jl 1976):97; R. W. Larson, NMHR, 51(Jan 1976):
     81-2.

Ellison, Mary. The Black Experience: American Blacks Since
     1865. New York: Barnes and Noble, 1974. Rev. by R. L.
     Zangrando, AHR, 81(Apr 1976):450-1.

Elovitz, Mark H. A Century of Jewish Life in Dixie: The Bir-
     mingham Experience. University: U Ala Press, 1974. S.
     F. Chyet, AHR, 81(Je 1976):680; W. Flynt, AlaR, 29(Oct
     1976):314-16; N. Lederer, ArkHQ, 35(Spr 1976):104-6.

Elrington, C. R., ed. Abstracts of Feet of Fines Relating to Wilt-
     shire for the Reign of Edward III. Devizes: Wiltshire Record
     Society, 1974. Rev. by J. R. Maddicott, EHR, 91(Jan 1976):
     180-1.

Elting, John R. The Battle of Bunker's Hill. Monmouth Beach,
     N.J.: Philip Freneau Press, 1975. Rev. by P. D. Nelson,
     MHM, 71(Sum 1976):272-3.

Elton, G. R. Studies in Tudor and Stuart Politics and Government:
     Papers and Reviews 1946-1972. Vols. I and II. Cambridge:
     Cam U Press, 1974. Rev. by E. W. Ives, History, 61(Feb

1976):106-7; J. W. Vardaman, JCS, 17(Spr 1975):342-3.

Elvin, Mark. The Pattern of the Chinese Past. Stanford, Cal.:
    Stanford U Press, 1973. Rev. by E. S. Rawski, JIH, 7(Sum
    1976):133-6.

_____ and G. William Skinner, eds. The Chinese City Between
    Two Worlds. Stanford, Cal.: Stanford U Press, 1975. Rev.
    by E. S. Rawski, CQ, Jan 1976, 128-31.

Elwitt, Sanford. The Making of the Third Republic: Class and
    Politics in France, 1868-1884. Baton Rouge: LSU Press,
    1975. Rev. by L. Loubère, AHR, 81(Je 1976):609-10; A. R.
    H. Copley, History, 61(Oct 1976):465.

Ely, James W., Jr. The Crisis of Conservative Virginia; The
    Byrd Organization and the Politics of Massive Resistance.
    Knoxville: U Tenn Press, 1976. Rev. by A. M. Burns,
    III, THQ, 35(Win 1976):426-8.

el-Zein, Abdul Hamid M. The Sacred Meadows. Evanston, Ill.:
    Northwestern U Press, 1974. Rev. by B. G. Martin, JAfH,
    17(Num 3, 1976):452-4.

Emden, A. B. A Biographical Register of the University of Ox-
    ford, A.D. 1501 to 1540. Oxford: Clarendon, 1974. Rev.
    by J. K. McConica, EHR, 91(Jan 1976):185-6; P. Collinson,
    JEccH, 27(Oct 1976):441-3.

Emerson, Dorothy. Among the Mescalero Apaches. The Story of
    Father Albert Braun, OFM. Tucson: U Ariz Press, 1973.
    Rev. by F. F. Fox, CaHR, 61(Jl 1976):520-1.

Empson, Donald. The Street Where You Live: A Guide to the
    Street Names of St. Paul. St. Paul: Witsend, 1975. Rev.
    by R. E. Hoag, MinnH, 45(Sum 1976):78.

Emy, H. V. Liberals, Radicals and Social Politics, 1892-1914.
    Cambridge: Cam U Press, 1973. Rev. by M. Freeden,
    JMH, 48(Sep 1976):547-52.

Endicott, S. L. Diplomacy and Enterprise: British China Policy,
    1933-1937. Manchester: Manchester U Press, 1975. Rev.
    by B. F. Beers, AHR, 81(Je 1976):595-6; I. Nish, EHR, 91
    (Oct 1976):938-9.

Endy, Melvin B., Jr. William Penn and Early Quakerism. Prince-
    ton, N.J.: Prin U Press, 1973. Rev. by H. Barbour, CaHR,
    62(Apr 1976):291-3; J. E. Illick, PH, 43(Jan 1976):82-3.

Engel, Lehman. The American Musical Theater. New York:
    Macmillan, n.d. Rev. by C. Anderson, Mankind, 5(Dec 1976):
    64.

Engelborghs-Bertels, Marthe. La Chine rurale: des villages aux Communes populaires. Brussels: L'Université de Bruxelles, 1974. Rev. by G. Étienne, CQ, Jan 1976, pp. 155-6.

Engel-Janosi, Friedrich, et al., eds. Denken über Geschichte: Aufsätze zur heutigen Situation des geschichtlichen Bewusstseins und der Geschichtswissenschaft. Munich: R. Oldenbourg Verlag, 1974. Rev. by G. G. Iggers, AHR, 81(Feb 1976):102-3.

_____. Vom Chaos zur Katastrophe: Vatikanische Gespräche, 1918 bis 1938. Vornehmlich auf Grund der Berichte der österreichischen Gesandten beim Heiligen Stuhl. Vienna: Verlag Herold, 1971. Rev. by G. O. Kent, AHR, 81(Feb 1976): 180.

Engels, Hans Werner. Gedichte und Lieder deutscher Jakobiner. Stuttgart: Metzler, 1971. Rev. by E. Tenner, JMH, 48(Mar 1976):162-4.

_____. Jakobinerschauspiel und Jakobinertheater. Stuttgart: Metzler, 1973. Rev. by E. Tenner, JMH, 48(Mar 1976): 162-4.

Engelsing, Rolf. Analphabetentum und Lekture: zur Sozialgeschichte des Lesens in Deutschland zwischen feudaler und industrieller Gesellschaft. Stuttgart: J. B. Metzlersche Verlag, 1973. Rev. by A. Lees, JSoH, 10(Fall 1976): 119-20.

Engerman, Stanley L. see Fogel, Robert W.

_____ and Eugene D. Genovese, eds. Race and Slavery in the Western Hemisphere: Quantitative Studies. Princeton, N.J.: Prin U Press, 1975. Rev. by M. J. MacLeod, AgH, 50(Apr 1976):437-9; A. J. R. Russell-Wood, AHR, 81(Apr 1976):355-7; H. J. Fisher, JAfH, 17(Num 1, 1976):141-2; R. Conrad, JAH, 63(Sep 1976):373-4; J. White, JAmS, 10(Apr 1976):113-17; F. W. Knight, JSoH, 10(Fall 1976):107-15; H. Hoetink, TAm, 33(Oct 1976):377-9.

Engle, Eloise and Lauri Paananen. The Winter War: The Russo-Finnish Conflict, 1939-40. New York: Scribner's, 1973. Rev. by H. P. Krosby, AHR, 81(Oct 1976):878-9.

Ennaïfer, Mongi, ed. see Alexander, Margaret A., ed.

Enrique de la Peña, José. With Santa Anna in Texas. College Station: Texas A & M U Press, 1975. Rev. by J. L. Pate, ChOk, 54(Fall 1976):408-9.

Epp, Frank. Mennonites in Canada 1786-1920: The History of a Separate People. Toronto: Macmillan, 1974. Rev. by V. Peters, CHR, 57(Je 1976):198-9; J. C. Wenger, IMH, 72 (Je 1976):168-70; J. C. Juhnke, JAH, 63(Je 1976):202-3.

EPSTEIN 116

Epstein, T. Scarlett. South India: Yesterday, Today and Tomorrow. London: Macmillan, 1973. Rev. by J. Manor, MAS, 10(Feb 1976):156-9.

Epton, Nina. Josephine: The Empress and Her Children. New York: Norton, 1976. Rev. by W. B. Kennedy, HRNB, 4(Aug 1976):203.

Erasmus. The Correspondence of Erasmus. Vol. I. Toronto: U Tor Press, 1974. Rev. by J. D. Tracy, AHR, 81(Feb 1976): 161.

_____. The Correspondence of Erasmus. Vol. 2. (R. A. Mynors, et al., trans.) Buffalo: U Tor Press, 1975. Rev. by F. G. Nuttall, JEccH, 27(Apr 1976):198-200.

Erb, Guy F. and Valeriana Kallab, eds. Beyond Dependency: The Developing World Speaks Out. New York: Praeger, 1975. Rev. by G. Rosen, JAS, 36(Nov 1976):117-19.

Eremenko, A. The Arduous Beginning. Moscow: Progress Publ'rs., 1966. Rev. by E. F. Ziemke, AHR, 81(Je 1976): 637-9.

Ericksen, E. E. The Psychological and Ethical Aspects of Mormon Group Life. Salt Lake City: U Utah Press, 1975. Rev. by R. Bailey, ChOk, 54(Sum 1976):283-4; H. M. Ward, JOW, 15(Jan 1976):136.

Erickson, Charlotte. Invisible Immigrants: The Adaptation of English and Scottish Immigrants in Nineteenth-Century America. Coral Gables, Fla.: U Miami Press, 1972. Rev. by E. R. Barkan, AS, 16(Fall 1975):93; R. J. Olney, Archives, 12(Atu 1976):198.

Erickson, John. The Road to Stalingrad. Vol. 1, Stalin's War with Germany. New York: Harper and Row, 1975. Rev. by M. Parrish, AHR, 81(Oct 1976):912.

Ernst, Eldon G. Moment of Truth for Protestant America: Inter-Church Campaigns Following World War One. Missoula, Mont.: Scholars Press, 1974. Rev. by P. D. Jordan, CH, 45(Mar 1976):122.

Ernst, Joseph Albert. Money and Politics in America, 1755-1775. Chapel Hill: UNC Press, 1973. Rev. by E. J. Perkins, Historian, 39(Mar 1976):144-5.

Esherick, Joseph W., ed. Last Chance in China: The World War II Dispatches of John S. Service. New York: Random, 1974. Rev. by J. C. Cheng, AHR, 81(Je 1976):687-8.

Essame, H. Patton: A Study in Command. New York: Scribner's,

1974. Rev. by D. G. Dayton, AHR, 81(Feb 1976):219.

Esslinger, Dean R. Immigrants and the City. Port Washington,
N. Y.: Kennikat, 1975. Rev. by R. Berthoff, AHR, 81(Oct
1976):982; S. T. McSeveney, HRNB, 4(Jan 1976):52; J. H.
Madison, IMH, 72(Je 1976):161-2; E. R. Kantowicz, JAH, 62
(Mar 1976):1016; I. Cohen, WMH, 60(Aut 1976):69.

Etchison, Don L. The United States and Militarism in Central
America. New York: Praeger, 1975. Rev. by T. Karnes,
HAHR, 56(May 1976):329-30; K. J. Grieb, TAm, 33(Oct
1976):369-70.

Ettinghausen, Richard. From Byzantium to Sasanian Iran and the
Islamic World. Leiden: E. J. Brill, 1972. Rev. by O.
Grabar, IJMES, 7(Apr 1976):293-6; D. Thompson, JNES, 35
(Jl 1976):199-201.

Ettlinger, Gerard H., ed. Theodoret of Cyrus, Eranistes: Critical
Text and Prolegomena. New York: Clarendon, 1975. Rev.
by F. W. Norris, CH, 45(Mar 1976):99-100.

Euler, Robert C., ed. see Gumerman, George J., ed.

Evans, Elizabeth. Weathering the Storm: Women of the American
Revolution. New York: Scribner's, 1975. Rev. by K. K.
Sklar, AHR, 81(Je 1976):672-3; M. M. Dunn, JSH, 42(Aug
1976):421-2; M. Gutheim, NEQ, 49(Mar 1976):138-40; M. J.
Morton, OH, 85(Sum 1976):266-7; M. M. Gordon, PH, 43(Oct
1976):368-9.

Evans, Emory G. Thomas Nelson of Yorktown: Revolutionary
Virginian. Charlottesville: U Press Va, 1975. Rev. by W.
M. Dabney, AHR, 81(Oct 1976):963-4; M. B. Sheldon, JAH,
63(Sep 1976):387-8; W. L. Shea, JSH, 42(Feb 1976):110-12;
E. Cometti, NCHR, 53(Win 1976):86-7; C. Collier, RAH, 4
(Mar 1976):53-8; J. J. Reardon, WMQ, 33(Jan 1976):165-6.

Evans, Frank B. and Harold T. Pinkett, eds. Research in the Administration of Public Policy. Washington, D.C.: Howard
U Press, 1975. Rev. by H. L. Calkin, AI, 43(Fall 1976):
480-2; G. D. Nash, JSH, 42(Feb 1976):138-9; R. W. Paul,
PHR, 45(Aug 1976):434-5.

Evans, George Ewart. The Days That We Have Seen. London:
Faber and Faber, 1975. Rev. by J. P. D. Dunbabin, EHR,
91(Jl 1976):615-18; A. Hawkins, History, 61(Oct 1976):486-7.

Evans, Michael. Karl Marx. London: Allen and Unwin, 1975.
Rev. by A. Ryan, HJ, 19(Je 1976):531-5.

Evans, J. W. Rudolf II and His World: A Study in Intellectual
History, 1576-1612. Oxford: Clarendon Press, 1973. Rev.

by D. Fenlon, HJ, 19(Sep 1976):787-92.

Evans, John G. The Environment of Early Man in the British Isles. London: Elek, 1975. Rev. by G. W. Dimbleby, Antiquity, 50(Mar 1976):81-2; R. J. Harrison, JEH, 36(Sep 1976):748-9.

Evans, R. J. W. Rudolf II and His World: A Study in Intellectual History, 1576-1612. New York: Oxford U Press, 1973. Rev. by J. P. Spielman, AHR, 81(Feb 1976):182-3; R. Bireley, CaHR, 62(Jan 1976):139-40.

Evans-Pritchard, E. E., ed. Man and Woman Among the Azande. London: Faber and Faber, 1974. Rev. by T. O. Beidelman, Africa, 46(Num 2, 1976):205-6.

Evergates, Theodore. Feudal Society in the Bailliage of Troyes Under the Counts of Champagne, 1152-1284. Baltimore: JHU Press, 1976. Rev. by A. R. Lewis, HRNB, 4(Apr 1976):134.

Evers, Hans-Dieter. Monks, Priests and Peasants. Leiden: E. J. Brill, 1972. Rev. by K. R. Norman, MAS, 10(Jl 1976):466-9.

Evitts, William. A Matter of Allegiances: Maryland from 1850-1861. Rev. by D. J. MacLeod, EHR, 91(Jl 1976):667-8.

Eyongetah, Tambi and Robert Brain. A History of the Cameroon. London: Longman, 1974. Rev. by E. M. Chilver, Africa, 46(Num 1, 1976):110-111; C. Fyfe, History, 61(Feb 1976): 154; P. Burnham, JAfH, 17(Num 3, 1976):476-7; H. O. H. Vernon-Jackson, JMAS, 14(Sep 1976):553-5.

Faderman, Lillian and Barbara Bradshaw, eds. Speaking for Ourselves: American Ethnic Writing. Glenview, Ill.: Scott, Foresman, 1975. Rev. by W. F. Smith, Jr., AIQ, 2(Sum 1975):153-5.

Fagan, B. see Oliver, R.

Fagan, Brian M. see Robinson, J. T.

Fage, J. D., ed. see Gray, Richard, ed.

Fagen, Richard, ed. see Cotler, Julio, ed.

Faherty, William Barnaby. Dream by the River. St. Louis: Piraeus, 1973. Rev. by N. A. Schneider, CaHR, 62(Jl 1976):481-3.

Fairbank, John K., ed. The Missionary Enterprise in China and America. Cambridge, Mass.: Har U Press, 1974. Rev. by Y. Shaw, AHR, 81(Oct 1976):934-6; M. H. Hunt, JAH, 62 (Mar 1976):1039-40; M. B. Young, JAS, 36(Nov 1976):132-5; P. W. Fay, PHR, 45(Feb 1976):141-2.

_____, ed. see Kierman, Frank A. , Jr. , ed.

Fairbanks, George R. The History and Antiquities of the City of
St. Augustine, Florida. Gainesville: U Presses Fla, 1975.
Rev. by L. R. Arana, AlaR, 29(Jl 1976):236-7.

Fairchilds, Cissie C. Poverty and Charity in Aix-en-Provence,
1640-1789. Baltimore: JHU Press, 1976. Rev. by M. H.
Schneider, HRNB, 5(Oct 1976):19.

Fairlie, Henry. The Spoiled Child of the Western World: The
Miscarriage of the American Idea of Our Time. New York:
Doubleday, 1976. Rev. by S. Weaver, Commentary, 61(Jl
1976):64-6, 68.

Fairmont Park Association. Sculpture of a City: Philadelphia's
Treasures in Bronze and Stone. New York: Walker, 1974.
Rev. by A. Lloyd, PH, 43(Apr 1976):188-9.

Falcoff, Mark and Ronald H. Dolkart, eds. Prologue to Peron:
Argentina in Depression and War, 1930-1943. Berkeley: U
Cal Press, 1976. Rev. by M. Navarro, HAHR, 56(Nov 1976):
660-1; E. P. Simmons, HRNB, 4(Sep 1976):221.

Falk, Richard A. A Study of Future Worlds. New York: Free
Press, 1975. Rev. by A. Lall, IQ, 32(Apr-Je 1976):226-30.

Falzone, Gaetano. La Sicilia nella Politica mediterranea delle
grandi potenze. Palermo: S. F. Flaccovio Editore, 1974.
Rev. by D. Koenig, AHR, 81(Je 1976):621-2.

Fantel, Hans. William Penn: Apostle of Dissent. New York:
Morrow, 1974. Rev. by J. E. Illick, PH, 43(Jan 1976):82-3.

Farber, Leslie H. Lying, Despair, Jealousy, Envy, Sex, Suicide,
Drugs, and the Good Life. New York: Basic Books, n. d.
Rev. by W. J. Dannhauser, Commentary, 62(Nov 1976):94, 96.

Farr, William. John Wycliff as Legal Reformer. Leiden: Brill,
1974. Rev. by M. Wilks, JEccH, 27(Oct 1976):432-3.

Farrant, Leda. Tippu Tip and the East African Slave Trade. London: Hamish Hamilton, 1975. Rev. by R. C. Bridges, History, 61(Feb 1976):158.

Farrell, Brian, ed. The Irish Parliamentary Tradition. New York:
Barnes and Noble, 1973. Rev. by H. Senior, AHR, 81(Feb
1976):150.

Farrell, James T. The Dunne Family. Garden City, N. Y.: Doubleday, n. d. Rev. by B. Wallenstein, Commentlry, 62(Dec
1976):82-5.

Fatica, Michele, ed. Le Relazioni diplomatiche fra lo Stato Ponti-
    ficio e la Francia. 2 vols. Rome: Istituto Storico Italiano,
    1971, 1972. Rev. by L. M. Case, AHR, 81(Apr 1976):377-8;
    A. J. Reinerman, CaHR, 62(Apr 1976):319-20.

Faulk, Odie B. Crimson Desert: Indian Wars of the American
    Southwest. New York: Oxford U Press, 1974. Rev. by W.
    S. Robinson, AHR, 81(Apr 1976):448; C. Trafzer, ChOk, 54
    (Sum 1976):284-5; J. P. Wilson, NMHR, 51(Jl 1976):253-4.

_____. The U. S. Camel Corps: An Army Experiment. New
    York: Oxford U Press, 1976. Rev. by M. E. Kroeker, JAH,
    63(Dec 1976):728-9; G. Thompson, JAriH, 17(Aut 1976):352-3;
    H. R. Grant, JSH, 42(Nov 1976):595-6; R. A. Trennert, Jr.,
    NMHR, 51(Oct 1976):346-7.

_____ and Joseph A. Stout, Jr. The Mexican War. Chicago:
    Swallow Press, 1974. Rev. by R. Burns, Mankind, 5(Aug
    1976):9, 58.

Fausold, Martin L. James W. Wadsworth, Jr.: The Gentleman
    from New York. Syracuse: Syracuse U Press, 1975. Rev.
    by E. L. Schapsmeier, HRNB, 4(Jan 1976):53-4; R. Lowitt,
    JAH, 63(Je 1976):178-80; L. Gould, RAH, 4(Mar 1976):105-9.

_____ and George T. Mazuzan, eds. The Hoover Presidency:
    A Reappraisal. Albany: SUNY Press, 1974. Rev. by R. H.
    Zeiger, AHR, 81(Oct 1976):800-10.

Favreau, Marie-Luise. Studien zur Frühgeschichte des Deutschen
    Ordens. Stuttgart: Ernst Klett Verlag, 1975. Rev. by P.
    W. Edbury, EHR, 91(Oct 1976):889.

Favretti, Rudy J. Once Upon Quoketaug: The Biography of a Con-
    necticut Farm Family, 1712-1960. Storrs, Conn.: Parousia
    Press, 1974. Rev. by D. P. Kelsey, AgH, 50(Jan 1976):320-
    1.

Fay, Peter Ward. The Opium War 1840-1842. Chapel Hill: U NC
    Press, 1975. Rev. by B. Avery, JAS, 36(Nov 1976):131-2;
    E. V. Gulick, PHR, 45(May 1976):295-7.

Federn, Ernst, ed. see Nunberg, Herman, ed.

Fedorova, Svetlana G. Ethnic Processes in Russian America.
    Anchorage: Anchorage Historical and Fine Arts Museum,
    1975. Rev. by R. M. Croskey, PNQ, 67(Apr 1976):88.

Feierman, S. The Shambaa Kingdom: A History. Madison: U
    Wis Press, 1974. Rev. by T. O. Beidelman, Africa, 46
    (Num 2, 1976):207-8; C. S. Nicolls, History, 61(Feb 1976):
    158; R. van Zwanenberg, JAAS, 11(Jl-Oct 1976):240-1.

Feil, Ernst and Rudolph Weth, eds. Diskussion zur "Theologie der Revolution." Munich: Chr. Kaiser Verlag, 1969. Rev. by W. A. Mueller, JCS, 18(Aut 1976):576-9.

Feingold, Henry L. Zion in America: The Jewish Experience from Colonial Times to the Present. New York: Twayne, 1974. Rev. by P. A. M. Taylor, History, 61(Oct 1976):411-12; R. A. Rockaway, JAH, 62(Mar 1976):858-9.

Feinstein, Alan. African Revolutionary: The Life and Times of Nigeria's Aminu Kano. Devizes, Wiltshire: Davidson, 1973. Rev. by F. A. Salamone, JMAS, 14(Mar 1976):172-3.

Feiwel, George R. The Intellectual Capital of Michal Kalecki, A Study in Economic Theory and Policy. Knoxville: U Tenn Press, 1975. Rev. by M. Bronfenbrenner, JEH, 36(Je 1976): 464-6.

Feldberg, Michael. The Philadelphia Riots of 1844: A Study in Ethnic Conflict. Westport, Conn.: Greenwood, 1975. Rev. by J. Schwartz, AHR, 81(Oct 1976):967-8; T. M. Hammett, JAH, 63(Sep 1976):411.

Feldman, Herbert. The End and the Beginning--Pakistan 1969-71. New Delhi: Oxford U Press, 1975. Rev. by B. B. Verghese, IQ, 32(Jl-Sep 1976):348-50.

Felldin, Jeanne Robey. Index to the 1820 Census of Virginia. Baltimore: Genealogical Publishing Co., 1976. Rev. by W. K. Winfree, VMHB, 84(Oct 1976):501.

Felmly, Bradford K. see Grady, John C.

Fenning, Hugh. The Undoing of the Friars of Ireland: A Study of the Novitiate Question in the Eighteenth Century. Louvain: Publications Universitaires, 1972. Rev. by J. Dollard, CaHR, 62(Apr 1976):299-301.

Fenyö, Mario O. Hitler, Horthy, and Hungary: German-Hungarian Relations 1941-1944. New Haven, Conn.: Yale U Press, 1972. Rev. by G. Ranki, ESR, 6(Jl 1976):402-3.

Ferguson, E. James. The Papers of Robert Morris. Pittsburgh: U Pittsburgh Press, 1975. Rev. by C. F. Hobson, NCHR, 53(Spr 1976):228-9; H. H. Miller, VMHB, 84(Apr 1976):207-9.

Ferguson, George Ekem. The Papers of George Ekem Ferguson. (Kwame Arhin, ed.) Cambridge: African Studies Centre, 1974. Rev. by M. Johnson, JAfH, 17(Num 4, 1976):638.

Fernández-Armesto, Felipe. Ferdinand and Isabella. New York: Taplinger, 1975. Rev. by J. N. Hillgarth, HAHR, 56(Aug 1976):468-9.

Ferns, H. S. The Argentine Republic 1516-1971. New York: Barnes and Noble, 1973. Rev. by P. Ranis, TAm, 32(Apr 1976):646-7.

Ferrell, Robert H., ed. America in a Divided World 1945-1972. Columbia: U SCar Press, 1975. Rev. by R. W. Sellen, HRNB, 4(Jl 1976):164.

Ferrier, Douglas M. and Mary Pearson, comp. and ed. Inventory of County Records: Hood County Courthouse. Austin: Texas State Library, 1974. Rev. by J. L. Mims, AmArc, 39(Jan 1976):54-6.

Ferris, Norman B. Desperate Diplomacy: William H. Seward's Foreign Policy, 1861. Knoxville: U Tenn Press, 1976. Rev. by W. F. Spencer, THQ, 35(Win 1976):428-9.

Fest, Joachim C. Hitler. London: Weidenfeld and Nicolson, 1974. Rev. by J. Caplan, EHR, 91(Apr 1976):460-1; J. Noakes, History, 61(Feb 1976):142-3.

Fetherling, Dale. Mother Jones, the Miners' Angel: a Portrait. Carbondale: S Ill U Press, 1974. Rev. by A. K. Powell, WHQ, 7(Jan 1976):66-7.

Feucht, Erika. Pektorale nichtköniglicher Personen. Wiesbaden: Harrassowitz, 1971. Rev. by P. L. Shinnie, JNES, 35(Jan 1976):55.

Feuchtwanger, E. J. Gladstone. New York: St. Martin's, 1975. Rev. by D. F. Schafer, HRNB, 4(Feb 1976):92-3.

Feuerwerker, Albert. Rebellion in Nineteenth Century China. Ann Arbor: U Mich, 1975. Rev. by P. Elmquist, AHR, 81(Oct 1976):936-7.

Fey, Harold E. With Sovereign Reverence: The First Twenty-Five Years of Americans United. Rockville, Md.: Roger Williams Press, 1974. Rev. by L. D. Newton, JCS, 17(Win 1975):154-5.

Field, Daniel. Rebels in the Name of the Tsar. Boston: Houghton Mifflin, 1976. Rev. by S. M. Horak, HRNB, 4(Aug 1976):205.

Field, Frank. Three French Writers and the Great War: Studies in the Rise of Communism and Fascism. New York: Cam U Press, 1975. Rev. by J. R. Censer, HRNB, 4(Mar 1976):110.

Field, John Osgood, ed. see Weiner, Myron, ed.

Fielder, Mildred. Sioux Indian Leaders. Seattle: Superior, 1975. Rev. by D. M. Shockley, NDH, 43(Sum 1976):44.

Fieldhouse, D. K. Economics and Empire 1830-1914. London:
    Weidenfeld and Nicolson, 1973. Rev. by I. M. Drummond,
    CHR, 57(Mar 1976):97-9.

Figueroa, Federico Brito. Historia económica y social de Venezuela:
    Una estructura para su estudio. Caracas: Universidad Cen-
    tral de Venezuela, 1974. Rev. by J. Nava, HAHR, 56(May
    1976):333-4.

Figueroa y Miranda, Miguel. Religión y política en la Cuba del
    siglo XIX: El Obispo Espada visto a la luz de los archivos
    romanos, 1802-1832. Miami: Ediciones Universal, 1975.
    Rev. by M. Crahan, HAHR, 56(Aug 1976):477-9.

Filho, Luís Viana. O governo Castello Branco. Rio de Janeiro:
    Livraria José Olympio Editora, 1975. Rev. by J. W. F.
    Dulles, HAHR, 56(May 1976):337-8.

Filler, Louis. Appointments at Armageddon: Muckraking and Pro-
    gressivism in the American Tradition. Westport, Conn.:
    Greenwood, 1976. Rev. by A. A. Ekirch, Jr., HRNB, 4(Sep
    1976):210.

Filliot, J.-M. La traite des esclaves vers les Mascareignes au
    XVIIIe siecle. Paris: ORSTOM, 1974. Rev. by H. Des-
    champs, Africa, 46(Num 2, 1976):208-9; N. R. Bennett, AHR,
    81(Je 1976):642-3; J. S. Bromley, EHR, 91(Jan 1976):205.

Finberg, H. P. R. Scandinavian England. Chichester: Phillimore,
    1975. Rev. by P. H. Blair, EHR, 91(Oct 1976):884.

Fine, John V. A., Jr. The Bosnian Church: A New Interpretation.
    New York: Columbia U Press, 1975. Rev. by R. Mojzes,
    CH, 45(Je 1976):251-2.

Fine, Lenore and Jesse A. Remington. The Corps of Engineers:
    Construction in the United States. Washington: Office of the
    Chief of Military History, U.S. Army, 1972. Rev. by C. W.
    Johnson, AHR, 81(Je 1976):689-90.

Fine, Sidney. Frank Murphy: The Detroit Years. Ann Arbor:
    U Mich Press, 1975. Rev. by D. A. Shannon, AHR, 81(Oct
    1976):994-5; J. L. Bates, JAH, 63(Je 1976):180-1; R. Dan-
    iels, RAH, 4(Mar 1976):110-14.

Fink, Gary and Milton Cantor, eds. Biographical Dictionary of
    American Labor Leaders. Westport, Conn.: Greenwood,
    1974. Rev. by W. M. Dick, CHR, 57(Je 1976):226-7.

Finkle, Lee. Forum for Protest: The Black Press During World
    War II. Rutherford, N.J.: Fairleigh Dickinson U Press,
    1975. Rev. by A. M. Osur, JAH, 63(Dec 1976):773-4.

Finlay, John L.   Canada in the North Atlantic Triangle: Two
    Centuries of Social Change.   New York: Oxford U Press,
    1975.   Rev. by H. S. Ferns, History, 61(Oct 1976):396-7.

Finlayson, Dale K. A., ed.   see   Borg, Dorothy, ed.

Finley, David Edward.   A Standard of Excellence: Andrew W.
    Mellon Founds the National Gallery of Art at Washington.
    Washington: Smithsonian Institution Press, 1973.   Rev. by
    J. M. Neil, JAH, 63(Je 1976):175-6.

Finley, M. I.   Democracy Ancient and Modern.   New Brunswick,
    N. J.:   Rutgers U Press, 1973.   Rev. by R. K. Sherk, AHR,
    81(Je 1976):558.

Finn, R. Welldon.   Domesday Book: A Guide.   Chichester: Phil-
    limore, 1973.   Rev. by B. Lyon, AHR, 81(Apr 1976):369;
    A. E. B. Owen, Archives, 12(Spr 1976):142-3.

Finster, Jerome, ed.   The National Archives and Urban Research.
    Athens: Ohio U Press, 1974.   Rev. by C. McL. Green, AHR,
    81(Feb 1976):201-2.

Finucane, James R.   Rural Development and Bureaucracy in Tan-
    zania: The Case of the Mwanza Region.   Uppsala: Scandinavi-
    an Institute of African Studies, 1974.   Rev. by R. Jeffries,
    AfAf, 75(Apr 1976):260-1; L. Mair, Africa, 46(Num 2, 1976):
    213; E. J. Keller, JMAS, 14(Sep 1976):536-9.

Fischer, Ernest G.   Robert Potter: Founder of the Texas Navy.
    Gretna, La.:   Pelican, 1976.   Rev. by S. E. Siegel, SWHQ,
    80(Oct 1976):245-6.

Fischer, Fritz.   World Power or Decline: The Controversy Over
    "Germany's Aims in the First World War."   New York: Nor-
    ton, 1974.   Rev. by H. W. Gatzke, AHR, 81(Feb 1976):167.

Fischer, Joachim.   Die sächsische Landeskirche im Kirchenkampf,
    1933-1937.   Göttingen: Vandenhoeck and Ruprecht, 1972.
    Rev. by W. A. Mueller, JCS, 17(Aut 1975):521-4.

Fischer, LeRoy H., ed.   The Civil War in Indian Territory.   Los
    Angeles: Morrison, 1974.   Rev. by C. N. Tyson, ChOk, 54
    (Spr 1976):156-7.

_____, ed.   Territorial Governors of Oklahoma.   Oklahoma City:
    Okla Historical Society, 1975.   Rev. by D. E. Green, ChOk,
    54(Spr 1976):163-4.

_____, ed.   "The Western States in the Civil War."   The Journal
    of the West, 14(Jan 1975).   Rev. by E. B. Long, CWTI, 15
    (Je 1976):49.

Fischer, Lewis A. and Philip E. Uren. The New Hungarian Agriculture. Montreal: McGill-Queen's U Press, 1973. Rev. by
N. F. Dreisziger, AgH, 50(Jan 1976):317-19.

Fischer, Richard and Gerhard Schäfer, comps. Landebischof D.
Wurm und der nationalsozialistische Staat, 1940-1945: Eine
Dokumentation. Stuttgart: Calwer Verlag, 1968. Rev. by
W. A. Mueller, JCS, 17(Aut 1975):521-4.

Fischer, Roger A. The Segregation Struggle in Louisiana, 1862-
77. Chicago: U Ill Press, 1974. Rev. by J. V. Reese,
SWHQ, 80(Jl 1976):123-4.

Fischer, Wolfram, ed. Beitrage zu Wirtschaftswachstum und Wirtschaftsstruktur in 16en und 19en Jahrhundert. Berlin: Duncker
& Humblot, 1971. Rev. by W. O. Henderson, ESR, 6(Jl
1976):383.

Fish, John Hall. Black Power/White Control: The Struggle of the
Woodlawn Organization in Chicago. Princeton, N.J.: Prin U
Press, 1973. Rev. by T. J. Ticknor, JISHS, 69(May 1976):
147-8.

Fisher, Louis. Presidential Spending Power. Princeton, N.J.:
Prin U Press, 1975. Rev. by J. E. Pluta, JAH, 63(Sep
1976):467-8.

Fisher, Roscoe Brown, ed. Michael Braun (Brown) of the Old
Stone House. Charlotte, N.C.: Privately printed, 1975.
Rev. by H. S. Stroupe, NCHR, 53(Spr 1976):221-3.

Fisher, W. B., ed. The Cambridge History of Iran. Vol. I.
Cambridge: Cam U Press, 1968. Rev. by T. C. Young,
IJMES, 7(Jan 1976):129-33.

Fisher, Wallace E. Politics, Poker, and Piety: A Perspective on
Cultural Religion in America. Nashville, Tenn: Abingdon,
1972. Rev. by G. W. Hull, JCS, 17(Spr 1975):331-3.

Fisk, Robert. The Point of No Return: The Strike Which Broke
the British Ulster. London: André Deutsch, 1975. Rev. by
G. Freyer, E-I, 11(Sum 1976):147-9.

Fiske, Turbese Lummis and Keith Lummis. Charles F. Lummis:
the Man and His West. Norman: U Ok Press, 1975. Rev.
by E. R. Bingham, A & W, 18(Win 1976):376-7; D. Gordon,
PHR, 45(Nov 1976):620-1; R. G. Lillard, SCQ, 58(Fall 1976):
438-9.

Fitzgerald, C. P. Mao Tse Tung and China. New York: Holmes
and Meier, 1976. Rev. in CurH, 71(Sep 1976):78.

Fitzhugh, Marie. Three Centuries Passed (The Fitzhugh Family).

San Antonio, Tex.: Naylor Co, 1975. Rev. by R. B. Davis, VMHB, 84(Jan 1976):103-4.

Fitzmyer, Joseph A. Essays on the Semitic Background of the New Testament. London: George Chapman, 1971. Rev. by J. C. Greenfield, JNES, 35(Jan 1976):59-61.

Fladeland, Betty. Men and Brothers: Anglo-American Antislavery Cooperation. Urbana: U Ill Press, 1972. Rev. by E. Noyes, JISHS, 69(May 1976):156-7.

Flannery, Austin P., ed. Documents of Vatican II. Grand Rapids, Mich.: Eerdmans, 1975. Rev. by R. A. Suelflow, CHIQ, 49(Spr 1976):46-7.

Fleisher, Martin. Radical Reform and Political Persuasion in the Life and Writings of Thomas More. Geneva: Librairie Droz, 1973. Rev. by J. H. Hexter, AHR, 81(Feb 1976):128.

Fleming, Thomas J. One Small Candle: The Pilgrims' First Year in America. New York: Norton, 1976. Rev. by C. W. Sorenson, HRNB, 4(Aug 1976):190.

_____. 1776: Year of Illusions. New York: Norton, 1975. Rev. by W. Moore, GHQ, 60(Spr 1976):79-80; P. F. Detweiler, JSH, 42(May 1976):275-6; W. F. Willingham, NCHR, 53(Win 1976):96-7; M. C. Steedman, SCHM, 77(Jl 1976):197-8.

Fletcher, Anthony. A County Community in Peace and War: Sussex, 1600-1660. New York: Longman, 1975. Rev. by B. Coward, JEccH, 27(Apr 1976):218-19.

Fletcher, Calvin see Thornbrough, Gayle, ed.

Fletcher, Marvin E. The Black Soldier and Officer in the United States Army, 1891-1917. Columbia, Mo.: U Mo Press, 1974. Rev. by W. A. Settle, Jr., ChOk, 54(Spr 1976):152-3; W. B. Gatewood, Jr., PHR, 45(Aug 1976):450-1; G. R. Woolfolk, PNQ, 67(Jan 1976):39.

Fletcher, William C. Religion and Soviet Foreign Policy, 1945-1970. New York: Oxford U Press, 1973. Rev. by D. J. Dunn, CaHR, 62(Oct 1976):672.

Flexner, Eleanor. Century of Struggle: The Woman's Rights Movement in the United States. Cambridge: Harvard U Press, 1975. Rev. by J. K. Ehrlich, NEQ, 49(Je 1976):297-9.

Flexner, James Thomas. Washington: The Indispensable Man. Boston: Little, Brown, 1974. Rev. by R. E. Brown, AHR, 81(Je 1976):655.

Flink, James J. The Car Culture. Cambridge, Mass.: MIT Press,

1975. Rev. by A. F. Wertheim, HT, 10(Nov 1976):158-9;
R. D. Gray, JAH, 62(Mar 1976):1042-3.

Flood, David. Peter Olivi's Rule Commentary. Wiesbaden:
Franz Steiner Verlag, 1972. Rev. by D. Burr, CaHR, 62
(Jan 1976):94-5.

Florescano, Enrique, ed. Haciendas, latifundios y plantaciones
en America Latina. Mexico: Siglo Veintiuno Editores, 1975.
Rev. by C. Gibson, HAHR, 56(Nov 1976):632-4.

Florin, Lambert. Backyard Classic: An Adventure in Nostalgia.
Seattle: Superior Publishing, 1975. Rev. by D. Pitcaithley,
JOW, 15(Apr 1976):134.

Florovsky, Georges. Christianity and Culture. Boston: Nordland,
1974. Rev. by A. C. Outler, JCS, 18(Aut 1976):569-71.

Floud, Roderick. An Introduction to Quantitative Methods for Historians. Princeton: Prin U Press, 1975. Rev. by J. M.
Allswang, HRNB, 4(May/Je 1976):149.

Fodale, Salvatore. La politica napolitana di'Urbano VI. Caltanis-
seta-Rome: Sciascia, 1973. Rev. by J. K. Hyde, EHR,
91(Jan 1976):182.

Fogarty, Gerald P. The Vatican and the Americanist Crisis:
Denis J. O'Connell, American Agent in Rome, 1885-1903.
Rome: Universita Gregoriana Editrice, 1974. Rev. by F.
T. Reuter, AHR, 81(Feb 1976):213-14; T. E. Wangler, CaHR,
62(Jl 1976):512-14; A. E. Firth, EHR, 91(Jan 1976):225-6;
R. T. Handy, JCS, 17(Win 1975):123-5.

Fogel, Robert W., ed. see Aydelotte, W. O., ed.

_____ and Stanley L. Engerman. Time on the Cross. 2 vols.
Boston: Little, Brown, 1974. Rev. by H. S. Smith, CH,
45(Je 1976):263-4.

Folda, Jaroslav. Crusader Manuscript Illumination at Saint-Jean
d'Arc, 1275-1291. Princeton, N.J.: Prin U Press, 1976.
Rev. by E. J. Polak, HRNB, 4(Sep 1976):228.

Folland, H. F. see Adamson, J. H.

Follmann, Anna-Barbara. Corpus Vasorum Antiquorum, Deutschland 34, Hannover Kastner-Museum I. Munich: C. H. Beck,
1971. Rev. by S. R. Roberts, AJA, 80(Sum 1976):314-15.

Folsom, Robert S. Attic Black-Figured Pottery. Park Ridge,
N.J.: Noyes, 1975. Rev. by R. M. Cook, Antiquity, 50
(Mar 1976):71-2.

Folz, Robert. The Coronation of Charlemagne, 25 December 800.
Boston: Routledge and Kegan Paul, 1975. Rev. by P. Munz,
AHR, 81(Nov 1976):836.

Foner, Philip S. American Labor Songs of the Nineteenth Century.
Urbana: U Ill Press, 1975. Rev. by R. M. Benson, JAH,
63(Sep 1976):436-7; S. J. Rosswurm, NDH, 43(Win 1976):41-2.

_____. History of Black Americans. Westport, Conn.: Green-
wood, 1975. Rev. by M. M. Kranz, HRNB, 4(Feb 1976):77;
W. H. Harris, IMH, 72(Dec 1976):374-6; J. L. Franklin, JAH,
63(Sep 1976):374; R. L. Harris, Jr., JNH, 61(Oct 1976):410-
12; A. E. Strickland, JSH, 42(Aug 1976):423-4.

_____. Organized Labor and the Black Worker: 1619-1973.
New York: Praeger, 1975. Rev. by G. E. Osborne, Crisis,
83(Jan 1976):33-4.

Foot, M. R. D. and H. C. G. Matthew, eds. The Gladstone Diaries. Vols. 3 and 4. Oxford: Clarendon Press, 1974.
Rev. by A. Ramm, EHR, 91(Apr 1976):397-400.

Foote, Shelby. The Civil War: A Narrative. Vol. 3. Red River
to Appomattox. New York: Random House, 1974. Rev. by
R. Hartje, AHR, 81(Oct 1976):975-6; Rev. by J. L. Mc-
Donough, THQ, 35(Spr 1976):108-10.

Foote, Wilder, ed. see Cordier, Andrew W., ed.

Forbes, Duncan. Hume's Philosophical Politics. New York: Cam
U Press, 1975. Rev. by L. B. Zimmer, HRNB, 4(May/Je
1976):150.

Forbes, Edwin. Life Studies of the Great Army. San Francisco:
Dunderave, 1975. Rev. by F. Ray, CWTI, 15(May 1976):49.

Forbes, John Douglas. Stettinius, Sr.: Portrait of a Morgan
Business Partner. Charlottesville: U Press Va, 1974.
Rev. by E. J. Perkins, AHR, 81(Je 1976):684.

Forbes, Stanton M. Lucy M. Stanton, Artist. Atlanta: Emory U
Press, 1975. Rev. by N. C. Carpenter, GHQ, 60(Sum 1976):
196-8.

Forbis, William H. Japan Today: People, Places, Power. New
York: Harper and Row, 1975. Rev. by S. K. Johnson, JJS,
2(Sum 1976):437-48.

Ford, Hugh. Published in Paris: American and British Writers,
Printers, and Publishers in Paris, 1920-1939. New York:
Macmillan, 1975. Rev. by R. Sklar, HRNB, 4(Mar 1976):109-
10.

Fordham, Monroe. Major Themes in Northern Black Religious Thought, 1800-1860. Hicksville, N.Y.: Exposition, 1975. Rev. by T. D. Morris, JAH, 63(Je 1976):120-1; J. R. Washington, Jr., JNH, 61(Jl 1976):318-20.

Forman, Shepard. The Brazilian Peasantry. New York: Columbia U Press, 1975. Rev. by S. Leacock, HAHR, 56(Nov 1976): 689-90.

Forrest, A. C. The Unholy Land. Old Greenwich, Conn.: Devin-Adair, 1972. Rev. by E. J. Vardaman, JCS, 17(Spr 1975): 354-5.

Forrest, Alan. Society and Politics in Revolutionary Bordeaux. London: Oxford U Press, 1975. Rev. by P. M. Jones, History, 61(Oct 1976):457-8.

Forrest, D. W. Francis Galton: The Life and Work of a Victorian Genius. New York: Taplinger, 1975. Rev. by S. Herbert, AHR, 81(Je 1976):592-3.

Forsey, Eugene. Freedom and Order: Collected Essays. Toronto: McClelland and Stewart, 1974. Rev. by A. Smith, CHR, 57 (Je 1976):189-91.

Förster, Jürgen. Stalingrad Risse im Bündnis, 1942-43. Freiburg: Verlag Rombach, 1975. Rev. by E. F. Ziemke, AHR, 81(Je 1976):638-9.

Forster, Robert and Orest Ranum, eds. Biology of Man in History. Baltimore: JHU Press, 1975. Rev. by K. A. R. Kennedy, HRNB, 4(Apr 1976):130-1; J. D. Post, JEH, 36(Je 1976):466-8.

Forte, Dieter. Martin Luther und Thomas Müntzer oder die Einführung der Buchhaltung. Berlin: Verlag Klaus Wagenbach, 1971. Rev. by H. Loewen, MQR, 50(Apr 1976):144-5.

Fortes, Meyer and Sheila Patterson, eds. Studies in African Social Anthropology. London: Academic Press, 1975. Rev. by A. O. Sanda, JMAS, 14(Sep 1976):550-3.

Fossett, Frank. Colorado. Glorieta, N.M.: Rio Grande, 1976. Rev. by M. F. Taylor, A & W, 18(Win 1976):375-6.

Foster, Edward Halsey. The Civilized Wilderness: Backgrounds to American Romantic Literature, 1817-1860. New York: Free Press, 1975. Rev. by N. H. Hostetler, AS, 16(Fall 1975): 92-3; B. Kuklick, JAH, 63(Je 1976):118.

Foster, James Caldwell. The Union Politic: The CIO Political Action Committee. Columbia: U Mo Press, 1975. Rev. by J.B., AS, 16(Fall 1975):101-2; D. Brody, JAH, 63(Je 1976): 200-1.

Foster, John.   Class Struggle and the Industrial Revolution: Early
    Industrial Capitalism in Three English Towns.   New York:
    St. Martin's, 1975.   Rev. by C. B. Cone, AHR, 81(Oct 1976):
    859.

Foster, Walter Roland.   The Church Before the Covenants: The
    Church of Scotland 1596-1638.   Edinburgh: Scottish Academic
    Press, 1975.   Rev. by W. S. Reid, CH, 45(Sep 1976):387-8.

Fowler, James W.   To See the Kingdom: The Theological Vision of
    H. Richard Niebuhr.   Nashville, Tenn.:   Abingdon, 1974.
    Rev. by T. B. Maston, JCS, 18(Spr 1976):341-4.

Fowler, Melvin L.   see   Robinson, J. T.

Fowler, P. J., ed.   see   Branigan, Keith, ed.

Fowler, William M., Jr.   Rebels Under Sail.   New York: Scrib-
    ner's, 1976.   Rev. by E. M. Eller, AHI, 11(Dec 1976):50;
    E. M. Eller, VMHB, 84(Oct 1976):492-4.

_____.   William Ellery: A Rhode Island Politico and Lord of Ad-
    miralty.   Metuchen, N.J.:   Scarecrow, 1973.   Rev. by W. E.
    A. Bernhard, JAH, 62(Mar 1976):971-2.

Fox, Francis L.   Luis María Peralta and His Adobe.   San Jose:
    Smith-McKay Printing, 1975.   Rev. by B. F. Gilbert, WHQ,
    7(Oct 1976):433.

Fox, Marvin, ed.   Modern Jewish Ethics.   Columbus, Ohio: Ohio
    St U Press, 1975.   Rev. by L. A. Olan, Judaism, 25(Win
    1976):121-3.

Fox, William Lloyd, ed.   see   Walsh, Richard, ed.

Foy, Leslie T.   The City Bountiful: Utah's Second Settlement
    from Pioneers to Present.   Bountiful, Utah: Horizon,
    1975.   Rev. by G. M. Leonard, UHQ, 44(Fall 1976):405-6.

Frank, Fedora Samall.   Beginnings on Market Street (Nashville and
    Her Jewry 1861-1901).   Nashville, Tenn: n.p., 1976.   Rev.
    by R. M. McBride, THQ, 35(Spr 1976):112-13.

Fraenkel, Heinrich   see   Manvell, Roger

Francis, A. D.   The Wine Trade.   New York: Harper and Row,
    1973.   Rev. by B. W. E. Alfrod, JEH, 36(Sep 1976):749-50.

Franciscan Institute.   Franciscan Studies.   Vol. 33.   New York:
    St. Bonaventure U, 1973.   Rev. by H. S. Offler, History, 61
    (Feb 1976):101-2.

Franda, Marcus F.   Radical Politics in West Bengal.   Cambridge,

Mass.: MIT Press, 1971. Rev. by R. Guha, MAS, 10(Feb 1976):146-9.

Frank, Isaiah, ed. The Japanese Economy in International Perspective. Baltimore: JHU Press, 1975. Rev. by S. B. Levine, JAS, 36(Nov 1976):155-7.

Frank, Larry and Francis B. Harlow. Historic Pottery of the Pueblo Indians, 1600-1880. New York: Graphic Society, 1975. Rev. by F. H. Ellis, JAriH, 17(Sum 1976):239-40.

Franke, Wolfgang, ed. China Handbuch. Düsseldorf: Bertelsmann, 1974. Rev. by W. Klatt, CQ, May 1976, pp. 402-3.

Franklin, John Hope. A Southern Odyssey: Travelers in the Antebellum North. Baton Rouge: LSU Press, 1976. Rev. by C. E. Wynes, GHQ, 60(Sum 1976):191-3; G. H. Callcott, JNH, 61(Oct 1976):404-5.

Frantz, Constantin. Briefe. Wiesbaden: Franz Steiner Verlag GmbH, 1974. Rev. by A. Dorpalen, AHR, 81(Oct 1976): 881-2.

Fraser, Antonia. Cromwell: Our Chief of Men. London: Weidenfeld and Nicolson, 1973. Rev. by N. Tyacke, History, 61 (Je 1976):288.

Fraser, Russell. The Dark Ages & the Age of Gold. Princeton, N.J.: Prin U Press, 1973. Rev. by J. E. Wrigley, AHR, 81(Feb 1976):108-9.

Frassanito, William A. Gettysburg: A Journey in Time. New York: Scribner's, 1975. Rev. by R. D. Hoffsommer, AHI, 11(May 1976):48; S. Hart, Smithsonian, 6(Jl 1975):109-10.

Frêche, Georges. Toulouse et la région Midi-Pyrénées au siècle des lumières (vers 1670-1789). Paris: Editions Cujas, 1975. Rev. by L. R. Berlanstein, AHR, 81(Je 1976):600; R. Forster, JMH, 48(Sep 1976):552-5.

Fredrickson, George M., ed. A Nation Divided: Problems and Issues of the Civil War and Reconstruction. Minneapolis: Burgess, 1975. Rev. by J. K. Folmar, HT, 10(Nov 1976): 145-6.

Frei, Hans W. The Eclipse of Biblical Narrative: A Study in 18th- and 19th-Century Hermeneutics. New Haven, Conn.: Yale U Press, 1974. Rev. by J. H. Lehmann, Commentary, 61(Jl 1976):75-8.

Freidel, Frank, ed. Harvard Guide to American History. 2 vols. Cambridge, Mass.: Harvard U Press, 1974. Rev. by W. Rundell, Jr., AHR, 81(Feb 1976):200-1.

Freidzon, V. I., ed. Problems of the Initial Accumulation of Capital and National Movements in Slavic Countries. Moscow: Izdatel'stvo "Nauka," 1972. Rev. by N. Spulber, AHR, 81(Apr 1976):418.

Frend, W. H. C. The Rise of the Monophysite Movement: Chapters in the History of the Church in the Fifth and Sixth Centuries. Cambridge: Cam U Press, 1972. Rev. by K. Ware, EHR, 91(Apr 1976):354-6.

Freyer-Schauenburg, Brigitte. Samos XI: Bildwerke der Archaischen Zeit und des Strengen Stils. Bonn: Rudolf Habelt Verlag, 1974. Rev. by B. S. Ridgway, AJA, 80(Spr 1976):207-9.

Fridensen, Patrick. Histoire des Usines Renault. Vol. I. Paris: Editions du Seuil, 1972. Rev. by C. E. Freedeman, JEH, 36 (Sep 1976):750-1.

Fried, Richard M. Men Against McCarthy. New York: Columbia U Press, 1976. Rev. by A. Theoharis, HRNB, 4(Sep 1976): 214.

Friedl, Joseph. A History of Education in McDowell County, West Virginia, 1858-1976. Parsons, W. Va.: McClain, 1975. Rev. by D. P. Ruggles, WVH, 38(Oct 1976):68-9.

Friedlander, Marc, ed. see Butterfield, L. H., ed.

Friedlander, Peter. The Emergence of a UAW Local, 1936-1939: A Study in Class and Culture. Pittsburgh: U Pittsburgh Press, 1975. Rev. by R. Asher, BHR, 50(Sum 1976):244-6; M. Green, HRNB, 4(Mar 1976):100; R. H. Zieger, JAH, 63(Sep 1976): 456-7; D. Brody, RAH, 4(Je 1976):262-7.

Friedländer, Saul. Histoire et psychoanalyse: Essai sur les possibilités et les limites de la psychohistoire. Paris: Editions du Seuil, 1975. Rev. by P. Loewenberg, AHR, 81(Oct 1976): 821-2.

_____ and Mahmoud Hussein. Arabs and Israelis: A Dialogue. New York: Holmes and Meier, 1975. Rev. by R. G. Lewis, Commentary, 61(Jan 1976):89-92, 94.

Friedman, Bernard. Smuts: A Reappraisal. New York: St. Martin's, 1976. Rev. by L. E. Meyer, HRNB, 4(Jl 1976):168.

Friedman, Edward. Backward Toward Revolution: The Chinese Revolutionary Party. Berkeley: U Cal Press, 1974. Rev. by Hungo-Mao Tien, CQ, Jan 1976, pp. 132-7.

Friedman, Lawrence J. Inventors of the Promised Land. New York: Knopf, 1975. Rev. by G. M. Fredrickson, AHR, 81 (Je 1976):659-60; A. A. Ekirch, Jr., JAH, 63(Je 1976):128-9;

P. C. Nagel, JSH, 42(Feb 1976):115-16; M. Fellman, RAH,
4(Je 1976):189-94; R. W. VanAlstyne, WMQ, 33(Apr 1976):
345-6.

Friedman, Lenemaja. Shirley Jackson. Boston: Twayne, 1975.
Rev. by E. Dwyer, VH, 44(Sum 1976):179-80.

Friedman, Saul S. No Haven for the Oppressed: United States
Policy Toward Jewish Refugees, 1938-1945. Detroit: Wayne
St U Press, 1973. Rev. by K. J. Carey, JCS, 17(Win 1975):
127-9.

Frigg, Carolyn, ed. Inventory of County Records: Ector County
Courthouse. Austin: Texas St Library, 1973. Rev. by J.
L. Mims, AmArc, 39(Jan 1976):54-6.

Friguglietti, James. Albert Mathiez: Historien révolutionnaire
(1874-1932). Paris: Société des Etudes Robespierristes,
1974. Rev. by W. R. Keylor, AHR, 81(Oct 1976):871-2.

Frijhoff, Willem and Dominique Julia. École et société dans la
France d'Ancien Régime: Quatre exemples Auch, Avallon,
Condom et Gisors. Paris: Librairie Armand Colin, 1975.
Rev. by S. J. Idzerda, AHR, 81(Je 1976):604-5; F. K. Ringer,
JIH, 7(Aut 1976):322-4.

Frisch, Morton J. Franklin D. Roosevelt: The Contribution of the
New Deal to American Political Thought and Practice. Boston:
Twayne, 1975. Rev. by S. Weiss, JAH, 63(Sep 1976):453-4.

Fritz, Paul S. The English Ministers & Jacobitism Between the
Rebellions of 1715 and 1745. Toronto: U Tor Press, 1975.
Rev. by L. Colley, HJ, 19(Dec 1976) 1030-3.

Frodsham, J. D. , trans. The First Chinese Embassy to the West:
The Journals of Kuo Sung-t'ao, Liu Hsi-hung, and Chang Te-
yi. New York: Oxford U Press, 1974. Rev. by M. Gasster,
AHR, 81(Feb 1976):194.

Frohman, Charles E. Rebels on Lake Erie: The Piracy, the
Conspiracy, Prison Life. Columbus: Ohio Historical Society,
1975. Rev. by P. R. Shriver, CWH, 22(Mar 1976):91-2.

Frost, J. William. The Quaker Family in Colonial America: A
Portrait of the Society of Friends. New York: St. Martin's,
1973. Rev. by M. B. Endy, Jr., CH, 45(Sep 1976):390-1;
S. L. Horst, MQR, 50(Apr 1976):138-40.

Frowein, Peter. Philipp Hedderich, 1744-1808: Ein rhenischer
Kanonist aus dem Minoritenorden im zeitalter der Aufklärung.
Cologne: Böhlau Verlag, 1973. Rev. by W. C. Schrader, III,
CaHR, 62(Apr 1976):306-7.

Fuller, Paul E. Laura Clay and the Woman's Rights Movement.
Lexington: U Press Ky, 1975. Rev. by V. L. Bullough,
AHR, 81(Je 1976):669-70; J. S. Chase, ArkHQ, 35(Spr 1976):
101-2; B. J. Brandon, GHQ, 60(Spr 1975):76-7; M. L. Rossiter, IMH, 72(Je 1976):176-8; S. H. Strom, JAH, 63(Je
1976):152-3; K. R. Johnson, JSH, 42(Feb 1976):129-31; J. L.
Dubbert, OH, 85(Spr 1976):170-1.

Funk, Arthur Layton. The Politics of TORCH: The Allied Land-
ings and the Algiers Putsch, 1942. Lawrence: U Press of
Kan, 1974. Rev. by H. L. Coles, PNQ, 67(Jan 1976):43.

Funnell, Charles E. By the Beautiful Sea. New York: Knopf,
1975. Rev. by L. C. Wade, JAH, 63(Dec 1976):745-6.

Furman, Necah Stewart. Walter Prescott Webb: His Life and Im-
pact. Albuquerque: U NM Press, 1976. Rev. by D. K.
Pickens, HRNB, 4(Aug 1976):187; A. C. Ashcraft, JOW, 15
(Jl 1976):97; F. H. Schapsmeier, JSH, 42(Nov 1976):573-5;
NMHR, 51(Oct 1976):338-40; W. Rundell, Jr., SWHQ, 80(Oct
1976):238-9.

Furnas, J. C. Great Times: An Informal Social History of the
United States, 1914-1929. New York: Putnam's, 1975. Rev.
by M. Olmert, Smithsonian, 6(Mar 1975):114-15.

Furner, Mary O. Advocacy and Objectivity: A Crisis in the Pro-
fessionalization of American Social Science, 1865-1905. Lexington: U Ky Press, 1975. Rev. by H. P. Segal, Historian,
39(Nov 1976):153-4; W. T. K. Nugent, IMH, 72(Dec 1976):
377-9; R. R. Dykstra, JAH, 63(Je 1976):142-3; D. Ross, JEH,
36(Je 1976):468-70; D. H. Calhoun, JIH, 7(Aut 1976):362-4;
A. R. Travis, MiA, 58(Oct 1976):189-92; B. G. Rader, PNQ,
67(Oct 1976):178-9.

Furness, Eric L. Money and Credit in Developing Africa. London: Heinemann, 1975. Rev. by R. M. Lawson, JMAS, 14
(Je 1976):354-5.

Furst, Peter, ed. Flesh of the Gods: The Ritual Use of Hallucino-
gens. New York: Praeger, 1972. Rev. by A. J. Rubel,
AA, 78(Je 1976):394-5.

Fusero, Clemente. The Borgias. New York: Praeger, 1972.
Rev. by E. Cochrane, AHR, 81(Feb 1976):175-7; J. J. Byrne,
CaHR, 62(Jan 1976):115-16.

Fusonie, Alan and Donna Jean Fusoni, comps. A Selected Bibliography on George Washington's Interest in Agriculture.
Davis, Cal.: U Cal, 1976. Rev. by Editor, NDH, 43(Sum
1976):46-7.

Gabert, Glen. In Hoc Signo? A Brief History of Catholic Parochi-

GÄBLER

al Education in America. Port Washington, N.Y.: Kennikat, 1973. Rev. by T. J. Donaghy, CaHR, 62(Jl 1976):483-4.

Gäbler, Ulrich and Erland Herkenrath, eds. Heinrich Bullinger, 1504-1575: Gesammelte Aufsätze zum 400 Todestag. Zürich: Theologischer Verlag, 1975. Rev. by G. R. Potter, JEccH, 27(Apr 1976):203-4.

Gabre-Selassie, Zewde. Yohannes IV of Ethiopia: A Political Biography. London: Oxford U Press, 1975. Rev. by J.M., AfAf, 75(Jl 1976):401-2; H. Marcus, AHR, 81(Oct 1976):928-9; C. J. Jaenen, HRNB, 4(Jl 1976):169-70; D. Crummey, JAfH, 17(Num 4, 1976):633-4.

Gaddy, C. Welton. Proclaim Liberty. Nashville, Tenn.: Broadman, 1975. Rev. by B. E. White, Jr., BHH, 10(Oct 1975): 253.

Gager, John G. Kingdom and Community: The Social World of Early Christianity. Englewood Cliffs, N.J.: Prentice-Hall, 1975. Rev. by B. Drewery, JEccH, 27(Oct 1976):413-4.

Gailey, Harry A. Sir Donald Cameron: Colonial Governor. Stanford, Cal.: Stanford U Press, 1974. Rev. by W. B. Cohen, AHR, 81(Oct 1976):299; R. T. Brown, JAAS, 11(Jan-Apr, 1976):121.

Galambos, Louis. The Public Image of Big Business in America, 1880-1940. Baltimore: JHU Press, 1975. Rev. by R. M. Abrams, BHR, 50(Sum 1976):223-5; W. F. Holmes, GHQ, 60 (Sum 1976):198; R. P. Swierenga, Historian, 39(Nov 1976): 156-7; J. W. Gowaskie, HRNB, 4(Apr 1976):124; J. M. Kousser, JAH, 63(Sep 1976):437-8; G. N. Grob, JSH, 42(May 1976):294-5; G. D. Nash, RAH, 4(Je 1976):237-43.

Galbraith, John Kenneth. Money: Whence It Came, Where It Went. Boston: Houghton Mifflin, 1975. Rev. by J. Boughton, AHR, 81(Oct 1976):815-16.

Galbraith, John S. Crown and Charter: The Early Years of the British South Africa Company. Berkeley: U Cal Press, 1974. Rev. by I. R. Phimister, AfAf, 75(Jan 1976):120-2; D. K. Fieldhouse, EHR, 91(Jl 1976):677-8; R. Brown, JAfH, 17(Num 3, 1976):463; R. Kubicek, JIH, 7(Aut 1976):372-3.

Galbraith, V. H. Domesday Book: Its Place in Administrative History. New York: Oxford U Press, 1974. Rev. by B. Lyon, AHR, 81(Apr 1976):369; H. R. Loyn, History, 61(Feb 1976): 97-8.

Galishoff, Stuart. Safeguarding the Public Health: Newark, 1895-1918. Westport, Conn.: Greenwood, 1975. Rev. by D. L. Cowen, AHR, 81(Je 1976):675-6; M. V. Melosi, Historian,

39(Nov 1976):155-6; A. I. Marcus, HRNB, 4(Mar 1976):100-1;
J. H. Jones, JAH, 63(Sep 1976):438-9; J. W. Leavitt, RAH,
4(Je 1976):150-7.

Gallaher, John G. The Iron Marshal: A Biography of Louis N.
Davout. Carbondale: S Ill U Press, 1976. Rev. by A. R.
Sunseri, HRNB, 4(Aug 1976):202-3.

Gallo, Patrick J. Ethnic Alienation: The Italian Americans.
Rutherford, N. J.: Fairleigh Dickinson U Press, 1974. Rev.
by J. Bodnar, PH, 43(Jl 1976):275-6.

Galston, William A. Kant and the Problem of History. Chicago:
U Chicago Press, 1975. Rev. by R. Anchor, AHR, 81(Oct
1976):813.

Cambasin, Angelo. Parroci e contadini nel Veneto alla fine dell'Ottocento. Rome: Edizioni di Storia e Letteratura, 1973. Rev.
by R. Grew, AHR, 81(Je 1976):624-5.

Ganguly, H. C. Foreign Students: The Indian Experience. New
Delhi: Sterling, 1975. Rev. by C. S. Ramakrishman, IQ,
32(Jl-Sep 1976):368.

Gann, L. H., ed. see Duignan, Peter, ed.

Ganshof, F.-L., ed. Le Polyptyque de l'Abbeye de Saint-Berlin
(844-859). Paris: Académie des Inscriptions et Belles-
Lettres, 1975. Rev. by J. M. Wallace-Hadrill, EHR, 91
(Oct 1976):884-5.

García Soriano, Manuel. El periodismo tucumano (1817-1900):
Ensayo de investigación sobre un aspecto de la cultura de
Tucumán durante el siglo XIX. Tucumán: Universidad Na-
cional de Tucumán, 1972. Rev. by J. T. Criscenti, AHR, 81
(Oct 1976):1013.

Gardiner, C. Harvey. The Japanese and Peru 1873-1973. Albuquerque: U NM Press, 1975. Rev. by R. Dingman, HRNB,
5(Oct 1976):15.

Gardiner, Dorothy A., ed. A Calendar of Early Chancery Proceedings Relating to West Country Shipping 1388-1493. n. p.:
Devon and Cornwall Record Society, 1976. Rev. by O. Coleman, Archives, 12(Aut 1976):192-3.

Gardiner, Robert W. The Cool Arm of Destruction. Philadelphia:
Westminster Press, 1974. Rev. by J. A. Wood, JCS, 18
(Aut 1976):573-6.

Gardiner, Stephen. Evolution of the House: An Introduction. New
York: Macmillan, 1974. Rev. by W. Seale, AHR, 81(Oct
1976):814-15.

Gardner, R. F. R. Abortion: The Personal Dilemma: A Christian
Gynecologist Examines the Medical, Social, and Spiritual Is-
sues. Grand Rapids, Mich.: Eerdmans, 1972. Rev. by D.
B. McGee, JCS, 18(Win 1976):134-6.

Garlan, Yvon. Recherches de Poliorcétique Grecque. Paris:
Ecole française d'Athens, 1974. Rev. by F. E. Winter, AJA,
80(Win 1976):92-3.

Garlínski, Józef. Fighting Auschwitz: The Resistance Movement
in the Concentration Camp. London: Julian Friedmann, 1975.
Rev. by H. A. Arnold, HRNB, 4(Apr 1976):133.

Garraty, John A., ed. Encyclopedia of American Biography. New
York: Harper and Row, 1974. Rev. by W. Rundell, Jr.,
AHR, 81(Feb 1976):200-1.

Garraza, Rodrigo Rodríguez. Tensiones de Navarra con la Ad-
ministración central (1778-1808). Pamplona: Institución
Príncipe de Viana, 1974. Rev. by V. G. Kiernan, EHR, 91
(Jl 1976):652-3.

Garrett, Clarke. Respectable Folly: Millenarians and the French
Revolution in France and England. Baltimore: JHU Press,
1975. Rev. by R. F. Necheles, AHR, 81(Oct 1976):843; R.
M. Golden, CH, 45(Mar 1976):116-17; N. Hampson, JEccH,
27(Apr 1976):207-8; L. I. Sweet, JIH, 7(Aut 1976):338-9.

Garrett, James Les, Jr. Baptist Relations with Other Christians.
Valley Forge, Pa.: Judson Press, 1974. Rev. by C. G.
Rutenben, JCS, 18(Aut 1976):591-2.

Garrow, Patrick H. The Mattamuskeet Documents. Raleigh: NC
Div Archives and History, 1975. Rev. by D. J. Spindel,
NCHR, 53(Spr 1976):234.

Garson, Robert A. The Democratic Party and the Politics of Sectionalism, 1941-1948. Baton Rouge: LSU Press, 1974. Rev.
by A. L. Hamby, AHR, 81(Feb 1976):219-20; W. C. Havard,
FHQ, 55(Jl 1976):100-2; A. Yarnell, PNQ, 67(Jan 1976):44-5;
A. D. Harper, RAH, 4(Je 1976):284-90.

Garzetti, Albino. From Tiberius to the Antonines: A History of
the Roman Empire, A.D. 14-192. New York: Barnes and
Noble, 1974. Rev. by M. Hammond, AHR, 81(Feb 1976):
107-8; J. J. Wilkes, History, 61(Oct 1976):435.

Gash, Norman. Peel. New York: Longman, 1976. Rev. by R.
Howell, Jr., HRNB, 5(Oct 1976):22.

Gasquet, Emile. Le Courant machiavelien dans la pensée et la
littérature anglaises du XVIe siècle. Montreal: Didier, 1975.
Rev. by G. R. Elton, EHR, 91(Oct 1976):904-5.

Gastaldelli, Gerruccio, ed. Geoffrey of Auxerre: Expositio in Cantica Canticorum. 2 vols. Rome: Edizioni di Storia e Letteratura, 1974. Rev. by D. H. Miller, CH, 45(Mar 1976): 103.

Gastaldi, Patrizia, ed. see Modesti, Gianni Bailo, ed.

Gates, Paul W. Landlords and Tenants on the Prairie Frontier. Studies in American Land Policy. Ithaca, N. Y.: Cornell U Press, 1973. Rev. by M. Walsh, JAmS, 10(Aug 1976):273-4.

Gatewood, Willard B., Jr. Black Americans and the White Man's Burden, 1898-1903. Urbana: U Ill Press, 1975. Rev. by P. S. Foner, AHR, 81(Je 1976):676-7; W. B. Weare, ArkHQ, 35(Spr 1976):99-101; R. Garson, History, 61(Oct 1976):414; R. M. Johnson, IMH, 72(Je 1976):277-8; E. L. Thornbrough, JAH, 63(Je 1976):156-7; R. Sherer, JNH, 61(Oct 1976):409-10; T. H. Buckley, JSH, 42(May 1976):295-6; J. P. Maddox, NCHR, 53(Win 1976):102-3; R. F. Weston, OH, 85(Win 1976): 92-3; R. E. Welch, Jr., PHR, 45(Nov 1976):625-6; J. Stein, RAH, 4(Mar 1976):88-92.

Gaudon, J., ed. see Charlton, D. G., ed.

Gauldie, Enid. Cruel Habitations: A History of Working-Class Housing, 1780-1918. New York: Barnes and Noble, 1974. Rev. by R. M. Gutchen, AHR, 81(Feb 1976):135-6; R. G. Rodger, BH, 17(Jl 1975):208-11; R. E. Quinault, EHR, 91 (Jl 1976):654-5; R. Smith, History, 61(Feb 1976):127.

Gaunt, David. Utbildning till statens tjänst. Stockholm: Almqvist and Wiksell, 1975. Rev. by M. Roberts, EHR, 91(Jl 1976): 642-3.

Gaustad, Edwin S. Dissent in American Religion. Chicago: U Chicago Press, 1973. Rev. by C. P. St. Amant, JCS, 17 (Aut 1975):517-20.

_____, ed. The Rise of Adventism. Religion and Society in Mid-Nineteenth-Century America. New York: Harper & Row, 1974. Rev. by C. N. Kraus, CH, 45(Mar 1976):121-2.

Gauthier, Philippe. Symbola: Les étrangers et la justice dans les cités grecques. Nancy: Université de Nancy, 1972. Rev. by C. D. Hamilton, AHR, 81(Feb 1976):105.

Gavin, R. J. Aden Under British Rule, 1839-1967. New York: Barnes and Noble, 1975. Rev. by K. E. Dunlop, AHR, 81(Oct 1976):917-18.

Gawlikowski, Michał. Palmyre VI. Le Temple Palmyrenien. Etude d'épigraphie et de Topographie Historique. Warsaw: Państwowe Wydawnictwo Naukowe, 1973. Rev. by G. M. Cohen, AJA, 80(Win 1976):107-8.

Gay, Peter, ed. Eighteenth-Century Studies Presented to Arthur
M. Wilson. Hanover, N. H.: U Press New England, 1972.
Rev. by R. Grimsley, AHR, 81(Je 1976):576.

_____. Style in History. New York: Basic Books, 1974.
Rev. by J. Johnson, AHR, 81(Apr 1976):352; M. Curti, PHR,
45(May 1976):276-8.

Gaydon, A. T., ed. Victoria County History of Shropshire. Vol.
II. Oxford: Oxford U Press, 1973. Rev. by J. F. A. Mason, History, 61(Feb 1976):79.

Gebhard, David and Harriette Von Breton. L. A. in the Thirties.
Salt Lake City: Peregrine Smith, 1975. Rev. by M. Pros-
kauer, CHQ, 55(Spr 1975):89-90.

Geduld, Harry M. The Birth of the Talkies. Bloomington: Ind U
Press, 1975. Rev. by J. Markus, Smithsonian, 6(Nov 1975):
160-3.

Geelan, Agnes. The Dakota Maverick: The Political Life of William Langer. Fargo, N. D.: The Author, 1975. Rev. by
G. H. Smith, NDH, 43(Spr 1976):102-4.

Geelan, P. J. M. and D. C. Twitchett, eds. The Times Atlas of
China. London: Times Books, 1974. Rev. by M. Free-
berne, CQ, Jan 1976, pp. 144-6; J. F. Jenner, MAS, 10(Jl
1976):449-50.

Gehm, Katherine. Sarah Winnemucca: A Most Extraordinary
Woman of the Paiute Nation. Phoenix: O'Sullivan Woodside
and Co., 1975. Rev. by V. E. Tiller, A & W, 18(Aut 1976):
294-5.

Geiger, Reed G. The Anzin Coal Company, 1800-1833: Big Business in the Early Stages of the French Industrial. Newark,
N. J.: Temple U Press, 1975. Rev. by F. E. Dykema, AHR,
81(Je 1976):606.

Geiger, Theodore and Frances Geiger. Tales of Two City-States:
The Development and Progress of Hong Kong and Singapore.
Washington, D. C.: Nation Planning Assn., 1973. Rev. by D.
Feeny, JEH, 36(Sep 1976):760-1.

Geiss, Imanuel. The Pan-African Movement. London: Methuen,
1974. Rev. by A. H. M. Kirk-Greene, Africa, 46(Num 2,
1976):209-10; C. Fyfe, EHR, 91(Jan 1976):155-7.

_____ and Bernd Jürgen Wendt, eds. Deutschland in der Weltpolitik des 19. und 20. Jahrhunderts. Gutersloh: Bertelsmann Universitätsverlag, 1973. Rev. by G. A. Craig, AHR,
81(Apr 1976):403-4; H. Trotnow, ESR, 6(Jl 1976):393-5.

Gelber, Steven M.   Black Men and Businessmen: The Growing
    Awareness of a Social Responsibility.   Port Washington, N. Y.:
    Kennikat, 1974.   Rev. by A. M. Johnson, JEH, 36(Sep 1976):
    751-2.

Gelfand, Mark I.   A Nation of Cities: the Federal Government and
    Urban America, 1933-1965.   New York: Oxford U Press,
    1975.   Rev. by 'J. Teaford, RAH, 4(Je 1976):272-6.

Gellately, Robert.   The Politics of Economic Despair: Shopkeepers
    and German Politics, 1890-1914.   Beverly Hills, Cal.:   Sage,
    1974.   Rev. by G. G. Field, AHR, 81(Je 1976):615-16.

Geller, Lawrence D. and Peter J. Gomes.   The Books of the Pil-
    grims.   New York: Garland, 1975.   Rev. by E. R. Taylor,
    NEQ, 49(Mar 1976):157-8.

Gellman, Irwin F.   Roosevelt and Batista: Good Neighbor Diplomacy
    in Cuba, 1933-1945.   Albuquerque: U NM Press, 1973.   Rev.
    by N. Valdés, JAH, 63(Sep 1976):457-9.

Gelpi, Albert.   The Tenth Muse: The Psyche of the American Poet.
    Cambridge: Harvard U Press, 1975.   Rev. by L. Buell, NEQ,
    49(Mar 1976):130-4.

Genovese, Eugene D.   Roll Jordan Roll: The World the Slaves
    Made.   New York: Pantheon, 1974.   Rev. by B. I. Wiley,
    AHI, 11(May 1976):48; M. Kilson, AHR, 81(Feb 1976):209-10;
    H. S. Smith, CH, 45(Je 1976):264-5; R. A. Wooster, ETHJ,
    14(Spr 1976):58-9; J. D. Anderson, JNH, 61(Jan 1976):99-114;
    M. Marable, NYHSQ, 60(Jan/Apr 1976):83-5; A. Zilversmit,
    WMQ, 33(Jan 1976):161-3.

_____, ed.   see   Engerman, Stanley L. , ed.

George, Alexander L. and Richard Smoke.   Deterrence in American
    Foreign Policy: Theory and Practice.   New York: Columbia
    U Press, 1974.   Rev. by J. L. Clayton, AHR, 81(Oct 1976):
    1002-3.

George, Carol V. R. , ed.   "Remember the Ladies":   New Perspec-
    tives on Women in American History: Essays in Honor of Nel-
    son Manfred Blake.   Syracuse, N. Y.:   Syracuse U Press, 1975.
    Rev. by S. H. Strom, JAH, 63(Dec 1976):677-8; V. V. Hamil-
    ton, JSH, 42(Aug 1976):447-8.

Gerald of Wales.   A Mirror of Two Men.   n. p.:   U Wales, 1974.
    Rev. by B. Smalley, EHR, 91(Jan 1976):177-8.

Gerber, William.   American Liberalism: Laudable End, Contro-
    versial Means.   Boston: Twayne, 1975.   Rev. by P. A. Cer-
    ter, JAH, 63(Sep 1976):466-7.

Gerdts, William H.   The Great American Nude: A History in Art.
New York: Praeger, 1974. Rev. by L. B. Miller, AHR, 81
(Feb 1976):202-3.

Gerloff, Sabine.   The Early Bronze-Age Daggers in Great Britain
and a Reconsideration of the Wessex Culture. Munich: Beck,
1975. Rev. by F. Lynch, Antiquity, 50(Sep-Dec 1976):246-7.

Ġērmanis, Uldis.   Oberst Vācietis und die lettischen Schützen im
Weltkrieg und in der Oktoberrevolution. Stockholm: Ålmqvist
and Wiksell, 1974. Rev. by A. Ezergailis, AHR, 81(Je 1976):
630-1.

Gerson, Jack J.   Horatio Nelson Lay and Sino-British Relations,
1854-1864. Cambridge, Mass: Harvard U Press, 1972. Rev.
by R. L. Bennett, MAS, 10(Apr 1976):303-4.

Gertzel, Cherry.   Party and Locality in Northern Uganda, 1945-
1962. London: Athlone, 1974. Rev. by A. King, JAfH, 17
(Num 1, 1976):149-50.

Getzler, Israel.   Neither Toleration nor Favour: The Australian
Chapter of Jewish Emancipation. Carlton, Victoria: Melbourne U Press, JCS, 17(Aut 1975):515-17.

Ghai, Dharam P. , ed. see Court, David, ed.

Ghebali, Victor Yves and Catherine Ghebali. A Repertoire of
League of Nations. 2 vols. Dobbs Ferry, N.Y.: Oceana,
1973. Rev. by W. F. Kuehl, AmArc, 39(Jan 1976):51-2.

Gheddo, Piero. Why Is the Third World Poor? Maryknoll, N.Y.:
Orbis, 1973. Rev. by H. W. Osborne, JSC, 18(Win 1976):
142-3.

Giacchero, Marta.   Edictum Diocletiani et Collegarum de pretiis
rerum Venalium. Genoa: Istituto di Storia Antica e Scienze
Ausiliare, 1974. Rev. by S. S. Frere, EHR, 91(Jl 1976):
619-20.

Giap, Vo Nguyen.   Unforgettable Months and Years. Ithaca, N.Y.:
Cornell U, 1975. Rev. by P. D. Caine, AHR, 81(Oct 1976):
944-5.

Gibb, Sir Hamilton.   The Life of Saladin. Oxford: Clarendon
Press, 1973. Rev. by M. W. Dols, IJMES, 7(Apr 1976):
298-9.

Gibbs, Donald A. , et al.   A Bibliography of Studies and Translations
of Modern Chinese Literature, 1918-1942. Cambridge, Mass.:
Harvard U Press, 1975. Rev. by F. P. Brandauer, JAS, 36
(Nov 1976):140-1.

Gibert, Anne Caroline. Pierre Gibert, Esq. The Devoted Huguen-
ot: A History of the French Settlement of New Bordeaux,
South Carolina. Columbia, S.C.: Privately Printed, 1976.
Rev. by L. B. Jones, SCHM, 77(Oct 1976):269-70.

Gibney, Frank. Japan: The Fragile Superpower. New York: Norton, 1975. Rev. by S. K. Johnson, JJS, 2(Sum 1976):437-48.

Gibson, Arrell M., ed. Frontier Historian: The Life and Work of
Edward Everett Dale. Norman: U Ok Press, 1975. Rev.
by J. W. Caughey, A & W, 18(Aut 1976):307-8; L. H. Fisher,
ChOk, 54(Fall 1976):413-14; W. Rundell, Jr., HRNB, 4(Apr
1976):120.

_____. The West in the Life of the Nation. Lexington, Mass.:
D. C. Heath, 1976. Rev. by D. C. Cutter, HRNB, 5(Oct
1976):5.

Gibson, James R. Imperial Russia in Frontier America: The
Changing Geography of Supply of Russian America, 1784-1867.
New York: Oxford U Press, 1976. Rev. by L. L. Morrison,
JOW, 15(Apr 1976):126; E. A. P. Crownhart-Vaughan, OrHQ,
77(Sep 1976):293.

Gibson, M. T., ed. see Alexander, J. J. G., ed.

Gibson, Tom. The Maori Wars: The British Army in New Zealand, 1840-1872. Hamden, Conn.: Shoe String, 1974. Rev.
by P. J. Coleman, AHR, 81(Feb 1976):200.

Gidney, James B. see Pieper, Thomas I.

Giglio, Carlo. Colonizzazione e Decolonizzazione. Cremona:
Padus Editrice, 1971. Rev. by A. Sbacchi, JMAS, 14(Mar
1976):164-6.

_____ and Elio Lodolini, eds. Guida delle Fonti per la Storia
dell'Africa a Sud del Sahara esistenti in Italia. Vol. II.
Zug: Inter Documentation Co., 1974. Rev. by R. Gray,
JAfH, 17(Num 3, 1976):447-8.

Gilbert, Felix, ed. see Hintze, Otto

Gilbert, James. Designing the Industrial State: The Intellectual
Pursuit of Collectivism in America, 1880-1940. Chicago:
Quadrangle, 1972. Rev. by K. McNaught, AHR, 81(Oct
1976):984-5.

Gilbert, Martin. Winston S. Churchill. Vol. IV. Boston: Houghton Mifflin, 1975. Rev. by J. M. Hernon, Jr., AHR, 81(Oct
1976):865-6; H. Pelling, EHR, 91(Jl 1976):611-13.

Gildner, Gary and Judith Gildner, eds. Out of This World: Poems

from the Hawkeye State. Ames: Ia St U Press, 1975. Rev.
by T. Garst, AI, 43(Sum 1976):396-8.

Gildrie, Richard P. Salem, Massachusetts, 1626-1683: A Covenant
Community. Charlottesville: U Press Va, 1975. Rev. by D.
B. Rutman, AHR, 81(Oct 1976):958-9; P. Boyer, JAH, 63(Je
1976):101-2; M. G. Williams, NEQ, 49(Sep 1976):486-8.

Giliomee, Hermann. Die Kaap tydens die Eerste Britse Bewind
1795-1803. Cape Town: Hollandsch Afrikaansche Uitgevers
Maatschappij, 1975. Rev. by W. M. Freund, JAfH, 17(Num
3, 1976):454-6.

Gilkes, Patrick. The Dying Lion. London: Julian Friedmann,
1975. Rev. by H. Erlich, JAfH, 17(Num 4, 1976):634-6.

Gill, Harold B., Jr. The Gunsmith in Colonial Virginia. Williamsburg, Va.: Colonial Williamsburg Foundation, 1974.
Rev. by E. A. Battison, JAH, 63(Dec 1976):687-8.

Gilliam, Olivia L., ed. see Morey, Sylvester M., ed.

Gillis, John R. Youth and History: Tradition and Change in European Age Relations 1770-Present. New York: Academic
Press, 1974. Rev. by T. K. Hareven, AHR, 81(Feb 1976):
121-2; H. Moller, JIH, 7(Aut 1976):324-5.

Gilmore, Al-Tony. Bad Nigger: The National Impact of Jack John-
son. Port Washington, N.Y.: Kennikat, 1975. Rev. by
I. A. Newby, AHR, 81(Je 1976):684-5; W. C. Farrell, Jr.,
JNH, 61(Apr 1976):224-7.

Gimaret, Daniel, ed. Kitâb Bilawhar wa Bûdhâsf. Beirut: Dar
el-Machreq, 1972. Rev. by I. K. Poonawala, JNES, 35(Oct
1976):294-5.

Gimbel, John. The Origins of the Marshall Plan. Stanford, Cal.:
Stanford U Press, 1976. Rev. by R. J. Tensen, HRNB, 5
(Oct 1976):12.

Gintis, Herbert see Bowles, Samuel

Giorgini, Michela Schiff, et al. Soleb. Vol. 2. Florence: Sansoni, 1971. Rev. by Zabkar, JNES, 35(Jan 1976):50-3.

Giraud, Marcel. Histoire de la Louisiane française. Vol. IV.
Paris: Presses U France, 1974. Rev. by H. C. Bezou,
AHR, 81(Apr 1976):439-40.

_____. A History of French Louisiana. Vol. I. Baton Rouge:
LSU Press, 1974. Rev. by C. J. Jaenen, CaHR, 62(Jl 1976):
478-80; E. J. Gum, ETHJ, 14(Spr 1976):74.

Girault, Rene. Eprunts russes et investissments français en Russie, 1887-1914. Paris: Armand Colin, 1973. Rev. by W. J. Kelley, JEH, 36(Je 1976):470-2.

Gisevius, Hans-Friedrich. Zur Vorgeschichte des Preussisch-Sachsischen Eisenbahnkrieges. Berlin: Duncker and Humblot, 1971. Rev. by W. O. Henderson, ESR, 6(Jl 1976):393.

Gitelman, Howard M. Workingmen of Waltham: Mobility in American Urban Industrial Development, 1850-1890. Baltimore: JHU Press, 1974. Rev. by E. Batteson, AHR, 81(Je 1976): 590; AS, 16(Fall 1975):101; C. Griffen, JIH, 7(Aut 1976):341-2.

Giudice, Filippo. Corpus Vasorum Antiquorum, Italy fasc. LIV, Gela, Museo Archeologico III. Rome: "L'Erma" di Bretschneider, 1974. Rev. by W. R. Biers, AJA, 80(Win 1976):94.

Gladen, Albin. Geschichte der Sozialpolitik in Deutschland: Eine Analyse ihrer Bedingungen, Formen zeilsetzungen und Auswirkungen. Wiesbaden: Franz Steiner Verlag, 1974. Rev. by D. G. Rohr, 81(Je 1976):614-15.

Glanz, Rudolf. The Jewish Woman in America: Two Female Immigrant Generations, 1820-1929. Vol. I. New York: KTAV, 1976. Rev. by E. S. Shapiro, JAH, 63(Dec 1976):733-4.

Glasscock, Robin E., ed. The Lay Subsidy of 1334. London: Oxford U Press, 1975. Rev. by G. A. Holmes, EHR, 91(Oct 1976):899; J. R. Maddicott, History, 61(Je 1976):261; R. D. Face, JEH, 36(Sep 1976):752-3.

Glazer, Nathan. Affirmative Discrimination: Ethnic Inequality and Public Policy. New York: Basic Books, 1976. Rev. by W. Petersen, Commentary, 61(May 1976):78-80.

Gleason, Abbot. European and Muscovite: Ivan Kireyersky and the Origins of Slavophilism. Cambridge, Mass.: Harvard U Press, 1972. Rev. by M. C. Chapman, ESR, 6(Apr 1976): 261-3.

Glick, Thomas F., ed. The Comparative Reception of Darwinism. Austin: U Texas Press, 1974. Rev. by W. F. Cannon, AHR, 81(Je 1976):559-61.

Glover, Betty Shropshire see Wilson, Reba Shorpshire

Göbl, Robert. Der Sâsânidische Siegelkanon: Handbücher der Mittelasiatischen Numismatik. Vol. 4. Braunsweig: Klinkhardt and Biermann, 1973. Rev. by J. Lerner, IJMES, 7(Apr 1976):313-15.

Godfrey, Aaron Austin. Government Operation of the Railroads:

145   GODFREY

Its Necessity, Success, and Consequences, 1918-1920. Austin, Tex.: Jenkins, 1974. Rev. by K. A. Kerr, AHR, 81
(Apr 1976):461-2.

Godfrey, Eleanor S. The Development of English Glassmaking
1560-1640. Chapel Hill: U NC Press, 1976. Rev. by G.
F. Frick, HRNB, 4(Sep 1976):227.

Goedicke, Hans and J. J. M. Roberts, eds. Unity and Diversity:
Essays in the History, Literature, and Religion of the Ancient
Near East. Baltimore: JHU Press, 1975. Rev. by J. E.
Seaver, HRNB, 4(Feb 1976):83.

Goerke, Heinz. Linnaeus. New York: Scribner's, 1973. Rev.
by G. H. M. Lawrence, AHR, 81(Je 1976):612.

Goertz, Hans-Jürgen, ed. Umstrittenes Täufertum, 1525-1975:
Neue Forschungen. Göttingen: Vandenhoeck & Ruprecht,
1975. Rev. by J. J. Kiwiet, CH, 45(Sep 1976):383-4; E. A.
Payne, JEccH, 27(Jan 1976):92-3.

Goetting, Hans, ed. Germania Sacra, neue Folge 8: Die Bistümer
der Kirchenprovinz Mainz. Das Bistum Hildesheim 2. Berlin: Walter de Gruyter, 1974. Rev. by H. S. Offler, EHR,
91(Apr 1976):366-9.

Goff, Frederick R. The Delights of a Rare Book Librarian. Boston: Boston Public Library, 1975. Rev. by J. R. Bentley,
FCHQ, 50(Jan 1976):79-80.

Goff, John H. Placenames of Georgia: Essays of John H. Goff.
(Francis L. Utley and Marion R. Hemperly, eds.) Athens,
Ga.: U Ga Press, 1975. Rev. by J. A. Morris, FHQ, 55
(Jl 1976):104-5; J. E. Talmadge, GHQ, 60(Spr 1976):68-9.

Goff, John S. Arizona Territorial Officials I: The Supreme Court
Justices, 1863-1912. Cave Creek: Ariz.: Black Mountain
Press, 1975. Rev. by C. B. Clark, A & W, 18(Sum 1976):
199-201; R. D. Hunt, JOW, 15(Apr 1976):128; M. B. Cooley,
WHQ, 7(Oct 1976):435.

Goffart, Walter. Caput and Colonate: Towards a History of Late
Roman Taxation. Buffalo: U Tor Press, 1974. Rev. by R.
E. Mitchell, AHR, 81(Oct 1976):831-2; J. C. Murdock, JEH,
36(Sep 1976):753-5.

Goitein, S. D. Letters of Medieval Jewish Traders. Princeton,
N.J.: Prin U Press, 1973. Rev. by R. W. Bulliet, IJMES,
7(Jl 1976):457-9; J. R. Strayer, JIH, 7(Sum 1976):131-3.

_____. A Mediterranean Society: The Jewish Communities of
the Arab World as Portrayed in the Documents of the Cairo
Geniza. Vol. II. The Community. Berkeley: U Cal Press,

1971. Rev. by M. A. Cook, History, 61(Je 1976):255.

Golan, Galia. Reform Rule in Czechoslovakia: The Dubcek Era 1968-1969. Cambridge: Cam U Press, 1972. Rev. by K. Reyman, EE, 24(May 1975):30-1.

Goldenberg, Joseph A. Shipbuilding in Colonial America. Charlottesville: U Press Va, 1976. Rev. by V. B. Platt, NCHR, 53(Aut 1976):406-7.

Goldhurst, Richard. Many Are the Hearts: The Agony and the Triumph of Ulysses S. Grant. New York: Reader's Digest Press, 1975. Rev. by K. G. Larew, HRNB, 4(Jan 1976): 55-6.

Goldner, Orville and George E. Turner. The Making of King Kong. New York: A. S. Barnes, 1975. Rev. by C. Anderson, Mankind, 5(Apr 1976):9-10.

Goldsmith, William M. The Growth of Presidential Power: A Documented History. 3 vols. New York: Chelsea House/ Bowker, 1974. Rev. by H. M. Hyman, JAH, 62(Mar 1976): 953-4.

Goldstein, Doris S. Trial of Faith: Religion and Politics in Tocqueville's Thought. New York: Elsevier, 1975. Rev. by J. W. Padberg, AHR, 81(Oct 1976):872; S. J. Stein, JAH, 63(Je 1976):129-30.

Goldstein, Leon J. Historical Knowing. Austin: U Texas Press, 1976. Rev. by S. Bailey, AHR, 81(Oct 1976):811-12; B. T. Wilkins, JSH, 42(Nov 1976):572-3.

Goldthwaite, Richard A., ed. see Baldwin, John W., ed.

Goll, Rinehold W. Valley Forge Rebel. Philadelphia: Dorrance, 1974. Rev. by J. C. Morton, PH, 43(Oct 1976):383.

Golte, Jürgen. Bauern in Peru: Entwicklungsfaktoren in der Wirtschafts-und Sozialgeschichte der Indianischen Landbevölkerung von der Inka-zeit bis Heute. Berlin: Gebr. Mann Verlag, 1973. Rev. by M. Mörner, HAHR, 56(Aug 1976):464-5.

Golvin, Lucien. Essai sur l'Architecture Musalmane. Vol. 3. Paris: n.p., 1974. Rev. by O. Grabar, IJMES, 7(Oct 1976):607-8.

Gomez, David F. Somos Chicanos: Strangers in Our Own Land. Boston: Beacon, 1973. Rev. by J. Sanchez, HAHR, 56(Nov 1976):684-6; E. Hernandez-Alarcon, WHQ, 7(Jan 1976):76-7.

Gómez-Quiñones, Juan. Sembradores Ricardo Flores Magnon y el Partido Liberal Mexicano: A Eulogy and Critique. Los An-

geles: U Cal Press, 1973. Rev. by V. C. Dahl, JOW,
15(Apr 1976):133-4; G. E. Miranda, SCQ, 58(Sum 1976):257-
9.

Góngora, Mario. Encomenderos y estancieros. Santiago de Chile:
Universidad de Chile at Valparaiso, 1970. Rev. by A. J.
Bauer, HAHR, 56(Feb 1976):130-2.

_____. Studies in the Colonial History of Spanish America.
Cambridge: Cam U Press, 1975. Rev. by I. A. Leonard,
HAHR, 56(May 1976):312-13; J. S. Cummins, History, 61(Oct
1976):425-6; R. Pike, HRNB, 4(Jan 1976):59-60; E. Tandeter,
JEH, 36(Sep 1976):755-6; H. Pietschmann, TAm, 33(Oct 1976):
367-9.

Gonnet, Jean and Amedeo Molnar. Les Vaudois au Moyen Age.
Torino: Claudiana, 1974. Rev. by J. H. Yoder, MQR, 50
(Apr 1976):137-8.

González, Edward. Cuba Under Castro: The Limits of Charisma.
Boston: Houghton Mifflin, 1974. Rev. by L. A. Perez, Jr.,
TAm, 32(Jan 1976):488-90.

González, Justo L. A History of Christian Thought. Vol. 3. New
York: Abingdon, 1975. Rev. by R. Mackenzie, CH, 45(Mar
1976):108-9.

Gonzalez-Wippler, Migene. Santeria: African Magic in Latin
America. New York: Julian, 1974. Rev. by C. Winters,
JMAS, 14(Mar 1976):175-7.

González Y Gonzalez, Luis. Invitación a la microhistoria. Mexico:
SepSentas, 1973. Rev. by C. A. Hale, HAHR, 56(Nov 1976):
637-8.

Gooch, John. The Plans of War: The General Staff and British
Military Strategy c. 1900-1916. New York: Wiley, 1974.
Rev. by P. Guinn, AHR, 81(Feb 1976):145; Z. Steiner, EHR,
91(Jan 1976):230-1.

Goode, Kenneth G. From Africa to the United States and Then ...
A Concise Afro-American History. Glenview, Ill.: Scott,
Foresman, 1976. Rev. by B. J. Gardner, JNH, 61(Jl 1976):
313.

Goodman, Felicitas D., et al. Trance, Healing and Hallucination:
Three Field Studies in Religious Experience. New York:
Wiley, 1974. Rev. by E. M. Schepers, AA, 78(Mar 1976):
145-6.

Goodman, Lenn Evan. Ibn Tufayl's Hayy Ibn Yaqzān. New York:
Twayne, 1972. Rev. by A. C. Hess, 81(Oct 1976):788-99.

Goodsell, Charles T. American Corporations and Peruvian Politics. Cambridge, Mass: Harvard U Press, 1974. Rev. by J. C. Carey, PHR, 45(May 1976):297-8.

Goodsell, James Nelson, ed. Fidel Castro's Personal Revolution in Cuba: 1959-1973. New York: Knopf, 1975. Rev. by D. M. Coerver, TAm, 33(Oct 1976):375-6.

Goody, Jack, ed. The Character of Kinship. London: Cam U Press, 1974. Rev. by N. H. H. Graburn, AA, 78(Je 1976): 400.

_____ and S. J. Tambiah. Bridewealth and Dowry. Cambridge: Cam U Press, 1973. Rev. by E. P. Skinner, CSSH, 18(Apr 1976):271-5.

Gopal, Sarvepalli. Jawaharlal Nehru: A Biography. Vol. I, 1889-1947. Cambridge, Mass.: Harvard U Press, 1976. Rev. by D. R. SarDesai, HRNB, 4(Sep 1976):222.

_____, ed. Selected Works of Jawaharlal Nehru. Vol. I. Columbia, Mo.: South Asia Books, 1972. Rev. by L. A. Gordon, AHR, 81(Apr 1976):436-7.

Gordimer, Nadine. The Black Interpreters: Notes on African Writing. Johannesburg: Spro-Cas/Ravan, 1973. Rev. by A. Ricard, JMAS, 14(Mar 1976):178-80.

Gordon, Barry. Economic Analysis Before Adam Smith: Hesiod to Lessius. New York: Barnes and Noble, 1975. Rev. by F. E. Dykema, AHR, 81(Oct 1976):840.

Gordon, Leonard A. Bengal: The Nationalist Movement 1876-1940. New York: Columbia U Press, 1974. Rev. by R. K. Ray, MAS, 10(Feb 1976):139-46.

Gordon, Peter. The Victorian School Manager. London: Woburn Press, 1974. Rev. by R. Johnson, History, 61(Oct 1976): 481-2.

_____, ed. see Howard, Christopher, ed.

Gordon, Phyllis Walter Goodhart, trans. and ed. Two Renaissance Book Hunters: The Letters of Poggius Bracciolini to Nicolaus de Niccolis. New York: Columbia U Press, 1974. Rev. by H. L. Oerter, AHR, 81(Oct 1976):891.

Gordon, Sydney see Allan, Ted

Gorenstein, Shirley. Not Forever on Earth: Prehistory of Mexico. New York: Scribner's, 1975. Rev. by E. Cadenhead, ChOk, 54(Sum 1976):286-7; F. A. Peterson, HAHR, 56(Aug 1976): 469-70.

Gori, Cesare see Borgiotti, Alberto

Gornall, Thomas, ed. see Dessain, Charles Stephen, ed.

Goss, Robert C. The San Xavier Altarpiece. Tucson: U Ariz
Press, 1974. Rev. by B. Bunting, CaHR, 62(Jl 1976):521-2.

Gössmann, Elisabeth. Antiqui und Moderni im Mittelalter: eine
geschichtliche Standort bestimmung. Vienna: Schönigh, 1974.
Rev. by W. Ullman, JEccH, 27(Jan 1976):88.

Gottlieb, Gerald. Early Children's Books and Their Illustrations.
Boston: David Godine, 1975. Rev. by W. Claire, Smithsonian, 6(Feb 1976):127-9.

Gottschalk, Stephen. The Emergence of Christian Science in American Religious Life. Berkeley: U Cal Press, 1973. Rev. by
R. J. Cunningham, CaHR, 62(Jl 1976):508-9.

Goubert, Pierre. L'Ancien Régime. Vol. II. Paris: Armand
Colin, 1973. Rev. by O. Ranum, AHR, 81(Feb 1976):152-3.

Gough, Michael. The Origins of Christian Art. New York:
Praeger, 1973. Rev. by H. C. Kee, Archaeology, 29(Jan
1976):61.

Goulart, Maurício. A escravidão africana no Brazil. São Paulo:
Editora Alfa-Omega, 1975. Rev. by G. Cardosa, HAHR, 56
(Nov 1976):641-2.

Gould, Jean. Amy. New York: Dodd, Mead, 1975. Rev. by J.
D. Baker, OH, 85(Aut 1976):341-2.

Gould, Lewis L., ed. The Progressive Era. Syracuse: Syracuse
U Press, 1974. Rev. by L. S. Theisen, PNQ, 67(Jan 1976):
37-8.

Goure, Leon and Morris Rothenberg. Soviet Penetration of Latin
America. Coral Gables, Fla.: U Miami Press, 1975. Rev.
by W. S. Smith, HAHR, 56(Feb 1976):121-2.

Gowans, Fred R. and Eugene E. Campbell. Fort Bridger: Island
in the Wilderness. Provo, Utah: BYU Press, 1975. Rev. by
E. F. Raines, Jr., A & W, 18(Sum 1976):185-7; S. R. Davison, JOW, 15(Jan 1976):134-5; R. A. Murray, UHQ, 44(Win
1976):98-9; W. N. Davis, Jr., WHQ, 7(Jan 1976):80.

Gowing, Margaret. Independence and Deterrence: Britain and
Atomic Energy, 1945-1952. 2 vols. London: Macmillan,
1974. Rev. by F. S. Northedge, History, 61(Oct 1976):476-7.

Goyon, Jean-Claude. Rituels funéraires de l'ancienne Egypte.
Paris: Les Editions du Cerf, 1972. Rev. by L. H. Lesko,
JNES, 35(Jan 1976):57-8.

Grab, Walter. V. Leben und Werker norddeutscher Jakobiner.
Stuttgart: Metzler, 1973. Rev. by E. Tenner, JMH, 48(Mar
1976):162-4.

Grace, John. Domestic Slavery in West Africa: With Particular
Reference to the Sierra Leone Protectorate, 1896-1927. New
York: Barnes and Noble, 1975. Rev. by M. A. Klein, AHR,
81(Oct 1976):923; P. E. H. Hair, EHR, 91(Oct 1976):929-30.

Grady, John C. and Bradford K. Felmly. Suffering to Silence:
29th Texas Cavalry, CSA Regimental History. Quanah, Texas:
Nortex, 1975. Rev. by R. D. Hoffsommer, CWTI, 15(Aug
1976):49; H. B. Simpson, Texana, 12(Num 4, 1976):383-4.

Graebner, Alan. Uncertain Saints: The Laity in the Lutheran
Church--Missouri Synod 1900-1970. Westport, Conn.: Greenwood, 1975. Rev. by M. E. Marty, CaHR, 62(Oct 1976):677-
8; J. H. Tietjen, CH, 45(Sep 1976):394; R. M. Miller, JAH,
63(Je 1976):168-9.

Graebner, Norman A. see DeBoe, David C.

Graebner, William. Coal-Mining Safety in the Progressive Period:
The Political Economy of Reform. Lexington: U Press Ky,
1976. Rev. by D. B. Shaffer, WVH, 38(Oct 1976):69-72.

Graetz, Heinrich. The Structure of Jewish History. New York:
KTAV, 1975. Rev. by F. Rosenthal, HRNB, 4(Apr 1976):
131-2.

Graf, LeRoy P., ed. see Johnson, Andrew

Graglio, Lino. Disaster by Decree: The Supreme Court Decisions
on Race and the Schools. Ithaca, N. Y.: Cornell U Press,
n. d. Rev. by E. Abrams, Commentary, 62(Nov 1976):84-6.

Graham, Hugh D. see Bartley, Numan V.

Graham, Ian and Eric von Euw. Corpus of Maya Hieroglyphic Inscriptions. Cambridge, Mass.: Harvard U Press, 1975.
Rev. by G. H. S. Bushnell, Antiquity, 50(Sep-Dec 1976):253-4.

Graham, Kenneth. Henry James: The Drama of Fulfillment. An
Approach to the Novels. Oxford: Clarendon Press, 1975.
Rev. by P. Grover, JAmS, 10(Apr 1976):127-8.

Graham, Patricia Albjerg. Community and Class in American Education, 1865-1918. New York: Wiley, 1974. Rev. by J.
Messerli, AHR, 81(Je 1976):666-7.

Graham, Richard and Peter H. Smith, eds. New Approaches to
Latin American History. Austin: U Texas Press, 1976.
Rev. by S. L. Baily, AHR, 81(Oct 1976):1008-9; A. T. Bryan,
TAm, 32(Jan 1976):482.

Graham, Roger, ed. see Heick, W. H. , ed.

Granatstein, J. L. Canada's War: The Politics of the Mackenzie
King Government, 1939-1945. New York: Oxford U Press,
1975. Rev. by G. F. G. Stanley, AHR, 81(Je 1976):698-9;
J. A. Gibson, CHR, 57(Je 1976):218-20.

Grange, Henri. Les Idées de Necker. Paris: Librairie C. Klincksieck, 1974. Rev. by H. Vyverberg, AHR, 81(Je 1976):604;
J. McManners, EHR, 91(Oct 1976):861-4.

Gransden, Antonia. Historical Writing in England c. 500 to c. 1307.
Ithaca, N. Y.: Cornell U Press, 1974. Rev. by M. McC.
Gatch, CH, 45(Mar 1976):101-2; D. J. A. Matthew, History,
61(Je 1976):249-50; E. C. Blake, JEccH, 27(Jan 1976):75-6.

Grant, Carolyn, ed. see Wakeman, Frederic, Jr. , ed.

Grant, H. Roger and L. Edward Purcell, eds. Years of Struggle:
The Farm Diary of Elmer G. Powers, 1931-1936. Ames:
Ia St U Press, 1975. Rev. by G. L. Wall, ChOk, 54(Win
1976):529-30; R. V. Scott, HRNB, 4(Jan 1976):126.

Grant, Julia Dent. The Personal Memoirs of Julia Dent Grant.
(John Y. Simon, ed.) New York: Putnam's, 1975. Rev. by
B. I. Wiley, AHI, 10(Feb 1976):50; V. L. Bullough, AHR, 81
(Je 1976):669-70.

Grant, Michael. The Army of the Caesars. New York: Scribner's,
1974. Rev. by M. P. Speidel, AHR, 81(Feb 1976):106-7.

_____. The Fall of the Roman Empire: A Reappraisal. New
York: Nelson, n. d. Rev. by S. Perowne, HTo, 26(Jl 1976):
475-6.

_____. Saint Paul. New York: Scribner's, n. d. Rev. by H.
Maccoby, Commentary, 62(Dec 1976):74, 76-9.

_____. The Twelve Caesars. New York: Scribner's, 1975.
Rev. by J. P. Cavarnos, HRNB, 4(Jan 1976):63.

Grantham, Dewey W. The United States Since 1945: The Ordeal
of Power. New York: McGraw-Hill, 1976. Rev. by G. T.
Mazuzan, JAH, 63(Dec 1976):776-7.

Grassotti, Hilda. Don Rodrigo Ximénez de Rada, gran señor y
hombre de negocios en la Castilla del siglo XIII. Buenos
Aires: Instituto de Historia de España, 1973. Rev. by P. A.
Linehan, EHR, 91(Jl 1976):631.

Gravely, William B. Gilbert Haven, Methodist Abolitionist. 1850-
1880. New York: Abingdon, 1973. Rev. by R. F. Hildebrand, HMPEC, 45(Dec 1976):460-2; J. M. Mulder, JCS, 18
(Win 1976):126-7.

Graves, Edgar B., ed. A Bibliography of English History to 1485. New York: Oxford U Press, 1975. Rev. by R. H. C. Davis, History, 61(Je 1976):250; A. Z. Freeman, HRNB, 4(May/Je 1976):153.

Graves, John. Texas Heartland: A Hill Country Year. College Station: Texas A & M U Press, 1975. Rev. by T. J. Sommers, ETHJ, 14(Fall 1976):72; E. S. Branda, SWHQ, 80(Jl 1976):113-14.

Gray, Ralph D. Stellite: A History of the Haynes Stellite Company, 1912-1972. Kokoma, Ind.: Cabot, 1974. Rev. by P. F. Erwin, JAH, 62(Mar 1976):1034-5.

Gray, Richard, J. D. Fage and R. Oliver, eds. The Cambridge History of Africa. Vol. IV. Cambridge: Cam U Press, 1975. Rev. by P. Duignan, Historian, 39(Nov 1976):138; J. D. Hargreaves, HJ, 19(Dec 1976):1033-6; J. Vansina, JAfH, 17(Num 3, 1976):441-5.

Gray, Robert S. A Visit to Texas in 1831. Houston, Texas: Cordovan, 1975. Rev. by J. M. Day, A & W, 18(Aut 1976): 303-4.

Grechko, Andrei. Battle for the Caucasus. Moscow: Progress Publ'rs., 1971. Rev. by E. F. Ziemke, AHR, 81(Je 1976): 638-9.

Green, Martin. Children of the Sun: A Narrative of "Decadence" in England after 1918. New York: Basic Books, 1976. Rev. by R. Alter, Commentary, 61(Je 1976):75-6; 78-80; W. H. Maehl, Jr., HRNB, 4(Jl 1976):178.

Green, V. H. H. A History of Oxford University. London: Batsford, 1974. Rev. by A. B. Cobban, EHR, 91(Jan 1976):178-9; J. M. Fletcher, History, 61(Feb 1976):82.

Green, William A. British Slave Emancipation: The Sugar Colonies and the Great Experiment, 1830-1865. New York: Oxford U Press, 1976. Rev. by W. H. Pease, HRNB, 4(Sep 1976):225-6.

Greenbaum, Fred. Robert Marion La Follette. Boston: Twayne, 1975. Rev. by H. F. Margulies, JAH, 63(Je 1976):162-3.

Greenbaum, Louis S. Talleyrand, Statesman Priest. Washington, D.C.: Catholic U Press, 1970. Rev. by M. E. Goldstein, JMH, 48(Mar 1976):132-5.

Greenblatt, Stephen J. Sir Walter Raleigh: The Renaissance Man and His Roles. New Haven, Conn.: Yale U Press, 1973. Rev. by L. A. Knafla, CHR, 57(Mar 1976):68-9.

Greene, Victor. For God and Country: The Rise of Polish and
    Lithuanian Ethnic Consciousness in America, 1860-1910.
    Madison: St Historical Society of Wis, 1975. Rev. by G. J.
    Bobango, HRNB, 4(Apr 1976):118-19; E. R. Kantowicz, JAH,
    63(Sep 1976):433; J. M. Allswang, WMH, 60(Aut 1976):69-71.

Greenhalgh, P. A. L. The Year of the Four Emperors. New York:
    Barnes and Noble, 1975. Rev. by J. Linderski, AHR, 81(Oct
    1976):830-1.

Greenhill, Ralph, et al. Ontario Towns. Toronto: Oberon, 1974.
    Rev. by G. de T. Glazebrook, CHR, 57(Je 1976):205-6.

Greenlaw, Ralph W. The Social Origins of the French Revolution:
    The Debate on the Role of the Middle Classes. Lexington,
    Mass.: Heath, 1975. Rev. by J. E. Brink, HT, 10(Nov
    1976):135-6.

Greenleaf, Richard E. and Michael C. Meyer. Research in Mexican
    History: Topics, Methodology, Sources, and a Practical Guide
    to Field Research. Lincoln: U Neb Press, 1973. Rev. by
    P. Hadley, HAHR, 56(Aug 1976):505.

Greenlee, Douglas. Peirce's Concept of Sign. The Hague: Mou-
    ton, 1973. Rev. by H. S. Thayer, JHP, 14(Jan 1976):115-17.

Greenwood, Gordon. Approaches to Asia: Australian Postwar
    Policies and Attitudes. Sydney: McGraw-Hill, 1975. Rev.
    by S. Krishnamurthi, IQ, 32(Apr-Je 1976):245-6.

Greenwood, John Ormerod. Quaker Encounters, Vol. I. New
    York: Wm. Sessions, 1975. Rev. by G. Best, History, 61
    (Oct 1976):496.

Gregor, A. James. The Fascist Persuasion in Radical Politics.
    Princeton: Prin U Press, 1974. Rev. by C. Gershman,
    Commentary, 61(Jan 1976):86-8.

Gregory, Frances W. Nathan Appleton: Merchant and Entrepreneur,
    1779-1861. Charlottesville: U Press Va., 1975. Rev. by
    R. F. Oaks, NEQ, 49(Sep 1976):485-6.

Greifenhagen, Adolf. Schmuckarbeiten in Edelmetall, Band II.
    Berlin: Gebrüder Mann Verlag, 1975. Rev. by W. Rudolf,
    AJA, 80(Fall 1976):438-9.

Grekov, I. B. Eastern Europe and the Downfall of the Golden
    Horde (at the Turn of the Fourteenth and Fifteenth Centuries).
    Moscow: Izdatel'stvo "Nauka," 1975. Rev. by C. J. Hal-
    perin, AHR, 81(Je 1976):626-7.

Grele, Ronald J., ed. Envelopes of Sound. Chicago: Precedent,
    1975. Rev. by L. J. Hackman, AmArc, 39(Apr 1976):208-9;
    B. M. Stave, JAH, 62(Mar 1976):1052-3.

Grelot, Pierre. Documents arameens d'Egypte. Paris: Les Editions au Cerf, 1972. Rev. by J. Teixidor, JNES, 35(Jl 1976): 217-18.

Gribbin, William. The Churches Militant: The War of 1812 and American Religion. New Haven, Conn.: Yale U Press, 1973. Rev. by L. L. Brown, HMPEC, 45(Sep 1976):350-1; G. W. Hull, JCS, 17(Aut 1975):511-12.

Grierson, Philip. Numismatics. Oxford: Oxford U Press, 1975. Rev. by R. A. G. Carson, Antiquity, 50(Mar 1976):73.

Griffith, James S. see Eckhart, George B.

Griffith, Kenneth. Thank God We Kept the Flag Flying. New York: Viking, 1975. Rev. by R. Higham, Historian, 39(Nov 1976): 121.

Griffith, Ralph A. and Roger S. Thomas. The Principality of Wales in the Later Middle Ages. Vol. I. Cardiff: U Wales Press, 1972. Rev. by P. Williams, EHR, 91(Jl 1976):632-3.

Griffiths, D. R. The New Testament and the Roman State. Swansea, U.K.: John Penry Press, 1970. Rev. by E. J. Vardaman, JCS, 17(Spr 1975):340-1.

Griffiths, Sir Percival. A Licence to Trade: A History of the English Chartered Companies. London: Ernest Benn, 1974. Rev. by D. K. Fieldhouse, History, 61(Feb 1976):85-6.

Grigg, D. B. The Agricultural Systems of the World: An Evolutionary Approach. London: Cam U Press, 1974. Rev. by W. C. Van Deventer, AgH, 50(Jl 1976):525-6; V. W. Ruttan, JEH, 36(Sep 1976):756-8.

Grillmeier, Aloys. Christ in Christian Tradition. I. Oxford: Mowbray, 1975. Rev. by M. Wiles, JEccH, 27(Jl 1976):307-8.

Grimstead, Patricia Kennedy. Archives and Manuscript Repositories in the USSR; Moscow and Leningrad. Princeton, N.J.: Prin U Press, 1972. Rev. by B. Hollingsworth, ESR, 6(Apr 1976):257-8.

Grindhammer, Lucille Wrubel. Art and the Public: The Democratization of the Fine Arts in the United States, 1830-1860. Stuttgart: J. B. Metzlersche, 1975. Rev. by N. Harris, AHR, 81(Oct 1976):973.

Grossman, Jill. Revelations of New England Architecture. New York: Grossman, n.d. Rev. by C. Page, Smithsonian, 7 (Mar 1976):105-7.

Grossman, Julian. Echo of a Distant Drum: Winslow Homer and the Civil War. New York: Abrams, 1974. Rev. by B. L. Bassham, CWH, 22(Je 1976):181-2.

Grossman, Lawrence. The Democratic Party and the Negro: Northern and National Politics, 1868-92. Urbana: U Ill Press, 1976. Rev. by R. A. Gerber, HRNB, 5(Oct 1976):9-10; K. I. Polakoff, HT, 10(Nov 1976):155-8; J. T. Doyle, JAH, 63(Dec 1976):725-6.

Grossman, Maria. Humanism in Wittenberg, 1485-1517. Nieuwkoop: De Graaf, 1975. Rev. by R. W. Scribner, JEccH, 27(Jl 1976):316-18.

Grossmann, Peter. S. Michele in Africiso zu Ravenna. Baugeschichtliche Untersuchungen. Mainz: Verlag Philipp von Zabern, 1973. Rev. by J. Morganstern, AJA, 80(Win 1976): 108-9.

Grove, Pearce, Becky J. Barnett and Sandra J. Hansen, ed. New Mexico Newspapers: A Comprehensive Guide to Bibliographical Entries and Locations. Albuquerque: U NM Press, 1975. Rev. by N. S. Furman, NMHR, 51(Jan 1976):87-8.

Gruber, Carol S. Mars and Minerva: World War I and the Uses of the Higher Learning in America. Baton Rouge: LSU Press, 1976. Rev. by R. D. Cohen, HRNB, 4(May/Je 1976):141-2; S. J. Whitfield, JAH, 63(Dec 1976):753-4; L. E. Gelfand, JSH, 42(Nov 1976):601-2.

Gruber, Howard E. Darwin on Man: A Psychological Study of Scientific Creativity. New York: Dutton, 1974. Rev. by M. Rase, JIH, 7(Aut 1976):351-4.

Grugel, Lee E. George Jacob Holyoake: A Study in the Evolution of a Victorian Radical. Philadelphia: Porcupine, 1976. Rev. by J. A. Casada, HRNB, 5(Oct 1976):20.

Grun, Bernard. The Timetables of History: A Horizontal Linkage of People and Events. New York: Simon and Schuster, 1975. Rev. by R. Rinehart, HRNB, 4(Mar 1976):107.

Grundy, Kenneth W. Confrontation and Accommodation in Southern Africa: The Limits of Independence. Berkeley: U Cal Press, 1973. Rev. by R. Dale, JAAS, 11(Jl-Oct 1976):239-40.

_____. Guerilla Struggle in Africa: An Analysis and Preview. New York: Grossman, 1971. Rev. by D. G. Anglin, JAAS, 11(Jan-Apr 1976):113-14.

Grunsfeld, Mary Jane see Hamblin, Dora Jane

Guberlet, Muriel L. The Windows to His World: The Story of

Trevor Kincaid. Palo Alto, Cal.: Pacific Books, 1975.
Rev. by A. Svihla, PNQ, 67(Oct 1976):180-1.

Gudde, Erwin G. California Gold Camps. Berkeley: U Cal Press,
1975. Rev. by D. J. Pisani, A & W, 18(Spr 1976):98-9;
K. M. Johnson, JOW, 15(Apr 1976):144; J. Caughey, PHR,
45(Nov 1976):40-4; O. E. Young, Jr., SCQ, 58(Sum 1976):
255-6.

Gudea, Nicolae see Chirilá, Eugen

Guerber, Jean. Le Ralliement du clergé français à la morale
liquorienne. L'Abbé Gousset et ses précurseurs (1785-1832).
Rome: Universitá Gregoriana Editrice, 1973. Rev. by C. B.
O'Keefe, CaHR, 62(Apr 1976):307-8.

Guest, Francis F. Fermin Francisco de Lasuén (1736-1803): A
Biography. Washington: Academy of American Franciscan
History, 1973. Rev. by J. Caughey, AHR, 81(Je 1976):652-3.

Guidry, Mary Gabriella. The Southern Negro Nun: An Autobiography.
New York: Exposition, 1974. Rev. by T. E. Brown, CaHR,
62(Jl 1976):522-3.

Guilford, Nancy see Brandt, Patricia

Guillaume, H. 'Les Nomades interrompus': introduction à l'étude
du canton twareg de l'Imanan. Niamey, CNRSH, 1974. Rev.
by C. Oxby, Africa, 46(Num 2, 1976):206.

Guilmartin, John Francis, Jr. Gunpowder and Galleys: Changing
Technology and Mediterranean Warfare at Sea in the Sixteenth
Century. Cambridge: Cam U Press, 1975. Rev. by A. C.
Hess, AHR, 81(Apr 1976):357; P. Earle, EHR, 91(Oct 1976):
843-5; G. Parker, History, 61(Je 1976):267.

Gulvin, Clifford. The Tweedmakers: A History of the Scottish
Fancy Woollen Industry, 1600-1914. Newton Abbot: David
and Charles, 1973. Rev. by J. R. Hume, History, 61(Feb
1976):83.

Gumerman, George J. and Robert C. Euler, eds. Papers on the
Archaeology of Black Mesa, Arizona. Carbondale, Ill.: S
Ill U Press, 1976. Rev. by W. Smith, JAriH, 17(Sum 1976):
240-1.

Gunn, Drewey Wayne. American and British Writers in Mexico
1556-1973. Austin: U Texas Press, 1974. Rev. by C. H.
Gardiner, TAm, 32(Apr 1976):652-3.

Gunnerson, Dolores A. The Jicarilla Apaches: A Study in Survival.
DeKalb: N Ill U Press, 1974. Rev. by D. E. Worcester,
PHR, 45(May 1976):278-9.

Gupta, Anirudha. Government and Politics in Africa. Delhi:
    Vikas, 1975. Rev. by R. R. Ramachandani, IQ, 32(Jan-Mar
    1976):93-5.

Gupta, Karunakar. The Hidden History of the Sino-Indian Frontier.
    Calcutta: Minerva, 1974. Rev. by A. Lamb, CQ, May 1976,
    pp. 386-8.

Gupta, Partha Sarathi. Imperialism and the British Labour Move-
    ment, 1914-1964. New York: Holmes and Meier, 1975. Rev.
    by M. Naidis, AHR, 81(Je 1976):595; J. M. Winter, History,
    61(Oct 1976):495; B. Spangenberg, JAS, 36(Nov 1976):177-9.

Gupta, R. S. History of Modern China. New Delhi: Sterling,
    1974. Rev. by S. Swarup, IQ, 32(Jan-Mar 1976):90-2.

Guralnick, Stanley M. Science and the Ante-Bellum American Col-
    lege. Philadelphia: American Philosophical Society, 1975.
    Rev. by D. B. Potts, JAH, 63(Dec 1976):714-15.

Guratzsch, Dankwart. Macht durch organisation: Die Grundlegung
    des Hugenbergschen Presseimperiums. Gütersloh: Bertels-
    mann Universitätsverlag, 1974. Rev. by T. S. Hamerow,
    AHR, 81(Feb 1976):167-8.

Guss, Brian H. see Snyder, Frank E.

Gustafson, Milton O., ed. The National Archives and Foreign Rela-
    tions Research. Athens: Ohio U Press, 1975. Rev. by D.
    M. Smith, PHR, 45(Feb 1976):118-9.

Guthman, William H. March to Massacre. New York: McGraw-
    Hill, 1975. Rev. by R. T. Smith, ChOk, 54(Sum 1976):281.

Gutkind, Lee. The Best Seat in Baseball, but You Have to Stand:
    The Game as Umpires See It. New York: Dial, 1975. Rev.
    by W. F. Clare, Smithsonian, 6(Aug 1975):96-8.

Gutman, Herbert G. Slavery and the Numbers Game: A Critique
    of Time on the Cross. Urbana: U Ill Press, 1975. Rev.
    by R. L. Ransom, AgH, 50(Apr 1976):435-7; F. W. Knight,
    AHR, 81(Oct 1976):949-50; in CWH, 22(Mar 1976):93; by R. B.
    Campbell, Historian, 39(Nov 1976):149-50; L. Filler, HRNB,
    4(Jan 1976):50; M. P. Johnson, HT, 10(Nov 1976):153-5; H. D.
    Woodman, IMH, 72(Je 1976):275-6; G. Sorin, JAH, 63(Je 1976):
    133-5; W. K. Scarborough, JMiH, 38(Nov 1976):376-8; P. Kol-
    shin, JSoH, 10(Fall 1976):107-9; N. R. Yetman, RAH, 4(Je
    1976):195-202; T. R. Waring, SCHM, 77(Jl 1976):196-7.

Gutteridge, W. F. Military Regimes in Africa. London: Methuen,
    1975. Rev. by C. Clapham, AfAf, 75(Jl 1976):391.

Gutton, Jean-Pierre. L'État et la mendicité dans la première moitié du XVIIIe siècle: Auvergne, Beaujolais, Forez, Lyonnais. Lyon: Centre d'études Foreziennes, 1973. Rev. by T. M. Adams, AHR, 81(Je 1976):600-1.

_____. La Société et les pauvres en Europe (XVIe-XVIIIe siècles). Paris: Presses Universitaires de France, 1974. Rev. by T. M. Adams, AHR, 81(Je 1976):600-1.

_____. La Société et les pauvres, 1534-1789. Paris: Société d'édition "Les Belles Lettres," 1971. Rev. by T. M. Adams, AHR, 81(Je 1976):600-1.

Guzzo, Piero G. Le Fibule in Etruria dal VI al I Secolo. Florence: Sansoni Editore, 1972. Rev. by E. Nielsen, AJA, 80(Win 1976):98.

Gwyn, Julian. The Enterprising Admiral: The Personal Fortune of Admiral Sir Peter Warren. Montreal: McGill-Queens U Press, 1974. Rev. by J. J. McCusker, AHR, 81(Je 1976): 585; N. Varga, NYHSQ, 60(Jan/Apr 1976):68-70.

Haas, Edward F. DeLesseps S. Morrison and the Image of Reform: New Orleans Politics, 1946-1961. Baton Rouge: LSU Press, 1975. Rev. by G. Osborn, AHR, 81(Oct 1976):995.

Haas, Martin, ed. Quellen zur Geschichte der Taufer in der Schweiz, IV Bd. Zürich: Theologischer Verlag, 1974. Rev. by W. Klaassen, MQR, 50(Jan 1976):77.

Haase, Carl. Ernst Brandes 1758-1810. 2 vols. Hildesheim: August Lax, 1973, 1974. Rev. by T. C. W. Blanning, EHR, 91(Jan 1976):209-10.

Haase, Ynez D. see Beck, Warren A.

Hachey, Thomas E., ed. Anglo-Vatican Relations, 1914-1939: Confidential Reports of the British Ministers to the Holy See. Boston: G. K. Hall, 1972. Rev. by R. A. Graham, CaHR, 62(Oct 1976):649-50; J. W. Vardaman, JCS, 17(Win 1975): 153.

Hacking, Ian. The Emergence of Probability. New York: Cam U Press, 1975. Rev. by J. M. Vickers, JHP, 14(Jl 1976): 366-7.

Haddad, Robert M. Syrian Christians in Muslim Society: An Interpretation. Princeton, N.J.: Prin U Press, 1970. Rev. by F. M. Graham, JCS, 17(Spr 1975):327-9.

Hadingham, Evan. Stone Circles--Standing Stones. London: Heineman, 1975. Rev. by E. Mackie, Antiquity, 50(Je 1976): 169-70.

Haeger, John W., ed. Crisis and Prosperity in Sung China. Tucson: U Ariz Press, 1975. Rev. by R. Taylor, HRNB, 4(Feb 1976):85; C. A. Johnson, JAS, 36(Nov 1976):127-9.

Haeny, G., ed. Beiträge zur ägyptischen Bauforschung und Altertumskunde, zum 70. Wiesbaden: n.p., 1971. Rev. by A. M. Badawy, JNES, 35(Jan 1976):47-50.

Haffenden, Philip S. New England in the English Nation, 1689-1713. Oxford: Clarendon Press, 1974. Rev. by C. Brooks, EHR, 91(Jan 1976):203-4.

Hager, Georgie M., comp. Index to the Journals of the North Dakota Historical Society: 1971-1975. Bismarck: St Library Commission, 1976. Rev. by Editor, NDH, 43(Sum 1976):46.

Hagopian, Mark N. The Phenomenon of Revolution. New York: Dodd, Mead, 1974. Rev. by D. Goodspeed, CHR, 57(Je 1976): 171-3.

Haigh, Christopher. Reformation and Resistance in Tudor Lancashire. New York: Cam U Press, 1975. Rev. by V. F. Snow, AHR, 81(Je 1976):582; F. H. Thompsett, CH, 45(Mar 1976):112-13; M. E. James, EHR, 91(Jl 1976):638-9; C. Cross, History, 61(Feb 1976):109.

Haimson, Leopold H., ed. The Mensheviks: From the Revolution of 1917 to the Second World War. Chicago: U Chi Press, 1975. Rev. by V. D. Medlin, AHR, 81(Oct 1976):910-11.

Haines, Francis. The Plains Indians: Their Origins, Migration, and Cultural Development. New York: Crowell, 1976. Rev. by R. E. Smith, JOW, 15(Jl 1976):99; E. L. Holland, NDH, 43(Fall 1976):42-3.

Haites, Erik F., et al. Western River Transportation. Baltimore: JHU Press, 1975. Rev. by M. Walsh, History, 61 (Oct 1976):404-5; V. G. Spence, HRNB, 4(Feb 1976):80; R. M. Jellison, IMH, 72(Je 1976):267-8; H. D. Woodman, JAH, 63(Dec 1976):711-12; J. G. Clark, JSH, 42(Aug 1976):427-8; J. F. Stover, PHQ, 7(Oct 1976):428-9.

Halecki, Oskar. Un empereur de Byzance à Rome. Vingt ans de travail pour l'union des églises et pour la défense de l'empire d'Orient, 1355-1375. London: Variorum Reprints, 1972. Rev. by G. T. Dennis, CaHR, 62(Jan 1976):102-4.

Halévy, Daniel. The End of the Notables. Middletown, Conn.: Wesleyan U Press, 1974. Rev. by A. R. H. Copley, History, 61(Feb 1976):137-8.

Haley, Alex. Roots: The Saga of an American Family. Garden

City, N. Y.: Doubleday, 1976. Rev. by D. H. Donald, Commentary, 62(Dec 1976):70, 72-4.

Haley, James L. The Buffalo War: The History of the Red River Indian Uprising of 1874. Garden City, N. Y.: Doubleday, 1976. Rev. by L. E. Oliva, HRNB, 4(May/Je 1976):144-5.

Halfpenny, Frances G. , ed. Dictionary of Canadian Biography. Toronto: U Tor Press, 1974. Rev. by A. F. McC. Madden, EHR, 91(Apr 1976):435.

Halicz, Emanuel. Partisan Warfare in 19th-Century Poland. Odense: Odense U Press, 1975. Rev. by P. S. Wandycz, AHR, 81(Oct 1976):900; R. F. Leslie, History, 61(Oct 1976): 463-4.

Halkin, Léon-E. Initiation à la critique historique. Paris: Librairie Armand Colin, 1973. Rev. by A. Scham, AHR, 81 (Oct 1976):812-13.

Hall, A. R. and M. Boas Hall, eds. and trans. The Correspondence of Henry Oldenburg. Madison: U Wis Press, 1973. Rev. by C. Hill, CHR, 91(Jl 1976):645-6.

Hall, D. G. E. Henry Burney: A Political Biography. Oxford: Oxford U Press, 1974. Rev. by M. Caldwell, History, 61 (Feb 1976):166.

Hall, Ivan Parker. Mori Arinori. Cambridge, Mass. : Harvard U Press, 1973. Rev. by K. B. Pyle, AHR, 81(Oct 1976):941; J. E. Hunter, MAS, 10(Oct 1976):622-9.

Hall, Kermit L. , ed. see Polk, James K.

Hall, Richard. Stanley: An Adventurer Explored. Boston: Houghton Mifflin, 1975. Rev. by R. Beeston, Smithsonian, 6(Feb 1975):122-3.

Hall, Sharlot M. Sharlot Hall on the Arizona Strip: a Diary of a Journey Through Northern Arizona in 1911. (C. Gregory Crampton, ed.) Flagstaff, Ariz.: Northland Press, 1975. Rev. by B. M. Goldwater, 44(Win 1976):101-2.

Haller, Mark H. , ed. see Davis, Allen F. , ed.

Hallett, Robin. Africa Since 1875. Ann Arbor: U Mich Press, 1974. Rev. by J. McCracken, JAfH, 17(Num 4, 1976):631-2.

Hallgarten, George W. F. and Joachim Radkau. Deutsche Industrie und Politik: Von Bismarck bis Heute. Frankfort am Main: Europäische Verlagsanstalt, 1974. Rev. by P. Pulzer, AHR, 81(Apr 1976):407-8.

Halpenny, Francess G. , ed. Dictionary of Canadian Biography.
Toronto: U Toronto Press, 1974. Rev. by J. L. Sturgis,
History, 61(Oct 1976):395.

Halperín-Donghi, Tulio. Politics, Economics, and Society in
Argentina in the Revolutionary Period. Cambridge: Cam U
Press, 1975. Rev. by H. S. Ferns, History, 61(Oct 1976):
429-30; C. Solberg, JEH, 36(Sep 1976):758-9.

Halpern, Paul G. , ed. The Keyes Papers: Selections from the
Private and Official Correspondence of Admiral of the Fleet
Baron Keyes of Zeebrugge. Vol. I, 1914-1918. London:
Navy Records Society, 1972. Rev. by A. Marder, AHR, 81
(Apr 1976):390.

_____. The Mediterranean Naval Situation 1908-1914. Cam-
bridge, Mass.: Harvard U Press, 1971. Rev. by J. Gooch,
ESR, 6(Jl 1976):396-8.

Hamblin, Dora Jane and Mary Jane Grunsfeld. The Appian Way.
New York: Random, 1974. Rev. by R. Rinehart, Smithsonian, 6(Feb 1975):123-5.

Hamelin, Marcel. Les Premières Années du parlementarisme
québécois (1867-1878). Portland, Ore.: International
Scholarly Book Services, 1974. Rev. by C. Nish, AHR, 81
(Apr 1976):471-2.

Hamerow, Theodore S. The Social Foundations of German Unifica-
tion 1858-1871: Struggles and Accomplishments. Princeton,
N.J.: Prin U Press, 1972. Rev. by D. Geary, ESR, 6(Jl
1976):387-9.

Hamil, James H. and Harold Hamil. Farmland, U.S.A. Kansas
City: Lowell, 1975. Rev. by F. H. Schapsmeier, JOW, 15
(Apr 1976):139.

Hamilton, Alexander. The Papers of Alexander Hamilton. Vol.
20. (Harold C. Syrett, et al., eds.) New York: Columbia
U Press, 1974. Rev. by J. Pancake, AHR, 81(Feb 1976):
207; E. J. Ferguson, JAH, 63(Sep 1976):368-9.

Hamilton, Carl. In No Time at All. Ames: Ia St U Press, 1974.
Rev. by P. L. Petersen, AgH, 50(Jl 1976):551-2.

Hamilton, David. The Diary of Sir David Hamilton, 1709-1714.
(Philip Roberts, ed.) Oxford: Clarendon, 1975. Rev. by
G. V. Bennett, EHR, 91(Oct 1976):913-14; A. McInnes, His-
tory, 61(Je 1976):293-4.

Hamilton, James. The Power to Probe: A Study of Congressional
Investigations. New York: Random House, 1976. Rev. by
H. M. Hyman, JAH, 63(Dec 1976):785-6.

Hamilton, Milton W. Sir William Johnson: Colonial American, 1715-1763. Port Washington, N. Y.: Kennikat Press, 1976. Rev. by R. P. Gildrie, HRNB, 4(Sep 1976):218-9.

Hammer, Kenneth, ed. see Camp, Walter

Hammett, Hugh B. Hilary Abner Herbert: A Southerner Returns to the Union. Philadelphia: American Philosophical Society, 1976. Rev. by R. H. Woody, JAH, 63(Dec 1976):723; D. W. Southern, JSH, 42(Nov 1976):597-8.

Hammond, N. G. L. see Edwards, I. E. S.

Hammond, Norman, et al. Archaeology in Northern Belize. Cambridge: Cam U Press, 1976. Rev. by G. H. S. Bushnell, Antiquity, 50(Sep-Dec 1976):253-4.

_____. Mesoamerican Archaeology: New Approaches. Austin: U Texas Press, 1974. Rev. by D. M. Pendergast, Archaeology, 29(Apr 1976):142.

Hammond-Tooke, W. D. , ed. The Bantu Speaking Peoples of Southern Africa. Boston: Routledge and Kegan Paul, 1974. Rev. by A. W. Southall, JAAS, 11(Jl-Oct 1976):219-22.

Hampson, Norman. The French Revolution. London: Thames and Hudson, 1975. Rev. by P. M. Jones, History, 61(Oct 1976): 457-8.

_____. The Life and Opinions of Maximilien Robespierre. London: Duckworth, 1974. Rev. by A. Forrest, EHR, 91 (Jan 1976):211; G. Lewis, History, 61(Feb 1976):120-1.

Hancock, W. K. Discovering Monaro: A Study of Man's Impact on His Environment. New York: Cam U Press, 1972. Rev. by S. C. McCulloch, AHR, 81(Oct 1976):948-9.

Handelman, Howard. Struggle in the Andes: Peasant Political Mobilization in Peru. Austin: U Texas Press, 1975. Rev. by B. Orlove, AgH, 50(Jl 1976):528-32; H. F. Dobyns, HAHR, 56(Nov 1976):692-3.

Handler, Andrew. The Zirids of Granada. Coral Gables: U Miami Press, 1974. Rev. by R. I. Burns, AHR, 81(Je 1976):570.

Handler, Jerome S. The Unappropriated People: Freedmen in the Slave Society of Barbados. Baltimore: JHU Press, 1974. Rev. by J. A. Borome, AHR, 81(Apr 1976):473-4.

Handlin, Oscar and Mary F. Handlin. The Wealth of the American People: A History of American Affluence. New York: McGraw-Hill, 1975. Rev. by G. C. Fite, HRNB, 4(Feb 1976):

74; R. E. Gallman, JSH, 42(Aug 1976):446-7; D. Lindstrom,
WMH, 60(Aut 1976):63-4.

Hanfmann, George M. A. From Croesus to Constantine: The
Cities of Western Asia Minor and Their Arts in Greek and
Roman Times. Ann Arbor: U Mich Press, 1975. Rev. by
M. J. Mellink, AJA, 80(Fall 1976):439-40.

Hanham, Alison. Richard III and His Early Historians, 1483-1535.
New York: Clarendon Press, 1975. Rev. by J. M. Hernon,
Jr., AHR, 81(Oct 1976):852-3; A. R. Myers, History, 61(Je
1976):264-5.

Hanke, Lewis. All Mankind Is One: A Study of the Disputation Between Bartolomé de Las Casas and Juan Ginés de Sepúlveda
in 1550 on the Intellectual and Religious Capacity of the American Indians. DeKalb: N Ill U Press, 1974. Rev. by W. S.
Maltby, AHR, 81(Apr 1976):473; M. V. Gannon, FHQ, 54(Jan
1976):387-90.

Hannaway, Owen. The Chemists and the Word: The Didactic Ori-
gins of Chemistry. Baltimore: JHU Press, 1975. Rev. by
A. B. Davis, AHR, 81(Oct 1976):813-14; H. A. Barnes,
HRNB, 4(Feb 1976):86-7.

Hansen, Arthur A. and Betty E. Mitson, eds. Voices Long Silent:
An Oral Inquiry into the Japanese American Evacuation. Ful-
lerton: Cal St U Japanese American Project, 1974. Rev. by
R. Daniels, PHR, 45(Aug 1976):452-3.

Hansen, Helen M. At Home in Early Sandusky. Sandusky, Ohio:
Sandusky Library Assn, 1975. Rev. by K. Davison, OH, 85
(Aut 1976):335-6.

Hansen, Mogens Herman see Isager, Signe

Hansen, Sandra J., ed. see Grove, Pearce, ed.

Hanser, Richard. The Glorious Hour of Lt. Monroe. New York:
Atheneum, 1976. Rev. by W. N. Murphy, HT, 10(Nov 1976):
153.

Hanson, Harry. The Canal Boatmen 1760-1914. Manchester:
Manchester U Press, 1975. Rev. by F. Duckham, History,
61(Oct 1976):480-1.

Hanson, James Austin. Metal Weapons, Tools, and Ornaments of
the Teton Dakota Indians. Lincoln: U Neb Press, 1975.
Rev. by A. R. Woolworth, MinnH, 45(Sum 1976):79-80; N.
G. Franke, NDH, 43(Spr 1976):105.

Hanson, Lee and Dick Ping Hsu. Casements and Cannonballs:
Archaeological Investigations at Fort Stanwix, Rome, New York.

Washington, D. C.: National Park Service, 1975. Rev. by
D. P. Heldman, Archaeology, 29(Jl 1976):210-11.

Hansot, Elisabeth. Perfection and Progress: Two Modes of
Utopian Thought. Cambridge, Mass.: MIT Press, 1974.
Rev. by M. S. De Pillis, AHR, 81(Oct 1976):841-2.

Harap, Louis. The Image of the Jew in American Literature:
From Early Republic to Mass Immigration. Philadelphia:
Jewish Publication Society, 1975. Rev. by E. Grumet, Com-
mentary, 61(Mar 1976):68-71.

Haraszti, E. H. Treaty-Breakers or 'Realpolitiker'? The Anglo-
German Naval Agreement of June 1935. Boppard am Rhein:
Boldt, 1974. Rev. by K. Robbins, History, 61(Feb 1976):143-
4.

Harder, Leland see Kauffman, J. Howard

Hardin, Herschel. A Nation Unaware: The Canadian Economic
Culture. Vancouver: J. J. Douglas, 1974. Rev. by R. W.
Pollay, BHR, 50(Spr 1976):112-13.

Harding, D. W. The Iron Age in Lowland Britain. London:
Routledge and Kegan Paul, 1974. Rev. by J. V. S. Megaw,
History, 61(Oct 1976):432-3.

Hardoy, Jorge, ed. Urbanization in Latin America. Garden City,
N. Y.: Anchor, 1975. Rev. by C. Sargent, HAHR, 56(Nov
1976):636-7.

Hardtwig, Wolfgang. Geschichtsschreibung zwischen Alteurope und
moderner Welt: Jacob Burckhardt in seiner Zeit. Göttingen:
Vandenhoeck and Ruprecht, 1974. Rev. by C. H. O'Brien,
AHR, 81(Je 1976):613-14.

Hardy, Peter. The Muslims of British India. Cambridge: Cam U
Press, 1972. Rev. by G. Minault, AHR, 81(Je 1976):645-7;
A. E. Meyers, JAAS, 11(Jan-Apr 1976):124-5.

Hargreaves, John D. West Africa Partitioned. Vol. 1. The
Loaded Pause, 1885-1889. Madison: U Wis Press, 1975.
Rev. by D. H. Jones, AfAf, 75(Jan 1976):112-13; P. Gifford,
AHR, 81(Oct 1976):921-2; C. Newbury, JAfH, 17(Num 3, 1976):
460-1.

Harik, Iliya F. The Political Mobilization of Peasants: A Study
of an Egyptian Community. Bloomington: Ind U Press, 1974.
Rev. by A. Rassam, AA, 78(Je 1976):413-14.

Harker, Douglas E. The Dukes. Vancouver, B. C.: Mitchell
Press, 1974. Rev. by R. H. Roy, PNQ, 67(Oct 1976):181.

Harkey, Ira. Pioneer Bush Pilot: The Story of Noel Wien. Seattle: U Wash Press, 1974. Rev. by N. E. Williams, JOW,
15(Apr 1976):135; S. Haycox, PNQ, 67(Jan 1976):45-6.

Harle, James. Gupta Sculpture. Oxford: Oxford U Press, 1974.
Rev. by M. W. Meister, JAS, 36(Nov 1976):166-7.

Harlow, Francis B. see Frank, Larry

Harney, Robert F. and Harold Troper. Immigrants: A Portrait
of the Urban Experience, 1890-1930. Toronto: Van Nostrand
Reinhold, 1975. Rev. by R. H. Bayor, HRNB, 5(Oct 1976):
12-13; V. R. Greene, JAH, 63(Dec 1976):736.

Harootunian, H. D., ed. see Silberman, Bernard, ed.

Harper, George Mills. Yeats: The Golden Dawn. New York:
Barnes and Noble, 1974. Rev. by A. O. Ceallaigh, E-I, 11
(Sum 1976):151-2.

Harrell, David Edwin, Jr. All Things Are Possible: The Healing
& Charismatic Revivals in Modern America. Bloomington:
Ind U Press, 1976. Rev. by E. R. Sandeen, AHR, 81(Oct
1976):1004; G. Wacker, Jr., CH, 45(Sep 1976):397; J. M.
Mulder, HRNB, 4(May/Je 1976):142; P. A. Carter, JAH, 63
(Dec 1976):759-60; W. C. Martin, JSH, 42(Nov 1976):603-4.

_____. The Social Sources of Division in the Disciples of Christ,
1865-1900. Athens, Ga.: Publishing Systems, 1973. Rev.
by T. E. Brown, CaHR, 62(Jl 1976):509-10; R. M. Pope,
JCS, 17(Win 1975):121-3.

Harrell-Bond, R. E. Modern Marriage in Sierra Leone: A Study
of the Professional Group. The Hague: Mouton, 1975. Rev.
by L. Mair, AfAf, 75(Jl 1976):395-6.

Harriman, W. Averell and Elie Abel. Special Envoy to Churchill
and Stalin, 1941-1946. New York: Random House, 1975.
Rev. by G. C. Herring, AHR, 81(Oct 1976):999-1000.

Harrington-Müller, Diethild. Der Fortschrittsklub im Abgeordneten-
haus des Österreichischen Reichsrats, 1873-1910. Vienna:
Hermann Böhlaus Nachf., 1972. Rev. by H. G. Dittmar,
AHR, 81(Feb 1976):174.

Harris, Charles H., III. A Mexican Family Empire: The Latifundio of the Sanchez Navarros, 1765-1867. Austin: U Texas
Press, 1975. Rev. by D. M. Vigness, A & W, 18(Spr 1976):
89-90; C. G. Hale, HAHR, 56(May 1976):279-301; J. D.
Riley, TAm, 33(Jl 1976):177-8.

Harris, Leon. Upton Sinclair: American Rebel. New York:
Crowell, 1975. Rev. by F. Annunziata, HRNB, 4(Feb 1976):

79-80; C. C. Alexander, OH, 85(Aut 1976):342-3; F. A.
Warren, RAH, 4(Je 1976):251-7.

Harris, P. R., ed. Douai College Documents, 1639-1794. London: Catholic Record Society, 1972. Rev. by J. J. Silke,
CaHR, 62(Apr 1976):279-80.

Harrison, Kenneth. The Framework of Anglo-Saxon History to
A. D. 900. New York: Cam U Press, 1976. Rev. by B. W.
Scholz, HRNB, 4(Jl 1976):177-8.

Harrison, Lowell H. The Civil War in Kentucky. Lexington:
U Press Ky, 1975. Rev. by D. Lindsey, JAH, 63(Je 1976):
136.

Harriss, G. L. King, Parliament and Public Finance in Medieval
England to 1369. Oxford: Oxford U Press, 1975. Rev. by
E. Miller, EHR, 91(Oct 1976):841-3; M. Prestwich, History,
61(Je 1976):260-1.

Hart, C. R. The Early Charters of Northern England and the
North Midlands. Leicester: Leicester U Press, 1975. Rev.
by R. H. C. Davis, History, 61(Oct 1976):438-9.

Hart, Roger L. Redeemers, Bourbons, and Populists: Tennessee,
1870-1896. Baton Rouge: LSU Press, 1975. Rev. by J.
M. Kousser, JAH, 62(Mar 1976):1005-6; I. Unger, JSH, 42
(May 1976):291-2; J. H. Cartwright, THQ, 35(Spr 1976):106-8.

Hartley, Shirley Foster. Illegitimacy. Berkeley: U Cal Press,
1975. Rev. by D. S. Smith, JSoH, 10(Fall 1976):106-7.

Harvey, John. Early Nurserymen. Chichester: Phillimore, 1974.
Rev. by J. Varley, Archives, 12(Spr 1976):149.

_____. The Medieval Architect. London: Wayland, 1972.
Rev. by D. McLees, History, 61(Oct 1976):441-2.

_____. Medieval Craftsmen. London: Batsford, 1975. Rev.
by D. McLees, History, 61(Oct 1976):441-2.

Harwell, Richard B. Confederate Imprints at the Georgia Historical Society. Savannah, Ga.: The Society, 1975. Rev.
by W. P. Kellam, GHQ, 60(Spr 1976):83-4.

Harwood, Jonathan see Banton, Michael

Haskins, Ralph W., ed. see Johnson, Andrew

Hasquin, Hervé. Une mutation: Le "Pays de Charleroi" aux
XVIIe et XVIIIe siècles. Aux origines de la Révolution in-
dustrielle en Belgique. Brussels: Editions de l'Institut de
Sociologie, Université Libre de Bruxelles, 1971. Rev. by
F. F. Mendels, AHR, 81(Oct 1976):877.

167   HASWELL

Haswell, Jock. James II: Soldier and Sailor. New York: St.
  Martin's, 1972. Rev. by R. E. Boyer, CaHR, 62(Apr 1976):
  290-1.

Hatcher, John and T. C. Barker. A History of British Pewter.
  London: Longman, 1974. Rev. by P. Ramsey, EHR, 91(Apr
  1976):415-16.

Hatfield, Charles, ed. The Scientist and Ethical Decision. Downers Grove, Ill.: Intervarsity, 1973. Rev. by C. M. Smith,
  JCS, 17(Win 1975):142-4.

Hattaway, Herman. General Stephen D. Lee. Jackson: U Miss
  Press, 1976. Rev. by F. A. Dennis, JMiH, 38(Nov 1976):
  378-9.

Hattendorf, John B., ed. see Hayes, John D., ed.

Hauberg, Clifford A. Puerto Rico and the Puerto Ricans. New
  York: Twayne, 1974. Rev. by M. K. Vaughn, HAHR, 56
  (Feb 1976):165-6; F. O. Gatell, JAH, 63(Je 1976):198-9.

Haugh, R. Photius and the Carolingians: The Trinitarian Controversy. Belmont, Mass.: Nordland, 1975. Rev. by R. A.
  Markus, JEccH, 27(Apr 1976):213.

Haupt, Georges. Socialism and the Great War: The Collapse of
  the Second International. New York: Oxford U Press, 1972.
  Rev. by C. Landauer, AHR, 81(Apr 1976):379-80.

Havens, Thomas R. H. Farm and Nation in Modern Japan:
  Agrarian Nationalism, 1870-1940. Princeton, N.J.: Prin U
  Press, 1974. Rev. by A. Stone, AgH, 50(Jl 1976):535-6; H.
  D. Smith, II, JJS, 2(Aut 1975):131-46.

Havighurst, Alfred F. Radical Journalist: H. W. Massingham
  (1860-1924). New York: Cam U Press, 1974. Rev. by P.
  F. Clarke, AHR, 81(Feb 1976):143-4; J. D. Dunbabin, EHR,
  91(Apr 1976):449-50.

Havinden, M. A., ed. see Chalklin, C. W., ed.

Havran, Martin J. Caroline Courtier: The Life of Lord Cottington. Columbia: U SCar Press, 1973. Rev. by A. J. Loom-
  ie, CaHR, 62(Apr 1976):278-9.

Hawke, David Freeman. Franklin. New York: Harper and Row,
  1976. Rev. by R. J. Chaffin, HRNB, 4(Sep 1976):217-28.

_____. Paine. New York: Harper and Row, 1974. Rev. by
  T. Parsons, Jr., NYHSQ, 60(Jan/Apr 1976):72-4.

Hawkins, John N. Mao Tse-tung and Education: His Thoughts and
  Teachings. Hamden, Conn.: Linnet Books, 1974. Rev. by

R. F. Price, JAAS, 11(Jl-Oct 1976):227-9.

Hay, D., et al., eds. Albion's Fatal Tree: Crime and Society
in Eighteenth-Century England. London: Allen Lane, 1975.
Rev. by J. Cannon, History, 61(Oct 1976):451-3.

Hay, J. R. The Origins of Liberal Welfare Reform. London:
Macmillan, 1975. Rev. by E. P. Hennock, EHR, 91(Oct
1976):931; M. Bruce, History, 61(Je 1976):312.

Hayami, Yujiro, et al. A Century of Agricultural Growth in Japan.
Minneapolis: U Minn Press, 1975. Rev. by K. Yamamura,
JEH, 36(Sep 1976):759-60.

Hayes, Alden C. The Four Churches of Pecos. Albuquerque: U
NM Press, 1974. Rev. by J. L. Kessell, CaHR, 62(Jl 1976):
523-4.

Hayes, Grace P. World War I: A Compact History. New York:
Hawthorn, 1972. Rev. by L. L. Farrar, Jr., AHR, 81(Oct
1976):847.

Hayes, John D. and John B. Hattendorf, eds. The Writings of
Stephen B. Luce. Newport, R.I.: Naval War College, 1975.
Rev. by A. Hoogenboom, JAH, 62(Mar 1976):1028-9.

Hayes, Paul. The Nineteenth Century: 1814-80. New York: St.
Martin's, 1975. Rev. by W. D. Jones, AHR, 81(Oct 1976):
860-1; A. F. Peterson, HRNB, 4(Feb 1976):95.

_____. Quisling: The Career and Political Ideas of Vidkun
Quisling, 1887-1945. Bloomington: Ind U Press, 1972. Rev.
by H. E. Ellersieck, AHR, 81(Feb 1976):164.

Haynes, D. E. L. The Portland Vase. London: British Museum,
1975. Rev. by R. Nicholls, Antiquity, 50(Sep-Dec 1976):249-
50.

Haynes, Donald, ed. Virginiana in the Printed Book Collections of
the Virginia State Library. 2 vols. Richmond: Va St Library, 1975. Rev. by C. M. Gibson, JSH, 42(Feb 1976):
137-8; J. Meehan, VMHB, 84(Apr 1976):218-19.

Hays, H. R. Children of the Raven: The Seven Indian Nations of
the Northwest Coast. New York: McGraw-Hill, 1975. Rev.
by W. E. Unrau, A-I, 43(Spr 1976):305-6; D. L. Smith, OH,
85(Sum 1976):274.

Hayter, Earl W. Education in Transition: The History of Northern Illinois University, 1899-1974. De Kalb: N Ill Press,
1974. Rev. by M. Brickford, JISHS, 69(May 1976):153-4.

Hazard, H. W., ed. The Fourteenth and Fifteenth Centuries.

Vol. III. Madison: U Wis Press, 1975. Rev. by D. E. Queller, AHR, 81(Oct 1976):833; P. W. Edbury, EHR, 91(Jl 1976):603-6.

Hazlewood, Arthur. Economic Integration: The East African Experience. London: Heinemann, 1975. Rev. by P. Mosley, JMAS, 14(Je 1976):356-7.

Head, Sydney, W., ed. Broadcasting in Africa: A Continental Survey of Radio and Television. Philadelphia: Temple U Press, 1974. Rev. by R. G. Willis, Africa, 46(Num 1, 1976):107.

Headlam-Morley, James. A Memoir of the Paris Peace Conference, 1919. New York: Barnes and Noble, 1972. Rev. by H. N. Howard, AHR, 81(Apr 1976):380-1.

Headlee, Thomas J., Jr. Journal of the Senate of Virginia: November Session, 1795. Richmond: Va St Library, 1975. Rev. by J. A. Goldenberg, VMHB, 84(Jl 1976):376-7.

Heal, Felicity, ed. see O'Day, Rosemary, ed.

Healey, Robert M. The French Achievement: Private School Aid, a Lesson for America. New York: Paulist Press, 1974. Rev. by A. J. Menendoz, JCS, 18(Aut 1976):563-5.

Healy, Ann Erickson. The Russian Autocracy in Crisis, 1905-1907. Hamden, Conn.: Shoe String, 1976. Rev. by G. J. Bobango, HRNB, 5(Oct 1976):17.

Healy, David. Gunboat Diplomacy in the Wilson Era: The U.S. Navy in Haiti, 1915-1916. Madison: U Wis Press, 1976. Rev. by R. G. O'Connor, HRNB, 4(Aug 1976):191.

Healy, Kathleen. Frances Warde: American Founder of the Sisters of Mercy. New York: Seabury, 1973. Rev. by H. W. Casper, CaHR, 62(Jl 1976):486-7.

Hearder, H. and H. R. Loyn, eds. British Government and Administration. Cardiff: U Wales Press, 1974. Rev. by G. L. Harriss, EHR, 91(Apr 1976):475.

Heath, Jim F. Decade of Disillusionment: The Kennedy-Johnson Years. Bloomington: Ind U Press, 1975. Rev. by H. Parmet, AHR, 81(Je 1976):692-3; R. Griffith, JAH, 63(Dec 1976): 779-80; L. H. Curry, Jr., JSH, 42(May 1976):297-8.

Hebert, Robert F. see Ekelund, Robert B., Jr.

Hechinger, Fred M. and Grace Hechinger. Growing Up in America. New York: McGraw-Hill, 1975. Rev. by J. C. Kiger, JSH, 42(Aug 1976):449-50; R. D. Cohen, RAH, 4(Je 1976):158-63.

Hechter, Michael. Internal Colonialism: The Celtic Fringe in British National Development, 1536-1966. Berkeley: U Cal Press, 1975. Rev. by S. E. Prall, HRNB, 4(Apr 1976):135.

Heckart, Beverly. From Bassermann to Bebel: The Grand Bloc's Quest for Reform in the Kaiserreich, 1900-1914. New Haven, Conn.: Yale U Press, 1974. Rev. by E.-T. Wilke, AHR, 81 (Apr 1976):408-9; G. Eley, HJ, 19(Mar 1976):299-302.

Heeger, G. A. The Politics of Underdevelopment. New York: Macmillan, 1974. Rev. by F. Stewart, AfAf, 75(Apr 1976): 253-4.

Heermance, J. Noel. Charles W. Chesnutt, America's First Great Black Novelist. Hamden, Conn.: Archon, 1974. Rev. by F. R. Keller, AHR, 81(Feb 1976):215; N. Flusche, NCHR, 53 (Win 1976):83-4.

Heers, Jacques. Le Clan familial au Moyen Age. Paris: Presses U France, 1974. Rev. by J. R. Strayer, AHR, 81(Feb 1976): 109-10; P. S. Lewis, EHR, 91(Jan 1976):179-80.

Hégy, Pierre. L'Autorité dans le Catholicisme contemporain, du Syllabus à Vatican II. Paris Beauchesne, 1975. Rev. by J.-J. D'Aoust, CH, 45(Mar 1976):122-3.

Heick, W. H. and Roger Graham, eds. His Own Man: Essays in Honour of Reginald Marsden Lower. Montreal: McGill-Queens U Press, 1974. Rev. by S. M. Trofimenkoff, CHR, 57(Je 1976):188-9.

Heidhues, Mary F. Somers. Southeast Asia's Chinese Minorities. Hawthorne, Victoria, Australia: Longman, 1974. Rev. by M. Freedman, CQ, Jan 1976, pp. 141-2; D. Feeny, JEH, 36 (Sep 1976):760-1.

Heikal, Mohammed. The Road to Ramadan. New York: Quadrangle, 1975. Rev. by J. Shattan, Commentary, 61(Apr 1976):94-6.

Heisler, Helmuth. Urbanization and the Government of Migration: The Inter-relation of Urban and Rural Life in Zambia. New York: St. Martin's, 1974. Rev. by H. H. Werlin, AHR, 81 (Je 1976):641; D. M. Boswell, JAfH, 17(Num 1, 1976):159-60; B. Magubane, JMAS, 14(Dec 1976):719-21.

Heizer, Robert F. Elizabethan California. Ramona, Cal.: Ballena Press, 1974. Rev. by M. L. Heyman, Jr., JOW, 15 (Jan 1976):130-1.

Hekmat, Forough. Folk Tales of Ancient Persia. New York: Scholar's Facsimiles & Reprints, 1974. Rev. by J. R. Perry, JNES, 35(Oct 1976):298.

171   HELCK

Helck, Wolfgang and Eberhard Otto, eds. Lexikon der Agyptologie.
Vol. 1. Wiesbaden: Otto Harrassowtiz, 1972, 1973. Rev. by
P. L. Shinnie, JNES, 35(Jan 1976):54-5.

Held, Joseph, ed. see Winters, Stanley B., ed.

Hellman, Ronald G. and H. Jon Rosenbaum, eds. Latin America:
The Search for a New International Role. New York: Halstead, 1975. Rev. by R. Roett, HAHR, 56(Nov 1976):668-9.

Helmcken, John Sebastian. The Reminiscences of Doctor John Se-
bastian Helmcken. (Dorothy Blakey Smigh, ed.) Vancouver:
U British Columbia Press, 1975. Rev. by M. Clark, Jr.,
OrHQ, 77(Sep 1976):294.

Helmer, John. Bringing the War Home: The American Soldier in
Vietnam and After. London: Collier-Macmillan, 1974. Rev.
by E. Ranson, JAmS, 10(Apr 1976):122-4.

Helmholz, R. H. Marriage Litigation in Medieval England. New
York: Cam U Press, 1975. Rev. by W. H. Dunham, Jr.,
AHR, 81(Apr 1976):369-70; R. E. Reynolds, CH, 45(Mar
1976):106.

Helmreich, Paul C. From Paris to Sevres: The Partition of the
Ottoman Empire at the Peace Conference of 1919-1920. Co-
lumbus: Ohio St U Press, 1974. Rev. by A. Williams,
EHR, 91(Jl 1976):686; D. Dakin, History, 61(Feb 1976):141.

Helms, Mary W. Middle America: A Culture History of Heartland
and Frontiers. Englewood Cliffs, N.J.: Prentice-Hall, 1975.
Rev. by R. C. Padden, AHR, 81(Apr 1976):472-3.

Hemesath, Caroline. From Slave to Priest. Chicago: Franciscan
Herald, 1974. Rev. by E. Misch, CaHR, 62(Jl 1976):524.

Hemperly, Marion R., ed. see Goff, John H.

_____, ed. see Utley, Francis Lee, ed.

Hemphill, W. Edwin, ed. see Calhoun, John C.

Henderson, H. James. Party Politics in the Continental Congress.
New York: McGraw-Hill, 1974. Rev. by P. H. Smith, FHQ,
54(Jan 1976):391-3; E. J. Ferguson, JAH, 62(Mar 1976):980-
1; O. S. Ireland, PH, 43(Oct 1976):377-9.

Henderson, Harry B., III. Versions of the Past: The Historical
Imagination in American Fiction. New York: Oxford U Press,
1974. Rev. by H. N. Smith, AHR, 81(Apr 1976):438-9; H.
Brogan, History, 61(Oct 1976):423-4.

Henderson, P. D. India: The Energy Sector. Delhi: Oxford U

Press, 1975. Rev. by Sreedhar, IQ, 32(Apr-Je 1976):254-5.

Henderson, Richard N. The King in Every Man: Evolutionary Trends in Omitsha Ibo Society. New Haven, Conn.: Yale U Press, 1972. Rev. by E. P. Skinner, CSSH, 18(Apr 1976): 271-5.

Henderson, W. O. The Rise of German Industrial Power 1834-1914. Berkeley: U Cal Press, 1976. Rev. by A. P. Krammer, Historian, 39(Nov 1976):130-1; W. Braatz, HRNB, 4(Aug 1976): 205.

Hendricks, Gordon. Eadweard Muybridge: The Father of the Motion Picture. New York: Grossman, 1975. Rev. by D. Longwell, Smithsonian, 6(Jl 1975):104-5.

Henige, David. African Chronology. Oxford: Oxford U Press, 1973. Rev. by G. S. P. Freeman-Grenville, AfAf, 75(Jan 1976):104-8.

_____. The Chronology of Oral Tradition: Quest for a Chimera. New York: Oxford U Press, 1974. Rev. by D. L. Newman, AmArc, 39(Jan 1976):61-2; R. C. C. L., JAfH, 17(Num 2, 1976):308-9.

Henke, J. England in Hitler's Politischen Kalkül 1935-1939. Boppard am Rhein: Boldt, 1973. Rev. by K. Robbins, History, 61(Feb 1976):143-4.

Henke, Warren A., comp. Prairie Politics: Parties and Platforms in North Dakota, 1889-1914. Bismarck: St Historical Society of ND, 1974. Rev. by D. F. Rylance, NDH, 43(Spr 1976):102.

Hennschke, Ekkehard. Landesherrschaft und Bergbauwirtshaft. Berlin: Dunker und Humblot, 1974. Rev. by R. Knauerhase, JEH, 36(Je 1976):472-6.

Henri, Florette. Black Migration: Movement North, 1900-1920. Garden City, N.Y.: Anchor, 1975. Rev. by N. J. Weiss, AHR, 81(Je 1976):681-2; W. H. Harris, IMH, 72(Mar 1976): 85-6; G. W. Reid, JSH, 42(Feb 1976):131-2; R. Gavins, NCHR, 53(Win 1976):103-4.

Henriksen, Georg. Hunters in the Barrens: The Naskapi on the Edge of the White Man's World. n.p.: Memorial U of Newfoundland, 1973. Rev. by H. F. McGee, Jr., AA, 78(Mar 1976):157.

Henry, Frances. Forgotten Canadians: The Blacks of Nova Scotia. Ontario: Longman Canada, 1973. Rev. by N. E. Whitten and D. S. Whitten, AA, 78(Mar 1976):159-60.

Henry, Stuart C. Unvanquished Puritan: A Portrait of Lyman
    Beecher. Grand Rapids, Mich.: Eerdmans, 1973. Rev. by
    M. H. Rice, CaHR, 62(Jl 1976):488-9.

Henry, Will. Tom Horn. Philadelphia: Lippincott, 1975. Rev.
    by L. Metz, JAriH, 17(Spr 1976):114-15.

Henson, Margaret Swett. Samuel May Williams: Early Texas
    Entrepreneur. College Station: Texas A and M U Press,
    1976. Rev. by L. J. White, JSH, 42(Nov 1976):592-3.

Her Majesty's Stationery Office. Calendar of Inquisitions Post Mor-
    tem. Vol. XVI: 7-15 Richard II. London: HMSO, 1974.
    Rev. by D. M. Owen, Archives, 12(Spr 1976):144.

_____. Calendar of the Patent Rolls, Elizabeth I, Vol. VI,
    1572-1573. London: HMSO, 1973. Rev. by J. Hurstfield,
    EHR, 91(Jan 1976):127-9.

_____. Documents on British Foreign Policy 1919-1939, Series
    IA, Vol. IV, European and Security Questions 1927-8. Lon-
    don: HMSO, 1971. Rev. by W. V. Wallace, EHR, 91(Jl
    1976):684.

Herbert, Eugenia W. see Lopez, Claude-Anne

Hercules, Frank. American Society and Black Revolution. New
    York: Harcourt, Brace, Jovanovich, n. d. Rev. by D. L.
    Watson, Crisis, 83(May 1976):165-6.

Herkenrath, Erland, ed. see Gäbler, Ulrich, ed.

Herm, Gerhard. The Phoenicians: The Purple Empire of the An-
    cient World. New York: Morrow, 1975. Rev. by M. Ham-
    mond, Mankind, 5(Oct 1976):58-9.

Hermann, A. H. A History of the Czechs. London: Allen Lane,
    1975. Rev. by W. V. Wallace, History, 61(Feb 1976):88-9.

Hermann, Isaac. Memoirs of a Confederate Veteran, 1861-1865.
    Lakemont, Ga.: CSA Press, 1974. Rev. by R. D. Hoffsom-
    mer, CWTI, 15(Je 1976):49-50.

Hermann, Ruth. Gold and Silver Colossus: William Morris Stewart
    and His Southern Bride. Sparks, Nev.: Davis, 1975. Rev.
    by J. V. Hawks, JMiH, 38(Aug 1976):321-2.

Hermanns, Matthias. Die Oraon. Wiesbaden: Franz Steiner, 1973.
    Rev. by C. S. Littleton, AA, 78(Je 1976):397-8.

Hero, Alfred O., Jr. American Religious Groups View Foreign
    Policy. Durham, N.C.: Duke U Press, 1973. Rev. by P.
    McNeal, CaHR, 62(Oct 1976):683-5.

Herold, Joyce see McKee, Barbara and Edwin

Herring, George C., ed. see Campbell, Thomas M., ed.

Herring, Reuben. The Baptist Almanac. Nashville, Tenn.: Broadman, 1976. Rev. in BHH, 11(Jan 1976):64.

Herrmann, Georgina see Mallowan, Max

Hervey, Maurice. Días oscuros en Chile. Buenos Aires: Editorial Francisco de Aguirre, 1974. Rev. by T. M. Bader, HAHR, 56(Aug 1976):494.

Herwig, Holger H. The German Naval Officer Corps: A Social and Political History, 1890-1918. London: Oxford U Press, 1973. Rev. by J. Gooch, ESR, 6(Jl 1976):396-8; M. Kitchen, JMH, 48(Je 1976):348-50.

Herzeld, Hans. Berlin in der Weltpolitik 1945-1970. New York: Walter de Gruyter, 1973. Rev. by R. Spencer, CHR, 57(Mar 1976):105.

Herzog, Chaim. The War of Atonement. Boston: Little, Brown, n.d. Rev. by J. Shattam, Commentary, 61(Apr 1976):94-6.

Hessen, Robert. Steel Titan: The Life of Charles M. Schwab. New York: Oxford U Press, 1975. Rev. by G. G. Eggert, AHR, 81(Oct 1976):986-7.

Hewes, Laurence. Rural Development: World Frontiers. Ames: Ia St U Press, 1974. Rev. by R. D. Stevens, AgH, 50(Jl 1976):526-7.

Hewlett, Richard G. and Francis Duncan. Nuclear Navy, 1946-1962. Chicago: U Chicago Press, 1974. Rev. by R. G. O'Connor, AHR, 81(Je 1976):695-6 ; G. E. Wheeler, PHR, 45 (Aug 1976):460-1.

Hewson, M. Anthony. Giles of Rome and the Medieval Theory of Conception. London: Athlone, 1975. Rev. by J. Dunbabin, History, 61(Je 1976):261-2.

Hexter, J. H. The Vision of Politics on the Eve of the Reformation. London: Allen Lane, 1973. Rev. by R. J. Knecht, History, 61(Feb 1976):107.

Hey, David G. An English Rural Community: Myddle Under the Tudors and Stuarts. Atlantic Highlands, N.J.: Humanities-Hillary, 1974. Rev. by C. Z. Wiener, AHR, 81(Apr 1976): 383-4; A. Woolrych, EHR, 91(Jan 1976):198-9.

Heyck, Thomas William. The Dimensions of British Radicalism: The Case of Ireland, 1874-95. Urbana: U Ill Press, 1974.

Rev. by M. V. Hazel, JMH, 48(Mar 1976):143-5.

Heyd, Uriel. Studies in Old Ottoman Criminal Law. Oxford:
    Clarendon Press, 1973. Rev. by F. Iz, JNES, 35(Oct 1976):
    291-3.

Heyman, Abigail. Growing Up Female: A Personal Photojournal.
    New York: Holt, Rinehart and Winston, 1974. Rev. by K.
    Noble, AA, 78(Mar 1976):153-4.

Hiernaux, Jean. The People of Africa. London: Weidenfeld and
    Nicolson, 1974. Rev. by D. F. Roberts, JAfH, 17(Num 3,
    1976):445-7.

Higgs, Robert J. and Ambrose N. Manning, eds. Voices from the
    Hills. New York: Ungar, 1975. Rev. by J. E. Stealey, III,
    NCHR, 53(Sum 1976):323-4.

Higham, Charles. Warner Brothers. New York: Scribner's, 1975.
    Rev. by W. Hughes, JAH, 63(Je 1976):176-7.

Higham, John. Send These to Me: Jews and Other Immigrants in
    Urban America. New York: Atheneum, 1975. Rev. by R.
    D. Marcus, JAH, 63(Sep 1976):444-5.

Higham, Robin, ed. Intervention or Abstention: The Dilemma of
    American Foreign Policy. Lexington: U Press Ky, 1975.
    Rev. by R. H. Ferrell, JAH, 63(Sep 1976):461; W. O. Walk-
    er, III, PHR, 45(Nov 1976):631-2.

Highwater, Jamake. Indian America. New York: McKay, 1975.
    Rev. by A. Silberman, ChOk, 54(Spr 1976):153-4.

Higounet, Charles, et al., eds. La seigneurie et le vignoble de
    Chateau Latour: Histoire d'un grand cru du Médoc (XIVe-XXe
    siècle). Vols. I and II. Bordeaux: Fédération historique
    du Sud-Ouest, 1974. Rev. by C. K. Warner, AHR, 81(Apr
    1976):393-4.

Hildebrand, Klaus. The Foreign Policy of the Third Reich. Lon-
    don: Batsford, 1973. Rev. by E. Hahn, CHR, 57(Mar 1976):
    104-5.

Hill, Christopher. Change and Continuity in Seventeenth-Century
    England. London: Weidenfeld and Nicolson, 1975. Rev. by
    A. Woolrych, History, 61(Feb 1976):113-14.

Hill, Derek Ingram. Christ's Glorious Church: The Story of
    Canterbury Cathedral. London: S. P. C. K., 1976. Rev. by
    H. T. Lewis, HMPEC, 45(Dec 1976):463-4.

Hill, Sir Francis. Victorian Lincoln. Cambridge: Cam U Press,
    1975. Rev. by R. G. Wilson, History, 61(Je 1976):304-5.

HILL 176

Hill, John Hugh and Lauritia L. Hill, trans. Peter Tudebode. Philadelphia: American Philosophical Society, 1974. Rev. by R. H. C. Davis, EHR, 91(Jan 1976):175-6.

Hill, L. M. , ed. The Ancient State Authoritie and Proceedings of the Court of Requests by Sir Julius Caesar. Cambridge: Cam U Press, 1975. Rev. by S. E. Prall, AHR, 81(Je 1976):582-3; E. W. Ives, History, 61(Je 1976):283-4; F. L. Cheyette, HRNB, 4(Jan 1976):65.

Hill, Leonidas. Die Weizsächer Papiere 1933-1950. Berlin: Propyläen Verlag, 1974. Rev. by K. Robbins, EHR, 91(Apr 1976):466-7; V. R. Berghahn, History, 61(Oct 1976):473-4.

Hill, M. S. see Oaks, D. H.

Hill, Richard, ed. see Toniolo, Elias, ed.

Hill, Rosalind M. T., ed. The Rolls and Register of Bishop Oliver Sutton, Vol. VII. Lincoln: Lincoln Record Society, 1975. Rev. by K. Edwards, EHR, 91(Oct 1976):896-7.

Hill, W. Speed, ed. Studies in Richard Hooker: Essays Preliminary to an Edition of His Works. Cleveland, Ohio: Press of Case Western Reserve U, 1972. Rev. by L. H. Carlson, AHR, 81(Feb 1976):129-30.

Hillerbrand, Hans J. The World of the Reformation. London: Dent, 1975. Rev. by H. G. Koenigsberger, History, 61(Je 1976):276.

Hillers, Delbert R. Lamentations. Garden City, N.Y.: Doubleday, 1972. Rev. by J. H. Tigay, JNES, 35(Apr 1976):140-3.

Hillman, Eugene. Polygamy Reconsidered: African Plural Marriage and the Christian Churches. Maryknoll, N.Y.: Orbis, 1975. Rev. by C. O. Nwanunobi, JMAS, 14(Dec 1976):729-30.

Hillman, Jordan Jay. The Parliamentary Structuring of British Road-Rail Freight Coordination. Evanston, Ill.: Northwestern U, 1973. Rev. by D. H. Aldcroft, JTH, 3(Sep 1976):300.

Hilton, R. H. The English Peasantry in the Later Middle Ages. New York: Oxford U Press, 1975. Rev. by W. O. Ault, AHR, 81(Je 1976):571-2; B. Dobson, History, 61(Je 1976):262-4.

Hilton, Rodney. Bond Men Made Free: Medieval Peasant Movements and the English Rising of 1381. London: Temple Smith, 1973. Rev. by P. R. Hyams, EHR, 91(Jl 1976):634-5.

Hilton, Stanley E. Brazil and the Great Powers, 1930-1939: The Politics of Trade Rivalry. Austin: U Texas Press, 1975.

Rev. by F. D. McCann, HAHR, 56(Nov 1976):670-3; T. Blossom, HRNB, 4(Feb 1976):81-2; R. M. Levine, TAm, 33(Oct 1976):371-2.

Himmelfarb, Gertrude. On Liberty and Liberalism: The Case of John Stuart Mill. New York: Knopf, 1974. Rev. by A. Ryan, AHR, 81(Feb 1976):139-40.

Hinde, Wendy. George Canning. London: Collins, 1973. Rev. by M. E. Goldstein, JMH, 48(Mar 1976):132-5.

Hindess, Barry and Paul Q. Hirst. Pre-Capitalist Modes of Production. Boston: Routledge and Kegan Paul, 1975. Rev. by M. Bronfenbrenner, JEH, 36(Sep 1976):761-3; M. Dobb, History, 61(Feb 1976):91.

Hindle, Brooke, ed. America's Wooden Age: Aspects of Its Early Technology. Tarrytown, N.Y.: Sleepy Hollow Restorations, 1975. Rev. by T. J. Donaghy, JAH, 63(Je 1976):114-5.

Hindle, G. B. Provision for the Relief of the Poor in Manchester 1754-1826. Manchester: Manchester U Press, 1975. Rev. by D. Bythell, EHR, 91(Oct 1976):917-18.

Hines, Donald M. An Index of Archived Resources for a Folklife and Cultural History of the Inland Pacific Northwest Frontier. Ann Arbor: University Microfilms, 1976. Rev. by C. de Lorge, OrHQ, 77(Sep 1976):297.

Hines, Thomas S. Burnham of Chicago: Architect and Planner. New York: Oxford U Press, 1974. Rev. by K. T. Jackson, AHR, 81(Feb 1976):215.

Hingley, Ronald. Joseph Stalin: Man and Legend. New York: McGraw-Hill, 1974. Rev. by S. M. Horak, AHR, 81(Feb 1976):189.

Hinnebusch, William A. The History of the Dominican Order. Vol. 2. New York: Alba House, 1973. Rev. by D. Knowles, CaHR, 62(Jan 1976):92-3.

Hinshaw, Robert E. Panajachel: A Guatemalan Town in Thirty-Year Perspective. Pittsburgh: U Pittsburgh Press, 1975. Rev. by B. Saler, HAHR, 56(Aug 1976):497-8.

Hintze, Otto. The Historical Essays of Otto Hintze. (Felix Gilbert, ed.) London: Oxford U Press, 1975. Rev. by H. M. Scott, History, 61(Oct 1976):454-6.

Hirschmeier, Johannes and Tsunehiko Yui. The Development of Japanese Business 1600-1973. Cambridge: Har U Press, 1975. Rev. by K. Yamamura, BHR, 50(Spr 1976):101-3; K. Taira, JEH, 36(Sep 1976):764-5.

Hirst, Derek. The Representative of the People?: Voters and Voting in England Under the Early Stuarts. Cambridge: Cam U Press, 1975. Rev. by L. G. Schwoerer, AHR, 81(Oct 1976):854-5; R. Ashton, EHR, 91(Oct 1976):848-50; A. Woolrych, History, 61(Oct 1976):285-6; B. Worden, HJ, 19(Je 1976):546-9.

Hirst, Paul Q. see Hindess, Barry

Hiskett, Mervyn. The Sword of Truth: The Life and Times of the Shehu Usuman Dan Fodio. New York: Oxford U Press, 1973. Rev. by J. R. Willis, JAfH, 17(Num 2, 1976):313-15.

Hitchcock, James. The Decline and Fall of Radical Catholicism. New York: Doubleday, 1971. Rev. by J. L. Garrett, Jr., JCS, 17(Spr 1975):335-8.

Hitti, Philip K. Capital Cities of Arab Islam. Minneapolis: U Minn Press, 1973. Rev. by A. C. Hess, AHR, 81(Oct 1976): 788-99.

Hix, John. The Glass House. Cambridge, Mass.: MIT Press, 1974. Rev. by B. C. Hacker, AHR, 81(Oct 1976):815.

Hixson, William B. Moorfield Storey and the Abolitionist Tradition. New York: Oxford U Press, 1972. Rev. by R. D. Marcus, JAH, 63(Dec 1976):754-5.

Ho, Ping-T. The Cradle of the East: An Inquiry into the In-digenous Origins of Techniques and Ideas of Neolithic and Early Historic China, 5000-1000 B.C. Chicago: U Chicago Press, 1976. Rev. by R. Taylor, HRNB, 4(Aug 1976):198.

Hoak, D. E. The King's Council in the Reign of Edward VI. New York: Cam U Press, 1976. Rev. by J. W. Zophy, HRNB, 5(Oct 1976):20-1.

Hoberg, Hermann, ed. Die Einnahmen der Apostolischen Kammer unter Innozenz VI. Paderborn: Ferdinand Schoningh Verlag, 1972. Rev. by J. E. Weakland, CaHR, 62(Jan 1976):100-2.

Hobsbawm, E. J. The Age of Capitalism, 1848-1875. New York: Scribner's, 1976. Rev. by W. L. Langer, AHR, 81(Oct 1976): 817; M. Berger, HRNB, 4(May/Je 1976):150-1.

Hockey, S. F., ed. The Beaulieu Cartulary. Southampton: Southampton U Press, 1974. Rev. by R. H. Hilton, EHR, 91(Oct 1976):892-3; E. Mason, JEccH, 27(Jan 1976):91.

Hoda, Mansur. Problems of Unemployment. New Delhi: Allied Publishers, 1974. Rev. by H. Venkatasubbiah, IQ, 32(Jan-Mar 1976):113-14.

Hodgson, Marshall G. S.   The Venture of Islam: Conscience and
History in a World Civilization.   3 vols.   Chicago: U Chicago
Press, 1974.   Rev. by A. C. Hess, AHR, 81(Oct 1976):788-
99; C. E. Dawn, Historian, 39(Nov 1976):113-15.

Hoensch, Jörg.   Sozialverfassung und politische Reform.   Cologne:
Böhlau Verlag, 1973.   Rev. by E. K. Bacon, JMH, 48(Mar
1976):169-71.

Hoffman, Abraham.   Unwanted Mexican Americans in the Great
Depression: Repatriation Pressures, 1929-1939.   Tucson:
U Ariz Press, 1974.   Rev. by D. S. Chandler, ETHJ, 14
(Spr 1976):69-70; M. T. Garcia, HAHR, 56(Feb 1976):158-61;
M. P. Servin, JAH, 62(Mar 1976):1044-5.

Hoffman, Gerhard and Wilhelm Wille, eds.   World Mission and
World Communism.   Richmond, Va.:   John Knox Press, 1971.
Rev. by J. C. Anderson, JCS, 17(Aut 1975):537-8.

Hoffman, Ross J. S.   The Marquis: A Study of Lord Rockingham
1730-1832.   New York: Fordham U Press, 1973.   Rev. by
C. B. Cone, CaHR, 62(Apr 1976):303-4; S. W. Jackson, CHR,
57(Mar 1976):69-71.

Hoffmann, Alfred, et al.   Bauernland Oberösterreich: Entwicklungsgeschichte seiner Land- und Forstwirtschaft.   Linz, Austria:
Rudolf Trauner Verlag, 1974.   Rev. by F. A. J. Szabo, JEH,
36(Je 1976):476-7.

Hoffmann, Donald.   The Architecture of John Wellborn Root.   Baltimore: JHU Press, 1973.   Rev. by W. Weisman, JAH, 62
(Mar 1976):1027-8.

Hoffmann, Stanley.   Decline or Renewal?   France Since the 1930's.
New York: Viking, 1974.   Rev. by G. Wright, JMH, 48(Mar
1976):154-5.

Hoffmeister, John Edward.   Land from the Sea: The Geologic Story
of South Florida.   Coral Gables: U Miami Press, 1974.
Rev. by H. K. Brooks, FHQ, 54(Jan 1976):385.

Höflechner, Walter.   Die Gesandten der europäischen Mächte,
vornehmlich des Kaisers und des Reiches, 1490-1500.   Vienna:
Hermann Böhlaus Nachf., 1972.   Rev. by G. E. Rothenberg,
AHR, 81(Feb 1976):115.

Hofmann, George F.   The Super Sixth: History of the 6th Armored
Division in World War II and Its Post-War Associaton.   Louis-
ville, Ky.:   Sixth Armored Division Assn., 1975.   Rev. by M.
Blumenson, JAH, 63(Dec 1976):774.

Hofsommer, Donovan L.   Katy Northwest: The Story of a Branch
Line Railroad.   Boulder, Colo.:   Pruett, 1976.   Rev. by A.

M. Gibson, NMHR, 51(Oct 1976):345-6.

_____. Prairie Oasis: The Railroads, Steamboats and Resorts of Iowa's Spirit Lake Country. Des Moines: Waukon and Mississippi Press, 1975. Rev. by H. R. Grant, AI, 43(Win 1976):234-5.

Hoge, Dean R. Commitment on Campus: Changes in Religion and Values Over Five Decades. Philadelphia: Westminster Press, 1974. Rev. by R. B. Flowers, JCS, 18(Win 1976):136-8.

Hogg, James, ed. Rubricae Cartusiae Gosnayensis. Salzburg, Austria: Institut für Englische Sprache, 1974. Rev. by R. Kay, CH, 45(Je 1976):250-1.

Holand, Robert Charles. The Hermeneutics of Peter Riedeman (1506-1556). Basel: Fredrich Reinhardt Kommissionsverlag, 1970. Rev. by H. Poettcker, MQR, 50(Apr 1976):140-2.

Holcombe, Lee. Victorian Ladies at Work. Hamden, Conn.: Shoe String, 1973. Rev. by C. Thomas, CHR, 57(Mar 1976): 76-8.

Holden, William Curry. Alton Huston: Reminiscences of a South Plains Youth. San Antonio, Tex.: Trinity U Press, n.d. Rev. by D. G. Muckelroy, ETHJ, 14(Spr 1976):63; B. Procter, NMHR, 51(Apr 1976):164-5; F. W. Rathjen, SWHQ, 80(Oct 1976):241-2.

Holeczek, Heinz. Humanistische Bibelphilologie als Reformproblem bei Erasmus von Rotterdam, Thomas More und William Tyndale. Leiden: Brill, 1975. Rev. by S. L. Greenslade, JEccH, 27(Apr 1976):197-8.

Holifield, E. Brooks. The Covenant Sealed: The Development of Puritan Sacramental Theology in Old and New England, 1570-1720. New Haven, Conn.: Yale U Press, 1974. Rev. by F. J. Bremer, AHR, 81(Oct 1976):956-7; T. A. Schafer, CH, 45(Sep 1976):387.

Holland, James C., ed. see Altholz, Josef L., ed.

Hollenweger, Walter J. The Pentecostals: The Charismatic Movement in the Churches. Minneapolis: Augusburg, 1972. Rev. by B. E. Patterson, JCS, 18(Spr 1976):339-41.

Holley, Donald. Uncle Sam's Farmers: The New Deal Communities in the Lower Mississippi Valley. Urbana: U Ill Press, 1975. Rev. by W. W. Rogers, AHR, 81(Oct 1976):997; D. E. Schob, Historian, 39(Nov 1976):160-1; J. L. Shover, JAH, 63(Sep 1976):455-6; M. V. Namorato, JMiH, 38(May 1976):230-2; D. H. Grubbs, JSH, 42(May 1976):296-7; W. D. Aeschbacher, OH, 85(Aut 1976):338.

181   HOLLINGER

Hollinger, David A. Morris R. Cohen and the Scientific Ideal.
Cambridge, Mass.: MIT Press, 1975. Rev. by E. A. Purcell, Jr., JAH, 63(Dec 1976):763-4; B. Kuklick, RAH, 4(Je
1976):258-61.

Hollis, Patricia, ed. Pressure from Without in Early Victorian
England. New York: St. Martin's, 1974. Rev. by F. M.
Leventhal, AHR, 81(Apr 1976):387-8; N. Gash, EHR, 91(Jan
1976):215-16; N. McCord, History, 61(Feb 1976):125-6.

Hollon, Eugene. The Great American Desert, Then and Now. Lincoln: U Neb Press, 1975. Rev. by E. L. Schapsmeier, JOW,
15(Jan 1976):122.

Holloway, Thomas H. The Brazilian Coffee Valorization of 1906:
Regional Politics and Economic Dependence. Madison: State
Historical Society of Wisconsin, 1975. Rev. by C. M. Peláez,
BHR, 50(Spr 1976):110-11; A. Wright, HAHR, 56(Aug 1976):
495; D. E. Worcester, HRNB, 4(Jan 1976):61.

Holmes, Clive. The Eastern Association in the English Civil War.
New York: Cam U Press, 1974. Rev. by P. H. Hardacre,
AHR, 81(Je 1976):583; S. R. Smith, Historian, 38(Feb 1976):
332-3; D. H. Pennington, History, 61(Je 1976):287; D. Under-
down, JMH, 48(Je 1976):324-6.

Holmes, George. Europe: Hierarchy and Revolt 1320-1450. London: Fontana, 1975. Rev. by J. Larner, History, 61(Je
1976):262.

_____. The Good Parliament. New York: Oxford U Press,
1975. Rev. by A. R. Myers, EHR, 91(Oct 1976):901-2; F.
L. Cheyette, HRNB, 4(Mar 1976):113.

Holmes, Michael S. The New Deal in Georgia: An Administrative
History. Westport, Conn.: Greenwood, 1975. Rev. by J.
C. Cobb, AHR, 81(Oct 1976):997-8.

Hölscher, Fernande. Corpus Vasorum Antiquorum, Deutschland
39, Würzburg, Martin von Wagner Museum I. Munich: C.
H. Beck'sche Verlagsbuchhandlung, 1975. Rev. by J. W.
Hayes, AJA, 80(Fall 1976):432-3.

Holt, P. M. Studies in the History of the Near East. London:
Frank Cass, 1973. Rev. by J. A. Crabbs, Jr., JNES, 35
(Oct 1976):295-6.

Holzhueter, John O. Madeline Island and the Chequamegon Region.
Madison: St Historical Society Wis, 1974. Rev. by R. R.
Gilman, MinnH, 45(Spr 1976):35.

Hood, Miriam. Gunboat Diplomacy: Great Power Pressure in
Venezuela, 1895-1905. London: Allen and Unwin, 1975.
Rev. by J. Smith, History, 61(Oct 1976):428-9.

Hoogenboom, Ari and Olive Hoogenboom. A History of the ICC:
    From Panacea to Palliative. New York: Norton, 1976. Rev.
    by R. E. Shaw, HRNB, 4(May/Je 1976):145-6; T. K. McGraw,
    JAH, 63(Dec 1976):740-1; E. D. Odom, JSH, 42(Nov 1976):
    599-600.

Hooker, J. R.   Henry Sylvester Williams: Imperial Pan-Africanist.
    London: Rex Collings, 1975. Rev. by M. C. Fierce, JMAS,
    14(Mar 1976):173-5.

Hooker, Thomas. Thomas Hooker: Writings in England and Hol-
    land, 1626-1633. (George H. Williams and Norman Petit,
    eds.). Cambridge: Harvard U Press, 1975. Rev. by E.
    Emerson, NEQ, 49(Sep 1976):468-70.

Hooper, Edwin Bickford. Mobility, Support, Endurance: A Story
    of Naval Operational Logistics in the Vietnam War, 1965-1968.
    Washington: Naval History Div., Dept. of Navy, 1972. Rev.
    by R. D. O'Connor, AHR, 81(Je 1976):695-6.

Hoopes, Alban W.   The Road to the Little Big Horn--and Beyond.
    New York: Vantage, 1975. Rev. by R. M. Utley, AHR, 81
    (Oct 1976):981; R. N. Ellis, JAH, 62(Mar 1976):1010-11.

Hoopes, Donnelson F.   see   Moure, Nancy Wall

Hoover, John P.   Sucre, soldado y revolucionario. Cumana,
    Venezuela: Editorial de la Universidad de Oriente, 1975.
    Rev. by J. de Grummond, HAHR, 56(May 1976):322-3.

Hopkins, Joseph.   The Armstrong Empire: A Look at the World-
    wide Church of God. Grand Rapids, Mich.: Eerdmans, 1974.
    Rev. by B. L. Lanning, JCS, 17(Spr 1975):347-8.

Hopsommer, Donovan L.   Prairie Oasis. Des Moines, Ia.:
    Waukon and Mississippi Press, 1975. Rev. by L. K. Dyson,
    NDH, 43(Win 1976):43.

Horgan, Paul.   Lamy of Sante Fe: His Life and Times. New
    York: Farrar, Straus and Giroux, 1975. Rev. by V. West-
    phall, A & W, 18(Sum 1976):207-8; J. L. Kessell, CaHR, 62
    (Jl 1976):501-2; R. H. Vigil, NMHR, 51(Jan 1976):76-8.

Horn, Huston.   The Pioneers. New York: Time-Life, 1974. Rev.
    by J. W. Franks, ChOk, 54(Sum 1976):292.

Horton, Adey.   The Child Jesus. New York: Dial, n.d. Rev. by
    W. Kramer, Mankind, 5(Je 1976):12-13.

Horton, Louise.   In the Hills of the Pennyroyal: A History of Allen
    County, Kentucky, from 1815 to 1888. Austin, Tx.: White
    Cross, 1975. Rev. by R. Mathis, HRNB, 4(Apr 1976):120-1.

Horvat, Branko, Mihailo Marković and Rudi Supek, eds. Self-
Governing Socialism, a Reader. 2 vols. New York: Interna-
tional Arts and Sciences Press, 1975. Rev. by K. Amdur,
JEH, 36(Sep 1976):766.

Hosford, David H. Nottingham, Nobles, and the North: Aspects of
the Revolution of 1688. Hamden, Conn.: Archon, 1976. Rev.
by H. S. Reinmuth, Jr., HRNB, 4(Aug 1976):207.

Hosking, Geoffrey A. The Russian Constitutional Experiment:
Government and Duma, 1907-1914. New York: Cam U Press,
1973. Rev. by B.-C. Pinchuk, AHR, 81(Apr 1976):427-8.

Hostetler, John A. Hutterite Society. Baltimore: JHU Press, 1974.
Rev. by V. Peters, AgH, 50(Jl 1976):548-9; J. W. Jolliff,
JCS, 18(Win 1976):122-3.

Houghton, Samuel G. A Trace of Desert Waters: The Great Basin
Story. Glendale, Cal.: A. H. Clark, 1976. Rev. by J. E.
Edwards, A & W, 18(Win 1976):390-2; D. D. Evans, JAriH,
17(Aut 1976):349.

Hourani, George F. Islamic Rationalism: The Ethics of 'Abd al-
Jabbar. Oxford: Clarendon Press, 1971. Rev. by L. V.
Berman, IJMES, 7(Apr 1976):316-9.

Hovannisian, Richard G. The Republic of Armenia. Vol. I.
Berkeley: U Cal Press, 1971. Rev. by F. Kazemzadeh,
IJMES, 7(Apr 1976):308-9.

Hovi, Kalervo. The Emergence of the New French Eastern European
Alliance Policy, 1971-1919. Turku: Turun Yliopisto, 1975.
Rev. by M. C. Siney, AHR, 81(Je 1976):610-11.

Howard, Christopher. Britain and the "Casus Belli," 1822-1902:
A Study of Britain's International Position from Canning to
Salisbury. Atlantic Highlands, N.J.: Humanities Press, 1974.
Rev. by R. A. Cosgrove, AHR, 81(Feb 1976):137; K. Bourne,
History, 61(Feb 1976):130.

_____ and Peter Gordon, eds. The Cabinet Journal of Dudley
Ryder, Viscount Sandon, 1878. London: Institute of Historical
Research, 1974. Rev. by J. P. Prest, EHR, 91(Jan 1976):
222; A. Ramm, History, 61(Feb 1976):132-3.

Howard, Deborah. Jacopo Sansovino: Architecture and Patronage
in Renaissance Venice. New Haven: Yale U Press, 1975.
Rev. by T. A. Fabiano, AHR, 81(Oct 1976):892; D. S. Chambers, EHR, 90(Oct 1976):903-4; K. H. Dannenfeldt, HRNB, 4
(Feb 1976):87; C. Page, Smithsonian, 6(Jan 1976):109-110.

Howard, Harry N. Turkey, the Straits and U.S. Policy. Baltimore: JHU Press, 1975. Rev. by R. R. Trask, AHR, 81
(Oct 1976):917; J. A. DeNovo, PHR, 45(Aug 1976):454-5.

Howard, McHenry. Recollections of a Maryland Confederate Soldier
and Staff Officer Under Johnston, Jackson and Lee. Dayton,
Ohio: Morningside Bookshop, 1975. Rev. in CWH, 22(Mar
1976):92-3; by B. I. Wiley, CWTI, 15(Aug 1976):49; R. R.
Duncan, VMHB, 84(Apr 1976):214-15.

Howe, Irving. World of Our Fathers. New York: Harcourt Brace
Jovanovich, n. d. Rev. by R. Alter, Commentary, 61(Apr
1976):83-6.

Howe, James W., et al. The U. S. and the Developing World:
Agenda for Action 1974. New York: Praeger, 1974. Rev.
by R. M. Finley, AgH, 50(Jl 1976):527-8.

Howe, Leroy T., ed. see Deschner, John, ed.

Howe, Ron. Darlington Municipal Transport. Darlington: Darlington Corp., 1972. Rev. by R. W. Brash, JTH, 3(Sep 1976):
299-300.

Howse, Derek. Francis Place and the Early History of the Greenwich Observatory. n. p. : Science History Publications, n. d.
Rev. by O. Gingerich, Smithsonian, 6(Oct 1975):142-4.

Hoyt, Edwin P. The Damndest Yankees: Ethan Allen and His Clan.
Brattleboro, Vt. : Stephen Greene Press, 1976. Rev. by
P. L. Thomas, VH, 44(Sum 1976):176-7.

Hsiao, Gene T., ed. Sino-American Detente and Its Policy Implica-
tions. New York: Praeger, 1974. Rev. by W. A. C. Adie,
CQ, Jan 1976, pp. 150-1.

Hsiao, Katharine Huang. Money and Monetary Policy in Communist
China. New York: Columbia U Press, 1971. Rev. by J. C.
Liu, MAS, 10(Oct 1976):640.

Hsiao, King-Ch'uan. A Modern China and a New World: K'ang Yu-
wei, Reformer and Utopian, 1858-1927. Seattle: U Wash
Press, 1975. Rev. by J. Israel, HRNB, 4(Mar 1976):103-4.

Hsiao, Liang-lin. China's Foreign Trade Statistics, 1864-1949.
Cambridge, Mass. : Harvard U Press, 1974. Rev. by R. F.
Dernberger, CQ, May 1976, pp. 382-4.

Hsieh, Winston. Chinese Historiography on the Revolution of 1911:
A Critical Survey and a Selected Bibliography. Stanford,
Cal. : Stanford U, 1975. Rev. by E. Rhoads, AHR, 81(Oct
1976):937-8; E. Friedman, JAS, 36(Nov 1976):135-6.

Hsu, Dick Ping see Hanson, Lee

Hsü, Francis L. K. see Hsü-Balzer, Eileen

Hsü, Immanuel C. Y.   The Rise of Modern China. New York:
    Oxford U Press, 1975. Rev. by J. H. Bailey, HRNB, 4(Apr
    1976):129.

Hsü-Balzer, Eileen, Richard J. Balzer and Francis L. K. Hsu.
    China Day by Day. New Haven, Conn.: Yale U Press, 1974.
    Rev. by D. S. G. Goodman, CQ, Jan 1976, pp. 156-7.

Huan T'an see Pokora, Timoteus, trans.

Huang, Philip C.   Liang Ch'i-ch'ao and Modern Chinese Liberalism.
    Seattle: U Wash Press, 1972. Rev. by L. A. Schneider,
    AHR, 81(Oct 1976):936.

Huang, Ray. Taxation and Governmental Finance in Sixteenth-Cen-
    tury Ming China. New York: Cam U Press, 1975. Rev. by
    E-tu zen Sun, HRNB, 4(Feb 1976):84-5.

Hubatsch, Walther.   Frederick the Great: Absolutism and Adminis-
    tration. London: Thames and Hudson, 1975. Rev. by H.
    M. Scott, History, 61(Oct 1976):454-6; T. C. W. Blanning,
    HJ, 19(Sep 1976):799-800.

Hubbell, John T., ed.   Battles Lost and Won: Essays from Civil
    War History. Westport, Conn.: Greenwood, 1976. Rev. by
    B. F. Cooling, HRNB, 4(Aug 1976):188.

Huber, Leonard V.   Louisiana: A Pictorial History. New York:
    Scribner's, 1975. Rev. by C. Peterson, ETHJ, 14(Fall 1976):
    74-5.

Hubscher, Arthur.   Denker gegen den Strom/Schopenhauer. Bonn:
    Bouvier Verlag Herbert Grumdmann, 1973. Rev. by J. Min-
    nich, JHP, 14(Apr 1976):241-4.

Hucker, Charles O.   China's Imperial Past: An Introduction to
    Chinese History and Culture. Stanford, Cal.: Stanford U
    Press, 1975. Rev. by H. B. Avery, Historian, 39(Nov 1976):
    140-1; J. Dardess, HRNB, 4(Mar 1976):103; A. Taten, Man-
    kind, 5(Dec 1976):60, 63.

Hudson, Charles M., ed.   Four Centuries of Southern Indians.
    Athens: U Ga Press, 1975. Rev. by W. S. Robinson, AHR,
    81(Oct 1976):951; N. Lederer, ChOk, 54(Fall 1976):417-19;
    J. T. Milanich, FHQ, 54(Jan 1976):402-5; G. W. Pilcher,
    HRNB, 4(Mar 1976):102; R. N. Ellis, JSH, 42(May 1976):267-
    8; P. Garrow, NCHR, 53(Sum 1976):326-7; K. R. Morrison,
    PHR, 45(Nov 1976):607-9.

Hudson, Kenneth.   Patriotism with Profit: British Agricultural
    Societies in the 18th and 19th Centuries. New York: British
    Book Centre, 1975. Rev. by Glenn Hueckel, JEH, 36(Je
    1976):478-9.

Hudson, Patricia, ed. The West Riding Wool Textile Industry: A
Catalogue of Business Records from the 16th to the 20th Cen-
turies. Edington, Wiltshire: Pasold Research Fund, 1975.
Rev. by W. Noblett, Archives, 12(Spr 1976):147-8; R. W.
Lovett, BHR, 50(Sum 1976):257-8.

Huffman, Benjamin L. Getting Around Vermont: A Study of Twenty
Years of Highway Building in Vermont, with Respect to Economics, Automotive Travel, Community Patterns, and the Future. Burlington, Vt.: U Vt, 1974. Rev. by C. H. Liebs,
VH, 44(Win 1976):49-50.

Hufton, Olwen H. The Poor of Eighteenth-Century France, 1750-
1789. New York: Oxford U Press, 1974. Rev. by T. M.
Adams, AHR, 81(Je 1976):600-1.

Huggett, Frank E. The Land Question and European Society Since
1650. New York: Harcourt Brace Jovanovich, 1975. Rev.
by J. Bilello, V. Buscareno and R. Russo, HT, 10(Nov 1976):
134-5.

Hughes, Charles C. Eskimo Boyhood: An Autobiography in Psycho-
social Perspective. Lexington: U Press Ky, 1974. Rev. by
T. Johnston, AA, 78(Mar 1976):158-9; M. Lantis, AIQ, 2(Sum
1975):161-3.

Hughes, H. Stuart. The Sea Change: The Migration of Social
Thought, 1930-1965. New York: Harper and Row, 1975.
Rev. by R. N. Soffer, AHR, 81(Je 1976):563-4.

Hughes, J. Donald. Ecology in Ancient Civilisations. Albuquerque:
U NM Press, 1975. Rev. by E. Higgs, Antiquity, 50(Mar
1976):78-9.

Hughes, Paul L., ed. see Larkin, James F., ed.

Huizinga, J. H. The Making of a Saint: The Tragi-Comedy of
Jean-Jacques Rousseau. London: Hamish Hamilton, 1976.
Rev. by N. Hampson, History, 61(Oct 1976):456.

Hull, Raymond, Gordon Soules and Christine Soules. Vancouver's
Past. Seattle: U Wash Press, 1974. Rev. by H. A. Fleming, JOW, 15(Jan 1976):131.

Humble, Richard. The Fall of Saxon England. New York: St.
Martin's, n.d. Rev. by E. Searle, Mankind, 5(Dec 1976):7,
58.

_____. Napoleon's Peninsular Marshals: A Reassessment.
New York: Taplinger, 1975. Rev. by D. D. Horward, AHR,
81(Je 1976):607-8.

Hume, Ivor Noel, ed. Five Artifact Studies. Charlottesville:

U Press Va, 1974. Rev. by S. South, AmAnt, 41(Jan 1976):
121-2.

Hunczak, Taras, ed. Russian Imperialism from Ivan the Great to
the Revolution. New Brunswick, N.J.: Rutgers U Press,
1974. Rev. by M. M. Luther, AHR, 81(Je 1976):631-2.

Hundley, Norris, Jr., ed. The Asian American: The Historical
Experience. Santa Barbara, Cal.: American Bibliographical
Center, 1976. Rev. by M. Rischin, HRNB, 5(Oct 1976):7.

_____, ed. The Chicano. Santa Barbara, Cal.: Clio, 1975.
Rev. by J. Gómez-Quiñones, CHQ, 55(Sum 1976):187-8; J.
Sanchez, HAHR, 56(Nov 1976):684-6; A. DeLeon, HRNB, 4(Feb
1976):78.

_____. Water and the West. Berkeley: U Cal Press, 1975.
Rev. by W. D. Rowley, A & W, 18(Aut 1976):288-9; C. C.
Colley, AgH, 50(Jl 1976):554-6; W. Rundell, Jr., AHR, 81
(Je 1976):683-4; P. S. Taylor, CHQ, 55(Spr 1976):84; I. G.
Clark, JAH, 63(Je 1976):177-8; R. Nash, NMHR, 51(Apr
1976):158-9; R. V. Hine, PHR, 45(May 1976):294-5; R. Romo,
RAH, 4(Mar 1976):32-7; G. M. Bakken, RAH, 4(Je 1976):
268-71; W. T. Jackson, SCQ, 58(Spr 1976):132-4; D. E.
Green, SWHQ, 80(Jl 1976):122-3; N. G. Bringhurst, UHQ, 44
(Spr 1976):190-1; G. D. Nash, WHQ, 7(Jl 1976):310-11.

Hunt, Richard N. The Political Ideas of Marx and Engels. Vol.
I. Pittsburgh: U Pittsburgh Press, 1974. Rev. by P.
Avrich, AHR, 81(Feb 1976):124-5; K. Nield, History, 61(Oct
1976):462-3; A. Ryan, HJ, 19(Je 1976):531-5; G. S. Sher,
JMH, 48(Je 1976):346-8.

Hunt, William R. Arctic Passage: The Turbulent History of the
Land and People of the Bering Sea 1697-1975. New York:
Scribner's, 1976. Rev. by P. D. Thomas, HRNB, 4(Aug
1976):197.

_____. North of 53 Degrees: The Wild Days of the Alaska-
Yukon Mining Frontier, 1870-1914. New York: Macmillan,
1974. Rev. by M. Sherwood, PHR, 45(Feb 1976):131-2; F.
E. Buske, PNQ, 67(Oct 1976):180.

Hunter, C. Bruce. A Guide to Ancient Maya Ruins. Norman:
U Ok Press, 1975. Rev. by N. Hammond, Antiqutiy, 50
(Mar 1976):76-7; W. Madsen, HAHR, 56(Feb 1976):162-3.

Hunter, Guy and Anthony F. Botterall, eds. Serving the Small
Farmer: Policy Choices in Indian Agricultural Development.
Hyderabad: National Institute of Community Development,
1974. Rev. by T. Singh, IQ, 32(Jan-Mar 1976):111-13.

Hunter, Michael. John Aubrey and the Realm of Learning. New

York: Science History, 1975. Rev. by S. Piggott, Antiquity,
50(Mar 1976):69-70; S. E. Lehmberg, HRNB, 4(Jl 1976):175-
6.

Hurd, John L.   Weathersfield, Century One.   Canaan, N.H.:
Phoenix Pub. Co., 1975.   Rev. by R. Teagle, VH, 44(Fall
1976):239-42.

Hurt, John.   Education in Evolution: Church, State, Society and
Popular Education 1800-1870. London: Hart-Davis, 1971.
Rev. by G. Sutherland, EHR, 91(Jl 1976):663-4.

Hurwitz, Edith F.   Politics and the Public Conscience: Slave
Emancipation and the Abolitionist Movement in Britain. New
York: Barnes and Noble, 1973.   Rev. by A. H. Adamson,
AHR, 81(Feb 1976):137-8.

Huson, Hobart.   Captain Phillip Dimmit's Commandancy of Goliad
(October 15, 1835-January 17, 1836). Austin: Von Boeck-
mann-Jones, 1974.   Rev. by H. B. Simpson, Texana, 12
(Num 4, 1976):382-3.

Hussain, Mehmood.   The Palestine Liberation Organisation.   Delhi:
University Publishers, 1975.   Rev. by A. J. Dastur, IQ,
32(Jl-Sep 1976):350-1.

Hussein, Mahmoud see Friedlander, Saul

Hutchinson, Joseph, ed.   Evolutionary Studies in World Crops:
Diversity and Change in the Indian Subcontinent. New York:
Cam U Press, 1974.   Rev. by W. C. Van Deventer, AgH,
50(Apr 1976):424-5.

Hutchison, Alan.   China's African Revolution.   London: Hutchinson,
1975.   Rev. by M. Bailey, AfAf, 75(Apr 1976):251-2; T. H.
Henriksen, JMAS, 14(Je 1976):350-3.

Hutchison, William R.   The Modernist Impulse in American Protestantism.   Cambridge, Mass.:   Harvard U Press, 1976.
Rev. by F. P. Weisenburger, HRNB, 4(Jl 1976):165-6.

Huthmacher, J. Joseph and Warren I. Susman, eds.   Herbert
Hoover and the Crisis of American Capitalism. Cambridge,
Mass.:   Schenkman, 1973.   Rev. by R. H. Zeiger, AHR, 81
(Oct 1976):800-10.

Huttenback, Robert A.   Racism and Empire: White Settlers and
Colored Immigrants in the British Self-Governing Colonies
1830-1910. Ithaca, N.Y.: Cornell U Press, 1976. Rev. by
I. V. Brown, HRNB, 4(Jl 1976):180.

Huxley, Elspeth.   Florence Nightingale.   London: Weidenfeld and
Nicolson, 1975.   Rev. by O. Anderson, History, 61(Je 1976):
307-8.

189   HVIDT

Hvidt, Kristian. Flight to America: The Social Background of
    300,000 Danish Emigrants. New York: Academic Press,
    1975. Rev. by K. O. Bjork, AHR, 81(Je 1976):670-2; C. C.
    Qualey, MinnH, 45(Spr 1976):37.

Hyam, Ronald and Ged Martin. Reappraisals in British Imperial
    History. London: Macmillan, 1975. Rev. by J. D. Har-
    greaves, JAfH, 17(Num 3, 1976):461-2.

Hyams, Edward. Terrorists and Terrorism. London: Dent, 1975.
    Rev. by P. Calvert, History, 61(Feb 1976):93-4.

Hyde, Francis E. Cunard and the North Atlantic, 1840-1973.
    London: Macmillan, 1975. Rev. by R. E. Coons, BHR, 50
    (Sum 1976):258-9; R. Davis, EHR, 91(Oct 1976):927-8; B.
    McGill, HRNB, 4(Apr 1976):131; C. I. Hamilton, HJ, 19(Mar
    1976):290-2; P. A. M. Taylor, JAmS, 10(Apr 1976):120-1.

Hyde, George E. Spotted Tail's Folk: A History of the Brulé
    Sioux. Norman: U Ok Press, 1974. Rev. by J. C. Olson,
    AIQ, 2(Spr 1975):31-2.

Hyde, J. K. Society and Politics in Medieval Italy: The Evolution
    of the Civil Life, 1000-1350. New York: St. Martin's, 1973.
    Rev. by D. Park, Jr., Historian, 38(Feb 1976):323-4.

Hydén, Göran see Rweyemanu, Anthony H.

_____, Robert Jackson, and John Okumu, eds. Development
    Administration: The Kenya Experience. Nairobi: Oxford U
    Press, 1970. Rev. by E. J. Keller, JMAS, 14(Sep 1976):
    536-9.

Hyman, Paula see Baum, Charlotte

Hynding, Alan. The Public Life of Eugene Semple: Promoter and
    Politician of the Pacific Northwest. Seattle: U Wash Press,
    1973. Rev. by T. C. Hinckley, AHR, 81(Feb 1976):212-13.

Ianni, Octávio. La formación del estado populista en América
    Latina. Mexico: Ediciones Era, 1975. Rev. by B. Loveman,
    HAHR, 56(Nov 1976):664-6.

Iazhborovskaia, I. S. The Ideological Development of the Polish
    Revolutionary Workers' Movement. Moscow: Izdatel'stvo
    "Nauka," 1973. Rev. by N. M. Naimark, AHR, 81(Oct 1976):
    901-2.

Ichioka, Yuji, Yasuo Sakata, Nobuya Tsuchida, and Eri Yasuhara.
    A Buried Past: An Annotated Bibliography of the Japanese
    American Research Project Collection. Berkeley: U Cal
    Press, 1974. Rev. by T. S. Miyakawa, PHR, 45(Feb 1976):
    133-4.

Idang, Gordon J.   Nigeria: Internal Politics and Foreign Policy
    1960-1966. Ibadan: Ibadan U Press, 1973. Rev. by A. H.
    M. Kirk-Greene, AfAf, 75(Apr 1976):258-9; T. M. Shaw,
    JAAS, 11(Jl-Oct 1976):241-3.

Iggers, Georg G.   New Directions in European Historiography.
    Middletown, Conn.: Wesleyan U Press, 1975. Rev. by L.
    Krieger, AHR, 81(Oct 1976):851.

Ike, Nabutake. Japan: The New Superstate. San Francisco: W.
    H. Freeman, 1973. Rev. by S. Vishwanathan, IQ, 32(Jan-
    Mar 1976):92.

Ikime, Obaro, ed.   Leadership in 19th-Century Africa. London:
    Longman, 1974. Rev. by H. J. Fisher, History, 61(Feb
    1976):151-2; D. Killingray, JAfH, 17(Num 3, 1976):458-9.

Illick, Joseph E.   Colonial Pennsylvania: A History. New York:
    Scribner's, 1976. Rev. by G. S. Rowe, HRNB, 4(Sep 1976):
    219.

Imam, Zafar.   Ideology and Reality in Soviet Policy in Asia: Indo-
    Soviet Relations, 1947-60. Dalhi: Kalyani, 1975. Rev. by
    V. S. Budhraj, IQ, 32(Apr-Je 1976):247-9.

_____, ed. Muslims in India. New Delhi: Orient Longman,
    1975. Rev. by M. Ram, IQ, 32(Jan-Mar 1976):97-8.

Inden, Ronald B.   Marriage and Rank in Bengali Culture: A History
    of Caste and Clan in Middle Period Bengal. Berkeley: U Cal
    Press, 1976. Rev. by G. R. G. Hambly, HRNB, 4(Jl 1976):
    173-4.

Indian Council of Social Science Research, The. A Survey of Re-
    search in Geography. Bombay: Popular Prakashan, 1972.
    Rev. by B. H. Farmer, MAS, 10(Feb 1976):159-60.

Ingalls, Robert P. Herbert H. Lehman and New York's Little New
    Deal. New York: NYU Press, 1975. Rev. by J. L. Shover,
    JAH, 63(Dec 1976):768-9.

Ingham, Kenneth. The Kingdom of the Toro, Uganda. London:
    Methuen, 1975. Rev. by M. L. Pirouet, AfAf, 75(Jan 1976):
    114-15; O. W. Furley, History, 61(Feb 1976):160-1.

Inglis, Alex I., ed. see Munro, John A., ed.

Inglis, Brian. The Forbidden Game: A Social History of Drugs.
    New York: Scribner's, 1975. Rev. by G. H. Breiger, HRNB,
    4(Feb 1976):87; S. Gershgoren, Mankind, 5(Aug 1976):8-9.

Inglis, K. S. The Australian Colonists: An Exploration of Social
    History 1788-1870. Portland, Ore.: International Scholarly

191INGRAM

Book Services, 1975.   Rev. by S. C. McCulloch, AHR, 81
(Apr 1976):437-8.

Ingram, George M.   Expropriation of U.S. Property in South Amer-
ica: Nationalization of Oil and Copper Companies in Peru,
Bolivia, and Chile.   New York: Praeger, 1974.   Rev. by R.
Weinert, HAHR, 56(May 1976):356-7.

Ingrams, Doreen, ed.   Palestine Papers, 1917-1922: Seeds of Conflict.   New York: George Braziller, 1973.   Rev. by R. H.
Davison, IJMES, 7(Apr 1976):319-20.

Innis, Ben.   Bloody Knife: Custer's Favorite Scout.   Ft. Collins,
Col.: Old Army Press, 1973.   Rev. by H. T. Hoover, AIQ,
2(Sum 1975):158-61.

Institute for Balkan Studies.   Symposium L'Epoque Phanariote:
21-25 Octobre 1970.   Thessaloniki: Inst. Balkan Studies,
1974.   Rev. by J. S. Counelis, CH, 45(Je 1976):259-60.

Institute of World History of the Academy of Science.   Materials
of the First Symposium of Soviet Americanists (November 30-
December 3, 1971).   Moscow: Institute of World History of
the Academy of Science, 1973.   Rev. by M. P. Trauth, JAH,
63(Sep 1976):462-3.

International Band of Reconstruction and Development.   Senegal:
Tradition, Diversification and Economic Development; A Re-
port.   Washington, D.C.: International Bank, 1974.   Rev. by
D. C. O'Brien, AfAf, 75(Jan 1976):113.

International Economic History Conference.   Third International
Conference of Economic History 1965, Part V.   Paris: Mouton, 1974.   Rev. by G. D. Ramsay, History, 61(Je 1976):
268-9.

Iredale, David.   Enjoying Archives.   Newton Abbot: David and
Charles, 1973.   Rev. by C. F. Slade, History, 61(Feb 1976):
77.

Iriye, Akira.   Mutual Images: Essays in American-Japanese Relations.   Cambridge, Mass.: Harvard U Press, 1975.   Rev.
by C. E. Neu, JAH, 63(Sep 1976):464-5; S. K. Johnson, JJS,
2(Sum 1976):437-8.

Irving, R. E. M.   The First Indochina War: French and American
Policy, 1945-54.   New York: Crane, Russak, 1975.   Rev. by
P. D. Caine, AHR, 81(Oct 1976):944-5.

Isaac de l'Etoile.   Sermons, 2(18-39).   Paris: Les Editions du
Ceri, 1974.   Rev. by J. F. Kelly, CH, 45(Mar 1976):102-3.

Isaac, Rael.   Israel Divided: Ideological Politics in the Jewish

State. Baltimore: JHU, n.d. Rev. by J. Shattan, Commentary, 62(Sep 1976):120-3.

Isaacs, Harold R. Idols of the Tribe. New York: Harper and Row, n.d. Rev. by D. Ravitch, Commentary, 61(Feb 1976): 79, 82-3.

_____, ed. Straw Sandals: Chinese Short Stories 1918-1933. Cambridge, Mass.: MIT Press, 1974. Rev. by W. A. Lyell, CQ, May 1976, pp. 390-2.

Isaak, Robert A. Individuals and World Politics. North Scituate, Mass.: Duxbury, 1975. Rev. by E. Gulick, AHR, 81(Oct 1976):819-20.

Isager, Signe and Mogens Herman Hansen. Aspects of Athenian Society in the Fourth Century B.C. Odense: Odense U Press, 1975. Rev. by O. W. Reinmuth, AHR, 81(Oct 1976):827.

Isichei, Elizabeth. A History of the Igbo People. New York: St. Martin's, 1976. Rev. by V. M. Smith, HRNB, 4(Jl 1976): 169.

Isler, Hans Peter. Corpus Vasorum Antiquorum, Schweiz 2, Zurich 1. Bern: Verlag Herbert Lang, 1973. Rev. by I. D. McPhee and A. D. Trendall, AJA, 80(Fall 1976):431-2.

Israel, J. I. Race, Class and Politics in Colonial Mexico, 1610-1670. New York: Oxford U Press, 1975. Rev. by C. Gibson, AHR, 81(Je 1976):701; S. B. Liebman, HAHR, 56(Feb 1976):122-3; B. R. Hammett, History, 61(Oct 1976):426-7.

Israel, John and Donald W. Klein. Rebels and Bureaucrats: China's December 9'ers. Berkeley: U Cal Press, 1976. Rev. by M. Patoski, HRNB, 4(Sep 1976):221-2.

Isser, Natalie. The Second Empire and the Press. A Study of Government Inspired Brochures on French Foreign Policy in Their Propaganda Milieu. The Hague: Martinus Nijhoff, 1974. Rev. by M. Palmer, EHR, 91(Jan 1976):224; I. Collins, History, 61(Je 1976):299.

Isserlin, B. S. J. and Joan du Plat Taylor. Motya, a Phoenician City in Sicily. Vol. I. Leiden: E. J. Brill, 1974. Rev. by J. Teixidor, AJA, 80(Spr 1976):206-7.

Issraeljan, Victor. The Anti-Hitler Coalition: Diplomatic Cooperation Between the USSR, USA, and Britain During the Second World War, 1941-1945. Moscow: Progress Publishers, 1971. Rev. by W. A. Fletcher, AHR, 81(Oct 1976):884-7.

Istituto per la Storia del Risorgimento Italiano. La Fine del Potere Temporale e il Ricongiungimento di Roma all'Italia.

Rome: Istituto per la Storia del Risorgimento Italiano, 1972. Rev. by D. Koenig, CaHR, 62(Oct 1976):635-6.

Istituto per la Storia dell'Università de Padova. Quaderni per la storia dell'Universita di Padova. 6 vols. Padua: Editrice Antenore, 1968-74. Rev. by J. K. Hyde, EHR, 91(Oct 1976): 900-1.

Iurato, Giovanni. Pietro Taglialatela. Turin: Libreria Editrice Claudiana, 1972. Rev. by P. Sylvain, CaHR, 62(Oct 1976): 637-9.

Ivers, Larry. British Drums on the Southern Frontier: The Military Colonization of Georgia, 1733-1749. New York: Oxford U Press, 1974. Rev. by B. Wood, History, 61(Oct 1976): 397-8.

Izumo, Takeda and Miyoshi Shoraku, and Namiki Senryn. The Treasury of Loyal Retainers. New York: Columbia U Press, 1971. Rev. by D. E. Mills, MAS, 10(Apr 1976):311-15.

Jackson, John W. The Pennsylvania Navy, 1775-1781. New Brunswick, N.J.: Rutgers U Press, 1974. Rev. by P. S. Haffenden, History, 61(Oct 1976):402; S. S. Cohen, PH, 43(Jan 1976):79-80.

Jackson, M. H. and C. de Beer. Eighteenth-Century Gunfounding: The Verbruggens at the Royal Brass Foundary, a Chapter in the History of Technology. Newton Abbot: David and Charles, 1974. Rev. by G. F. Hammersley, History, 61(Feb 1976): 118.

Jackson, Robert, ed. see Hyden, Göran, ed.

Jackson, Samuel B. 200 Trails to Gold: A Guide to Promising Old Mines and Hidden Lodes Throughout the West. New York: Doubleday, 1976. Rev. by D. A. Smith, NMHR, 51(Oct 1976): 348-9.

Jacobs, David Michael. The UFO Controversy in America. Bloomington: Ind U Press, 1975. Rev. by R. Tobey, RAH, 4(Mar 1976):128-31.

Jacobs, Mike. One Time Harvest. Jamestown, N.D.: ND Farmers Union, 1975. Rev. by D. H. Johnson, NDH, 43(Spr 1976): 101-2.

Jacobsen, J. N. see Downey, Fairfax

Jacoby, Johann. Briefwechsel, 1816-1849. Hanover: Fackelträger Verlag, 1974. Rev. by A. Schuetz, AHR, 81(Je 1976):614.

Jacoby, Neil H. Multinational Oil. New York: Macmillan, n.d. Rev. by J. Marsh, Commentary, 61(Apr 1976):86-90.

Jacquart, Jean. La crise rurale en Ile-De-France: 1550-1670. Paris: Librairie Armand Colin, 1974. Rev. by R. Forster, AHR, 81(Apr 1976):394.

Jaeger, Henrik. Henrik Ibsen, 1828-1888: A Critical Biography. New York: Benjamin Blom, 1972. Rev. by L. A. Muinzer, ESR, 6(Jan 1976):159-60.

Jaffe, Irma B. John Trumbull: Patriot-Artist of the American Revolution. Boston: N. Y. Graphic Society, 1975. Rev. by R. Paulson, GR, 30(Sum 1976):460-7; P. R. Baker, JAH, 63 (Dec 1976):698-9.

Jaffe, Julian F. Crusade Against Radicalism. Port Washington, N. Y.: Kennikat, 1972. Rev. by J. A. Thompson, HJ, 19 (Mar 1976):257-74.

Jäger, Otto A. and Ivy Pearce. Antiquities of North Ethiopia: A Guide. Stuttgart: F. A. Brockhaus, 1974. Rev. by D. Buxton, Antiquity, 50(Je 1976):154.

Jahoda, Gloria. Florida: A Bicentennial History. New York: Norton, 1976. Rev. by H. S. Marks, HRNB, 5(Oct 1976):4.

_____. The Trail of Tears. New York: Holt, Rinehart and Winston, 1975. Rev. by F. P. Prucha, WMH, 60(Aut 1976): 67-8.

Jain, D. C. Parliamentary Privileges Under the Indian Constitution. New Delhi: Sterling, 1975. Rev. by S. L. Shakdher, IQ, 32 (Jan-Mar 1976):104-6.

Jain, J. P. After Mao What? Army Party and Group Rivalries in China. New Delhi: Radiant, 1975. Rev. by M. Mohanty, IQ, 32(Apr-Je 1976):242-3.

_____. China, Pakistan, and Bangladesh. New Delhi: Radiant, 1974. Rev. by A. Lamb, CQ, Jan 1976, pp. 148-50.

James, Coy Hilton. Silas Deane--Patriot or Traitor? East Lansing: Mich St U Press, 1975. Rev. by W. Stinchcombe, JAH, 63 (Sep 1976):389-90.

James, D. Clayton. The Years of MacArthur. Vol. II, 1941-1945. Boston: Houghton Mifflin, 1975. Rev. by F. F. Pogue, AHR, 81(Je 1976):689; D. MacIsaac, Historian, 39(Nov 1976):166-7.

James, Edward T., ed. Dictionary of American Biography, Supplement Three, 1941-1945. New York: Scribner's, 1973. Rev. by D. K. Adams, EHR, 91(Apr 1976):463.

_____, Janet Wilson James, and Paul Boyer, eds. Notable American Women, 1607-1950: A Biographical Dictionary.

3 vols. Cambridge, Mass.: Harv U Press, 1971. Rev. by M. B. Akin, CH, 45(Mar 1976):117-18; O. E. S., CurH, 70 (May 1976):228.

James, F. G. Ireland in the Empire, 1688-1770. Cambridge, Mass.: Harvard U Press, 1973. Rev. by G. D. Ramsay, EHR, 91(Jan 1976):133-4.

James, Harry C. Pages from Hopi History. Tucson: U Ariz Press, 1974. Rev. by W. S. Robinson, AHR, 81(Apr 1976): 448: S. K. Gragert, JOW, 15(Jl 1976):104.

James, Mervyn. Family, Lineage, and Civil Society: A Study of Society, Politics, and Mentality in the Durham Region, 1500-1640. New York: Oxford U Press, 1974. Rev. by R. Howell, Jr., AHR, 81(Feb 1976):127-8; G. E. Aylmer, EHR, 91(Jan 1976):190-1.

James, Sydney V. Colonial Rhode Island: A History. New York: Scribner's, 1975. Rev. by N. S. Cohen, HRNB, 4(Sep 1976): 215-16.

Janeski, Paul F. see Margraff, William F.

Janik, Allan and Stephen Toulmin. Wittgenstein's Vienna. New York: Simon and Schuster, 1973. Rev. by C. Henderson, JHP, 14(Jan 1976):118-21.

Janke, Peter. Mendizabal y la Instauración de la Monarquia Constitucional en españa 1790-1853. Madrid: Siglo XXI, 1974. Rev. by R. A. H. Robinson, History, 61(Oct 1976):461.

Jankuhn, Herbert, et al., eds. Vor- und Frühformen der europäischen Stadt im Mittelalter: Bericht über ein Symposium in Reinhausen bei Göttingen in der Zeit vom 18. bis 24. April 1972. Vol. 2. Göttingen: Vandenhoeck and Ruprecht, 1974. Rev. by K.-U. Jäschke, AHR, 81(Apr 1976):371-2; J. M. Wallace-Hadrill, EHR, 91(Apr 1976):405-6.

Jannuzi, F. Tomasson. Agrarian Crisis in India: The Case of Bihar. New York: U Texas Press, 1974. Rev. by D. Rodnick, AA, 78(Je 1976):410-11.

Janos, Andrew C. and William B. Slottman, eds. Revolution in Perspective: Essays on the Hungarian Soviet Republic of 1919. Berkeley: U Cal Press, 1971. Rev. by R. V. Burks, AHR, 81(Oct 1976):899.

Jansen, Marius B. Japan and China: From War to Peace, 1894-1972. Chicago: Rand McNally, 1975. Rev. by C. Johnson, JJS, 2(Aut 1975):147-52.

Jansen, P. Arnauld d'Andilly: Défenseur de Port-Royal (1654-

1659). Paris: Librairie Philosophique J. Vren, 1973. Rev. by F. E. Weaver, CaHR, 62(Apr 1976):281-2.

Janssen, Koen, ed. and trans. see Bontinck, François, ed. and trans.

Jardine, Lisa. Francis Bacon: Discovery and the Art of Discourse. Cambridge: Cam U Press, 1974. Rev. by H. F. Kearney, EHR, 91(Jl 1976):641-2.

Jaspert, Bernd and Eugene Manning, eds. Regulae Benedicti Studia: Annuarium Internationale. Hildesheim: Gerstenberg, 1973. Rev. by F. Hockey, JEccH, 28(Apr 1976):186-7.

Jay, Martin. The Dialectical Imagination: A History of the Frankfurt School and the Institute of Social Research, 1923-1950. Boston: Little, Brown, 1973. Rev. by W. W. Wagar, AHR, 81(Oct 1976):818-19.

Jedin, Hubert, ed. Handbuch der Kirchengeschichte. Band VI. Freiberg: Verlag Herder, 1973. Rev. by J. Hennesey, CaHR, 62(Oct 1976):640-1.

Jedrzejewicz, Janusz. In the Service of an Idea: Memoirs and Writings. New York: Pilsudski Institute of America, 1972. Rev. by K. F. Lewalski, AHR, 81(Oct 1976):902.

Jefferson, Thomas. Thomas Jefferson: A Biography in His Own Words. (Newsweek Editors, eds.) New York: Harper and Row, 1974. Rev. by R. McColley, PH, 43(Jan 1976):84-6.

Jeffery, L. H. Archaic Greece: The City-States c. 700-500 B.C. New York: St. Martin's Press, 1976. Rev. by E. S. Gruen, HRNB, 4(Sep 1976):223.

Jeffrey, David L. The Early English Lyric and Franciscan Spirituality. Lincoln: U Neb Press, 1975. Rev. by E. R. Daniel, CH, 45(Mar 1976):104-5.

Jelinek, Yeshayaher. The Parish Republic: Hlinka's Slovak People's Party, 1939-1945. Boulder, Col.: East European Quarterly, 1976. Rev. by E. C. Helmreich, HRNB, 4(Aug 1976): 203-4.

Jenkins, Brian. Britain and the War for the Union. Vol. I. Montreal: McGill-Queen's U Press, 1974. Rev. by A. O'Rourke, AHR, 81(Je 1976):592; M. Ellison, EHR, 91(Apr 1976):448-9.

Jenkins, D. T. The West Riding Wool Textile Industry 1770-1835. Edington: Pasold Research Fund, 1975. Rev. by R. A. Church, History, 61(Oct 1976):480.

Jenkins, Elizabeth. The Mystery of Arthur. London: Michael

Joseph, 1975. Rev. by P. Rahtz, Antiquity, 50(Je 1976):
161-3.

Jenkins, John H., ed. The Papers of the Texas Revolution, 1835-
1836. 10 vols. Austin, Tx.: Presidial, 1973. Rev. by B.
Procter, JAH, 63(Je 1976):93-4; A. C. Ashcraft, JOW, 15
(Jl 1976):79-83.

Jenkins, Myra Ellen and Albert H. Schroeder. A Brief History of
New Mexico. Albuquerque: U NM Press, 1974. Rev. by M.
Simmons, JOW, 15(Jan 1976):124.

Jennings, Francis. The Invasion of America: Indians, Colonialism,
and the Cant of Conquest. Chapel Hill: U NC Press, 1975.
Rev. by G. W. Pilcher, HRNB, 4(Mar 1976):102-3; B. W.
Sheehan, JAH, 63(Sep 1976):378-9; R. D. Cohen, JSH, 42(May
1976):266-7; N. Salisbury, NEQ, 49(Mar 1976):158-61; A. T.
Vaughan, WHQ, 7(Oct 1976):421-2.

Jennison, Peter S., ed. The 1976-1977 Official Vermont Bicentennial Guide. Taftsville, Vt: Countryman Press, 1976. Rev.
by M. Hanagan, VH, 44(Sum 1976):182-4.

Jensen, De Lamar. Confrontation at Worms: Martin Luther and
the Diet of Worms. Provo, Utah: BYU Press, 1973. Rev.
by P. L. Kintner, CaHR, 62(Jan 1976):121-3.

Jensen, John R., ed. Journal and Letter Book of Nicholas Buckeridge, 1651-1654. Minneapolis: U Minn Press, 1973. Rev.
by E. A. Alpers, JAfH, 17(Num 1, 1976):156.

Jensen, Merrill. The American Revolution Within America. New
York: New York U Press, 1974. Rev. by J. R. Pole, WMQ,
33(Jan 1976):156-8.

_____, ed. The Documentary History of the Ratification of the
Constitution. 2 vols. Madison: St Historical Society of Wis,
1976. Rev. by J. May, HRNB, 4(Sep 1976):212.

Jensen, Oliver O. The American Heritage History of Railroads in
America. New York: American Heritage, 1975. Rev. by H.
R. Grant, OH, 85(Spr 1976):177-8; S. L. Carr, UHQ, 44
(Sum 1976):309-10.

Jensen, Ronald J. The Alaska Purchase and Russian-American Relations. Seattle: U Wash Press, 1975. Rev. by H. I. Kushner, JAH, 63(Je 1976):139-40; M. E. Wheeler, WHQ, 7(Jl
1976):311-14.

Jensen, Vernon H. Strife on the Waterfront. Ithaca, N.Y.: Cornell U Press, 1974. Rev. by J. M. Gowaskie, PH, 43(Jl
1976):283-5.

Jeppesen, Kristian. Neues zum Rätsel des Grand Camée de France. Copenhagen: Ejnar Munksgaard, 1974. Rev. by U. W. Hiesinger, AJA, 80(Spr 1976):217-18.

Jessee, Dean C. Letters of Brigham Young to His Sons. Salt Lake City: Deseret, 1974. Rev. by J. Ships, JAH, 62(Mar 1976): 1007-8.

Jessup, Philip C. The Birth of Nations. New York: Columbia U Press, 1974. Rev. by T. P. Peardon, AHR, 81(Apr 1976): 365.

Jewett, Robert. The Captain America Complex: The Dilemma of Zealous Nationalism. Philadelphia: Westminster, 1973. Rev. by J. A. Lindsey, JCS, 17(Win 1975):138-40.

Jha, Jata Shankar. Beginnings of Modern Education in Mithila. Patna: Jayaswal Research Institute, 1972. Rev. by C. Dewey, MAS, 10(Jl 1976):453-60.

_____. History of Darbhanga Raj. Patna: Research Society of Bihar, 1966. Rev. by C. Dewey, MAS, 10(Jl 1976):453-60.

_____. Maharaja Lakshmiswar Singh of Darbhanga. Patna: Maharaja Lakshmishwar Singh Smarak Samiti, 1972. Rev. by C. Dewey, MAS, 10(Jl 1976):453-60.

Jick, Leon A. The Americanization of the Synagogue 1820-1870. Hanover, N.H.: U Press New England, 1976. Rev. by H. P. Segal, HRNB, 5(Oct 1976):2-3.

Joffe, Ellis. Between Two Plenums: China's Intraleadership Conflict, 1959-1962. Ann Arbor: U Mich, 1975. Rev. by P. Elmquist, AHR, 81(Oct 1976):936-7.

John, Elizabeth A. H. Storms Brewed in Other Men's Worlds. College Station: Texas A & M Press, 1975. Rev. by J. P. Sanchez, A & W, 18(Aut 1976):304-5; H. P. Hinton, HAHR, 56(Aug 1976):476-7; D. E. Berge, JAH, 63(Sep 1976):376-7; D. E. Chipman, JSH, 42(May 1976):269-70; A. P. Nasatir, NMHR, 51(Jan 1976):78-9; A. B. Thomas, PHR, 45(Nov 1976): 606-7; R. S. Weddle, SWHQ, 80(Jl 1976):114-16; J. F. Bannon, WHQ, 7(Jl 1976):318-19.

John of Paris. On Royal Order and Power. New York: Columbia U Press, 1974. Rev. by H. M. MacDonald, JCS, 18(Aut 1976):550-2.

Johnson, A. Ross. The Transformation of Communist Ideology: The Yugoslav Case, 1945-1953. Cambridge, Mass.: MIT Press, n.d. Rev. by K. Reyman, EE, 24(May 1975):30-1.

Johnson, Andrew. The Papers of Andrew Johnson, Vol. IV. 1860-

1861. (LeRoy P. Graf and Ralph W. Haskins, eds.) Knoxville, U Tenn Press, 1976. Rev. by F. B. Williams, Jr.,
THQ, 35(Sum 1976):225-6.

Johnson, Christopher H. Utopian Communism in France: Cabet
and the Icarians 1839-1851. Ithaca, N.Y.: Cornell U Press,
1974. Rev. by L. Loubere, AHR, 81(Apr 1976):399; R.
Price, History, 61(Je 1976):297-8.

Johnson, Donald J. and E. Jean Johnson, eds. Through Indian
Eyes. 2 vols. New York: Praeger, 1974. Rev. by Tyabji,
IQ, 32(Jan-Mar 1976):107-8.

Johnson, Edward C. Walker River Paiutes: A Tribal History.
Salt Lake City: U Utah Press, 1974. Rev. by R. Wilson,
A & W, 18(Sum 1976):204-5; R. F. Heizer, CHQ, 55(Spr
1976):87-8; C. S. Fowler, UHQ, 44(Win 1976):102-3; E. B.
Patterson, WHQ, 7(Apr 1976):208-9.

Johnson, Elden, ed. Aspects of Upper Great Lakes Anthropology.
St. Paul: Minn Historical Society, 1974. Rev. by D. C.
Anderson, AI, 43(Sum 1976):388-90; D. Ozker, AmAnt, 41
(Apr 1976):248-9.

Johnson, Gordon. Provincial Politics and Indian Nationalism.
Cambridge: Cam U Press, 1973. Rev. by B. N. Pandey,
EHR, 91(Jan 1976):227-8.

Johnson, Herbert A., ed. The Papers of John Marshall. Vol. I.
Chapel Hill: U NC Press, 1974. Rev. by M. K. Bonsteel
Tachau, FCHQ, 50(Jan 1976):72-3; R. K. Faulkner, WMQ,
33(Jan 1976):154-6.

Johnson, Hubert C. Frederick the Great and His Officials. New
Haven, Conn.: Yale U Press, 1975. Rev. by M. S. Anderson, EHR, 91(Oct 1976):915-16; H. M. Scott, History, 61(Oct
1976):454-6; T. C. W. Blanning, JMH, 48(Sep 1976):562-4.

Johnson, James Turner. Ideology, Reason and the Limitation of
War: Religious and Secular Concepts, 1200-1740. Princeton,
N.J.: Prin U Press, 1975. Rev. by G. Parker, History,
61(Je 1976):267-8.

Johnson, Patricia Givens. James Patton and the Appalachian
Colonists. Verona, Va.: McClure, 1973. Rev. by D. A.
Williams, JAH, 63(Sep 1976):386.

Johnson, Paul. Elizabeth: A Study in Power and Intellect. London: Weidenfeld and Nicolson, 1974. Rev. by P. McGrath,
EHR, 91(Jan 1976):195.

Johnson, Sheila K. American Attitudes Toward Japan, 1941-1975.
Stanford, Cal.: Hoover Institution, 1975. Rev. by A. Iriye,
JJS, 2(Sum 1976):449-51.

Johnson, William see Peck, Ira

Johnson, William Weber. Cortés. Boston: Little, Brown, 1975.
Rev. by H. C. Schmidt, SWHQ, 80(Jl 1976):120-1.

_____. The Forty-Niners. New York: Time-Life, 1974. Rev.
by K. A. Franks, ChOk, 54(Sum 1976):295-6.

Johnston, E. M. Ireland in the Eighteenth Century. Dublin: Gill
and Macmillan, 1974. Rev. by H. F. Kearney, History, 61
(Je 1976):294.

Johnston, William M. The Austrian Mind: An Intellectual and Social History 1848-1938. Berkeley: U Cal Press, 1972. Rev.
by E. Wangerman, EHR, 91(Jl 1976):674-5.

Johnstone, Paul. The Archaeology of Ships. New York: Henry Z.
Walck, 1974. Rev. by N. Stavrolakes, Archaeology, 29(Jan
1976):65-7.

Joiner, Charles A. The Politics of Massacre: Political Processes
in South Vietnam. Philadelphia: Temple U Press, 1974.
Rev. by D. Wurfel, AHR, 81(Feb 1976):197-8.

Jones, A. H. M. The Roman Economy. Oxford: Blackwell, 1974.
Rev. by P. J. Cuff, EHR, 91(Jan 1976):169.

Jones, Alfred Hayworth. Roosevelt's Image Brokers: Poets, Playwrights, and the Use of the Lincoln Symbol. Port Washington,
N.Y.: Kennikat, 1974. Rev. by J.B., AS, 16(Fall 1975):
97-8.

Jones, Benjamin Washington. Under the Stars and Bars: A History
of the Surry Light Artillery; Recollections of a Private Soldier
in the War Between the States. Dayton, Ohio: Morningside
Bookshop, 1975. Rev. by J. I. Robertson, Jr., VMHB, 84
(Jan 1976):112-14.

Jones, Charles Edwin. Perfectionist Persuasion: The Holiness
Movement and American Methodism, 1867-1936. Metuchen,
N.J.: Scarecrow, 1974. Rev. by D. W. Dayton, CH, 45(Mar
1976):120-1.

Jones, Dave. The Western Horse: Advice and Training. Norman:
U Ok Press, 1974. Rev. by W. E. McFarland, ChOk, 54
(Win 1976):540.

Jones, David. Chartism and the Chartists. London: Allen Lane,
1975. Rev. by F. C. Mather, History, 61(Oct 1976):484-5;
W. H. Maehl, Jr., HRNB, 4(Feb 1976):91-2.

_____. A Journal of Two Visits Made to Some Nations of Indians
on the West Side of the River Ohio, in the Years 1772 and

<u>1773</u>. Fairfield, Wash.: Ye Galleon Press, 1973. Rev. by
J. P. Ronda, AIQ, 2(Sum 1975):149-50.

Jones, E. L. <u>Agriculture and the Industrial Revolution</u>. Oxford:
Basil Blackwell, 1975. Rev. by F. M. L. Thompson, History, 61(Je 1976):303.

Jones, Eric L., ed. <u>see</u> Parker, William N., ed.

Jones, Howard Mumford. <u>Revolution and Romanticism</u>. Cambridge,
Mass.: Harvard U Press, 1974. Rev. by K. D. Wren, ESR,
6(Jan 1976):151-3; C. Breunig, JMH, 48(Mar 1976):125-9.

Jones, J. R. <u>The Revolution of 1688 in England</u>. New York: Norton, 1972. Rev. by J. E. Farnell, JMH, 48(Mar 1976):142-3.

Jones, James W. <u>The Shattered Synthesis: New England Puritanism Before the Great Awakening</u>. New Haven, Conn.: Yale
U Press, 1973. Rev. by E. K. Brown, CaHR, 62(Jl 1976):
474-5.

Jones, Lewis Pinckney. <u>Stormy Petrel: N. G. Gonzales and His</u>
<u>State</u>. Columbia, S.C.: U SCar Press, 1973. Rev. by R.
B. Jones, JSH, 42(May 1976):292-3.

Jones, Maldwyn A. <u>Destination America</u>. New York: Holt, Rinehart and Winston, 1976. Rev. by E. R. Barkan, JAH, 63
(Dec 1976):732-3; A. H., Hto, 26(Jl 1976):478-9.

Jones, Michael Wynn. <u>The Cartoon History of the American</u>
<u>Revolution</u>. New York: Putnam's, 1975. Rev. by R. Paulson, GR, 30(Sum 1976):460-7.

Jones, Peter d'A. <u>Since Columbus: Poverty and Pluralism in the</u>
<u>History of the Americas</u>. Totowa, N.J.: Rowman and Littlefield, 1976. Rev. by P. E. Kuhl, HRNB, 5(Oct 1976):11.

_____. <u>The U.S.A.: A History of Its People and Society</u>.
Homewood, Ill.: Dorsey, 1976. Rev. by P. R. Rulon, HT,
10(Nov 1976):138-9.

Jones, Whitney R. D. <u>The Mid-Tudor Crisis, 1539-1563</u>. London:
Macmillan, 1973. Rev. by F. D. Price, EHR, 91(Apr 1976):
417-18.

Jones, Wilbur Devereux. <u>The American Problem in British Diplomacy, 1841-1861</u>. London: Macmillan, 1974. Rev. by K.
Bourne, History, 61(Feb 1976):131-2; R. E. May, PNQ, 67
(Apr 1976):88-9.

Jones, William C., et al. <u>Mile-High Trolleys</u>. Boulder, Colo.:
Pruett, 1975. Rev. by J. L. Dodson, JOW, 15(Jan 1976):
121-2.

Jordan, Weymouth T., Jr. North Carolina Troops, 1861-1865, a Roster. Vol. 5. Raleigh: NC Division Archives and History, 1975. Rev. by E. L. Hill, AmArc, 39(Apr 1976):203-4; B. I. Wiley, NCHR, 53(Win 1976):80-1.

Josephson, Hannah. Jeannette Rankin: First Lady in Congress. Indianapolis: Bobbs-Merrill, 1974. Rev. by M. P. Malone, PHR, 45(Feb 1976):149-50; L. E. Zimmerman, PNQ, 67(Apr 1976):90-1.

Josephson, Harold. James T. Shotwell and the Rise of Internationalism in America. Rutherford, N.J.: Fairleigh Dickinson U Press, 1975. Rev. by S. R. Herman, PNQ, 67(Oct 1976): 176-7.

Josephy, Alvin M., Jr. History of the Congress of the United States. New York: McGraw Hill, 1975. Rev. by V. de Keyserling, ETHJ, 14(Fall 1976):76-7; H. B. Asher, OH, 85 (Sum 1976):268-9.

Joshi, Arun. Lola Shri Ram: A Study in Entrepreneurship and Industrial Management. New Delhi: Orient Longman, 1975. Rev. by H. Venkatasubbiah, IQ, 32(Jan-Mar 1976):114-15.

Joshi, Nirmala. Foundations of Indo-Soviet Relations. New Delhi: Radiant Publishers, 1975. Rev. by M. Murlidhara, IQ, 32 (Jl-Sep 1976):358-61.

Joshi, P. M., ed. see Sherwani, H. K., ed.

Jozef, B., ed. Scripta Hierosolymitana. Vol. XXVI. Jerusalem: Magnes, 1974. Rev. by I. A. Leonard, HAHR, 56(Feb 1976): 120-1.

Judd, Jacob, ed. see East, Robert A., ed.

Judd, Walter F. Palaces and Forts of the Hawaiian Kingdom: From Thatch to American Florentine. Palo Alto, Cal.: Pacific, 1975. Rev. by J. H, Kemble, JAH, 63(Dec 1976): 728.

Juhnke, James C. A People of Two Kingdoms: The Political Acculturation of the Kansas Mennonites. Newton, Kan.: Faith and Life, 1975. Rev. by D. F. Durnbaugh, CH, 45(Mar 1976): 119-20; F. Luebke, JAH, 62(Mar 1976):1021-2; P. Yoder, IMH, 72(Je 1976):167-8; R. J. Sawatsky, MQR, 50(Jan 1976):72-3.

Jukes, Geoffrey. The Soviet Union in Asia. Berkeley: U Cal Press, 1973. Rev. by M. Rossabi, JAAS, 11(Jan-Apr 1976): 126-7.

Julien, Charles-Andre, et al. Perspectives nouvelles sur le passé de l'Afrique noire et de Madagascar. n.p.: Publications de

203   JULIEN

la Sorbonne, 1974. Rev. by J. D. Hargreaves, JAfH, 17
(Num 2, 1976):319-20.

Julien, Michele see Lavallee, Danielle

July, Robert W. Precolonial Africa: An Economic and Social History. New York: Scribners, 1975. Rev. by N. R. Bennett,
HRNB, 4(Feb 1976):82.

Junkin, Edward Dixon. Religion versus Revolution: The Interpretation of the French Revolution by German Protestant Churchmen,
1789-1799. 2 vols. Austin, Tx.: Austin Presbyterian Theological Seminary, 1974. Rev. by J. McManners, JEccH, 27
(Jl 1976):320-1.

Justman, Dorothy E. German Colonists and Their Descendants in
Houston, Including Usener and Allied Families. Quanah, Tx.:
Nortex, 1974. Rev. by W. L. Taylor, ETHJ, 14(Spr 1976):
68-9.

Jutikkala, Eino and Kauko Pirinen. A History of Finland. New
York: Praeger, 1974. Rev. by O. E. S., CurH, 70(Apr
1976):177-8.

Kaarsted, Tage. President of the Concil C. Th. Zahle's Diary
1914-1917. Aarhus: Universitelsforlaget, 1974. Rev. by E.
J. Friis, AHR, 81(Feb 1976):163.

_____. Storbritannien og Danmark, 1914-20. Odense: Odense U
Press, 1974. Rev. by P. M. Hayes, EHR, 91(Apr 1976):456.

Kaba, Lansiné. The Wahhabiyya: Islamic Reform and Politics in
French West Africa. Evanston: Northwestern U Press, 1974.
Rev. by H. J. Fisher, JAfH, 17(Num 1, 1976):147-9.

Kabanov, V. V. The October Revolution and Cooperative Societies
(1917-March 1919). Moscow: Izdatel'stvo "Nauka," 1973.
Rev. by W. G. Rosenberg, AHR, 81(Je 1976):633.

Kagan, Paul. New World Utopias. New York: Penguin, 1976.
Rev. by D. Lindsey, Mankind, 5(Feb 1976):8-9.

Kagan, Richard L. Students and Society in Early Modern Spain.
Baltimore: JHU Press, 1974. Rev. by D. R. Ringrose,
AHR, 81(Apr 1976):400; J. R. L. Highfield, EHR, 91(Jl
1976):639-40; J. Lynch, History, 61(Je 1976):280-1.

Kahler, Erich. The Germans. Princeton, N.J.: Prin U Press,
1974. Rev. by M. Ermarth, AHR, 81(Feb 1976):164-5; J. C.
Fout, CH, 45(Mar 1976):112.

Kahn, E. J., Jr. The China Hands: America's Foreign Service
Officers and What Befell Them. New York: Viking Press,
1975. Rev. by G. May, RAH, 4(Mar 1976):120-7.

Kahn, Herman, William Brown and Leon Martel. The Next 200 Years: A Scenario for America and the World. New York: Morrow, n. d. Rev. by B. Kovner, Commentary, 62(Dec 1976):85-8.

Kahrl, Stanley J. Traditions of Medieval English Drama. Pittsburgh: U Pittsburgh Press, 1975. Rev. by M. McC. Gatch, CH, 45(Sep 1976):378.

Kaiser, Robert G. Russia, the People and the Power. London: Secker and Warburg, n. d. Rev. by M. Latey, HTo, 26(Jl 1976):475.

Kalicki, J. H. The Pattern of Sino-American Crises. Cambridge: Cambridge U Press, 1975. Rev. by E. Ions, History, 61(Oct 1976):418-19.

Kallab, Valeriana, ed. see Erb, Guy F., ed.

Kamenka, Eugene and R. S. Neale, eds. Feudalism, Capitalism and Beyond. New York: St. Martin's, 1976. Rev. by J. T. Fuhrmann, HRNB, 5(Oct 1976):15-16.

Kammen, Michael. Colonial New York: A History. New York: Scribner's, 1975. Rev. by L. H. Leder, AHR, 81(Oct 1976): 955; J. Sosin, Historian, 39(Nov 1976):142-3; D. T. Konig, HRNB, 4(Mar 1976):98; J. Judd, JAH, 63(Dec 1976):681-2.

Kammler, Hans. Die Feudalmonarchien. Cologne/Vienna: Böhlau, 1974. Rev. by E. O. Blake, EHR, 91(Jl 1976):626.

Kamp, Norbert. Kirche und Monarchie im staufischen Konigreich Sizilien. 2 vols. Munich: Fink, 1975. Rev. by D. S. H. Abulafia, JEccH, 27(Jan 1976):89-90.

Kämpf, Helmut, ed. Canossa als Wende: Ausgewählte Aufsätze zur Neuren Forschung. Darmstadt: Wissenschaftliche Buchgesellschaft, 1969. Rev. by W. A. Mueller, JCS, 17(Spr 1975):341-2.

Kane, Elizabeth Wood. Twelve Mormon Homes Visited in Succession on a Journey Through Utah to Arizona. Salt Lake City: U Utah Library, 1974. Rev. by B. D. Blumell, PNQ, 67(Jl 1976):133.

Kang, Shin T. Sumerian Economic Texts from the Umma Archive. Urbana: U Ill Press, 1973. Rev. by D. I. Owen, JNES, 35 (Jl 1976):206-8.

Kann, Robert A. A History of the Habsburg Empire, 1526-1918. Berkeley: U Cal Press, 1974. Rev. by P. F. Sugar, AHR, 81(Oct 1976):888-9; R. J. W. Evans, EHR, 91(Apr 1976): 383-6.

205   KANTOWICZ

Kantowicz, Edward R. Polish-American Politics in Chicago, 1888-
1940. Chicago: U Chicago Press, 1975. Rev. by AS, 16(Fall
1975):95; M. Ridge, IMH, 72(Je 1972):163-5; E. J. Watts,
JAH, 63(Je 1976):158-9; M. H. Ebner, JISHS, 69(May 1976):
154-5; H. P. Chudacoff, RAH, 4(Mar 1976):99-104.

Kaplan, Justin. Lincoln Steffens: A Biography. New York: Simon and Schuster, 1974. Rev. by H. Shapiro, PNQ, 67(Jan
1976):36-7.

Kapp, Robert A. Szechwan and the Chinese Republic: Provincial
Militarism and Central Power, 1911-1938. New Haven, Conn.:
Yale U Press, 1973. Rev. by D. G. Gillin, AHR, 81(Apr
1976):432.

Kapungu, Leonard. Rhodesia: The Struggle for Freedom. Maryknoll, N.Y.: Orbis, 1974. Rev. by T. I. Matthews, AfAf,
75(Jan 1976):115-17.

Kapur, Harish. China in World Politics. New Delhi: India International Centre, 1975. Rev. by K. P. S. Menon, IQ, 32(Jan-
Mar 1976):88-90.

Karageorghis, Vassos. Kition: Mycenaean and Phoenician Dis-
coveries in Cyprus. London: Thames and Hudson, 1976.
Rev. by V. A. Wilson, Antiquity, 50(Sep-Dec 1976):252-3.

_____. Salamis. Vol. 5. Nicosia, Cyprus: Dept Antiquities,
1973/4. Rev. by O. W. Muscarella, Archaeology, 29(Jan
1976):67-9.

_____ and J. des Gagniers. La céramique Chypriote de style
figure. 2 vols. Rome: Istituto per gli Studi Micenei ed
Egeo-Anatolici, 1974, 1975. Rev. by F. H. Stubbings, Antiquity, 50(Sep-Dec 1976):254-5.

_____ see Buchholz, Hans-Günter

Karff, Samuel E., ed. Hebrew Union College--Jewish Institute of
Religion at One Hundred Years. Cincinnati: Hebrew Union
College Press, 1976. Rev. by N. W. Cohen, JAH, 63(Dec
1976):716-18.

Karl, Barry D. Charles E. Merriam and the Study of Politics.
Chicago: U Chicago Press, 1974. Rev. in AS, 16(Fall
1975):97; P. B. Fischer, JISHS, 69(May 1976):152; H. A.
Bone, PNQ, 67(Jan 1976):43-4.

Karlin, Jules A. Joseph M. Dixon of Montana. Missoula: U
Montana Press, 1974. Rev. by R. B. Roeder, AHR, 81(Je
1976):677; J. A. Brennan, JAH, 63(Sep 1976):449-50; J.
Waksmundski, MiA, 58(Oct 1976):193-4; M. P. Malone, PHR,
45(May 1976):288-90.

Karnani, Chetan. Nissim Ezekiel. New Delhi: Arnold Heinemann (India), 1975. Rev. by K. Schomer, JAS, 36(Nov 1976):165.

Karol, K. S. The Second Chinese Revolution. New York: Hill and Wang, 1974. Rev. by R. Baum, CQ, May 1976, pp. 372-5.

Karp, Mark, ed. African Dimensions: Essays in Honor of William O. Brown. New York: Africana, 1975. Rev. by A. D. R., JAfH, 17(Num 3, 1976):477; G. Maasdorf, JMAS, 14(Je 1976): 353-4.

Karr, Clarence. The Canada Land Company: The Early Years. Toronto: Ontario Historical Society, 1974. Rev. by K. Kelly, CHR, 57(Je 1976):194-5.

Karst, Kenneth L., Murray L. Schwartz and Audrey J. Schwartz. The Evolution of Law in the Barrios of Caracas. Los Angeles: U Cal Press, 1973. Rev. by T. Ray, HAHR, 56 (Feb 1976):184-5.

Karsten, Detlev. The Economics of Handicrafts in Traditional Societies. Munchen: Weltform Verlag, 1972. Rev. by T. T. W. Baxter, Africa, 46(Num 1, 1976):102-3.

Kartodirdjo, Sartono. Protest Movements in Rural Java. New York: Oxford U Press, 1973. Rev. by R. T. McVey, AHR, 81(Feb 1976):198-9.

Kas'ianenko, O. E., et al., eds. History of the Cities and Villages of the Ukrainian SSR. 7 vols. Kiev: Institut Istorii Akademii Nauk URSR, 1972-1974. Rev. by J. A. Armstrong, AHR, 81(Feb 1976):189-90.

Kasson, John F. Civilizing the Machine: Technology and Republican Values in America, 1776-1900. New York: Grossman, 1976. Rev. by H. A. Barnes, HRNB, 5(Oct 1976):2.

Kastrup, Allan. The Swedish Heritage in America. n. p.: Swedish Council of America, n. d. Rev. by F. R. Di Federico, Smithsonian, 7(Sep 1976):162, 164, 166; M. Brook, MinnH, 45(Sum 1976):77.

Kataoka, Tetsuya. Resistance and Revolution in China: The Communists and the Second United Front. Berkeley: U Cal Press, 1974. Rev. by S. M. Goldstein, CQ, May 1976, pp. 365-9.

Katcher, Philip. Armies of the American Wars, 1753-1815. New York: Hastings, n. d. Rev. by R. Burns, Mankind, 5(Aug 1976):9, 58.

Kater-Sibbes, G. J. F. and M. J. Vermaseren. Apis, I. The

Monuments of the Hellenistic-Roman Period from Egypt. II. Leiden: E. J. Brill, 1975. Rev. by P. N. Boulter, AJA, 80(Fall 1976):441.

Katz, Jonathan. Resistance at Christiana: The Fugitive Slave Rebellion, Christiana, Pennsylvania, September 11, 1851. New York: Crowell, 1974. Rev. by P. M. Mitchell, AHR, 81(Feb 1976):210-11; T. R. Kline, PH, 43(Jan 1976):90-2.

Katz, Michael B. The People of Hamilton, Canada West: Family and Class in a Mid-Nineteenth Century City. Cambridge, Mass.: Harvard U Press, 1976. Rev. by E. Pessen, JAH, 63(Sep 1976):472-4; M. Frisch, JIH, 7(Aut 1976):346-9.

Katz, Robert. The Fall of the House of Savoy. New York: Macmillan, 1971. Rev. by E. Carrillo, AHR, 81(Apr 1976):415.

Katzenellenbogen, S. E. Railways and the Copper Mines of Katanga. Oxford: Clarendon, 1973. Rev. by P. E. H. Hair, BH, 17 (Jl 1975):203; P. Musgrave, JTH, 3(Sep 1976):301-2.

Katzenstein, Peter J. Disjoined Partners: Austria and Germany Since 1815. Berkeley: U Cal Press, 1976. Rev. by A. Dorpalen, HRNB, 5(Oct 1976):23.

Kauffman, J. Howard and Leland Harder. Anabaptists Four Centuries Later. Scottdale: Herald Press, 1975. Rev. by D. E. Smucker, MQR, 50(Apr 1976):150-3; C. Redekop, MQR, 50(Apr 1976):153-5.

Kaufman, Burton I. Efficiency and Expansion: Foreign Trade Organization in the Wilson Administration 1913-1921. Westport, Conn.: Greenwood, 1974. Rev. by E. F. Trani, AHR, 81(Je 1976):682-3; M. Horacek, IMH, 72(Mar 1976):86-7; J. W. Osborne, PH, 43(Je 1976):93-4; L. E. Glefand, PNQ, 67 (Jan 1976):42.

Kaufman, Stuart Bruce. Samuel Gompers and the Origins of the American Federation of Labor 1848-1896. Westport, Conn.: Greenwood, 1973. Rev. by D. K. Adams, EHR, 91(Jl 1976): 667.

Kayaloff, Jacques. The Battle of Sardarabad. The Hague: Mouton, 1973. Rev. by R. G. Hovannisian, IJMES, 7(Oct 1976): 603-5.

Kearney, Robert N. The Politics of Ceylon (Sri Lanka). Ithaca, N.Y.: Cornell U Press, 1973. Rev. by B. H. Farmer, MAS, 10(Apr 1976):319-20.

Kearns, Doris. Lyndon Johnson and the American Dream. New York: Harper and Row, 1976. Rev. by J. Kirkpatrick, Commentary, 62(Aug 1976):75-6, 78, 80.

Keating, Rex. Nubian Rescue. New York: Hawthorn Books, 1975.
Rev. by B. Trigger, Antiquity, 50(Mar 1976):72.

Keddie, Nikki R. Sayyid Jamāl ad-Dīn "al-Afghani: A Political
Biography. Berkeley: U Cal Press, 1972. Rev. by A. C.
Hess, AHR, 81(Oct 1976):788-99.

_____, ed. Scholars, Saints and Sifis: Muslim Religious Insti-
tutions in the Middle East Since 1500. Berkeley: U Cal Press,
1972. Rev. by J. Kritzeck, CaHR, 62(Apr 1976):270-1; A.
Schimmel, IJMES, 7(Jl 1976):453-6.

Kedourie, Elie. In the Anglo-Arab Labyrinth: The McMahon-
Husayn Correspondence and Its Interpretations of 1914-1939.
New York: Cambridge U Press, 1976. Rev. by R. Davison,
HRNB, 4(Aug 1976):195.

Kee, Robert. The Green Flag: A History of Irish Nationalism.
New York: Delacourt, 1972. Rev. by M. R. O'Connell,
CaHR, 62(Apr 1976):309-10.

Keel, John A. The Mothman Prophecies. New York: Dutton,
1975. Rev. by J. K. Long, AA, 78(Je 1976):403-4.

Keen, M. H. England in the Later Middle Ages. London:
Methuen, 1973. Rev. by C. M. Barron, History, 61(Feb
1976):102-4.

Kegan, Elizabeth Hamer, comp. Leadership in the American Revolution. Washington: Library of Congress, 1974. Rev. by J.
K. Martin, MHM, 71(Sum 1976):264-6.

Kehrig, Manfred. Stalingrad, Analyse und Dokumentation einer
Schlacht. Stuttgart: Deutsche Verlags-Anstalt, 1974. Rev.
by E. F. Ziemke, AHR, 81(Je 1976):638-9.

Keim, Albert N., ed. Compulsory Education and the Amish: The
Right Not to Be Modern. Boston: Beacon, 1975. Rev. by
J. L. Garrett, Jr., CH, 45(Sep 1976):397-8; J. W. Fretz,
MQR, 50(Oct 1976):300.

Keith, Agnes Newton. Before the Blossoms Fall: Life and Death
in Japan. Boston: Atlantic Monthly-Little, Brown, 1975.
Rev. by S. K. Johnson, JJS, 2(Sum 1976):437-48.

Keith, Brendan see Cook, Chris

Kellenbenz, Herman, ed. Schwerpunkte der Eisengewinnung und
Eisenverarbeitung in Europa 1500-1650. Cologne: Böhlau
Verlag, 1974. Rev. by R. Knauerhase, JEH, 36(Je 1976):
472-6.

_____ and Klara van Eyll. Die Geschichte der Unternehmerischen

Selbstverwaltung in Köln 1797-1914.   Köln: Rheinisch-Westfälisches Wirtschaftsarchiv, 1972.   Rev. by J. Kocka, BHR,
50(Spr 1976):104-6.

Keller, Karl.   The Example of Edward Taylor.   Amherst: U Mass
Press, 1975.   Rev. by F. Murphy, NEQ, 49(Je 1976):323-5;
S. Bush, WMQ, 33(Apr 1976):346-8.

Kelley, Allen C., Jeffrey G. Williamson, and Russell J. Cheetham.
Dualistic Economic Development, Theory and History.   Chi-
cago: U Chicago Press, 1972.   Rev. by S. Chakravarty,
IESHR, 13(Jan-Mar 1976):109-11.

Kelley, Darwin.   Milligan's Fight Against Lincoln.   New York:
Exposition, 1972.   Rev. by M. Klein, CWTI, 15(May 1976):
46-8.

Kelley, Donald R.   François Hotman: A Revolutionary's Ordeal.
Princeton, N.J.:   Prin U Press, 1973.   Rev. by R. F.
Kierstead, AHR, 81(Apr 1976):395-6.

Kelly, Alfred H., et al.   Library of Congress Symposia on the
American Revolution, May 9 and 10, 1974.   Washington: Li-
brary of Congress, 1974.   Rev. by K. Coleman, FHQ, 54
(Jan 1976):390-1; L. G. Bowman, Historian, 30(Nov 1976):
145-6; T. Colbourn, IMH, 72(Je 1976):171-3; R. M. Calhoon,
JAH, 63(Je 1976):112; G. G. Shackelford, JSH, 42(Feb 1976):
109-10; A. E. Matthews, NCHR, 53(Win 1976):94-5; G. W.
Knepper, OH, 85(Win 1976):86-7.

Kelly, Celsus and Gerard Bushell, eds.   Austrialia Franciscana.
Vols. V and VI.   Madrid: Archivo Ibero Americano, 1971-
1973.   Rev. by A. Gschaedler, TAm, 33(Jl 1976):181-2.

Kelly, Henry Ansgar.   The Matrimonial Trials of Henry VIII.
Stanford: Stan U Press, 1976.   Rev. by B. L. Beer, AHR,
81(Oct 1976):853; J. W. Ferguson, HRNB, 4(May/Je 1976):
153.

Kelly, J. N. D.   Jerome: His Life, Writings and Controversies.
New York: Harper and Row, 1975.   Rev. by R. L. Wilken,
CH, 45(Sep 1976):376; G. Bonner, JEccH, 27(Apr 1976):184.

Kelly, R. Gordon.   Mother Was a Lady: Self and Society in Selected
American Children's Periodicals 1865-1890.   Westport, Conn.:
Greenwood, 1974.   Rev. by B. W. Wishy, AHR, 81(Feb 1976):
211-12.

Kendall, Dorothy Steinbomer and Carmen Perry.   Gentilz: Artist
of the Old Southwest.   Austin: U Texas Press, 1974.   Rev.
by J. H. Jenkins, WHQ, 7(Oct 1976):432-3.

Kendle, John E.   The Round Table Movement and Imperial Union.

Buffalo, N.Y.: U Toronto Press, 1975. Rev. by D. C. Gordon, AHR, 81(Oct 1976):864-5.

Kendrick, Alexander. The Wound Within: America in the Vietnam Years, 1945-1974. Boston: Little, Brown, 1974. Rev. by B. J. Bernstein, AHR, 81(Apr 1976):470.

Kennedy, Gavin. The Economics of Defense. Totowa, N.J.: Rowman and Littlefield, 1975. Rev. by W. W. Lindsay, JEH, 36(Je 1976):479-80.

Kennedy, Paul M. The Samoan Tangle: A Study in Anglo-German-American Relations, 1878-1900. New York: Barnes and Noble, 1974. Rev. by P. S. Holbo, AHR, 81(Apr 1976):361; D. K. Fieldhouse, EHR, 91(Jan 1976):223-4; C. Howard, History, 61(Je 1976):311; M. Tate, PHR, 45(Feb 1976):144-5.

Kennedy, Thomas C. Charles A. Beard and American Foreign Policy. Gainesville: U Presses Fla, 1975. Rev. by B. Kuklick, AHR, 81(Je 1976):688; L. Gardner, History, 61(Oct 1976):424; C. J. Phillips, IMH, 72(Je 1976):180-1; W. S. Cole, JAH, 63(Je 1976):184-5; R. N. Current, PHR, 45(Aug 1976):435-6.

Kennett, Lee and James Laverne Anderson. The Gun in America: The Origins of a National Dilemma. Westport, Conn.: Greenwood, 1975. Rev. by S. E. Ambrose, AHR, 81(Oct 1976): 1006-7; J. W. Carson, JOW, 15(Jan 1976):133; W. E. Hollon, WHQ, 7(Apr 1976):211-12.

Kenney, E. J. The Classical Text. Berkeley: U Cal Press, 1974. Rev. by J. D. Woodbridge, CH, 45(Mar 1976):107-8.

Kenney, Edwin J. Elizabeth Bowen. Lewisburg, Pa.: Bucknell U Press, 1975. Rev. by C. W. Barrow, E-I, 11(Sum 1976): 155-6.

Kent, Harold Winfield. Dr. Hyde and Mr. Stevenson. Rutland, Vt.: Tuttle, 1973. Rev. by J. B. McGloin, CaHR, 62(Jl 1976):505-6.

Kent, Sherman. The Election of 1827 in France. Cambridge, Mass.: Harvard U Press, 1976. Rev. by E. L. Newman, AHR, 81(Oct 1976):869-70; M. S. Hartman, Historian, 39 (Nov 1976):125-7; G. Fasel, HRNB, 4(Jan 1976):65-6.

Kern, Richard. John Winebrenner: Nineteenth-Century Reformer. Harrisburg, Pa.: Central Publishing House, 1974. Rev. by D. E. Harrell, Jr., AHR, 81(Apr 1976):446; I. V. Brown, PH, 43(Jan 1976):87-9.

Kern, Stephen. Anatomy and Destiny. Indianapolis: Bobbs-Merrill, 1975. Rev. by V. L. Bullough, AHR, 81(Oct 1976):814; E. H. Baruch, Commentary, 61(Je 1976):84-8.

Kernek, S. J. Distractions of Peace During War. Philadelphia:
    American Philosophical Society, 1975. Rev. by K. Robbins,
    EHR, 91(Oct 1976):934; V. H. Rothwell, HJ, 19(Mar 1976):
    304-5.

Kerr, Malcolm H., ed. The Elusive Peace in the Middle East.
    Albany: SUNY Press, 1975. Rev. by R. G. Landen, HRNB,
    4(Feb 1976):86.

Kersey, Harry A., Jr. Pelts, Plumes, and Hides. Gainesville:
    U Presses Fla, 1975. Rev. by C. Hudson, GHQ, 60(Sum
    1976):194-5; J. W. Bailey, JSH, 42(Nov 1976):596-7.

Kershaw, Gordon E. "Gentlemen of Large Property & Judicious
    Men:" The Kennebeck Proprietors, 1749-1775. Sommers-
    worth, N.H.: New Hampshire Pub. Co., 1975. Rev. by
    R. F. Banks, WMQ, 33(Apr 1976):348-50.

Kessen, William, ed. Childhood in China. New Haven, Conn.:
    Yale U Press, 1975. Rev. by N. J. Olsen, JAS, 36(Nov
    1976):141-2.

Kessinger, Tom G. Vilyatpur, 1848-1968: Social and Economic
    Change in a North Indian Village. Berkeley: U Cal Press,
    1974. Rev. by J. Adams, JAAS, 11(Jl-Oct 1976):231-3; C.
    Dewey, MAS, 10(Feb 1976):131-8.

Ketcham, Ralph. From Colony to Country ... 1750-1820. New
    York: Macmillan, 1974. Rev. by J. M. Bumsted, NYHSQ,
    60(Jan/Apr 1976):71-2; J. A. Neuenschwander, PH, 43(Oct
    1976):382.

Ketchum, Richard M. Decisive Day: The Battle for Bunker Hill.
    Garden City, N.Y.: Doubleday, 1974. Rev. by P. D. Nel-
    son, MHM, 71(Sum 1971):272-3.

_____. The World of George Washington. New York: American
    Heritage, 1974. Rev. by E. Park, Smithsonian, 6(Feb 1975):
    125-6.

Keyser, Marja, comp. Dirk Philips, 1504-1568: A Catalogue of
    His Printed Works in the University Library of Amsterdam.
    Nieuwkoop: B. DeGraaf, 1975. Rev. by R. S. Armour, CH,
    45(Sep 1976):383.

Khalidi, Tarif. Islamic Historiography. Albany: SUNY Press,
    1975. Rev. by D. W. Littlefield, HRNB, 4(Feb 1976):83-4.

Khoo, Kay Kim. The Western Malay States, 1850-1873: The Ef-
    fects of Commercial Development on Malay Politics. New
    York: Oxford U Press, 1972. Rev. by R. Van Niel, AHR,
    81(Oct 1976):946-7.

Kibler, William W., ed. Eleanor of Aquitaine. Austin: U

Texas Press, 1976. Rev. by J. L. Shneidman, HRNB, 4(Sep 1976):229-30.

Kierman, Frank A., Jr. and John K. Fairbank, eds. Chinese Ways in Warfare. Cambridge, Mass.: Harvard U Press, 1974. Rev. by R. Taylor, AHR, 81(Feb 1976):193.

Kiernan, V. G. Marxism and Imperialism. New York: St. Martin's, 1975. Rev. by R. W. Winks, AHR, 81(Je 1976):561-2; P. J. Cain, History, 61(Oct 1976):466-8.

Kierstead, Raymond F., ed. State and Society in Seventeenth-Century France. New York: New Viewpoints, 1975. Rev. by L. Martines, HRNB, 4(Mar 1976):111.

Kieve, J. L. The Electric Telegraph: A Social and Economic History. Newton Abbot: David and Charles, 1973. Rev. by W. H. Chaloner, BH, 17(Jan 1975):86-7.

Kiewe, Heinz Edgar. Civilization on Loan. Oxford: A. N. I., 1973. Rev. by T. N. Foss, JMH, 48(Mar 1976):118-19.

Kilian, Klaus. Fibeln in Thessalien. München: C. H. Beck, 1975. Rev. by A. M. Snodgrass, Antiquity, 50(Mar 1976): 75-6.

Killion, Ronald G. and Charles T. Waller. Georgia and the Revolution. Atlanta: Cherokee, 1975. Rev. by G. R. Lamplugh, JSH, 42(Feb 1976):112.

Killmer, Richard L. and Charles P. Lutz. The Draft and the Rest of Your Life. Minneapolis: Augsburg, 1972. Rev. by R. L. Uzzel, JCS, 17(Spr 1975):347.

Kilmer, Kenton and Donald Sweig. The Fairfax Family in Fairfax County: A Brief History. Fairfax: Fairfax County Office of Comprehensive Planning, 1975. Rev. by S. E. Brown, Jr., VMHB, 84(Jan 1976):102-3.

Kilson, Marion. African Urban Kinsman: The Ga of Central Accra. London: Hurst, 1974. Rev. by K. Hart, AfAf, 75 (Jl 1976):396-7; L. Mair, Africa, 46(Num 1, 1976):207.

Kimambo, I. N., ed. see Ranger, T. O., ed.

Kimball, Solon T. and James T. Watson, eds. Crossing Cultural Boundaries. n. p.: Chandler, 1972. Rev. by R. H. Wax, AA, 78(Mar 1976):151.

Kinch, Sam and Stuart Long. Allan Shivers: The Pied Piper of Texas Politics. Austin: Shoal Creek, 1975. Rev. by A. Barr, A & W, 18(Aut 1976):299-300.

Kinchen, Oscar A. Women Who Spied for the Blue and the Gray.
Philadelphia: Dorrance, 1972. Rev. by R. D. Hoffsommer,
CWTI, 15(May 1976):46-7.

King, Edmund. Peterborough Abbey 1086-1310: A Study in the
Land Market. Cambridge: Cam U Press, 1973. Rev. by
P. R. Hyams, History, 61(Je 1976):257; J. H. Munro, JEH,
36(Sep 1976):767.

King, James T. and Walker D. Wyman. Centennial History: The
University of Wisconsin-River Falls, 1874-1974. River Falls:
U Wisconsin-River Falls Press, 1975. Rev. by J. Lankford,
WMH, 60(Aut 1976):57-8.

King, Preston. The Ideology of Order: A Comparative Analysis
of Jean Bodin and Thomas Hobbes. New York: Barnes and
Noble, 1974. Rev. by W. F. Church, AHR, 81(Apr 1976):
374-5.

King, Robert R. and Robert W. Dean, eds. East European Per-
spectives on European Security and Cooperation. New York:
Praeger, 1974. Rev. by W. C. Clemens, Jr., EEQ, 10
(Mar 1976):133-5.

Kinnamon, Keneth, ed. James Baldwin. Englewood Cliffs, N. J.:
Prentice-Hall, 1974. Rev. in Crisis, 83(Mar 1976):102.

Kinney, John M., comp. Index to Applications for Texas Confederate Pensions. Austin: Texas St Library, 1975. Rev.
by R. S. Lackey, AmArc, 39(Jan 1976):56-7.

Kinsbrunner, Jay. Chile: A Historical Interpretation. New York:
Harper and Row, 1974. Rev. by G. Matyoka, TAm, 32(Jan
1976):486-8.

Kinsley, David R. The Sword and the Flute. Berkeley: U Cal
Press, 1975. Rev. by J. T. O'Connell, JAS, 36(Nov 1976):
170-1.

Kiple, Kenneth F. Blacks in Colonial Cuba, 1774-1899. Gainesville: U Presses Fla, 1976. Rev. by F. W. Knight, HAHR,
56(Nov 1976):647-8.

Király, Bela K., ed. Tolerance and Movements of Religious Dissent in Eastern Europe. Boulder, Col.: East European
Quarterly, 1976. Rev. by J. F. Zacek, HRNB, 4(Aug 1976):
201.

Kirby, R. G. and A. E. Musson. The Voice of the People: John
Doherty, Trade Unionist, Radical and Factory Reformer.
Manchester: Manchester U Press, 1975. Rev. by G. B. A.
M. Finlayson, History, 61(Oct 1976):484.

Kirkbride, Alec. From the Wings. London: Frank Cass, n. d.
Rev. by T. Prittie, HTo, 26(Jl 1976):481-2.

Kirkman, James. Fort Jesus: A Portuguese Fortress on the East
African Coast. Oxford: Oxford U Press, 1974. Rev. by M.
S. Bisson, Archaeology, 29(Apr 1976):142.

Kirsch, A. Thomas, ed. see Skinner, G. William, ed.

Kirstein, Lincoln. Nijinsky Dancing. New York: Knopf, 1975.
Rev. by G. Gelles, Smithsonian, 7(Feb 1976):124, 126-7.

Kitagawa, Hiroshi and Bruce T. Tsuchida, trans. The Tale of
the Heike. Tokyo: U Tokyo Press, 1975. Rev. by H. C.
McCullough, JJS, 2(Sum 1976):460-70.

Kitchen, Kenneth A. The Third Intermediate Period in Egypt
(1100-650 B.C.). Warminster: Aris & Phillips, 1973.
Rev. by E. F. Wente, JNES, 35(Oct 1976):275-8.

Kitchen, Martin. A Military History of Germany from the
Eighteenth Century to the Present Day. Bloomington: Ind U
Press, 1975. Rev. by G. A. Craig, AHR, 81(Je 1976):613;
W. Carr, History, 61(Je 1976):322-3.

Kitchen, Paddy. A Most Unsettling Person: The Life and Ideas
of Patrick Geddes. New York: Saturday Review, 1976.
Rev. by J. S. Rosenberg, Smithsonian, 7(May 1976):122,
124-6.

Kitsikis, Dimitri. Le rôle des experts à la Conference de la Paix
de 1919. Ottawa: Editions de l'Université d'Ottawa, 1972.
Rev. by H. N. Howard, AHR, 81(Apr 1976):380-1; H. Nelson, CHR, 57(Mar 1976):100-2.

Kittelson, James M. Wolfgang Capito: From Humanist to Reformer. Leiden: E. J. Brill, 1975. Rev. by R. L. Harrison, Jr. , CH, 45(Je 1976):258.

Kleimola, Ann M. Justice in Medieval Russia: Muscovite Judgment Charters (Pravye Gramoty) of the Fifteenth and Sixteenth
Centuries. Philadelphia: American Philosophical Society,
1975. Rev. by R. Hellie, AHR, 81(Oct 1976):904.

Klein, Donald W. see Israel, John

Klein, Milton M. New York in the Revolution: A Bibliography.
Albany: NY St American Revolution Bicentennial Commission,
1974. Rev. by J. Judd, NYHSQ, 60(Jan/Apr 1976):67.

_____. Politics of Diversity. Port Washington, N. Y. : Ken-
nikat, 1974. Rev. by D. Greenberg, NYHSQ, 60(Jan/Apr
1976):61-2; D. C. Humphrey, PH, 43(Jl 1976):272-3.

215   KLEIN

Klein, Randolph Shipley.   Portrait of an Early American Family:
   The Shippens of Pennsylvania Across Five Generations.
   Philadelphia: U Pa Press, 1975. Rev. by N. S. Cohen,
   JAH, 63(Dec 1976):688-9; R. E. Paulson, RAH, 4(Je 1976):
   171-7.   •

Klein, Robert A.   Sovereign Equality Among States.   Toronto: U
   Tor Press, 1974. Rev. by S. E. Cooper, AHR, 81(Je 1976):
   566.

Klessman, Christoph.   Die Selbstbehauptung einer Nation: Nationalsozialistische Kulturpolitik und polnische Widerstands-
   bewegung im Generalgouvernement, 1939-1945. [Düsseldorf]:
   Bertelsmann Universitätsverlag, 1971. Rev. by Y. Jelinek,
   AHR, 81(Oct 1976):903.

Klindt-Jensen, Ole.   A History of Scandinavian Archaeology.   London: Thames and Hudson, 1975. Rev. by D. M. Wilson,
   Antiquity, 50(Mar 1976):70.

Kline, Mary-Jo, ed.   see Butterfield, L. H. , ed.

Klingaman, David C. and Richard K. Vedder, eds.   Essays in
   Nineteenth-Century Economic History. Athens: Ohio U Press,
   1975. Rev. by H. N. Scheiber, AHR, 81(Je 1976):662-3;
   W. Graebner, OH, 85(Spr 1976):164-6; G. Wright, RAH, 4
   (Mar 1976):73-7.

Kluger, Richard.   Simple Justice.   New York: Knopf, 1976.
   Rev. by C. E. Finn, Jr. , Commentary, 61(Apr 1976):78-82.

Knapp, Vincent J.   Europe in the Era of Social Transformation:
   1700--Present. Englewood Cliffs, N.J.: Prentice-Hall, 1976.
   Rev. by J. B. Ridley, HRNB, 4(Mar 1976):108.

Kneer, Warren G.   Great Britain and the Caribbean, 1901-1913:
   A Study in Anglo-American Relations. East Lansing: Mich
   St U Press, 1975. Rev. by W. D. Jones, AHR, 81(Oct 1976):
   1010-11; M. T. Gilderhus, HAHR, 56(Feb 1976):148-9.

Knight, David.   Sources for the History of Science, 1660-1914.
   Ithaca, N.Y.: Cornell U Press, 1975. Rev. by S. G.
   Brush, AHR, 81(Je 1976):558-9.

Knight, Franklin W.   The African Dimension in Latin American
   Societies. New York: Macmillan, 1974. Rev. by C. Winters, JMAS, 14(Mar 1976):175-7.

Knightley, Phillip.   The First Casualty: The War Correspondent
   as Hero, Propagandist, and Myth-Maker. New York: Harcourt, Brace, Jovanovich, 1975. Rev. by L. R. Bisceglia,
   HRNB, 4(Apr 1976):130.

Knipping, Franz. Die amerikanische Russlandpolitik in der Zeit des Hitler-Stalin-Pakts 1939-1941. Tübingen: J. C. B. Mohr, 1974. Rev. by U. Sautter, AHR, 81(Apr 1976):465.

Knoles, George H., ed. Essays and Assays: California History Reappraised. San Francisco: Cal Historical Society, 1973. Rev. by W. W. Cordray, JOW, 15(Jan 1976):125.

Knollenberg, Bernhard. Growth of the American Revolution, 1766-1775. New York: Free Press, 1975. Rev. by J. P. Greene, AHR, 81(Je 1976):653-4; A. L. Stoeckel, IMH, 72(Mar 1976): 68-9; R. J. Champagne, JAH, 63(Sep 1976):395-6; A. S. Brown, JSH, 42(Feb 1976):105-7; M. M. Merwin, NCHR, 53 (Win 1976):91-2; J. E. Cooke, PH, 43(Oct 1976):367-8; M. Freiberg, NEQ, 49(Mar 1976):165-7; R. R. Johnson, PNQ, (Jl 1976):130.

Koblick, Steven, ed. Sweden's Development from Poverty to Affluence, 1750-1970. Minneapolis: U Minn Press, 1975. Rev. by P. V. Thorson, Historian, 39(Nov 1976):137; F. J. Bowman, HRNB, 4(Mar 1976):111.

Kocka, Jürgen. Klassengesellschaft im Krieg 1914-1918. Göttingen: Vandenhoeck and Rupprecht, 1973. Rev. by G. Feldman, JIH, 7(Sum 1976):164-9.

Kofos, Evangelos. Greece and the Eastern Crisis, 1875-1878. Thesseloniki: Institute for Balkan Studies, 1975. Rev. by D. G. Kousoulas, AHR, 81(Oct 1976):895.

Köhler, Joachim. Das Ringen um die tridentinische Erneuerung im Bistum Breslau. Cologne: Verlag Böhlau, 1973. Rev. by D. Miller, CaHR, 62(Jan 1976):130-2.

Kohler, Par Jean-Marie. Activités agricoles et changements sociaux dans l'ouest mossi. Paris: Orstrom, 1971. Rev. by B. W. Hodder, Africa, 46(Num 1, 1976):100.

Kohli, Suresh, ed. Modern Indian Short Stories. New Delhi: Arnold Heinemann (India), 1974. Rev. by S. Dulai, JAS, 36(Nov 1976):164-5.

Kohlstedt, Sally Gregory. The Formation of the American Scientific Community. Urbana: U Ill Press, n.d. Rev. by R. C. Post, Smithsonian, 7(May 1976):108-10.

Kohn, Richard H. Eagle and Sword: The Federalists and the Creation of the Military Establishment in America, 1783-1802. New York: Free Press, 1975. Rev. by R. M. Rollins, AHR, 81(Oct 1976):964; T. E. Templin, FCHQ, 50(Jl 1976):326-7; J. F. Stegeman, GHQ, 60(Spr 1976):84-5; C. B. Smith, HRNB, 4(Jan 1976):60; W. M. Fowler, Jr., IMH, 72(Dec 1976):366-7; A. A. Ekirch, Jr., JAH, 63(Je 1976):107-8; L.

217   KOLINSKY

Morton, JSH, 42(May 1976):277-9; R. Burns, Mankind, 5(Aug 1976):9, 58; D. Higginbotham, NCHR, 53(Sum 1976):328-9; L. Reed, Smithsonian, 6(Oct 1975):148, 150, 152; R. F. Weigley, RAH, 4(Mar 1976):59-63.

Kolinsky, Martin. Continuity and Change in European Society. New York: St. Martin's, 1974. Rev. by J. Colton, AHR, 81(Oct 1976):849-50; M. Larkin, History, 61(Feb 1976):140.

Kolodziej, Edward A. French International Policy Under De Gaulle and Pompidou. Ithaca, N.Y.: Cornell U Press, 1974. Rev. by W. R. Keylor, JMH, 48(Mar 1976):155-7.

Koloskov, B. T. see Borisov, O. B.

Komlos, John H. Louis Kossuth in America, 1851-1852. Buffalo, N.Y.: East European Institute, 1973. Rev. by J. M. Bergquist, AHR, 81(Oct 1976):974.

Konev, I. S. The Great March of Liberation. Moscow: Progress Publ'rs, 1972. Rev. by E. F. Ziemke, AHR, 81(Je 1976): 638-9.

Koob, C. Albert and Russell Shaw. S.O.S. for Catholic Schools. New York: Holt, Rinehart and Winston, 1970. Rev. by E. D. Wynot, Jr., JCS, 18(Aut 1976):571-3.

Köpecki, Béla and E. H. Balázs, eds. Paysannerie Française, Paysannerie Hongroise XVIe-XXe siecles. Budapest: Akademiai Kiado, 1973. Rev. by R. J. W. Evans, History, 61 (Feb 1976):92.

Kopylov, A. N. Essays on the Cultural Life of Siberia from the 17th to the Beginning of the 19th Century. Novosibirsk: Izdatel'stvo "Nauka," 1974. Rev. by S. Watrous, AHR, 81 (Oct 1976):905-6.

Korn, Bertram Wallace. The Early Jews of New Orleans. Waltham, Mass.: American Jewish Historical Society, 1969. Rev. by C. L. Howe, Jr., JCS, 17(Spr 1975):312-14.

Korn, Francis. Elementary Structures Reconsidered. Berkeley: U Cal Press, 1973. Rev. by I. Rossi, AA, 78(Mar 1976): 145.

Körner, Alfred. Die Wiener Jakobiner: Schriften und Dokumente. Stuttgart: Metzler, 1972. Rev. by E. Tenner, JMH, 48(Mar 1976):162-4.

Kornrumpf, Hans-Jürgen and Miterbeit von Jutta Kornrumpf. Osmanische Bibliographie mit Besonderer Berucksichtigung der Türkei in Europa. Leiden-Köln: E. J. Brill, 1973. Rev. by J. P. Jankowski, EEQ, 10(Mar 1976):126-7.

KORNWEIBEL 218

Kornweibel, Theodore, Jr. No Crystal Stair. Westport, Conn.:
Greenwood, 1975. Rev. by M. M. Kranz, HRNB, 4(Jl 1976):
163; W. H. Harris, JAH, 63(Dec 1976):755-7.

Korr, Charles P. Cromwell and the New Model Foreign Policy.
Berkeley: U Cal Press, 1975. Rev. by W. K. Hackmann,
AHR, 81(Oct 1976):855; A. Woolrych, History, 61(Oct 1976):
450-1.

Kors, Alan Charles. D'Holbach's Coterie: An Enlightenment in
Paris. Princeton, N.J.: Prin U Press, 1976. Rev. by D.
Bitton, HRNB, 4(Sep 1976):228.

Korsok, Albert J. see Noble, Allen G.

Koselleck, Reinhart. Kritik und Krise. Frankfurt: Suhrkamp
Verlag, 1973. Rev. by B. Loewenstein, JMH, 48(Mar 1976):
122-4.

Koss, Stephen. Nonconformity in Modern British Politics. Hamden,
Conn.: Archon, 1975. Rev. by K. O. Morgan, HJ, 19(Mar
1976):296-9; N. J. Richards, JCS, 18(Aut 1976):556-8.

Kossmann, E. H. and A. F. Mellink. Texts Concerning the Revolt
of the Netherlands. Cambridge: Cam U Press, 1974. Rev.
by G. Parker, History, 61(Feb 1976):112.

Koster, John see Burnette, Robert

Koszeliwec, Iwan. Mykola Skrypnyk. New York: Suchasnist
Publ'rs, 1972. Rev. by M. Bohachevsky-Chomiak, AHR, 81
(Je 1976):635-6.

Kothari, Rajni. Footsteps into the Future. New York: Free
Press, 1974. Rev. by A. Lall, IQ, 32(Apr-Je 1976):226-30.

Koumoulides, J. T. A. Cyprus and the War of Greek Independence,
1821-1829. London: Zeno, 1974. Rev. by R. Albrecht-
Carrié, AHR, 81(Apr 1976):417; R. Clogg, History, 61(Feb
1976):122.

Kouri, R. , ed. see Nelson, J. G. , ed.

Kousser, J. Morgan. The Shaping of Southern Politics. New
Haven, Conn.: Yale U Press, 1974. Rev. by J. Williamson,
AHR, 81(Apr 1976):457-8; J. R. Pole, HJ, 19(Sep 1976):802-
5; K. I. Polakoff, HT, 10(Nov 1976):155-8; A. S. Link, JIH,
7(Sum 1976):178-81.

Kovaleff, Theodore P. , ed. see Cannistraro, Philip V. , ed.

Kozik, Jan. Between Reaction and Revolution. Cracow: Universy-
tet Jagiellónskiego, n.d. Rev. by M. Bohachevsky-Chomiak,
AHR, 81(Oct 1976):900-1.

Kozlowski, Stefan Karol <u>see</u> Krzysztof, Janusz

Kraay, Colin M. <u>see</u> Davis, Norman

Kraft, Herbert C., ed. <u>A Delaware Indian Symposium.</u> Harrisburg: Pennsylvania Historical and Museum Commission, 1974. Rev. by N. M. Belting, AHR, 81(Oct 1976):950-1; J. Miller, AmAnt, 41(Apr 1976):245-8; D. L. Smith, JAH, 63(Je 1976): 100-1.

Krailsheimer, A. J. <u>Armand-Jean de Rancé, Abbot of La Trappe.</u> New York: Oxford U Press, 1974. Rev. by N. Ravitch, AHR, 81(Feb 1976):155-6; B. Plongeron, EHR, 91(Jl 1976): 645; D. Fenlon, HJ, 19(Sep 1976):787-92.

Kranz, Peter and Reinhard Lullies. <u>Corpus Vasorum Antiquorum, Deutschland 38.</u> Munich: C. H. Beck, 1975. Rev. by A. H. Ashmead, AJA, 80(Sum 1976):315-16.

Krassowski, A. <u>Development and the Debt Trap: Economic Planning and External Borrowing in Ghana.</u> London: Croom Helm, 1974. Rev. by F. Stewart, AfAf, 75(Jan 1976):108-9.

Krausse, Alexis. <u>Russia in Asia: A Record and a Study, 1558-1899.</u> New York: Barnes and Noble, 1973. Rev. by M. Rossabi, JAAS, 11(Jl-Oct 1976):223-4.

Krautscheidt, Joseph and Heiner Marre, eds. <u>Essener Gespräche zum Thema Staat und Kirche.</u> Münster: Aschendorff, 1969. Rev. by W. A. Mueller, JCS, 16(Spr 1976):352-5.

Kravets', M. M. <u>Ivan Franko--Historian of the Ukraine.</u> L'viv: Vydavnytstvo L'vivskoho Universytetu, 1971. Rev. by V. D. Medlin, AHR, 81(Je 1976):639-40.

Kravic, Frank J. <u>see</u> Neuman, George C.

Kreidberg, Marjorie. <u>Food on the Frontier.</u> St. Paul: Minn Historical Society, 1975. Rev. by E. Jones, MinnH, 45(Spr 1976):34-5.

Krick, Robert K. <u>Parker's Virginia Battery, C.S.A.</u> Berryville, Va.: Va Book Co., 1975. Rev. by J. I. Robertson, Jr., CWTI, 15(May 1976):49; M. Stuart, VMHB, 84(Jl 1976):365-7.

Krickus, Richard. <u>Pursuing the American Dream.</u> Garden City, N.Y.: Anchor, 1976. Rev. by N. Lederer, Mankind, 5(Oct 1976):55, 57.

Kring, Walter Donald. <u>Liberals Among the Orthodox.</u> Boston: Beacon, 1974. Rev. by D. W. Howe, AHR, 81(Feb 1976): 208.

Krisch, Henry. <u>German Politics Under Soviet Occupation.</u> New

York: Columbia U Press, 1974. Rev. by A. H. Price,
AHR, 81(Oct 1976):887.

Kroeker, Marvin E. Great Plains Command: William B. Hazen in
the Frontier West. Norman: U Ok Press, 1976. Rev. by
R. N. Ellis, JAH, 63(Dec 1976):730-1; B. Farwell, Smithsonian, 7(Aug 1976):95-6.

Krohn, Helga. Die Juden in Hamburg. Hamburg: Hans Christians
Verlag, 1974. Rev. by G. R. Mork, AHR, 81(Feb 1976):
166-7.

Kromer, William M., ed. The American West and the Religious
Experience. Los Angeles: Western American, 1972. Rev.
by D. L. Thrapp, JAriH, 17(Sum 1976):243-4.

Krüger, Gerda. Die Rechtsstellung der Vorkonstantinischen Kirchen.
Amsterdam: Rodopi, 1969. Rev. by W. A. Mueller, JCS,
18(Aut 1976):582-3.

Krusen, Jessie Ball Thompson. Tuckahoe Plantation. Richmond:
Whittet & Shepperson, 1975. Rev. by M. Lester, VMHB,
84(Jan 1976):99-100.

Krzysztof, Janusz and Stefan Karol Kozlowski. Pradzieje Europy
ad XL do IV tysiaclecia. Warsaw: Panstowe Wydawnictwo
Naukowe, 1975. Rev. by P. Allsworth-Jones, Antiquity, 50
(Je 1976):152-4.

Kuhlman, James A., ed. see Mensonides, Louis, ed.

Kuiper, Gerard J. The Pseudo-Jonathan Targum and Its Relationship to Targum Onkelos. Rome: Institutum Patristicum, 1972.
Rev. by S. A. Kaufman, JNES, 35(Jan 1976):61-2.

Kuklick, Bruce. American Policy and the Division of Germany.
London: Cornell U Press, 1972. Rev. by E. Ions, History,
61(Feb 1976):148.

Kulczykowski, Mariusz. The Textile Center of Andrychow in the
18th and 19th Centuries. Cracow: Zaklad Narodowy imienia
Ossolińskich, Wydawnictwo Polskiej Akademii Nauk., 1972.
Rev. by S. Dabrowski, AHR, 81(Oct 1976):899-900.

Kull, Andrew. New England Cemeteries. n. p.: Stephen Greene,
1975. Rev. by R. Rinehart, Smithsonian, 6(Aug 1975):92-4.

Kunin, Madeline and Marilyn Stout. The Big Green Book: A Four-
Season Guide to Vermont. Barre, Mass.: Barre Publishing,
1976. Rev. by M. Hanagan, VH, 44(Sum 1976):182-4.

Kup, A. P. Sierra Leone. New York: St. Martin's, 1975. Rev.
by V. M. Smith, HRNB, 4(Feb 1976):82-3.

221   KUPCHINSKY

Kupchinsky, Roman, comp. The Nationalities Question in the USSR:
A Collection of Documents. Munich: Suchasnist, 1975. Rev.
by R. Solchanyk, AHR, 81(Oct 1976):911.

Kuper, Leo. Race, Class, and Power. London: Duckworth, 1974.
Rev. by T. O. Odetola, JMAS, 14(Sep 1976):548-50.

Kurgan, G. and P. Moureaux. La Quantification en Histoire.
Brussels: Editions de l'Universite de Bruxelles, 1973. Rev.
by R. Schofield, History, 61(Feb 1976):75-6.

Kurland, Philip B., ed. The Supreme Court Review: 1973.
Chicago: U Chicago Press, 1974. Rev. by W. H. Peterson,
JCS, 17(Win 1975):134-6.

Kurtz, Donna Carol. Athenian White Lekythoi. Oxford: Clarendon
Press, 1975. Rev. by B. F. Cook, Antiquity, 50(Je 1976):
171.

Kurze, Wilhelm. Codex diplomaticus Amiatinus I (736-951).
Tubingen: Max Niemeyer Verlag, 1974. Rev. by D. A.
Bullough, EHR, 91(Jl 1976):623-4.

Kurzman, Paul A. Harry Hopkins and the New Deal. Fair Lawn,
N.J.: Burdick, 1974. Rev. by F. J. Rader, AI, 43(Spr
1976):303-5.

Kushner, Howard I. Conflict on the Northwest Coast: American-
Russian Rivalry in the Pacific Northwest, 1790-1867. Westport, Conn.: Greenwood, 1975. Rev. by R. E. MacMaster,
NEQ, 49(Mar 1976):128-30; E. A. P. Crownhart-Vaughan,
OrHQ, 77(Mar 1976):85-6; M. E. Wheeler, WHQ, 7(Jl 1976):
311-14; C. B. O'Brien, CHQ, 55(Spr 1976):88-9; W. J. Morgan, HRNB, 4(Jan 1976):59; S. B. Rolland, JAH, 63(Sep
1976):405-6.

Kusmer, Kenneth L. A Ghetto Takes Shape: Black Cleveland
1870-1930. Urbana: U Ill Press, 1976. Rev. by R. Davis,
JNH, 61(Oct 1976):407-9.

Kuuse, Jan. Interaction Between Agriculture and Industry. Gothenburg: U Gothenburg, 1974. Rev. by S. B. Saul, History, 61
(Feb 1976):92-3.

Kwamena-Poh, M. A. see McWilliam, H. O. A.

Labaree, Benjamin W., ed. The Atlantic World of Robert G. Albion. Middletown, Conn.: Wesleyan U Press, 1975. Rev.
by C. McKee, JAH, 63(Dec 1976):678-80.

_____ see Christie, Ian R.

Labbe, John T. see Carranco, Lynwood

Labrecque, Yvette see Tran Tam Tinh, V.

Lacy, Leslie Alexander. The Soil Soldiers: The Civilian Conservation Corps in the Great Depression. Radnor, Pa.: Chilton, 1976. Rev. by M. S. Holmes, JSH, 42(Nov 1976):603.

Ladd, Everett Carll, Jr. Transformations of the American Party System. New York: Norton, 1975. Rev. by P. T. David, AHR, 81(Oct 1976):998; J. A. Kentleton, History, 61(Oct 1976): 420-1.

_____ and Seymour Martin Lipset. The Divided Academy: Professors and Politics. New York: McGraw-Hill, 1975. Rev. by Veysey, JAH, 62(Mar 1976):1051-2.

Ladons, Regis. L'Abbé Portal et al Campagne Anglo-Romaine 1890-1912. Grenoble: Presses U Grenoble, 1973. Rev. by H. J. Ryan, CaHR, 62(Oct 1976):642-3.

Ladurie, Emmanuel Le Roy. The Peasants of Languedoc. Urbana: U Ill Press, 1974. Rev. by T. W. Margadant, AgH, 50(Apr 1976):429-31; J. L. Goldsmith, CHR, 57(Je 1976): 229-30.

Laffin, John. The French Foreign Legion. London: Dent, 1974. Rev. by H. R. Kedward, History, 61(Je 1976):319.

La Fontaine, Charles see Angell, Charles

La Fore, Laurence. American Classic. Iowa City: Ia State Historical Society, 1975. Rev. by J. McDonald, AI, 43(Win 1976):222-4; D. Zimmer, IMH, 72(Je 1976):170-1; K. Davison, OH, 85(Aut 1976):335-6; C. Page, Smithsonian, 7(Mar 1976): 105-7.

La Forte, Robert Sherman. Leaders of Reform: Progressive Republicans in Kansas, 1900-1916. Lawrence: U Press Kan, 1974. Rev. by H. S. Merrill, AHR, 81(Oct 1976):989-90.

Lagarrigue, Georges, ed. Salvien de Marseille, Oeuvres Tome II: Du gouvernement de Dieu. Paris: Editions du Ceri, 1975. Rev. by R. M. Grant, CH, 45(Je 1976):247.

La Gumina, Salvatore J., ed. WOP! A Documentary History of Anti-Italian Discrimination in the United States. San Francisco: Arrow Books, 1973. Rev. by S. M. Tomasi, CaHR, 62(Jl 1976):525-6.

Laird, Carobeth. Encounter with an Angry God. Banning, Cal.: Malki Museum, 1975. Rev. by M. E. Opler, A & W, 18 (Win 1976):371-4; W. E. Washburn, Smithsonian, 7(Apr 1976): 126, 128.

Lal, Sheo Kumar. The Urban Elite. Delhi: Thomson, 1974.
Rev. by C. N. Venugopal, IQ, 32(Jan-Mar 1976):110-11.

Laloux-Jain, Genevieve. Les manuels d'histoire du Canada au
Québec et en Ontario (de 1867 à 1914). Portland, Ore.:
International Scholarly Book Services, 1974. Rev. by C.
Nish, AHR, 81(Feb 1976):224.

Lamb, Curt. Political Power in Poor Neighborhoods. New York:
Wiley, 1975. Rev. by N. V. Bartley, JAH, 63(Dec 1976):
784-5.

Lamberg-Karlovsky, C. C., ed. see Sabloff, Jeremy A., ed.

Lampton, David M. Health, Conflict and the Chinese Political System. Ann Arbor: U Mich, 1974. Rev. by J. G. Lutz, AHR,
81(Oct 1976):939-40.

Lanckoronska, Carolina, ed. Elementa ad Fontium Editiones.
Vols. XXIX to XXXV. Rome: Institutum Historicom
Polonicum, 1972-1975. Rev. by T. J. Szatkowski, CaHR,
62(Apr 1976):267-9.

Landau, Jacob M. Radical Politics in Modern Turkey. Leiden:
E. J. Brill, 1974. Rev. by W. F. Weiker, IJMES, 7(Apr
1976):302-5.

Landau, Peter. Ius Patronatus: Studien zur Entwicklung des
Patronats im Dekretalenrecht und der Kanonistik des 12. und
13. Jahrhunderts. Cologne: Böhlau Verlag, 1975. Rev. by
W. Ullmann, EHR, 91(Oct 1976):890-1.

Landsberger, Henry A., ed. Rural Protest: Peasant Movements
and Social Change. New York: Barnes and Noble, 1973.
Rev. by J. W. Cole, JMH, 48(Je 1976):358-60.

Landuyt, Ariane. Le sinistre e l'Aventino. Milan: Franco Angeli
Editore, 1973. Rev. by R. Sarti, AHR, 81(Apr 1976):416-17.

Lane, Frederic C. Venice: A Maritime Republic. Baltimore:
JHU Press, 1974. Rev. by D. S. Chambers, History, 61(Feb
1976):87-8.

Lane, James B. Jacob A. Riis and the American City. Port
Washington, N.Y.: Kennikat, 1974. Rev. by D. M. Reimers,
AHR, 81(Je 1976):677-8.

Lane, Mills, ed. General Oglethorpe's Georgia: Colonial Letters,
1733-1743. 2 vols. Savannah, Ga.: Beehive, 1975. Rev.
by K. Coleman, GHQ, 60(Spr 1976):82-3.

Lang, James. Conquest and Commerce; Spain and England in the
Americas. Nashville, Tenn.: Academic Press, 1975. Rev.

by T. Teaters, ETHJ, 14(Fall 1976):75-6; J. L. Phelan,
HAHR, 56(May 1976):314-15; K. R. Andrews, History, 61
(Feb 1976):108-9; D. Greenberg, JAH, 62(Mar 1976):957-8.

Langbein, John H. Prosecuting Crime in the Renaissance. Cambridge, Mass.: Harvard U Press, 1974. Rev. by J. H.
Baker, EHR, 91(Jan 1976):192-3.

Lange, Charles H., Carroll L. Riley, and Elizabeth M. Lange,
eds. The Southwestern Journals of Adolph F. Bandelier,
1885-1888. Albuquerque: U NM Press, 1976. Rev. by E.
B. McCluney, HRNB, 5(Oct 1976):8-9.

Lange, Elizabeth M., ed. see Lange, Charles H.

Langford, J. I. Staffordshire and Worcestershire Canal. n. p.
Goose and Son, 1974. Rev. by M. G. Miller, JTH, 3(Sep
1976):297-8.

Langford, J. O. Big Bend: A Homesteader's Story. Austin:
U Texas Press, 1973. Rev. by G. Starnes, ChOk, 54(Spr
1976):154-5.

Langford, Paul. The Excise Crisis: Society and Politics in the
Age of Walpole. New York: Oxford U Press, 1975. Rev.
by E. A. Reitan, AHR, 81(Oct 1976):857-8; W. A. Speck,
EHR, 91(Oct 1976):859-60.

Langley, Harold D., ed. To Utah with the Dragoons; and
Glimpses of Life in Arizona and California, 1858-1859.
Salt Lake City: U Utah Press, 1974. Rev. by M. J.
Mattes, PHR, 45(Nov 1975):617-18; D. R. Moorman, WHQ,
7(Jan 1976):75.

Langley, J. Ayodele. Pan-Africanism and Nationalism in West
Africa 1900-1945. Oxford: Clarendon, 1973. Rev. by A.
H. M. Kirk-Greene, Africa, 46(Num 2, 1976):209-10.

Langley, Joan and Wright Langley. Yesterday's Asheville. Miami:
Seemann, 1975. Rev. by R. M. Topkins, NCHR, 53(Spr
1976):220-1.

Langley, Lester D. Struggle for the American Mediterranean:
United States-European Rivalry in the Gulf-Caribbean, 1776-
1904. Athens: U Ga Press, 1976. Rev. by E. D. Fitchen,
HRNB, 4(May/Je 1976):147; K. J. Grieb, JAH, 63(Dec 1976):
701-2; W. H. Beezley, JSH, 42(Nov 1976):584-5.

Langworthy, H. W. Zambia Before 1890. London: Longmans,
1973. Rev. by D. Killingray, JAfH, 17(Num 3, 1976):458-9.

Lannie, Vincent P., ed. On the Side of Truth, George N. Shuster.
Notre Dame, Ind.: U Notre Dame Press, 1974. Rev. by
J. T. Ellis, CaHR, 62(Oct 1976):679-81.

Lanning, John Tate. Pedro de la Torre: Doctor to Conquerors.
Baton Rouge: LSU Press, 1974. Rev. by C. Gibson, AHR,
81(Apr 1976):473.

Lansden, John M. A History of the City of Cairo, Illinois. Carbondale: S Ill U Press, 1976. Rev. by R. G. Miller, HRNB,
5(Oct 1976):7-8.

Lansing, John Stephen. Evil in the Morning of the World. Ann
Arbor: U Mich, 1974. Rev. by R. Krulfeld, AA, 78(Je
1976):407.

Lapati, Americo D. Education and the Federal Government. New
York: Mason/Charter, 1975. Rev. by W. L. Fox, AHR, 81
(Je 1976):673-4; P. D. Lambert, CaHR, 62(Oct 1976):678-9.

Lapchick, Richard Edward. The Politics of Race and International
Sport: The Case of South Africa. Westport, Conn.: Green-
wood, 1975. Rev. by I. A. Newby, AHR, 81(Je 1976):684-5;
S. J. Morse, JMAS, 14(Dec 1976):731-2.

Laplante, Marc see Tremblay, Marc Abelard

Laqueur, Walter. Weimar: A Cultural History 1918-1933. London: Weidenfeld and Nicolson, 1974. Rev. by F. Field, History, 61(Feb 1976):141.

Larkin, Emmet. The Roman Catholic Church and the Creation of
the Modern Irish State, 1878-1886. Philadelphia: American
Philosophical Assn., 1975. Rev. by J. L. Altholz, JMH, 48
(Sep 1976):544-5.

Larkin, James F. and Paul L. Hughes, eds. Stuart Royal Proclamations. Vol. I. Oxford, Clarendon, 1973. Rev. by J. P.
Cooper, EHR, 91(Oct 1976):850-2.

Larkin, John A. The Pampangans: Colonial Society in a Philippine
Province. Berkeley: U Cal Press, 1972. Rev. by M. P.
Onorato, AHR, 81(Oct 1976):945.

Larkin, Maurice. Church and State After the Dreyfus Affair. New
York: Barnes and Noble, 1974. Rev. by J. N. Moody, CaHR,
62(Oct 1976):643-5; R. L. Lynn, JCS, 18(Win 1976):127-9.

Larrie, Reginald R. Corners of Black History. New York: Vantage, 1971. Rev. by G. E. Osborne, Crisis, 83(Jan 1976):
33.

Larson, David R., et al., eds. Guide to Manuscripts Collections
and Institutional Records in Ohio. Bowling Green: Society of
Ohio Archivists, 1974. Rev. by L. Alig, IMH, 72(Je 1976):
162-3.

Larson, Robert W. New Mexico Populism. Boulder, Colo.: Associated U Press, 1974. Rev. by D. H. Stratton, A & W, 18(Spr 1976):102-3; R. H. Williams, AHR, 81(Je 1976):678-9; W. T. K. Nugent, JEH, 36(Sep 1976):769; H. A. DeWitt, JOW, 15(Apr 1976):139; G. L. Seligman, Jr., NMHR, 51(Jan 1976):84-5; R. Ridgley, WHQ, 7(Apr 1976):213-14.

Lary, Diana. Region and Nation: The Kwangsi Clique in Chinese Politics, 1925-1937. New York: Cam U Press, 1975. Rev. by D. Deal, AHR, 81(Oct 1976):938; A. J. Nathan, CQ, May 1976, pp. 369-70.

Las Casas, Bartolomé de. In Defense of the Indians. DeKalb: N Ill U Press, 1974. Rev. by W. S. Maltby, AHR, 81(Apr 1976):473.

Lash, Joseph P. From the Diaries of Felix Frankfurter. New York: Norton, 1975. Rev. by F. Freidel, AHR, 81(Oct 1976):1002; D. Roper, Historian, 39(Nov 1976):164-6; J. S. Auerbach, JAH, 62(Mar 1976):1038-9; R. A. Maidment, JAmS, 10(Apr 1976):124-5; D. L. Sterling, OH, 85(Aut 1976): 336-8; E. A. Purcell, Jr., NEQ, 49(Je 1976):314-17; M. E. Parrish, RAH, 4(Je 1976):277-83.

Lash, Nicholas. Newman on Development: The Search for an Explanation in History. Shepherdstown, W. Va.: Patmos Press, 1975. Rev. by J. L. Altholz, CH, 45(Je 1976):261-2.

Laslett, John H. M. and Seymour Martin Lipset, eds. Failure of a Dream? Garden City, N. Y.: Anchor/Doubleday, 1974. Rev. by J. Braeman, CHR, 57(Je 1976):224-5.

László, Gyula. The Art of the Migration Period. Coral Gables, Fla.: U Miami Press, 1974. Rev. by S. Foltiny, Archaeology, 29(Apr 1976):139-41.

Latham, R. E. Dictionary of Medieval Latin From British Sources. Oxford: Oxford U Press, 1975. Rev. by F. Barlow, EHR, 91(Oct 1976):882.

Latorre, Felipe A. and Delores L. Latorre. The Mexican Kickapoo Indians. Austin: U Texas Press, 1976. Rev. by E. J. Hindman, ChOk, 54(Win 1976):542-4; J. Kelley, HAHR, 56(Nov 1976):677-8; G. Kincaid, SWHQ, 80(Oct 1976):234-6.

Lattimore, Owen. History and Revolution in China. Lund: Scandinavian Institute of Asian Studies, 1970. Rev. by S. Uhalley, Jr., JAAS, 11(Jl-Oct 1976):229-31.

Lātūkefu, Sione. Church and State in Tonga. Honolulu: U Press Hawaii, 1974. Rev. by D. R. Sardesai, AHR, 81(Feb 1976): 199-200.

Latzer, Beth Good. Myrtleville: A Canadian Farm and Family,

1837-1967. Carbondale: S Ill U Press, 1976. Rev. by M.
B. Cohen, HRNB, 4(Sep 1976):220.

Laubscher, Hans Peter. Der Reliefschmuck des Galeriusbogens in
Thessaloniki. Berlin: Gebr. Mann Verlag, 1975. Rev. by
M. S. P. Rothman, AJA, 80(Fall 1976):441-4.

Laudonnière, René. Three Voyages. Gainesville: U Presses Fla,
1975. Rev. by N. M. Belting, AHR, 81(Oct 1976):954; R. A.
Matter, FHQ, 54(Jan 1976):379-80; L. E. Breeze, JSH, 42
(May 1976):271; P. L. Barbour, WMQ, 33(Apr 1976):352-4.

Lavallee, Danielle and Michele Julien. Les establissements asto
à l'époque préhispanique. Vol. I. Lima: Institut Français
d'Etudes Andiennes, 1973. Rev. by L. Vallée, HAHR, 56(Feb
1976):185-6.

Lavan, Spencer. The Ahmadiyah Movement. Columbia, Mo.:
South Asia Books, 1974. Rev. by K. R. Stunkel, AHR, 81
(Apr 1976):434-5.

Lavender, David. Nothing Seemed Impossible. Palo Alto, Cal.:
West, 1975. Rev. by G. Stanley, A & W, 18(Aut 1976):
301-2; M. G. Blackford, BHR, 50(Sum 1976):230-1; T. F.
Andrews, HRNB, 4(Aug 1976):189-90; W. T. Jackson, JAH,
63(Sep 1976):416-18; R. E. Smith, JOW, 15(Apr 1976):140-1.

Laverychev, V. Ia. Tsarism and the Labor Question in Russia
(1861-1917). Moscow: Izdatel'stvo "Mysl," 1972. Rev. by
R. V. Layton, Jr., AHR, 81(Feb 1976):185.

Lawson, John and Harold Silver. A Social History of Education in
England. London: Methuen, 1973. Rev. by G. Sutherland,
History, 61(Feb 1976):81-2.

Lawton, James, ed. Shop Talk. Boston: Boston Public Library,
1976. Rev. by R. A. Shiff, AmArc, 39(Apr 1976):206-8.

Leab, Daniel J. From Sambo to Superspade: The Black Experience
in Motion Pictures. Boston: Houghton Mifflin, 1975. Rev.
by J. E. DiMeglio, JAH, 63(Sep 1976):451-2.

Leadabrand, Russ, Shelly Lowenkopf, and Bryce Patterson. Yesterday's California. Miami: E. A. Seeman, 1975. Rev. by
J. L. Dodson, JOW, 15(Jl 1976):108.

Lebergott, Stanley. The American Economy. Princeton, N.J.:
Prin U Press, 1976. Rev. by S. L. Engerman, JEH, 36
(Sep 1976):770-2.

_____. Wealth and Want. Princeton: Prin U Press, 1975.
Rev. by S. L. Engerman, JEH, 36(Sep 1976):770-2.

LE BRUN 228

Le Brun, François. Les hommes et la mort in Anjou aux 17e et 18e siècles. Paris: Mouton, 1971. Rev. by R. I. Boss, AHR, 80(Oct 1976):866-7.

Le Brun, Jacques. La Spiritualité de Bossuet. Paris: Librairie C. Klincksieck, 1972. Rev. by G. D. Balsama, CaHR, 62 (Apr 1976):284-7.

Leca, Ange-Pierre. La Médecine égyptienne au temps des pharaons. Paris: Les Editions Roger Dacosta, 1971. Rev. by K. R. Weeks, JNES, 35(Jan 1976):43-6.

Lecourt, Dominique. Marxism and Epistemology: Bachelard, Canguilhem, Foucault. Atlantic Highlands, N. J.: Humanities, 1975. Rev. by R. D'Amico, JMH, 48(Je 1976):334-7.

Ledeen, Michael Arthur. Universal Fascism: The Theory and Practice of the Fascist International, 1928-1936. New York: Fertig, 1972. Rev. by F. R. Willis, AHR, 81(Oct 1976): 848-9.

Lederer, Ivo J. and Wayne S. Vucinich, eds. The Soviet Union and the Middle East. Stanford, Cal.: Hoover Institution, 1974. Rev. by P. Jabber, IJMES, 7(Oct 1976):605-7.

Lee, Chae-jin. Japan Faces China. Baltimore: JHU Press, 1976. Rev. in CurH, 71(Sep 1976):78.

Lee, D. N. and H. C. Woodhouse. Art on the Rocks of Southern Africa. New York: Scribner's, n.d. Rev. by B. Forgey, Smithsonian, 6(May 1975):105-7.

Lee, Dwight E. Europe's Crucial Years: The Diplomatic Background of World War I, 1902-1914. Hanover, N. H.: U Press New England, 1974. Rev. by G. E. Silberstein, AHR, 81(Feb 1976):125-6.

Lee, Oey Hong, ed. Indonesia After the 1971 Elections. London: Oxford U Press, 1974. Rev. by W. H. Frederick, JAAS, 11 (Jan and Apr 1976):128-9.

Lee, Örlan and T. A. Robertson. "Moral Order" and the Criminal Law: Reform Efforts in the United States and West Germany. The Hague: Martinus Nijhoff, 1973. Rev. by H. D. Wendorf, JCS, 17(Spr 1975):329-31.

Lee, Robert E. Blackbeard the Pirate. Winston-Salem, N. C.: John F. Blair, 1974. Rev. by J. L. Wright, Jr., AHR, 81 (Je 1976):652.

Leeb, I. Leonard. The Ideological Origins of the Batavian Revolution. The Hague: Martinus Nijoff, 1973. Rev. by H. H. Rowen, CHR, 57(Mar 1976):96-7.

Lees, Andrew. Revolution and Reflection: Intellectual Change in Germany During the 1850's. The Hague: Martinus Nijhoff, 1974. Rev. by R. Southard, JMH, 48(Mar 1976):166-8.

Lees-Milne, James. William Beckford. n. p. : Compton Russell, n. d. Rev. by P. Q., HTo, 26(Jl 1976):480-1.

Legeza, Laszlo see Rawson, Philip

Legge, J. D. Sukarno: A Political Biography. New York: Praeger, 1972. Rev. by T. Friend, AHR, 81(Oct 1976): 947-8.

Le Hérissier, R. G. The Development of the Government of Jersey 1771-1972. Jersey: States Greffe, 1974. Rev. by D. Read, History, 61(Feb 1976):149.

Leifer, Michael. The Philippine Claim to Sabah. IDC, Switzerland: Hull Monographs, 1968. Rev. by B. Powell, MAS, 10(Feb 1976):149-54.

Leigh, Michael. The Rising Moon. Portland, Ore.: Scholarly Book Service, 1974. Rev. by A. R. Maxwell, AA, 78(Je 1976):405-6.

Lemarchand, René and David Martin. Selective Genocide in Burundi. London: Minority Rights Group, 1974. Rev. by W. Weinstein, JMAS, 14(Mar 1976):161-3.

Lemarié, Charles. Etudes sur les missionnaires bretone dans le middle West Americain. Tome I. Angers: The Author, 1973. Rev. by T. W. Spalding, CaHR, 62(Jl 1976):489-90.

_____. Les Missionnaires bretons de l'Indiana au XIXe siècle. Angers: The Author, 1973. Rev. by E. Logan, CaHR, 62 (Jl 1976):492-3.

_____. Monseigneur Bruté de Rémur. Paris: Librairie C. Klincksieck, 1974. Rev. by A. M. Melville, CaHR, 62(Jl 1976):490-2.

Lemasters, E. E. Blue-Collar Aristocrats: Life-Styles at a Working-Class Tavern. Madison: U Wis Press, 1975. Rev. by J. Corzine, AS, 16(Fall 1975):102.

Lenczowski, George. Soviet Advances in the Middle East. Washington, D. C.: American Enterprise Institute for Public Policy Research, 1972. Rev. by R. H. Dekmejian, AHR, 81(Oct 1976):913-14.

Lenihan, John. Human Engineering. New York: Braziller, 1975. Rev. by J. N. Tuck, Smithsonian, 6(Jl 1975):105, 107, 108.

Lensen, George Alexander. The Damned Inheritance: The Soviet
    Union and the Manchurian Crises, 1924-1935. Tallahassee,
    Fla.: Diplomatic Press, 1974. Rev. by D. C. Price, AHR,
    81(Oct 1976):911-12.

Lentricchia, Frank. Robert Frost: Modern Poetics and the Land-
    scapes of Self. Durham, N.C.: Duke U Press, 1975. Rev.
    by P. J. Stanlis, NEQ, 49(Je 1976):320-2.

Lentz, Perry. It Must Be Now the Kingdom Coming. New York:
    Crown, 1973. Rev. by R. Ashley, CWTI, 15(Apr 1976):45-6.

Léon, Pierre. Géographie de la Fortune et Structures Sociales à
    Lyon au XIXe siècle (1815-1914). Lyon: Centre d'histoire
    economique, 1974. Rev. by M. Palmer, EHR, 91(Jl 1976):
    661-3.

Leone, Mark P., ed. see Zaretsky, Irving I., ed.

Leopold, Wanda and Zbigniew Stolarek. / Antologia Poezji Afrykan-
    skiej. Warsaw: Ludwowa Spoldzielnia Wydawnicza, 1974.
    Rev. by B. W. Andrzejewski, Africa, 46(Num 1, 1976):107-8.

Lepelley, Claude. L'Empire romain et le christianisme. Paris:
    Flammarion, 1969. Rev. by R. M. Golden, JCS, 18(Aut
    1976):581-2.

Leruez, Jacques. Economic Planning and Politics in Britain. New
    York: Barnes and Noble, 1976. Rev. by L. Hannah, JEH,
    36(Sep 1976):772-3.

Lesser, Charles H., ed. The Sinews of Independence. Chicago:
    U Chicago Press, 1976. Rev. by C. W. Troxler, NCHR, 53
    (Aut 1976):409-11; M. L. Cann, SCHM, 77(Oct 1976):268; H.
    F. Rankin, VMHB, 84(Jl 1976):375-6.

Lester, Richard I. Confederate Finance and Purchasing in Great
    Britain. Charlottesville: U Press Va, 1975. Rev. by W. W.
    Hassler, Jr., JAH, 62(Mar 1976):1000-1; J. F. Gentry, JSH,
    42(May 1976):287-8; W. F. Spencer, VMHB, 84(Jan 1976):117-
    18.

Levenson, Joseph R. Revolution and Cosmopolitanism. Berkeley:
    U Cal Press, 1971. Rev. by C. M. Lewis, AHR, 81(Je
    1976):644-5.

Leventhal, Herbert. In the Shadow of the Enlightenment. New
    York: NYU Press, 1976. Rev. by P. D. Jordan, HRNB, 4
    (Sep 1976):210.

Levin, David, ed. Emerson: Prophecy, Metamorphosis, and Influ-
    ence. New York: Columbia U Press, 1975. Rev. by B.
    Wood, NEQ, 49(Je 1976):330-2.

Levine, Donald M. Greater Ethiopia. Chicago: U Chicago Press, 1974. Rev. by F. C. Gamst, AA, 78(Je 1976):414-15.

Levine, Norman. The Tragic Deception. Santa Barbara, Cal.: Clio, 1975. Rev. by J. Seigel, AHR, 81(Oct 1976):845-6; K. Seshadri, IQ, 32(Apr-Je 1976):233-6.

Le Vine, Victor T. Political Corruption: The Ghana Case. Stanford, Cal.: Hoover Institution, 1975. Rev. by R. Crook, AfAf, 75(Jan 1976):113-14.

_____ and Roger P. Nye. Historical Dictionary of the Cameroon. Metuchen, N.J.: Scarecrow, 1974. Rev. by H. O. H. Vernon-Jackson, JMAS, 14(Sep 1976):553-5.

Levine-Meyer, Rosa. Levine: The Life of a Revolutionary. New York: Atheneum, 1973. Rev. by L. A. Feldman, AHR, 81 (Oct 1976):883-4.

Levi-Strauss, Claude. Anthropologie structurale deux. Paris: Plon, 1973. Rev. by I. Rossi, AA, 78(Mar 1976):145.

Levitan, Sar A. and Karen A. Cleary. Old Wars Remain Unfinished. Baltimore: JHU Press, 1974. Rev. by E. Ranson, JAmS, 10(Apr 1976):122-4.

Levitas, Gloria, Frank P. Vivelo and Jacqueline J. Vivelo, eds. American Indian Prose and Poetry. New York: Putnam's, 1974. Rev. by T. E. Sanders, AIQ, 2(Spr 1975):33-5.

Lévy, Claude. Les Nouveaux Temps et l'idéologie de la collaboration. Paris: Armand Colin, 1974. Rev. by M. Palmer, EHR, 91(Jl 1976):689-90.

Levy, David, ed. see Brandeis, Louis

Levy, David W. , ed. see Urofsky, Melvin I. , ed.

Levy, Lester S. Flashes of Merriment: A Century of Humorous Songs in America, 1805-1905. Norman: U Ok Press, 1971. Rev. by D. H. Gordon, VMHB, 84(Oct 1976):488-9.

_____ . "Give Me Yesterday." Norman: U Ok Press, 1975. Rev. by G. Schaade, ETHJ, 14(Fall 1976):76; P. W. Filby, MHM, 71(Spr 1976):107; D. H. Gordon, VMHB, 84(Oct 1976): 488-9.

Levy, Richard S. The Downfall and the Anti-Semitic Political Parties in Imperial Germany. New Haven, Conn.: Yale U Press, 1975. Rev. by R. H. Phelps, Historian, 39(Nov 1976): 129-30; R. E. Neil, HRNB, 4(Jan 1976):69.

LeWarne, Charles P. Utopias on Puget Sound. Seattle: U Wash

Press, 1975. Rev. by J. R. Finger, A & W, 10(Spr 1976):
92-3; H. R. Grant, AHR, 81(Oct 1976):985-6; R. V. Hine,
JAH, 62(Mar 1976):1024-5; S. Tanasoca, OrHQ, 77(Sep 1976):
294-5; K. L. Murray, PNG, 67(Oct 1976):174-5; P. Kagan,
WHQ, 7(Jl 1976):324-5.

Lewels, Francisco J., Jr. The Uses of Media by the Chicano
Movement. New York: Praeger, 1974. Rev. by M. T.
Garcia, HAHR, 56(Feb 1976):158-61.

Lewicki, Tadeusz. West African Food in the Middle Ages, Ac-
cording to Arabic Sources. New York: Cam U Press, 1974.
Rev. by M. Miracle, AHR, 81(Oct 1976):921; R. A. Austen,
JNES, 35(Oct 1976):297-8.

Lewin, Moshe. Political Undercurrents in Soviet Economic Debates.
Princeton, N.J.: Prin U Press, 1974. Rev. by B. Katz,
JEH, 36(Sep 1976):773-4.

_____. Russian Peasants and Soviet Power: A Study of Col-
lectivization. New York: Norton, 1975. Rev. by N. Spulber, AHR, 81(Je 1976):637.

Lewinson, Edwin R. Black Politics in New York City. New York:
Twayne, 1974. Rev. by S. M. Scheiner, AHR, 81(Oct 1976):
950.

Lewis, Bernard. History: Remembered, Recovered, Invented.
Princeton, N.J.: Prin U Press, 1975. Rev. by S. Bailey,
AHR, 81(Oct 1976):811-12; J. Johnson, AmArc 39(Jan 1976):
59-60; E. N. Luttwak, Commentary, 61(May 1976):86-9; J.
S. F. Parker, History, 61(Feb 1976):75; W. H. McNeill,
JIH, 7(Aut 1976):350.

_____. Islamic History: Ideas, Men and Events in the Middle
East. La Salle, Ill.: Library Press, 1973. Rev. by M.
W. Dols, IJMES, 7(Apr 1976):297-8.

_____, ed. and trans. Islam from the Prophet Muhammed to
the Capture of Constantinople. 2 vols. London: Harper and
Row, 1974. Rev. by W. M. Watt, History, 61(Feb 1976):
161-2.

Lewis, Bessie. They Called Their Town Darien. Darien, Ga.:
Darien News, 1975. Rev. by J. C. Bonner, GHQ, 60(Spr
1976):77-8.

Lewis, Gordon K. Notes on the Puerto Rican Revolution. New
York: Monthly Review, 1974. Rev. by M. K. Vaughn,
HAHR, 56(Feb 1976):165-6.

Lewis, Marianna O., ed. The Foundation Directory. New York:
Columbia U Press, 1975. Rev. by L. L. Morrison, JOW,
15(Jan 1976):139.

233   LEWIS

Lewis, Taylor, Jr. Spirit Up the People. Birmingham, Ala.:
    Oxmoor House, 1975. Rev. by H. G. Jones, NCHR, 53(Spr
    1976):217-18.

Lewis, Thomas S. W., ed. Letters of Hart Crane and His Family.
    New York: Columbia U Press, 1974. Rev. by C. E. Eaton,
    GR, 30(Sum 1976):447-60.

Lewis, W. S., et al., eds. see Walpole, Horace

Ley, Francis. Alexandre 1er et sa Sainte-Alliance (1811-1825).
    Paris: Librairie Fischbacher, 1975. Rev. by E. J. Knapton,
    AHR, 81(Oct 1976):907-8.

Leys, Colin. Underdevelopment in Kenya. London: Heinemann,
    1975. Rev. by J. F. Munro, JAfH, 17(Num 1, 1976):151-2.

Leys, Simon. Ombres Chinoises. Paris: Union General d'Edi-
    tions, 1974. Rev. by L. Bianco, CQ, May 1976, pp. 377-8.

Li, Lincoln. The Japanese Army in North China, 1937-1941.
    Tokyo: Oxford U Press, 1975. Rev. by CurH, 71(Sep 1976):
    77-8; A. D. Coox, HRNB, 5(Oct 1976):14; R. A. Kapp, JAS,
    36(Nov 1976):136-7.

Library of Congress. Symposia on the American Revolution, May
    10 and 11, 1973. Washington: Library of Congress, 1973.
    Rev. by I. D. Gruber, JAH, 62(Mar 1976):968-70.

Lichtheim, Miriam. Ancient Egyptian Literature. Vol. 1. The
    Old and Middle Kingdoms. Los Angeles: U Cal Press, 1973.
    Rev. by D. Mueller, JNES, 35(Apr 1976):139-40.

Liebeschuetz, J. H. W. G. Antioch: City and Imperial Adminis-
    tration in the Later Roman Empire. New York: Oxford U
    Press, 1972. Rev. by G. W. Bowersock, AHR, 81(Oct 1976):
    831.

Liebeschütz, Hans. Von Georg Simmel zu Franz Rosenzweig.
    Tübingen: J. C. B. Mohr (Paul Siebeck), 1970. Rev. by
    B. D. Weinryb, AHR, 81(Apr 1976):404-5.

Liebman, Seymour B. The Inquisitors and the Jews in the New
    World. Coral Gables, Fla.: U Miami Press, 1974. Rev.
    by E. B. Alams, Historian, 39(Nov 1976):168.

Lievsay, John Leon. Venetian Phoenix. Lawrence: U Press Kan,
    1973. Rev. by A. C. Outler, JCS, 18(Aut 1976):584-5.

Ligeti, Louis, ed. Researches in Altaic Languages. Budapest:
    Akademiai Kiado, 1975. Rev. by J. Street, JAS, 36(Nov
    1976):121-3.

Lill, Rudolf. Die Wende im Kulturkampf. Tübingen: Max Niemeyer Verlag, 1973. Rev. by J. Zeender, CaHR, 62(Oct
1976):619-22; O. Chadwick, EHR, 91(Jan 1976):222-3.

Lillibridge, G. D. Images of American Society. New York:
Houghton Mifflin, 1975. Rev. by T. M. Ruddy, HT, 10(Nov
1976):140-1.

Lindemann, Albert S. The 'Red Years': European Socialism versus
Bolshevism, 1919-1921. Berkeley: U Cal Press, 1974. Rev.
by P. Hollander, AHR, 81(Je 1976):634-5.

Linden, Ian and Jane Linden. Catholics, Peasants and Chewa Resistance in Nyasaland, 1889-1939. London: Heinemann, 1974.
Rev. by R. I. Rotberg, AHR, 81(Je 1976):643; B. Wilson,
EHR, 91(Apr 1976):451; J. McCracken, JAfH, 17(Num 3,
1976):465-6.

Linderman, Frank B. Pretty Shield: Medicine Woman of the
Crows. Lincoln: U Neb Press, 1974. Rev. by N. E. Williams, JOW, 15(Jl 1976):99.

Linderman, Gerald F. The Mirror of War: American Society and
the Spanish-American War. Ann Arbor: U Mich Press, 1974.
Rev. by R. L. Beisner, AHR, 81(Oct 1976):988; P. S. Foner,
PHR, 45(May 1976):298-9.

Lindfors, Bernth. Folklore in Nigerian Literature. New York:
Africana, 1973. Rev. by A. Ricard, JMAS, 14(Mar 1976):
178-80.

Lindgren, Margareta. The People of Pylos. Prosopographical and
Methodological Studies in the Pylos Archives. Uppsala:
Studies in Ancient Mediterranean and Near Eastern Civiliza-
tions, 1973. Rev. by M. L. Lang, AJA, 80(Spr 1976):204-5.

Lindley, Harlow, ed. Fort Meigs and the War of 1812: Orderly
Book of Cushing's Company, 2nd U.S. Artillery, April, 1813-
February, 1814 and Personal Diary of Daniel Cushing, October, 1812-July, 1813. Columbus: Ohio Historical Society,
1975. Rev. by A. R. Gilpin, AHR, 81(Oct 1976):978-9.

Lindquist, Emory. Bethany in Kansas. Lindsborg, Kan.: Bethany
College, 1975. Rev. by C. H. Chrislock, JAH, 63(Sep 1976):
427-8.

_____. An Immigrant's American Odyssey. Rock Island, Ill.:
Augustana Historical Society, 1974. Rev. by K. O. Bjork,
AHR, 81(Je 1976):670-2; W. Johnson, PNQ, 67(Oct 1976):
179-80.

Lingenfelter, Richard E. The Hardrock Miners. Berkeley: U
Cal Press, 1974. Rev. by R. C. Brown, AHR, 81(Je 1976):

672; C. Erickson, History, 61(Oct 1976):412-14; R. A. Burchell, JAmS, 10(Aug 1976):278; M. G. Burlingame, PHR, 45(Feb 1976):128-9.

Link, Arthur S., et al. Wilson's Diplomacy. Morristown, N. J.: General Learning Press, 1973. Rev. by E. P. Trani, AHR, 81(Je 1976):682-3.

_____, eds. see Wilson, Woodrow

Linkh, Richard M. American Catholicism and European Immigrants (1900-1924). Staten Island, N. Y.: Center for Migration Studies, 1975. Rev. by J. Scarpaci, JAH, 62(Mar 1976): 1019-20.

Lipp, Solomon. Three Chilean Thinkers. Waterloo, Canada: Wilfred Laurier U Press, 1975. Rev. by P. J. Sehlinger, HAHR, 56(Aug 1976):493.

Lippelt, Helmut. Thietmar von Merseburg. Cologne: Böhlau Verlag, 1973. Rev. by J. M. Bak, AHR, 81(Feb 1976):114.

Lipset, Seymour Martin and David Riesman. Education and Politics at Harvard. New York: McGraw-Hill, 1975. Rev. by D. J. Leab, NEQ, 49(Je 1976):310-12.

_____ see Ladd, Everett Carll, Jr.

_____, ed. see Laslett, John H. M., ed.

Lipshires, Sidney. Herbert Marcuse: From Marx to Freud and Beyond. Cambridge, Mass.: Schenkman, 1974. Rev. by C. Bay, CHR, 57(Je 1976):179-80.

Lisanti, Luis. Negocios coloniais. São Paulo: Ministério da Fazenda, 1973. Rev. by B. W. Diffie, HAHR, 56(Feb 1976): 129-30.

Lisio, Donald J. The President and Protest. Columbia, Mo.: U Mo Press, 1974. Rev. by T. H. Greer, AHR, 81(Apr 1976):463-4.

Liska, George. Beyond Kissinger. Baltimore: JHU Press, n. d. Rev. by V. Baras, Commentary, 61(Mar 1976):74-6.

Liss, Peggy K. Mexico Under Spain 1521-1556. Chicago: U Chicago Press, 1975. Rev. by CurH, 70(Feb 1976):78; W. L. Sherman, HAHR, 56(May 1976):315-17; U. Lamb, TAm, 33 (Jl 1976):179-80.

Lissington, M. P. New Zealand and the United States, 1840-1944. Wellington, New Zealand: A. R. Shearer, Government Printer, 1972. Rev. by C. H. Grattan, PHR, 45(Feb 1976):139-40.

Listowel, Judith. The Other Livingstone. London: Julian Fried-
    man, 1974. Rev. by A. F. McC. Madden, EHR, 91(Jan 1976):
    220; J. A. Casada, Historian, 39(Nov 1976):138-9.

Liszkowski, Uwe, ed. Russland und Deutschland. Stuttgart: Ernst
    Klett Verlag, 1974. Rev. by G. L. Weinberg, AHR, 81(Je
    1976):832-3.

Littell, Franklin H. The Crucifixion of the Jews. New York:
    Harper & Row, 1975. Rev. by S. Sandmel, Judaism, 25(Win
    1976):123-5.

_____ and Hubert G. Locke, eds. The German Church Struggle
    and the Holocaust. Detroit: Wayne St U Press, 1974. Rev.
    by L. D. Walker, CaHR, 62(Oct 1976):665-7; J. S. Wozniak,
    JCS, 17(Spr 1975):324-5.

Little, Kenneth. Urbanization as a Social Process. Boston:
    Routledge and Kegan Paul, 1974. Rev. by B. T. Nkemdirim,
    JMAS, 14(Dec 1976):716-19.

Littman, R. J. The Greek Experience: Imperialism and Social
    Conflict, 800-400 B. C. London: Thames and Hudson, 1974.
    Rev. by C. Rodewald, History, 61(Oct 1976):431-2.

Litvinoff, Barnet see Weizmann, Chaim

Liu, Alan P. L. Communications and National Integration in Com-
    munist China. Berkeley: U Cal Press, 1971. Rev. by A.
    J. Watson, MAS, 10(Apr 1976):308-10.

Liu, Tai. Discord in Zion. The Hague: Martinus Nijhoff, 1973.
    Rev. by G. Drake, CaHR, 62(Apr 1976):280-1.

Livesay, Harold C. Andrew Carnegie and the Rise of Big Business.
    Boston: Little, Brown, 1975. Rev. by L. L. Murray, BHR,
    50(Spr 1976):119-21; P. H. Tedesco, HT, 10(Nov 1976):146-7;
    A. Martin, JAH, 62(Mar 1976):1012-13.

Livingston, Bernard. Zoo Animals, People, Places. New York:
    Arbor House, 1974. Rev. by F. Sartwell, Smithsonian, 6
    (Jan 1975):102-4.

Livingstone, I. , et al. The Teaching of Economics in Africa.
    Sussex: Sussex U Press, 1973. Rev. by T. D. Williams,
    AfAf, 75(Jan 1976):109-11.

Lloyd, P. C. Power and Independence. Boston: Routledge and
    Kegan Paul, 1974. Rev. by B. A. Nkemdirim, JMAS, 14
    (Dec 1976):716-19.

Lo, Winston Wan. The Life and Thought of Yeh Shih. Hong Kong:
    U Presses Fla, 1974. Rev. by G. Hatch, JAS, 36(Nov 1976):
    126-7.

237   LO BELLO

Lo Bello, Nino. Vatican, U.S.A. New York: Trident, 1972.
Rev. by J. E. Rouse, Jr., JCS, 17(Win 1975):140-2.

Locke, Hubert G., ed. see Littell, Franklin H., ed.

Locke, Robert R. French Legitimists and the Politics of Moral
Order in the Early Third Republic. Princeton, N.J.: Princeton U Press, 1974. Rev. by M. Larkin, EHR, 91(Jan 1976):
224-5; A. R. H. Copley, History, 61(Feb 1976):137-8.

Lockhart, James and Enrique Otte, eds. and trans. Letters and
People of the Spanish Indies: Sixteenth Century. New York:
Cam U Press, 1976. Rev. by R. Pike, HRNB, 4(Jl 1976):
167.

Lockridge, Kenneth A. Literacy in Colonial New England. New
York: Norton, 1974. Rev. by D. Cressy, AHR, 81(Feb
1976):203-4.

Lodge, George C. The New American Ideology. New York:
Knopf, 1975. Rev. by S. Engelbourg, BHR, 50(Sum 1976):
241-2.

Lodolini, Elio, ed. see Giglio, Carlo, ed.

Loemker, Leroy E. Struggle for Synthesis: The Seventeenth Century Background of Leibniz's Synthesis of Order and Freedom.
Cambridge, Mass.: Harvard U Press, 1972. Rev. by W.
von Leyden, JHP, 14(Apr 1976):233-5.

Loewen, Harry. Luther and the Radicals: Another Look at Some
Aspects of the Struggle Between Luther and the Radical Re-
formers. Waterloo, Ontario: Wilfrid Laurier U, 1974. Rev.
by G. Harland, MQR, 50(Apr 1976):143-4.

Loftis, Anne. California--Where the Twain Did Meet. New York:
Macmillan, 1973. Rev. by H. A. DeWitt, JOW, 15(Jan
1976):129.

Lomax, Alfred L. Later Woolen Mills in Oregon. Portland, Ore.:
Binfords and Mort, 1974. Rev. by L. Nash, ORHQ, 77(Je
1976):193-4; W. J. Baboury, WHQ, 7(Jan 1976):64-5.

Lombard, Maurice. The Golden Age of Islam. New York:
American Elsevier, 1975. Rev. by A. C. Hess, AHR, 81
(Oct 1976):788-99; W. M. Watt, History, 61(Oct 1976):436-7.

Lombardi, Mary. Brazilian Serial Documents. Bloomington: Ind
U Press, 1974. Rev. by C. J. Pencheff, TAm, 32(Jan 1976):
482-3.

London, Joan. Jack London and His Times. Seattle: U Wash
Press, 1939, 1974. Rev. by S. Black, JOW, 15(Jan 1976):
132.

Loney, Martin. Rhodesia: White Racism and Imperial Response.
New York: Penguin, 1975. Rev. by T. I. Matthews, AfAf,
75(Jan 1976):115-17.

Long, Charlotte R. The Ayia Triadha Sarcophagus. A Study of
Late Minoan and Mycenaean Funerary Practises and Beliefs.
Göteborg: Paul Aströms Förlag, 1974. Rev. by J. S. Soles,
AJA, 80(Spr 1976):203-4.

Long, Stuart see Kinch, Sam

Longacre, Edward G. Mounted Raids of the Civil War. New York:
A. S. Barnes, 1975. Rev. by J. P. Cullen, CWTI, 15(Jl
1976):49; D. T. Cornish, JAH, 63(Sep 1976):424-5; M. S.
Miller, JSH, 42(Aug 1976):436-7.

Longford, Elizabeth. Wellington, Pillar of State. New York:
Harper and Row, 1972. Rev. by M. E. Goldstein, JMH, 48
(Mar 1976):132-5.

_____. Wellington, the Years of the Sword. New York:
Harper and Row, 1969. Rev. by M. E. Goldstein, JMH,
48(Mar 1976):132-5.

Longford, Lord. Abraham Lincoln. New York: Putnam's, 1975.
Rev. by R. D. Hoffsommer, AHI, 11(Oct 1976):49.

Long-Hsuen, Hsu and Chang Ming-Kai, comps. History of the Sino-
Japanese War (1937-1945). Taipei: Chung Wu, 1972. Rev.
by P. Chu, AHR, 81(Apr 1976):433.

Longmate, Norman. The G. I. 's: The Americans in Britain 1942-
1945. New York: Scribner's, 1976. Rev. by E. M. Coff-
man, HRNB, 4(Sep 1976):211-12.

Longworth, Philip. The Rise and Fall of Venice. London: Constable, 1974. Rev. by D. S. Chambers, History, 61(Feb
1976):88.

Lopez, Adalberto and James Petras, eds. Puerto Rico and the
Puerto Ricans. New York: Schenkman, 1974. Rev. by S.
Bhana, AS, 16(Fall 1975):90-2.

Lopez, Claude-Anne and Eugenia W. Herbert. The Private Franklin. New York: Norton, 1975. Rev. by G. S. Wood, JAH,
63(Sep 1976):386-7; E. Wolf, MHM, 71(Sum 1976):270-2; A.
O. Aldridge, NEQ, 49(Je 1976):295-7.

Lord, Barry. The History of Painting in Canada. Toronto: n. p. ,
1974. Rev. by A. Davis, CHR, 57(Mar 1976):40-7.

Lotchin, Roger W. San Francisco, 1846-1856. New York: Oxford
U Press, 1974. Rev. by W. S. Glazer, AHR, 81(Feb 1976):

239   LOTTER

210; M. H. Frisch, JAH, 63(Je 1976):122-3; K. N. Conzen,
JEH, 36(Sep 1976):775.

Lotter, Friedrich. Der Brief des Priesters Gerhard an den
Erzbishof Friedrich von Mainz. Sigmaringen: Thorbecke,
1975. Rev. by W. Ullmann, JEccH, 27(Jl 1976):309-10.

Lottinville, Savoie. The Rhetoric of History. Norman: U Ok
Press, 1976. Rev. by A. J. Going, JSH, 42(Nov 1976):612.

Loubère, Leo. Radicalism in Mediterranean France. Albany:
SUNY Press, 1974. Rev. by A. Sedgwick, CHR, 57(Je 1976):
232-3; R. Magraw, EHR, 91(Jan 1976):218-19.

Lough, John. The Contributors to the Encyclopedie. London:
Grand and Cutler, 1973. Rev. by W. H. Williams, AHR, 81
(Je 1976):602.

Louis, Ray Baldwin. Child of the Hogan. Provo, Utah: BYU
Press, 1975. Rev. by R. Wilson, JAriH, 17(Spr 1976):117-
18.

Louisville Abstract and Loan Assn. Atlas of the City of Louisville,
Ky., 1876. Louisville: Standard Printing, 1974. Rev. by
M. F. Schmidt, FCHQ, 50(Apr 1976):90-1.

Lovett, Robert W., ed. Harvard College Records: Part IV,
Documents from the Harvard University Archives 1638-1722;
Part V, Documents from the Harvard University Archives
1722-1750. Boston: Colonial Society of Mass., 1975. Rev.
by R. E. Welch, Jr., NEQ, 49(Mar 1976):169-72.

Lovoll, Odd Sverre. The "Bygdelag" in America. Boston:
Twayne, 1975. Rev. by A. W. Andersen, JAH, 62(Mar
1976):1022-3; R. Nelson, NDH, 43(Spr 1976):106.

Low, Alfred D. The Anschluss Movement, 1918-1919 and the Paris
Peace Conference. Philadelphia: American Philosophical Society, 1974. Rev. by F. Dumin, AHR, 81(Je 1976):617.

Low, D. A. Lion Rampant. Portland, Ore.: International Scholarly Book Service, 1973. Rev. by A. P. Thornton, AHR, 81
(Feb 1976):140-1.

Low, Victor N. Three Nigerian Emirates. Evanston: Northwestern U Press, 1972. Rev. by R. Cohen, AHR, 81(Je
1976):640-1.

Lowance, Mason I., Jr. Increase Mather. New York: Twayne,
1974. Rev. by R. G. Pope, JAH, 62(Mar 1976):963-4; P.
J. Gomes, NEQ, 49(Mar 1976):121-6.

Lowe, C. J. and F. Marzari. Italian Foreign Policy, 1870-1940.

Boston: Routledge and Kegan Paul, 1975. Rev. by A. Cassels, AHR, 81(Je 1976):622-3; J. Whittam, EHR, 91(Jl 1976): 675-6; C. Seton-Watson, History, 61(Oct 1976):468-70.

Lowe, David. Lost Chicago. Boston: Houghton Mifflin, 1975. Rev. by P. E. Sprague, WMH, 60(Aug 1976):71-2.

Lowe, Don and Roberta Lowe. Mount Hood. Caldwell, Ida.: Caxton, 1975. Rev. by L. L. Morrison, JOW, 15(Jan 1976): 132-3; L. L. McArthur, OrHQ, 77(Mar 1976):87-8.

Lowe, Heinz. Die Karolinger von Verdun bis zum Herrschaftsantrett der Herrscher aus dem Sächsischen Hause. Weimar: Bohlau, 1973. Rev. by P. Wormald, EHR, 91(Jl 1976):622-3.

Lowenkopf, Shelly see Leadabrand, Russ

Lowenthal, Abraham F., ed. The Peruvian Experiment: Continuity and Change Under Military Rule. Princeton, N.J.: Prin U Press, 1976. Rev. by F. B. Pike, AHR, 81(Oct 1976): 1012.

Lowman, Al. Printing Arts in Texas. Austin, Tx.: Roger Beacham, 1975. Rev. by J. S. Mayfield, SWHQ, 80(Jl 1976):117-18.

Lowrie, Ernest Benson. The Shape of the Puritan Mind: The Thought of Samuel Willard. New Haven, Conn.: Yale U Press, 1974. Rev. by A. O. Aldridge, AHR, 81(Je 1976): 651-2.

Loy, Ursula F. and Pauline Marion Worthy, eds. Washington and the Pamlico. Washington, N.C.: Washington-Beaufort County Bicentennial Commission, 1976. Rev. by C. L. Paul, NCHR, 53(Aut 1976):401-2.

Loyn, H. R. and John Percival, eds. The Reign of Charlemagne. London: Arnold, 1975. Rev. by R. A. Markus, JEccH, 27 (Jl 1976):327-8.

_____, ed. see Hearder, H., ed.

Lubin, Maurice A. Afrique et Politique. Paris: La Pensée Universelle, 1974. Rev. by J. Philips, Américas, 28(May 1976):23.

Lucas, Noah. The Modern History of Israel. London: Weidenfeld and Nicolson, 1975. Rev. by L. Kochan, History, 61 (Feb 1976):162-3.

Lucas, Paul R. Valley of Discord. Hanover, N.H.: U Press New England, 1976. Rev. by F. J. Bremer, HRNB, 5(Oct 1976):3.

Luce, J. V. see Stanford, W. B.

Lucia, Ellis. The Big Woods: Logging and Lumbering ... in the
  Pacific Northwest. Garden City, N. Y.: Doubleday, 1975.
  Rev. by J. T. Labbe, OrHQ, 77(Mar 1976):86-7.

Ludlum, David. The Country Journal New England Weather Book.
  Boston: Houghton Mifflin, 1976. Rev. by M. Hanagan, VH,
  44(Sum 1976):183-4.

Ludwig, Charles. Levi Coffin and the Underground Railroad.
  Scottdale, Pa.: Herald, 1975. Rev. by J. L. Nethers, OH,
  85(Sum 1976):269-70.

Lukacs, John. The Last European War. Garden City, N. Y.:
  Anchor/Doubleday, 1976. Rev. by J. Shattan, Commentary,
  62(Aug 1976):68, 70-2; J. M. Block, HRNB, 4(May/Je 1976):
  158-9; G. R. Kleinfeld, HRNB, 4(Sep 1976):231.

Lullies, Reinhard see Kranz, Peter

Lumbreras, Luis G. The Peoples and Cultures of Ancient Peru.
  Washington, D. C.: Smithsonian, 1974. Rev. by M. E.
  Moseley, TAm, 33(Jl 1976):165-7.

Lumholtz, Carl. Unknown Mexico. Glorieta, N. M.: Rio Grande
  Press, 1975. Rev. by J. Griffith, A & W, 18(Win 1976):
  377-8.

Lummis, Keith see Fiske, Turbesé Lummis

Lumpkin, Katharine Du Pre. The Emancipation of Angelina
  Grimké. Chapel Hill: U NC Press, 1974. Rev. by B.
  Wyatt-Brown, AHR, 81(Apr 1976):446-7; N. Walker, AS, 16
  (Fall 1975):100-1; W. H. Pease, JAH, 62(Mar 1976):992-3.

Lundeberg, Philip K. Samuel Colt's Submarine Battery. Washington, D. C.: Smithsonian, 1974. Rev. by R. W. Donnelly,
  JSH, 42(Feb 1976):136-7.

Lundestad, Geir. The American Non-Policy Towards Eastern
  Europe, 1943-1947: Universalism in an Area Not of Essential Interest to the United States. New York: Humanities
  Press, 1975. Rev. by B. Kovrig, AHR, 81(Oct 1976):1001-
  2; L. C. Gardner, JAH, 62(Mar 1976):1045-6.

Lunt, James. John Burgoyne of Saratoga. New York: Harcourt
  Brace Jovanovich, 1975. Rev. by W. F. Ricketson, Jr.,
  HRNB, 4(Mar 1976):111-12; D. Lindsey, Mankind, 5(Je
  1976):60; D. K. Martin, VH, 44(Spr 1976):116-19.

Lupold, Harry Forrest. The Forgotten People. Hicksville, N. Y.:
  Exposition, 1975. Rev. by H. J. Viola, JAH, 63(Dec 1976):
  686.

LUPPOV 242

Luppov, S. P. The Book in Russia in the First Quarter of the
18th Century. Leningrad: Izdatel'stvo "Nauka," 1973. Rev.
by C. B. O'Brien, AHR, 81(Feb 1976):183-4.

Lupul, Manoly R. The Roman Catholic Church and the North-West
School Question. Toronto: U Tor Press, 1974. Rev. by
J. R. Miller, CHR, 57(Je 1976):200-2.

Lurie, Edward. Nature and the American Mind: Louis Agassiz
and the Culture of Science. New York: Science History
Publ., 1974. Rev. by H.C., AS, 16(Fall 1975):92.

Lutaud, Olivier. Des Révolutions d'Angleterre à la Révolution
française. The Hague: Martinus Nijhoff, 1973. Rev. by
A. L. Moote, JMH, 48(Mar 1976):120-1.

Lutheran Historical Conference. Lutheran Historical Conference,
19-20 October 1972. St. Louis, Mo.: Lutheran Historical
Conference, 1974. Rev. by A. Graebner, JAH, 63(Sep 1976):
432-3.

Lutz, Charles P. see Killmer, Richard L.

Luyken, Jan. The Drama of the Martyrs. Lancaster, Pa.: Mennonite Historical Associates, 1975. Rev. by V. Burnett,
MQR, 50(Apr 1976):158-60.

Luza, Radomir. Austro-German Relations in the Anschluss Era.
Princeton, N.J.: Prin U Press, 1975. Rev. by J. Remak,
EEQ, 10(Mar 1976):132-3; H. A. Arnold, HRNB, 4(Feb 1976):
90-1.

Lyday, Leon F. and George W. Woodyard, eds. Dramatists in
Revolt: The New Latin American Theatre. Austin: U Tex
Press, 1976. Rev. by K. F. Nigro, HAHR, 56(Nov 1976):
693-4.

Lynam, Shevawn. Humanity Dick, 1754-1834. London: Hamish
Hamilton, 1975. Rev. by D. Large, History, 61(Je 1976):
301-2.

Lyon, Martyn. France Under the Directory. Cambridge: Cam U
Press, 1975. Rev. by C. Lucas, EHR, 91(Oct 1976):922;
G. Cavanaugh, HRNB, 4(Feb 1976):87-8; W. B. Kennedy, HT,
10(Nov 1976):162-3.

Lyon, Peter. Eisenhower: Portrait of the Hero. Boston: Little,
Brown, 1974. Rev. by A. Yarnell, PHR, 45(Feb 1976):154-5.

Lyttelton, Margaret. Baroque Architecture in Classical Antiquity.
Ithaca, N.Y.: Cornell U Press, 1974. Rev. by J. B.
Ward-Perkins, AJA, 80(Sum 1976):322-4; A. Frazer, Archae-
ology, 29(Jan 1976):61-2.

Mabry, Donald J.   Mexico's Acción Nacional: A Catholic Alterna-
tive to Revolution.   Syracuse, N.Y.:   Syracuse U Press, 1973.
Rev. by W. D. Raat, AHR, 81(Feb 1976):226; H. D. Joseph,
JCS, 17(Win 1975):125-7.

McAllister, Lester G. and Willism E. Tucker.   Journey in Faith.
St. Louis, Mo.:   Bethany, 1975.   Rev. by L. P. Donovan,
ArkHQ, 35(Spr 1976):103-4; W. C. Gilpin, CH, 45(Je 1976):
266; B. Luckingham, ChOk, 54(Fall 1976):411-12; G. L. Hart-
man, IMH, 72(Je 1976):271-2; P. E. Million, Jr., JAH, 63
(Sep 1976):413-14; H. W. Bowden, JSH, 42(Aug 1976):451-2;
D. T. Stokes, NCHR, 53(Sum 1976):333-4; I. L. M. Duncan,
THQ, 35(Spr 1976):110-11; W. H. Daniel, VMHB, 84(Apr
1976):209-11.

Macauley, Neill.   The Prestes Column Revolution in Brazil.   New
York: New Viewpoints, 1974.   Rev. by J. D. Wirth, TAm,
33(Jl 1976):169-70.

McBride, Theresa M.   The Domestic Revolution: The Modernization
of Household Service in England and France 1820-1920.   New
York: Holmes and Meier, 1976.   Rev. by P. McCandless,
HRNB, 4(Sep 1976):228-9.

McCaffrey, Lawrence J.   The Irish Diaspora in America.   Bloomington: Ind U Press, 1976.   Rev. by R. N. Current, HRNB,
4(Sep 1976):216.

McCann, Frank D., Jr.   The Brazilian-American Alliance 1937-
1945.   Princeton, N.J.:   Prin U Press, 1973.   Rev. by
J.-S. Tulchin, CHR, 57(Mar 1976):89-91.

McCarthy, Patrick.   Céline.   London: Allen Lane, 1975.   Rev.
by F. Field, History, 61(Oct 1976):474.

McCaughey, Robert A.   Josiah Quincy, 1772-1864:   The Last
Federalist.   Cambridge, Mass.:   Harvard U Press, 1974.
Rev. by S. Nathans, CWH, 22(Mar 1976):83-5.

McClelland, Charles E.   The German Historians and England.
Cambridge: Cam U Press, 1971.   Rev. by W. M. Medlicott,
ESR, 6(Jan 1976):156-7.

McClelland, John M., Jr.   R. A. Long's Planned City: The Story
of Longview.   Longview, Washington: Longview Pub. Co.,
1976.   Rev. by G. G. Macnab, OrHQ, 77(Dec 1976):381-2.

McClelland, Peter D.   Casual Explanation and Model Building in
History, Economics, and the New Economic History.   Ithaca,
N.Y.:   Cornell U Press, 1975.   Rev. by A. J. Field, BHR,
50(Spr 1976):96-9; W. O. Wagnon, Jr., HRNB, 4(May/Je
1976):149.

McCloskey, Donald N. Economic Maturity and Entrepreneurial Decline: British Iron and Steel, 1870-1913. Cambridge, Mass.: Harvard U Press, 1973. Rev. by M. W. Flinn, BH, 17(Jan 1975):73-5; C. H. Feinstein, JMH, 48(Je 1976):326-7.

McConal, Jon see Stricklin, Al

MacCormack, John R. Revolutionary Politics in the Long Parliament. Cambridge, Mass.: Harvard U Press, 1974. Rev. by C. Russell, EHR, 91(Jl 1976):644.

McCormmach, Russell, ed. Historical Studies in the Physical Sciences. Vol. 5. Princeton, N.J.: Prin U Press, 1975. Rev. by R. Olson, AHR, 81(Oct 1976):813.

McCoy, Donald R. Coming of Age: The United States 1920-1930. Harmondsworth: Penguin, 1975. Rev. by J. Potter, History, 61(Oct 1976):417.

McCoy, F. N. Robert Baillie and the Second Scots Reformation. Berkeley: U Cal Press, 1974. Rev. by T. S. Colahan, AHR, 81(Apr 1976):392-3.

McCreary, Guy Weddington. From Glory to Oblivion: The Real Truth About the Mexican Revolution. New York: Vantage, 1974. Rev. by R. Mohan, JOW, 15(Jl 1976):102; P. J. Vanderwood, SCQ, 58(Win 1976):539-42; D. B. Adams, SWHQ, 80(Oct 1976):242-3.

McDermott, John Francis, ed. The Spanish in the Mississippi Valley, 1762-1804. Urbana: U Ill Press, 1974. Rev. by J. L. Wright, Jr., PHR, 45(Aug 1976):438-9.

McDermott, Robert A., ed. Six Pillars: Introductions to the Major Works of Sri Aurobindo. Chambersburg, Pa.: Wilson, 1974. Rev. by S. Lavan, JAS, 36(Nov 1976):174-5.

MacDonald, Charles B. The Last Offensive. Washington, D.C.: Office of Chief of Military History, U.S. Army, 1973. Rev. by D. G. Dayton, AHR, 81(Feb 1976):219.

MacDonald, Edith Fox. Rebellion in the Mountains: The Story of Universalism and Unitarianism in Vermont. Concord, N.H.: New Hampshire Vermont District of the Unitarian Universalist Association, 1976. Rev. by W. A. Cate, Jr., VH, 44(Sum 1976):184-5.

McDonald, Forrest. The Presidency of George Washington. Lawrence: U Press Kan, 1974. Rev. by R. F. Jones, NYHSQ, 60(Jan/Apr 1976):76-8.

McDonald, Margaret Simms. White Already to Harvest. Sewanee, Tenn.: U Press Sewanee, 1975. Rev. by W. L. Brown, ArkHQ, 35(Sum 1976):144-7.

McDonald, William A. and George R. Rapp, Jr. The Minnesota
Messenia Expedition. Minneapolis: U Minn Press, 1972.
Rev. by T. W. Jacobsen, Archaeology, 29(Apr 1976):136-7.

MacDonald, William L. Northampton Massachusetts: Architecture
and Buildings. Northampton, Mass.: Northampton Bicentennial Committee, 1975. Rev. by R. B. Stein, JAH, 63(Dec
1976):708-9.

MacDougall, H. A., ed. Lord Acton on Papal Power. London:
Sheed and Ward, 1973. Rev. by J. C. Holland, CaHR, 62
(Oct 1976):629-30.

Macebuh, Stanley. James Baldwin: A Critical Study. New York:
Third Press, 1973. Rev. by G. E. Osborne, Crisis, 83(Mar
1976):102.

McElrath, Damian. Richard Simpson, 1820-1876. Louvain:
Universitaires de Louvain, 1972. Rev. by R. J. Schiefen,
CaHR, 62(Oct 1976):626-8.

_____, ed. see Altholz, Josef L., ed.

McFarland, Keith D. Harry H. Woodring. Lawrence: U Press
Kan, 1975. Rev. by A. A. Ekirch, Jr., HRNB, 4(Mar 1976):
98-9; E. L. Schapsmeier, JAH, 63(Je 1976):182-3; A. B.
Sageser, JOW, 15(Apr 1976):142.

McFarlane, I. D. A Literary History of France. New York:
Barnes and Noble, 1974. Rev. by D. Bitton, AHR, 81(Feb
1976):151-2.

McFarlane, K. B. Lancastrian Kings and Lollard Knights. New
York: Oxford U Press, 1972. Rev. by M. Aston, CaHR,
62(Jan 1976):106-8.

MacFarquhar, Roderick. The Origins of the Cultural Revolution.
New York: Columbia U Press, 1974. Rev. by S. Uhalley,
Jr., JAAS, 11(Jl-Oct 1976):229-31.

MacGaffey, Wyatt. Custom and Government in the Lower Congo.
Berkeley: U Cal Press, 1970. Rev. by D. Birmingham,
AfAf, 75(Jl 1976):400-1.

MacGillivray, Royce. Restoration Historians and the English Civil
War. The Hague: Martinus Nijhoff, 1974. Rev. by C. A.
Edie, AHR, 81(Oct 1976):855-6.

McGimsey, Charles R., III. Public Archaeology. New York:
Seminar Press, 1972. Rev. by T. E. King, AmAnt, 41(Apr
1976):236-8.

McGinnis, Vera. Rodeo Road: My Life as a Pioneer Cowgirl.

New York: Hastings, 1974. Rev. by D. F. Kee, JOW, 15 (Jl 1976):103.

MacGowan, J. The Imperial History of China. New York: Harper and Row, 1973. Rev. by E-tu Zen Sun, JAAS, 11(Jan-Apr 1976):131-2.

McGrade, Arthur Stephen. The Political Thought of William of Ockham. New York: Cam U Press, 1974. Rev. by B. D. Hill, AHR, 81(Feb 1976):112-13; H. S. Offler, History, 61(Feb 1976):101-2; J. H. Hallowell, JCS, 17(Win 1975):115-17; C. Vasoli, JHP, 14(Apr 1976):230-3.

McGrath, William J. Dionysian Art and Populist Politics in Austria. New Haven, Conn.: Yale U Press, 1974. Rev. by A. G. Whiteside, AHR, 81(Feb 1976):173-4; C. E. Williams, JMH, 48(Je 1976):356-8.

Maciel, David and Patricia Bueno. Aztlan: Historia del Pueblo Chicano (1848-1910). Mexico: D. F., Sep/Setentas, 1975. Rev. by O. J. Martinez, PHR, 45(Aug 1976):444-5.

McIntosh, James T., ed. see Davis, Jefferson

McKale, Donald M. The Nazi Party Courts. Lawrence: U Press Kan, 1974. Rev. by G. G. Field, AHR, 81(Feb 1976):170; W. Sweet, JMH, 48(Je 1976):352-6.

McKay, A. G. Houses, Villas, and Palaces in the Roman World. London: Thames and Hudson, 1975. Rev. by J. Liversidge, Antiquity, 50(Je 1976):155-6.

McKay, David P. and Richard Crawford. William Billings of Boston. Princeton, N.J.: Prin U Press, 1975. Rev. by T. Wendel, AHR, 81(Je 1976):656-7; H. Norden, NEQ, 49 (Je 1976):327-8.

Mackay, Ruddock F. Fisher of Kilverstone. New York: Oxford U Press, 1974. Rev. by A. N. Ryan, History, 61(Feb 1976): 134-5.

McKee, Barbara, Edwin McKee and Joyce Herold. Havasupai Baskets and Their Makers: 1930-1940. Flagstaff, Ariz.: Northland, 1975. Rev. by C. L. Tanner, JAriH, 17(Spr 1976):110-12.

McKee, John De Witt. William Allen White: Maverick on Main Street. Westport, Conn.: Greenwood, 1975. Rev. by L. L. Ashby, AHR, 81(Je 1976):681; P. A. Brooks, AS, 16(Fall 1975):95; E. H. Ziegner, IMH, 72(Je 1976):280-1; P. W. Glad, JAH, 63(Je 1976):164-5; J. Mushkat, NDH, 43(Win 1976):40-1.

McKee, Russell. The Last West: A History of the Great Plains of
    North America. New York: Crowell, 1974. Rev. by C. F.
    Kraenzel, WHQ, 7(Apr 1976):214-15.

Macken, Raymond. "La Lectura Odinaria Super Scripturam."
    Paris: Nauwelaerts, 1972. Rev. by J. Dunbabin, EHR, 91
    (Jan 1976):179.

McKendrick, Neil, ed. Historical Perspectives. New York: In-
    ternational Publications, 1974. Rev. by R. K. Webb, AHR,
    81(Oct 1976):856-7; H. T. Dickinson, History, 61(Feb 1976):
    70.

MacKendrick, Paul. The Dacian Stones Speak. Chapel Hill, S.C.:
    U NCar Press, 1975. Rev. by S. L. Dyson, AHR, 81(Oct
    1976):829-30.

MacKenzie, David. The Lion of Tashkent. Athens, Ga.: U Ga
    Press, 1974. Rev. by T. B. Rainey, AHR, 81(Feb 1976):
    185-7; P. Dukes, EHR, 91(Jl 1976):676-7.

McKenzie, Robert H., ed. Southern Universities and the South.
    University: U Ala Press, 1976. Rev. by W. B. Gatewood,
    Jr., NCHR, 53(Aut 1976):405-6.

Mackesy, Piers. Statesmen at War. London: Longman, 1974.
    Rev. by S. Ross, AHR, 81(Feb 1976):135-6.

Mackey, Carol J. see Moseley, Michael Edward

McKibbin, Ross. The Evolution of the Labour Party, 1910-1924.
    New York: Oxford U Press, 1974. Rev. by H. R. Winkler,
    AHR, 81(Je 1976):594-5; P. F. Clarke, EHR, 91(Jan 1976):
    157-63; J. Brown, History, 61(Oct 1976):494; M. Freeden,
    JMH, 48(Sep 1976):547-52.

Mackie, J. A. C. Konfrontasi: The Indonesia-Malaysia Dispute
    1963-1966. Kuala Lumpur: Oxford U Press, 1974. Rev. by
    F. Bunnell, JAS, 36(Nov 1976):186-7.

McKinstry, Bruce L. The California Gold Rush Overland Diary
    of Byron N. McKinstry, 1850-1852. Glendale, Cal.: Arthur
    H. Clark, 1975. Rev. by J. E. King, A & W, 18(Sum 1976):
    195-6.

McKitrich, Eric, ed. see Elkins, Stanley, ed.

McKown, Dave R. The Dean, the Life of Julien C. Monnet. Nor-
    man: U Ok Press, 1973. Rev. by G. H. Shirk, ChOk, 54
    (Sum 1976):289.

Mackrell, J. Q. C. The Attack on "Feudalism" in Eighteenth-
    Century France. London: Routledge and Kegan Paul, 1973.
    Rev. by C. M. Greene, CHR, 57(Mar 1976):95-6.

MacLachlan, Colin M. Criminal Justice in Eighteenth-Century
Mexico. Berkeley: U Cal Press, 1974. Rev. by W. Dusenberry, HAHR, 56(Feb 1976):123-4; B. R. Hamnett, History,
61(Oct 1976):426-7; R. Pike, TAm, 33(Jl 1976):175-6.

MacLaren, A. Allen. Religion and Social Class: The Disruption
Years in Aberdeen. London: Routledge and Kegan Paul,
1974. Rev. by D. M. Thompson, History, 61(Oct 1976):485.

McLean, E., ed. see Oluwasanmi, E., ed.

McLean, Iain. Keir Hardie. New York: St. Martin's, 1975.
Rev. by D. F. Schafer, HRNB, 4(May/Je 1976):152-3.

McLean, Malcolm D., ed. Papers Concerning Robertson's Colony
in Texas. Vols. I and II. Fort Worth: TCU Press, 1975.
Rev. by A. P. Nasatir, A & W, 18(Sum 1976):201-2; J. M.
Nance, AHR, 81(Je 1976):656; D. J. Weber, JAH, 63(Dec
1976):670; M. S. Henson, JSH, 42(Feb 1976):116-17; M. S.
Henson, JSH, 42(Aug 1976):428-9; F. D. Almaraz, Jr.,
NMHR, 51(Oct 1976):341-3.

MacLean, R. A. see Campbell, D.

McLeish, Kenneth, comp. and trans. see Nichols, Roger, comp.
and trans.

MacLeod, Anne Scott. A Moral Tale. Hamden, Conn.: Archon,
1975. Rev. by K. Jeffrey, HRNB, 4(Mar 1976):101; R.
Welter, JAH, 63(Sep 1976):408.

MacLeod, Duncan J. Slavery, Race and the American Revolution.
New York: Cam U Press, 1974. Rev. by P. M. Mitchell,
AHR, 81(Je 1976):655-6; B. Wood, History, 61(Oct 1976):
403; J. White, JAmS, 10(Apr 1976):113-17; R. J. Christen,
JSH, 42(Feb 1976):108-9.

McLeod, Hugh. Class and Religion in the Late Victorian City.
London: Croom Helm, 1974. Rev. by P. Marsh, AHR, 81
(Je 1976):593; J. Kent, History, 61(Je 1976):310.

McLeod, Joseph A. see Brewster, John W.

McManners, John. Church and State in France, 1870-1914.
New York: Harper and Row, 1973. Rev. by R. J. Schiefen,
JCS, 17(Spr 1975):316-18.

MacMaster, Richard K. see Copeland, Pamela C.

McMath, Robert C., Jr. Populist Vanguard: A History of the
Southern Farmers' Alliance. Chapel Hill: U NC Press,
1976. Rev. by F. H. Schapsmeier, HRNB, 4(May/Je 1976):
139-40; R. V. Scott, JSH, 42(Aug 1976):440-1.

McMillan, Malcolm C. Yesterday's Birmingham. Miami, Fla.:
  E. A. Seeman, 1975. Rev. by H. C. Bailey, AlaR, 29
  (Apr 1976):155.

Macmillan, W. M. My South African Years. Cape Town: David
  Philip, 1975. Rev. by P. Lewsen, JAfH, 17(Num 3, 1976):
  469-70.

MacMullan, Ramsay. Roman Social Relations 50 B.C. to A.D.
  284. New Haven, Conn.: Yale U Press, 1974. Rev. by
  J. H. D'Arms, JIH, 7(Sum 1976):126-9.

McMullen, Roy. Mona Lisa--The Picture and the Myth. Boston:
  Houghton Mifflin, n.d. Rev. by R. L. Lowe, Mankind, 5
  (Je 1976):58.

McNab, Gordon. A Century of News and People in the East
  Oregonian, 1875-1975. Pendleton: East Oregonian, 1975.
  Rev. by R. B. Frazier, OrHQ, 77(Je 1976):192-3.

Macnab, Roy. The French Colonel. New York: Oxford U Press,
  1976. Rev. by J. J. Cook, HRNB, 4(Jl 1976):181.

McNamara, Robert F. Catholic Sunday Preaching. Washington,
  D.C.: Word of God Institute, 1975. Rev. by R. Trisco,
  CaHR, 62(Jl 1976):526-7.

McNaught, Kenneth and David J. Bercuson. The Winnipeg Strike:
  1919. Don Mills, Ont.: Longman, 1974. Rev. by N. Penner, CHR, 57(Mar 1976):61-3; M. Dubofsky, JAH, 63(Je
  1976):205.

McNeil, David O. Guillaume Budé and Humanism in the Reign of
  Francis I. Geneva: Droz, 1975. Rev. by R. J. Knecht,
  History, 61(Oct 1976):446-7.

McNeill, William H. The Shape of European History. New York:
  Oxford U Press, 1974. Rev. by M. B. Becker, AHR, 81
  (Oct 1976):839-40; D. Hay, History, 61(Feb 1976):87.

_____. Venice: The Hinge of Europe, 1081-1797. Chicago:
  U Chicago Press, 1974. Rev. by S. Chojnacki, AHR, 81
  (Feb 1976):99-100.

MacNeish, Richard S., ed. The Prehistory of the Tehuacan Valley. Vol. 5. Austin: U Texas Press, 1975. Rev. by E.
  B. McCluney, HRNB, 4(Feb 1976):82; B. J. Meggers, TAm,
  33(Oct 1976):366-7.

McPherson, A., ed. History of the Free Presbyterian Church of
  Scotland (1893-1970). Inverness: Free Presbyterian Church
  of Scotland, 1973. Rev. by L. A. Dralle, CH, 45(Je 1976):
  268.

McPherson, James M. The Abolitionist Legacy: From Reconstruction to the NAACP. Princeton: Prin U Press, 1976. Rev.
by J. B. Stewart, HRNB, 4(May/Je 1976):139; E. L. Thornbrough, JAH, 63(Dec 1976):723-4; W. F. Holmes, NCHR, 53
(Sum 1976):329-30; R. E. Luker, NEQ, 49(Sep 1976):483-5.

MacQueen, J. G. The Hittites and Their Contemporaries in Asia
Minor. Boulder, Colo.: Westview Press, 1976. Rev. by
J. G. Pritchard, AHR, 81(Oct 1976):915; S. Kosak, Antiquity,
50(Je 1976):168-9.

McQuire, William, ed. The Freud/Jung Letters. London: Hogarth,
1974. Rev. by A. Cunningham, ESR, 6(Jan 1976):160-3.

McSeveney, Samuel T. The Politics of Depression. New York:
Oxford U Press, 1972. Rev. by J. A. Thompson, HJ, 19
(Mar 1976):257-74.

McShane, Clay. Technology and Reform: Street Railways and the
Growth of Milwaukee, 1887-1900. Madison: U Wis, 1975.
Rev. by J. F. Stover, AHR, 81(Je 1976):674-5.

McWilliam, H. O. A. and M. A. Kwamena-Poh. The Development
of Education in Ghana. London: Longman, 1975. Rev. by
B. Lindsay, JMAS, 14(Dec 1976):721-2.

McWilliams, Wilson Carey. The Idea of Fraternity in America.
Berkeley: U Cal Press, 1973. Rev. by M. McKenna, CHR,
57(Mar 1976):81-3.

Maddicott, J. R. The English Peasantry and the Demands of the
Crown, 1294-1341. Oxford: Past and Present Society, 1975.
Rev. by E. Miller, EHR, 91(Oct 1976):897-8.

Madison, James. The Papers of James Madison. Vol. 9. (Robert
A. Rutland, et al., eds.) Chicago: U Chicago Press, 1975.
Rev. by J. B. Whisker, HRNB, 4(Apr 1976):122; R. L.
Ketcham, JSH, 42(May 1976):276-7.

Madsen, David. Early National Education: 1776-1830. New
York: Wiley, 1974. Rev. by J. Messerli, AHR, 81(Je
1976):666-7.

Maestro, Marcello. Cesare Beccaria and the Origins of Penal Reform. Philadelphia: Temple U Press, 1973. Rev. by L.
F. Barmann, AHR, 81(Oct 1976):842-3.

Magnussen, Daniel O., ed. Peter Thompson's Narrative to the
Little Bighorn Campaign, 1876: A Critical Analysis of an
Eyewitness Account of the Custer Debacle. Glendale, Cal.:
Arthur H. Clark Co., 1974. Rev. by R. M. Utley, PHR,
45(May 1976):290.

Magoulias, Harry J. , trans. Decline and Fall of Byzantium to
the Ottoman Turks. Detroit: Wayne St. U Press, 1975.
Rev. by W. S. Vucinich, AHR, 81(Oct 1976):839; P. D.
Thomas, HRNB, 4(Mar 1976):106.

Mahon, John K. , ed. Indians of the Lower South. Pensacola:
Gulf Coast History Conference, 1975. Rev. by C. Hudson,
FHQ, 54(Jan 1975):407-8; J. H. O'Donnell, JAH, 63(Sep
1976):380-1; R. M. Miller, JOS, 15(Jan 1976):128-9; K. R.
Morrison, PHR, 45(Nov 1976):607-9.

Mahoney, Barry see Westin, Alan F.

Mahoney, Irene. Madame Catharine. New York: Coward, McCann
and Geoghegan, 1976. Rev. by S. Gershgoren, Mankind, 5(Feb
1976):6.

Mahoney, Michael Sean. The Mathematical Career of Pierre de
Fermat (1601-1665). Princeton: Prin U Press, 1973. Rev.
by N. T. Gridgeman, AHR, 81(Oct 1976):840-1.

Maier, Charles S. Recasting Bourgeois Europe. Princeton, N. J. :
Prin U Press, 1975. Rev. by J. Colton, AHR, 81(Oct 1976):
849-50; R. Wohl, JIH, 7(Aut 1976):366-70.

Mails, Thomas E. Dog Soldiers, Bear Men and Buffalo Women.
Englewood Cliffs, N. J. : Prentice-Hall, 1973. Rev. by J. F.
Hamburg, AIQ, 2(Spr 1975):29-31.

Main, Jackson Turner. The Sovereign States 1775-1783. London:
Croom Helm, 1974. Rev. by C. C. Bonwick, History, 61
(Oct 1976):400-1.

Mair, Lucy. African Societies. Cambridge: Cam U Press, 1974.
Rev. by R. G. Willis, Africa, 46(Num 1, 1976):105.

Majkowski, Joseph. Saint Stanislaus Kostka. Rome: Papal Institute of Ecclesiastical Studies, 1972. Rev. by E. D. McShane,
CaHR, 62(Jan 1976):137-8.

Majno, Guido. The Healing Hand: Man and Wound in the Ancient
World. Cambridge, Mass. : Harvard U Press, 1974. Rev.
by J. N. Tuck, Smithsonian, 7(May 1976):120.

Makarova, Raisa V. Russians on the Pacific, 1743-1799. Kingston, Ontario: Limestone Press, 1975. Rev. by R. H.
Fisher, PHR, 45(Nov 1976):611-13.

Makkreel, Rudolf A. Dilthey: Philosopher of the Human Studies.
Princeton: Prin U Press, 1975. Rev. by I. N. Bulhof,
AHR, 81(Oct 1976):823-4.

Makonnen, Ras. Pan-Africanism from Within. Nairobi: Oxford

U Press, n.d. Rev. by A. H. M. Kirk-Greene, Africa, 46 (Num 2, 1976):209-10.

Malagón y Barceló, Javier. Código Negro Carolino. Santo Domingo, R.D.: Editora Taller, 1974. Rev. by R. W. Logan, TAm, 33(Jl 1976):168-9.

Malcomson, Robert W. Popular Recreations in English Society 1700-1850. New York: Cam U Press, 1973. Rev. by N. Harris, JIH, 7(Sum 1976):71-7.

Malin, James C. Doctors, Devils and the Woman: Fort Scott, Kansas, 1870-1890. Lawrence, Kan.: Coronado, 1975. Rev. by H. E. Socolofsky, JAH, 63(Je 1976):148-9; D. A. Clary, WHQ, 7(Jl 1976):330.

Malina, Jaroslav see Stelcl, Jinurich

Malinvaud, E. see Carré, J.-J.

Mallinckrodt, Anita M. see Starrels, John M.

Mallowan, Max and Georgina Herrmann. Ivories from Nimrud (1949-1963), Fascicule III: Furniture from SW7 Fort Shalmaneser. Aberdeen: British School of Archaeology in Iraq, 1974. Rev. by I. J. Winter, AJA, 80(Spr 1976):201-3; O. W. Muscarella, JNES, 35(Jl 1976):208-10.

Malone, Dumas. Jefferson the President: Second Term, 1805-1909. Boston: Little, Brown, 1974. Rev. by J. R. Sharp, AHR, 81(Apr 1976):445-6.

Malval, Jean. Essai de chronologie tchadienne (1707-1940). Paris: Ed. C.N.R.S., n.d. Rev. by E. Conte, Africa, 46(Num 1, 1976):108-9.

Manchester, William. The Glory and the Dream. Boston: Little, Brown, 1973. Rev. by D. K. Adams, History, 61(Oct 1976): 419-20; C. Anderson, Mankind, 5(Feb 1976):68-9.

Mandrou, Robert. Introduction to Modern France, 1500-1640: An Essay in Historical Psychology. London: Edward Arnold, 1975. Rev. by R. J. Knecht, History, 61(Je 1976):278-9.

Manfred, Frederick, ed. Conversations with Frederick Manfred. (John R. Milton, moderator.) Salt Lake City: U Utah Press, 1974. Rev. by J. T. Flanagan, MinnH, 45(Spr 1976):36-7.

Manitius, Karl, ed. Eupolemius das Bibelgedicht. Weimar: Bohlaus Nachfolger, 1973. Rev. by B. Smalley, JEccH, 27 (Jan 1976):90-1.

Mann, Hans-Dieter. Lucien Febvre. Paris: Librairie Armand

Colin, 1971. Rev. by M. Siegel, AHR, 81(Apr 1976):399-400.

Manning, Ambrose N., ed. see Higgs, Robert J., ed.

Manning, Brian. The English People and the English Revolution
  1640-1649. London: Heinemann, n.d. Rev. by A. L. Rowse,
  HTo, 26(Jl 1976):478.

_____, ed. Politics, Religion and the English Civil War. New
  York: St. Martin's, 1973. Rev. by C. Robbins, AHR, 81
  (Feb 1976):131-2.

Manning, Eugene, ed. see Jaspert, Bernd, ed.

Mannion, John J. Irish Settlements in Eastern Canada. Buffalo,
  N.Y.: U Tor Press, 1974. Rev. by D. A. McQuillan, AgH,
  50(Jl 1976):545-8.

Mansergh, Nicholas, ed. The Transfer of Power, 1942-7. Vols.
  4 and 5. Palo Alto, Cal.: Pendragon, 1973, 1974. Rev.
  by R. E. Frykenberg, AHR, 81(Feb 1976):196-7; R. E. Frykenberg, AHR, 81(Je 1976):648-9; J. M. Brown, EHR, 91(Oct
  1976):877-9; W. Golant, History, 61(Feb 1976):165-6.

Mantell, Martin E. Johnson, Grant, and the Politics of Reconstruction. New York: Columbia U Press, 1973. Rev. in
  AS, 16(Spr 1975):75.

Mantou, Reine, ed. Le censier d'Herchies de 1267. Brussels:
  Royale d'Historie, 1974. Rev. by P. D. A. Harvey, EHR,
  91(Oct 1976):894.

Manuel, Frank E. The Religion of Isaac Newton. New York: Oxford U Press, 1974. Rev. by R. Stromberg, AHR, 81(Apr
  1976):386; D. F. Walker, EHR, 91(Apr 1976):428-9; D. Fenlon, HJ, 19(Sep 1976):787-92.

Manvel, Roger and Heinrich Fraenkel. The Hundred Days to Hitler.
  London: Dent, 1974. Rev. by J. Noakes, History, 61(Feb
  1976):142-3.

Mapp, Alf J., Jr. The Golden Dragon: Alfred the Great and His
  Times. LaSalle, Ill.: Open Court, 1974. Rev. by J. D. A.
  Ogilvy, AHR, 81(Apr 1976):368-9; B. Farwell, Smithsonian,
  6(Mar 1975):108, 110, 112.

Marasinghe, M. M. J. Gods in Early Buddhism. Kelaniya: U
  Sri Lanka, 1974. Rev. by R. Gombrich, JAS, 36(Nov 1976):
  175-6.

Marchione, Margherita, ed. Philip Mazzei: Jefferson's "Zealous
  Whig." New York: American Institute of Italian Studies,
  1975. Rev. by E. Cometti, VMHB, 84(Oct 1976):496-8.

Marcus, Harold G. The Life and Times of Menelik II: Ethiopia
    1844-1913. Oxford: Clarendon Press, 1975. Rev. by D.
    Crummey, EHR, 91(Oct 1976):928-9; R. A. Caulk, JAfH, 17
    (Num 3, 1976):464-5.

Marcus, Robert D. A Brief History of the United States Since
    1945. New York: St. Martins, 1975. Rev. by D. R. McCoy,
    JAH, 63(Je 1976):195-6.

Marder, Arthur J. From the Dardanelles to Oran. New York:
    Oxford U Press, 1974. Rev. by T. Ropp, AHR, 81(Feb
    1976):146; M. L. Dockrill, EHR, 91(Jl 1976):688; E. J.
    Grove, History, 61(Feb 1976):146.

_____. Operation "Menace." New York: Oxford U Press,
    1976. Rev. by P. Guinn, HRNB, 4(Jl 1976):179-80.

Marens, Sheldon. Father Coughlin. Boston: Little, Brown, 1973.
    Rev. by C. J. Tull, CaHR, 62(Oct 1976):681-2.

Margolies, Barbara Luise. Princes of the Earth: Subcultural
    Diversity in a Mexican Municipality. Washington, D. C.: Am.
    Anthropological Assoc., 1975. Rev. by G. Foster, HAHR,
    56(Nov 1976):678-80.

Margolin, Jean Claude, ed. Colloquia Erasmiana Turonesia.
    Toronto: U Tor Press, 1973. Rev. by J. K. McConica,
    EHR, 91(Jan 1976):187-8.

Margraff, William F. A Civil War Soldier Soldier's Last Letters.
    New York: Vantage, 1975. Rev. by R. D. Hoffsommer,
    CWTI, 15(Jl 1976):49-50.

Marius, Richard. Luther: A Biography. Philadelphia: Lippin-
    cott, 1974. Rev. by H. Schuessler, AHR, 81(Je 1976):611-
    12; G. G. Krodel, CH, 45(Je 1976):255.

Markakis, John. Ethiopia: Anatomy of a Traditional Policy.
    Oxford: Clarendon Press, 1974. Rev. by C. Clapham,
    JAfH, 17(Num 1, 1976):152-4.

Markham, Felix. The Bonapartes. New York: Taplinger, 1975.
    Rev. by R. B. Holtman, AHR, 81(Oct 1976):868-9.

Markovic̆, Mihailo see Horvat, Branko

Marquess of Anglesey, The. A History of the British Cavalry,
    1816-1919. Vol. 2. Hamden, Conn.: Archon, 1975. Rev.
    by S. J. Stearns, AHR, 81(Je 1976):591.

Marquette, J.-B. Le Trésor des Chartes d'Albret, I. Paris:
    Bibliothèque Nationale, 1973. Rev. by M. G. A. Vale,
    EHR, 91(Jan 1976):181-2.

Márquez, Jesús Velasco. La guerra del '47 y la opinión pública, 1845-1848. Mexico: SepSetentas, 1975. Rev. by D. M. Pletcher, HAHR, 56(Nov 1976):657-9.

Marquis, Arnold. A Guide to America's Indians. Norman: U Ok Press, 1974. Rev. by B. Satcher, ChOk, 54(Win 1976):541-2.

Marquis, Thomas B. Keep the Last Bullet for Yourself. n. p. : Two Continents, n. d. Rev. by M. Kernan, Smithsonian, 7 (Je 1976):106-8.

Marre, Heiner, ed. see Krautscheidt, Joseph, ed.

Marrero, Levi. Cuba: Economía y sociedad. 2 vols. Rio Piedras, P. R. : Editorial San Juan, 1972, 1974. Rev. by M. J. MacLeod, HAHR, 56(Aug 1976):480-2.

Marrin, Albert. The Last Crusade. Durham, N. C. : Duke U Press, 1974. Rev. by P. T. Marsh, CaHR, 62(Oct 1976): 650-1; F. Sugeno, HMPEC, 45(Mar 1976):103-5; T. L. Auffenberg, JCS, 18(Spr 1976):331-3.

Marriott, Alice and Carol K. Rachlin, eds. American Indian Mythology. New York: Crowell, 1968. Rev. by L. Vantine, NDH, 43(Fall 1976):40.

_____ and _____. Plains Indian Mythology. New York: Crowell, 1975. Rev. by L. S. Theisen, ChOk, 54(Win 1976): 534-5; H. Prado, Mankind, 5(Aug 1976):59; E. Holland, NDH, 43(Spr 1976):105-6; G. C. Stein, NMHR, 51(Oct 1976):344-5.

Marrone, Giovanni. La Schiavitù nella società Siciliana dell'età moderna. Caltanissetta: Edizioni Salvatore Sciascia, 1972. Rev. by J. Renaldo, JMH, 48(Mar 1976):157-9.

Marrou, Henri-Irénée, et al. Monseigneur Duchesne et son temps. Rome: Ecole Française de Rome, 1975. Rev. by M. Simon, JEccH, 27(Apr 1976):209-11.

Marsden, George and Frank Roberts, eds. A Christian View of History? Grand Rapids, Mich. : Eerdmans, 1975. Rev. by D. Pals, CH, 45(Sep 1976):402-3; R. A. Suelflow, CHIQ, 49 (Spr 1976):45-6.

Marshall, D. Bruce. The French Colonial Myth and Constitution-Making in the Fourth Republic. New Haven, Conn. : Yale U Press, 1973. Rev. by D. H. Pinkney, AHR, 81(Je 1976):611.

Marshall, Douglas W. and Howard H. Marshall. Campaigns of the American Revolution: An Atlas of Manuscript Maps. Ann Arbor: U Mich Press, 1976. Rev. by D. C. Skaggs, WVH, 38(Oct 1976):72-3.

Martel, Leon see Kahn, Herman

Martelli, Mario. L'altro Niccolò di Bernardo Machiavelli.
    Florence: G. C. Sansoni Editore, 1975. Rev. by J. Kirsh-
    ner, JMH, 48(Je 1976):337-8.

Martí, José. Inside the Monster: Writings on the United States
    and American Imperialism. New York: Monthly Review
    Press, 1975. Rev. by M. S. Stabb, HAHR, 56(Nov 1976):
    663-4.

Martin, A. Lynn. Henry III and the Jesuit Politicians. Geneva:
    Librairie Droz, 1973. Rev. by N. L. Roelker, CaHR, 62
    (Jan 1976):138-9.

Martin, Bernd. Friedensinitiativen und Machtpolitik im zweiten
    Weltkrieg 1939-1942. Düsseldorf: Droste Verlag, 1974.
    Rev. by W. A. Fletcher, AHR, 81(Apr 1976):364.

Martin, Charles H. The Angelo Herndon Case and Southern Justice.
    Baton Rouge: LSU Press, 1976. Rev. by A. T. Stephens,
    THQ, 35(Fall 1976):339-41.

Martin, Curt. North Carolina Legislators: 1976. Atlanta:
    Southern Regional Council, 1976. Rev. by M. F. Mitchell,
    NCHR, 53(Aut 1976):402-3.

Martin, David see Lemarchand, René

Martin, Ged see Hyam, Ronald

Martin, George. Madam Secretary: Frances Perkins. Boston:
    Houghton Mifflin, 1976. Rev. by S. M. Hartmann, HRNB, 4
    (Jl 1976):164-5.

Martin, James Kirby, ed. The Human Dimensions of Nation
    Making. Madison: St Historical Society Wis, 1976. Rev.
    by B. Henry, HRNB, 4(Sep 1976):216-7; E. P. Douglas,
    NCHR, 53(Aut 1976):407-8.

Martin, John Bartlow. Adlai Stevenson of Illinois. Garden City,
    N.Y.: Doubleday, 1976. Rev. by J. T. Patterson, HRNB,
    4(Aut 1976):191-2; E. H. Ziegner, IMH, 72(Dec 1976):380-1;
    D. Lindsey, Mankind, 5(Dec 1976):6; J. M. Cooper, Jr.,
    WMH, 60(Aut 1976):72-4.

Martin, Luis. The Kingdom of the Sun: A Short History of Peru.
    New York: Scribner's, 1974. Rev. by J. Klaiber, TAm, 33
    (Jl 1976):167-8.

Martin, M. Kay and Barbara Voorhies. Female of the Species.
    New York: Columbia U Press, 1974. Rev. by K. Cassill,
    Smithsonian, 6(Sep 1975):112, 114.

Martin, Paul S. and Fred Plog. The Archaeology of Arizona.
Garden City, N.Y.: Doubleday, 1973. Rev. by D. K. Washburn, AmAnt, 41(Apr 1976):243-5.

Martina, Giacomo. Pio IX (1846-1850). Rome: Universita Gregoriana Editrice, 1974. Rev. by N. Blakiston, EHR, 91(Jan
1976):217-18.

Martinez-Alier, Verena. Marriage, Class and Colour in Nineteenth-
Century Cuba. New York: Cam U Press, 1974. Rev. by F.
W. Knight, TAm, 33(Jl 1976):170-1.

Marucco, Dora. Arturo Labriola e il sindacalismo rivoluzionario
in Italia. Turin: Fondazione Luigi Einaudi, 1970. Rev. by
J. M. Cammett, AHR, 81(Je 1976):623-4.

Marwick, Arthur. War and Social Change in the Twentieth Century.
New York: St. Martin's, 1975. Rev. by K. G. Larew, AHR,
81(Je 1976):566; P. F. Clarke, EHR, 91(Jan 1976):228-9.

Marwil, Jonathan. The Trials of Counsel: Francis Bacon in 1621.
Detroit: Wayne St U Press, 1976. Rev. by W. G. Simon,
HRNB, 4(Jl 1976):179.

Marx, Roland. La Révolution et les classes sociales en Basse-
Alsace. Paris: Bibliothèque Nationale, 1974. Rev. by P.
Dawson, AHR, 81(Je 1976):604.

Marzari, F. see Lowe, C. J.

Marzulla, Elene, ed. Pictorial Treasury of U. S. Stamps. Omaha:
Collectors Institute, 1974. Rev. in ETHJ, 14(Spr 1976):76-8.

Mason, Philip. A Matter of Honour. New York: Holt, Rinehart
and Winston, 1974. Rev. by J. Tottenham, AHR, 81(Feb
1976):195-6; K. Ballhatchet, History, 61(Feb 1976):163-4.

Massa-Gille, Genevieve. Histoire des emprunts de la ville de
Paris (1814-1875). Paris: Commission des Travaux historiques, 1973. Rev. by G. Ellis, EHR, 91(Jl 1976):660-1.

Massell, Gregory J. The Surrogate Proletariat. Princeton, N. J.:
Prin U Press, 1974. Rev. by B. B. Farnsworth, AHR, 81
(Apr 1976):429.

Massey, Joseph A. Youth and Politics in Japan. Lexington,
Mass.: Lexington Books, 1976. Rev. by E. S. Krauss,
JAS, 36(Nov 1976):154-5.

Mathes, W. Michael, ed. California III: Documentos para la
Historia de Transformacion Colonizadora de California (1679-
1686). Madrid: Ediciones José Porrúa Turanzas, 1974.

Rev. by B. E. Bobb, PHR, 45(May 1976):279-80; M. Geiger,
SCQ, 58(Spr 1976):127-8; D. C. Cutter, TAm, 33(Oct 1976):
372-3.

Matheson, Sylvia A. Persia: An Archaeological Guide. Park
Ridge, N. J.: Noyes Press, 1973. Rev. by E. Carter,
JNES, 35(Jl 1976):202-3.

Mathias, Frank Furlong. Albert D. Kirwan. Lexington: U Press
Ky, 1975. Rev. by R. F. Sexton, FCHQ, 50(Apr 1976):91-2;
T. R. Crane, JAH, 62(Mar 1976):1050-1.

_____, ed. Incidents and Experiences in the Life of Thomas W.
Parsons from 1826-1900. Lexington: U Press Ky, 1975.
Rev. by L. H. Harrison, FCHQ, 50(Jan 1976):73-5; Q. B.
Keen, JAH, 62(Mar 1976):987-8.

Matrat, Jean. Robespierre, or the Tyranny of the Majority.
London: Angus and Robertson, 1975. Rev. by G. Lewis,
History, 61(Oct 1976):456-7.

Matthew, H. C. G. The Liberal Imperialists. Oxford: Oxford
U Press, 1973. Rev. by M. Freeden, JMH, 48(Sep 1976):
547-52.

_____, ed. see Foot, M. R. D., ed.

Matthews, Herbert L. Revolution in Cuba. New York: Scribner's, 1975. Rev. by R. E. Ruiz, HAHR, 56(Aug 1976):
490-2.

Matthews, John. Western Aristocracies and Imperial Court, A. D.
364-425. Oxford: Clarendon Press, 1975. Rev. by W. Goffart, EHR, 91(Apr 1976):351-4.

Matthews, Noel. Guides to Materials for African History in European Archives. London: U London, 1973. Rev. by D. H.
Jones, JAfH, 17(Num 1, 1976):154-5.

Matthews, Robert J. "A Plainer Translation:" Joseph Smith's
Translation of the Bible--A History and Commentary. Provo:
BYU Press, 1975. Rev. by L. Petersen, UHQ, 44(Win 1976):
95-6.

Mattingly, Paul H. The Classless Profession: American Schoolmen in the Nineteenth Century. New York: NYU Press,
1975. Rev. by D. Calhoun, AHR, 81(Je 1976):666; D. Tyack,
JAH, 63(Je 1976):127-8.

Matz, Friedrich and Hans-Gunter Buchholz, eds. Archaeologia
Homerica: Die Denkmaler und das Fruhgriechische Epos.
Vol. I, G: "Seewesen," by Dorothea Gray. Göttingen:
Vandenhoeck and Ruprecht, 1974. Rev. by S. Alexiou, AJA,
80(Spr 1976):205-6.

259   MATZ

_____ and Ingo Pini, eds. Corpus der Minoischen und Myken-
ischen Siegel. Berlin: Gebr. Mann Verlag, 1974. Rev. by
M. H. Wiencke, AJA, 80(Fall 1976):429-31.

Maunder, Elwood R. Dr. Richard E. McArdle. Santa Cruz,
Cal.: Forest Historical Society, 1975. Rev. by H. T.
Pinkett, AmArc, 39(Apr 1976):209-10.

_____. Twentieth-Century Businessman. Santa Cruz, Cal.:
Forest History Society, 1974. Rev. by D. C. Smith, BHR,
50(Sum 1976):237-8.

Maurer, Ilse. Reichsfinanzen und Grosse Koalition. Bern: Herbert Lang, 1973. Rev. by H. C. Meyer, AHR, 81(Feb 1976):
170-1.

Maxey, Kees. The Fight for Rhodesia. London: Rex Collings,
1975. Rev. by T. Ranger, AfAf, 75(Jan 1976):117-19.

Maxwell, John Francis. Slavery and the Catholic Church. London:
Barry Rose, 1975. Rev. by D. A. Johnson, CH, 45(Sep
1976):398-9.

May, Ernest R. Lessons of the Past: The Use and Misuse of
History in American Foreign Policy. New York: Oxford U
Press, 1973. Rev. by K. Eagles, CHR, 57(Mar 1976):91-2.

_____. The Making of the Monroe Doctrine. Cambridge, Mass.:
Harvard U Press, 1975. Rev. by CurH, 70(Feb 1976):77;
B. B. Solnick, HAHR, 56(Nov 1976):639-40; J. May, HRNB,
4(Mar 1976):98; M. J. Heale, JAmS, 10(Dec 1976):389; A. V.
Huff, Jr., JSH, 42(Nov 1976):588-9.

May, Georg, ed. see Scheuerman, Audomar, ed.

May, George S. A Most Unique Machine: The Michigan Origins
of the American Automibile Industry. Grand Rapids, Mich.:
Eerdmans, 1975. Rev. by J. W. Eastman, BHR, 50(Sum
1976):235-7; R. D. Gray, IMH, 72(Mar 1976):83-5.

Mayer, Cornelius Petrus and Willigis Eckermann. Scientia Augustiniana. Würzburg: Augustinus-Verlag, 1975. Rev. by
H. E. J. Cowdrey, JEccH, 27(Apr 1976):185-6.

Mayer, Martin. Today and Tomorrow in America. New York:
Harper and Row, 1976. Rev. by C. E. Finn, Jr., Commentary, 62(Sep 1976):126-8.

Mayer, Vicente V., Jr. Utah: A Hispanic History. Salt Lake
City: U Utah, 1975. Rev. by A. A. Ávila, UHQ, 44(Sum
1976):304-5.

Mayer, Vincent, Jr. The Black on New Spain's Northern Fron-

tier: San José de Parral, 1631-1641. Durango: Fort Lewis
College, 1974. Rev. by P. Boyd-Bowman, HAHR, 56(Feb
1976):175-6.

Mayhew, Alan. Rural Settlement and Farming in Germany. New
York: Barnes and Noble, 1973. Rev. by M. Walker, AHR,
81(Oct 1976):879.

Mazlish, Bruce. James and John Stuart Mill. New York: Basic
Books, 1975. Rev. by S. Rothblatt, AHR, 81(Oct 1976):861-
3.

Mazrui, Ali A. Soldiers and Kinsmen in Uganda. Beverly Hills,
Cal.: Sage, 1975. Rev. by F. J. Ravenhill, JMAS, 14(Dec
1976):725-8.

_____. World Culture and the Black Experience. Seattle: U
Wash Press, 1974. Rev. by S. S. Nyang, JAAS, 11(Jan
and Apr 1976):118-20.

Mazuzan, George T., ed. see Fausold, George T., ed.

Mazzei, Philip. Researches on the United States. Charlottesville: U Press Va, 1976. Rev. by E. Cometti, VMHB,
84(Oct 1976):496-8.

Meade, C. Wake. Road to Babylon. Leiden: E. J. Brill, 1974.
Rev. by S. J. Lieberman, Archaeology, 29(Apr 1976):137-8.

Meadows, A. J. Science and Controversy. Cambridge, Mass.:
MIT Press, 1972. Rev. by H. I. Sharlin, AHR, 81(Oct
1976):863.

Meaker, Gerald H. The Revolutionary Left in Spain, 1914-1923.
Stanford, Cal.: Stanford U Press, 1974. Rev. by J. C.
Ullman, AHR, 81(Feb 1976):160-1; G. Jackson, CHR, 57
(Je 1976):233-4; M. Blinkhorn, History, 61(Oct 1976):471-2;
D. Smyth, HJ, 19(Mar 1976):302-4.

Medina, Pedro de. A Navigator's Universe: The "Libro de
Cosmographia" of 1538. Chicago: U Chicago Press, 1972.
Rev. by K. R. Andrews, AHR, 81(Je 1976):611-12.

Medlin, Virgil D. and Stephen L. Parsons, eds. V. D. Nabokov
and the Russian Provisional Government, 1917. New Haven,
Conn.: Yale U Press, 1976. Rev. by S. D. Spector, HRNB,
4(Jl 1976):183.

Medvedev, Zhores A. Ten Years After Ivan Denisovich. New
York: Random, 1974. Rev. by F. Harvey, JCS, 16(Spr
1976):350-2.

Mee, Graham. Aristocratic Enterprise. London: Blackie, 1975.
Rev. by D. Spring, BHR, 50(Sum 1976):256-7.

261   MEEK

Meek, Ronald L., ed. Turgot on Progress, Sociology, and Economics. Cambridge: Cam U Press, 1973. Rev. by H.
Höpfl, ESR, 6(Jan 1976):147-9.

_____. Social Science and the Ignoble Savage. Cambridge: Cam
U Press, 1976. Rev. by C. D. W. Goodwin, JEH, 36(Sep
1976):776-7.

Meeks, Harold A. The Geographic Regions of Vermont. Dartmouth, N.H.: Geography Publications at Dartmouth, 1975.
Rev. by R. Illick and V. H. Malmstrom, VH, 44(Fall 1976):
236-8.

Mehta, Prayag. Election Campagin: Anatomy of Mass Influence.
Delhi: National Publishing, 1975. Rev. by C. P. Bhambhri,
IQ, 32(Apr-Je 1976):250-1.

Meier, Golda. My Life. New York: Putnam's, 1975. Rev. by S.
Bhutani, IQ, 32(Jl-Sep 1976):351-3.

Meier, Matt S. and Feliciano Rivera, eds. Readings on La Raza.
New York: Hill and Wang, 1974. Rev. by F. P. Hebblethwaite, Américas, 28(Apr 1976):23.

Melady, Thomas Patrick. Burundi: The Tragic Years. Maryknoll,
N.Y.: Orbis, 1974. Rev. by M. White, JCS, 18(Aut 1976):
589-90; W. Weinstein, JMAS, 14(Mar 1976):161-3.

Mellaart, James. The Neolithic of the Near East. London:
Thames and Hudson, 1975. Rev. by J. Oates, Antiquity, 50
(Sep-Dec 1976):244-5.

Mellafe, Rolando. Negro Slavery in Latin America. Berkeley:
U Cal Press, 1975. Rev. by R. B. Toplin, Historian, 39
(Nov 1976):168-9; A. J. R. Russell-Wood, HRNB, 4(Apr
1976):127-8; F. W. Knight, JEH, 36(Sep 1976):777-9; P.
Boyd-Bowman, TAm, 33(Oct 1976):376-7.

Mellink, A. F. see Kossmann, E. H.

_____, ed. Documenta Anabaptistica Neerlandica. Part 1.
Leiden: E. J. Brill, 1975. Rev. by W. Keeney, MQR, 50
(Oct 1976):304-5.

Mellor, Roy E. H. Eastern Europe: A Geography of the Comecon
Countries. London: Macmillan, 1975. Rev. by A. Teichova,
History, 61(Oct 1976):477-8.

Melograni, Piero. Gli industriali e Mussolini. Milan: Longanesi,
1972. Rev. by S. B. Clough, AHR, 81(Apr 1976):415-16.

Mendelson, E. Michael. Sangha and State in Burma. Ithaca,
N.Y.: Cornell U Press, 1975. Rev. by C. F. Keyes, JAS,
36(Nov 1976):183-4.

Mendlovitz, Saul H. On the Creation of a Just World Order. New
York: Free Press, 1975. Rev. by A. Lall, IQ, 32(Apr-
Je 1976):226-30.

Menges, Karl H. Altajische Studien II. Japanisch und Altajisch.
Wiesbaden: Kommissionsverlag Franz Steiner GMBH, 1975.
Rev. by N. Poppe, JJS, 2(Sum 1976):470-4.

Mensonides, Louis and James A. Kuhlman, eds. The Future of
Inter-Bloc Relations in Europe. New York: Praeger, 1974.
Rev. by W. C. Clemens, Jr., EEQ, 10(Mar 1976):133-4.

Menton, Seymour. Prose Fiction of the Cuban Revolution. Austin:
U Tex Press, 1975. Rev. by E. Rivero, HAHR, 56(Nov
1976):686-7.

Menzel, Brigitte. Textilien aus Westafrika. 3 vols. Berlin:
Museum für Völkerkunde, 1972-1973. Rev. by M. V, Gilbert,
Africa, 46(Num 1, 1976):101.

Mercer, Eric. English Vernacular Houses. London: HMSO, 1975.
Rev. by I. C. Peate, Antiquity, 50(Sep-Dec 1976):250-1.

Mercer, John. Spanish Sahara. London: Allen and Unwin, 1976.
R. J. Harrison Church, AfAf, 75(Jl 1976):391-2.

Meredith, Howard L. The Native American Factor. New York:
Seabury, 1973. Rev. by M. R. Patrick, JCS, 18(Aut 1976):
592-3.

Meredith, William. Hazard, the Painter. New York: Knopf, 1975.
Rev. by R. Howard, GR, 30(Spr 1976):205-11.

Meretskov, K. A. City Invincible. Moscow: Progress Publ'rs,
1970. Rev. by E. F. Ziemke, AHR, 81(Je 1976):637-9.

_____. Serving the People. Moscow: Progress Publ'rs, 1971.
Rev. by E. F. Ziemke, AHR, 81(Je 1976):637-9.

Meritt, Benjamin D. and John S. Traill. The Athenian Agora, XV.
Princeton, N.J.: American School of Classical Studies, 1974.
Rev. by D. J. Geagan, AJA, 80(Spr 1976):211-12.

Meriwether, James B. South Carolina Journals and Journalists.
Columbia: U SCar, 1974. Rev. by A. D. Watson, NCHR,
53(Spr 1976):223-4.

Merkes, Manfred. Die deutsche Politik im spanischen Bürgerkrieg,
1936-1939. Bonn: L. Rohrscheid Verlag, 1969. Rev. by G.
Jackson, JMH, 48(Mar 1976):135-8.

Merkl, Peter H. German Foreign Policies, West and East. Santa
Barbara, Cal.: Clio, 1974. Rev. by B. Tyabji, IQ, 32(Apr-
Je 1976):236-7.

_____. Political Violence Under the Swastika. Princeton,
N.J.: Prin U Press, 1975. Rev. by D. J. Schnall, JSoH,
10(Fall 1976):120-4.

Merrill, Perry H. Vermont Under Four Flags, a History of the
Green Mountain State, 1635-1975. Montpelier, Vt.: the
author, 1975. Rev. by C. Cheney, VH, 44(Win 1976):48-9.

Merrill, William C., et al. Panama's Economic Development: The
Role of Agriculture. Ames: Ia St U Press, 1975. Rev. by
G. Anguizola, HAHR, 56(Feb 1976):184.

Merrillees, R. S. Trade and Transcendence in the Bronze Age
Levant. Göteborg: Aströms Forlag, 1974. Rev. by G.
Cadogan, AJA, 80(Sum 1976):309-10.

Merwick, Donna. Boston Priests, 1848-1910. Cambridge, Mass.:
Harvard U Press, 1973. Rev. by G. P. Fogarty, CaHR, 62
(Jl 1976):498-9.

Mesch, Barry. Studies in Joseph ibn Caspi. Leiden: E. J. Brill,
1974. Rev. by N. Samuelson, JHP, 14(Jan 1976):105-9.

Meseguer Illán, Diego. José Carlos Mariátegui y su pensamiento
revolucionario. Lima, Peru: Instituto de Estudios Peruanos,
1974. Rev. by T. M. Davies, Jr., HAHR, 56(Nov 1976):662.

Meshcheriuk, I. I. The Socioeconomic Development of Bulgar and
Gaguzi Villages in Southern Bessarabia (1808-1856). Kishinev:
Redaktsionno-izdatel'skii Otdel Akademii Nauk Moldavskoi SSR,
1970. Rev. by K. Hitchins, AHR, 81(Apr 1976):418-19.

Metcalf, E. W., Jr. Paul Laurence Dunbar. Metuchen, N.J.:
Scarecrow, 1975. Rev. by G. H. Hudson, OH, 85(Win 1976):
90-2.

Metz, Johannes, ed. Faith and the World of Politics. New York:
Paulist Press, 1968. Rev. by W. A. Mueller, JCS, 18(Aut
1976):576-9.

Metz, Leon C. Pat Garrett: The Story of a Western Lawman.
Norman: U Ok Press, 1974. Rev. by W. H. Hutchinson,
PHR, 45(Feb 1976):130.

Meyendorff, John. Byzantine Theology: Historical Trends and
Doctrinal Themes. New York: Fordham U Press, 1974.
Rev. by J. E. Rexine, AHR, 81(Apr 1976):372-3.

Meyer, Donald H. The Democratic Enlightenment. New York:
Putnam's, 1976. Rev. by R. J. Brugger, JSH, 42(Nov 1976):
579-80.

Meyer, Henry Cord. The Long Generation: Germany from Em-

pire to Ruin, 1913-1945. New York: Walker, n.d. Rev. by
H. K. Rosenthal, EE, 24(Je 1975):31.

Meyer, Howard N. The Amendment That Refused to Die. Radnor,
Pa.: Chilton, 1973. Rev. by A. M. Paul, AHR, 81(Je
1976):669; W. S. Jackson, JNH, 61(Apr 1976):218-19.

Meyer, Jean. Apocalypse et Révolution au Mexique. Paris: Editions Gallimard/Julliard, 1974. Rev. by D. C. Bailey,
HAHR, 56(Feb 1976):145-7.

_____. La Cristiada. 3 vols. Mexico: Siglo Veintiuno, 1974.
Rev. by D. C. Bailey, HAHR, 56(Feb 1976):145-7.

Meyer, Larry L. Shadow of a Continent. Palo Alto, Cal.:
American West, 1975. Rev. by B. A. Storey, JOW, 15(Apr
1976):135.

Meyer, Michael C. see Greenleaf, Richard E.

Meyers, Rose. A History of Baton Rouge, 1699-1812. Baton
Rouge: LSU Press, 1976. Rev. by P. D. Uzee, JSH, 42
(Nov 1976):614.

Michel, Henri. The Shadow War: European Resistance 1939-1945.
New York: Harper and Row, 1972. Rev. by R. O. Paxton,
AHR, 81(Apr 1976):382-3.

Michel, Sonya see Baum, Charlotte

Michener, James A. Centennial. New York: Random House,
1974. Rev. by S. L. Eaton, JOW, 15(Jl 1976):96; J. A.
Brennan, WHQ, 7(Jan 1976):78; J. A. Brennan, WHQ, 7(Jan
1976):78.

Middleton, Drew. Can America Win the Next War? New York:
Scribner's, n.d. Rev. by J. Q. Wilson, Commentary, 61
(Feb 1976):76, 78-9.

Midgley, Graham. The Life of Orator Henley. New York: Oxford U Press, 1973. Rev. by B. H. Davis, AHR, 81(Feb
1976):132-3.

Miers, Suzanne. Britain and the Ending of the Slave Trade. New
York: Africana, 1975. Rev. by J. H. Gleason, HRNB, 4
(Jl 1976):176-7.

Milazzo, Matteo J. The Chetnik Movement and the Yugoslav Resistance. Baltimore: JHU Press, 1975. Rev. by J. C.
Campbell, AHR, 81(Oct 1976):897-9.

Milet, Jean. Bergson et le calcul infinitésimal: ou, la raison et
le temps. Paris: Presses U. de France, 1974. Rev. by
P. A. Y. Gunter, JHP, 14(Apr 1976):244-7.

265   MILIC

Milic, Louis T. , ed. The Modernity of the Eighteenth Century.
    Cleveland: Press CWRU, 1971. Rev. by V. G. Wexler, AHR,
    81(Apr 1976):375-6.

Milits, Alex. Tro och Makt i Sovjet. Orebro, Sweden: Tryck-
    centralen, 1973. Rev. by D. B. Westerlund, JCS, 18(Win
    1976):145-6.

Mill, James. The History of British India. Chicago: U Chicago
    Press, 1975. Rev. by E. B. Jones, AHR, 81(Oct 1976):943-4.

Miller, Charles. Battle for the Bundu: The First World War in
    East Africa. New York: Macmillan, 1974. Rev. by K. A.
    Jackson, Jr., AHR, 81(Apr 1976):361-2.

Miller, David E. and Della S. Miller. Nauvoo: The City of
    Joseph. Salt Lake City: Peregrine Smith, 1974. Rev. by
    D. L. Lythgoe, AHR, 81(Apr 1976):447; S. J. Layton, JOW,
    15(Jan 1976):130.

Miller, David W. Church, State and Nation in Ireland, 1898-1921.
    Pittsburgh: U Pittsburgh, 1973. Rev. by L. J. McCaffrey,
    CaHR, 62(Oct 1976):651-2.

Miller, Ernest C. Horn's Fort. Philadelphia: Dorrance, 1976.
    Rev. by D. C. Cutter, HRNB, 4(Apr 1976):125-6.

Miller, Floyd J. The Search for a Black Nationality: Black
    Emigration and Colonization, 1787-1863. Urbana: U Ill
    Press, 1975. Rev. by H. R. Lynch, AHR, 81(Oct 1976):
    966-7; R. Gavins, JSH, 42(Aug 1976):424-5; S. Gershgoren,
    Mankind, 5(Apr 1976):10; L. H. Fishel, Jr., OH, 85(Spr
    1976):167-8; L. S. Gerteis, RAH, 4(Mar 1976):83-7.

Miller, Helen Hill. George Mason: Gentleman Revolutionary.
    Chapel Hill: U NC Press, 1975. Rev. by F. J. Bremer,
    HRNB, 4(Feb 1976):75; R. R. Beeman, JAH, 63(Sep 1976):
    388-9; B. J. Newcomb, JSH, 42(Aug 1976):419-21; C. F.
    Hobson, VMHB, 84(Apr 1976):203-4.

Miller, John. Popery and Politics in England, 1660-1688. New
    York: Cam U Press, 1973. Rev. by J. A. Williams, CaHR,
    62(Apr 1976):289-90.

Miller, Lillian B. "The Dye Is Now Cast": The Road to American
    Independence, 1774-1776. Washington: Smithsonian Institution,
    1975. Rev. by B. W. Labaree, JAH, 63(Sep 1976):397-8.

Miller, Lynn H. and Ronald W. Pruessen, eds. Reflections on the
    Cold War. Philadelphia: Temple U Press, 1974. Rev. by
    R. A. Esthus, AHR, 81(Feb 1976):220-1.

Miller, Marshall Lee. Bulgaria During the Second World War.
    Stanford, Cal.: Stanford U Press, 1975. Rev. by P. E.

MILLER 266

Michelson, Historian, 39(Nov 1976):134.

Miller, Orlando W. The Frontier in Alaska and the Matanuska Colony. New Haven, Conn.: Yale U Press, 1975. Rev. by M. Walsh, History, 61(Oct 1976):417-18; M. Sherwood, JAH, 62(Mar 1976):1009; J. H. Shideler, PHR, 45(Aug 1976):448-9; J. C. Foster, WHQ, 7(Jl 1976):325-6.

Miller, S. J. Peter Richard Kenrick, Bishop and Archbishop of St. Louis 1806-1896. Philadelphia: Cath Historical Society, 1973. Rev. by J. Hennesey, CaHR, 62(Jl 1976):497-8.

Miller, Susanne. Burgfrieden und Klassenkampf. Düsseldorf: Droste Verlag, 1974. Rev. by C. Landauer, AHR, 81(Je 1976):616-17; F. L. Carsten, EHR, 91(Apr 1976):456-7; M. Nolan, JMH, 48(Je 1976):350-2.

Miller, William D. A Harsh and Dreadful Love. New York: Liveright, 1973. Rev. by R. Van Allen, CaHR, 62(Oct 1976): 682-3.

Millett, Allan R. The General: Robert L. Bullard and Officership in the United States Army, 1881-1925. Westport, Conn.: Greenwood, 1975. Rev. by J. D. Hill, HRNB, 4(Apr 1976): 122-3; S. L. Falk, JAH, 63(Sep 1976):447-8.

Milligan, Edward A. Dakota Twilight: The Standing Rock Sioux, 1874-1890. Hicksville, N.Y.: Exposition, 1976. Rev. by T. P. Wilson, JAH, 63(Dec 1976):731-2; H. R. Grant, NDH, 43(Fall 1976):39.

Millon, René, ed. Urbanization at Teotihuacán, Mexico. Vol. I. Austin: U Texas Press, 1973. Rev. by R. A. Diehl, AmAn, 41(Jl 1976):405-7; M. D. Coe, TAm, 32(Jan 1976):494-6.

Milton, John R. Conversations with Frederick Manfred. Salt Lake City: U Utah Press, 1974. Rev. by B. L. Blackburn, JOW, 15(Jl 1976):102.

_____, moderator see Manfred, Frederick, ed.

Miners, N. J. The Government and Politics of Hong Kong. New York: Oxford U Press, 1976. Rev. by O.E.S., CurH, 71 (Sep 1976):79.

Mines, Mattison. Muslim Merchants. New Delhi: Shri Ram Centre, 1972. Rev. by L. M. Bookman, AA, 78(Je 1976):409-10.

Minge, Ward Alan. Acoma: Pueblo in the Sky. Albuquerque: U NM Press, 1976. Rev. by G. W. Pilcher, HRNB, 4(Sep 1976):218.

Minger, Ralph Eldin. William Howard Taft and the United States

Foreign Policy₀ Urbana: U Ill Press, 1975. Rev₀ by R. A.
Esthus, AHR, 81(Je 1976):680-1; J₀ Braeman, JAH, 63(Je
1976):163-4; L. L. Gould, OH, 85(Aut 1976):333-4.

Minick, Bob₀ Hills of Home: The Rural Ozarks of Arkansas.
San Francisco: Scrimshaw, 1975. Rev. by M. Kernan,
Smithsonian, 6(Dec 1975):132-3.

Minogue, Kenneth, ed₀ see De Crespigny, Anthony, ed₀

Mintz, Sidney W. , ed. Slavery, Colonialism, and Racism. New
York: Norton, 1975₀ Rev₀ by J₀ White, JAmS, 10(Apr
1976):113-17₀

Mishra, D. P. Living an Era: India's March to Freedom. Vol₀
I. Delhi: Vikas, 1975₀ Rev. by N. C₀ Bhattacharya, IQ,
32(Jl-Sep 1976):339-41.

Miskimin, H₀ A. The Economy of Early Renaissance Europe,
1300-1460. Cambridge: Cam U Press, 1975₀ Rev₀ by R.
H. Hilton, History, 61(Je 1976):244-5.

Misra, J₀ P. The Administration of India Under Lord Lansdowne
(1888-94). New Delhi: Sterling, 1975. Rev. by S. V.
Desikachar, IQ, 32(Apr-Je 1976):253-4.

Mitchell, B. R. European Historical Statistics 1750-1970₀ London: Macmillan, 1975₀ Rev. by P₀ Mathias, EHR, 91(Jan
1976):135-9.

Mitchell, Broadus. Alexander Hamilton. New York: Oxford U
Press, 1976. Rev₀ by A. H. Bowman, JSH, 42(Nov 1976):
581-2.

Mitchell, Yvonne. Colette: A Taste for Life₀ New York: Harcourt Brace Jovanovich, n. d. Rev. by E. Wakerman, Mankind, 5(Dec 1976):63-4₀

Mitson, Betty E. , ed. see Hansen, Arthur A. , ed.

Mittelman, James H. Ideology and Politics in Uganda. Ithaca,
N. Y₀: Cornell U Press, 1975₀ Rev. by F₀ J. Ravenhill,
JMAS, 14(Dec 1976):725-8.

Modell, John, ed. The Kikuchi Diary. Urbana: U Ill Press,
1973. Rev. in AHI, 11(Oct 1976):50.

Modesti, Gianni Bailo, Bruno d'Agostino, Patrizia Gastaldi, eds₀
Seconda Mostra della Preistoria e della Protostoria nel
Salernitano. Salerno: Pietro Laveglia, 1974₀ Rev. by N.
H₀ Ramage, AJA, 80(Win 1976):96-7.

Moeller, Bernd₀ Imperial Cities and the Reformation: Three Essays. Philadelphia: Fortress, 1972. Rev. by J. S. Oyer, MQR, 50(Oct 1976):308-9.

Mohl, Raymond A. Poverty in New York, 1783-1825. New York: Oxford U Press, 1971. Rev. by D. W. Hoover, JAH, 62 (Mar 1976):981-2.

Mohr, James C., ed. Radical Republicans in the North. Baltimore: JHU Press, 1976. Rev. by J. V. Merring, HRNB, 4(Sep 1976):212; O. H. Olsen, NCHR, 53(Aut 1976):417-18.

Mollat, Michel, ed. Etudes Sur L'Histoire de la Pauvreté (Moyen Age-XVIe Siécle). Paris: Publications de la Sorbonne, 1974. Rev. by R. H. Hilton, History, 61(Je 1976):245-6.

Möller, Horst. Aufklärung in Preussen. Berlin: Colloquium Verlag, 1974. Rev. by T. C. W. Blanning, EHR, 91(Oct 1976): 914-15.

Molnar, Amedeo see Gonnet, Jean

Moltmann, Günter. Atlantische Blockpolitik im 19. Jahrhundert. Dusseldorf: Droste Verlag, 1973. Rev. by T. Schoonover, AHR, 81(Apr 1976):360.

Momaday, N. Scott. The Way to Rainy Mountain. Albuquerque: U NM Press, 1969. Rev. by D. Wynn, NMHR, 51(Jl 1976): 259-60.

Mommsen, Hans, Dietmar Petzina and Bernd Weisbrod, eds. Industrielles System und politische Entwicklung in der Weimarer Republik. Düsseldorf: Droste Verlag, 1974. Rev. by V. R. Berghahn, EHR, 91(Jl 1976):685-6.

Mommsen, Heide. Der Affecter. 2 vols. Mayence: Philipp von Zabern, 1975. Rev. by D. von Bothmer, AJA, 80(Feb 1976): 433-8.

Monaco, Michele. Il "De Officio Collectoris in Regno Angliae" di Pietro Griffi da Pisa (1469-1516). Rome: Edizioni di Storia e Letteratura, 1973. Rev. by P. Partner, CaHR, 62(Jan 1976):112-13.

Monjarás-Ruiz, Jesús, trans. Los primeros días de la Revolución. Mexico: SepSetentas, 1975. Rev. by P. J. Vanderwood, HAHR, 56(Nov 1976):653-4.

Monkkonen, Eric H. The Dangerous Class. Cambridge, Mass.: Harvard U Press, 1975. Rev. by E. J. Watts, BHR, 50(Sum 1976):225-7; R. C. Johnson, JAH, 63(Dec 1976):738-9; R. Lane, RAH, 4(Je 1976):212-17.

Monluc, Blaise de. The Habsburg-Valois Wars and the French

War of Religion. Hamden, Conn.: Archon, 1972. Rev. by
P. M. Ascoli, AHR, 81(Je 1976):598-9.

Montaigne, Sanford H. Blood Over Texas. New Rochelle, N.Y.:
Arlington, 1976. Rev. by J. M. Smallwood, JSH, 42(Nov
1976):613-14.

Montell, William Lynwood. Ghosts Along the Cumberland. Knoxville: U Tenn Press, 1975. Rev. by F. R. Johnson, NCHR,
53(Win 1976):87-8.

Montgomery, James W. Liberated Woman: A Life of May Arkwright Hutton. Spokane: Gingko House, 1974. Rev. by S.
B. Rolland, PNQ, 67(Jan 1976):40-1.

Montgomery, John Warwick. Cross and Crucible. 2 vols. The
Hague: Martinus Nijhoff, 1973. Rev. by J. E. Groh, CaHR,
62(Apr 1976):276-8; W. J. Bouwsma, JMH, 48(Mar 1976):
160-1.

Montgomery-Massingberd, Hugh, ed. Burke's Presidential Families
of the United States of America. London: Burke's Peerage
Ltd., 1975. Rev. by G. G. Shackelford, VMHB, 84(Jan
1976):121-3.

Monz, Heinz. Karl Marx. Trier: NCO--Verlag, 1973. Rev. by
D. McLellan, EHR, 91(Jl 1976):665-6.

Moodie, T. Dunbar. The Rise of Afrikanerdom. Berkeley: U
Cal Press, 1975. Rev. by P. R. Dekar, CH, 45(Je 1976):
268-9.

Moody, Michael E., ed. see Cole, C. Robert, ed.

Moody, Robert E., ed. The Saltonstall Papers, 1607-1815. Boston: Mass Historical Society, 1974. Rev. by A. T. Vaughan,
JAH, 62(Mar 1976):947-8; E. M. Walsh, WMQ, 33(Jan 1976):
171-3.

Moody, T. W. The Ulster Question, 1603-1973. Cork: Mercier,
1974. Rev. by P. Bucklund, History, 61(Feb 1976):84.

Moon, Penderal, ed. Wavell: The Viceroy's Journal. London:
Oxford U Press, 1973. Rev. by B. Prasad, IQ, 32(Jan-
Mar 1976):101-3; B. S. Rao, MAS, 10(Jl 1976):463-6.

Mooney, James. Historical Sketch of the Cherokee. Chicago:
Aldine, 1975. Rev. by G. Harrison, GHQ, 60(Sum 1976):
190-1; D. M. Hufhines, JOW, 15(Jl 1976):100; A. M. Gibson,
JSH, 42(Nov 1976):608-9; J. H. O'Donnell, III, NCHR, 53(Sum
1976):325-6.

Mooney, Michael M., ed. George Catlin: Letters and Notes on the

North American Indian. New York: Clarkson N. Potter, 1975. Rev. by J. T. Forrest, WHQ, 7(Jl 1976):319-20.

Moore, Daniel G. Shoot Me a Biscuit. Tucson: U Ariz Press, 1974. Rev. by D. Welsh, NDH, 43(Sum 1976):45.

Moore, Gerald. Wole Soyinka. Modern African Writers. New York: Africana, 1972. Rev. by M. Dorsinville, JAAS, 11 (Jl-Oct 1976):245-7.

Moore, James Tice. Two Paths to the New South. Lexington: U Press, Ky, 1974. Rev. by J. P. Maddex, Jr., AHR, 81 (Apr 1976):455.

Moore, Jerome A. Texas Christian University: A Hundred Years of History. Fort Worth: TCU Press, 1974. Rev. by M. M. Thomas, AHR, 81(Apr 1976):457.

Moore, Maxine. That Lonely Game: Melville, Mardi, and the Almanac. Columbia, Mo.: U Missouri Press, 1975. Rev. by B. Rosenthal, NEQ, 49(Sep 1976):488-90.

Moore, R. I., ed. The Birth of Popular Heresy. London: Edward Arnold, 1975. Rev. by C. Morris, History, 61(Oct 1976):442-3; F. L. Cheyette, HRNB, 4(Aug 1976):202.

Moore, R. J. The Crisis of Indian Unity, 1917-1940. New York: Oxford U. Press, 1974. Rev. by A. T. Embree, AHR, 81(Je 1976):647-8; P. Robb, MAS, 10(Jl 1976):460-3.

Moorhead, Max L. The Presidio: Bastion of the Spanish Borderlands. Norman: U Ok Press, 1975. Rev. by J. Fireman, A & W, 18(Aut 1976):297-8; E. A. Beilharz, AHR, 81(Oct 1976):1010; W. F. Strobridge, CHQ, 55(Spr 1976):84-5; T. H. Kreneck, ETHJ, 14(Spr 1976):56; J. F. Bannon, HAHR, 56 (Feb 1976):132-4; O. B. Faulk, JAH, 63(Je 1976):98-9; F. D. Almaraz, Jr., JOW, 15(Apr 1976):129; D. M. Vigness, JSH, 42(Feb 1976):104-5; D. C. Cutter, NMHR, 51(Jl 1976):261-2; W. M. Mathes, WHQ, 7(Apr 1976):195-7.

Moran, Theodore H. Multinational Corporations and the Politics of Dependence: Copper in Chile. Princeton, N.J.: Prin U Press, 1975. Rev. by R. Dix, AHR, 81(Oct 1976):1015; R. H. Chilcote, HAHR, 56(Nov 1976):690-2.

Morange, J. and J. F. Chassaing. Le Mouvement de réforme de l'enseignement en France, 1760-1798. Paris: Presses Universitaires de France, 1974. Rev. by J. K. Burton, JMH, 48(Sep 1976):555-7.

Moravia, Sergio. Il pensiero degli Idéologues: Scienza e filosofia in Francia (1780-1815). Firenze: La Nuova Italia, 1974. Rev. by M. S. Staum, JHP, 14(Jl 1976):378-80.

Morawetz, David. The Andean Group. Cambridge, Mass.: MIT
Press, 1974. Rev. by M. S. Wionczek, HAHR, 56(Feb 1976):
168-70.

Morenz, Siegfried. Egyptian Religion. New York: Cornell U
Press, 1973. Rev. by L. H. Lesko, JNES, 35(Oct 1976):
281-2.

Morey, Sylvester M. and Olivia L. Gilliam, eds. Respect for Life.
Garden City, N.Y.: Waldorf, 1974. Rev. by C. Vaughan,
JOW, 15(Jl 1976):101.

Morgan, Arthur E. The Making of the TVA. Buffalo: Prometheus,
1974. Rev. by T. H. Goode, AHR, 81(Je 1976):686-7; J. P.
Moeller, HJ, 19(Mar 1976):308-12.

Morgan, David. Suffragists and Liberals. Totowa, N.J.: Rowman
and Littlefield, 1975. Rev. by A. Robson, AHR, 81(Oct
1976):864.

_____ see also Cotterell, Arthur

Morgan, David W. The Socialist Left and the German Revolution.
Ithaca, N.Y.: Cornell U Press, 1975. Rev. by P. Becker,
HRNB, 4(Apr 1976):132.

Morgan, E. P., ed. The Administration of Change in Africa.
New York: Dunellan, 1974. Rev. by G. Glentworth, AfAf,
75(Apr 1976):265-6.

Morgan, Edmund S. American Slavery, American Freedom: The
Ordeal of Colonial Virginia. New York: Norton, 1975. Rev.
by O. Handlin, AHR, 81(Oct 1976):957-8; L. Filler, HRNB,
4(May/Je 1976):138-9; R. R. Menard, JAH, 63(Sep 1976):
371-3; D. J. MacLeod, JAmS, 10(Aug 1976):271-2; M. G.
Kammen, JSH, 42(May 1976):271-3; R. Isaac, RAH, 4(Mar
1976):46-52.

Morgan, Kenneth O. Keir Hardie: Radical and Socialist. London:
Weidenfeld and Nicolson, 1975. Rev. by B. B. Gilbert, AHR,
81(Apr 1976):389-90; P. Smith, EHR, 91(Oct 1976):933; J.
Hinton, History, 61(Oct 1976):492-4; M. Freeden, JMH, 48
(Sep 1976):547-52.

_____, ed. Lloyd George: Family Letters, 1885-1936. Cardiff:
U Wales Press, 1973. Rev. by T. Lloyd, CHR, 57(Mar 1976):
78.

Morgan, Richard E. The Supreme Court and Religion. New York:
Free Press, 1972. Rev. by J. L. Powers, CaHR, 62(Jl
1976):527-8.

Morgan, Roger. The United States and West Germany, 1945-1973.

London: Oxford U Press, 1974. Rev. by J. May, AHR, 81 (Je 1976):693-4.

Morgan, William see Thomas, Samuel W.

Morison, Elting E. From Know-How to Nowhere. New York: Basic Books, 1975. Rev. by K. Birr, AHR, 81(Je 1976): 661-2; B. Sinclair, BHR, 50(Spr 1976):128-9.

Morison, Samuel Eliot. The European Discovery of America: The Northern Voyages, A.D. 500-1600. New York: Oxford U Press, 1971. Rev. by D. Alden, PNQ, 67(Jan 1976):32-3.

_____. The European Discovery of America: The Southern Voyages, A.D. 1492-1616. New York: Oxford U Press, 1974. Rev. by D. B. Quinn, AHR, 81(Feb 1976):100-1; U. Lamb, FHQ, 54(Jan 1976):385-7; D. Alden, PNQ, 67(Jan 1976):32-3.

Morley, Morris see Petras, James

Morrill, George P. Snow, Stars and Wild Honey. Philadelphia: Lippincott, 1975. Rev. by J. S. Peters, VH, 44(Win 1976): 54-5.

Morrill, J. S. Cheshire 1630-1660. New York: Oxford U Press, 1974. Rev. by W. T. MacCaffrey, AHR, 81(Feb 1976):130-1.

Morris, A. J. A., ed. Edwardian Radicalism 1900-1914. Boston: Routledge and Kegan Paul, 1974. Rev. by A. Marrin, AHR, 81(Je 1976):594; H. Pelling, EHR, 91(Jan 1976):232; P. F. Clarke, History, 61(Je 1976):312-14; M. Freeden, JMH, 48 (Sep 1976):547-52.

Morris, John, ed. Domesday Book. Vols. 3, 11, 19. Chichester: Phillimore, 1975. Rev. by H. R. Lyon, History, 61(Oct 1976):439-41.

Morris, Paul C. Four Masted Schooners of the East Coast. Orleans, Mass.: Lower Cape Publishing, 1975. Rev. by A. A. Fahrner, NCHR, 53(Sum 1976):334-5.

Morris, Richard B., ed. see Commager, Henry Steele, ed.

Morris, Robert see Ferguson, E. James, ed.

Morris, Roger, et al. Passing By. New York: Carnegie Endowment for International Peace, 1973. Rev. by W. Weinstein, JMAS, 14(Mar 1976):161-3.

Morrison, James L., Jr., ed. The Memoirs of Henry Heth. Westport, Conn.: Greenwood, 1974. Rev. by H. Schindler, UHQ, 44(Spr 1976):189-90.

273 MORRISON

Morrison, Theodore. Chautauqua: A Center for Education, Religion, and the Arts in America. Chicago: U Chicago Press, 1974. Rev. by R. W. Johannsen, JISHS, 69(Feb 1976):77-8.

Morse, Edward L. Foreign Policy and Interdependence in Gaullist France. Princeton, N.J.: Prin U Press, 1973. Rev. by W. R. Keylor, JMH, 48(Mar 1976):155-7.

Morse, Richard M., ed. From Community to Metropolis: A Biography of São Paulo, Brazil. New York: Octagon, 1974. Rev. by T. E. Skidmore, HAHR, 56(May 1976):336-7.

_____. Las ciudades latinoamericanas. 2 vols. Mexico: Sepsetentas, 1973. Rev. by C. J. Savio, HAHR, 56(Nov 1976): 634-6.

Morsy, Magali. Les Ahansala: Examen du rôle historique d'une famille maraboutique de l'Atlas Marocain. Paris: Mouton, 1972. Rev. by W. S. Hopkins, IJMES, 7(Jan 1976):143-4.

Mortensen, Peder. Tell Shimshara. Copenhagen: Munksgaard, 1970. Rev. by McG. Gibson, JNES, 35(Jan 1976):65-7.

Morton, Desmond. The Canadian General: Sir William Otter. Toronto: Halkert, 1974. Rev. by W. A. B. Douglas, CHR, 57(Mar 1976):55-7.

_____. The Queen v. Louis Riel. Toronto: U Tor Press, 1974. Rev. by H. Bowsfield, CHR, 57(Je 1976):211-12.

Moseley, Michael Edward and Carol J. Mackey. Twenty-Four Architectural Plans of Chan Chan, Peru. Cambridge, Mass.: Harvard U Press, 1974. Rev. by C. Morris, AmAn, 41(Jl 1976):407-8; R. Millon, Antiquity, 50(Sep-Dec 1976):243-4.

Moses, John A. The Politics of Illusion. New York: Barnes and Noble, 1975. Rev. by C. W. Sydnor, Jr., Historian, 39(Nov 1976):133-4; G. G. Iggers, HT, 10(Nov 1976):163-4.

Mosley, D. J. see Adcock, Frank

Moss, Bernard H. The Origins of the French Labor Movement, 1830-1914. Berkeley: U Cal Press, 1976. Rev. by A. F. Peterson, HRNB, 5(Oct 1976):19.

Moss, Howard. Buried City. New York: Atheneum, 1975. Rev. by R. Howard, GR, 30(Spr 1976):205-11.

Moss, R. P. and R. J. A. R. Rathbone, eds. The Population Factor in African Studies. London: U London Press, 1975. Rev. by A. Adepoju, AfAf, 75(Jl 1976):386-8; K. D. Patterson, JAfH, 17(Num 2, 1976):307-8.

Mosse, George L.   The Nationalization of the Masses.   New York:
   Fertig, 1975.   Rev. by R. W. Lougee, AHR, 81(Apr 1976):
   404.

_____, ed.   see also   Vago, Bela, ed.

Mosse, W. E.   Liberal Europe: The Age of the Bourgeois Liberalism, 1848-1875.   London: Thames and Hudson, 1974.   Rev.
   by I. Collins, History, 61(Je 1976):297.

Motherall, Elva, ed.   see   Wilson, Keith, ed.

Motley, Mary Penick, comp. and ed.   The Invisible Soldier: The
   Experience of the Black Soldier, World War II.   Detroit:
   Wayne St U Press, 1975.   Rev. by C. G. Contee, HRNB,
   4(Apr 1976):120.

Moulinas, René.   L'imprimerie, la librairie, et la presse à
   Avignon au XVIIIe siècle.   Grenoble: Presses Universitaires
   de Grenoble, 1974.   Rev. by R. Birn, AHR, 81(Feb 1976):
   156.

Moure, Nancy Wall and Donnelson F. Hoopes.   American Narrative
   Painting.   New York: Praeger, 1974.   Rev. by L. B. Miller, AHR, 81(Feb 1976):202-3.

Moureaux, P.   see   Kurgan, G.

Mousnier, Roland.   The Assassination of Henry IV.   New York:
   Scribner's, 1973.   Rev. by M. K. Becker, CaHR, 62(Apr
   1976):272-3.

_____.   Les Institutions de la France sous la monarchie absolue,
   1598-1789.   Paris: Presses Universitaires de France, 1974.
   Rev. by W. F. Church, AHR, 81(Feb 1976):153-4; R. M. Hat-
   ton, History, 61(Feb 1976):107-8.

Mouton, Pierre.   Social Security in Africa.   Geneva: International
   Labour Office, 1975.   Rev. by M. A. Tribe, AfAf, 75(Jl
   1976):410-11.

Moya Pons, Frank.   La dominación haitiana, 1822-1844.   Santiago,
   D. R.: Universidad Católica Madre y Maestra, 1972.   Rev.
   by T. Mathews, HAHR, 56(Aug 1976):467-8.

Mozingo, David.   Chinese Policy Toward Indonesia, 1949-1967.
   Ithaca, N. Y.: Cornell U Press, 1976.   Rev. by F. H. Tucker, HRNB, 4(Jl 1976):172-3.

Muckermann, Friedrich.   Im Kampf zwischen Epochen.   Mainz:
   Matthias-Grünewald, 1973.   Rev. by T. A. Knapp, CaHR, 62
   (Oct 1976):662-3.

275 MUDROCH

Mudroch, Vaclav and G. S. Couse, eds. Essays on the Reconstruction of Medieval History. Montreal: McGill-Queen's U Press, 1974. Rev. by F. Oakley, AHR, 81(Feb 1976):109.

Mueller, Jerry E. Restless River: International Law and the Behavior of the Rio Grande. El Paso: Texas Western Press, 1975. Rev. by S. B. Liss, HAHR, 56(Aug 1976):489-90.

Mui, Hoh-Cheung and Lorna H. Mui, eds. William Melrose in China 1845-1855. n. p.: Scottish History Society, 1973. Rev. by S. Marriner, BH, 17(Jan 1975):87-8.

Muir, John and John Earl. John Muir's Longest Walk. Garden City, N. Y.: Doubleday, 1975. Rev. by F. H. Q., 54(Jan 1975):412; C. S. Brown, GHQ, 60(Spr 1976):75-6.

Mukherjee, Ramkrishna. The Rise and Fall of the East India Company. New York: Monthly Review Press, 1974. Rev. by K. K. Datta, IQ, 32(Jan-Mar 1976):89-100.

Mullen, Robert James. Dominican Architecture in Sixteenth-Century Oaxaca. Tempe, Ariz.: Ariz St U, 1975. Rev. by L. Castedo, HAHR, 56(Aug 1976):475-6; J. H. De Sandoval, TAm, 32(Apr 1976):654-7.

Muller, Alexander V., ed. and trans. The Spiritual Regulation of Peter the Great. Seattle: U Wash Press, 1972. Rev. by G. L. Bissonnette, CaHR, 62(Apr 1976):301-2.

Müller, Gerhard, ed. see Osiander, Andreas

Müller, Hans Wolfgang. Staatliche Sammlung ägyptischer Kunst in der Müncher Residenz am Hofgarten. Munich: Hans Holzinger, 1972. Rev. by W. H. Peck, JNES, 35(Jan 1976):58-9.

Müller-Karpe, Hermann, ed. Beiträge zu Italienischen und greichischen Bronzefunde. München: C. H. Beck'sche Verlagsbuchhandlung, 1974. Rev. by H. L. Thomas, AJA, 80(Win 1976): 88-9.

Mullin, Michael, ed. American Negro Slavery. Columbia: U SCar Press, 1976. Rev. by P. Davidson, NCHR, 53 (Aut 1976):415-16.

Muminov, I. M., et al. History of Samarkand. 2 vols. Tashkent: Izdatel'stvo, 1971. Rev. by D. C. Montgomery, AHR, 81(Oct 1976):914-15.

Muncy, Raymond Lee. Sex and Marriage in Utopian Communities. Bloomington: Ind U Press, 1973. Rev. by R. Francis, JAmS, 10(Dec 1976):390-3.

Munro, Dana G. The U. S. and the Caribbean Republics, 1921-1933.

Princeton, N. J.: Prin U Press, 1974. Rev. by S. Bhana, AS, 16(Fall 1975):90-2.

Munro, J. Forbes. Colonial Rule and the Kamba. London: Oxford U Press, 1975. Rev. by R. Waller, AfAf, 75(Jl 1976):402-3; J. Lamphear, AHR, 81(Oct 1976):927-8; O. B. Pollak, HRNB, 4(Apr 1976):128.

Munro, John A. and Alex I. Inglis, eds. Mike: The Memoirs of the Right Honourable Lester B. Pearson. Vol. 3. New York: Quadrangel, 1976. Rev. by R. Bothwell, CHR, 57(Je 1976):222-4; J. Boudreau, HRNB, 4(Jl 1976):166.

Munro, John H. A. Wool, Cloth, and Gold. Toronto: U Tor Press, 1973. Rev. by H. L. Misbach, JIH, 7(Sum 1976): 130-1.

Muraskin, William A. Middle-Class Blacks in a White Society. Berkeley: U Cal Press, 1975. Rev. by R. Wolters, JAH, 63(Sep 1976):375-6.

Muriuki, Godfrey. A History of the Kikuyu, 1500-1900. New York: Oxford U Press, 1974. Rev. by C. F. Holmes, AHR, 81(Oct 1976):926.

Murphy, John A. Ireland in the Twentieth Century. Dublin: Gill and Macmillan, 1975. Rev. by P. Buckland, History, 61(Je 1976):315.

Murphy, Paul L. The Passaic Textile Strike of 1926. Belmont, Cal.: Wadsworth, 1974. Rev. by J. M. Gowaskie, BHR, 50 (Sum 1976):243.

Murra, John V. Formaciones economicas y politicas del mundo andino. Lima: Instituto de Estudios Peruanos, 1975. Rev. by A. J. Bauer, HAHR, 56(Aug 1976):472-3.

Murray, David R., ed. Documents of Canadian External Relations. Vol. 7, part 1, 1939-1941. Ottowa: Dept. External Affairs, 1974. Rev. by R. A. Preston, AHR, 81(Je 1976):697-8.

Murray, James G. Henry Adams. New York: Twayne, 1974. Rev. by H. C. Miner, JAH, 63(Dec 1976):742-3.

Murray, Robert K. The Politics of Normalcy: Governmental Theory and Practice in the Harding-Coolidge Era. New York: Norton, 1973. Rev. by D. H. Stratton, PNQ, 67(Apr 1976): 91.

Muscarella, Oscar White, ed. Ancient Art: The Norbert Schimmel Collection. Mainz: Verlag Philipp von Zabern, 1974. Rev. by W. K. Simpson, AJA, 80(Sum 1976):317-19.

Muscatine, Doris. Old San Francisco. New York: Putnam's,
1975. Rev. by C. Wollenberg, CHQ, 55(Sum 1976):186.

Musson, A. E. Trade Union and Social History. Portland, Ore.: International Scholarly Book Services, 1974. Rev. by R. G.
Cowherd, AHR, 81(Je 1976):562; N. McCord, EHR, 91(Jan
1976):213-14; R. Harrison, History, 61(Feb 1976):127-8.

_____ see also Kirby, R. G.

Mutasa, Didymus. Rhodesian Black Behind Bars. n. p.: Mow-
brays, 1974. Rev. by T. I. Matthews, AfAf, 75(Jan 1976):
115-17.

Mutibwa, Phares M. The Malagasy and the Europeans. Atlantic
Highlands, N. J.: Humanities Press, 1975. Rev. by N. R.
Bennett, AHR, 81(Je 1976):642-3.

Myers, A. R. Parliaments and Estates in Europe to 1789. London: Thames and Hudson, 1975. Rev. by H. G. Koenigsberger, History, 61(Oct 1976):445.

Myers, Andrew B., ed. The Knickerbocker Tradition. Tarrytown, N. Y.: Sleepy Hollow Restorations, 1974. Rev. by M.
W. Bowden, NYHSQ, 60(Jan/Apr 1976):81-2.

Myers, Robert Manson. A Georgian at Princeton. New York:
Harcourt Brace Jovanovich, 1976. Rev. by D. G. Matthews,
NCHR, 53(Aut 1976):404-5.

Myrick, David F. Railroads of Arizona. Vol. 1. Berkeley,
Howell-North, 1975. Rev. by J. E. Sherman, A & W, 18
(Sum 1976):192-3; B. M. Fireman, JAriH, 17(Sum 1976):245-7.

Na'aman, S. Die Konstituierung der deutschen Arbeiterbewegung
1862/3 Darstellung und Dokumentation. Assen: Van Gorcum,
1975. Rev. by W. Carr, EHR, 91(Oct 1976):870-3.

Nackman, Mark E. A Nation Within a Nation: The Rise of Texas
Nationalism. Port Washington, N. Y.: Kennikat, 1975. Rev.
by J. M. Day, A & W, 18(Aut 1976):303-4; S. E. Siegel,
AHR, 81(Oct 1976):973; H. S. Marks, HRNB, 4(May/Je
1976):140; B. D. Ledbetter, JSH, 42(Nov 1976):609-10.

Nadal, Jordi. El fracaso de la revolución industrial en España,
1814-1913. Barcelona: Editorial Ariel, 1975. Rev. by S.
G. Payne, JEH, 36(Sep 1976):779-80.

Nagarkan, V. V. Genesis of Pakistan. Columbia, Mo.: South
Asia Books, 1975. Rev. by A. D. Lopaten, HRNB, 4(Aug
1976):194-5.

Nam, Koon Woo. The North Korean Communist Leadership, 1945-

65. University, Ala.: U Ala Press, 1974. Rev. by R. R. Krishnan, IQ, 32(Jan-Mar 1976):84-6.

Nanda, B. R. Gokhale, Gandhi, and the Nehrus. New York: St. Martin's, 1974. Rev. by L. A. Gordon, AHR, 81(Apr 1976): 436-7.

_____, ed. Socialism in India. New York: Barnes and Noble, 1972. Rev. by A. A. Yang, AHR, 81(Apr 1976):435-6.

Nandy, Pritish, ed. Modern Indian Poetry. New Delhi: Heinemann (India), 1974. Rev. by S. Dulai, JAS, 36(Nov 1976): 164-5.

Napoleoni, Claudio. Smith, Ricardo, Marx: Observations on the History of Economic Thought. New York: Halsted, 1976. Rev. by D. Felix, HRNB, 4(Aug 1976):196.

Nardi, Paolo. Mariano Sozzini, Giureconsulto Senese del Quattrocento. Milan: A Giuffrê Editore, 1974. Rev. by R. Bennett, EHR, 91(Jan 1976):126-7.

Naroll, Raoul and Frada Naroll, eds. Main Currents in Cultural Anthropology. New York: Appleton-Century-Crofts, 1973. Rev. by R. Darnell, AA, 78(Je 1976):387-8.

_____, Vern L. Bullough, and Frada Naroll. Military Deterrence in History. Albany: SUNY Press, 1974. Rev. by S. E. Ambrose, JIH, 7(Sum 1976):123-4.

Nasatir, Abraham P. Borderland in Retreat. Albuquerque: U NM Press, 1976. Rev. by R. A. Bartlett, HRNB, 5(Oct 1976):9.

Nash, George H. The Conservative Intellectual Movement in America Since 1945. New York: Basic Books, 1975. Rev. by N. W. Polsby, Commentary, 62(Aug 1976):62-5; J. J. Hanus, HRNB, 4(Jl 1976):162; L. M. Simms, Jr., HRNB, 4(Aug 1976):186; J. T. Gay, HRNB, 4(Sep 1976):213-14.

Nash, Hope. Royalton, Vermont. Royaltown, Vermont: Stinehour Press, 1975. Rev. by R. Teagle, VH, 44(Fall 1976):239-42.

Nash, Manning. Peasant Citizens: Politics, Religion, and Modernization in Kelantan, Malaysia. Athens, Ohio: Ohio U Press, 1974. Rev. by D. J. Banks, AA, 78(Je 1976):407-9.

Natarajan, B. The City of the Cosmic Dance: Chidambaram. New Delhi: Orient Longmans, 1974. Rev. by M. W. Meister, JAS, 36(Nov 1976):167-8.

Natella, Arthur A., Jr., comp. and ed. The Spanish in America, 1513-1974. Dobbs Ferry, N.Y.: Oceana, 1975. Rev. by J. Sánchez, HAHR, 56(Nov 1976):684-6.

Nath, Tribhuvan. The Nepalese Dilemma. New Delhi: Sterling, 1975. Rev. by S. D. Muni, IQ, 32(Apr-Je 1976):239-42.

Nathan, John. Mishima: A Biography. London: Hanish Hamilton. Rev. by H. Yamanouchi, MAS, 10(Oct 1976):632-7.

National Archives and Records Service. Public Papers of the Presidents of the United States: Herbert Hoover. Washington: Government Printing Office, 1974. Rev. by R. H. Zieger, AHR, 81(Oct 1976):800-10.

_____. Public Papers of the Presidents of the United States: Richard Nixon. Washington, D.C.: Government Printing Office, 1974. Rev. by W. C. Berman, AHR, 81(Feb 1976): 222-3.

Naval Historical Foundation, The. Naval Historical Foundation Manuscript Collections: A Catalog. Washington: Library of Congress, 1974. Rev. by K. J. Bauer, AmArc, 39(Je 1976):50-1.

Naylor, Thomas H. and James Clotfelter. Strategies for Change in the South. Chapel Hill: U NC Press, 1975. Rev. by F. R. Marshall, JSH, 42(Feb 1976):147-8.

Neale, R. S., ed. see Kamenka, Eugene, ed.

Nebenzahl, Kenneth. A Bibliography of Printed Battle Plans of the American Revolution, 1775-1795. Chicago: U Chicago Press, 1975. Rev. by P. D. McLaughlin, AmArc, 39(Jan 1976):47-8; T. R. Adams, VMHB, 84(Jan 1976):106-8.

Nechkina, M. V., et al., eds. The Revolutionary Situation in Russia, 1859-1861. Moscow: Izdatel'stvo "Nauka," 1974. Rev. by A. J. Rieber, AHR, 81(Apr 1976):425-6.

Needham, D. E. Iron Age to Independence: A History of Central Africa. London: Longmans, 1974. Rev. by D. Killingray, JAfH, 17(Num 3, 1976):458-9.

Needham, Joseph. Science and Civilisation in China. Vol. 5. London: Cam U Press, 1974. Rev. by C. Cullen, CQ, Jan 1976, pp. 143-4.

Neidhardt, W. S. Fenianism in North America. University Park: Pa St U Press, 1975. Rev. by J. A. Howrigan, VH, 44(Spr 1976):115-16.

Neighbours, Kenneth F. Robert Simpson Neighbors and the Texas Frontier, 1836-1859. Waco: Texian Press, 1975. Rev. by J. Holt, ETHJ, 14(Fall 1976):71.

Neilan, Edward and Charles R. Smith. The Future of the China

Market. Stanford, Cal.: Hoover Institution, 1974. Rev. by
S. B. Lubman, CQ, May 1976, pp. 379-82.

Nelles, H. V. The Politics of Development. Hamden, Conn.:
Archon, 1974. Rev. by M. Prang, AHR, 81(Feb 1976):223-4.

Nelsen, Hart M. and Anne Kusener Nelsen. Black Church in the
Sixties. Lexington: U Press Ky, 1975. Rev. by R. L.
Zangrando, JAH, 63(Je 1976):202; N. G. Sapper, JSH, 42
(May 1976):299-300.

Nelson, Daniel. Managers and Workers: Origins of the New Factory System in the United States, 1880-1920. Madison: U
Wis Press, 1975. Rev. by D. Montgomery, JAH, 63(Dec
1976):739-40.

Nelson, Douglas W. Heart Mountain. Madison: U Wis Press,
1976. Rev. by P. Knuth, OrHQ, 77(Sep 1976):297-8.

Nelson, E. Clifford, ed. A Pioneer Churchman. New York:
Twayne, 1973. Rev. by G. McDonald, CaHR, 62(Jl 1976):
494-5.

Nelson, J. G., R. C. Scace, and R. Kouri, eds. Canadian Public
Land Use in Perspective. Ottawa: Social Science Research
Council, 1974. Rev. by N. Semple, CHR, 57(Je 1976):196-7.

Nelson, Keith L. Victors Divided: America and the Allies in Ger-
many, 1918-1923. Berkeley: U Cal Press, 1975. Rev. by
M. W. Kerr, AHR, 81(Oct 1976):992-3; P. C. Helmreich,
HRNB, 4(Jan 1976):51-2; R. H. Ferrell, JAH, 63(Sep 1976):
446-7; S. J. Kneeshaw, MiA, 58(Apr/Jl 1976):130-1; N. G.
Levin, Jr., PHR, 45(May 1976):299-300.

Nelson, Paul David. General Horatio Gates: A Biography. Baton
Rouge: LSU Press, 1976. Rev. by C. R. Allen, Jr., NCHR,
53(Aut 1976):408-9; D. Higginbotham, VMHB, 84(Oct 1976):
495-6.

Nelson, William E. Americanization of the Common Law. Cambridge, Mass.: Harvard U Press, 1975. Rev. by K. Preyer,
JAH, 63(Dec 1976):692-3.

Neré, J. The Foreign Policy of France from 1914 to 1945. Boston: Routledge and Kegan Paul, 1975. Rev. by M. C. Siney,
AHR, 81(Je 1976):610-11; A. S. Turner, EHR, 91(Apr 1976):
472-3; A. Adamthwaite, History, 61(Je 1960):320.

Neruda, Pablo. Confieso que he vivido, memorias. Barcelona:
Editorial Seix Barral, 1974. Rev. by M. G. de Gallo,
Américas, 28(Oct 1976):25-6.

Netamuxwe Bock, William Sauts. The First Americans. Wallingford, Pa.: Middle Atlantic Press, 1974. Rev. by C. A. Weslager, AIQ, 2(Spr 1975):29.

Neuenschwander, John A. The Middle Colonies and the American Revolution. Port Washington, N.Y.: Kennikat, 1973. Rev. by A. Tully, Historian, 39(Nov 1976):146-8; J. V. Jezierski, PH, 43(Oct 1976):374-5.

Neuman, George C. and Frank J. Kravic. Collectors' Illustrated Encyclopedia of the American Revolution. Harrisburg, Pa.: Stackpole, 1975. Rev. by H. L. Peterson, AHI, 11(Oct 1976):49; R. A. Howard, PH, 43(Oct 1976):371-2.

Neumüller, Michael. Liberalismus und Revolution. Düsseldorf: Pädagogischer Verlag Schwann, 1973. Rev. by R. Southard, JMH, 48(Mar 1976):164-6.

Neveu, Bruno, ed. Correspondance du Nonce en France: Angelo Ranuzzi (1683-1689); Tome I and II. Rome: Editions de l'Université Gregorienne, 1973. Rev. by W. H. Williams, CaHR, 62(Apr 1976):287-8.

Nevin, David. The Expressmen. New York: Time-Life, 1974. Rev. by J. Campbell, ChOk, 54(Sum 1976):293-4.

Nevins, Allan. Allan Nevins on History. (Ray Allen Billington, comp.) New York: Scribner's, 1975. Rev. by W. U. Solberg, HRNB, 4(Apr 1976):118.

Newell, R. R. and A. P. J. Vroomans. Automatic Artifact Registration Systems for Archaeological Analysis with the Phillips P1100 Computer. New York: Humanities Press, 1972. Rev. by D. F. Green, AmAnt, 41(Jan 1976):120.

Newitt, M. D. D. Portuguese Settlement of the Zambesi. London: Longman, 1973. Rev. by K. Ingham, History, 61(Feb 1976):156-7.

Newman, Ralph Geoffrey. Abraham Lincoln: His Story in His Own Words. Garden City, N.Y.: Doubleday, 1975. Rev. by R. D. Hoffsommer, AHI, 11(May 1976):49; J. E. Suppiger, JISHS, 69(Feb 1976):76-7.

Newsome, David. Two Classes of Man: Platonism and English Romantic Thought. London: John Murray, 1974. Rev. by O. Anderson, History, 61(Feb 1976):124.

Ngugi, James. Homecoming. Essays on African and Caribbean Literature, Culture and Politics. New York: Lawrence Hill, 1973. Rev. by M. Dorsinville, JAAS, 11(Jl-Oct 1976):245-7.

Nibbi, Alessandra. The Sea Peoples and Egypt. Park Ridge, N.J.: Noyes, 1975. Rev. by M. L. Bierbrier, Antiquity, 50(Sep-Dec 1976):245-6.

Ničev, Alexandre. L'Enigme de la catharsis tragique dans Aristotle. Sofia: Editions de l'Academie Bulgare des Sciences, 1970. Rev. by W. Trimpi, JHP, 14(Jan 1976):101-4.

Nicholas, H. G. The United States and Britain. Chicago: U Chicago Press, 1975. Rev. by C. J. Bartlett, History, 61 (Oct 1976):424-5; K. J. Cook, HRNB, 4(Jan 1976):53; B. Perkins, JAH, 62(Mar 1976):979; H. C. Randall, NEQ, 49(Mar 1976):153-5.

Nicholls, David. The Pluralist State. London: Macmillan, 1975. Rev. by D. Read, History, 61(Oct 1976):492.

Nichols, Kenneth. Yesterday's Akron. Miami: E. A. Semman, 1975. Rev. by J. W. Heuener, OH, 85(Win 1976):95-6.

Nichols, Roger and Kenneth McLeish, comps. and trans. Through Greek Eyes. Cambridge: Cam U Press, 1974. Rev. by R. G. Kenworthy, HT, 10(Nov 1976):133-4.

Nicholson, Ranald₀ Scotland: The Later Middle Ages. Edinburgh: Oliver and Boyd, 1974. Rev. by J. Collins, Historian, 38(Feb 1976):327-9; G. W. S. Barrow, History, 61(Je 1976):252-3.

Nicholson, Robert Lawrence. Joscelyn III and the Fall of the Crusader States. Leiden: E. J. Brill, 1973. Rev. by J. H. Hill, CaHR, 62(Jan 1976):80-2; D. J. A₀ Matthew, EHR, 91 (Jl 1976):629; C. R. Young, Historian, 38(Feb 1976):321-2₀

Nicol, Donald M. Meteora: The Rock Monasteries of Thessaly. London: Variorum Reprints, 1975. Rev. by P. Hammond, JEccH, 27(Apr 1976):212-13.

Nicolas, Guy. Dynamique Sociale et Appréhension du Monde au Sein d'une Société Hausa. Paris: Institute d'Ethnologie, 1975. Rev. by M. Last, AfAf, 75(Jl 1976):397-8.

Nicolson, John, ed. The Arizona of Joseph Pratt Allyn: Letters from a Pioneer Judge. Tucson: U Ariz Press, 1974. Rev. by C. Trafzer, ChOk, 54(Win 1976):530-1.

Nicolson, Nigel. Alex: The Life of Field Marshal Earl Alexander of Tunis. New York: Atheneum, 1973. Rev. by R. Higham, AHR, 81(Je 1976):596-7.

Niemeijer, Albert Christiaan. The Khilofat Movement in India, 1919-1924. The Hague: Smits, n.d. Rev. by G. Minault, AHR, 81(Je 1976):645-7.

Niemeyer, E. V., Jr. Revolution at Querétaro. Austin: U Texas Press, 1974. Rev. by R. N. Sinkin, TAm, 32(Jan 1976): 496-7₀

Niemi, Albert W. , Jr.   State and Regional Patterns in American
Manufacturing, 1860-1900.   Westport, Conn. :   Greenwood,
1974.   Rev. by J. H. Madison, AHR, 81(Oct 1976):983-4.

Nipperdey, Thomas.   Reformation, Revolution, Utopie: Studien zum
16. Jahrhundert.   Göttingen: Vandenhoeck & Ruprecht, 1975.
Rev. by B. C. Weber, CH, 45(Je 1976):255-6.

Nisbet, Robert.   The Social Philosophers.   New York: Crowell,
1973. Rev. by D. Hymes, AA, 78(Mar 1976):149-51.

_____. Twilight of Authority.   Oxford: Oxford U Press, n. d.
Rev. by P. P. Witonski, Commentary, 61(Mar 1976):78-80.

Nixson, F. I.   Economic Integration and Industrial Location.   London: Longman, 1973.   Rev. by P. Mosley, JMAS, 14(Je
1976):356-7.

Noble, Allen G. and Albert J. Korsok.   Ohio--An American Heartland.   Columbus: Ohio Div of Geological Survey, 1975.   Rev.
by H. L. Hunker, OH, 85(Spr 1976):173-5.

Noble, Donald R. and Joab L. Thomas, eds.   The Rising South.
Vol. I.   University: U Ala Press, 1976.   Rev. by W. B.
Gatewood, Jr. , 53(Aut 1976):405-6.

Noble, Harold Joyce.   Embassy at War.   Seattle: U Wash Press,
1975. Rev. by N. Pugach, AHR, 81(Oct 1976):1004-5; R. R.
Simmons, PNQ, 67(Oct 1976):177.

Noggle, Burl.   Into the Twenties.   Urbana: U Ill Press, 1974.
Rev. by A. J. Lichtman, AHR, 81(Je 1976):686; J. B. , AS,
16(Spr 1975):76; J. D. Doenecke, OH, 85(Win 1976):94-5; D.
H. Stratton, PNQ, 67(Apr 1976):91.

Nolde, O. Frederick.   The Churches and the Nations.   Philadelphia:
Fortress, 1970.   Rev. by C. P. St. Amant, JCS, 17(Win
1975):150-1.

Nöldeke, Th.   Geschichte der Perser und Araber zur Zeit der
Sasaniden.   Graz: Akademische Druck-U Verlagsanstalt, 1973.
Rev. by M. G. Morony, IJMES, 7(Oct 1976):602-3.

Nolte, Ernst.   Deutschland und der Kalte Krieg.   Munich: R.
Piper, 1974.   Rev. by F. Gilbert, AHR, 81(Je 1976):618-20.

Nolutshungu, Sam C.   South Africa in Africa.   Manchester: Manchester U Press, 1975.   Rev. by O. Geyser, AfAf, 75(Jl
1976):405-6.

Noonan, John T. , Jr.   Power to Dissolve: Lawyers and Marriages
in the Courts of the Roman Curia.   Cambridge, Mass. : Bel-
knap (Harvard U Press), 1972.   Rev. by H. G. J. Beck, AHR,
81(Feb 1976):98-9.

Norbu, Dawa. Red Star Over Tibet. London: Collins, 1974. Rev. by G. Patterson, CQ, May 1976, pp. 400-2.

Nordin, D. Sven. Rich Harvest: A History of the Grange, 1867-1900. Jackson: U Press Miss, 1974. Rev. by R. Sherman, AgH, 50(Jan 1976):323-5; N. Pollack, AHR, 81(Apr 1976):454-5; D. Crosson, AI, 43(Win 1976):228-9; D. J. Berthrong, IMH, 72(Mar 1976):81-3.

Northcott, Cecil. David Livingstone: His Triumph, Decline and Fall. Philadelphia: Westminster Press, 1973. Rev. by E. E. Beauregard, CaHR, 62(Oct 1976):625-6.

Norton, Thomas Elliot. The Fur Trade in Colonial New York, 1686-1776. Madison: U Wis Press, 1974. Rev. by J. Sosin, PHR, 45(Feb 1976):121-2.

Norwood, Frederick A. The Story of American Methodism. Nashville: Abingdon, 1974. Rev. by W. B. Posey, JCS, 18(Spr 1976):336-9.

Nossiter, T. J. Influence, Opinion and Political Idioms in Reformed England. Brighton: Harvester, 1975. Rev. by V. M. Batzel, AHR, 81(Je 1976):591-2; N. Gash, EHR, 91(Oct 1976):924-5; N. McCord, History, 61(Je 1976):306-7; A. J. Heesom, HJ, 19(Mar 1976):289-90.

Nouailhat, Yves-Henri. Les Americans à Nantes et Saint-Nazaire, 1917-1919. Paris: Les Belles Lettres, 1972. Rev. by T. Ropp, AHR, 81(Je 1976):683.

Novak, Maximillian E., ed. see Dudley, Edward, ed.

Novak, Michael. The Joy of Sports. New York: Basic Books, n.d. Rev. by W. J. Bennett, Commentary, 62(Oct 1976): 85-7.

Novales, Alberto Gil. Las sociedades patrioticas 1820-1823. 2 vols. Madrid: Editorial Tecnos, 1975. Rev. by P. Janke, History, 61(Oct 1976):460.

Nove, Alec. Stalinism and After. London: George Allen and Unwin, 1975. Rev. by W. J. Lavery, HRNB, 4(Jan 1976):67.

Novinsky, Anita. Cristãos novos na Babia. São Paulo: Editora Perspectiva, 1972. Rev. by D. E. Levi, TAm, 32(Apr 1976):649-50.

Nugent, Donald. Ecumenism in the Age of the Reformation. Cambridge, Mass.: Harvard U Press, 1974. Rev. by R. J. Knecht, History, 61(Feb 1976):111; W. D. J. Cargill Thompson, JEccH, 27(Apr 1976):204-5; P. M. Ascoli, JMH, 48 (Mar 1976):145-6.

Nunberg, Herman and Ernst Federn, eds. Minutes of the Vienna
    Psychoanalytic Society. Vol. 4, 1912-1918. New York: In-
    ternational Universities Press, 1975. Rev. by R. L. Schoen-
    wald, AHR, 81(Apr 1976):411-12.

Nunis, Doyce B., Jr., ed. Los Angeles and Its Environs in the
    Twentieth Century: A Bibliography of a Metropolis. Los
    Angeles: Ward Ritchie Press, 1973. Rev. by J. Caughey,
    PHR, 45(Feb 1976):136-7.

Nwabueze, B. O. Presidentialism in Commonwealth Africa. Lon-
    don: Hurst, 1974. Rev. by T. V. Sathyamurthy, AfAf, 75
    (Jl 1976):390-1; R. Martin, JMAS, 14(Sep 1976):531-3.

Nwulie, Moses D. E. Britain and Slavery in East Africa. Wash-
    ington, D.C.: Three Continents Press, 1975. Rev. by M. S.
    Tsomondo, JNH, 61(Jl 1976):316-18.

Nye, Robert A. The Origins of Crowd Psychology. Beverly Hills,
    Cal.: Sage, 1975. Rev. by R. L. Geiger, JMH, 48(Sep
    1976):557-60.

Nye, Roger P. see Le Vine, Victor T.

Nyerere, Julius K. Freedom and Development. London: Oxford
    U Press, 1973. Rev. by J. H. Konter, JMAS, 14(Mar 1976):
    171-2.

Oakley, Ann. Woman's Work: The Housewife, Past and Present.
    New York: Pantheon, 1975. Rev. by S. J. Kleinberg, JSoH,
    10(Fall 1976):99-103; K. Cassill, Smithsonian, 6(Sep 1975):
    112, 114.

Oakley, Francis. The Medieval Experience. New York: Scrib-
    ner's, 1974. Rev. by W. J. Courtenay, CH, 45(Mar 1976):
    107.

Oaks, D. H. and M. S. Hill. Carthage Conspiracy. Urbana: U
    Ill Press, 1975. Rev. by J. D. W. Guice, A & W, 18(Sum
    1976):184-5; W. C. Ringenberg, HRNB, 4(Feb 1976):77; C. S.
    Peterson, JAH, 63(Sep 1976):415; E. H. Ellis, WHQ, 7(Oct
    1976):433-4.

Oates, Stephen B. The Fires of Jubilee: Nat Turner's Fierce Re-
    bellion. New York: Harper and Row, 1975. Rev. by H.
    Aptheker, AHR, 81(Je 1976):660.

O'Ballance, Edgar. Arab Guerilla Power, 1967-1972. Hamden,
    Conn.: Archon, 1973. Rev. by C. W. Dawn, AHR, 81(Oct
    1976):919.

_____. The Electronic War in the Middle East, 1968-70. Ham-
    den, Conn.: Archon, 1974. Rev. by D. R. Tahtinen, AHR,
    81(Oct 1976):919-20.

Obermann, Heiko A. , ed. Luther and the Dawn of the Modern Era.
Leiden: E. J. Brill, 1974. Rev. by W. D. J. Cargill
Thompson, JEccH, 27(Oct 1976):433-5.

Obiozor, George see Butler, William J.

Obojski, Robert. Bush League: A History of Minor League Baseball. New York: Macmillan, 1975. Rev. by W. F. Clare,
Smithsonian, 6(Aug 1975):96-8.

O'Brien, Francis William, ed. Hoover-Wilson Correspondence,
September 24, 1914 to November 11, 1918. Ames: Ia St U
Press, 1974. Rev. by R. H. Zieger, AHR, 81(Oct 1976):
800-10.

O'Brien, George Dennis. Hegel on Reason and History: A Contemporary Interpretation. Chicago: U Chi Press, 1975. Rev.
by G. G. Iggers, AHR, 81(Oct 1976):843-4.

O'Brien, Joseph V. William O'Brien and the Course of Irish Politics 1881-1918. Berkeley: U Cal Press, 1976. Rev. by S.
H. Palmer, HRNB, 4(Jl 1976):180.

O'Callaghan, Joseph F. A History of Medieval Spain. Ithaca,
N.Y.: Cornell U Press, 1975. Rev. by T. N. Bisson, AHR,
81(Je 1976):569-70; U. L. , HAHR, 56(Feb 1976):172; D. W.
Lomax, History, 61(Je 1976):253-4; A. G. Biggs, TAm, 32
(Apr 1976):643-4.

Ochse, Orpha C. The History of the Organ in the United States.
Bloomington: Ind U Press, 1975. Rev. by P. D. Petersen,
CH, 45(Mar 1976):126-8.

O'Connell, Daniel. The Correspondence of Daniel O'Connell. 3
vols. (Maurice R. O'Connell, ed.). New York: Barnes and
Noble, 1973, 1974. Rev. by D. H. Akenson, AHR, 81(Je
1976):598; W. D. Griffin, CaHR, 62(Apr 1976):310-12; E.
Larkin, JMH, 48(Sep 1976):540-3.

O'Connell, Marvin R. The Counter Reformation, 1559-1610. New
York: Harper and Row, 1974. Rev. by J. Bossy, CaHR, 62
(Jan 1976):132-3.

O'Connell, Maurice R. , ed. see Daniel O'Connell

Odaka, Kunio. Toward Industrial Democracy: Management and
Workers in Modern Japan. Cambridge, Mass.: Harvard U
Press, 1975. Rev. by K. Azumi, JAS, 36(Nov 1976):157-8.

O'Day, Rosemary and Felicity Heal, eds. Continuity and Change:
Personnel and Administration of the Church in England 1500-
1642. Leicester: Leicester U Press, 1976. Rev. by W. T.
MacCaffrey, Archives, 12(Aut 1976):193-4.

Oded, Arye. Islam in Uganda. New York: Wiley, 1974. Rev. by G. S. Ibingira, AHR, 81(Je 1976):641-2.

O'Fahey, R. S. and J. E. Spaulding. Kingdoms of the Sudan. London: Methuen, 1974. Rev. by J. S. F. Parker, History, 61(Feb 1976):161.

O'Farrell, Patrick. England and Ireland Since 1800. New York: Oxford U Press, 1975. Rev. by G. Costigan, HRNB, 4(Feb 1976):93.

O'Gorman, Edmundo. Cuatro historiadores de Indias, siglo XVI. Mexico: SepSetentas, 1972. Rev. by P. K. Liss, HAHR, 56(Nov 1976):651-2.

O'Gorman, Frank. The Rise of Party in England: The Rockingham Whigs, 1760-1782. London: Allen and Unwin, 1975. Rev. by I. R. Christie, EHR, 91(Apr 1976):390-3.

Ogunsanwo, Alaba. China's Policy in Africa, 1958-1971. Cambridge: Cam U Press, 1974. Rev. by P. Lyon, AfAf, 75 (Apr 1976):252-3; A. L. Segal, JAAS, 11(Jan and Apr 1976): 114-15.

Okamoto, Shumpei, ed. see Borg, Dorothy, ed.

Okoso-Amaa, K. Rice Marketing in Ghana. Uppsala: Scandinavian Institute of African Studies, 1975. Rev. by P. Hill, AfAf, 75(Apr 1976):257-8.

Okumu, John, ed. see Hyden, Göran, ed.

Old, Hughes Oliphant. The Patristic Roots of Reformed Worship. Zurich: Theologischer Verlag, 1975. Rev. by G. J. Cuming, JEccH, 27(Oct 1976):440-1.

Oldfield, John J. The Problem of Tolerance and Social Existence in the Writings of Félicité Lamennais 1809-1831. Leiden: Brill, 1973. Rev. by G. de Bertier, CaHR, 62(Apr 1976): 113-14.

O'Leary, Cornelius see Budge, Ian

Oleson, Alexandra and Sanborn C. Brown, eds. The Pursuit of Knowledge in the Early American Republic. Baltimore: JH U Press, 1976. Rev. by W. U. Solberg, HRNB, 4(Sep 1976):216.

Olinder, Björn. Porticus Octavia in Circo Flaminio. Topographical Studies in the Campus Region of Rome. Lund: Paul Astroms, 1974. Rev. by D. M. Robathan, AJA, 80(Win 1976):98-9.

Olivella, Manuel Zapata. El Hombre Colombiano. Bogota: Fundación Colombiana de Investigaciones Folclóricas, 1974. Rev.
by V. G. Stoddard, Américas, 28(Aug 1976):22.

Oliver, R. and B. Fagan. Africa in the Iron Age: c. 500 B.C.
to 1400 A.D. Cambridge: Cam U Press, 1975. Rev. by J.
F. Addison, AfAf, 75(Jl 1976):384-5; H. G. Soff, HRNB, 4
(Mar 1976):105-6; M. Posmansky, JAfH, 17(Num 4, 1976):
629-31.

_____, ed. see also Gray, Richard, ed.

Olla, Paola Brundu. Le origini diplomatiche dell'accordo navale
anglo-tedesco del giugno 1935. Milan: Giuffrè Editore, 1974.
Rev. by A. Cassels, AHR, 81(Feb 1976):146-7.

Olney, James. Tell Me Africa. Princeton, N.J.: Prin U Press,
1973. Rev. by M. M. Mahood, AfAf, 75(Apr 1976):262-4;
A. Ricard, JMAS, 14(Mar 1976):178-80.

Olsberg, R. Nicholas, ed. The Journal of the Commons House of
Assembly, 23 April 1750-31 August 1751. Columbia, S.C.:
U SCar Press, 1974. Rev. by C. L. VerSteeg, JSH, 42(Feb
1976):105; A. Scherr, SCHM, 77(Jan 1976):52-5.

Olsen, V. Norskov. John Foxe and the Elizabethan Church. Berkeley: U Cal Press, 1973. Rev. by J. Hurstfield, CaHR, 62
(Jan 1976):134-5; K. L. Spunger, MQR, 50(Apr 1976):145-6.

Olson, Gary L. U.S. Foreign Policy and the Third World Peasant.
New York: Praeger, 1974. Rev. by S. L. Forman, HAHR,
56(Feb 1976):157-8.

Olson, Keith W. The G.I. Bill, the Veterans, and the Colleges.
Lexington: U Press Ky, 1974. Rev. by E. Ranson, JAmS,
10(Apr 1976):122-4.

Olton, Charles S. Artisans for Independence: Philadelphia Mechanics and the American Revolution. Syracuse, N.Y.: Syracuse U Press, 1975. Rev. by R. Walsh, AHR, 81(Oct 1976):
962; B. Friedman, JAH, 63(Sep 1976):392-3.

Oluwasanmi, E., E. Mc Lean, and H. Zell, eds. Publishing in
Africa in the 70's. Ife: U Life Press, 1975. Rev. by D.
H. Simpson, AfAf, 75(Jl 1976):409-10.

O'Meara, John J. and Ludwig Bieler, eds. The Mind of Eriugena.
Dublin: Irish U Press, 1973. Rev. by D. Luscombe, JEccH,
27(Jl 1976):310-11.

O'Neil, Robert M. Discriminating Against Discrimination. Bloomington: Ind U Press, n.d. Rev. by W. Petersen, Commentary, 61(Je 1976):88.

_____. The Price of Dependency: Civil Liberties in the Welfare State. New York: Dutton, 1970. Rev. by J. D. Bragg, JCS, 18(Win 1976):141-2.

O'Neill, P. G. Essential Kanji. New York: Weatherhill, 1973. Rev. by J. Silverman, MAS, 10(Apr 1976):316-19.

O'Neill, William L. The Progressive Years: America Comes of Age. New York: Dodd, Mead, 1975. Rev. by O. A. Pease, AHR, 81(Oct 1976):988-9; R. C. Bannister, JAH, 63(Je 1976): 159-60.

Onuf, Peter S., ed. Maryland and the Empire, 1773. Baltimore: JHU Press, 1974. Rev. by T. O'B. Hanley, CaHR, 62(Jl 1976):477-8.

Onwuejeogwu, M. Angulu. The Social Anthropology of Africa. London: Heineman, 1975. Rev. by L. Mair, AfAf, 75(Jl 1976):386.

Ooms, Herman. Charismatic Bureaucrat: A Political Biography of Matsudaira Sadanobu, 1758-1829. Chicago: U Chicago Press, 1975. Rev. by R. M. Spaulding, AHR, 81(Oct 1976):940-1; E. B. Lee, HRNB, 4(Jan 1976):62; H. Bolitho, JJS, 2(Aut 1975):152-5.

Oppong, Christine. Marriage Among a Matrilineal Elite. London: Cam U Press, 1974. Rev. by D. D. Vellenga, JAAS, 11(Jan and Apr 1976):117-18.

Ordnance Survey. Britain Before the Norman Conquest. Southampton: Ordnance Survey, 1973. Rev. by A. P. Smith, EHR, 91(Apr 1976):407-8.

Organization of American States. Situación Económica, Principales, Problemas y Perspectivas de Desarrollo de Colombia. Washington, D. C.: Organization of American States, 1975. Rev. by F. P. Hebblethwaite, Américas, 28(May 1976):20, 21.

Orieux, Jean. Talleyrand. New York: Knopf, 1974. Rev. by M. E. Goldstein, JMH, 48(Mar 1976):132-5.

Orimalade, Oluronke O., comp. Bibliography on Labour in Nigeria, 1910-1970. Lagos: Nat'l Library of Nigeria, 1974. Rev. by S. E. Moses, AfAf, 75(Jl 1976):399-400.

Orlik, O. V. Progressive Russia and Revolutionary France in the First Half of the 19th Century. Moscow: Izdatel'stvo "Nauka," 1973. Rev. by R. F. Byrnes, AHR, 81(Feb 1976):123.

Ormond, Leonée and Richard Ormond. Lord Leighton. New Haven, Conn.: Yale U Press, n. d. Rev. by R. Watson, Smithsonian, 7(Mar 1976):102-3.

Ortiz Oderigo, Nestor. Aspectos de la cultura africana en el Río de la Plata. Buenos Aires: Editorial PLUS ULTRA. 1974. Rev. by V. Peloso, JNH, 61(Apr 1976):224-5.

Orum, Anthony M. Black Students in Protest. Washington, D.C.: American Sociological Assn., 1972. Rev. by W. M. King, JNH, 61(Oct 1976):406-7.

Osbat, Luciano. L'Inquisizione a Napoli. Rome: Edizioni di Storia e Letteratura, 1974. Rev. by W. J. Bonwsma, CaHR, 62(Apr 1976):293-5.

Osborn, George Coleman. John James Tigert: American Educator. Gainesville: U Presses Fla, 1974. Rev. by H. L. Swint, FHQ, 54(Jan 1976):382-5.

Oshinsky, David M. Senator Joseph McCarthy and the American Labor Movement. Columbia, Mo.: U Mo Press, 1976. Rev. by T. C. Reeves, JAH, 63(Dec 1976):778-9.

Osiander, Andreas. Andreas Osiander d. A. Gesamtausgabe. Vol. I: Schriften und Briefe 1522 bis März 1525. (Gerhard Müller and Gottfried Seebass, eds.) Güttersloh: Verlagshaus Gerd Mohn, 1975. Rev. by H. J. Grimm, CH, 45(Je 1976):257-8.

Osterloh, Kark-Heinz. Joseph von Sonnenfels und die österreichische Reformbewegung im Zeitalter des aufgeklärten. Lubeck: Historische Studien, 1970. Rev. by E. Wangermann, ESR, 6(Jl 1976):383-5.

Osterweis, Rollin G. The Myth of the Lost Cause, 1865-1900. Hamden, Conn.: Archon, 1973. Rev. by W. L. Richter, ETHJ, 14(Spr 1976):64-6.

Oteo, Guadalupe Nava. Cabildos y ayuntamientos de la Nueva España en 1808. Mexico: SepSetentas, 1973. Rev. by N. L. Benson, HAHR, 56(Nov 1976):650-1.

Otte, Enrique, ed. and trans. see Lockhart, James, ed. and trans.

Otto, Eberhard, ed. see Helck, Wolfgang

Outland, Charles F. Stagecoaching on El Camino Real. Glendale, Cal.: A. H. Clark, 1973. Rev. by W. R. Wilson, ChOk, 54(Spr 1976):158-60.

Owen, Dorothy M., ed. John Lydford's Book. London: HMSO, 1974. Rev. by J. H. Denton, EHR, 91(Jl 1976):633-4; F. D. Logan, Archives, 12(Aut 1976):191-2; J. R. L. Highfield, JEccH, 27(Jan 1976):79-80.

Owen, Edgar Wesley. Trek of the Oil Finders: A History of Ex-

ploration for Petroleum. Tulsa: American Association of
Petroleum Geologists, 1975. Rev. by P. H. Giddens, AHR,
81(Oct 1976):822; A. M. Johnson, JAH, 63(Je 1976):153-4;
H. M. Larson, JEH, 36(Sep 1976):781-2.

Owen, John B. The Eighteenth Century, 1714-1815. Totowa, N.J.:
Rowman and Littlefield, 1975. Rev. by E. C. Black, AHR,
81(Oct 1976):858-9.

Owens, Leslie Howard. This Species of Property: Slave Life and
Culture in the Old South. New York: Oxford U Press, 1976.
Rev. by N. Thorburn, HRNB, 4(May/Je 1976):147; R. M.
Johnson, JSH, 42(Nov 1976):575-6.

Owens, William A. A Fair and Happy Land. New York: Scrib-
ner's, 1975. Rev. by D. L. Smith, JAH, 63(Sep 1976):406;
R. E. Paulson, JSH, 42(Aug 1976):450-1; J. W. Goodrich,
WHQ, 7(Oct 1976):419.

Oxnam, Robert B. Ruling from Horseback: Manchu Politics in
the Oboi Regency, 1661-1669. Chicago: U Chicago Press,
1975. Rev. by L. D. Kessler, AHR, 81(Oct 1976):932-3; M.
Patoski, HRNB, 4(Jan 1976):62; H. L. Miller, JAS, 36(Nov
1976):130-1.

Ozment, Steven E. The Reformation in the Cities. New Haven,
Conn.: Yale U Press, 1975. Rev. by L. W. Spitz, CH, 45
(Je 1976):254-5; E. R. Monter, Historian, 39(Nov 1976):115-
16; H. J. Cohn, History, 61(Oct 1976):446; H. T. Blethen,
HRNB, 4(Feb 1976):91; A. G. Dickens, JEccH, 27(Apr 1976):
200-1.

Paananen, Lauri see Engle, Lauri

Pacaut, Marcel and Paul M. Bouju, eds. Le Monde Contemporain
1945-1973. Paris: Armand Colin, 1974. Rev. by P. J. V.
Rolo, History, 61(Feb 1976):150.

Pachter, Henry M. The Fall and Rise of Europe. New York:
Praeger, 1975. Rev. by E. P. Noether, HRNB, 4(Jan 1976):
64.

Paden, John N. Religion and Political Culture in Kano. Berkeley:
U Cal Press, 1973. Rev. by F. A. Salamone, JMAS, 14
(Mar 1976):172-3.

Palau, A. Arribas, et al. Excavaciones en al Poblado de la Edad
del Bronce "Cerro de la Encina" Monachil. Madrid: Excavaciones Arqueologicas en Espana, 1971. Rev. by R. W.
Chapman, Antiquity, 50(Mar 1976):73-4.

Palmer, Alan. Alexander I: Tsar of War and Peace. London:
Weidenfeld and Nicolson, 1974. Rev. by P. Dukes, History,
61(Feb 1976):121-2.

_____. Bismarck. London: Weidenfeld and Nicolson, n. d.
Rev. by J. Richardson, HTo, 26(Jl 1976):479-80.

_____. Metternich. New York: Harper and Row, 1972. Rev.
by M. E. Goldstein, JMH, 48(Mar 1976):132-5.

Palmer, Colin A. Slaves of the White God: Blacks in Mexico,
1570-1650. Cambridge, Mass.: Harvard U Press, 1976.
Rev. by E. D. Fitchen, HRNB, 5(Oct 1976):12.

Palmer, Dave Richard. The Way of the Fox. Westport, Conn.:
Greenwood, 1975. Rev. by J. K. Martin, PH, 43(Oct 1976):
369-70.

Palmer, J. J. N. England, France and Christendom, 1377-99.
London: Routledge and Kegan Paul, 1972. Rev. by J. W.
Sherborne, History, 61(Feb 1976):104-5.

Palmer, R. R., ed. and trans. The School of the French Revolution. Princeton, N. J.: Prin U Press, 1975. Rev. by C.
Tilly, AHR, 81(Je 1976):604; N. Hampson, History, 61(Oct
1976):459; D. Outram, HJ, 19(Mar 1976):283-7; J. K. Burton,
JMH, 48(Sep 1976):555-7.

Palmore, Erdman. The Honorable Elders. Durham, N. C.: Duke
U Press, 1975. Rev. by L. E. Rosensweig, JAS, 36(Nov
1976):152-3.

Paludon, Phillip S. A Covenant with Death. Urbana: U Ill Press,
1975. Rev. by B. W. Collins, HJ, 19(Je 1976):555-8; L. S.
Gerteis, JAH, 62(Mar 1976):999-1000; L. Gara, JISHS, 69
(Aug 1976):238; W. M. Wiecek, JSH, 42(Feb 1976):123-4.

Pamlényi, Ervin, ed. A History of Hungary. London: Collet's,
1975. Rev. by I. Deak, AHR, 81(Apr 1976):420-1.

_____, ed. Social-Economic Researches on the History of East-
Central Europe. Budapest: Akadémiai Kiadó, 1970. Rev. by
J. R. Lampe, AHR, 81(Je 1976):627.

Pampaloni, Guido, ed. Firenze al tempo di Dante. Rome: Pubbli-
cazioni degli Archivi di Stato, 1973. Rev. by J. K. Hyde,
Archives, 12(Aut 1976):189.

Pandey, S. M. Development of Marginal Farmers and Agriculture
Labourers. New Delhi: Shri Ram Centre for Industrial Rela-
tions and Human Resources, 1974. Rev. by M. T. R. Sarma,
IQ, 32(Jl-Sep 1976):372-4.

Pannabecker, S. F. Open Doors: A History of the General Conference Mennonite Church. Newton, Kan.: Faith and Life
Press, 1975. Rev. by F. H. Epp, MQR, 50(Apr 1976):156-8.

293   PANNEL

Pannel, J. P. M. Techniques of Industrial Archaeology. North
Pomfret, Vt.: David and Charles, 1974. Rev. by M. Olmert, Smithsonian, 6(Je 1975):103, 104.

Papachristou, Judith. Women Together. New York: Knopf, 1976.
Rev. by E. I. Perry, HRNB, 5(Oct 1976):10-11.

Papenfuse, Edward C. In Pursuit of Profit: The Annapolis
Merchants in the Era of the American Revolution, 1763-1805.
Baltimore: JHU Press, 1975. Rev. by J. M. Price, AHR,
81(Apr 1976):442; R. Walsh, AmArc, 39(Apr 1976):211; R.
F. Oaks, JAH, 62(Mar 1976):970-1; N. Risjord, MHM, 71
(Sum 1976):273-5; R. G. Miller, PH, 43(Oct 1976):380-2;
M. Egnal, WMQ, 33(Jan 1976):158-60.

Paper, Lewis J. The Promise and the Performance: The Leadership of John F. Kennedy. New York: Crown, 1975. Rev.
by H. S. Parmet, AHR, 81(Oct 1976):1005-6; R. M. Dalfiume,
JAH, 63(Dec 1976):780-1.

Parakatil, Francis. India and United Nation Peace Keeping Opera-
tions. New Delhi: S. Chand, 1975. Rev. by K. P. Saksena,
IQ, 32(Jl-Sep 1976):356-7.

Parish, Peter J. The American Civil War. New York: Holmes
and Meier, 1975. Rev. by B. I. Wiley, AHR, 81(Oct 1976):
976-7; H. G. Pitt, EHR, 91(Jl 1976):608-9; S. G. F. Spackman, History, 61(Oct 1976):408-9; L. H. Johnson, III, JAH,
62(Mar 1976):996-8; E. Ranson, JAmS, 10(Dec 1976):395-6;
J. A. Rawley, JSH, 42(Feb 1976):125-6.

Parker, Derek. Familiar to All: William Lilly and Astrology in
the Seventeenth Century. London: Jonathan Cape, 1975.
Rev. by I. Roots, History, 61(Oct 1976):450.

Parker, Geoffrey. The Army of Flanders and the Spanish Road,
1567-1659: The Logistics of Spanish Victory and Defeat in
the Low Countries' Wars. New York: Cam U Press, 1972.
Rev. by J. X. Evans, AHR, 81(Oct 1976):874-5.

Parker, John, ed. The Journals of Jonathan Carver. St. Paul,
Minn.: Minn Historical Society, 1976. Rev. by L. E.
Oliva, HRNB, 5(Oct 1976):8.

_____ and Carol Urness, eds. The American Revolution: A
Heritage of Change. Minneapolis: U Minn, 1975. Rev. by
R. J. Chaffin, HRNB, 4(Apr 1976):123; P. Goodman, JAH,
63(Sep 1976):391-2; J. K. Martin, MHM, 71(Sum 1976):264-
6; H. H. Jackson, NCHR, 53(Win 1976):95-6.

Parker, Olive. For the Family's Sake. Folkestone: Bailey,
1975. Rev. by R. Hillyer, JEccH, 27(Apr 1976):220.

Parker, R. H., comp. see Pryce-Jones, Janet, comp.

Parker, Robert A. C. Coke of Norfolk. New York: Oxford U Press, 1975. Rev. by A. C. Land, HRNB, 4(Sep 1976):226.

Parker, William N. and Eric L. Jones. European Peasants and Their Markets. Princeton, N.J.: Prin U Press, 1976. Rev. by G. Kish, HRNB, 4(Jl 1976):182-3; P. M. Hohenberg, JEH, 36(Sep 1976):782-4.

Parkinson, Roger. Blood, Toil, Tears and Sweat. New York: David McKay, 1973. Rev. by R. Callahan, AHR, 81(Apr 1976):391-2.

————. Zapata. New York: Stein and Day, 1975. Rev. by J. Hart, HAHR, 56(May 1976):323-4.

Parkman, Aubrey. David Jayne Hill and the Problem of World Peace. Lewisburg, Pa.: Bucknell U Press, 1975. Rev. by R. L. Beisner, JAH, 63(Je 1976):169-70.

Parman, Donald L. The Navajos and the New Deal. New Haven, Conn.: Yale U Press, 1976. Rev. by G. D. Nash, A & W, 18(Win 1976):387-9; J. Hodges, HRNB, 4(May/Je 1976):146-7; N. Lederer, JAriH, 17(Sum 1976):234-5.

Parmet, Herbert S. The Democrats: The Years After FDR. New York: Macmillan, 1976. Rev. by A. Erlebacher, HRNB, 4(Jl 1976):162; K. I. Polakoff, HT, 10(Nov 1976):155-8; R. Griffith, JAH, 63(Dec 1976):777-8; J. D. Doenecke, JSH, 42 (Nov 1976):605-6; D. Lindsey, Mankind, 5(Dec 1976):6.

Parramore, Thomas C. Launching the Craft. Raleigh: Grand Lodge of NCA.F. and A.M., 1975. Rev. by F. Gatton, Jr., NCHR, 53(Sum 1976):320.

Parry, Ellwood. The Image of the Indian and the Black Man in American Art, 1590-1900. New York: George Braziller, 1974. Rev. by J. H. Jenkins, WHQ, 7(Jl 1976):320-1.

Parry, J. H. The Discovery of the Sea. New York: Dial, 1974. Rev. by C. R. Boxer, AHR, 81(Apr 1976):354-5; K. R. Andrews, History, 61(Je 1976):265-6.

Parry, Noel and Jose Parry. The Rise of the Medical Profession. New York: International Publications, 1976. Rev. by M. H. Saffron, HRNB, 4(Aug 1976):206-7.

Parry, V. J. and M. E. Yapp, eds. War, Technology and Society in the Middle East. New York: Oxford U Press, 1975. Rev. by A. C. Hess, AHR, 81(Oct 1976):788-99.

Parsons, Stephen L., ed. see Medlin, Virgil D., ed.

295   PARTLOW

Partlow, Miriam. Liberty, Liberty County, and the Atascosito District. Austin, Tex.: Pemberton, 1974. Rev. by P. R. Scott, ETHJ, 14(Spr 1976):67-8; J. V. Reese, JSH, 42(Feb 1976): 143-4.

Partner, Peter. The Lands of St. Peter. Berkeley: U Cal Press, 1972. Rev. by D. E. Queller, AHR, 81(Oct 1976): 838-9.

Pasler, Rudolph J. and Margaret C. Pasler. The New Jersey Federalists. Rutherford, N. J.: Fairleigh Dickinson U Press, 1975. Rev. by D. B. Cole, AHR, 81(Oct 1976):965.

Pastore, Alessandro. Nella Valtellina del tardo cinquecento: fede, cultura, società. Milan: Sugarco 5e Edizioni, 1975. Rev. by D. Fenlon, HJ, 19(Dec 1976):1023-4.

Pastore, Carlos. La lucha por la tierra en el Paraguay. Montevideo: Editorial Antequera, 1972. Rev. by H. G. Warren, HAHR, 56(Aug 1976):465-6.

Paterson, Thomas G., ed. American Imperialism and Anti-Imperialism. New York: Crowell, 1973. Rev. by J. E. Pluta, HAHR, 56(Feb 1976):155.

Patschovsky, Alexander. Die Anfänge einer ständigen Inquisition in Böhmen. New York: Walter de Gruyter, 1975. Rev. by P. W. Knoll, CH, 45(Je 1976):252.

Patterson, A. Temple. Tyrwhitt of the Harwich Force. London: Macdonald, 1973. Rev. by A. N. Ryan, History, 61(Feb 1976):134-5.

Patterson, Bryce see Leadabrand, Russ

Patterson, James T. America in the Twentieth Century. New York: Harcourt Brace Jovanovich, 1976. Rev. by J. D. Doenecke, HT, 10(Nov 1976):147-50.

Patterson, K. David. The Northern Gabon Coast to 1875. Oxford: Oxford U Press, 1975. Rev. by D. Birmingham, History, 61(Feb 1976):154; P. M. Martin, JAfH, 17(Num 3, 1976): 454-5.

Patterson, R. B. Earldom of Gloucester Charters. Oxford: Oxford U Press, 1973. Rev. by D. J. A. Matthew, EHR, 91 (Jl 1976):599-601; R. R. Davies, History, 61(Feb 1976):98-9.

Patterson, Sheila, ed. see Fortes, Meyer, ed.

Paul, John. Mozambique: Memoirs of a Revolution. New York: Penguin, 1975. Rev. by D. Birmingham, AfAf, 75(Jan 1976): 119-20.

PAWLEY 296

Pawley, Bernard and Margaret Pawley. Rome and Canterbury
Through Four Centuries: A Study of the Relations Between
the Church of Rome and the Anglican Churches, 1530-1973.
New York: Seabury Press, 1975. Rev. by W. A. Johnson,
CH, 45(Sep 1976):403-5; F. E. Sugeno, HMPEC, 45(Sep 1976):
347-8.

Pawson, Michael and David Buisseret. Port Royal, Jamaica. New
York: Oxford U Press, 1975. Rev. by M. J. MacLeod,
HRNB, 4(Mar 1976):103.

Payne, Darwin. The Man of Only Yesterday: Frederick Lewis Allen. New York: Harper and Row, 1975. Rev. by N. M.
Blake, AHR, 81(Je 1976):688-9; B. K. Zobrist, JAH, 62(Mar
1976):1041-2.

Payne, Ernest A. Out of Great Tribulation: Baptists in the
U. S. S. R. London: Baptist Union of Great Britain and Ireland, 1974. Rev. by F. H. Thomas, Jr., BHH, 10(Jl 1975):
182, 186; J. L. Garrett, Jr., JCS, 18(Win 1976):146-7.

Payne, Harry C. The Philosophers and the People. New Haven:
Yale U Press, 1976. Rev. by S. M. Bolkosky, HRNB, 5(Oct
1976):14-15.

Payne, P. L. British Entrepreneurship in the Nineteenth Century.
London: Macmillan, 1974. Rev. by B. E. Supple, BH, 17
(Jan 1975):76-7; R. A. Church, History, 61(Feb 1976):129-30.

Payne, Stanley G. Basque Nationalism. Reno: U Nevada Press,
1975. Rev. by R. D. Tinnell, AHR, 81(Oct 1976):874; V. R.
Pilapil, HAHR, 56(Aug 1976):496-7.

Pearce, Ivy see Jäger, Otto A.

Pearlman, Moshe. The Maccabees. New York: Macmillan, 1973.
Rev. by E. J. Vardaman, JCS, 17(Win 1975):151-2.

Pearson, Keith L. The Indian in American History. New York:
Harcourt Brace Jovanovich, 1973. Rev. by L. Robbins, AA,
78(Mar 1976):156-7.

Pearson, M. N. Merchants and Rulers in Gujarat. Berkeley: U
Cal Press, 1976. Rev. by A. D. Gupta, JAS, 36(Nov 1976):
158-60.

Pearson, Mary, ed. see Ferrier, Douglas M., comp.

Pearson, R. E. see Ruddock, J. G.

Pease, Jane H. and William H. Pease. Bound with Them in
Chains. Westport, Conn.: Greenwood, 1972. Rev. by M.
K. Bonsteel Tachau, FCHQ, 50(Apr 1976):92-4.

297   PEASE

_____ and _____. They Who Would Be Free. New York:
Atheneum, 1974. Rev. by B. Wyatt-Brown, AHR, 81(Apr
1976):446-7; D. M. Jacobs, NYHSQ, 60(Jan/Apr 1976):82-3.

Peattie, Mark R. Ishiwara Kanji and Japan's Confrontation with the
West. Princeton, N.J.: Prin U Press, 1975. Rev. by J.
C. Lebra, AHR, 81(Oct 1976):942-3; G. M. Berger, JJS, 2
(Aut 1975):156-69.

Peck, Ira, William Johnson and Frances Plotkin. Scholastic World
History Program. 4 vols. New York: Scholastic Book Service, 1976. Rev. by J. F. Marran, HT, 10(Nov 1976):126-7.

Pedler, F. The Lion and the Unicorn in Africa. London: Heineman, 1974. Rev. by M. Johnson, Africa, 46(Num 2, 1976):
209; P. E. H. Hair, History, 61(Feb 1976):152-3.

Peel, Lynnette J. Rural Industry in the Port Philip Region, 1835-
1880. Melbourne: Melbourne U Press, 1974. Rev. by P.
Parry, AgH, 50(Jl 1976):534-5.

Pei Huang. Autocracy at Work: A Study of the Yung-cheng Period,
1723-1735. Bloomington: Ind U Press ... 1975. Rev. by
J. Spence, AHR, 81(Oct 1976):933-4.

Pelenski, Jaroslaw. Russia and Kazan. The Hague: Mouton,
1974. Rev. by D. C. Matuszewski, AHR, 81(Feb 1976):183.

Pelikan, Jaroslav. The Christian Tradition. Vol. 2. Chicago: U
Chicago Press, 1974. Rev. by J. E. Rexine, AHR, 81(Feb
1976):119-20.

Pelon, Olivier, comp. Mallia, Plan du site, plans du palais
indices. Paris: Paul Geuthner, 1974. Rev. by J. W.
Graham, AJA, 80(Fall 1976):429.

Pendry, E. D. Elizabethan Prisons and Prison Scenes. Salzburg:
U Salzburg, 1974. Rev. by J. Goring, EHR, 91(Apr 1976):
419; E. W. Ives, History, 61(Je 1976):283-4.

Penney, Sherry. Patrician in Politics: Daniel Dewey Barnard of
New York. Port Washington, N.Y.: Kennikat, 1974. Rev.
by P. Levine, AHR, 81(Oct 1976):971-2.

Penrose, E. F., ed. European Imperialism and the Partition of
Africa. London: Cass, 1975. Rev. by J. D. Hargreaves,
JAfH, 17(Num 3, 1976):461-2.

Penzel, Klaus see Deschner, John, ed.

Percival, John, ed. see Loyn, H. R., ed.

Perez i Ferrer, Francisco. Notes Historiques: Aportació a la

historia de Soller. Palma de Mallorca: Graficas Miramar,
1974. Rev. by N. Holub, TAm, 33(Jl 1976):182-3.

Perkins, David and Norman Tanis, comps. Native Americans of
North America. Northridge, Cal.: Cal St U, 1975. Rev.
by H. G. Jordan, JOW, 15(Jan 1976):126-7.

Perkins, Dwight H., ed. China's Modern Economy in Historical
Perspective. Stanford, Cal.: Stanford U Press, 1975. Rev.
by G. Cochran, JAS, 36(Nov 1976):142-5.

Perkins, Edwin J. Financing Anglo-American Trade: The House
of Brown, 1800-1880. Cambridge, Mass.: Harvard U Press,
1975. Rev. by P. J. Coleman, AHR, 81(Oct 1976):967; R.
Sylla, BHR, 50(Spr 1976):116-18; L. E. Ambrosius, HRNB,
4(Jan 1976):53; S. Bruchey, JAH, 63(Sep 1976):406-7; T. P.
Govan, WMH, 60(Aut 1976):65-6.

Perrigo, Lynn I. La Reunión: A Personal Chronicle of the Munici-
ple Consolidation of Las Vegas, New Mexico. Peralta, New
Mexico: Yguado Press, 1975. Rev. by D. W. Whisenhunt,
NMHR, 51(Apr 1976):162-3.

Perrot, D., ed. see Wilson, F., ed.

Perrot, Michelle. Les Ouvriers en Grève: France 1871-1890.
Paris: Mouton, 1974. Rev. by E. Schulkind, History, 61
(Feb 1976):138.

Perry, John and Cassandra Perry, comps. A Chief Is a Chief by
the People: The Autobiography of Stimela Jason Jingoes.
London: Oxford U Press, 1975. Rev. by P. Spray, JMAS,
14(Je 1976):368-9.

Perry, P. J. British Farming in the Great Depression, 1870-1914.
Newton Abbot: David and Charles, 1974. Rev. by R. Perren,
History, 61(Feb 1976):129.

Perry, Rosalie Sandra. Charles Ives and the American Mind.
Kent, Ohio: Kent St U Press, 1974. Rev. by P. R. Baker,
JAH, 62(Mar 1976):1031.

Persons, Stow. The Decline of American Gentility. New York:
Columbia U Press, 1973. Rev. by F. H. Matthews, CHR,
57(Mar 1976):83-6.

Pescatello, Ann. Female and Male in Latin America. Pittsburgh:
U Pittsburgh Press, 1973. Rev. by C. Bausch, AA, 78(Je
1976):402.

Pessen, Edward. Riches, Class and Power Before the Civil War.
Lexington, Mass.: Heath, 1973. Rev. by J. A. Tarr, JIH,
7(Sum 1976):172-8.

Peterkiewicz, Jerzy. The Third Adam. Oxford: Oxford U Press, 1975. Rev. by R. F. Leslie, History, 61(Je 1976):326.

Peters, Edward, ed. Monks, Bishops and Pagans. Philadelphia: U Pa Press, 1975. Rev. by H. Rosenberg, CH, 45(Mar 1976):101; B. Hamilton, JEccH, 27(Oct 1976):417-18.

Peters, F. E. Allah's Commonwealth: A History of Islam in the Near East 600-1100 A. D. New York: Simon and Schuster, 1974. Rev. by G. F. Hourani, JNES, 35(Oct 1976):296-7.

Peterson, Charles S. Look to the Mountains. Provo, Utah: BYU Press, 1975. Rev. by C. J. Bayard, A & W, 18(Spr 1976): 93-4; L. B. Lee, JAH, 62(Mar 1976):1010; J. M. Haymond, UHQ, 44(Spr 1976):181.

Peterson, Mendel. The Funnel of Gold. Boston: Little, Brown, 1975. Rev. by R. Pike, AHR, 81(Oct 1976):1009-10; E. Lyon, FHQ, 55(Jl 1976):80-1; C. R. Boxer, HAHR, 56(Nov 1976):645-7.

Pethybridge, Roger. The Social Prelude to Stalinism. New York: St. Martin's, 1974. Rev. by A. Dallin, AHR, 81(Feb 1976): 188.

Petit, Norman, ed. see Hooker, Thomas

Petit, Ramon, ed. see de Epalza, Miguel, ed.

Petras, James and Morris Morley. The United States and Chile: Imperialism and the Overthrow of the Allende Government. New York: Monthly Review, 1975. Rev. by F. N. Nunn, HAHR, 56(Feb 1976):149-51; M. Fleet, PHR, 45(Nov 1976): 634-5.

_____, ed. see Lopez, Adalberto, ed.

Pettit, Arthur G. Mark Twain and the South. Lexington: U Press Ky, 1974. Rev. by P. Fatout, AHR, 81(Apr 1976):457; E. W. Hirshberg, FHQ, 54(Jan 1976):408-10.

Petz, Weldon E. In the Presence of Abraham Lincoln. Harrogate, Tenn.: Lincoln Memorial U, 1973. Rev. by R. D. Rietveld, JISHS, 69(Aug 1976):238-9.

Petzina, Dietmar, ed. see Mommsen, Hans, ed.

Pfeffer, Leo. God, Caesar, and the Constitution. Boston: Beacon, 1975. Rev. by R. T. Miller, JCS, 18(Spr 1976):327-30.

Pfeiffer, Heinrich. Zur Ikonographie von Raffaels Disputa. Rome: Università Gregoriana Editrice, 1975. Rev. by M. P. Gilmore, CaHR, 62(Jan 1976):116-18.

Pfister, Rudolf. Kirchengeschichte der Schweiz. Vol. 2. Zürich: Theologischer Verlag, 1974. Rev. by H. A. Oberman, CH, 45(Sep 1976):381-2.

Pflug, Warner W., ed. A Guide to the Archives of Labor History and Urban Affairs: Wayne State University. Detroit: Wayne St U Press, 1974. Rev. by K. Winn, PNQ, 67(Jan 1976):46.

Phelps, Gilbert. Tragedy of Paraguay. New York: St. Martin's, 1975. Rev. by H. G. Warren, HAHR, 56(Feb 1976):144-5; J. H. Williams, TAm, 32(Apr 1976):659-60.

Phillips, Cabell. The 1940s: Decade of Triumph and Trouble. New York: Macmillan, 1975. Rev. by A. Theoharis, AHR, 81(Oct 1976):999; R. Polenberg, HRNB, 4(Jan 1976):51.

Phillips, E. D. Aspects of Greek Medicine. New York: St. Martin's, 1973. Rev. by W. D. Smith, AHR, 81(Feb 1976): 104.

Phillips, George Harwood. Chiefs and Challengers: Indian Resistance and Cooperation in Southern California. Berkeley: U Cal Press, 1975. Rev. by M. P. Servin, AHR, 81(Oct 1976):975; R. F. Heizer, CHQ, 55(Spr 1976):87-8; D. C. Cutter, HAHR, 56(May 1976):328-9; D. B. Nunis, JAH, 63 (Je 1976):126-7; J. Caughey, PHR, 45(Aug 1976):443-4; H. Kelsey, SCQ, 58(Spr 1976):128-9; E. H. Howes, WHQ, 7(Oct 1976):422-4.

Phillips, John. The Reformation of Images: Destruction of Art in England 1535-1660. Berkeley: U Cal Press, 1973. Rev. by C. Russell, EHR, 91(Apr 1976):416-17.

Phillips, Nigel, ed. and trans. see Sweeney, Amin, ed. and trans.

Phillips, P. Lee. Notes on the Life and Works of Bernard Romans. Gainesville: U Presses Fla, 1975. Rev. by L. De Vorsey, Jr., GHQ, 60(Sum 1976):187-8.

Phillips, Patricia. Early Farmers of West Mediterranean Europe. London: Hutchinson, 1975. Rev. by R. D. Whitehouse, Antiquity, 50(Je 1976):165-6.

Phippen, George. The Life of a Cowboy. Tucson: U Ariz Press, 1975. Rev. by F. Olds, ChOk, 54(Sum 1976):285-6.

Pickens, William, comp. A List of References for the History of Apiculture and Sericulture in America. Davis, Cal.: U Cal Press, 1976. Rev. by Editor, NDH, 43(Sum 1976):47.

Pickering, James H., ed. The World Turned Upside Down: Prose and Poetry of the American Revolution. Port Washington,

N. Y.: Kennikat, 1975. Rev. by D. R. Jamieson, HRNB, 4 (Jan 1976):54-5.

Pickl, Othmar, ed. Die Wirtschaftlichen Auswirkungen der Türken Kriege. Groz: Universitat Groz, 1971. Rev. by R. Knauerhause, JEH, 36(Jl 1976):472-6.

Pieper, Thomas I. and James B. Gidney. Fort Laurens, 1778-79. Kent, Ohio: Kent St U Press, 1976. Rev. by L. H. Harrison, AHI, 11(Dec 1976):50.

Pierce, Neil R. The Border South States: People, Politics, and Power in the Five Border South States. New York: Norton, 1975. Rev. by W. W. Holt, Jr., VMHB, 84(Apr 1976):216-18.

Pierce, Richard D., ed. The Records of the First Church in Salem, Massachusetts 1629-1736. Salem: Essex Institute, 1974. Rev. by G. E. Kershaw, NEQ, 49(Mar 1976):142-4; G. Selement, WMQ, 33(Jan 1976):173-4.

Pike, Fredrick B. and Thomas Stritch, eds. The New Corporatism. Notre Dame, Inc.: U Notre Dame Press, 1974. Rev. by L. E. Aguilar, HAHR, 56(Feb 1976):116-18.

Pike, Kermit J. Guide to Shaker Manuscripts. Cleveland: Western Reserve Historical Society, 1974. Rev. by A. R. Suelflow, AmArc, 39(Jan 1976):48.

Pike, Robert E. Drama on the Connecticut. Eatontown, N.J.: H-H Press, 1975. Rev. by S. R. Waterman, VH, 44(Sum 1976):180-2.

Pilch, Andrzej. The Student Political Movement in Poland, 1932-1939. Cracow: Universytetu Jagiellonskiego, 1972. Rev. by G. J. Lerski, AHR, 81(Je 1976):629-30.

Pilcher, William W. The Portland Longshoremen. New York: Holt, Rinehart and Winston, 1972. Rev. by L. D. Borman, AA, 78(Mar 1976):161.

Pilkington, John, ed. Stark Young. 2 vols. Baton Rouge: LSU Press, 1975. Rev. by W. W. Wooden, JMiH, 38(Aug 1976): 317-20.

Pilsudski, Jozef. Year 1920 and Its Climax. New York: Pilsudski Institute, 1972. Rev. by B. Dmytryshyn, AHR, 81(Je 1976): 629.

Pimlott, J. A. R. The Englishman's Holiday. New York: International Publications Service, 1976. Rev. by J. P. Zaccano, Jr., HRNB, 5(Oct 1976):20.

Pincherle, Marcella. Moderatismo politico e riforma religioso in

Terenzio Mamiani. Milan: Dott. A. Giuffre Editore, 1973. Rev. by R. Grew, AHR, 81(Feb 1976):178.

Pines, Jim. Blacks in Films. London: Studio Vista, 1975. Rev. by R. Willett, JAmS, 10(Apr 1976):128.

Pini, Ingo, ed. see Matz, Friedrich, ed.

Pinkett, Harold T., ed. see Evans, Frank B., ed.

Pinney, Thomas, ed. The Letters of Thomas Babington Macaulay. Vols. I and II. New York: Cam U Press, 1974. Rev. by W. Thomas, EHR, 91(Oct 1976):868-9; N. Gash, History, 61 (Feb 1976):123-4.

Pino Iturrieta, Elías, ed. Castro: epistolaria presidencial. Caracas: Universidad Central de Venezuela, 1974. Rev. by W. J. Burggraaff, HAHR, 56(May 1976):332-3.

Pipes, Richard. Russia Under the Old Regime. London: Weidenfeld and Nicolson, 1974. Rev. by D. Atkinson, AHR, 81(Apr 1976):423-4; I. De Madariaga, History, 61(Feb 1976):89-91; R. F. Drew, HRNB, 4(Jan 1976):67.

Pippert, Wesley. Memo for 1976: Some Political Options. Downers Grove, Ill.: Intervarsity Press, 1974. Rev. by G. R. Avant, JCS, 17(Spr 1975):349-50.

Pirinen, Kauko see Jutikkala, Eino

Piscitelli, Enzo, et al. Italia 1945-48: Le Origini della Repubblica. Turin: Giappichelli, 1974. Rev. by M. Clark, EHR, 91(Apr 1976):470-1; R. A. H. Robinson, History, 61(Je 1976): 331-2.

Pitkin, Thomas M. Keepers of the Gate: A History of Ellis Island. New York: NYU Press, 1975. Rev. by C. C. Qualey, JAH, 62(Mar 1976):1020-1.

Pivar, David J. Purity Crusade. Westport, Conn.: Greenwood, 1973. Rev. by F. L. Beach, CaHR, 62(Jl 1976):507-8.

Plaschka, Richard Georg, Horst Haselsteiner and Arnold Suppan. Innere Front, Militärassistenz, Widerstand und Umsturz in der Donaumonarchie 1918. 2 vols. Munich: R. Oldenbourg Verlag, 1974. Rev. by F. L. Carsten, EHR, 91(Jl 1976): 613-15.

Plath, David W., ed. Adult Episdoes in Japan. Leiden: E. J. Brill, 1975. Rev. by H. Wagatsuma, JAS, 36(Nov 1976): 153-4.

Platonov, S. F. Moscow and the West. Hattiesburg, Miss.:

303   PLATT

Academic International, 1972. Rev. by J. T. Fuhrmann,
CaHR, 62(Apr 1976):269-70.

Platt, Colin. The English Medieval Town. London: Secker and
Warburg, 1976. Rev. by R. Swanson, Archives, 12(Aut 1976):
189-90.

_____, et al. Excavations in Medieval Southampton, 1953-1969.
2 vols. Leicester: U Press, 1975. Rev. by T. Hassall,
Antiquity, 50(Sep-Dec 1976):248-9.

Pletcher, David M. The Diplomacy of Annexation: Texas, Oregon
and the Mexican War. Columbia: U Mo Press, 1973. Rev.
by S. F. Wells, Jr., CHR, 57(Mar 1976):86-87; W. D. Jones,
PNQ, 67(Jan 1976):35.

Plog, Fred see Martin, Paul S.

Plongeron, Bernard. Théologie et politique au siècle des lumières
(1770-1820). Geneva: Librairie Droz, 1973. Rev. by A. C.
Kors, JMH, 48(Mar 1976):146-9.

Plotkin, Frances see Peck, Ira

Plum, Gunter. Gesellschaftsstruktur und politisches Bewusstsein
in einer katholischen Region, 1928-1933. Stuttgart: Deutsche
Verlags-Anstalt, 1972. Rev. by J. S. Conway, AHR, 81(Feb
1976):171.

Pocock, J. G. A. The Machiavellian Moment: Florentine Political
Thought and the Atlantic Republican Tradition. Princeton,
N.J.: Prin U Press, 1975. Rev. by M. M. Goldsmith,
AHR, 81(Oct 1976):890-1; D. Forbes, HJ, 19(Je 1976):553-6;
C. Robbins, WMQ, 33(Apr 1976):335-7.

Pokora, Timoteus, trans. Hsin-lun (New Treatise) and Other
Writings by Huan T'an. Ann Arbor: U Mich Press, 1975.
Rev. by D. R. Knechtges, JAS, 36(Nov 1976):138-9.

Pokrovskii, N. N. Documentary Sources on the History of Taxable
State Ownership of Land in Russia from the 14th to the Be-
ginning of the 16th Century. Novosibirsk: Izdatel'stvo
"Nauka," 1973. Rev. by G. Alef, AHR, 81(Feb 1976):118-19.

Poliakov, Léon. The Aryan Myth: A History of Racist and Nationalist Ideas in Europe. London: Sussex U Press, 1974.
Rev. by M. D. Biddiss, History, 61(Je 1976):296.

_____. The History of Anti-Semitism. 3 vols. London:
Routledge and Kegan Paul, 1975. Rev. by M. D. Biddiss,
History, 61(Je 1976):296; R. I. Moore, History, 61(Oct 1976):
436.

POLK   304

Polk, James K. Correspondence of James K. Polk. Vol. III.
(Herbert Weaver and Kermit L. Hall, eds.) Nashville:
Vanderbilt U Press, 1975. Rev. by J. N. Riismandel, AI,
43(Spr 1976):309-10; E. C. Nagy, ETHJ, 14(Fall 1976):73-4;
J. H. Parks, FHQ, 55(Jl 1976):90-1; J. O. M. Werner, IMH,
72(Je 1976):174-6; R. V. Remini, JAH, 62(Mar 1976):949-50;
H. C. Coles, JMiH, 38(Feb 1976):121-2; E. A. Miles, JSH,
42(May 1976):284-5.

Pollins, Harold. Britain's Railways. Newton Abbot: David and
Charles, 1971. Rev. by M. C. Reed, BH, 17(Jan 1975):82-3.

Poltavskii, M. A. The Austrian People and the Anschluss, 1938.
Moscow: Izdatel'stvo "Nauka," 1971. Rev. by S. B. Winters,
AHR, 81(Feb 1976):174-5.

Polzer, Charles W. Rules and Precepts of the Jesuit Missions of
Northwestern New Spain. Tucson: U Ariz Press, 1976.
Rev. by P. O'Grady, HRNB, 5(Oct 1976):3-4; N. S. Furman,
JOW, 15(Jl 1976):105-6.

Pomeroy, Earl. The Pacific Slope. Seattle: U Wash Press, 1973.
Rev. by T. B. Colbert, JOW, 15(Apr 1976):127.

Pomeroy, Sarah B. Goddesses, Whores, Wives, and Slaves:
Women in Classical Antiquity. New York: Schocken, 1975.
Rev. by M. C. Horowitz, AHR, 81(Oct 1976):825; C. C.
Patsavos, Historian, 39(Nov 1976):112-13; E. Stansfield, Man-
kind, 5(Oct 1976):55.

Pompa, Leon. Vico. Cambridge: Cam U Press, 1975. Rev. by
P. Gardiner, History, 61(Feb 1976):72-3.

Poniatowski, Elena. Massacre in Mexico. New York: Viking,
1975. Rev. by P. Kelso, HAHR, 56(Aug 1976):509.

Ponko, Vincent, Jr. Ships, Seas, and Scientists: U. S. Naval
Exploration in the Nineteenth Century. Annapolis: Naval Institute Press, 1974. Rev. by W. Stanton, PHR, 45(Nov 1976):
613-14.

Pons, Frank Moya. Historia colonial de Santo Domingo. Santiago:
Universidad Catolica Madre y Maestra, 1974. Rev. by W.
Borah, HAHR, 56(May 1976):317-19.

Pontgieter, Hermina and James Taylor Dunn, eds. Gopher Reader,
II. St. Paul: Minn Historical Society, 1975. Rev. by M.
Kaplan, NDH, 43(Win 1976):42-3.

Pool, William C. A Historical Atlas of Texas. Austin, Tx: Encino Press, 1975. Rev. by T. R. Young, A & W, 18(Sum
1976):183-4.

Poole, Stafford. A History of the Congregation of the Mission, 1625-1843. Camarillo, Cal.: Author, 1973. Rev. by L. J. Lekai, CaHR, 62(Apr 1976):275-6.

_____, ed. see de Las Casas, Bartolomé

Porter, Bernard. The Lion's Share: A Short History of British Imperialism, 1850-1976. New York: Longman, 1976. Rev. by L. R. Bisceglia, HRNB, 5(Oct 1976):21; G. Douds, HTo, 26(Jl 1976):476-8.

Porter, Jonathan. Tseng Kuo-fan's Private Bureaucracy. Berkeley: U Cal Press, 1972. Rev. by S. Wu, AHR, 81(Oct 1976):934.

Post, Kenneth and Michael Vickers. Structure and Conflict in Nigeria 1960-1966. Madison: U Wis Press, 1973. Rev. by F. Chalk, AHR, 81(Feb 1976):192-3.

Postel, Rainer. Johann Martin Lappenberg: Ein Beitrag zur Geschichte der Geschichtswissenschaft im 19. Jahrhundert. Lübeck: Matthiesen Verlag, 1972. Rev. by R. A. Pois, AHR, 81(Oct 1976):880.

Potter, David M. The Impending Crisis, 1848-1861. New York: Harper & Row, 1976. Rev. by E. Pessen, HRNB, 4(May/Je 1976):138; M. G. Baxter, JAH, 63(Dec 1976):719-20.

Potter, Jim. The American Economy Between the World Wars. New York: Wiley, 1975. Rev. by R. Higgs, AHR, 81(Je 1976):685-6; H. G. Nicholas, EHR, 91(Apr 1976):459-60.

Potts, Richard, ed. A Calendar of Cornish Glebe Terriers, 1673-1735. Torquay, England: Devonshire Press, 1974. Rev. by A. Jewell, AgH, 50(Apr 1976):426-7.

Poulantzas, Nicos. Fascism and Dictatorship. Atlantic Highlands, N.J.: Humanities, 1975. Rev. by F. R. Willis, AHR, 81 (Oct 1976):848-9.

Poulose, T. T., ed. Indian Ocean Power Rivalry. New Delhi: Young Asia Publications, 1974. Rev. by B. R. Babu, IQ, 32(Apr-Je 1976):243-5.

_____. Succession in International Law. New Delhi: Orient Longman, 1974. Rev. by V. Baxi, IQ, 32(Jl-Sep 1976):393-5.

Poulsen, Vagn. Les Portraits Romains II. Copenhagen: Glyptothèque Ny Carlsberg, 1974. Rev. by R. Brilliant, AJA, 80 (Spr 1976):218-19.

Pounds, N. J. G. An Economic History of Medieval Europe. London: Longmans, 1974. Rev. by K. F. Drew, AHR, 81(Apr 1976):368; R. H. Hilton, History, 61(Je 1976):244-5.

Powell, Philip Wayne. Soldiers, Indians and Silver: North America's First Frontier War. Tempe, Ariz.: Ariz St U, 1975. Rev. by E. A. Beilharz, AHR, 81(Oct 1976):1010.

Powell, W. R., ed. Victoria County History of Essex. Vol. VI. London: Oxford U Press, 1973. Rev. by R. Ashton, EHR, 91(Jan 1976):170; J. L. Bolton, History, 61(Feb 1976):78-9.

Power, Eileen. Medieval Women. New York: Cam U Press, 1976. Rev. by K. F. Drew, AHR, 81(Oct 1976):833-4; J. W. Baldwin, HRNB, 4(Jl 1976):182.

Powicke, Michael R. The Community of the Realm. New York: Knopf, 1973. Rev. by B. Lyon, AHR, 81(Feb 1976):111-12.

Powley, Edward B. The Naval Side of King William's War. Hamden, Conn.: Archon, 1972. Rev. by D. A. Baugh, AHR, 81(Je 1976):584.

Poznanskii, V. S. Essays on the Armed Struggle of the Siberian Soviets Against the Counterrevolution, 1917-1918. Novosibirsk: Izdatel'stvo "Nauka," 1973. Rev. by C. F. Smith, AHR, 81 (Feb 1976):187.

Pradervand, Marcel. A Century of Service: A History of the World Alliance of Reformed Churches, 1875-1975. Grand Rapids, Mich.: Eerdmans, 1975. Rev. by P. D. Jordan, CH, 45(Sep 1976):392-3.

Prain, Ronald. Copper: The Anatomy of an Industry. London: Mining Journal Books, 1975. Rev. by C. Perrings, JAfH, 17(Num 2, 1976):318-19.

Prang, Margaret. N. W. Rowell: Ontario Nationalist. Buffalo: U Tor Press, 1975. Rev. by T. Faulkner, CH, 45(Je 1976): 267-8.

Pratt, Cranford. The Critical Phase in Tanzania 1945-1968. New York: Cambridge U Press, 1976. Rev. by R. Yeager, HRNB, 4(Jl 1976):170-1.

Pratt, Davis, ed. The Photographic Eye of Ben Shahn. Cambridge, Mass.: Harvard U Press, 1975. Rev. by G. Porter, BHR, 50(Spr 1976):122-3.

Pratt, Lawrence R. East of Malta, West of Suez. New York: Cam U Press, 1975. Rev. by K. E. Dunlop, AHR, 81(Oct 1976):917-18; E. B. Scovill, HRNB, 4(May/Je 1976):151-2.

Prauss, Gerold. Kant und das Problem der Dinge an sich. Bonn: Bouvier Verlag H. Grundmann, 1974. Rev. by R. B. Pippin, JHP, 14(Jl 1976):374-8.

307   PRED

Pred, Allan R. Urban Growth and the Circulation of Information.
 Cambridge, Mass.: Harvard U Press, 1973. Rev. by J. A.
 Tarr, JIH, 7(Sum 1976):172-8.

Press, Irwin. Tradition and Adaptation: Life in a Modern Yucatan
 Maya Village. Westport, Conn.: Greenwood, 1975. Rev. by
 G. Foster, HAHR, 56(Nov 1976):678-80.

Preston, R. H., ed. Technology and Social Justice: A Symposium
 Sponsored by the International Humanum Foundation. Valley
 Forge, Pa.: Judson, 1971. Rev. by T. B. Maston, JCS,
 17(Aut 1975):533-5.

Preston, Richard Arthur, ed. For Friends at Home. Montreal:
 McGill-Queens U Press, 1974. Rev. by J. J. Talman, AHR,
 81(Je 1976):696; W. T. Jackson, JAH, 63(Je 1976):119-20;
 P. A. M. Taylor, JAmS, 10(Aug 1976):274-5; J. A. Brown,
 JOW, 15(Apr 1976):133; J. M. Bumsted, WHQ, 7(Jl 1976):
 322-3.

Price, J. L. Culture and Society in the Dutch Republic During the
 Seventeenth Century. New York: Scribner's, 1974. Rev. by
 G. D. Homan, Historian, 38(Feb 1976):330-2; G. C. Gibbs,
 History, 61(Je 1976):291-2.

Price, Jacob M. France and the Chesapeake. 2 vols. Ann Arbor:
 U Mich Press, 1973. Rev. by J. F. Bosher, CHR, 57(Mar
 1976):93-5; P. G. M. Dickson, EHR, 91(Jan 1976):132-3.

Price, Roger. The Economic Modernization of France, 1730-1880.
 New York: Wiley, 1975. Rev. by C. Fairchilds, BHR, 50
 (Sum 1976):250-1; D. P. Resnick, HRNB, 4(Apr 1976):134-5.

Pridham, Geoffrey. Hitler's Rise to Power. London: Hart-Davis,
 MacGibbon, 1973. Rev. by K. E. War, ESR, 6(Jl 1976):
 401-2.

Priestley, Raymond E. Antarctic Adventure. n.p.: Stephen
 Greene, 1975. Rev. by R. Beeston, Smithsonian, 6(Jan
 1976):102, 104, 106.

Prill, Felician. Ireland, Britain and Germany, 1871-1914. New
 York: Barnes and Noble, 1975. Rev. by J. M. Hernon, Jr.,
 AHR, 81(Oct 1976):846-7; P. M. Kennedy, EHR, 91(Oct 1976):
 928; M. J. Lyons, Historian, 39(Nov 1976):122.

Pringle, Robert. Rajahs and Rebels. Ithaca, N.Y.: Cornell U
 Press, 1970. Rev. by M. Clarke, AHR, 81(Apr 1976):437.

Printila, L. A. The Political History of Finland 1809-1966.
 London: Heineman, 1976. Rev. by J. I. Kolehmainen,
 HRNB, 4(Jl 1976):181-2.

Pritchard, R. M. Housing and the Spatial Structure of the City. New York: Cam U Press, 1976. Rev. by R. J. Helmstadter, HRNB, 5(Oct 1976):23.

Proctor, Samuel, ed. Eighteenth-Century Florida and Its Borderlands. Gainesville: U Presses Fla., 1975. Rev. by R. L. Gold, JAH, 63(Dec 1976):683-4; R. K. Murdoch, JSH, 42(Feb 1976):102-3.

Proudfoot, Mary. British Politics and Government, 1951-1970. Atlantic Highlands, N.J.: Humanities, 1974. Rev. by T. J. Spinner, Jr., AHR, 81(Je 1976):596.

Provencher, Ronald. Mainland Southeast Asia. Pacific Palisades, Cal.: Goodyear, 1975. Rev. by A. T. Kirsch, JAS, 36(Nov 1976):181-2.

Prucha, Francis Paul, ed. Americanizing the American Indians. Cambridge, Mass.: Harvard U Press, 1973. Rev. by L. Robbins, AA, 78(Mar 1976):156-7.

_____, ed. Documents of United States Indian Policy. Lincoln: U Neb Press, 1975. Rev. by R. L. Nichols, A & W, 18(Aut 1976):295-7; D. A. Walker, NDH, 43(Sum 1976):46.

Pruessen, Ronald W., ed. see Miller, Lynn H., ed.

Pryce-Jones, Janet and R. H. Parket, comps. Accounting in Scotland. n.p.: Institute of Chartered Accountants of Scotland, 1974. Rev. by S. Marriner, BH, 17(Jl 1975):205-6.

Pugh, A. R., ed. see Charlton, D. G., ed.

Pullan, Brian. A History of Early Renaissance. New York: St. Martin's, 1972. Rev. by R. C. Trexler, CaHR, 62(Jan 1976):96-7.

Puppi, Lionello. Andrea Palladio. New York: Graphic Society, 1975. Rev. by C. Page, Smithsonian, 6(Jan 1976):109-10.

Purcell, L. Edward, ed. see Grant, H. Roger, ed.

Purcell, Susan Kaufman. The Mexican Profit-Sharing Decision. Berkeley: U Cal Press, 1975. Rev. by V. Padgett, HAHR, 56(Nov 1976):683-4.

Puryear, Pamela Ashworth and Nath Winfield, Jr. Sandbars and Sternwheelers. College Station: Texas A & M Press, 1976. Rev. by W. E. Hollon, JAH, 63(Dec 1976):712-13.

Pustarnakov, V. F. K. Marx's "Capital" and Philosophical Thought in Russia. Moscow: Izdatel'stvo "Nauka," 1974. Rev. by P. Avrich, AHR, 81(Feb 1976):124-5.

309   QUALE

Quale, G. Robina. Eastern Civilization. Englewood Cliffs, N.J.:
Prentice-Hall, 1975. Rev. by E. C. Lydon, HT, 10(Nov
1976):127-8.

Quarles, Benjamin. Allies for Freedom: Blacks and John Brown.
New York: Oxford U Press, 1974. Rev. by J. M. Richard-
son, FHQ, 54(Jan 1976):396-7; D. J. MacLeod, History, 61
(Oct 1976):407; L. J. Friedman, OH, 85(Spr 1976):169-70.

_____, ed. Blacks on John Brown. Urbana: U Ill Press, 1972.
Rev. by E. Noyes, JISHS, 69(May 1976):156-7.

Quecke, Hans, ed. Die Briefe Pachoms. Regensburg: Pustet,
1975. Rev. by R. McL. Wilson, JEccH, 27(Jl 1976):308-9.

Quesada, M. A. Ladero. Andalucía en el siglo XV. Madrid:
Consejo Superior de Investigaciones Cientifícas, 1973. Rev.
by A. Mackay, EHR, 91(Jan 1976):183-4.

Quinn, D. B., ed. The Hakluyt Handbook. London: Hakluyt Society, 1974. Rev. by J. T. Juricek, WMQ, 33(Jan 1976):168-70.

Quinn, David Beers. England and the Discovery of America 1481-
1620. London: Allen and Unwin, 1974. Rev. by G. V.
Scammell, History, 61(Oct 1976):447-8.

_____, ed. The Last Voyage of Thomas Cavendish, 1591-1592.
Chicago: U Chicago Press, 1975. Rev. by S. Sternlicht,
HRNB, 4(Apr 1976):135.

_____ and Neil M. Cheshire, eds. The New Found Land of
Stephen Parmenius. Toronto: U Tor Press, 1972. Rev. by
S. B. Vardy, AHR, 81(Apr 1976):421-2.

Quinn, Jane. Minorcans in Florida. St. Augustine, Fla: Mission
Press, 1975. Rev. by O. G. Ganong, CaHR, 62(Jl 1976):
475-6.

Quint, Howard and Milton Cantor, eds. Men, Women, and Issues
in American History. Homewood, Ill.: Dorsey, 1975. Rev.
by R. Lewis, History, 61(Oct 1976):421-2; J. F. Marran, HT,
10(Nov 1976):143-4.

Quitslund, Sonya A. Beauduin. A Prophet Vindicated. New York:
Newman, 1973. Rev. by G. H. Tavard, CaHR, 62(Oct
1976):656-7.

Rabiah, Labid Ibn. The Golden Ode. Chicago: U Chicago Press,
1974. Rev. by I. Shahîd, IJMES, 7(Apr 1976):299-302.

Rabushka, Alvin. Race and Politics in Urban Malaya. Stanford,
Cal.: Hoover Institution, 1973. Rev. by C. H. Enloe, JAAS,
11(Jl-Oct 1976):236-9.

RACHLIN 310

Rachlin, Carol K. see Marriott, Alice

Radetski, Marian. Aid and Development. New York: Praeger, 1973. Rev. by F. Stewart, AfAf, 75(Jan 1976):108-9.

Radford, C. A. and Michael J. Swanton. Arthurian Sites in the West. Exeter: U Exeter, 1975. Rev. by P. Rahtz, Anquity, 50(Je 1976):161-3.

Radkau, Joachim see Hallgarten, George W. F.

Radosh, Ronald. Prophets on the Right. New York: Simon and Schuster, 1975. Rev. by S. Adler, AHR, 81(Apr 1976):464-5.

Rae, T. I., ed. The Union of 1707: Its Impact on Scotland. Edinburgh: Blackie, 1974. Rev. by R. Mitchison, EHR, 91 (Jan 1976):204-5.

Rafnsson, S. Studier i Landnámabók. Lund: Gleerup, 1974. Rev. by A. P. Smith, EHR, 91(Jan 1976):173-4.

Raftis, J. A. Assart Data and Land Values. Toronto: Pontifical Institute, 1974. Rev. by P. D. A. Harvey, Archives, 12(Aut 1976):188-9; C. Dyer, History, 61(Feb 1976):99.

Raftis, J. Ambrose. Warboys. Toronto: Pontifical Institute, 1974. Rev. by B. Harvey, EHR, 91(Oct 1976):893-4.

Rahul, Ram. Politics of Central Asia. New York: Barnes & Noble, 1974. Rev. by M. Rossabi, JAAS, 11(Jl-Oct 1976): 223-4.

Raman, K. Venkata. The Ways of the Peacemaker. New York: UNITAR, 1975. Rev. by K. P. Saksena, IQ, 32(Jl-Sept 1976):342-3.

Rampp, Donald and Lary Rampp. The Civil War in Indian Territory. Austin, Tex.: Presidial Press, 1975. Rev. by C. N. Tyson, A & W, 18(Sum 1976):191-2; J. W. Bailey, JOW, 15 (Jan 1976):134.

Ramsay, G. D. The City of London in International Politics at the Accession of Elizabeth Tudor. Totowa, N.J.: Rowman Littlefield, 1975. Rev. by M. C. Rosenfield, AHR, 81(Oct 1976):853-4.

Rand, Christopher T. Making Democracy Safe for Oil. Boston: Atlantic-Little, Brown, 1975. Rev. by J. Marsh, Commentary, 61(Apr 1976):86-90.

Randles, W. G. L. L'Empire du Monomotapa du XVe au XIXe Siecle. Paris: Mouton, 1975. Rev. by M. Newitt, History, 61(Feb 1976):157-8; D. N. Beach, JAfH, 17(Num 2, 1976): 311-13.

Ranger, T. O. and I. N. Kimambo, eds. The Historical Study of
    African Religion. Berkeley: U Cal Press, 1972. Rev. by
    H. J. Fisher, AHR, 81(Apr 1976):430-1.

_____ and John Weller, eds. Themes in the Christian History
    of Central Africa. Berkeley: U Cal Press, 1975. Rev. by
    J. Mbiti, AHR, 81(Oct 1976):925; A. D. Roberts, History, 61
    (Feb 1976):155-6; R. Gray, JAfH, 17(Num 4, 1976):636-8.

Ranki, Gregori see Berend, Ivan T.

Rankin, Hugh F. Francis Marion: The Swamp Fox. New York:
    Thomas Y. Crowell, 1973. Rev. by L. G. Tyler, SCHM, 77
    (Jan 1976):57-8.

_____ see Cumming, William P.

Ransel, David L. The Politics of Catherinian Russia: The Panin
    Party. New Haven, Conn.: Yale U Press, 1975. Rev. by
    R. E. Jones, AHR, 81(Oct 1976):906-7; B. Lincoln, Histori-
    an, 39(Nov 1976):136; G. G. Govorchin, HRNB, 4(Mar 1976):
    113.

Ransom, P. J. G. Waterways Restored. London: Faber and Fa-
    ber, 1974. Rev. by M. G. Miller, JTH, 3(Sep 1976):303-4.

Ranum, Orest, ed. National Consciousness, History and Political
    Culture in Early-Modern Europe. Baltimore: JHU Press,
    1975. Rev. by A. Lossky, AHR, 81(Je 1976):575-6.

_____, ed. see Forster, Robert, ed.

Rao, Amiya and B. G. Rao. Six Thousand Days: Jawaharlal
    Nehru--Prime Minister. New Delhi: Sterling, 1974. Rev.
    by B. R. Nanda, IQ, 32(Jan-Mar 1976):100-1.

Rao, Kamala Gopal. Studies in Family Planning: India. New
    Delhi: Abhinav, 1974. Rev. by N. Nag, JAS, 36(Nov 1976):
    180-1.

Raphael, Paul and Maurice Gontard. Hippolyte Fortoul, 1841-1856:
    Un ministre de l'instruction publique sous l'Empire autoritaire.
    Paris: Presses Universitaires de France, 1975. Rev. by S.
    J. Idzerda, AHR, 81(Je 1976):605; R. D. Anderson, EHR,
    91(Oct 1976):926-7.

Rapp, Richard Tilden. Industry and Economic Decline in Seven-
    teenth-Century Venice. Cambridge, Mass.: Harvard U
    Press, 1976. Rev. by D. B. Epstein, HRNB, 4(Aug 1976):
    203.

Raptis, Michael. Revolution and Counter-Revolution in Chile. New
    York: St. Martin's, 1974. Rev. by J. Petras, HAHR, 56
    (May 1976):354-6.

Rasmussen, Poul, ed. Århus Domkapitlets Jordebøger II og III.
Copenhagen: Landbohistorisk Selskab, 1975. Rev. by S. P.
Oakley, EHR, 91(Oct 1976):900.

Rasmussen, Wayne D. Agriculture in the United States. New York:
Random House, 1975. Rev. by H. D. Woodman, JSH, 42(Nov
1976):606-7.

Rastogi, P. N. The Nature and Dynamics of Factional Conflict.
Delhi: Macmillan, 1975. Rev. by S. V. Kogekar, IQ, 32
(Apr-Je 1976):251-3.

Rathbone, R. J. A. R., ed. see Moss, R. P., ed.

Rathjen, Frederick W. The Texas Panhandle Frontier. Austin:
U Texas Press, 1973. Rev. by A. P. Nasatir, AgH, 50(Jan
1976):314-15.

Rauh, Horst Dieter. Das Bild des Antichrist im Mittelalter: Von
Tyconius zum Deutschen Symbolismus. Münster: Verlag
Aschendorff, 1973. Rev. by B. McGinn, CH, 45(Je 1976):
247-8.

Raulston, J. Leonard and James W. Livingood. Sequatchie: A
Story of the Southern Cumberlands. Knoxville: U Tenn Press,
1974. Rev. by W. Masterson, PHR, 45(Aug 1976):436-7.

Raven, Peter H. see Berlin, Brent

Ravensdale, J. R. Liable to Floods. Cambridge: Cam U Press,
1974. Rev. by J. R. Wordie, AgH, 50(Apr 1976):425-6; G.
C. F. Forster, AHR, 81(Oct 1976):851-2; C. Dyer, History,
61(Feb 1976):81; J. G. Gazley, JIH, 7(Aut 1976):327-9.

Rawson, Philip and Laszlo Legeza. Tao. London: Thames and
Hudson, 1973. Rev. by W. Chi-You, CQ, Jan 1976, pp. 157-
8.

Ray, Arthur J. Indians in the Fur Trade. Toronto: U Tor Press,
1974. Rev. by H. L. Carter, AHR, 81(Je 1976):651; S. Van
Kirk, CHR, 57(Mar 1976):50-1; C. Martin, JAH, 63(Dec
1976):729-30; J. C. Ewers, PHR, 45(Feb 1976):119-21; B.
W. Hodgins, WHQ, 7(Jan 1976):70-1.

Ray, Benjamin C. African Religions. Englewood Cliffs, N.J.:
Prentice-Hall, 1976. Rev. by S. Walker, JNH, 61(Oct 1976):
414-15.

Ray, Dorothy Jean. The Eskimos of Bering Strait, 1650-1898.
Seattle: U Wash Press, 1975. Rev. by D. Archibald, OrHQ,
77(Sep 1976):295-6.

Ray, Frederic E. Alfred R. Waud: Civil War Artist. New York:

Viking, 1974. Rev. by M. Schmitt, AHR, 81(Apr 1976):
449-50; B. L. Bassham, CWH, 22(Je 1976):181-2.

Rea, J. E. Bishop Alexander Macdonell and the Politics of Upper
Canada. Toronto: Ontario Historical Society, 1974. Rev.
by F. H. Armstrong, CHR, 57(Je 1976):197-8.

Read, Jan. The Moors in Spain and Portugal. Totowa, N.J.:
Rowman and Littlefield, 1975. Rev. by K. Kennelly, AHR,
81(Oct 1976):837.

Reader, W. J. Imperial Chemical Industries. Vol. 2. Oxford:
Oxford U Press, 1975. Rev. by M. Gowing, EHR, 91(Oct
1976):875-6.

Reale, Giovanni, trans. and ed. Aristotele: Trattato sul Cosmo
per Alessandro. Napoli: Luigi Loffredo, 1974. Rev. by A.
Preus, JHP, 14(Oct 1976):478-80.

Reardon, Bernard. Liberalism and Tradition. Cambridge: Cam
U Press, 1975. Rev. by A. Vidler, JEccH, 27(Apr 1976):
219-20.

Reardon, John J. Edmund Randolph: A Biography. New York:
Macmillan, 1974. Rev. by D. Higginbotham, JAH, 62(Mar
1976):973-4; J. M. Beeson, PH, 43(Oct 1976):383-5; L.
Reed, Smithsonian, 6(Je 1975):99-100.

Rearick, Charles. Beyond the Enlightenment. Bloomington: Ind
U Press, 1974. Rev. by J. Rothney, AHR, 81(Apr 1976):
397-8.

Rebuffat-Emmanuel, Denise. Le Miroir étrusque d'après la collection du cabinet des Médailles. Rome: Ecole Française de
Rome, 1974. Rev. by L. Bonfante, AJA, 80(Spr 1976):213-15.

Redemptorist Fathers. Two Hundred Years, 1773-1973: History
of the Catholic Church in St. Thomas. St. Thomas, U.S.
Virgin Islands: Redemptorist Fathers, 1973. Rev. by C. J.
Barry, CaHR, 62(Jl 1976):529.

Reece, R. H. W. Aborigines and Colonists: Aborigines and Co-
lonial Society in New South Wales in the 1830s and 1840s.
Sydney: Sydney U Press, 1975. Rev. by S. C. McCulloch,
AHR, 81(Oct 1976):948-9.

Reed, John Shelton. The Enduring South: Subcultural Persistence
in Mass Society. Chapel Hill: U NCar Press, 1975. Rev.
by C. P. Roland, AHR, 81(Oct 1976):953-4.

Reed, M. C. Investment in Railways in Britain, 1820-1844. New
York: Oxford U Press, 1975. Rev. by L. Williams, HRNB,
5(Oct 1976):21-2; G. R. Hawke, JEH, 36(Sep 1976):784-5.

Reeves, Marjorie and Beatrice Hirsch-Reich. The Figurae of
   Joachim of Fiore. New York: Oxford U Press, 1972. Rev.
   by B. McGinn, CaHR, 62(Jan 1976):86-8.

Reeves, Richard. A Ford, Not a Lincoln. New York: Harcourt
   Brace Jovanovich, n.d. Rev. by E. J. Epstein, Commentary,
   61(Jan 1976):79, 82.

Reeves, Thomas C. Gentleman Boss: The Life of Chester Alan
   Arthur. New York: Knopf, 1975. Rev. by H. S. Merrill,
   AHR, 81(Apr 1976):458-9.

Regenstein, Lewis. The Politics of Extinction. New York: Macmillan, 1975. Rev. by M. R. Huxley, Smithsonian, 6(Aug
   1975):98-9.

Reichard, Gary W. The Reaffirmation of Republicanism: Eisenhower and the Eighty-Third Congress. Knoxville: U Tenn
   Press, 1975. Rev. by K. W. Olson, AHR, 81(Oct 1976):
   1005; R. A. Lee, IMH, 72(Je 1976):181-2.

Reichert, William O. Partisans of Freedom. Bowling Green,
   Ohio: Bowling Green U Press, 1976. Rev. by R. J. Cooke,
   HRNB, 5(Oct 1976):8.

Reid, Alfred Sandlin. Furman University. Durham, N.C.: Duke
   U Press, 1976. Rev. by G. G. Parker, HRNB, 4(Sep 1976):
   213; C. W. Chessman, JAH, 63(Dec 1976):760-1.

Reid, B. L. The Lives of Roger Casement. New Haven, Conn.:
   Yale U Press, 1976. Rev. by G. Costigan, HRNB, 4(Sep
   1976):226-7.

Reid, J. W. History of the Fourth Regiment of S. C. Volunteers.
   Dayton, Ohio: Morningside, 1975. Rev. by J. I. Robertson,
   Jr., CWTI, 15(Jl 1976):49.

Reigelman, Milton M. The Midland: A Venture in Literary Re-
   gionalism. Iowa City: U Iowa Press, 1975. Rev. by B.
   Workman, AI, 43(Fall 1976):476-8.

Reiger, John F. American Sportsmen and the Origins of Conserva-
   tion. New York: Winchester, 1975. Rev. by G. Prescott,
   A & W, 18(Sum 1976):177-8; W. T. Doherty, Jr., AHR, 81
   (Oct 1976):968; P. D. Thomas, ChOk, 54(Win 1976):533-4;
   R. A. Bartlett, HRNB, 4(Jan 1976):58; A. A. Ekirch, Jr.,
   JAH, 63(Sep 1976):435-6; H. T. Pinkett, PHR, 45(Nov 1976):
   621-3; R. G. Lillard, WHQ, 7(Oct 1976):435-6.

Reill, Peter Hanns. The German Enlightenment and the Rise of
   Historicism. Berkeley: U Cal Press, 1975. Rev. by W. J.
   McGill, HRNB, 4(Mar 1976):115.

Reilly, Elizabeth Carroll. A Dictionary of Colonial American
    Printers' Ornaments and Illustrations. A Tribute to Alden
    Porter Johnson. Worcester: American Antiquarian Society,
    1975. Rev. by M. Freiberg, NEQ, 49(Sep 1976):476-8.

Reilly, Robin. The British at the Gates: The New Orleans Cam-
    paign in the War of 1812. New York: Putnam's, 1974. Rev.
    by F. L. Owsley, FHQ, 55(Jl 1976):87-8.

Reimers, David M. see Dinnerstein, Leonard

Reinert, Paul C. The Urban Catholic University. New York:
    Sheed & Ward, 1970. Rev. by E. O. Wynot, Jr., JCS, 18
    (Aut 1976):571-3.

Reinhardt, Klaus. Die Wende vor Moskau: Das Scheitern der
    Strategie Hitlers im Winter 1941/42. Stuttgart: Deutsche
    Verlags-Anstalt, 1972. Rev. by W. A. Fletcher, AHR, 81
    (Oct 1976):884-7.

Reinharz, Jehuda. Fatherland or Promised Land. Ann Arbor:
    U Mich Press, 1975. Rev. by S. A. Diamond, HRNB, 4(Mar
    1976):114-15.

Reinhold, Meyer, ed. The Classick Pages: Classical Reading of
    Eighteenth-Century Americans. University Park: Pa St U,
    1975. Rev. by T. Colbourn, WMQ, 33(Jan 1976):177-9.

Reinsch, D. Die Briefe des Matthias von Ephesos im Codex
    Vindobonensis Theol. gr. 174. Berlin: Mielke, 1974. Rev.
    by D. M. Nicol, JEccH, 27(Jan 1976):81-2.

Reiske, Heinz. Die USA in den berichten italienischer Reisender.
    Meisenheim am Glan: Verlag Anton Haim, 1971. Rev. by
    P. A. Spengler, JAH, 63(Dec 1976):736-8.

Reitman, Alan, ed. The Pulse of Freedom: American Liberties,
    1920-1970s. New York: Norton, 1975. Rev. by T. C.
    Reeves, AHR, 81(Oct 1976):992; J.B.A., CurH, 70(Jan 1976):
    31.

Rekers, Bernard. Benito Arias Montano (1527-1598). Leiden:
    E. J. Brill, 1972. Rev. by A. J. Loomis, CaHR, 62(Jan
    1976):136.

Remak, Joachim. The Origins of the Second World War. Engle-
    wood Cliffs, N.J.: Prentice-Hall, 1976. Rev. by P. C.
    Helmreich, HRNB, 4(Sep 1976):230.

Remington, Frederic. Stubble and Slough in Dakota. Fargo: Box
    Elder Bug Press, 1975. Rev. in NDH, 43(Sum 1976):47.

Remington, Jesse A. see Fine, Lenore

Remini, Robert V. The Revolutionary Age of Andrew Jackson.
New York: Harper & Row, 1976. Rev. by C. Jackson,
THQ, 35(Win 1976):418-19.

Render, Lorne E. The Mountains and the Sky. Calgary: McClelland and Stewart West, 1974. Rev. by A. Davis, CHR, 57
(Mar 1976):40-7.

Renoff, Richard and Stephen Reynolds, eds. Proceedings of the
Conference on the Carpatho-Ruthenian Immigration, 8 June
1974. Cambridge, Mass.: Harvard U, 1975. Rev. by J. S.
Pula, JAH, 63(Dec 1976):734-5.

Renou, Louis. Religions of Ancient India. New York: Schocken,
1968. Rev. by J. Breckenridge, JCS, 18(Win 1976):138-9.

Resch, Tyler. The Shires of Bennington: A Sampler of Green
Mountain Heritage. Bennington, Vt.: Bennington Banner,
1975. Rev. by C. Fish, VH, 44(Fall 1976):242-4.

Reynolds, Joyce, ed. Select Papers of the Late R. G. Goodchild.
London: Paul Elek, 1976. Rev. by J. J. Wilkes, Antiquity,
50(Sep-Dec 1976):255-6.

Reynolds, Stephen, ed. see Renoff, Richard, ed.

Rezneck, Samuel. Unrecognized Patriots: The Jews in the American Revolution. Westport, Conn.: Greenwood, 1975. Rev.
by W. R. Jacobs, HRNB, 4(Jl 1976):163-4; J. Weinberg,
JAH, 63(Je 1976):109-10; B. W. Korn, Judaism, 25(Sum
1976):383-4; M. L. Raphael, OH, 85(Sum 1976):267-8; R.
Detweiler, PH, 43(Oct 1976):379-80; N. M. Kaganoff, NEQ,
49(Je 1976):308-10.

Rhodes, Anthony. The Vatican in the Age of the Dictators (1922-
1945). New York: Holt, Rinehart and Winston, n. p. Rev.
by J. H. Nichols, CH, 45(Mar 1976):123-4.

Rice, C. Duncan. The Rise and Fall of Black Slavery. New
York: Harper and Row, 1975. Rev. by R. Anstey, EHR,
91(Jan 1976):141-8; R. T. Takaki, JAH, 63(Je 1976):131-2;
M. F. Berry, JNH, 61(Apr 1976):221-4; D. M. McFarland,
JSH, 42(May 1976):268-9.

Rice, Lee M. and Glenn R. Vernam. They Saddled the West.
Cambridge, Md.: Cornell Maritime Press, 1975. Rev. by
C. Black, JOW, 15(Apr 1976):141.

Rice, Otis K. Frontier Kentucky. Lexington: U Press Ky, 1975.
Rev. by C. G. Talbert, WHQ, 7(Jl 1976):314-15.

Rich, Norman. Hitler's War Aims. Vols. I and II. New York:
Norton, 1973, 1974. Rev. by D. E. Emerson, AHR, 81(Feb
1976):172-3.

Richard, Lucien Joseph. The Spirituality of John Calvin. Atlanta: John Knox Press, 1974. Rev. by J. H. Leith, CH, 45(Mar 1976):109.

Richards, D. H., ed. Islamic Civilisation, 950-1150. Oxford: Bruno Cassirer, 1973. Rev. by M. A. Cook, History, 61 (Feb 1976):162.

Richards, J. F. Mughal Administration in Golconda. London: Oxford U Press, 1975. Rev. by M. A. Ali, JAS, 36(Nov 1976): 160-1.

Richardson, Boyce. Strangers Devour the Land: A Chronicle of the Assault Upon the Last Coherent Hunting Culture in North America, the Cree Indians of Northern Quebec, and Their Vast Primeval Homelands. New York: Knopf, 1976. Rev. by L. M. Hauptman, WHQ, 7(Oct 1976):420.

Richardson, Frank. Napoleon's Death: An Inquest. London: William Kimber, 1975. Rev. by O. Connelly, AHR, 81(Je 1976):608.

Richardson, H. Edward. Cassius Marcellus Clay: Firebrand of Freedom. Lexington: U Press Ky, 1976. Rev. by N. F. Magruder, HRNB, 4(May/Je 1976):146; W. H. Pease, JAH, 63(Dec 1976):718-19.

Richardson, Otis Dunbar. The Phantom Homestead: A Circuit of Our People. Hicksville, N.Y.: Exposition, 1975. Rev. by R. C. Carriker, PNQ, 67(Jan 1976):45.

Richardson, W. C., ed. The Report of the Royal Commission of 1552. Morgantown: W Va U Library, 1974. Rev. by C. S. L. Davies, EHR, 91(Apr 1976):418-19; B. W. Beckingsale, History, 61(Je 1976):274.

Richey, Elinor. Eminent Women of the West. Berkeley: Howell-North Books, 1975. Rev. by M. Dinnerstein, A & W, 18(Aut 1976):306-7; M. M. Allen, WHQ, 7(Oct 1976):424-5.

Richmond, Hugh M. The Christian Revolutionary: John Milton. Berkeley: U Cal Press, 1974. Rev. by B. M. Levy, CH, 45(Mar 1976):115.

Richmond, Robert W. Kansas: A Land of Contrasts. St. Louis, Mo.: Forum, 1974. Rev. by J. L. Forsythe, AgH, 50(Jl 1976):549-50.

Richter, Heinz. Griechenland zwischen Revolution und Kounterrevolution (1936-1946). Cologne: Europäische Verlagsanstadt, 1973. Rev. by J. C. Campbell, AHR, 81(Feb 1976):181.

Richter, Michael, ed. Canterbury Professions. Torquay: Devon-

shire, 1973. Rev. by K. Edwards, JEccH, 27(Apr 1976):
189-91.

Ricklefs, M. C. Jogjakarta Under Sultan Mangkubumi, 1749-1792:
A History of the Division of Java. New York: Oxford U
Press, 1974. Rev. by R. Van Niel, AHR, 81(Oct 1976):
946-7.

Ridley, Jasper. Garibaldi. London: Constable, 1974. Rev. by
H. Hearder, EHR, 91(Jan 1976):216-17.

Rieger, Paul E., ed. Through One Man's Eyes ... Letters of
James G. Threaker. Mount Vernon: Printing Arts, 1974.
Rev. by J. Hubbell, OH, 85(Win 1976):89-90.

Rieser, Leonard M. see Brown, Sanborn C.

Riesman, David see Lipset, Seymour Martin

Riis, P. J. and Hendrik Thrane. Sūkās III. The Neolithic Periods. Köbenhavn: Munksgaard, 1974. Rev. by T. W. Jacob-
son, AJA, 80(Win 1976):85-6.

Riker, Dorothy L., ed. see Thornbrough, Gayle, ed.

Riley, Carroll L., ed. see Lange, Charles H., ed.

Riley-Smith, Jonathan. The Feudal Nobility and the Kingdom of
Jerusalem, 1174-1277. London: Macmillan, 1973. Rev. by
J. Chrysostomides, JEccH, 27(Oct 1976):422.

Rimlinger, Gaston V. Welfare Policy and Industrialization in
Europe, America, and Russia. New York: Wiley, 1971.
Rev. by J. P. McKay, JEH, 36(Sep 1976):785-6.

Rintoul, William. Spuddin In: Recollections of Pioneer Days in the
California Oil Fields. San Francisco: California Historical
Society, 1976. Rev. by R. C. Schwarzman, SCQ, 58(Win
1976):537-9.

Ripoll, Carlos. José Martí: Letras y huellas desconocidas. New
York: Eliseo Torres, 1976. Rev. by M. S. Stabb, HAHR,
56(Nov 1976):663-4.

Ritter, Archibald R. M. The Economic Development of Revolutionary Cuba. New York: Praeger, n.d. Rev. by L. A. Perez,
Jr., TAm, 32(Apr 1976):650-1.

Ritter, Gerhard A., ed. Gesellschaft, Parlement und Regierung:
zur Geschichte des Parlamentarismus in Deutschland. Düsseldorf: Droste Verlag, 1974. Rev. by L. Cecil, AHR, 81
(Apr 1976):405-7; J. J. Sheehan, JMH, 48(Sep 1976):564-7.

Robbins, Richard G., Jr. Famine in Russia, 1891-1892: The Imperial Government Responds to a Crisis. New York: Columbia U Press, 1975. Rev. by W. B. Lincoln, AHR, 81(Oct
1976):908-9.

Robé, Udo. Berner Oberland und Staat Bern. Bern: Stadt- und
Universitätsbibliothek Bern, 1972. Rev. by H. K. Meier,
AHR, 81(Apr 1976):412-13.

Roberts, Andrew D. A History of the Bemba: Political Growth
and Change in North-eastern Zambia Before 1900. Madison:
U Wis Press, 1973. Rev. by C. Potholm, AHR, 81(Oct 1976):
926; K. Ingman, EHR, 91(Apr 1976):473-4.

Roberts, Brian. The Zulu Kings. New York: Scribner's, 1975.
Rev. by L. H. Gann, AHR, 81(Je 1976):643-4.

Roberts, Frank, ed. see Marsden, George, ed.

Roberts, J. J. M., ed. see Goedicke, Hans, ed.

Roberts, J. M. History of the World. New York: Knopf, 1976.
Rev. by J. Bohnstedt, HT, 10(Nov 1976):124-6.

_____. The Mythology of the Secret Societies. New York:
Scribner's, 1972. Rev. by R. J. Rath, JMH, 48(Mar 1976):
124-5.

Roberts, John. Revolution and Improvement: The Western World
1775-1847. Berkeley: U Cal Press, 1976. Rev. by G. J.
Cavanaugh, HRNB, 4(Aug 1976):196-7.

Roberts, Leonard. Song Branch Settlers. Austin: U Texas Press,
1974. Rev. by S. W. Corrigan, AA, 78(Mar 1976):161-2.

Roberts, Martin. A Portrait of Europe, 1900-1973. New York:
Oxford U Press, 1975. Rev. by J. D. Startt, HT, 10(Nov
1976):137-8.

Roberts, Philip, ed. see Hamilton, David

Roberts, T. A. The Concept of Benevolence. Aspects of 18th
Century Moral Philosophy. New York: Humanities, 1973.
Rev. by J. King, JHP, 14(Jan 1976):109-12.

Roberts, Warren. Morality and Social Class in Eighteenth-Century
French Literature and Painting. Toronto: U Tor Press,
1974. Rev. by O. T. Murphy, AHR, 81(Je 1976):601-2; J.
M. Roberts, EHR, 91(Apr 1976):435-6; R. Birn, Historian,
39(Nov 1976):124-5; N. Hampson, History, 61(Feb 1976):115-
16; D. R. Thelander, JMH, 48(Je 1976):331-3.

Robertson, A. F. see Dunn, John

Robertson, Heard see Cashin, Edward J., Jr.

Robertson, Marian. Diamond Fever: South African Diamond History 1866-9, from Primary Sources. New York: Oxford U Press, 1974. Rev. by L. C. Duly, AHR, 81(Oct 1976):930.

Robertson, Martin. A History of Greek Art. Vols. 1 and 2. New York: Cam U Press, 1976. Rev. by R. Brilliant, HRNB, 4(Jl 1976):174.

Robertson, T. A. see Lee, Orlan

Robin, Martin. Pillars of Profit. Toronto: McClelland and Stewart, 1973. Rev. by J. T. Morley, CHR, 57(Mar 1976):64-6.

Robinson, David. Chiefs and Clerics: Abdul Bokar Kan and Futa Toro, 1853-1891. New York: Oxford U Press, 1975. Rev. by C. A. Quinn, AHR, 81(Oct 1976):923; J. H. Frye, HRNB, 4(Mar 1976):106.

Robinson, Edgar Eugene and Vaughn Davis Bornet. Herbert Hoover: President of the United States. Stanford, Cal.: Hoover Institution Press, 1975. Rev. by R. H. Zieger, AHR, 81(Oct 1976):800-10; G. D. Best, AI, 43(Spr 1976):302-3; R. H. Ferrell, HRNB, 4(Feb 1976):75; B. I. Kaufman, JSH, 42(Aug 1976):443-4.

Robinson, Francis. Separatism Among Indian Muslims. Cambridge: Cam U Press, 1974. Rev. by G. Minault, AHR, 81 (Je 1976):645-7; P. Hardy, History, 61(Feb 1976):164-5; G. Pandey, HJ, 19(Mar 1976):293-4.

Robinson, Glen O. The Forest Service. Baltimore: JHU Press, 1975. Rev. by G. Ogden, AgH, 50(Jl 1976):556-7; J. H. Moore, JSH, 42(Nov 1976):598-9.

Robinson, J. T., Melvin L. Fowler and Brian M. Fagan. Indiana Historical Society Lectures, 1973-1974: Human and Cultural Development. Indianapolis: Ind Historical Society, 1974. Rev. by J. A. Brown, IMH, 72(Mar 1976):66-8.

Robinson, Willard B. see Webb, Todd

Robock, Stefan H. Brazil. Lexington, Mass.: Heath, 1975. Rev. by W. G. Tyler, HAHR, 56(Aug 1976):500-1.

Roche, Kennedy F. Rousseau: Stoic and Romantic. New York: Barnes and Noble, 1974. Rev. by J. N. Shklar, AHR, 81 (Feb 1976):156-7.

Rochon, André, et al. Les Ecrivains et le pouvoir en Italie à l'époque de la Renaissance. Paris: Université de la Sorbonne Nouvelle, 1974. Rev. by A. Andrews, AHR, 81(Feb 1976):177.

Rock, David, ed. Argentina in the Twentieth Century. London: Duckworth, 1975. Rev. by C. E. Solberg, HAHR, 56(May 1976):344-6; R. Carr, History, 61(Oct 1976):430-1.

_____. Politics in Argentina 1890-1930. Cambridge: Cam U Press, 1975. Rev. by CurH, 70(Feb 1976):77-8; H. S. Ferns, History, 61(Oct 1976):429-30; P. E. Kuhl, HRNB, 4 (Aug 1976):194.

Rodrigues, José Honorio. O Parlemento e a evolução nacional. 5 vols. Brasilia: Senado Federal, 1972. Rev. by N. Holub, HAHR, 56(May 1976):340-2.

Rodríguez, Jaime E. The Emergence of Spanish America. London: U Cal Press, 1976. Rev. by J. Fisher, History, 61 (Oct 1976):428; F. MacD. Spindler, HRNB, 4(Apr 1976):126-7.

Rodríguez Gallad, Irene. El petroleo en la historiografía venezolana. Tomo II. Rev. by J. Nava, HAHR, 54(May 1976): 333-4.

Roe, Michael. Kenealy and the Tichborne Cause. Portland, Ore.: International Scholarly Book Services, 1974. Rev. by W. L. Arnstein, AHR, 81(Feb 1976):142.

Roebuck, Janet. The Making of Modern English Society from 1850. New York: Scribner's, 1973. Rev. by S. Meacham, AHR, 81(Feb 1976):138.

Roehrich, Kaye L., ed. Brevet's North Dakota Historical Markers and Sites. n.p.: Brevet Press, 1975. Rev. by Editor, NDH, 43(Win 1976):36-7.

Roemer, Kenneth M. The Obsolete Necessity: America in Utopian Writings, 1888-1900. Kent, Ohio: Kent St U Press, 1976. Rev. by J. B. Quandt, AHR, 81(Oct 1976):986; H. A. Barnes, HRNB, 4(May/Je 1976):145; A. F. Wertheim, JAH, 63(Dec 1976):743-4.

Roessel, Ruth and B. H. Johnson. Navajo Livestock Reduction. Tsaile, Ariz.: Navajo Community College Press, 1974. Rev. by K. P. Philp, A & W, 18(Spr 1976):99-101.

Roff, William R., ed. Kelantan: Religion, Society and Politics in a Malay State. London: Oxford U Press, 1974. Rev. by D. J. Banks, AA, 78(Je 1976):407-9; R. Van Niel, AHR, 81 (Oct 1976):946-7; B. B. R. Carey, EHR, 91(Jl 1976):693.

Rogers, Alan. Empire and Liberty: American Resistance to British Authority, 1755-1763. Berkeley: U Cal Press, 1974. Rev. by J. P. Greene, AHR, 81(Je 1976):653-4; I. R. Christie, EHR, 91(Jl 1976):651-2; G. Seed, History, 61(Oct 1976): 398; M. Klein, NYHSQ, 60(Jan/Apr 1976):62-4; A. G. Olson, WMQ, 33(Jan 1976):160-1.

Rogers, Earl M., comp. A List of References for the History of Agriculture in the Great Plains. Davis, Cal.: U Cal, 1976. Rev. by Editor, NDH, 43(Sum 1976):47.

Rogers, H. C. B. The Confederates and Federals at War. New York: Hippocrene, 1975. Rev. by J. T. Hubbell, JSH, 42 (Aug 1976):432-4.

Rogers, Patricia, ed. History of Guildhall, Vermont. Guildhall, Vt.: Bicentennial Committee, 1975. Rev. by R. Teagle, VH, 44(Fall 1976):239-42.

Roget, Jacques Petitjean, ed. Historie de l'Ile de Grenade en Amérique, 1649-1659. Montreal: Les Presses de l'Université de Montreal, 1975. Rev. by T. Mathews, HAHR, 56(Aug 1976):467-8; C. E. Dickson, JAH, 63(Sep 1976):377-8.

Rogin, Michael Paul. Fathers and Children: Andrew Jackson and the Subjugation of the American Indian. New York: Knopf, 1975. Rev. by R. N. Satz, AHR, 81(Je 1976):658-9; R. Mc-Colley, JAH, 62(Mar 1976):990-1; S. Botein, JIH, 7(Aut 1976): 360-2; A. F. C. Wallace, JISHS, 69(May 1976):148-9; H. L. Kushner, JSH, 42(Nov 1976):591-2; D. Lindsey, Mankind, 5 (Dec 1976):7.

Rohde, Horst. Das deutsche Wehrmachttransportwesen im Zweiten Weltkrieg: Entstehung--Organisation--Aufgaben. Stuttgart: Deutsche Verlags-Anstalt, 1971. Rev. by W. A. Fletcher, AHR, 81(Oct 1976):884-7.

Ro'i, Yaacov. From Encroachment to Involvement. New York: Wiley, 1974. Rev. by P. Jabber, IJMES, 7(Oct 1976):605-7.

Rojas, Armando. Las misiones diplomáticas de Guzmán Blanco. Caracas: Monte Avila Editores, 1972. Rev. by J. A. Rayfield, HAHR, 56(May 1976):335.

Rokossovsky, K. A Soldier's Duty. Moscow: Progress Publ'rs, 1970. Rev. by E. F. Ziemke, AHR, 81(Je 1976):637-9.

Roland, Charles P. The Improbable Era: The South Since World War II. Lexington: U Press Ky, 1975. Rev. by F. M. Wilhoit, AHR, 81(Oct 1976):1000; W. F. Holmes, GHQ, 60(Spr 1975):72-3; R. A. Divine, HRNB, 4(Aug 1976):186; K. K. Bailey, JAH, 63(Sep 1976):465-6; C. Sallis, JMiH, 38(Nov 1976):379-81; S. Proctor, JSH, 42(Nov 1976):571-2; R. S. Kirkendall, NCHR, 53(Sum 1976):336-7; J. M. Phillips, THQ, 35(Spr 1976):104-6.

Rolle, Andrew F. The American Italians. Belmont, Cal.: Wadsworth, 1972. Rev. by B. B. Caroli, JAH, 63(Je 1976):173-4.

Rolt, L. T. C. Victorian Engineering. Gretna, La.: Pelican, 1974. Rev. by A. E. Musson, JTH, 3(Sep 1976):296-7.

Romera Cabrera, Lilians Betty. José Miguel de Tagle. Cordoba: Universidad Nacional de Cordoba, 1973. Rev. by D.J.G., HAHR, 56(Feb 1976):176.

Ronen, Dov. Dahomey Between Tradition and Modernity. Ithaca, N.Y.: Cornell U Press, 1975. Rev. by M. Staniland, JAfH, 17(Num 1, 1976):160; S. Decalo, JMAS, 14(Je 1976):366-8.

Ronning, Chester. A Memoir of China in Revolution: From the Boxer Rebellion to the People's Republic. New York: Pantheon Books, 1974. Rev. by R. Harris, CQ, Jan 1976, pp. 137-8.

Rosario Natal, Carmelo. Puerto Rico y la crisis de la Guerra Hispanoamericana: 1895-1898. Hato Rey, P.R.: Ramallo, 1975. Rev. by D. T. Trask, HAHR, 56(May 1976):320-2.

Rose, Elliot. Cases of Conscience: Alternatives Open to Recusants and Puritans Under Elizabeth I and James I. Cambridge: Cam U Press, 1975. Rev. by J. D. Hanlon, AHR, 81(Apr 1976):384; D. D. Wallace, Jr., CH, 45(Mar 1976):114; C. Russell, EHR, 91(Apr 1976):421; C. Cross, History, 61(Feb 1976):110-11; J. Goring, JEccH, 27(Jan 1976):84-5.

Rose, Willie Lee, ed. A Documentary History of Slavery in North America. New York: Oxford U Press, 1976. Rev. by A. M. Kraut, HRNB, 4(Apr 1976):123-4; R. H. Haunton, JSH, 42(Nov 1976):576-7; W. H. Daniel, VMHB, 84(Jl 1976):377-8.

Rosen, Andrew. Rise Up, Women! The Militant Campaign of the Women's Social and Political Union 1903-1914. Boston: Routledge and Kegan Paul, 1974. Rev. by A. Robson, AHR, 81 (Oct 1976):864; H. C. G. Matthew, EHR, 91(Jl 1976):679; P. F. Clarke, History, 71(Je 1976):312-14.

Rosen, Charles. The Classical Style. New York: Viking, 1971. Rev. by R. K. Webb, AHR, 81(Apr 1976):376-7.

Rosen, George. From Medical Police to Social Medicine. New York: Science History, 1974. Rev. by J. B. Blake, AHR, 81(Je 1976):559.

_____. Preventive Medicine in the United States, 1900-1975. New York: Science History, 1975. Rev. by J. H. Young, JAH, 63(Dec 1976):749-50.

Rosenberg, Bruce A. Custer and the Epic of Defeat. University Park: Pa St U Press, 1974. Rev. by R. M. Utley, AHR, 81 (Oct 1976):981; H. R. Grant, JOW, 15(Jan 1976):127.

Rosenberg, Charles E., ed. The Family in History. Philadelphia: U Pa Press, 1975. Rev. by M. Matossian, AHR, 81(Oct 1976):822-3.

Rosenberg, Philip. The Seventh Hero. Cambridge, Mass.: Harvard U Press, 1974. Rev. by J. M. Robson, AHR, 81(Oct 1976):863.

Rosenberg, William G. Liberals in the Russian Revolution. Princeton, N.J.: Prin U Press, 1974. Rev. by R. A. Wade, AHR, 81(Apr 1976):428-9; R. Pethybridge, History, 61(Oct 1976):468; D. N. Collins, JMH, 48(Sep 1976):571-3.

Rosenberger, Homer T. Mountain Folks. Lock Haven: Annie Halenbake Ross Library, 1974. Rev. by J. A. Andrew, III, PH, 43(Jl 1976):282-3.

Rosenfeld, Clare see Wray, Elizabeth

Rosengarten, Frederick, Jr. Free Booters Must Die! The Life and Death William Walker, the Most Notorious Soldier of Fortune of the Nineteenth Century. Wayne, Pa.: Haverford House, 1976. Rev. by J. H. Neal, THQ, 35(Win 1976):419-20.

Rosengarten, Theodore. All God's Dangers: The Life of Nate Shaw. New York: Knopf, 1974. Rev. by J. M. Youngdale, AgH, 50(Jan 1976):321-3.

Rosenof, Theodore. Dogma, Depression, and the New Deal. Port Washington, N.Y.: Kennikat, 1975. Rev. by J. M. Skaggs, Historian, 39(Nov 1976):161-2; P. M. Buzanski, HRNB, 4 (Mar 1976):99; R. A. Mulder, JAH, 63(Sep 1976):454-5.

Rosenstone, Robert A. Romantic Revolutionary: A Biography of John Reed. New York: Knopf, 1975. Rev. by J. P. Diggins, JAH, 63(Je 1976):172-3; A. C. Spencer, III, OrHQ, 77 (Mar 1976):88-9.

Rosenthal, Franz. The Classical Heritage of Islam. Berkeley: U Cal Press, 1975. Rev. by A. C. Hess, AHR, 81(Oct 1976):788-99.

Rosenthal, Joel T. The Purchase of Paradise. Buffalo: U Tor Press, 1972. Rev. by J. H. Dahmus, CaHR, 62(Jan 1976): 97-8.

Roskell, John S., ed. see Taylor, Frank, ed.

Ross, Charles. Edward IV. Berkeley: U Cal Press, 1974. Rev. by J. R. Lander, AHR, 81(Je 1976):572-3; B. P. Wolffe, EHR, 91(Apr 1976):369-74; C. Richmond, History, 61(Feb 1976):105-6.

Ross, Dudley T. Devil on Horseback: A Biography of the "Notorious" Jack Powers. Fresno, Cal.: Valley Publishers, 1975. Rev. by R. F. Wood, SCQ, 58(Fall 1976):435-8.

Ross, Michael. Banners of the King: The War of the Vendée, 1793-4. London: Seeley, Service, 1975. Rev. by G. Lewis, History, 61(Oct 1976):456-7.

Ross, Ronald J. Beleaguered Tower: The Dilemma of Political Catholicism in Wilhelmine Germany. Notre Dame, Ind.: U Notre Dame Press, 1976. Rev. by R. E. Neil, HRNB, 4(Aug 1976):204.

Ross, Stanley R., ed. Is the Mexican Revolution Dead? Philadelphia: Temple U Press, 1975. Rev. by M. Bernstein, HAHR, 56(Nov 1976):675-7.

Rosselli, John. Lord William Bentinck. London: Sussex U Press, 1974. Rev. by G. Johnson, History, 61(Feb 1976):123.

Rossie, Jonathan Gregory. The Politics of Command in the American Revolution. Syracuse, N.Y.: Syracuse U Press, 1975. Rev. by G. W. Kyte, JAH, 63(Sep 1976):394-5.

Rossiter, Frank R. Charles Ives and His America. New York: Liveright, 1975. Rev. by J. Adams, NEQ, 49(Je 1976):313-14.

Rossiter, Margaret W. The Emergence of Agricultural Science. New Haven, Conn.: Yale U Press, 1975. Rev. by D. C. Brown, HRNB, 4(Apr 1976):124; W. D. Rasmussen, JAH, 63 (Dec 1976):713-14.

Rössler, Roman. Kirche und Revolution in Russland. Köln: Böhlau Verlag, 1969. Rev. by William A. Mueller, JCS, 17 (Spr 1975):320-2.

Rostagni, Carla Meneguzzi, ed. Il Carteggio Antonelli-Barli, 1859-1861. Rome: Istituto per la Storia del Risorgimento Italiano, 1973. Rev. by F. J. Coppa, CaHR, 62(Oct 1976):623-4.

Rostow, W. W. How It All Began: Origins of the Modern Economy. New York: McGraw-Hill, 1975. Rev. by J. A. Pratt, BHR, 50(Spr 1976):99-101; R. A. Church, History, 61(Oct 1976): 449-50; E. L. Jones, JEH, 36(Sep 1976):786-9.

Rotberg, Robert I., ed. see Chittick, H. Neville, ed.

Rothbard, Murray N. "Salutary Neglect": The American Colonies in the First Half of the Eighteenth Century. New Rochelle, N.Y.: Arlington, 1975. Rev. by G. F. Frick, HRNB, 4(Jan 1976):58; C. Ubbelohde, JSH, 42(Aug 1976):416-17.

Rothchild, John and Susan Wolf. The Children of the Counterculture. New York: Doubleday, 1976. Rev. by J. L. Crain, Commentary, 62(Aug 1976):72-5.

Rothenberg, Morris see Goure, Leon

Rothkirchen, Livia, ed. Yad Vashem Studies on the European Jewish Catastrophe and Resistance. New York: KTAV, 1974. Rev. by L. S. Dawidowicz, AHR, 81(Je 1976):579-80; D. J. Diephouse, JCS, 18(Aut 1976):558-60.

Rothman, David and Sheila Rothman, eds. Sources of the American Social Tradition. 2 vols. New York: Basic Books, 1975. Rev. by A. H. Scholl, HT, 10(Nov 1976):142-3.

Rothschild, Emma. Paradise Lost: The Decline of the Auto-Industrial Age. New York: Random House, 1973. Rev. by D. E. Robinson, PNQ, 67(Apr 1976):87-8.

Rothschild, Joseph. East Central Europe Between the Two World Wars. Seattle: U Wash Press, 1975. Rev. by V. S. Mamatey, AHR, 81(Je 1976):628.

Rothstein, Marion, trans. see Walzer, Michael, ed.

Rothstein, William G. American Physicians in the Nineteenth Century. Baltimore: JHU Press, 1972. Rev. by H. Fruchtbaum, AHR, 81(Apr 1976):444-5.

Rothwell, Harry, ed. English Historical Documents. Vol. III: 1189-1327. London: Eyre and Spottiswoode, 1975. Rev. by J. R. Maddicott, EHR, 91(Jl 1976):601-3; R. H. C. Davis, History, 61(Je 1976):258.

Rotondò, Antonio. Studi e ricerche di storia ereticale italiana del Cinquecento. Torino: Edizioni Giappichelli, 1974. Rev. by E. G. Gleason, CH, 45(Sep 1976):384-5; J. W. O'Malley, JMH, 48(Sep 1976):560-2.

Rouillard, Jacques. Les Travailleurs du Coton au Quebec 1900-1915. Montreal: Les Presses de Université du Quebec, 1974. Rev. by T. Copp, CHR, 57(Mar 1976):58-60.

Rouse, J. K. From Blowing Rock to Georgetown. Kannapolis, N.C.: Privately printed by Author, 1975. Rev. by R. M. Topkins, NCHR, 53(Win 1976):85.

Rouse, Parke, Jr. Virginia: A Pictorial History. New York: Scribner's, 1975. Rev. by J. P. Cullen, AHI, 11(Aug 1976):49; W. M. E. Rachal, NCHR, 53(Spr 1976):224-5; F. L. Berkeley, Jr., VMHB, 84(Apr 1976):204-6.

Rowbotham, Sheila. Hidden from History: Rediscovering Women

in History from the 17th Century to the Present. New York:
Pantheon, 1974. Rev. by B. S. Anderson, JMH, 48(Mar
1976):140-1; S. J. Kleinberg, JSoH, 10(Fall 1976):99-103.

Rowe, John. The Hard-Rock Men. Liverpool: Liverpool U Press,
1974. Rev. by C. Erickson, History, 61(Oct 1976):412-14;
P. Blessing, JIH, 7(Aut 1976):342-3.

Rowell, Geoffrey. Hell and the Victorians. Oxford: Clarendon,
1973. Rev. by S. Gilley, EHR, 91(Jan 1976):214-15.

Rowell, John W. Yankee Artillerymen. Knoxville: U Tenn Press,
1975. Rev. by J. L. McDonough, CWH, 22(Mar 1976):90-1;
R. D. Hoffsommer, CWTI, 15(May 1976):48-9; S. Davis, GHQ,
60(Spr 1976):81-2; A. L. Funk, IMH, 72(Je 1976):261-2; A.
Jones, JAH, 63(Sep 1976):425-6; J. T. Hubbell, JSH, 42(Aug
1976):432-4.

Rowlands, Marie B. Masters and Men in the West Midland Metal-
ware Trades Before the Industrial Revolution. Manchester:
Manchester U Press, 1975. Rev. by G. Hammersley, History, 61(Oct 1976):453-4.

Rowse, A. L. Sex and Society in Shakespeare's Age: Simon Forman the Astrologer. New York: Scribner's, 1976. Rev. by
E. I. Perry, HRNB, 3(May/Je 1976):153-4.

Royal Historical Society. Camden Miscellany, Vol. XXV. London:
University College, 1974. Rev. by C. W. Arnade, HAHR, 56
(Feb 1976):172-3.

Royce, Charles C. The Cherokee Nation of Indians. Chicago:
Aldine, 1975. Rev. by L. M. Hauptman, HRNB, 4(May/Je
1976):144; D. M. Hufhines, JOW, 15(Jl 1976):101; A. M.
Gibson, JSH, 42(Nov 1976):608-9; H. O'Donnell, III, NCHR,
53(Sum 1976):325-6.

Royle, Edward. Victorian Infidels. Totowa, N.J.: Rowman and
Littlefield, 1974. Rev. by R. A. Soloway, AHR, 81(Je 1976):
590-1; C. Binfield, History, 61(Feb 1976):125.

Rozhkov, B. A. The English Workers' Movement, 1859-1864.
Moscow: Izdatel'stvo "Nauka," 1973. Rev. by P. B. Johnson,
AHR, 81(Feb 1976):138-9.

Rozman, Gilbert. Urban Networks in Russia, 1750-1800. Princeton, N.J.: Prin U Press, 1976. Rev. by S. A. Zenkovsky,
HRNB, 4(Aug 1976):206.

Rubin, Stanley. Medieval English Medicine. New York: Barnes
and Noble, 1975. Rev. by E. A. Hammond, AHR, 81(Je
1976):570-1.

Rubinstein, Alvin Z., ed. Soviet and Chinese Influence in the Third World. New York: Praeger, 1975. Rev. by T. H. Henriksen, JMAS, 14(Je 1976):350-3.

Ruby, Robert H. and John A. Brown. Ferryboats on the Columbia River. Seattle: Superior, 1974. Rev. by E. W. Buehler, OrHQ, 77(Mar 1976):87.

Ruchames, Louis, ed. The Letters of William Lloyd Garrison. Vol. IV. Cambridge, Mass.: Harvard U Press, 1975. Rev. by M. L. Dillon, JSH, 42(Nov 1976):593-4.

Ruddock, J. G. and R. E. Pearson. The Railway History of Lincoln. n. p.: J. G. Ruddock, 1974. Rev. by F. Henthorn, JTH, 3(Sep 1976):295-6.

Rudé, George. Debate on Europe, 1815-1850. New York: Harper and Row, 1972. Rev. by E. A. Clark, AHR, 81(Je 1976): 576-7.

Ruelland, Suzanne. La fille sans mains. Paris: Société d'études linguistiques et anthropologiques de France, 1973. Rev. by J. Knappert, Africa, 46(Num 1, 1976):100-1.

Ruether, Rosemary. Faith and Fratricide: The Theological Roots of Anti-Semitism. New York: Seabury, 1974. Rev. by G. T. Miller, JCS, 16(Spr 1976):355-8.

Ruggle, Richard, ed. Some Men and Some Controversies. Erin, Ont.: Press Procepic, 1974. Rev. by J. S. Moir, CHR, 57 (Je 1976):199-200.

Ruhl, Klaus-Jörg. Spanien im Zweiten Weltkrieg: Franco, die Falange und das "Dritte Reich." Hamburg: Hoffman und Campe, 1975. Rev. by Stanley G. Payne, AHR, 81(Oct 1976): 876-7.

Ruiz, Ramon E. Labor and the Ambivalent Revolutionaries: Mexico, 1911-1933. Baltimore: JHU Press, 1976. Rev. by D. J. Mabry, HRNB, 4(Jl 1976):167-8.

Ruíz Rivera, Julian B. Encomienda y mita en Nueva Granada. Seville: Escuela de Estudios Hispanoamericanos de Seville, 1975. Rev. by J. L. Phelan, HAHR, 56(Aug 1976):482-3.

Rusco, Elmer. "Good Time Coming?" Westport, Conn.: Greenwood, 1976. Rev. by A. T. Gilmore, HRNB, 4(Sep 1976): 217; R. G. Coleman, UHQ, 44(Fall 1976):402-3.

Rush, John A. Witchcraft and Sorcery. Springfield, Ill.: C. C. Thomas, 1974. Rev. by A. B. Kehoe, AA, 78(Je 1976):399-400.

Rusho, W. L. and C. Gregory Crampton. Desert River Crossing.
Salt Lake City: Peregrine Smith, 1975. Rev. by B. M.
Fireman, JAriH, 17(Spr 1976):109-10; M. T. Smith, UHQ,
44(Spr 1976):186.

Russell, D. E. H. Rebellion, Revolution, and Armed Force. New
York: Academic, 1974. Rev. by A. Suárez, HAHR, 56(May
1976):348-9.

Russell, Don, ed. Trails of the Iron Horse. New York: Doubleday, 1975. Rev. by L. Carranco, JOW, 15(Apr 1976):140.

Russell, Francis. A City in Terror: 1919--The Boston Police
Strike. New York: Viking, 1975. Rev. by D. M. Reimers,
AHR, 81(Je 1976):677-8; J. T. Galvin, NEQ, 49(Sep 1976):
472-4.

Russell, Frank. The Pima Indians. Tucson: U Ariz Press, 1975.
Rev. by J. C. Winter, UHQ, 44(Spr 1976):192-3.

Russell, Frederick H. The Just War in the Middle Ages. Cambridge: Cam U Press, 1975. Rev. by C. L. Klausner, AHR,
81(Oct 1976):834; D. Eggenberger, HRNB, 4(Feb 1976):92;
G. R. Duncan, JEccH, 27(Apr 1976):193-5.

Russell-Wood, A. J. R., ed. From Colony to Nation. Baltimore:
JHU Press, 1975. Rev. by D. Alden, AHR, 81(Je 1976):
701-2; G. P. Browne, Historian, 39(Nov 1976):169-70.

Russett, Cynthia Eagle. Darwin in America. San Francisco:
Freeman, 1976. Rev. by W. T. Deininger, HRNB, 4(Aug
1976):188-9.

Russo, David J. Families and Communities. Nashville: American
Assn for State and Local History, 1975. Rev. by D. B. Dan-
bom, NDH, 43(Sum 1976):41-2.

Russu, Ioan I., ed. Introducere istorică şi epigraphică, diplomele
militare, tablițele cerate. Bucharest: Academiei Republicii
Socialiste România, 1975. Rev. by D. W. Wade, AHR, 81
(Oct 1976):828-9.

Ruth, John L. Conrad Grebel: Son of Zurich. Scottdale, Pa.:
Herald Press, 1975. Rev. by P. J. Klassen, CH, 45(Je
1976):257; R. Wiebe, MQR, 50(Apr 1976):149-50.

Rutland, Robert A., et al., eds. see Madison, James

Rweyemanu, Anthony H. and Göran Hydén. A Decade of Public Administration in Africa. Nairobi: E African Literature Bureau,
1975. Rev. by D. Hirschmann, JMAS, 14(Mar 1976):183-5.

Rweyemanu, Justinian F. Underdevelopment and Industrialization in Tanzania. London: Oxford U Press, 1973. Rev. by P. Mosley, JMAS, 14(Sep 1976):543-6.

Ryan, Alan. J. S. Mill. Boston: Routledge and Kegan Paul, 1975. Rev. by S. Rothblatt, AHR, 81(Oct 1976):861-3; J. Rees, EHR, 91(Jl 1976):666; K. Nield, History, 61(Je 1976): 306.

Ryan, Mary P. Womanhood in America. New York: New Viewpoints, 1975. Rev. by K. K. Sklar, AHR, 81(Je 1976):672-3; O.E.S., CurH, 70(May 1976):228; G. Lerner, JAH, 63(Je 1976):96-7.

Ryan, Paul B. see Bailey, Thomas Andrew

Ryder, A. J. Twentieth Century Germany: From Bismarck to Brandt. New York: Columbia U Press, 1972. Rev. by G. F. Botjer, AHR, 81(Apr 1976):408-9; H. K. Rosenthal, EE, 24(Je 1975):31.

Ryder, Rowland. Edith Cavell. London: Hamish Hamilton, 1975. Rev. by G. Best, History, 61(Oct 1976):496.

Ryley, Thomas W. A Little Group of Willful Men. Port Washington, N.Y.: Kennikat, 1975. Rev. by J. Brademas, IMH, 72 (Je 1976):281-3; J. G. Clifford, JAH, 63(Sep 1976):448-9.

Ryosetsu, Fujiwara. The Way to Nirvana. Tokyo: Kyoiku Shinchosha, 1974. Rev. by J. Pas, JAS, 36(Nov 1976):145-6.

Rystad, Goran. Ambiguous Imperialism. Stockholm: Esselte Studium, 1975. Rev. by J. A. Field, Jr., HRNB, 4(Jl 1976): 164.

Sabbatucci, G. I combattenti nel primo dopoguerra. Rome: Bari, 1974. Rev. by N. A. O. Lyttelton, EHR, 91(Jan 1976):163-5.

Sabloff, Jeremy A. and C. C. Lamberg-Karlovsky, eds. Ancient Civilization and Trade. Albuquerque: U NM Press, 1975. Rev. by C. Haselgrove, Antiquity, 50(Je 1976):160-1.

Sachse, William L. Lord Somers: A Political Portrait. Manchester: J. P. Kenyon, History, 61(Je 1976):289.

Sack, Ronald Herbert. Amel-Marduk 562-560 B.C. Neukirchen--Vluyn: Verlag Butzon und Bercker Kevelaer, 1972. Rev. by D. B. Weisberg, JNES, 35(Jan 1976):67-9.

Sackett, Everett B. New Hampshire's University: The Story of a New England Land Grant College. Somersworth: New Hampshire Publ. Co., 1974. Rev. by L. Ulrich, NEQ, 49 (Je 1976):325-7.

Safford, Frank. The Ideal of the Practical. Austin: U Texas Press, 1976. Rev. by C. Beyer, HRNB, 4(Aug 1976):193-4.

Saidi, Omar, ed. Kitab al-'Uyun wa-1-Hadaiq fi Akhbar al-Haqaiq. Damascus: Institut français de Demas, 1972. Rev. by M. G. Morony, IJMES, 7(Apr 1976):306-7.

Saint-Simon, Henri. Selected Writings on Science, Industry, and Social Organisation (1760-1825). New York: Holmes and Meier, 1975. Rev. by D. Bitton, HRNB, 4(Mar 1976):107-8.

Sakharov, Andrei D. My Country and the World. New York: Knopf, n.d. Rev. by J. Laber, Commentary, 61(Jan 1976): 94-6, 98.

Sale, Kirkpatrick. Power Shift. New York: Random House, n.d. Rev. by J. Kirkpatrick, Commentary, 61(May 1976):94-6.

Sales, Jane. Mission Stations and the Coloured Communities of the Eastern Cape 1800-1852. Cape Town: Balkema, 1975. Rev. by T. Kirk, JAfH, 17(Num 1, 1976):143-4.

Saletore, R. N. Early Indian Economic History. Totowa, N.J.: Rowman and Littlefield, 1975. Rev. by B. Stein, AHR, 81 (Oct 1976):943.

Sallagar, Frederick M. The Road to Total War. New York: Van Nostrand Reinhold, 1975. Rev. by A. Norman, AHR, 81(Oct 1976):824-5.

Salmon, J. H. M. Society in Crisis. New York: St. Martin's, 1976. Rev. by N. M. Sutherland, EHR, 91(Oct 1976):845-7; R. J. Knecht, History, 61(Je 1976):278-9; J. Davies, HJ, 19 (Dec 1976):1024-6; D. L. Jensen, HRNB, 4(Jl 1976):180-1.

Salusbury-Jones, G. T. Street Life in Medieval England. Totowa, N.J.: Rowman and Littlefield, 1975. Rev. by J. T. Rosenthal, AHR, 81(Je 1976):580.

Samoff, Joel. Tanzania: Local Politics and the Structure of Power. Madison: U Wis Press, 1974. Rev. by R. Jeffries, AfAf, 75(Apr 1976):260-1; S. F. Moore, Africa, 46(Num 2, 1976): 211-12.

Sampson, Anthony. The Seven Sisters. New York: Viking, 1975. Rev. by J. Marsh, Commentary, 61(Apr 1976):86-90; M. Wilkins, JEH, 36(Sep 1976):789-90.

Sampson, William R., ed. John McLoughlin's Business Correspondence, 1847-48. Seattle: U Wash Press, 1973. Rev. by M. A. Ormsby, CHR, 57(Mar 1976):88-9.

Samsonov, A. M. From the Volga to the Baltic. Moscow: Izdatel

SAMUEL 332

'stvo "Nauka, " 1973. Rev. by M. Parrish, AHR, 81(Apr 1976):429-30.

Samuel, Raphael, ed. Village Life and Labour. Boston: Routledge and Kegan Paul, 1975. Rev. by J. Roebuck, AHR, 81(Oct 1976):816; A. Howkins, History, 61(Oct 1976):486-7; D. N. Cannadine, JIH, 7(Aut 1976):329-32.

Samuelson, Myron. The Story of the Jewish Community of Burlington, Vermont. Burlington, Vt.: privately printed, 1976. Rev. by M. M. Kunn, VH, 44(Fall, 1976):244-6.

Samuelsson, Jan. Islam in Afghanistan Under King Muhammed Zahir Shah. Stockholm: n.p., 1975. Rev. by D. B. Westerlund, JCS, 18(Aut 1976):567-9.

Sanchez, Rodrigo see Alberti, Giorgio

Sánchez-Albornoz, Nicolás. The Population of Latin America. Berkeley: U Cal Press, 1974. Rev. by C. Gibson, AIQ, 2 (Spr 1975):25-6; W. M. Denevan, HAHR, 56(May 1976):297-9.

Sanchez-Saavedra, E. M. A Description of the Country: Virginia's Cartographers and Their Maps, 1607-1881. Richmond: Va St Library, 1975. Rev. by W. P. Cumming, VMHB, 84(Jl 1976):367-9.

Sandberg, Lars G. Lancashire in Decline. Columbus: Ohio St U Press, 1974. Rev. by D. A. Farnie, BH, 17(Jan 1975):83-4; P. F. Clarke, JIH, 7(Sum 1976):148-50.

Sandbrook, Richard. Proletarians and African Capitalism. Cambridge: Cam U Press, 1975. Rev. by T. Ranger, History, 61(Feb 1976):160.

Sanders, Harland. Finger Lickin' Good. Carol Stream, Ill.: Creation House, 1974. Rev. by S. E. Greene, BHR, 50(Spr 1976):123-4.

Sanders, Jack T. Ethics in the New Testament. Philadelphia: Fortress, 1975. Rev. by R. M. Grant, CH, 45(Sep 1976): 374.

Sanderson, Meredith, ed. see Abdallah, Yohanna B., comp.

Sandor, Istvan. Xántos János. Budapest: Maguető Könyvkiadó, 1970. Rev. by H. M. Madden, AHR, 81(Apr 1976):360-1.

Sankalia, H. D. The Prehistory and Protohistory of India and Pakistan. Poona: Deccan College ... 1974. Rev. by M. Wheeler, Antiquity, 50(Mar 1976):72-3; R. W. Butzer, Archaeology, 29(Apr 1976):141.

Sappington, Roger E. The Brethren in Virginia: The History of
the Church of the Brethren in Virginia. Harrisonburg, Va.:
Committee for Brethren History in Virginia, 1973. Rev. by
J. O. Lehman, MQR, 50(Apr 1976):147-8.

Sarkar, Sumit. The Swadeshi Movement in Bengal, 1903-1908.
New Delhi: People's Publishing House, 1973. Rev. by P. J.
Ray, IESHR, 13(Jan-Mar 1976):113-17.

Sartain, E. M. Jalal al-din al-Suyūti. 2 vols. Cambridge: Cam
U Press, 1975. Rev. by H. J. Fisher, JAfH, 17(Num 3,
1976):448-50.

Sastri, P. S. Ananda K. Coomaraswamy. New Delhi: Heinemann
(India), 1974. Rev. by R. A. Perry, JAS, 36(Nov 1976):
165-6.

Satyanarayana, J. Incentives and Productivity in Public Enterprises.
Bombay: Popular Prakashan, 1974. Rev. by D. L. Taub,
JAS, 36(Nov 1976):179-80.

Satyaparkash, comp. and ed. Pakistan: A Bibliography, 1962-74.
Gurgaon: Indian Documentation Service, 1975. Rev. by A. C.
Devi, IQ, 32(Jl-Sep 1976):353.

Satz, Ronald N. American Indian Policy in the Jacksonian Era.
Lincoln: U Neb Press, 1975. Rev. by R. L. Nichols, A &
W, 18(Aut 1976):295-7; M. Rogin, AHR, 81(Oct 1976):969-70;
R. E. Bieder, AIQ, 2(Spr 1976):27-8; E. C. Bearss, FHQ,
55(Jl 1976):91-2; W. H. Conser, Jr., IMH, 72(Dec 1976):
369-70; M. Young, WHQ, 7(Jan 1976):68-9.

Saul, J. S. see Arrighi, G.

Saunders, Christopher and Robin Derricourt, eds. Beyond the Cape
Frontier. London: Longman, 1975. Rev. by M. Newitt, History, 61(Feb 1976):155.

Savage, Donald C. see Clayton, Anthony

Savage, William W., Jr., ed. Cowboy Life: Reconstructing an
American Myth. Norman: U Ok Press, 1975. Rev. by O.
Sawey, WHQ, 7(Apr 1976):209-10.

Savelle, Max. Empires to Nations. Minneapolis: U Minn Press,
1974. Rev. by O. B. Pollak, AHR, 81(Apr 1976):358-9; G.
Williams, History, 61(Oct 1976):427-8; M. Kaups, JAH, 62
(Mar 1976):966-7; A. P. Nasatir, PNQ, 67(Jl 1976):129.

Saxton, Alexander. The Indispensable Enemy. Berkeley: U Cal
Press, 1971. Rev. by G. K. Renner, JOW, 15(Jan 1976):
140.

Sayles, G. O. The King's Parliament of England. London: Edward Arnold, 1975. Rev. by C. S. Sims, AHR, 81(Je 1976): 571; G. L. Harriss, EHR, 91(Jan 1976):124-6; E. Miller, History, 61(Je 1976):259-60.

Scace, R. C., ed. see Nelson, J. G., ed.

Scally, Robert J. The Origins of the Lloyd George Coalition. Princeton, N.J.: Prin U Press, 1975. Rev. by P. F. Clarke, EHR, 91(Oct 1976):873-5; B. McGill, HRNB, 4(Jan 1976):65.

Schachwacht, J. H. Schiffahrt und Güterverkehr zwischen Köln und Rotterdam, 1794-1850-51. Cologne: Rheinisch-Westfälisches, 1973. Rev. by R. Knauerhase, JEH, 36(Je 1976): 472-6.

Schäfer, Gerhard, comp. see Fischer, Richard, comp.

Schapera, I., ed. David Livingstone: South African Papers, 1849-1853. Cape Town: Van Riebeeck Society, 1974. Rev. by Q. N. Parsons, JAfH, 17(Num 3, 1976):456-8.

Schapsmeier, Edward L. and Frederick H. Schapsmeier. Encyclopedia of American Agricultural History. Westport, Conn.: Greenwood, 1976. Rev. by Editor, NDH, 43(Fall 1976):40-1; W. D. Barns, WVH, 38(Oct 1976):56-8.

Scheffbuch, Winrich. Christians Under the Hammer and Sickle. Grand Rapids, Mich.: Zondervan, 1974. Rev. by A. W. Wardin, Jr., JCS, 17(Spr 1975):352-3.

Scheiderman, Jeremiah. Sergei Zubatov and Revolutionary Marxism. Ithaca, N.Y.: Cornell U Press, 1976. Rev. by W. J. Lavery, HRNB, 4(Aug 1976):206.

Schell, Herbert S. History of South Dakota. Lincoln: U Neb Press, 1975. Rev. by H. R. Grant, NDH, 43(Win 1976):43.

Schenck, Carl Alwin. The Birth of Forestry in America: Biltmore Forest School, 1898-1913. Santa Cruz: Forest History Society and Appalachian Consortium, 1974. Rev. by R. S. Maxwell, PNQ, 67(Jan 1976):40.

Scherer, Lester B. Slavery and the Churches in Early America, 1619-1819. Grand Rapids, Mich.: Eerdmans, 1975. Rev. by M. L. Bradbury, AHR, 81(Oct 1976):958; D. J. MacLeod, Historian, 39(Nov 1976):149; S. J. Stein, IMH, 72(Je 1976): 173-4; E. S. Gaustad, JAH, 63(Dec 1976):680; S. C. Bolton, JSH, 42(May 1976):273-4; B. Wyatt-Brown, OH, 85(Spr 1976): 166-7.

Scherrer, Jutta. Die Petersburger Religios-Philosophischen Verein-

igungen. Berlin: Osteuropa-Institut an der Freien Universität Berlin, 1973. Rev. by M. Raeff, AHR, 81(Apr 1976):
426-7.

Scheuerman, Audomar and Georg May, eds. Ius Sacrum. Munich.
Paderborn, 1969. Rev. by W. A. Mueller, JCS, 18(Aut
1976):587-8.

Scheurer, Remy, ed. Correspondance du Cardinal Jean du Bellay.
Paris: Librairie C. Klinksieck, 1973. Rev. by D. Nugent,
CaHR, 62(Jan 1976):128-9.

Schieder, Theodor. Hermann Rauschnings "Gesprache mit Hitler"
als Geschichtsquelle. Opladen: Westdeutscher Verlag, 1972.
Rev. by B. F. Smith, AHR, 81(Je 1976):618.

Schiefel, Werner. Bernhard Dernburg 1865-1937. Zurich: Atlantis
Verlag, 1974. Rev. by A. J. Knoll, AHR, 81(Apr 1976):405;
J. Iliffe, JAfH, 17(Num 1, 1976):157-8.

Schindler, Herbert. Mosty und Dirschau 1939: Zwei Handstreiche
der Wehrmacht vor Beginn des Polenfeldzuges. Freiburg:
Verlag Rombach, 1971. Rev. by W. A. Fletcher, AHR, 81(Oct
1976):884-7.

Schlebecker, John T. Whereby We Thrive. Ames: Ia St U Press,
1975. Rev. by R. P. Swierenga, AI, 43(Win 1976):229-30; G.
Wright, BHR, 50(Sum 1976):233; P. W. Gates, IMH, 72(Mar
1976):79-81; M. W. M. Hargreaves, JAH, 63(Je 1976):97-8;
G. C. Fite, JSH, 42(Feb 1976):101; B. Weaver, NDH, 43(Win
1976):38; A. G. Bogue, PHR, 45(Nov 1976):610-11; J. W.
Whitaker, WHQ, 7(Oct 1976):426-7.

Schmid, Hans-Dieter. Täufertum und Obrigkeit in Nürnberg.
Nürnberg: Stadtarchiv Nürnberg, 1972. Rev. by J. S. Oyer,
MQR, 50(Oct 1976):305-8.

Schmidt, Fredrich W. Zum Begriff der Negativität bei Schelling
und Hegel. Stuttgart: J. B. Metzler, 1971. Rev. by D. E.
Christensen, JHP, 14(Apr 1976):240-1.

Schmidt, John D. Ramesses II: A Chronological Structure for His
Reign. Baltimore: JHU Press, 1973. Rev. by W. H. Shea,
JNES, 35(Oct 1976):282-3.

Schmithals, Walter. The Apocalyptic Movement. Nashville:
Abingdon, 1975. Rev. by H. Partrick, CH, 45(Mar 1976):97.

Schmitt, Karl M. Mexico and the United States, 1821-1973. New
York: Wiley, 1974. Rev. by T. Schoonover, ETHJ, 14(Spr
1976):57-8; K. J. Grieb, PHR, 45(Feb 1976):138-9.

Schmucher, Werner. Untersuchungen zu einigen Wichtigen Boden-

rechtlichen Konsequenzen der Islamischen Eroberungsbewegung.
Bonn: Selbstverlag des Orientalischen seminars der Universität, 1972. Rev. by M. G. Morony, IJMES, 7(Oct 1976):600-2.

Schnabel, James F. Policy and Direction: The First Year. Washington: Office of Chief of Military Hist., US Army, 1972.
Rev. by H. L. Coles, AHR, 81(Apr 1976):467-8.

Schnore, Leo F., ed. The New Urban History. Princeton, N.J.:
Prin U Press, 1975. Rev. by E. Pessen, AHR, 81(Apr 1976):
451-2; J.B., AS, 16(Fall 1975):99.

Schob, David E. Hired Hands and Plowboys. Urbana: U Ill
Press, 1975. Rev. by G. W. Wolff, CWH, 22(Je 1976):182-
4; H. E. Socolofsky, Historian, 39(Nov 1976):151-2; P. D.
Thomas, HRNB, 4(Jan 1976):55; H. N. Scheiber, IMH, 72(Mar
1976):269-70; G. C. Fite, JAH, 63(Je 1976):119; M. Walsh,
JAmS, 10(Aug 1976):273-4; E. D. Elbert, JISHS, 69(Aug
1976):240; M. W. M. Hargreaves, WHQ, 7(Jl 1976):315-16.

Schochet, Gordon J. Patriarchalism in Political Thought. Oxford:
Basil Blackwell, 1975. Rev. by B. Worden, EHR, 91(Oct
1976):911-12; J. P. Kenyon, History, 61(Feb 1976):115.

Schoder, Raymond V. Wings Over Hellas. New York: Oxford U
Press, 1974. Rev. by R. L. Pounder, AJA, 80(Fall 1976):
431.

Schoeps, Hans-Joachim. Ja-Nein-und Trotzdem. Mainz: Hase &
Koehler Verlag, 1974. Rev. by M. P. Fleischer, AHR, 81
(Apr 1976):409-10.

Schofer, Lawrence. The Formation of a Modern Labor Force: Upper Silesia, 1865-1914. Berkeley: U Cal Press, 1975. Rev.
by U. Nocken, BHR, 50(Sum 1976):246-8; M. Berger, HRNB,
4(Jan 1976):67-8; M. R. Haines, JEH, 36(Sep 1976):790-1.

Schölch, Alexander. Ägypten den Ägyptern! Die politische und
gesellschaftliche Krise der Jahre 1878-1882 in Agypten.
Zurich: Atlantis, 1972. Rev. by H. Fähndrich, AHR, 81(Oct
1976):920-1.

Scholem, Gershom. Sabbatai Sevi. Princeton, N.J.: Prin U
Press, 1973. Rev. by J. Neusner, JMH, 48(Je 1976):316-20.

Schorger, A. W. The Passenger Pigeon. Norman: U Ok Press,
1973. Rev. by D. E. Green, ChOk, 54(Sum 1976):290.

Schreiner, Peter, ed. Die byzantinischen Kleinchroniken, I. Vienna: Osterreichischen Akademie der Wissenschaften, 1975.
Rev. by D. M. Nicol, JEccH, 27(Apr 1976):187-8.

Schroder, Hans-Jurgen. Deutschland und die Vereinigten Staaten,

1933-1939: Wirtschaft und Politik in der Entwicklund des deutsch-Amerikanischen Gegensatzes. Wiesbaden, Germany: Franz Steiner Verlag, GmbH, 1970. Rev. by T. Schoonover, PHR, 45(May 1976):300-1.

Schröder, Karsten. Parlament und Aussenpolitik in England 1911-1914. Göttingen: Musterschmidt Verlag, 1974. Rev. by P. M. Kennedy, EHR, 91(Jl 1976):681.

Schroeder, G. P. Miracles of Grace and Judgment. Kingsport, Tenn.: Kingsport Press, 1974. Rev. by J. Toews, MQR, 50(Jan 1976):70-1.

Schroeder, John H. Mr. Polk's War: American Opposition and Dissent, 1846-1848. Madison: U Wis Press, 1973. Rev. by K. J. Bauer, NMHR, 51(Jl 1976):258; J. C. Curtis, PH, 43 (Jan 1976):89-90.

Schroeder, Paul W. Austria, Great Britain, and the Crimean War. Ithaca, N.Y.: Cornell U Press, 1972. Rev. by E. B. Segel, AHR, 81(Apr 1976):378-9.

Schroeder, William. The Bergthal Colony. Winnipeg: Canadian Mennonite Bible College, 1974. Rev. by W. Klaassen, MQR, 50(Jan 1976):68-9.

Schroth, Raymond A. The Eagle and Brooklyn. Westport, Conn.: Greenwood, 1974. Rev. by J. M. Harrison, AHR, 81(Je 1976):660-1.

Schubart, Hermanfrid. Die Kultur der Bronzezeit im Sudwesten der Iberischen Halbinsel. Berlin: de Gruyter, 1975. Rev. by R. J. Harrison, Antiquity, 50(Sep-Dec 1976):241-2.

Schulthess, Emil. Soviet Union. New York: Harper and Row, 1972. Rev. by R. Galligan, EE, 24(Je 1975):31-2.

Schultz, Charles R. and Mary Pearson, comp. and ed. Inventory of County Records: Lee County. Austin: Texas St Library, 1974. Rev. by J. L. Mims, AmArc, 30(Jan 1976):54-6.

Schulz, Charles M. Peanuts Jubilee. New York: Holt, Rinehart and Winston, 1975. Rev. by C. Kozlak, MinnH, 45(Sum 1976):78.

Schulz, Gerhard. Faschismus--Nationalsozialismus. Berlin: Propyläen, 1974. Rev. by F. R. Willis, AHR, 81(Oct 1976): 848-9.

Schulze-Bidlingmaier, Ingrid, ed. Die Kabinette Wirth I und II. Boppard am Rhein: Harald Boldt Verlag, 1973. Rev. by H. A. Turner, Jr., AHR, 81(Feb 1976):168-9.

Schulzinger, Robert D. The Making of the Diplomatic Mind: The Training, Outlook, and Style of United States Foreign Service Officers, 1908-1931. Middletown, Conn.: Wesleyan U Press, 1975. Rev. by C. E. Neu, AHR, 81(Oct 1976):990-1; W. H. Heinrichs, Jr., PHR, 45(Nov 1976):627-8.

Schumacher, Edward J. Politics, Bureaucracy and Rural Development in Senegal. Berkeley: U Cal Press, 1975. Rev. by D. C. O'Brien, AfAf, 75(Jl 1976):394.

Schumacher, John N. Father José Burgos. Manila: Ateneo U Press, 1972. Rev. by N. P. Cushner, CaHR, 62(Oct 1976): 639-40.

Schusky, Ernest L. The Forgotten Sioux. Chicago: Nelson-Hall, 1975. Rev. by J. C. Olson, A & W, 18(Spr 1976):101-2; J. W. Bailey, JAH, 63(Je 1976):144-5.

Schustereit, Hartmut. Linksliberalismus und Socialdemokratie in der Weimarer Republik 1919-1930. Düsseldorf: Schwann, 1975. Rev. by A. J. Ryder, History, 61(Je 1976):321.

Schwaab, Eugene L., ed. Travels in the Old South. Lexington: U Press Ky, 1973. Rev. by J. L. Nichols, ETHJ, 14(Spr 1976):59-60.

Schwab, Dieter. Die "Selbstverwaltungsidee" des Freiherrn vom Stein und ihre geistigen Grundlagen: Zugleich ein Beitrag zur Geschichte der politischen Ethik im 18. Jahrhundert. Frankfurt: Athenäum Verlag, 1971. Rev. by P. R. Sweet, AHR, 81(Oct 1976):879-80.

Schwartz, Benjamin I. Reflections on the May Fourth Movement. Cambridge, Mass.: Harvard U Press, 1972. Rev. by Young-Tsu Wong, MAS, 10(Apr 1976):305-8.

Schwartz, Bernard. The Law in America. New York: McGraw-Hill, 1974. Rev. by R. G. Russo, JCS, 18(Spr 1976):344-6.

Schwartz, Murray L. and Audrey J. see Karst, Kenneth L.

Schwarz, Hans-Peter, ed. Konrad Adenauer, Reden 1917-1967: Eine Auswahl. Stuttgart: Deutsche Verlags-Anstalt, 1975. Rev. by F. E. Hirsch, AHR, 81(Oct 1976):887-8.

Schwarzmaier, Hansmartin. Lucca und das Reich bis zum Ende des 11. Jahrhunderts. Tübingen: Max Niemeyer, 1972. Rev. by D. A. Bullough, EHR, 91(Jl 1976):624-5.

Schwieder, Elmer and Dorothy Schwieder. A Peculiar People. Ames: Ia St U Press, 1975. Rev. by P. D. Jordan, AI, 43(Sum 1976):385-7; A. Teichroew, IMH, 72(Dec 1976):376-7; J. C. Juhnke, JAH, 63(Sep 1976):431-2.

Schwoerer, Lois G.   "No Standing Armies!": The Antiarmy
     Ideology in Seventeenth-Century England. Baltimore: JHU
     Press, 1974. Rev. by S. J. Stearns, AHR, 81(Je 1976):
     584; A. Woolrych, History, 61(Je 1976):284-5.

Scott, A. F., ed. Everyone a Witness. New York: Crowell,
     1976. Rev. by J. J. Contreni, HT, 10(Nov 1976):134; E.
     Earle, Mankind, 5(Dec 1976):58.

Scott, Franklin D. Scandinavia. Cambridge, Mass.: Harvard U
     Press, 1975. Rev. by E. Anderson, HRNB, 4(Jan 1976):66.

Scott, J. Irving E. The Education of Black People in Florida.
     Philadelphia: Dorrance, 1974. Rev. by H. A. Kersey, Jr.,
     FHQ, 55(Jl 1976):83-4.

Scott, Joan Wallach. The Glassworkers of Carmaux. Cambridge,
     Mass.: Harvard U Press, 1974. Rev. by M. R. Marrus,
     CHR, 57(Je 1976):230-1; D. H. Pinkney, JIH, 7(Sep 1976):
     160-1.

Scott, John Anthony. Hard Trails on My Way. New York: Knopf,
     1974. Rev. by A. C. Ashcraft, JOW, 15(Jan 1976):127-8.

Scott, Roy V. and J. G. Shoalmire. The Public Career of Cully A.
     Cobb. Jackson: U and Coll Press Miss, 1973. Rev. by G.
     L. Baker, AgH, 50(Jan 1976):315-17; M. Rothstein, JSH, 42
     (Feb 1976):133-5.

Scott, W. S. Jeanne d'Arc. New York: Barnes and Noble, 1974.
     Rev. by P. M. Ascoli, AHR, 81(Je 1976):598-9.

Scribner, Robert L., ed. and comp. see Van Schreeven, William
     J., comp.

Scullard, H. H. The Elephant in the Greek and Roman World.
     Ithaca, N.Y.: Cornell U Press, 1974. Rev. by T. E.
     Philoon, Historian, 38(Feb 1976):319.

Seager, Robin. Tiberius. Berkeley: U Cal Press, 1972. Rev.
     by J. Linderski, AHR, 81(Oct 1976):830-1.

Searle, Eleanor. Lordship and Community. Toronto: Pontifical
     Institute, 1974. Rev. by J. R. Wright, CH, 45(Je 1976):
     249-50; B. Harvey, EHR, 91(Jan 1976):175; C. Dyer, History,
     61(Feb 1976):97.

Seaver, Paul S., ed. Seventeenth-Century England. New York:
     New Viewpoints, 1976. Rev. by A. Weikel, HRNB, 4(Jl
     1976):179.

Sechi, Salvatore. Dopoguerra e fascismo in Sardegna. Turin:
     Einaudi, 1969. Rev. by N. A. O. Lyttelton, EHR, 91(Jan
     1976):163-5.

Secor, Robert, ed. Pennsylvania, 1776. University Park: Pa St
    U Press, 1975. Rev. by R. P. Gildrie, HRNB, 4(May/Je
    1976):143-4.

Secretary of State of Missouri. A Guide to the Missouri State
    Archives. Jefferson City: Secretary of State of Mo., 1975.
    Rev. by W. N. Davis, Jr., AmArc, 39(Apr 1976):202-3.

Sedlak, Michael W. see Church, Robert L.

Seebass, Gottfried, ed. see Osiander, Andreas

Seibt, Ferdinand. Deutschland und die Tschechen. Munich: Paul
    List Verlag, 1974. Rev. by V. S. Mamatey, EEQ, 10(Mar
    1976):130-2.

Seidel, Robert N. Toward an Andean Common Market for Science
    and Technology. Ithaca, N. Y.: Cornell U Press, 1974. Rev.
    by G. Matyoka, TAm, 32(Apr 1976):657-9.

Seidl, Ursala. Gefässmarken von Bogazköy, Bogazköy Hattusa,
    Ergebnisse der Ausgrabungen des Deutschen Archäologischen
    Instituts und der Deutschen Orient-Gesellschaft. Berlin:
    Gebr. Mann Verlag, 1972. Rev. by J. V. Canby, AJA, 80
    (Fall 1976):428-9.

Selassie, Haile. The Autobiography of Emperor Haile Selassie.
    Vol. I. (Edward Ullendorff, trans.) New York: Oxford U
    Press, 1976. Rev. by C. J. Jaenen, HRNB, 5(Oct 1976):13.

Selby, John. The Road to Yorktown. New York: St. Martin's,
    1976. Rev. by P. D. Nelson, JAH, 63(Dec 1976):700-1;
    R. R. Beeman, VMHB, 84(Oct 1976):494-5.

Selcher, Wayne A. The Afro-Asian Dimension of Brazilian Foreign
    Policy, 1956-1972. Gainesville: U Presses Fla, 1974. Rev.
    by R. N. Schneider, HAHR, 56(Feb 1976):138-40.

Sellers, John R., et al., comps. Manuscript Sources in the Li-
    brary of Congress for Research on the American Revolution.
    Washington, D. C.: Library of Congress, 1975. Rev. by W.
    Dykeman, AmArc, 39(Jan 1976):46-7; L. G. Bowman, His-
    torian, 39(Nov 1976):145-6; T. W. Mitchell, NCHR, 53(Win
    1976):92-3; J. Cary, OH, 85(Spr 1976):160-1.

Selwyn, Percy, ed. Development Policy in Small Countries. Lon-
    don: Croom Helm, 1975. Rev. by P. Robson, JMAS, 14
    (Sep 1976):541-3.

_____. Industries in the Southern African Periphery. London:
    Croom Helm, 1975. Rev. by P. Robson, JMAS, 14(Sep
    1976):541-3; P. Mosley, JMAS, 14(Sep 1976):543-6.

Semanov, S. N. The Liquidation of the Anti-Soviet Kronstadt Revolt of 1921. Moscow: Izdatel'stvo "Nauka," 1973. Rev. by A. Dallin, AHR, 81(Feb 1976):188.

Semmel, Bernard. The Methodist Revolution. London: Heinemann, 1974. Rev. by H. D. Rack, EHR, 91(Apr 1976):438-9.

Semo, Enrique. Historia del capitalismo en Mexico, Los Origenes, 1521/1763. Mexico: Ediciones Era, S. A., 1973. Rev. by J. Tutino, TAm, 33(Oct 1976):382-3.

Sen, Bandhudas. The Green Revolution in India. New York: Wiley, 1974. Rev. by T. Singh, IQ, 32(Apr-Je 1976):249-50.

Sen, Debabrata. Basic Principles of Geopolitics and History. Delhi: Concept Publishing, 1975. Rev. by K. P. Misra, IQ, 32(Jl-Sep 1976):341-2.

Senado Federal. Diario da assemblea geral constituinte e legislativa do Imperio do Brasil, 1823. 2 vols. Brasilia: Senado General Centro Grafica, 1973. Rev. by D. Parker, HAHR, 56(Feb 1976):177.

Senn, Alfred Erich. Diplomacy and Revolution. Notre Dame, Ind.: U Notre Dame, 1974. Rev. by R. A. Wade, AHR, 81(Feb 1976):187-8.

Senryn, Namiki see Izumo, Takeda

Sepúlveda Amor, Bernardo, et al. Las empresas trasnacionales en Mexico. Mexico: El Colegio de Mexico, 1974. Rev. by R. L. Bennett, HAHR, 56(May 1976):327-8.

Serafim, Archimandrite. The Quest for Orthodox Church Unity in America. New York: Sts. Boris and Glebb Press, 1973. Rev. by G. J. Tsoumas, CaHR, 62(Jl 1976):514-15.

Serge, Victor and Natalia Sedova Trotsky. The Life and Death of Leon Trotsky. New York: Basic Books, 1975. Rev. by C. Gershman, Commentary, 61(Jl 1976):73-5; S. D. Spector, HRNB, 4(Feb 1976):89.

Sernett, Milton C. Black Religion and American Evangelicalism. Metuchen, N.J.: Scarecrow, 1975. Rev. by J. M. Washington, CH, 45(Mar 1976):118-19; D. M. Tucker, JAH, 62(Mar 1976):982-3.

Sessions, Gene A. Latter-Day Patriots. Salt Lake City: Deseret Book Co., 1975. Rev. by L. Foster, A & W, 18(Aut 1976): 290-1; D. L. Lythgoe, JAH, 63(Dec 1976):702-3.

Seton-Watson, Hugh. The "Sick Heart" of Modern Europe: The Problem of the Danubian Lands. Seattle: U Wash Press, 1973. Rev. by R. A. Kann, AHR, 81(Oct 1976):895-6.

Setton, K. M. Catalan Domination of Athens 1311-1388. London:
    Variorum, 1975. Rev. by P. W. Edbury, EHR, 91(Oct 1976):
    898-9.

Sevost'ianov, G. N., ed. Basic Problems in the History of the
    U. S. A. in American Historiography. Moscow: Izdatel'stvo
    "Nauka," 1971. Rev. by R. V. Allen, AHR, 81(Je 1976):
    667-8.

Seward, Desmond. The Monks of War: The Military Religious
    Orders. Hamden, Conn.: Archon, 1972. Rev. by E. G.
    Blanco, CaHR, 62(Jan 1976):79-80.

Sewell, Richard H. Ballots for Freedom. New York: Oxford U
    Press, 1976. Rev. by F. Blue, CWH, 22(Je 1976):184-6.

Shabaeva, M. F., ed. Essays on the History of Schools and Peda-
    gogical Thought of the Peoples of the USSR. Moscow:
    Izdatel'stvo "Pedagogika," 1973. Rev. by E. C. Thaden,
    AHR, 81(Feb 1976):184-5.

Shade, William Gerald. Banks or No Banks: The Money Issue in
    Western Politics, 1832-1865. Detroit: Wayne St U Press,
    1972. Rev. in AS, 16(Spr 1975):75.

Shade, William L. Social Change and the Electoral Process.
    Gainesville: U Fla Press, 1973. Rev. by J. Baker, JIH,
    7(Sum 1976):184-6.

Shaffer, Arthur H. The Politics of History: Writing the History of
    the American Revolution, 1783-1815. Chicago: Precedent,
    1975. Rev. by R. J. Rubanowice, HRNB, 4(Feb 1976):76;
    J. A. Schutz, JAH, 63(Sep 1976):399-400; L. H. Leder, JSH,
    42(May 1976):279-80; V. Sapio, NCHR, 53(Spr 1976):227-8;
    R. Ketcham, VMHB, 84(Oct 1976):498-9.

Shaffer, E. S. "Kubla Khan" and "The Fall of Jerusalem." Cam-
    bridge: Cam U Press, 1975. Rev. by J. H. Lehmann,
    Commentary, 61(Jl 1976):75-8.

Shah, Ghanshyam. Politics of Scheduled Castes and Tribes. Bom-
    bay: Vora Publishers, 1975. Rev. by P. N. Sheth, 32(Jl-
    Sep 1976):368-71.

Shaha, Rishikesh. Nepali Politics: Retrospect and Prospect.
    Delhi: Oxford U Press, 1975. Rev. by S. D. Muni, IQ,
    32(Apr-Je 1976):239-42.

Shanin, Teodor. The Awkward Class. Oxford: Clarendon Press,
    1972. Rev. by R. Pethybridge, ESR, 6(Apr 1976):269-71.

Sharf, Andrew. Byzantine Jewry from Justinian to the Fourth
    Crusade. New York: Schocken, 1971. Rev. by R. L. Reid,
    JCS, 18(Win 1976):139.

Sharma, J. N. The Union and the States. New Delhi: Sterling,
    1974. Rev. by S. Ranganathan, IQ, 32(Jan-Mar 1976):106-7.

Sharp, Robert L. Big Outfit: Ranching on the Baca Float. Tucson:
    U Ariz Press, 1974. Rev. by C. C. Boykin, AgH, 50(Apr
    1976):433-4.

Sharp, Tony. The Wartime Alliance and the Zonal Division of Ger-
    many. New York: Oxford U Press, 1975. Rev. by M.
    Howard, EHR, 91(Apr 1976):469-70; R. W. Sellen, HRNB, 4
    (Jan 1976):68-9; P. G. Boyle, History, 61(Je 1976):329-30.

Shaw, Duncan, ed. John Knox: A Quatercentenary Reappraisal.
    Edinburgh: Saint Andrew Press, 1975. Rev. by R. L.
    Greaves, CH, 45(Mar 1976):113-14.

Shaw, Peter. The Character of John Adams. Chapel Hill: U NC
    Press, 1976. Rev. by H. Belz, Commentary, 61(Jl 1976):
    78-80; L. L. Tucker, HRNB, 4(Jl 1976):166; S. G. Kurtz,
    JAH, 63(Dec 1976):703-4; J. M. Poteet, JSH, 42(Nov 1976):
    580-1; C. Schulz, MHM, 71(Sum 1976):269-70; G. L. Lint,
    NEQ, 49(Sep 1976):479-80.

Shaw, Russell see Koob, C. Albert

Shea, William R., ed. see Bonelli, M. L. Righini, ed.

Shebl, James M. King of the Mountains. Stockton, Cal.: Pacific
    Center for Western Historical Studies, 1974. Rev. by R.
    Nash, JAH, 62(Mar 1976):1008.

Sheerin, John B. Never Look Back: The Career and Concerns of
    John J. Burke. Paramus, N.J.: Paulist Press, 1975. Rev.
    by J. H. Plough, CH, 45(Sep 1976):394-5.

Shennan, J. H. The Origins of the Modern European State 1450-
    1725. London: Hutchinson, 1974. Rev. by H. J. Cohn,
    EHR, 91(Jan 1976):185.

Shepelev, L. E. Joint Stock Companies in Russia. Leningrad:
    Izdatel'stvo "Nauka," 1973. Rev. by W. L. Blackwell, AHR,
    81(Je 1976):632.

Shepherd, Jack. The Adams Chronicles. Boston: Little, Brown,
    n.d. Rev. by H. Belz, Commentary, 61(Jl 1976):78-80.

_____. The Forest Killers. New York: Weybright and Talley,
    1975. Rev. by R. T. Dennis, Smithsonian, 6(Sep 1975):108,
    110, 112.

Shepherd, James F. and Gary M. Walton. Shipping, Maritime
    Trade, and the Economic Development of Colonial North
    America. New York: Cam U Press, 1972. Rev. by W. S.
    Sachs, AHR, 81(Apr 1976):441-2.

Sheridan, James E. China in Disintegration. New York: Mac-
    millan, 1975. Rev. by O.E.S., CurH, 71(Sep 1976):77; G.
    F. Botjer, HRNB, 4(Feb 1976):85; D. H. Bays, HT, 10(Nov
    1976):128-9; S. Karnow, Smithsonian, 6(Jan 1976):106-8.

Sheridan, James J., ed. and trans. Alan of Lille. Toronto:
    Pontifical Institute, 1973. Rev. by M. Wilks, History, 61
    (Oct 1976):443-4.

Sherman, Joan R. Invisible Poets. Urbana: U Ill, 1974. Rev.
    by D. T. Turner, JNH, 61(Apr 1976):215-17.

Sherman, William T. War Is Hell! Savannah, Ga.: Beehive, 1974.
    Rev. by R. M. McMurry, CWTI, 15(May 1976):50.

Sherwani, H. K. and P. M. Joshi, eds. History of Medieval
    Deccan, 1295-1724. Vol. II. Andhra Pradesh: Government
    of Andhra Pradesh, 1974. Rev. by M. N. Peasson, JAS,
    36(Nov 1976):161-2.

Sherwin, Martin J. A World Destroyed. New York: Knopf, 1975.
    Rev. by S. L. Falk, JAH, 63(Je 1976):197-8.

Shideler, James H., ed. Agriculture in the Development of the
    Far West. Washington: Agricultural History Society, 1975.
    Rev. by P. W. Gates, CHQ, 55(Spr 1976):92-3; I. May, Jr.,
    JOW, 15(Apr 1976):136-7; H. E. Socolofsky, SCQ, 58(Spr
    1976):132; L. Scamehorn, UHQ, 44(Spr 1976):191-2.

Shihata, Ibrahim F. I. The Case for the Arab Oil Embargo.
    Beirut: Institute for Palestine Studies, 1975. Rev. by R.
    Khan, IQ, 32(Jan-Mar 1976):92-3.

Shipton, Clifford K. Biographical Sketches of Those Who Attended
    Harvard College in the Classes 1768-1771. Boston: Massa-
    chusetts Historical Society, 1975. Rev. by M. Savelle, NEQ,
    49(Sep 1976):464-7.

Shirley, Janet, trans. Garnier's Becket. Chichester: Phillimore,
    1975. Rev. by K. Edwards, JEccH, 27(Apr 1976):213-14.

Shirley, John W. Thomas Harriott: Renaissance Scientist. Ox-
    ford: Clarendon, 1974. Rev. by K. T. Hoppen, EHR, 91
    (Jan 1976):200.

Shoalmire, J. G. see Scott, Roy V.

Shockley, John Staples. Chicano Revolt in a Texas Town. Notre
    Dame, Ind.: Notre Dame Press, 1974. Rev. by J. Small-
    wood, ETHJ, 14(Spr 1976):70-1.

Shofner, Jerrell H. Nor Is It Over Yet: Florida in the Era of
    Reconstruction, 1863-1877. Gainesville: U Presses Fla,
    1974. Rev. by H. Hattaway, AHR, 81(Oct 1976):979-80.

Shorter, Edward. The Making of the Modern Family. New York: Basic Books, 1975. Rev. by M. Matossian, AHR, 81(Oct 1976):822-3.

_____ and Charles Tilly. Strikes in France: 1830-1968. New York: Cam U Press, 1974. Rev. by M. R. Waldman, AHR, 81(Feb 1976):159-60; E. Schulkind, History, 61(Feb 1976): 138-9; J. Laux, JEH, 36(Sep 1976):792-4; R. J. Bezucha, JIH, 7(Sum 1976):157-60.

Shoruku, Mujoshi see Izumo, Takeda

Shoufani, Elias. The Arab Institute for Research and Publishing. Toronto: U Tor Press, 1973. Rev. by R. W. Smith, AHR, 81(Feb 1976):190-1.

Showalter, Dennis E. Railroads and Rifles. Hamden, Conn.: Archon, 1975. Rev. by J. R. Dukes, HRNB, 4(Mar 1976): 115.

Shriver, George H., ed. Contemporary Reflections on the Medieval Christian Tradition. Durham, N.C.: Duke U Press, 1974. Rev. by R. Luman, CH, 45(Je 1976):248-9.

Shtemenko, S. M. The Soviet General Staff at War, 1941-1945. Moscow: Progress Pub., 1970. Rev. by E. F. Ziemke, AHR, 81(Je 1976):638-9.

Shtohryn, Dmytro, et al., eds. Ukrainians in North America: A Biographical Directory of Noteworthy Men and Women of Ukrainian Origin in the United States and Canada. Champaign, Ill.: Association for the Advancement of Ukrainian Studies, 1975. Rev. by A. Sydorenko, AHR, 81(Oct 1976):951-2.

Shukla, Ram L. Britain, India and the Turkish Empire, 1853-1882. New Delhi: People's Publishing House, 1973. Rev. by J. J. Malone, CHR, 57(Mar 1976):78-9.

Shulvass, Moses A. The Jews in the World Renaissance. Leiden: E. J. Brill, 1973. Rev. by R. H. Popkin, AHR, 81(Je 1976): 573-4.

Shy, John. A People Numerous and Armed. New York: Oxford U Press, 1976. Rev. by C. Ubbelohde, NCHR, 53(Aut 1976): 412-13; L. Griffith, VMHB, 84(Jl 1976):373-5.

Shyllon, F. O. Black Slaves in Britain. New York: Oxford U Press, 1974. Rev. by R. W. Winks, AHR, 81(Feb 1976): 134-5; R. Anstey, EHR, 91(Apr 1976):436-7.

Sichrovsky, Harry. Koreareport. Vienna: Europaverlag, 1973. Rev. by A. Schmid, CQ, Jan 1976, pp. 151-3.

Sichtermann, Hellmut and Guntram Koch. Griechische Mythen auf
Römischen Sarkophagen. Tübingen: Verlag Ernst Wasmuth,
1975. Rev. by G. M. A. Hanfmann, AJA, 80(Fall 1976):440-
1.

Sidel, Ruth. Families of Fengsheng. Baltimore: Penguin, 1974.
Rev. by R. Witke, CQ, May 1976, pp. 394-6.

Sidel, Victor W. and Ruth Sidel. Serve the People, Observations
on Medicine in the People's Republic of China. New York:
Josiah Macy, Jr. Foundation, 1973. Rev. by J. N. Hawkins,
JAAS, 11(Jl-Oct 1976):215-19.

Sider, Ronald J. Andreas Bodenstein von Karlstadt. Leiden:
E. J. Brill, 1974. Rev. by C. Douglas, CaHR, 62(Jan 1976):
120-1; U. Plath, JEccH, 27(Jan 1976):83-4; K. R. Davis,
MQR, 50(Jan 1976):75-7.

Sidey, Hugh. These United States. McLean, Va.: EPM, 1975.
Rev. by R. Beeston, Smithsonian, 6(Je 1975):98-9.

Sierra Nava-Lasa, Luis. El Cardenal Lorenzana y la Illustracion.
Madrid: Fundacion Universitaria Española, 1975. Rev. by
G. Addy, HAHR, 56(Aug 1976):473-4.

Sijes, B. A. Studies over Jodenvervolging. Assen: Van Gorcum,
1974. Rev. by W. Warmbrunn, AHR, 81(Oct 1976):877-8.

Silberman, Bernard and H. D. Harootunian, eds. Japan in Crisis.
Princeton, N.J.: Prin U Press, 1974. Rev. by J. E. Hoare,
MAS, 10(Apr 1976):315-16.

Silva, Héleo. O ciclo de Vargas. Vol. XIII. Rio de Janeiro:
Civilizacão Brasileira, 1974. Rev. by F. D. McCann, HAHR,
56(May 1976):342-3.

Silver, Abba Hillel. Where Judaism Differed. New York: Macmillan, 1972. Rev. by H. A. Friedman, JCS, 17(Win 1976):
153-4.

Silver, Harold see Lawson, John

Silver, Pamela and Harold Silver. The Education of the Poor: The
History of a National School 1824-1974. Boston: Routledge and
Kegan Paul, 1974. Rev. by R. K. Webb, AHR, 81(Apr 1976):
388-9; N. McCord, EHR, 91(Jan 1976):214; G. Sutherland,
History, 61(Je 1976):305.

Simmons, Marc. The Little Lion of the Southwest. Chicago:
Swallow, 1973. Rev. by C. Trafzer, JOW, 15(Jan 1976):
124-5.

_____. Witchcraft in the Southwest: Spanish and Indian Super-

naturalism on the Rio Grande. Flagstaff, Ariz: Northland
Press, 1974. Rev. by C. H. Lange, PHR, 45(Feb 1976):
125-6.

Simmons, Robert T. The Strained Alliance. New York: Free
Press, 1975. Rev. by L. Weiss, CQ, May 1976, pp. 384-6.

Simon, Brian and Ian Bradley, eds. The Victorian Public School.
Dublin: Gill and Macmillan, 1975. Rev. by G. Sutherland,
History, 61(Oct 1976):482-3.

Simon, Erika, ed. Führer durch die Antikenabteilung des Martin
von Wagner Museums der Universität Würzburg. Mainz:
Verlag Philipp von Zabern, 1975. Rev. by C. G. Boulter,
AJA, 80(Fall 1976):439.

Simon, Gerhard. Church, State and Opposition in the U.S.S.R.
Berkeley: U Cal Press, 1974. Rev. by W. C. Fletcher,
CaHR, 62(Oct 1976):670-1; N. Zernov, JCS, 17(Spr 1975):
325-7.

Simon, John Y., ed. see Grant, Julia Dent

Simonetti, Manlio, ed. Gregorio di Elvira, La Fede. Turin:
Società Editrice Internazionale, 1975. Rev. by G. Bonner,
JEccH, 27(Oct 1976):415-16.

Simonson, Harold P. Jonathan Edwards: Theologian of the Heart.
Grand Rapids, Mich.: Eerdman's, 1974. Rev. by W. R.
Ward, EHR, 91(Jl 1976):650.

Simpson, Lewis P. The Dispossessed Garden. Athens, Ga.: U
Ga Press, 1975. Rev. by E. S. Godbold, Jr., AHR, 81(Je
1976):649; C. W. Joyner, JSH, 42(Feb 1976):149-50.

Sims, Harold D. La Expulsión de los españoles de Mexico (1821-
1828). Mexico: Fondo de Cultura Economica, 1974. Rev.
by E. W. Harrell, TAm, 33(Oct 1976):181-2.

Sinclair, Bruce. Philadelphia's Philosopher Mechanics. Baltimore:
JHU Press, 1975. Rev. by K. Birr, AHR, 81(Je 1976):661-
2; A. C. Davies, History, 61(Oct 1976):405-6; W. B. Hen-
drickson, IMH, 72(Mar 1976):73-4; N. Lederer, PH, 43(Jan
1976):86-7.

Sinel, Allen. The Classroom and the Chancellery. Cambridge,
Mass.: Harvard U Press, 1973. Rev. by S. F. Starr, JMH,
48(Sep 1976):570-1.

Singh, Bawa Satinder. The Jammu Fox. Carbondale: S Ill U
Press, 1974. Rev. by N. Rabitoy, AHR, 81(Feb 1976):196;
J. Pemble, EHR, 91(Jan 1976):212-13.

Singh, Diwaker Prasad. American Attitude Towards the Indian Nationalist Movement. New Delhi: Munshiram Manocharial
Publishers, 1974. Rev. by Alan Raucher, PHR, 45(Aug 1976):
459-60.

Singleton, Fred. Twentieth-Century Yugoslavia. London: Macmillan, n.d. Rev. by S. Clissold, EHR, 91(Oct 1976):934-5.

Sinh, Raghubir, ed. Fort William--India House Correspondence.
New Delhi: Manager, Publications, Government of India,
1972. Rev. by E. W. AmArc, 39(Jan 1976):52-4; P. J.
Marshall, EHR, 91(Jl 1976):633-4.

Sinha, P. B. Indian National Liberation Movement and Russia,
1905-17. New Delhi: Sterling Publishers, 1975. Rev. by R.
Vaidyanath, IQ, 32(Jl-Sep 1976):361-2.

Sinha, S. N. Subah of Allahabad Under the Mughals (1580-1707).
New Delhi: Jamia Millia Islamia, 1974. Rev. by U. N. Day,
IESHR, 13(Jan-Mar 1976):120-3.

Siraisi, Nancy G. Arts and Sciences at Padua. Toronto: Pontifical
Institute, 1973. Rev. by J. K. Hyde, History, 61(Feb 1976):
99-100.

Sisson, Daniel. The American Revolution of 1800. New York:
Knopf, 1974. Rev. by J. Cooke, AHR, 81(Oct 1976):964-5.

Skardal, Dorothy Burton. The Divided Heart. Lincoln: U Neb
Press, 1974. Rev. by K. O. Bjork, AHR, 81(Je 1976):
670-2; L. E. Purcell, AI, 43(Spr 1976):299-302; P. A. M.
Taylor, EHR, 91(Jan 1976):221; C. Erickson, JAmS, 10(Apr
1976):117-18.

Skidelsky, Robert. Oswald Mosley. New York: Holt, Rinehart
and Winston, 1975. Rev. by R. I. McKibben, EHR, 91(Jan
1976):166-7; G. B. Beadle, JMH, 48(Je 1976):328-9.

Skidmore, Thomas E. Black into White. New York: Oxford U
Press, 1974. Rev. by T. W. Walker, JCS, 17(Spr 1975):
338-40.

Skinner, G. William and A. Thomas Kirsch, eds. Change and
Persistence in Thai Society. Ithaca, N.Y.: Cornell U Press,
1975. Rev. by J. M. Potter, JAS, 36(Nov 1976):184-5.

_____, ed. see Elvin, Mark, ed.

Sklar, Robert. Movie-Made America. New York: Random House,
1975. Rev. by J. Cawelti, JAH, 63(Sep 1976):450-1.

Skrynnikov, R. G. The Correspondence of Groznyi and Kurbskii:
The Paradoxes of Edward Keenan. Leningrad: Izdatel'stvo

"Nauka," 1973. Rev. by D. B. Miller, AHR, 81(Oct 1976): 904-5.

Skrypnyk, Mykola. Articles and Speeches on the Nationality Question. Munich: Suchasnist Publ'rs, 1974. Rev. by M. Bohachevsky-Chomiak, AHR, 81(Je 1976):635-6.

Sladkevich, N. G., ed. Problems of Social Thought and Economic Policy in Russia, 19th-20th Centuries. Leningrad: Izdatel'stvo Leningradskogo Universiteta, 1972. Rev. by M. S. Shatz, AHR, 81(Apr 1976):424.

Slaven, Anthony. The Development of the West of Scotland, 1750-1960. London: Routledge and Kegan Paul, 1975. Rev. by S. B. Saul, BHR, 50(Spr 1976):106-7; R. H. Campbell, History, 61(Oct 1976):478-80.

Slavin, Arthur. The Way of the West. Vols. A and B. Lexington, Mass.: Xerox College, 1975. Rev. by J. Hunt, HT, 10 (Nov 1976):131-3.

Slottman, William B., ed. see Janos, Andrew C., ed.

Slukhovskii, M. I. The Russian Library in the 16th and 17th Centuries. Moscow: Izdatel'stvo "Kniga," 1973. Rev. by C. B. O'Brien, AHR, 81(Feb 1976):183-4.

Smail, R. C. The Crusaders. New York: Praeger, 1974. Rev. by M. W. Baldwin, AHR, 81(Feb 1976):110-11.

Smalley, Beryl. Historians in the Middle Ages. London: Thames and Hudson, 1974. Rev. by D. Luscombe, History, 61(Je 1976):249.

Smallwood, Frank. Free and Independent: The Initiation of a College Professor into State Politics--Candid Look at How Our Laws Begin. Brattleboro, Vt.: Stephen Greene Press, 1976. Rev. by H. O. Moffett, VH, 44(Sum 1976):173-5.

Smart, William B. and Henry A. Smith, ed. Deseret, 1776-1976: A Bicentennial Illustrated History of Utah by the Deseret News. Salt Lake City: Deseret News, 1975. Rev. by I. S. Cooper, UHQ, 44(Spr 1976):183-5.

Smelser, Marshall. The Life That Ruth Built. New York: Quadrangle, 1975. Rev. by H. Seymour, JAH, 63(Dec 1976):762.

_____. The Winning of Independence. London: Croom Helm, 1974. Rev. by C. C. Bonwick, History, 61(Oct 1976):400-1.

Smelser, Ronald M. The Sudeten Problem 1933-1938: "Volkstumspolitik" and the Formulation of Nazi Foreign Policy. Folkestone: Dawson, 1975. Rev. by W. V. Wallace, History, 61 (Je 1976):323-4.

Smethurst, Richard J. A Social Basis for Prewar Japanese Militarism. Berkeley: U Cal Press, 1974. Rev. by M. Fletcher, AHR, 81(Je 1976):645; H. D. Smith, II, JJS, 2(Aut 1975): 131-46.

Smilie, Robert S. The Sonoma Mission: San Francisco Solano de Sonoma. Fresno, Cal.: Valley Publishers, 1975. Rev. by J. McCormick, A & W, 18(Aut 1976):305-6; R. J. Roske, WHQ, 7(Jan 1976):72-3.

Smith, A. C. H., et al. Paper Voices. Totowa, N.J.: Rowman and Littlefield, 1975. Rev. by C. A. Cline, AHR, 81(Oct 1976):865.

Smith, A. Hassell. County and Court: Government and Politics in Norfolk, 1558-1603. New York: Oxford U Press, 1974. Rev. by G. L. Owens, AHR, 81(Feb 1976):128-9; A. L. Rowse, EHR, 91(Jan 1976):193-5.

Smith, B., ed. see Constable, G., ed.

Smith, Barbara Sweetland. Preliminary Survey of Documents in the Archives of the Russian Orthodox Church in Alaska. Boulder, Colo.: Resources Development Internship Program, 1974. Rev. by T. C. Hinckley, PNQ, 67(Jl 1976):132.

Smith, Brooke Williams. Jacques Maritain: Antimodern or Ultramodern? New York: Elsevier, 1976. Rev. by R. Mathis, HRNB, 4(Aug 1976):201.

Smith, C. Earle, Jr., ed. Man and His Foods. University, Ala.: U Ala Press, 1973. Rev. by R. I. Ford, AmAnt, 41(Jl 1976):409.

Smith, Canfield F. Vladivostok Under Red and White Rule. Seattle: U Wash Press, 1976. Rev. by N. Saul, HRNB, 5(Oct 1976):17.

Smith, Charles R. Marines in the Revolution. Washington: U.S. Marine Corps, 1975. Rev. by H. H. Peckham, JAH, 63(Sep 1976):398-9; G. B. Smith, NCHR, 53(Aut 1976):411-12; B. Hall, SCHM, 77(Apr 1976):131-2.

_____ see Neilan, Edward

Smith, Denis Mack. Mussolini's Roman Empire. New York: Viking, 1976. Rev. by J. M. Block, HRNB, 5(Oct 1976):18.

Smith, Dorothy Blakey. The Reminiscences of Doctor John Sebastian Helmcken. Vancouver: U BC, 1975. Rev. by M. Clark, Jr., OHQ, 77(Sep 1976):294.

Smith, Duane A. Silver Saga. Boulder, Colo.: Pruett, 1974. Rev. by A. F. January, A & W, 18(Sum 1976):203-4.

Smith, Dwight L. , ed. Indians of the United States and Canada: A Bibliography. Santa Barbara, Cal.: Clio, 1974. Rev. by F. P. Prucha, ChOk, 54(Win 1976):532-3; A. M. Gibson, WHQ, 7(Apr 1976):203-4.

Smith, E. A. Whig Principles and Party Politics. Manchester: Manchester U Press, 1975. Rev. by J. Cannon, EHR, 91 (Oct 1976):917.

Smith, Elbert B. The Presidency of James Buchanan. Lawrence: U Press Kan, 1975. Rev. by J. George, Jr., AHR, 81(Apr 1976):449; R. E. Shaw, HRNB, 4(Jan 1976):57-8; D. E. Meerse, IMH, 72(Mar 1976):76-7; J. T. Hubbell, JAH, 63 (Sep 1976):420-1; L. H. Croce, JOW, 15(Apr 1976):136; K. L. Hall, JSH, 42(Feb 1976):121-2.

Smith, Elihu Hubbard. The Diary of Elihu Hubbard Smith (1771-1798). (James E. Cronin, ed.) Philadelphia: American Philosophical Society, 1973. Rev. by R. S. Klein, AHR, 81 (Je 1976):654-5; J. F. Beard, NYHSQ, 60(Jan/Apr 1976): 64-5.

Smith, Elwyn A. Religious Liberty in the United States. Philadelphia: Fortress Press, 1972. Rev. by O. C. Robison, JCS, 18(Win 1976):130-2.

Smith, F. B. Radical Artisan: William James Linton 1812-97. Manchester: Manchester U Press, 1973. Rev. by D. Hay, CHR, 57(Mar 1976):73-4.

Smith, Gary V. Zionism: The Dream and the Reality. New York: Barnes and Noble, 1974. Rev. by D. R. Divine, IJMES, 7(Apr 1976):305-6.

Smith, George L. Religion and Trade in New Netherlands. Ithaca, N.Y.: Cornell U Press, 1973. Rev. by H. M. Dunkak, CaHR, 62(Jl 1976):473-4; C. Brooks, EHR, 91(Jan 1976):204.

Smith, Gustavus Woodson. The Battle of Seven Pines. Dayton, Ohio: Morningside, 1974. Rev. by J. P. Cullen, CWTI, 15 (May 1976):48.

Smith, H. Shelton. In His Image, But: Racism in Southern Religion, 1780-1910. Durham: Duke U Press, 1972. Rev. by J. D. Bragg, JCS, 17(Spr 1975):314-16.

Smith, Henry DeWitt II. Japan's First Student Radicals. Cambridge, Mass.: Harvard U Press, 1972. Rev. by J. E. Hunter, MAS, 10(Oct 1976):629-32.

Smith, Jean Edward, ed. see Clay, Lucius D.

Smith, John Holland. Francis of Assisi. New York: Scribner's,

1972. Rev. by C. T. Davis, AHR, 81(Feb 1976):116-17;
J. J. Smith, CaHR, 62(Jan 1976):88-9.

Smith, Lacey Baldwin. Elizabeth Tudor: Portrait of a Queen.
Boston: Little, Brown, 1975. Rev. by M. M. Lomax, Historian, 39(Nov 1976):118-19.

Smith, Page. A New Age Now Begins. New York: McGraw-Hill,
1976. Rev. by R. Detweiler, HT, 10(Nov 1976):150-1; D. B.
Scheick, IMH, 72(Dec 1976):364-6.

Smith, Paul, ed. The Historian and Film. New York: Cam U
Press, 1976. Rev. by G. Porter, BHR, 50(Sum 1976):229-30;
E. Gordon, HRNB, 4(May/Je 1976):151; E. B. Burns, PHR,
45(Aug 1976):433-4.

Smith, Peter H. Argentina and the Failure of Democracy: Conflict
Among Political Elites, 1904-1955. Madison: U Wis Press,
1974. Rev. by P. B. Goodwin, Jr., AHR, 81(Oct 1976):
1013-14; R. A. Potash, HAHR, 56(Feb 1976):140-2.

_____, ed. see Graham, Richard

Smith, Rex Allan. Moon of Popping Trees. New York: Reader's
Digest/Crowell, 1975. Rev. by L. M. Hauptman, HRNB, 4
(Apr 1976):122.

Smith, Robert J. Ancestor Worship in Contemporary Japan. Stanford, Cal.: Stanford U Press, 1974. Rev. by H. Befu, JJS,
2(Aut 1975):172-7.

Smith, Roger see Sutcliffe, Anthony

Smith, Sidonie. Where I'm Bound. Westport, Conn.: Greenwood,
1974. Rev. by R. L. Zangrando, AHR, 81(Apr 1976):450-1;
H. Jones, AS, 16(Fall 1975):94.

Smith, T. Lynn. Brazilian Society. Albuquerque: U NM Press,
1975. Rev. by J. Saunders, Américas, 28(Feb 1976):44; C.
Wagley, HAHR, 56(Feb 1976):113-14.

Smith, Thomas H., ed. An Ohio Reader: 1750 to the Civil War.
Grand Rapids, Mich.: Eerdmans, 1975. Rev. by W. Giffin,
IMH, 72(Je 1976):263-4.

_____, ed. An Ohio Reader: Reconstruction to the Present.
Grand Rapids, Mich.: Eerdmans, 1975. Rev. by W. Giffin,
IMH, 72(Je 1976):263-4.

Smith, Van Mitchell see DeBoe, David C.

Smithson, Rulon Nephi. Augustin Thierry: Social and Political
Consciousness in the Evolution of a Historical Method. Gene-

va: Libraire Droz, 1972. Rev. by A. Scham, AHR, 81(Oct 1976):870-1.

Smoke, Richard see George, Alexander L.

Smolar, Boris. Soviet Jewry, Today and Tomorrow. New York: Macmillan, 1971. Rev. by A. W. Wardin, Jr., JCS, 17(Win 1975):144-5.

Smyth, Howard McGaw. Secrets of the Fascist Era. Carbondale: S Ill U Press, 1975. Rev. by J. E. Miller, AmArc, 39(Jan 1976):58-9; C. Seton-Wallace, History, 61(Oct 1976):468-70; F. C. Pogue, JAH, 63(Je 1976):189-90.

Snetsinger, John. Truman, the Jewish Vote, and the Creation of Israel. Stanford, Cal.: Hoover Institution Press, 1974. Rev. by R. T. Ruetten, JAH, 63(Je 1976):191-3.

Snyder, Charles M. The Lady and the President: The Letters of Dorothea Dix and Millard Fillmore. Lexington: U Press Ky, 1975. Rev. by L. Filler, JAH, 63(Dec 1976):720-1; C. Wilson, NCHR, 53(Sum 1976):332-3; R. E. Goerler, OH, 85(Sum 1976):271-3.

Snyder, Frank E. and Brian H. Guss. The District: A History of the Philadelphia District U.S. Army Corps of Engineers, 1866-1871. Philadelphia: US Army Engineer Dist., 1974. Rev. by D. H. Stapleton, PH, 43(Apr 1976):191-2.

So, Kwan-wai. Japanese Piracy in Ming China During the 16th Century. East Lansing: Mich St U Press, 1975. Rev. by E. L. Dreyer, JAS, 36(Nov 1976):129-30.

Sobel, Robert. The Entrepreneurs. New York: Weybright and Talley, 1974. Rev. by T. Freyes, BHR, 50(Sum 1976):234-5.

_____. N.Y.S.E.: A History of the New York Stock Exchange, 1935-1975. New York: Weybright and Talley, 1975. Rev. by B. Mitchell, AHR, 81(Oct 1976):998-9.

Société de l'histoire du Protestantisme français. Actes du Colloque l'admiral de coligny et son temps. Paris: Société de l'histoire du Protestantisme français, 1974. Rev. by D. Potter, EHR, 91(Jan 1976):197-8; R. J. Knecht, History, 61(Je 1976): 279-80.

Soelle, Dorothee. Political Theology. Philadelphia: Fortress, 1974. Rev. by M. D. Gustafson, JCS, 17(Aut 1975):526-8.

Soininen, Arvo M. Vanha maataloutemme. Helsinki: Historiallisia tutkimuksia 96, 1974. Rev. by D. Kirby, EHR, 91(Jl 1976): 652.

Soliday, Gerald L. A Community in Conflict: Frankfurt Society in
the Seventeenth and Early Eighteenth Centuries. Hanover,
N.H.: U Press New England, 1974. Rev. by T. C. W. Blanning, EHR, 91(Apr 1976):429; D. McKay, History, 61(Je 1976):
292.

Sollberger, E. see Edwards, I. E. S.

Solov'ev, A. A., et al., eds. Russian Internationalists in the
Struggle for the Hungarian Soviet Republic, 1919. Moscow:
Izdatel'stvo Politicheskoi Literatury, 1972. Rev. by I.
Avakumovic, AHR, 81(Feb 1976):126.

Soltow, Lee. Men and Wealth in the United States, 1850-1870.
New Haven, Conn.: Yale U Press, 1976. Rev. by S. L.
Engerman, BHR, 50(Spr 1976):118-19; M. Walsh, History,
61(Oct 1976):410; S. Lebergott, JEH, 36(Sep 1976):795-7.

Solyom, Garrett and Bronwen Solyom. Textiles of the Indonesian
Archipelago. Honolulu: U Hawaii Press, 1973. Rev. by H.
O'Neill, JAAS, 11(Jl-Oct 1976):223.

Solzhenitsyn, Alexsander I. The Gulag Archipelago, vol. II. New
York: Harper and Row, n.d. Rev. by L. Abel, Commentary,
61(Mar 1976):64-8.

Soman, Alfred, ed. The Massacre of St. Bartholomew. The
Hague: Martinus Nijhoff, 1974. Rev. by N. L. Roelker,
AHR, 81(Apr 1976):394-5; J. W. Brush, CH, 45(Mar 1976):
110; R. B. Wernham, EHR, 91(Oct 1976):906-7; R. J. Knecht,
History, 61(Je 1976):279-80.

Somekh, Sasson. The Changing Rhythm. Leiden: E. J. Brill,
1973. Rev. by R. Allen, IJMES, 7(Jan 1976):134-6.

Sommer, Lawrence J. The Heritage of Dubuque. Dubuque: First
National Bank, Dubuque, 1975. Rev. by M. S. Foster, JAH,
63(Dec 1976):709-10.

Sonnichsen, C. L. Colonel Greene and the Copper Skyrocket.
Tucson: U Ariz Press, 1974. Rev. by M. D. Bernstein,
PHR, 45(May 1976):291-2; B. Finch, WHQ, 7(Apr 1976):215-
16.

_____ see Chambers, G. W.

Sonnino, Sidney. Diario 1866-1922. 3 vols. Lawrence: U Press
Kan, 1972. Rev. by R. Albrecht-Carrié, AHR, 81(Je 1976):
622.

_____. Scritti e discorsi extraparlamentari. Lawrence: U
Press Kan, 1972. Rev. by R. Albrecht-Carrié, AHR, 81(Je
1976):622.

Sorauf, Frank J.   The Wall of Separation.   Princeton, N.J.:   Prin
U Press, 1976.   Rev. by P. L. Murphy, JAH, 63(Dec 1976):
781-2.

Sorsby, Arnold, ed.   Tenements of Clay.   London: Julian Friedmann, 1974.   Rev. by T. M. Brown, JIH, 7(Aut 1976):354-6.

Soules, Gordon and Christine   see   Hull, Raymond

Southgate, Donald, ed.   The Conservative Leadership, 1832-1932.
London: Macmillan, 1974.   Rev. by R. E. Quinault, EHR, 91
(Jl 1976):669-70; P. Smith, History, 61(Feb 1976):133-4.

Sowards, J. Kelley.   Desiderius Erasmus.   Boston: Twayne, 1975.
Rev. by A. Rabil, Jr., CH, 45(Je 1976):253-4.

Sowell, Thomas.   Race and Economics.   New York: David McKay,
1975.   Rev. by N. J. Weiss, AHR, 81(Je 1976):681-2.

Spadolini, Giovanni, ed.   Il Cardinale Gasparri e la Questione
Romana.   Florence: Felice Le Monnier, 1972.   Rev. by A.
C. O'Brien, CaHR, 62(Oct 1976):647-9.

Spalding, Ruth.   The Improbable Puritan.   London: Faber and Faber, 1975.   Rev. by I. Roots, EHR, 91(Apr 1976):425-6; A.
Woolrych, History, 61(Feb 1976):114.

Spalding, Thomas W.   Martin John Spalding: American Churchman.
Washington: Catholic U America Press, 1973.   Rev. by M.
V. Gannon, CaHR, 62(Jl 1976):495-6.

Spaulding, J. L.   see   O'Fahey, R. S.

Spear, Percival.   Master of Bengal: Clive and His India.   London:
Thames and Hudson, 1975.   Rev. by P. J. Marshall, History,
61(Feb 1976):163.

Speare, Jean E., ed.   The Days of Augusta.   North Pomfret, Vt.:
David and Charles, n.d.   Rev. by B. Schiff, Smithsonian, 6
(Jan 1975):99-101.

Speck, Paul.   Die Kaiserliche Universität von Konstantinopel.
Munich: C. H. Beck, 1974.   Rev. by D. M. Nicol, EHR,
91(Jan 1976):174.

Spector, Ronald.   Admiral of the New Empire: The Life and
Career of George Dewey.   Baton Rouge: LSU Press, 1974.
Rev. by H. W. Morgan, PHR, 45(Feb 1976):146-7.

Spence, Clark C.   Territorial Politics and Government in Montana
1864-89.   Urbana: U Ill Press, 1976.   Rev. by L. E. Ziewacz, HRNB, 4(May/Je 1976):144; K. N. Owens, JAH, 63(Dec
1976):726-7; S. R. Davison, JOW, 15(Apr 1976):128; D. M.

Shockley, NDH, 43(Fall 1976):43; S. R. Davison, UHQ, 44
(Sum 1976):307-8; M. P. Malone, WHQ, 7(Oct 1976):430-1.

Spencer, Charles Floyd. Wyoming Homestead Heritage. Hicksville,
N. Y.: Exposition, 1975. Rev. by M. B. Husband, JOW, 15
(Apr 1976):141-2.

Spencer, William. Algiers in the Age of the Corsairs. Norman:
U Ok Press, 1976. Rev. by D. W. Littlefield, HRNB, 4(Sep
1976):223-4.

Spengler, Joseph J. Population and America's Future. San Francisco: Freeman, 1975. Rev. by J. E. Eblen, JAH, 63(Sep
1976):469-70.

Spielman, Richard M. Bexley Hall: 150 Years. Rochester, N. Y.:
Colgate-Rochester Divinity School, 1974. Rev. by L. L.
Brown, HMPEC, 45(Sep 1976):350-1.

Spinka, Matthew, trans. The Letters of John Hus. Totowa, N. J.:
Rowman and Littlefield, 1972. Rev. by O. Odlozilik, CaHR,
62(Jan 1976):109-10.

Spinner, Thomas J., Jr. George Joachim Goschen. Cambridge:
Cam U Press, 1973. Rev. by A. Jones, HJ, 19(Mar 1976):
251-6.

Spira, György. A Hungarian Count in the Revolution of 1848. Budapest: Akademiai Kiadó, 1974. Rev. by P. I. Hidas, AHR,
81(Apr 1976):422.

Spitzer, Leo. The Creoles of Sierra Leone. Madison: U Wis
Press, 1974. Rev. by J. Peterson, ÅfAf, 75(Apr 1976):
256-7; C. Fyfe, JAfH, 17(Num 2, 1976):315-17.

Spotts, Frederic. The Churches and Politics in Germany. Middletown, Conn.: Wesleyan U Press, 1973. Rev. by J. H.
Spurk, CaHR, 62(Oct 1976):669-70; K. Penzel, JCS, 18(Aut
1976):561-3; G. C. Zahn, JMH, 48(Sep 1976):568-70.

Sprague, Marshall. So Vast So Beautiful a Land: Louisiana and
the Purchase. Boston: Little, Brown, 1974. Rev. by A.
P. Nasatir, PHR, 45(Aug 1976):440-1.

Spriano, Paolo. Storia di Torino Operaia e Socialista. Turin:
Giulio Einaudi Editore, 1972. Rev. by L. A. Tilly, JMH,
48(Je 1976):339-42.

Sprunger, Keith L., et al., eds. Voices Against War. North
Newton, Kan.: Bethel College, 1973. Rev. by R. J.
Sawatsky, MQR, 50(Jan 1976):69-70.

Spufford, Margaret. Contrasting Communities: English Villagers in the Sixteenth and Seventeenth Centuries. New York: Cam U Press, 1974. Rev. by D. Cressy, AHR, 81(Apr 1976): 383; K. Thomas, History, 61(Je 1976):271-2; W. T. McCaffrey, JIH, 7(Sum 1976):144-6; D. T. Courtwright, JSoH, 10 (Fall 1976):116-19.

Squarciapino, Maria Floriani. Sculture del Foro severiano di Leptis Magna. Rome: L'Erma di Bretschneider, 1974. Rev. by D. White, AJA, 80(Sum 1976):321-2.

Staar, Richard F., ed. Yearbook on International Communist Affairs, 1975. Stanford, Cal.: Hoover Institution Press, 1975. Rev. by K. M. Schmitt, HAHR, 56(Feb 1976):179-80.

Stacey, Margaret, et al. Power, Persistence and Change: A Second Study of Banbury. London: Routledge and Kegan Paul, 1975. Rev. by A. Warwick, History, 61(Oct 1976):497.

Stachura, Peter D. Nazi Youth in the Weimar Republic. Santa Barbara, Cal.: Clio, 1975. Rev. by T. A. Knapp, HRNB, 4(Mar 1976):113-14.

Stadelmann, Rudolph. Social and Political History of the German 1848 Revolution. Athens, Ohio: Ohio U Press, 1975. Rev. by W. Carr, History, 61(Oct 1976):463; C. M. Prelinger, HRNB, 4(Feb 1976):89-90.

Stafford, Irene, ed. see Cushing, Irene, ed.

Stahl, Michael. Ethiopia: Political Contradictions in Agricultural Development. Stockholm: Political Science Assn in Uppsala, 1974. Rev. by W. A. Shack, Africa, 46(Num 2, 1976):214.

Stahl, Wilhelm. Der Elitekreislauf in der Unternehmerschaft: Eine Empirische Untersuchung fur den Deutschsprachigen Raum. Frankfurt am Main: Deutsch, 1973. Rev. by J. Kocka, BHR, 50(Spr 1976):103-4.

Stairs, Denis. The Diplomacy of Constraint. Toronto: U Tor Press, 1974. Rev. by R. Bothwell, CHR, 57(Je 1976):220-2.

Standing Bear, Luther. My People the Sioux. Lincoln: U Neb, 1975. Rev. by G. Riley, AI, 43(Win 1976):224-7.

Stanford, G. H. To Serve the Community: The Story of Toronto's Board of Trade. Toronto: U Tor Press, 1974. Rev. by D. S. Macmillan, BH, 17(Jl 1975):211-12.

Stanford, W. B. and J. V. Luce. The Quest for Ulysses. New York: Praeger, 1974. Rev. by F. Stubbings, Antiquity, 50 (Mar 1976):77-8; N. Stravrolakes, Archaeology, 29(Jan 1976): 62-4.

STANIFORD   358

Staniford, Edward.   The Pattern of California History.   New York:
     Canfield, 1975.   Rev. by B. Luckingham, CHQ, 55(Sum 1976):
     186-7; H. B. Melendy, PNQ, 67(Oct 1976):178.

Stannard, David E., ed.   Death in America.   n.p.: U of Pa Press,
     1975.   Rev. by J. Kent, History, 61(Oct 1976):421.

Stanton, William.   The Great United States Exploring Expedition of
     1838-1842.   Berkeley: U Cal Press, 1975.   Rev. by J. H.
     Kemble, JAH, 63(Sep 1976):410; A. H. Dupree, PHR, 45(Nov
     1976):615-17.

Starck, Christian.   Verfassungsrecht in Fällen.   Baden-Baden:
     Nomes, 1968.   Rev. by W A. Mueller, JCS, 18(Win 1976):
     144-5.

Starobin, Robert S., ed.   Blacks in Bondage.   New York: New
     Viewpoints, 1974.   Rev. by E. Noyes, JISHS, 69(May 1976):
     156-7.

Starr, Kevin.   Americans and the California Dream, 1850-1915.
     New York: Oxford U Press, 1973.   Rev. by G. O. Nash,
     Historian, 39(Nov 1976):158-60.

Starr, S. Frederick.   Decentralization and Self-Government in Rus-
     sia 1830-1870.   Princeton, N.J.: Prin U Press, 1970.   Rev.
     by M. C. Chapman, ESR, 6(Apr 1976):258-60.

Starr, Steven Z.   Jennison's Jayhawkers.   Baton Rouge: LSU
     Press, 1973.   Rev. by R. D. Hoffsommer, CWTI, 15(May
     1976):50.

Starrels, John M. and Anita M. Mallinckrodt.   Politics in the Ger-
     man Democratic Republic.   New York: Praeger, 1975.   Rev.
     by O. E. S., CurH, 70(Mar 1976):123; M. Grote, EEQ, 10(Sum
     1976):270-2.

Stave, Bruce M., ed.   Socialism and the Cities.   Port Washington,
     N.Y.: Kennikat, 1975.   Rev. by H. F. Bedford, AHR, 81
     (Oct 1976):953.

Stavenhagen, Rodolfo.   Social Classes in Agrarian Societies.   Gar-
     den City, N.Y.: Anchor, 1975.   Rev. by M. Seligson, HAHR,
     56(Feb 1976):170-1.

Stayer, James M.   Anabaptists and the Sword.   Lawrence, Kan.:
     Coronado, 1973.   Rev. by H. J. Hillerbrand, CaHR, 62(Jan
     1976):125-7.

Stearns, Peter N.   1848: The Revolutionary Tide in Europe.   New
     York: Norton, 1974.   Rev. by J. Bowditch, AHR, 81(Oct
     1976):844-5.

359   STEARNS

_____. Lives of Labor: Work in a Maturing Industrial Society.
New York: Holmes and Meier, 1975. Rev. by J. W. Scott,
AHR, 81(Je 1976):565; D. Montgomery, JIH, 7(Aut 1976):326-
7; R. J. Bezucha, JMH, 48(Sep 1976):535-8.

Steckel, Charles W. Destruction and Survival. Los Angeles: Del-
mar, 1973. Rev. by D. Aronson, Judaism, 25(Spr 1976):255-
6.

Steel, Tom. The Life and Death of St. Kilda. London: Collins/
Fontana, 1975. Rev. by R. H. Campbell, History, 61(Oct
1976):478-80.

Steele, Colin. English Interpreters of the Iberian New World (1603-
1726). Oxford: Dolphin, 1975. Rev. by J. Lynch, EHR, 91
(Oct 1976):909; M. G. Hall, HAHR, 56(Feb 1976):174; J. S.
Cummins, History, 61(Je 1976):282; M. J. McLeod, TAm, 32
(Apr 1976):644-5.

Steele, E. D. Irish Land and British Politics. New York: Cam
U Press, 1974. Rev. by L. J. McCaffrey, AHR, 81(Feb
1976):150-1; M. Hurst, History, 61(Feb 1976):128-9.

Steelman, Joseph F. North Carolina's Role in the Spanish-American
War. Raleigh: NC Div Archives and History, 1975. Rev.
by W. B. Gatewood, NCHR, 53(Spr 1976):233-4.

Steensgaard, Niels. Carracks, Caravans and Companies. Copenhagen: Studentlitteratur, 1973. Rev. by R. A. McDaniel,
AHR, 81(Apr 1976):357-8; G. V. Scammell, HJ, 19(Je 1976):
545-6.

Steer, Francis, comp. The Archives of New College, Oxford.
Chichester: Phillimore, 1974. Rev. by D. M. Owen,
Archives, 12(Aut 1976):200.

Stegner, Wallace, ed. The Letters of Bernard De Voto. Garden
City, N.Y.: Doubleday, 1975. Rev. by B. Luckingham, AI,
43(Fall 1976):482-3; J. H. Levitt, UHQ, 44(Win 1976):96-7.

_____. The Uneasy Chair: A Biography of Bernard DeVoto.
Garden City: Doubleday, 1974. Rev. by R. W. Etulain, PNQ,
67(Apr 1976):93.

Stehkämper, Hugo, ed. Konrad Adenauer, Oberbürgermeister von
Köln. Köln: Rheinland-Verlag, 1976. Rev. by F. E. Hirsch,
AHR, 81(Oct 1976):887-8.

Stein, Roger B. Seascape and the American Imagination. New
York: Potter, 1975. Rev. by P. R. Baker, JAH, 63(Sep
1976):430-1.

Stein, Walter J. California and the Dust Bowl Migration. Westport, Conn.: Greenwood, 1973. Rev. by G. D. Nash, Historian, 39(Nov 1976):158-60.

Steinberg, Alfred. Sam Rayburn. New York: Hawthorn, 1975. Rev. by B. Procter, JSH, 42(Feb 1976):135-6.

Steiner, Bruce E. Samuel Seabury, 1729-1796. Athens, Ohio: Ohio U Press, 1972. Rev. by L. L. Brown, HMPEC, 45(Sep 1976):350-1; F. D. Schneider, JCS, 17(Spr 1975):307-8.

Stelcl, Jinurich and Jaroslav Malina. Zaklady petroarcheologie. Brno: J. E. Purkyne U, 1975. Rev. by S. J. Shennan, Antiquity, 50(Je 1976):157-8.

Stelling-Michard, S., et al., eds. Autour d'Alexandre Herzen. Geneva: Librairie Droz, 1973. Rev. by M. C. Chapman, ESR, 6(Jan 1976):159-60.

Steneck, Nicholas H. Science and Creation in the Middle Ages. Notre Dame, Ind.: U Notre Dame Press, 1976. Rev. by D. J. Wilcox, HRNB, 4(Sep 1976):224.

Stenehjem, Michele Flynn. An American First: John T. Flynn and the America First Committee. New Rochelle, N. Y.: Arlington House, 1976. Rev. by E. W. Chester, HRNB, 4(May/Je 1976):141.

Stenzel, Franz. James Madison Alden: Yankee Artist of the Pacific Coast, 1854-1860. Fort Worth: Amon Carter Museum, 1975. Rev. by R. B. Stein, JAH, 62(Mar 1976):995-6; R. R. Cotroneo, NDH, 43(Win 1976):37-8; B. Procter, PNQ, 67(Oct 1976):179.

Stephan, J. J. The Kuril Islands. Oxford: Clarendon, 1974. Rev. by I. Nish, EHR, 91(Apr 1976):450.

Stephens, Lester D. Probing the Past: A Guide to the Study and Teaching of History. Boston: Allyn and Bacon, 1974. Rev. by K. I. Polakoff, PHR, 45(Feb 1976):117-18.

Stephens, W. B. Sources for English Local History. Manchester: Manchester U Press, 1973. Rev. by C. F. Slade, History, 61(Feb 1976):77.

Stephenson, Terry E. Shadows of Old Saddleback. Orange, Cal.: Rasmussen, 1974. Rev. by K. Black, JOW, 15(Jan 1976): 135.

Sterling, Carlos Márquez and Manuel Marquez Sterling. Historia de la Isla de Cuba. New York: Regents, 1975. Rev. by G. de Zéndegui, Américas, 28(May 1976):19.

Sterling, Dorothy. The Trouble They Seen. Garden City, N. Y.:

Doubleday, 1976. Rev. by D. Gay, NCHR, 53(Aut 1976): 416-17.

Sterling, Keir B. Last of the Naturalists. New York: Arno, 1974. Rev. by H. Cravens, JAH, 63(Je 1976):156.

Sternsher, Bernard. Consensus, Conflict, and American Historians. Bloomington: Ind U Press, 1975. Rev. by C. V. Woodward, AHR, 81(Apr 1976):438-9; J. Higham, JAH, 62(Mar 1976): 1047-9.

Stettler, Bernhard, ed. Aegidius Tschudi Chronicon Helveticum. Bern: Stadt- und Universitätsbibliothek, 1974. Rev. by G. R. Potter, EHR, 91(Oct 1976):895-6.

Stevens, Christopher. The Soviet Union and Black Africa. New York: Holmes and Meier, 1976. Rev. by W. W. Schmokel, HRNB, 5(Oct 1976):17-18.

Stevens, R. A. Brecknock and Abergavenny and Monmouthshire Canals. n.p.: Goose, 1974. Rev. by M. G. Miller, JTH, 3(Sep 1976):297-8.

Stevens, Robert and Rosemary Stevens. Welfare Medicine in America. New York: Free Press, 1974. Rev. by G. H. Brieger, AHR, 81(Apr 1976):453-4.

Stevenson, Andrew see Allen, Kevin

Stevenson, David. The Scottish Revolution, 1637-1644. New York: St. Martin's, 1974. Rev. by R. P. Barnes, AHR, 81(Feb 1976):149-50; A. B. Birchler, Historian, 38(Feb 1976):329-30.

Steward, Dick. Trade and Hemisphere: The Good Neighbor Policy and Reciprocal Trade. Columbia: U Mo Press, 1975. Rev. by R. R. Trask, HAHR, 56(Nov 1976):666-7; P. A. Varg, PHR, 45(Aug 1976):457-8.

Stewart, Donald E. J., ed. Handbook of Latin American Studies, No. 36: Humanities. Gainesville: U Fla Press, 1974. Rev. by I. S. Wright, HAHR, 56(Nov 1976):631-2.

Stewart, James R. Tell el 'Ajjūl: The Middle Bronze Age Remains. Göteborg: P. Aströms Förlag, 1974. Rev. by B. Williams, AJA, 80(Spr 1976):199-200.

Stewart, Janet Ann. Arizona Ranch Houses. Tucson: Ariz Historical Assn., 1974. Rev. by C. C. Colley, A & W, 18(Spr 1976):91-2; B. Luckingham, AgH, 50(Jl 1976):550-1.

Stigler, George J. The Citizen and the State. Chicago: U Chicago Press, 1975. Rev. by A. R. Sanderson, JEH, 36(Sep 1976):797-8.

Stipanovich, Joseph.   The South Slavs in Utah.   Saratogo, Cal.:
    R and E Research Assn., 1975.   Rev. by J. Bodnar, JAH,
    63(Dec 1976):735; N. Lederer, UHQ, 44(Spr 1976):186-7.

Stockholm International Peace Research Institute.   Chemical Dis-
    armament.   Stockholm: Almquist and Wiksell, 1975.   Rev.
    by R. Rama Rao, IQ, 32(Jan-Mar 1976):78-80.

Stockholm International Peace Research Institute.   Incendiary
    Weapons.   Cambridge, Mass.: MIT Press, 1975.   Rev. by
    J. N. Chaudhuri, IQ, 32(Jan-Mar 1976):77-8.

Stoddard, Ellwyn R.   Mexican Americans.   New York: Random
    House, 1973.   Rev. by J. Gomez-Quinones, A & W, 18(Sum
    1976):196-8; C. N. Marín, NMHR, 51(Apr 1976):163-4.

Stoehr, C. Eric.   Bonanza Victorian.   Albuquerque: U NM Press,
    1975.   Rev. by F. Rochlin, JOW, 15(Jan 1976):121.

Stokes, Durward T. and William T. Scott.   A History of the Chris-
    tian Church in the South.   Burlington, N.C.: Southern Confer-
    ence of United Church of Christ, 1976.   Rev. by W. H. Dan-
    iel, VMHB, 84(Oct 1976):502-3.

Stokes, Gale.   Legitimacy Through Liberalism: Valdimir Jovanović
    and the Transformation of Serbian Politics.   Seattle: U Wash
    Press, 1975.   Rev. by W. S. Vucinich, AHR, 81(Oct 1976):
    897; D. McKenzie, Historian, 39(Nov 1976):135-6.

Stolarek, Zbigniew see Leopold, Wanda

Stoljar, S. J.   A History of Contract at Common Law.   Canberra:
    Australian National U Press, 1975.   Rev. by T. Freyer,
    BHR, 50(Spr 1976):124-6.

Stolleis, Michael.   Gemeinwohlformeln im nationalsozialistischen
    Recht.   Berlin: Schweitzer, 1974.   Rev. by B. Nicholas,
    EHR, 91(Jan 1976):238.

Stone, Christopher D.   Where the Law Ends.   New York: Harper
    and Row, 1975.   Rev. by R. A. Bauer, BHR, 50(Sum 1976):
    240-1.

Stone, Gerald.   The Smallest Slavonic Nation: The Sorbs of Lusatia.
    London: Athlone, 1972.   Rev. by S. D. Spector, AHR, 81
    (Oct 1976):887.

Stone, Lawrence.   Family and Fortune.   New York: Oxford U
    Press, 1973.   Rev. by B. Underdown, JEH, 36(Sep 1976):
    794-5.

_____, ed.   The University in Society.   Vols. I and II.   Prince-
    ton, N.J.: Prin U Press, 1975.   Rev. by D. Roselli, AHR,

81(Je 1976):573; W. R. Ward, EHR, 91(Apr 1976):378-81; R. Porter, HJ, 19(Je 1976):550-2; M. B. Katz, JIH, 7(Aut 1976): 319-22.

Stone, Lyle M. Fort Michilimackinac 1715-1781. East Lansing: Mich St U, 1974. Rev. by A. Pilling, AmAnt, 41(Apr 1976): 249-51; J. L. Cotter, Archaeology, 29(Jl 1976):210.

Stone, Norman. The Eastern Front, 1914-1917. New York: Scribner's, 1976. Rev. by P. Kenez, AHR, 81(Oct 1976): 909-10; R. F. Leslie, History, 61(Je 1976):317-18; D. Reinhartz, HRNB, 4(May/Je 1976):155-6.

Stookey, Robert W. America and the Arab States. New York: Wiley, 1975. Rev. by J. A. DeNovo, JAH, 63(Sep 1976): 461-2.

Stout, Joseph A., Jr. Apache Lightning. New York: Oxford U Press, 1974. Rev. by W. S. Robinson, AHR, 81(Apr 1976): 448; T. Wilson, ChOk, 54(Spr 1976):161-2; R. M. Utley, PHR, 45(Feb 1976):127-8.

_____ see also Faulk, Odie B.

Stover, John F. History of the Illinois Central Railroad. New York: Macmillan, 1975. Rev. by I. D. Neu, JSH, 42(Nov 1976):594-5.

Stover, Leon E. The Cultural Ecology of Chinese Civilization. New York: Pica Press, 1974. Rev. by S. F. Tobias, AA, 78(Je 1976):411-12.

Stratan, Ioan see Chirilă, Eugen

Strickland, Rennard. Fire and the Spirits: Cherokee Law from Clan to Court. Norman: U Ok Press, 1975. Rev. by G. E. Moulton, AHR, 81(Je 1976):657-8; R. O. Swimmer, ChOk, 54 (Sum 1976):291-2; M. Young, JAH, 63(Je 1976):125-6; D. E. Livingston-Little, JOW, 15(Jl 1976):108; J. H. O'Donnell, III, JSH, 42(Feb 1976):142-3; D. H. Corkran, PHR, 45(Nov 1976): 609-10.

Stricklin, Al and Jon McConal. My Years with Bob Wills. San Antonio, Texas: Naylor, 1976. Rev. by G. Shirley, ChOk, 54(Win 1976):531-2.

Stritch, Thomas, ed. see Pike, Fredrick, B., ed.

Stromberg, Roland N. After Everything: Western Intellectual History Since 1945. New York: St. Martin's, 1975. Rev. by G. G. Iggers, AHR, 81(Oct 1976):850-1.

Stuart, Graham H. and James L. Tigner. Latin America and the

STUBBS 364

United States. Englewood Cliffs, N.J.: Prentice-Hall, 1975.
Rev. by J. L. Mecham, HAHR, 56(Feb 1976):173.

Stubbs, Dacre. Prehistoric Art of Australia. New York: Scribner's, 1975. Rev. by B. Forgey, Smithsonian, 6(May 1976): 105-7.

Stucki, Heinzpeter. Bürgermeister Hans Rudolf Lavater, 1492-1557. Zürich: Theologischer Verlag, 1973. Rev. by G. Ruff, JEccH, 27(Jl 1976):318-19.

Stuewer, Roger H. The Compton Effect. New York: Science History, 1975. Rev. by G. Goldberg, AHR, 81(Je 1976):562-3.

Stultz, Newell M. Afrikaner Politics in South Africa, 1934-1948. Berkeley: U Cal Press, 1975. Rev. by A. W. Stadler, AfAf, 75(Jan 1976):122-3; R. Dale, JMAS, 14(Mar 1976):167-9.

Stupperich, Martin. Osiander in Preussen, 1549-1552. New York: Walter de Gruyter, 1973. Rev. by W. D. J. Cargill Thompson, JEccH, 27(Oct 1976):436-8.

Sturhahn, Joan. Carvaho: Portrait of a Forgotten American. Merrick, New York: Richwood, 1976. Rev. by M. L. Spence, A & W, 18(Win 1976):382-4.

Stürmer, Michael. Regierung und Reichstag im Bismarckstaat, 1871-1880. Düsseldorf: Droste Verlag, 1974. Rev. by L. Cecil, AHR, 81(Apr 1976):405-7; J. J. Sheehan, JMH, 48 (Sep 1976):564-7.

Stuttler, B. J. A. Kirche und Staat. Aschaffenburg: Paul Pattloch Verlag, 1969. Rev. by W. A. Mueller, JCS, 17(Aut 1975):538-9.

Subramanian, K. Brahmin Priest of Tamilnadu. Delhi: Wiley, 1947. Rev. by Umashankari, IESHR, 13(Jan-Mar 1976):118-20.

Subramanian, V. Parched Earth: Maharashtra Drought 1970-73. Bombay: Orient Longman, 1975. Rev. by D. T. Lakdawala, IQ, 32(Jan-Mar 1976):108-10.

Sully, Langdon. No Tears for the General. Palo Alto: Cal.: American West, 1974. Rev. by R. L. Kerby, AHR, 81(Apr 1976):447-8; R. D. Hoffsommer, CWTI, 15(May 1976):50; R. Roske, PHR, 45(Aug 1976):447-8.

Sulzer, Elmer G. Ghost Railroads of Tennessee. Indianapolis: Vane A. Jones, 1976. Rev. by J. Burt, THQ, 35(Spr 1976): 111-12.

Sumner, G. V. The Orators in Cicero's "Brutus." Toronto: U
Tor Press, 1973. Rev. by G. Downey, AHR, 81(Feb 1976):
106.

Sumners, Bill F., comp. Inventory of County Records: Palo Pinto
County. Austin: Texas St Library, 1976. Rev. by R. B.
Campbell, SWHQ, 80(Oct 1976):231-3.

Sumption, Jonathan. Pilgrimage: An Image of Medieval Religion.
Totowa, N.J.: Rowman and Littlefield, 1976. Rev. by R. I.
Burns, AHR, 81(Oct 1976):835; C. N. L. Brooke, History, 61
(Je 1976):248; J. Muldoon, HRNB, 4(May/Je 1976):158.

Sunar, Ilkay. State and Society in the Politics of Turkey's Development. Ankara: Ankara Universitesi Basimevi, 1974. Rev.
by P. T. Suzuki, AHR, 81(Oct 1976):916.

Sundström, Lars. The Exchange Economy of Pre-Colonial Tropical
Africa. London: C. Hurst, 1974. Rev. by A. Roberts,
AfAf, 75(Apr 1976):254-5; G. Dalton, Africa, 46(Num 1, 1976):
110; M. Johnson, JAfH, 17(Num 2, 1976):310-11.

Supek, Rudi see Horvat, Branko

Suppan, Arnold see Plaschka, Richard Georg

Susman, Warren I., ed. see Huthmacher, J. Joseph, ed.

Sutch, Victor D. Gilbert Sheldon. The Hague: Nijhoff, 1973.
Rev. by J. P. Kenyon, EHR, 91(Jan 1976):201; R. A. Beddard, HJ, 19(Dec 1976):1005-17.

Sutcliffe, Anthony, ed. Multi-Storey Living. New York: Barnes
and Noble, 1974. Rev. by R. M. Gutchen, AHR, 81(Feb
1976):135-6.

_____ and Roger Smith. Birmingham 1939-1970. New York:
Oxford U Press, 1974. Rev. by E. P. Hennock, AHR, 81
(Feb 1976):147-8; D. Cannadine, HJ, 19(Je 1976):536-44.

Sutherland, Gillian. Policy-Making in Elementary Education, 1870-
1895. New York: Oxford U Press, 1973. Rev. by F. M.
Schweitzer, AHR, 81(Feb 1976):142-3.

Sutherland, John. A General Systems Philosophy for the Social and
Behavioral Sciences. New York: Braziller, 1973. Rev. by
DeW. R. Middleton, AA, 78(Je 1976):388-9.

Sutton, Imre. Indian Land Tenure. New York: Clearwater, 1975.
Rev. by M. Zanger, JAH, 63(Sep 1976):381-2; W. T. Hagan,
NMHR, 51(Jl 1976):255.

Sutton, Robert C., Jr. The Sutton-Taylor Feud. Quanah, Tex.:

Nortex, 1974. Rev. by R. Ellison, ETHJ, 14(Spr 1976):
61-2.

Sutton, Robert M. see Brichford, Maynard J.

Swadesh, Frances Leon. Los Primeros Pobladores: Hispanic
Americans of Ute Frontier. Notre Dame: U Notre Dame
Press, 1974. Rev. by M. P. Servin, PHR, 45(May 1976):
281-2.

Swann, Don, Sr., and Don Swann, Jr. Colonial and Historic Homes
of Maryland. Baltimore: JHU Press, 1975. Rev. by J. G.
Guthrie, Jr., GHQ, 60(Spr 1976):78-9; J. R. Rivoire, NCHR,
53(Sum 1976):323.

Swanton, M. J. The Spearheads of the Anglo-Saxon Settlements.
London: Royal Archaeological Institute, 1973. Rev. by C.
Hills, Antiquity, 50(Sep-Dec 1976):251-2.

Swanton, Michael J. see Radford, C. A.

Swartz, Helen M. and Marvin Swartz, eds. Disraeli's Reminiscences. London: Hamish Hamilton, 1975. Rev. by P.
Smith, History, 61(Oct 1976):491.

Sweeney, Amin and Nigel Phillips, eds. and trans. The Voyages
of Mohamed Ibrahim Munshi. New York: Oxford U Press,
1976. Rev. by P. J. Coleman, HRNB, 4(Aug 1976):195.

Sweezy, Paul, et al. The Transition from Feudalism to Capitalism. Atlantic Highlands, N.J.: Humanities, 1976. Rev. by
H. S. Reinmuth, Jr., HRNB, 4(Aug 1976):200-1.

Swetz, Frank. Mathematics Education in China. Cambridge, Mass.:
MIT Press, 1974. Rev. by S. H. Gould, AHR, 81(Je 1976):
644; L. L. Yong, CQ, May 1976, pp. 396-8.

Swierenga, Robert P., ed. Beyond the Civil War Synthesis: Political Essays of the Civil War Era. Westport, Conn.:
Greenwood, 1975. Rev. by R. F. Durden, AHR, 81(Oct
1975):978-9; J. A. Carpenter, HRNB, 4(Apr 1976):121-2;
L. E. Tise, NCHR, 53(Sum 1976):331-2.

Swisher, Carl B. The Oliver Wendell Holmes Devise History of the
Supreme Court of the United States. New York: Macmillan,
1974. Rev. by R. W. Johannsen, PNQ, 67(Jan 1976):35-6.

Sword, Wiley. Shiloh: Bloody April. New York: Morrow, 1974.
Rev. by W. W. Hassler, Jr., AHR, 81(Apr 1976):450.

Sydenham, M. J. The First French Republic, 1792-1804. London:
Batsford, 1974. Rev. by G. Lewis, History, 61(Feb 1976):
120-1.

Sylvester, D. W. Robert Lowe and Education. New York: Cam U
    Press, 1974. Rev. by R. K. Webb, AHR, 81(Apr 1976):388-
    9.

Symcox, Geoffrey. The Crisis of French Sea Power, 1688-1697:
    From the Guerre D'Escadre to the Guerre De Course. The
    Hague: Martinus Nijhoff, 1974. Rev. by A. N. Ryan, EHR,
    91(Jl 1976):646-7; R. M. Hatton, History, 61(Je 1976):290-1.

Syrett, David, ed. see Balderston, Marion

Syrett, Harold C., et al., eds. see Hamilton, Alexander

Syrquin, Moises see Chenery, Hillis

Szajkowski, Zosa. Jews, Wars, and Communism. Vols. 1 and 2.
    New York: KTAV, 1974. Rev. by D. W. Levy, AHR, 81
    (Feb 1976):217; M. Rischin, JAH, 62(Mar 1976):1035-6; J.
    V. Clardy, JCS, 18(Aut 1976):560-1.

Szarnicki, Henry A. Michael O'Connor, First Catholic Bishop of
    Pittsburgh, 1843-1860. Pittsburgh: Wolfson, 1975. Rev. by
    J. F. Connelly, CaHR, 62(Jl 1976):487-8.

Szasz, Margaret. Education and the American Indian: The Road
    to Self-Determination, 1928-1973. Albuquerque: U NMex
    Press, 1974. Rev. by H. W. Hertzberg, AHR, 81(Oct 1976):
    993; A. M. Gibson, ChOk, 53(Spr 1976):164-5; M. L. Hey-
    man, Jr., JOW, 15(Jan 1976):126; A. W. Vogel, NMHR, 51
    (Jan 1976):82-4; L. M. Hauptman, PNQ, 67(Apr 1976):92;
    H. T. Hoover, WHQ, 7(Apr 1976):206-7.

Szramkiewicz, Romuald. Les Régents et censeurs de la Banque de
    France nommés sous le consulat et l'Empire. Geneva: Li-
    brairie Droz, 1974. Rev. by J. F. Bosher, AHR, 81(Apr
    1976):398-9; G. Ellis, EHR, 91(Jl 1976):657-9.

Szyliowicz, Joseph S. Education and Modernization in the Middle
    East. Ithaca, N.Y.: Cornell U Press, 1973. Rev. by W.
    W. Brickman, IJMES, 7(Jan 1976):138-41.

Tagliaferri, Amelio, ed. Pedestaria e Capitanato di Padova.
    Milan: Dott. A. Giuffre Editore, 1975. Rev. by L. B. Rob-
    bert, JEH, 36(Sep 1976):798-9.

Tal, Uriel. Christians and Jews in Germany: 1870-1914. Ithaca,
    N.Y.: Cornell U Press, 1975. Rev. by S. Beinfeld, AHR,
    81(Je 1976):615; O. Chadwick, HJ, 19(Je 1976):558-9.

Talbert, R. J. A. Timoleon and the Revival of Greek Sicily, 344-
    317 B.C. New York: Cambridge U Press, 1975. Rev. by
    M. Goldsberry, AHR, 81(Oct 1976):827-8.

Talbott, Robert D. A History of the Chilean Boundaries. Ames:
Ia St U Press, 1974. Rev. by D.J.C., HAHR, 56(Feb 1976):
176-7.

Talmon, Jacob L. Israel Among the Nations. New York: Macmillan, 1971. Rev. by D. L. Baker, JCS, 17(Win 1975):
145-50.

Tambiah, S. J. see Goody, Jack

Tamuno, Tekena N., ed. see Ajayi, J. F. Ade, ed.

Tanenbaum, Jan Karl. General Maurice Sarrail 1856-1929: The
French Army and Left-Wing Politics. Chapel Hill: UNO
Press, 1974. Rev. by D. B. Ralston, AHR, 81(Feb 1976):
160; H. R. Kedward, History, 61(Je 1976):319.

Tanis, Norman, comp. see Perkins, David, comp.

Tannenbaum, Frank. The Future of Democracy in Latin America.
New York: Knopf, 1974. Rev. by S. R. Ross, HAHR, 56
(May 1976):295-7; A. P. Whitaker, TAm, 32(Jan 1976):480-1.

Tanner, Annie Clark. A Biography of Ezra Thompson Clark. Salt
Lake City: U Utah Library, 1975. Rev. by L. Foster, A &
W, 18(Aut 1976):290-1; E. E. Campbell, UHQ, 44(Sum 1976):
303-4.

Tanner, Faun McConkie. The Far Country: A Regional History of
Moab and La Sal, Utah. Salt Lake City: Olympus Publ. Co.,
1976. Rev. by A. K. Powell, UHQ, 44(Fall 1976):399-400.

Tapie, Victor-Lucien. France in the Age of Louis XIII and
Richelieu. New York: Praeger, 1975. Rev. by M. Cummings, Historian, 38(Feb 1976):326-7.

Tappolet, Claude. La Vie musicale à Genève au dixneuvième
siècle (1814-1918). Geneva: Alex. Jullien publiés par la
Société d'histoire et d'archéologie de Genève, 1972. Rev. by
D. W. Hadley, AHR, 81(Oct 1976):889-90.

Taracena, Alfonso. Zapata: Fantasía y realidad. Mexico: B.
Costa-Amic, 1974. Rev. by W. Beezley, HAHR, 56(Nov
1976):659-60.

Tarn, John Nelson. Five Percent Philanthropy. Cambridge: Cam
U Press, 1973. Rev. by R. M. Gutchen, AHR, 81(Feb 1976):
135-6; S. Marriner, BH, 17(Jan 1975):79-82.

Tarradell, Miquel. Terracotas Punicasde Ibiza. Barcelona:
Gustavo Gili, 1974. Rev. by V. A. Wilson, Antiquity, 50
(Je 1976):163-4.

Tashjian, Dickran. Skyscraper Primitives: Dada and the American
    Avant-Garde, 1910-1925. Middletown, Conn.: Wesleyan U
    Press, 1975. Rev. by J. D. Mathews, AHR, 81(Oct 1976):
    991.

Taylor, A. J. P., ed. My Darling Pussy. London: Weidenfeld
    and Nicolson, 1975. Rev. by M. Bentley, History, 61(Je
    1976):316.

_____. The Second World War: An Illustrated History. Lon-
    don: Hamish Hamilton, 1975. Rev. by C. J. Bartlett, His-
    tory, 61(Oct 1976):474-5.

Taylor, Arnold H. American Diplomacy and the Narcotics Traffic,
    1900-1939. Durham, N.C.: Duke U Press, 1969. Rev. by
    D. F. Musto, JAH, 63(Je 1976):160-1.

Taylor, Arthur J., ed. The Standard of Living in Britain in the
    Industrial Revolution. London: Methuen, 1975. Rev. by T.
    M. Kemnitz, AHR, 81(Je 1976):587-8; C. K. Hyde, JEH, 36
    (Sep 1976):800-1.

Taylor, Barry, ed. see Darroch, Elizabeth, ed.

Taylor, Christopher. Fields in the English Landscape. London:
    Dent, 1975. Rev. by G. Whittington, Antiquity, 50(Je 1976):
    165.

Taylor, Clare, ed. British and American Abolitionists. Edin-
    burgh: Edinburgh U Press, 1975. Rev. by H. Temperley,
    EHR, 91(Oct 1976):925-6; C. D. Rice, JAH, 63(Je 1976):132-
    3; J. White, JAmS, 10(Apr 1976):113-17; P. C. Lipscomb,
    III, JSH, 42(May 1976):282-3.

Taylor, Colin. The Warriors of the Plains. New York: Arco,
    1975. Rev. by R. Conn, MinnH, 45(Sum 1976):78-9.

Taylor, Frank and John S. Roskell, eds. and trans. Gesta Henrici
    Quinti: The Deeds of Henry the Fifth. Oxford: Oxford U
    Press, 1975. Rev. by C. T. Allmand, History, 61(Je 1976):
    264; J. A. F. Thomson, JEccH, 27(Apr 1976):196-7.

Taylor, Gus, ed. Mexican-Americans Tomorrow. Albuquerque:
    U NM Press, 1975. Rev. by J. Gomez-Quinones, A & W,
    18(Aut 1976):291-2.

Taylor, Joan du Plat see Isserlin, B. S. J.

Taylor, Joe Gray. Louisiana Reconstructed, 1863-1877. Baton
    Rouge: LSU Press, 1974. Rev. by R. N. Current, FHQ,
    54(Jan 1976):399-400; M. J. Schott, GHQ, 60(Spr 1976):86-7.

Taylor, John R. M. The Philippine Insurrection Against the United

States. Vols. 1-5. Pasay City, Philippines: Eugenio Lopez
Foundation, 1971. Rev. by J. A. Larkin, AHR, 81(Oct 1976):
945-6.

Taylor, Lloyd C., Jr. The Medical Profession and the Social Reform, 1885-1945. New York: St. Martin's, 1974. Rev. by
G. H. Brieger, AHR, 81(Apr 1976):453-4; D. L. Hall, JIH,
7(Aut 1976):356-7.

Taylor, Lonn and David B. Warren. Texas Furniture. Austin:
U Tex Press, 1975. Rev. by A. Lowman, A & W, 18(Win
1976):389-90; M. M. Sibley, SWHQ, 80(Jl 1976):116-17.

Taylor, Robert. Lord Salisbury. New York: St. Martin's, 1975.
Rev. by M. R. Robinton, HRNB, 4(Feb 1976):94.

_____, ed. see Bogue, Allan G., ed.

Taylor, Robert R. The Word in Stone. Berkeley: U Cal Press,
1974. Rev. by R. Lenman, EHR, 91(Jan 1976):238-9.

Taylor, Ronald B. Chavez and the Farm Workers. Boston:
Beacon, 1975. Rev. by C. Wollenberg, CHQ, 55(Spr 1976):
86-7.

Taylor, Samuel W. The Kingdom or Nothing: The Life of John
Taylor, Militant Mormon. New York: Macmillan, 1976.
Rev. by D. R. Moorman, UHQ, 44(Fall 1976):403-5.

Taylor, Telford. Courts of Terror: Soviet Criminal Justice and
Jewish Emigration. New York: Knopf, n.d. Rev. by J.
Rubenstein, Commentary, 61(May 1976):82, 84, 86.

Taylor, Thomas Jones. A History of Madison County, and Incidentally of North Alabama, 1732-1840. University, Ala.:
Cherokee Printing Co., 1976. Rev. by R. M. McBride, THQ,
35(Win 1976):431.

Teaford, Jon C. The Municipal Revolution in America. Chicago:
U Chicago Press, 1975. Rev. by S. E. Hirsch, BHR, 50
(Spr 1976):115-16; H. P. Chudacoff, JAH, 63(Je 1976):102-3.

Teich, Mikuláš and Robert Young, ed. Changing Perspectives in
the History of Science. London: Heinemann, 1973. Rev. by
A. R. Hall, History, 61(Feb 1976):71-2.

Teichova, Alice. An Economic Background to Munich. New York:
Cam U Press, 1974. Rev. by M. L. Flaningam, AHR, 81
(Apr 1976):423; M. V. Wallace, History, 61(Feb 1976):145-6.

Telford, Shirley. Economic and Political Peace. Portland, Ore.:
William and Richards, 1975. Rev. by A. K. Dasgupta, IQ,
32(Apr-Je 1976):230-2.

Telle, Emile Y., ed. L'Erasmianus sive Ciceronia nus d'Etienne Dolet (1535). Geneva: Librairie Droz, 1974. Rev. by R. L. DeMolen, CaHR, 62(Jan 1976):127-8.

Temin, Peter. Causal Factors in American Economic Growth in the Nineteenth Century. London: Macmillan, 1975. Rev. by S. B. Saul, History, 61(Oct 1976):410.

_____. Did Monetary Forces Cause the Great Depression? New York: Norton, 1976. Rev. by E. Wicker, AHR, 81(Oct 1976):993-4; H. M. Burns, JAH, 63(Dec 1976):765-6.

Teng, S. Y. The Taiping Rebellion and the Western Powers. Oxford: Clarendon Press, 1971. Rev. by S. W. Barnett, JIH, 7(Sum 1976):136-40.

Terrell, John Upton. The Plains Apache. New York: Crowell, 1975. Rev. by R. N. Ellis, ChOk, 54(Fall 1976):419; R. Wilson, NDH, 43(Sum 1976):44-5; D. G. Gunnerson, SWHQ, 80(Oct 1976):236-7.

_____ and Donna M. Terrell. Indian Women of the Western Morning. New York: Dial, 1974. Rev. by S. Roggia, AIQ, 2(Sum 1975):152-3; B. B. Jensen, JOW, 15(Jan 1976):139-40.

Teuteberg, Hans J. and Günter Wiegelmann. Der Wandel der Nahrungsgewohnheiten unter dem Einfluss der Industrialisierung. Göttingen: Vandenhoeck and Ruprecht, 1972. Rev. by M. Mattmüller, JMH, 48(Je 1976):345-6.

Thatcher, Mary, ed. and comp. Cambridge South Asian Archive. London: Mansell, 1973. Rev. by L. J. Stout, AmArc, 39 (Apr 1976):205-6.

Thayer, Theodore. Colonial and Revolutionary Morris County. Morristown, N.J.: Morris County Heritage Commission, 1975. Rev. by W. C. Kiessel, JAH, 63(Dec 1976):698.

Thibault, Pierre. Savoir et Pouvoir. Quebec: Les Presses de l'Universite Loval, 1972. Rev. by J. Hennesey, CaHR, 62 (Oct 1976):641-2.

Thickett, D., ed. Estienne Pasquier. Geneva: Droz, 1974. Rev. by N. M. Sutherland, History, 61(Feb 1976):112.

Thomas, Abraham Vazhayil. Christians in Secular India. Rutherford, N.J.: Fairleigh Dickinson U Press, 1974. Rev. by C. M. Brown, JCS, 16(Spr 1976):348-50.

Thomas, Daniel H. and Lynn M. Case, eds. The New Guide to the Diplomatic Archives of Western Europe. Philadelphia: U Pa Press, 1975. Rev. by G. O. Kent, AmArc, 39(Apr 1976):204-5.

Thomas, Joab L., ed. see Noble, Donald R., ed.

Thomas, John N. The Institute of Pacific Relations. Seattle: U Wash Press, 1974. Rev. by J. A. Thompson, EHR, 91(Jl 1976):687-8.

Thomas, Lewis G., ed. The Prairie West to 1905. Toronto: Oxford U Press, 1975. Rev. by L. E. Ziewacz, HT, 10(Nov 1976):138.

Thomas, Lewis H. The Renaissance of Canadian History. Toronto: U Tor Press, 1975. Rev. by P. F. Sharp, JAH, 62(Mar 1976):1054-5.

Thomas, Lewis V. A Study of Naima. New York: NYU Press, 1972. Rev. by R. H. Davison, AHR, 81(Oct 1976):915-16.

Thomas, Mary Martha Hosford. Southern Methodist University: Fonding and Early Years. Dallas: SMU Press, 1974. Rev. by J. A. Moore, AHR, 81(Apr 1976):461.

Thomas, P. D. G. British Politics and the Stamp Act Crisis: The First Phase of the American Revolution, 1763-1767. New York: Clarendon, 1975. Rev. by C. Robbins, AHR, 81(Apr 1976):386-7; P. Langford, EHR, 91(Apr 1976):393-5; J. Cannon, History, 61(Feb 1976):116-17; J. J. Hecht, NEQ, 49 (Mar 1976):172-4.

_____. Lord North. New York: St. Martin's Press, 1975. Rev. by G. B. Cooper, HRNB, 4(Jl 1976):176.

Thomas, Roger S. see Griffith, Ralph A.

Thomas, S. Bernard. "Proletarian Hegemony" in the Chinese Revolution and the Canton Commune of 1927. Ann Arbor: U Mich, 1975. Rev. by P. Elmquist, AHR, 81(Oct 1976):936-7.

Thomas, Samuel W. and William Morgan. Old Louisville: The Victorian Era. Louisville: Data Courier, 1975. Rev. by T. Owen, FCHQ, 50(Jl 1976):323-4.

Thomasevich, Jozo. The Chetniks. London: Oxford U Press, n.d. Rev. by J. P. Moeller, HJ, 19(Mar 1976):308-12.

Thomis, Malcolm I. The Town Labourer and the Industrial Revolution. London: Batsford, 1974. Rev. by J. W. Osborne, AHR, 81(Je 1976):587; S. Pollard, EHR, 91(Apr 1976):440; T. C. Barker, History, 61(Je 1976):302-3.

Thompson, Craig R., ed. Inquisitio de Fide. Hamden, Conn.: Archon, 1975. Rev. by G. F. Nuttall, JEccH, 27(Apr 1976): 198-200.

Thompson, E. P. Whigs and Hunters. London: Allen Lane, 1975.
Rev. by J. Cannon, History, 61(Oct 1976):451-3; S. E. Prall,
HRNB, 4(Sep 1976):225.

Thompson, Edgar T. Plantation Societies, Race Relations, and the
South. Durham, N.C.: Duke U Press, 1975. Rev. by J.
Schor, AgH, 50(Apr 1976):440-1; F. C. Davidson, JSH, 42
(Feb 1976):118-19.

Thompson, F. M. L. Hampstead. Boston: Routledge and Kegan
Paul, 1974. Rev. by D. M. Fahey, AHR, 81(Apr 1976):384-5.

Thompson, Gerald. The Army and the Navajo. Tucson: U Ariz
Press, 1976. Rev. by R. M. Utley, A & W, 18(Win 1976):
374-5; T. P. Wilson, ChOk, 54(Win 1976):536-7; C. Trafzer,
JAriH, 17(Aut 1976):348-9.

Thompson, Hildegard. The Navajo's Long Walk for Education.
Tsaile, Ariz.: Navajo Community College Press, 1975.
Rev. by K. R. Philp, A & W, 18(Spr 1976):99-101.

Thompson, Jerry. Sabers on the Rio Grande. Austin, Tex.:
Presidal, 1974. Rev. by M. Darst, ETHJ, 14(Fall 1976):
70-1.

Thompson, Leonard. Survival in Two Worlds: Moshoe-shoe of
Lesotho, 1786-1870. London: Oxford U Press, 1975. Rev.
by L. H. Gann, AHR, 81(Oct 1976):929-30; E. V. Winams,
HRNB, 4(Apr 1976):128.

_____ and Jeffrey Butler, eds. Change in Contemporary South
Africa. Berkeley: U Cal Press, 1975. Rev. by R. G.
Southall, JMAS, 14(Sep 1976):546-8.

Thompson, Paul. The Edwardians. Bloomington: Ind U Press,
1975. Rev. by J. A. Casada, HRNB, 4(Feb 1976):93-4;
R. N. Soffer, Mankind, 5(Dec 1976):58, 60.

Thompson, Richard A. The Winds of Tomorrow. Chicago: U
Chicago Press, 1974. Rev. by C. E. Dibble, AIQ, 2(Sum
1975):140-1; W. Madsen, HAHR, 56(Feb 1976):162-3.

Thompson, Richard H. Lothar Franz von Schönborn and the Diplomacy of the Electorate of Mainz from the Treaty of Rys-
wick to the Outbreak of the War of the Spanish Succession.
The Hague: Martinus Nijhoff, 1973. Rev. by R. Wines,
CaHR, 62(Apr 1976):295-6.

Thompson, Roger. Women in Stuart England and America. Boston:
Routledge and Kegan Paul, 1974. Rev. by A. Missa, JAmS,
10(Apr 1976):110-11.

Thomsen, Robert. Bill W. New York: Harper and Row, 1975.

THOMSON 374

Rev. by J. H. Sweetland, HRNB, 4(Jan 1976):54; L. J. Issel-
hardt, VH, 44(Fall 1976):250-1.

Thomson, R. M., ed. and trans. The Chronicle of the Election of
Hugh, Abbot of Bury St Edmunds and Later Bishop of Ely.
Oxford: Oxford U Press, 1974. Rev. by W. L. Warren,
History, 61(Je 1976):258-9.

Thornbrough, Gayle and Dorothy L. Riker, eds. The Diary of
Calvin Fletcher. Vol. III. Indianapolis: Ind Historical Society, 1974. Rev. by I. D. Neu, IMH, 72(Je 1976):159-60.

_____, _____, and Paula Corpuz, eds. The Diary of Calvin
Fletcher. Vol. IV. Indianapolis: Ind Historical Society,
1975. Rev. by J. P. Stover, JAH, 63(Sep 1976):414-15.

Thorne, Christopher. The Limits of Foreign Policy. London:
Macmillan, 1973. Rev. by P. M. Kennedy, EHR, 91(Jan
1976):237-8.

Thrane, Hendrik see Riis, P. J.

Thrapp, Dan L. Victorio and the Mimbres Apaches. Norman: U
Ok Press, 1974. Rev. by M. L. Tate, AIQ, 2(Spr 1975):
26-7.

Tigerstedt, E. N. The Decline and Fall of the Neoplatonic Interpretation of Plato. Helsinki: Societas Scientiarum Fennica,
1974. Rev. by C. B. Schmitt, JHP, 14(Jl 1976):364-6.

Tigner, James L. see Stuart, Graham H.

Tignor, Robert L. The Colonial Transformation of Kenya: The
Kamba, Kikuyu, and Maasai from 1900 to 1939. Princeton,
N.J.: Prin U Press, 1976. Rev. by J. Lamphear, AHR, 81
(Oct 1976):927-8; D. M. McFarland, HRNB, 4(Jl 1976):168.

Tikhomirov, M. N. The Russian State During the 15th-17th Centuries. Moscow: Izdatel'stvo "Nauka," 1973. Rev. by G.
Alef, AHR, 81(Feb 1976):118-19.

Tilly, Charles see Shorter, Edward

_____, ed. The Formation of National States in Western Europe.
Princeton, N.J.: Prin U Press, 1975. Rev. by R. A. Le-
brun, AHR, 81(Je 1976):574-5.

_____, Louise Tilly, and Richard Tilly. The Rebellious Cen-
tury, 1830-1930. Cambridge, Mass.: Harvard U Press,
1975. Rev. by S. Elwitt, AHR, 81(Je 1976):577-8; P. H.
Amann, JIH, 7(Sum 1976):154-7.

Tindall, George Brown. The Persistent Tradition in New South

Politics. Baton Rouge: LSU Press, 1975. Rev. by H. D.
Graham, AHR, 81(Apr 1976):460; D. W. Grantham, FHQ, 55
(Jl 1976):97-8; W. F. Holmes, JAH, 62(Mar 1976):1004-5.

Tipton, I. C. Berkeley: The Philosophy of Immaterialism. London: Methuen; New York: Harper and Row, 1974. Rev. by
H. M. Bracken, JHP, 14(Apr 1976):235-6.

Tiryakian, Edward A., ed. On the Margin of the Visible. New
York: Wiley, 1974. Rev. by M. Kearney, AA, 78(Mar
1976):147-8.

Tite, C. G. C. Impeachment and Parliamentary Judicature in
Early Stuart England. Atlantic Highlands, N.J.: Humanities,
1974. Rev. by C. M. Gray, AHR, 81(Feb 1976):130; G. E.
Aylmer, EHR, 91(Jan 1976):130-1; E. W. Ives, History, 61
(Je 1976):283-4.

Titus, David Anson. Palace and Politics in Prewar Japan. New
York: Columbia U Press, 1974. Rev. by R. M. Spaulding,
JJS, 2(Aut 1975):177-84.

Tobey, Jeremy L. The History of Ideas: a bibliographical introduction. Volume 1, Classical Antiquity. Santa Barbara: Clio
Press, 1975. Rev. by T. S. Brown, AHR, 81(Oct 1976):826.

Tobias, J. J. Prince of the Fences: The Life and Crimes of Ikey
Solomons. London: Valentine Mitchell, 1975. Rev. by H.
McLeod, History, 61(Je 1976):302.

Todd, Frederick P., et al. American Military Equipage: 1851-
1872. n.p.: Military Historians, 1974. Rev. by T. Ray,
CWTI, 15(May 1976):49-50.

Todd, Malcolm. The Northern Barbarians 100 B.C.-A.D. 300.
London: Hutchinson, 1975. Rev. by A. E. Astin, History,
61(Oct 1976):435-6.

Toepperwein, Herman. Showdown: Western Gunfighters in Moments
of Truth. Austin, Texas: Madrona, 1974. Rev. by R. Ellison, ETHJ, 14(Spr 1976):61.

Toews, J. A. A History of the Mennonite Brethren Church: Pilgrims and Pioneers. Fresno, Cal.: Board of Christian
Literature, n.d. Rev. by P. Penner, MQR, 50(Jan 1976):
73-5.

Tokes, Rudolf L. Dissent in the USSR. Baltimore: JHU Press,
1975. Rev. by J. Laber, Commentary, 61(Jan 1976):94-6,
98.

Toland, John. Adolf Hitler. Garden City, N.Y.: Doubleday, n.d.
Rev. by J. Shattan, Commentary, 62(Dec 1976):79-82.

Toll, Robert C. Blacking Up: The Minstrel Show in Nineteenth-Century America. New York: Oxford U Press, 1974. Rev. by L. O. Saum, PNQ, 67(Jan 1976):39-40.

Tolson, Arthur. The Black Oklahomans. New Orleans: Edwards, 1972. Rev. by J. T. Hubbell, A & W, 18(Win 1976):379-80; J. L. Franklin, JNH, 61(Jan 1976):115-16.

Tolybekov, S. E. The Nomadic Society of Kazakhs in the Seventeenth to the Beginning of the Twentieth Century: A Political-Economic Analysis. Alma Ata: Izdatel'stvo "Nauka," 1971. Rev. by A. W. Fisher, AHR, 81(Oct 1976):906.

Tomasevich, Jozo. War and Revolution in Yugoslavia, 1941-1945: The Chetniks. Stanford, Cal.: Stanford U Press, 1975. Rev. by J. C. Campbell, AHR, 81(Oct 1976):897-9.

Tomasi, Silvano M. Piety and Power. Staten Island, N. Y.: Center for Migration Studies, 1975. Rev. by B. B. Caroli, JAH, 62(Mar 1976):1018-19.

Toniolo, Elias and Richard Hill, eds. The Opening of the Nile Basin. London: C. Hurst, 1974. Rev. by R. Gray, JAfH, 17(Num 3, 1976):474-5.

Toplin, Robert Brent, ed. Slavery and Race Relations in Latin America. Westport, Conn.: Greenwood, 1974. Rev. by C. N. Degler, AHR, 81(Je 1976):699-700; R. W. Logan, TAm, 33(Oct 1976):379-80.

_____. Unchallenged Violence. Westport, Conn.: Greenwood, 1975. Rev. by R. M. Brown, JAH, 63(Sep 1976):443.

Torgal, Luis Manuel Reis. Tradicionalismo e contra-revolução. Coimbra: Universidade de Coimbra, 1973. Rev. by M. Cardoza, HAHR, 56(Feb 1976):177-8.

Torstendahl, Rolf. Teknologins Nytta. Stockholm: Almqvist and Wiksell, 1975. Rev. by S. P. Oakley, EHR, 91(Oct 1976):923-4.

Toscano, Mario. Alto Adige--South Tyrol: Italy's Frontier with the German World. Baltimore: JHU Press, 1976. Rev. by G. R. Kleinfeld, HRNB, 4(Apr 1976):133.

Toson, Shimazaki. The Broken Commandment. Tokyo: U Tokyo Press, 1974. Rev. by E. McClellan, JJS, 2(Aut 1975):169-71.

Toth, Charles W., ed. The American Revolution and the West Indies. Port Washington, N. Y.: Kennikat, 1975. Rev. by L. R. Gerlach, HRNB, 4(Jan 1976):61.

Touati, Charles. La Pensée philosophique et théologique de

Gersonide. Paris: Les Editions De Minuit, 1973. Rev. by
S. Feldman, JHP, 14(Jl 1976):362-4.

Toubert, Pierre. Les Structures du Latium medieval. Rome:
Ecole Française de Rome, 1973. Rev. by D. Herlihy, AHR,
81(Feb 1976):115-16.

Trachtman, Paul. The Gunfighters. New York: Time-Life, 1974.
Rev. by M. Mobley, ChOk, 54(Spr 1976):155-6.

Traill, John S. The Political Organization of Attica. Princeton,
N.J.: American School of Classical Studies, 1975. Rev. by
D. M. Lewis, AJA, 80(Sum 1976):311-12.

_____ see Meritt, Benjamin D.

Tranoy, Alain, ed. Hydace, Chronique. 2 vols. Paris: Editions
du Cerf, 1974. Rev. by G. F. Chesnut, CH, 45(Sep 1976):
375; R. A. Markus, JEccH, 27(Jan 1976):74-5.

Tran Tam Tinh, V. and Yvette Labrecque. Isis Lactans. Corpus
des Monuments gréco-romains d'Isis allaitant Harpocrate.
Leyden: E. J. Brill, 1973. Rev. by L. Bonfante, AJA, 80
(Win 1976):104-5.

Trattner, Walter I. From Poor Law to Welfare State. New York:
Free Press, 1974. Rev. by D. A. Mohler, CaHR, 62(Oct
1976):674-5.

Treadgold, Donald W. The West in Russia and China. Vol. I.
Cambridge: Cam U Press, 1973. Rev. by G. Barraclough,
EHR, 91(Jl 1976):693-4; N. Zernov, JCS, 17(Win 1975):117-
19.

Trebiliani, Maria Luisa, ed. Cronaca di Roma, 1844-1870.
Vol. I. Rome: Istituto per la Storia del Risorgimento
Italiano, 1972. Rev. by R. L. Cummings, CaHR, 62(Apr
1976):318-19.

Trefousse, Hans L. The Radical Republicans: Lincoln's Vanguard
for Racial Justice. Baton Rouge: LSU Press, 1975. Rev.
by J. L. Barnidge, ChOk, 54(Fall 1976):409-10.

Treharne, R. F., and I. J. Sanders, ed. Documents of the
Baronial Movement of Reform and Rebellion 1258-1267.
Oxford: Clarendon, 1973. Rev. by J. C. Holt, EHR, 91
(Apr 1976):363-6.

Tremblay, Marc Abelard and Marc Laplante. Familie et parenté
en Acadie. Ottawa: National Museums of Canada, 1971.
Rev. by N. Sealy, AA, 78(Mar 1976):160-1.

Trenn, Thaddeus J. , ed. Radioactivity and Atomic Theory. New

York: Halsted Press, 1975. Rev. by M. J. Nye, AHR, 81(Oct 1976):817-18.

Trennert, Robert A. Alternative to Extinction. Philadelphia: Temple U Press, 1975. Rev. by L. O. Saum, A & W, 18 (Sum 1976):178-80; M. Rogin, AHR, 81(Oct 1976):969-70; B. W. Sheehan, IMH, 72(Dec 1976):370-1; B. A. Glasrud, JOW, 15(Apr 1976):130-1; R. N. Satz, WHQ, 7(Apr 1976):204-5; P. Stuart, WMH, 60(Aut 1976):68-9.

Treves, Renato. La dottrina sansimoniana nel pensiero italiano del Risorgimento. Turin: Edizioni Giappichelli, 1973. Rev. by R. S. Cunsolo, AHR, 81(Feb 1976):178-9.

Trexler, Richard C. The Spiritual Power. Leiden: E. J. Brill, 1974. Rev. by R. Brentano, CaHR, 62(Jan 1976):99-100; R. Starn, JCS, 18(Aut 1976):552-4.

Tripathi, Amales. Vidyasagar: The Traditional Modernizer. Calcutta: Orient Longman, 1974. Rev. by W. M. Gunderson, AHR, 81(Apr 1976):434-5.

Trithemius, Johannes. In Praise of Scribes. Lawrence, Kan.: Coronado, 1974. Rev. by D. Hay, EHR, 91(Jan 1976):187.

Troen, Selwyn K. The Public and the Schools. Columbia, Mo.: U Mo Press, 1975. Rev. by S. Schlossman, AHR, 81(Apr 1976):456; W. Issel, HRNB, 4(Feb 1976):78-9; W. A. Bullough, JAH, 62(Mar 1976):991-2; G. L. Gutek, JSH, 42(Feb 1976):141-2.

Troje, Hans Erich. Graeca Leguntur. Cologne: Böhlau Verlag, 1971. Rev. by W. Ullmann, JMH, 48(Sep 1976):531-2.

Trolander, Judith Ann. Settlement Houses and the Great Depression. Detroit: Wayne St U Press, 1975. Rev. by J. E. Johnson, JAH, 62(Mar 1975):1043-4; R. S. Kirkendall, JISHS, 69(Aug 1976):239; E. Gilman, MinnH, 45(Spr 1976):36.

Tronchon, J. L'Insurrection Malgache de 1947. Paris: Maspero, 1974. Rev. by R. Archer, AfAf, 75(Apr 1976):261-2.

Troper, Harold see Harney, Robert F.

Trotter, Ann. Britain and East Asia 1933-1937. Cambridge: Cam U Press, 1975. Rev. by P. Lowe, History, 61(Je 1976):326-7; J. C. Shakeshaft, MAS, 10(Jl 1976):450-3.

Troxler, Carole Watterson. The Loyalist Experience in North Carolina. Raleigh: NC Dept Cultural Resources, 1976. Rev. by R. M. Calhoon, NCHR, 53(Aut 1976):400-1.

Trudel, Marcel. Les Débuts du régime seigneurial. Montreal: Fides, 1974. Rev. by M. Allard, CHR, 57(Je 1976):193-4.

379   TRUDGILL

Trudgill, Eric. Madonnas and Magdalens. New York: Holmes
and Meier, 1976. Rev. by M. E. Francois, HRNB, 4(Jl
1976):177.

True, C. W. Meighan and Harvey Crew. Archaeological Investigations at Molpa, San Diego County, California. Berkeley: U
Cal Press, 1974. Rev. by J. A. Tainter, AmAnt, 41(Jan
1976):120-1.

Truffaut, François. Les Films de ma vie. Paris: Flammarion,
1975. Rev. by A. Sesonske, GR, 6(Spr 1976):211-15.

Tsuchida, Bruce T., trans. see Kitagawa, Hiroshi, trans.

Tucker, David M. Black Pastors and Leaders: The Memphis
Clergy, 1819-1972. Memphis, Tenn.: Memphis St U Press,
1975. Rev. by R. E. Luker, CaHR, 62(Jl 1976):528-9; N.
Thorburn, HRNB, 4(Jan 1976):58-9; W. B. Weare, JAH, 63
(Je 1976):130-1; M. Fordham, JNH, 61(Jan 1976):116-17;
C. H. Martin, JSH, 42(Feb 1976):140-1.

Tucker, Robert C. Stalin as Revolutionary: 1878-1929. New
York: Norton, 1973. Rev. by J. L. Black, CHR, 57(Mar
1976):99-100.

Tucker, William E. see McAllister, Lester G.

Tucker, William R. The Fascist Ego: A Political Biography of
Robert Brasillach. Berkeley: U Cal Press, 1975. Rev.
by A. L. Funk, AHR, 81(Oct 1976):872-3; E. Weber, Historian, 39(Nov 1976):127-8.

Tugwell, Franklin. The Politics of Oil in Venezuela. Stanford,
Cal.: Stanford U Press, 1975. Rev. by E. Lieuwen, HAHR,
56(May 1976):353-4.

Tugwell, Rexford G. The Compromising of the Constitution.
Notre Dame, Ind.: U Notre Dame Press, 1976. Rev. by
D. O. Dewey, HRNB, 5(Oct 1976):5-6.

Tulchin, Joseph S., ed. Latin America in the Year 2000. Reading, Mass.: Addison-Wesley, 1975. Rev. by G. MacEoin,
HAHR, 56(May 1976):351-3.

Tung, William L. The Chinese in America, 1820-1973. Dobbs
Ferry, N.Y.: Oceana, 1974. Rev. by W. E. Willmott, CQ,
May 1976):pp. 398-9.

Turnbull, Pauline. May Lansfield Keller: Life and Letters.
Verona, Va.: McClure, 1975. Rev. by F. Farmer, VMHB,
84(Apr 1976):215-16.

Turner, Eldon. Pathways to the Present. New York: Harper and
Row, 1976. Rev. by E. Bonkalo, HT, 10(Nov 1976):141-2.

Turner, Frank Miller. Between Science and Religion. London:
    Yale U Press, 1974. Rev. by K. Nield, History, 61(Feb
    1976):134.

Turner, Frederick W. , II, ed. The Portable North American Indian
    Reader. New York: Viking, 1973. Rev. by A. R. Velie,
    AIQ, 2(Sum 1975):150-1.

Turner, George E. see Goldner, Orville

Turner, Robert F. Vietnamese Communism: Its Origins and De-
    velopment. Stanford, Cal.: Hoover Institution Press, Stan-
    ford U, 1975. Rev. by P. D. Caine, AHR, 81(Oct 1976):944-
    5.

Turner, Robert P. Up to the Front of the Line. Port Washington,
    N. Y.: Kennikat, 1975. Rev. by R. D. Ralston, JSH, 42
    (May 1976):298-9.

Turner, Thomas B. Heritage of Excellence: The Johns Hopkins
    Medical Institutions, 1914-1947. Baltimore: JHU Press,
    1974. Rev. by S. Benison, AHR, 81(Feb 1976):216.

Tuska, Jon. The Filming of the West. Garden City, N. Y.:
    Doubleday, 1976. Rev. by L. D. Hill, SWHQ, 80(Oct 1976):
    240-1.

Tuveson, Ernest Lee. Redeemer Nation. Chicago: U Chicago
    Press, 1974. Rev. by R. V. Pierard, JCS, 17(Spr 1975):
    344-5.

Twaddle, Michael, ed. Expulsion of a Minority. London: Athlone,
    1975. Rev. by V. Jamal, JMAS, 14(Je 1976):357-61.

Twichell, Heath, Jr. Allen: The Biography of an Army Officer,
    1859-1930. New Brunswick, N.J.: Rutgers U Press, 1974.
    Rev. by V. Hicken, AHR, 81(Apr 1976):459-60.

Twining, Charles E. Downriver: Orrin H. Ingram and the Empire
    Lumber Company. Madison: State Historical Society of Wis-
    consin, 1975. Rev. by T. F. Gedosch, AHR, 81(Oct 1976):
    985; B. E. Benson, IMH, 72(Je 1976):165-6; L. M. Kane,
    JAH, 63(Je 1976):145-6; C. M. Becker, OH, 85(Aut 1976):
    334-5; R. S. Maxwell, PNQ, 67(Oct 1976):175-6.

Twitchett, D. C. , ed. see Geelan, P. J. M. , ed.

Tyack, David B. The One Best System. Cambridge, Mass.: Har-
    vard U Press, 1974. Rev. by S. Schlossman, AHR, 81(Apr
    1976):456; H. A. Larrabee, NEQ, 49(Mar 1976):155-7.

Tyagi, Sushila. Indo-Nepalise Relations. Delhi: D. K. Publishing
    House, 1974. Rev. by S. K. Jha, IQ, 32(Jl-Sep 1976):357-8.

Tyler, Hamilton A. Pueblo Animals and Myths. Norman: U Ok Press, 1975. Rev. by H. E. Chrisman, A & W, 18(Spr 1976):88-9; W. D. Laird, JAriH, 17(Spr 1976):115-17.

Tyler, Ronnie C. The Big Bend. Washington: National Park Service, 1975. Rev. by T. R. Young, A & W, 18(Sum 1976): 183-4; L. E. Oliva, HRNB, 4(Jan 1976):54; W. B. Hughes, JAH, 63(Sep 1976):418; L. S. Theisen, JOW, 15(Apr 1976): 138; D. M. Vigness, NMHR, 51(Jl 1976):256-7; J. R. Jameson, SWHQ, 80(Oct 1976):233-4.

Tyler, Stephen A. India: An Anthropological Perspective. Pacific Palisades, Cal.: Goodyear, 1973. Rev. by P. Kolenda, JAS, 36(Nov 1976):176-7.

Udovitch, Abraham L. Partnership and Profit in Medieval Islam. Princeton, N.J.: Prin U Press, 1970. Rev. by R. W. Bulliet, IJMES, 7(Oct 1976):599-600.

Ulam, Adam B. Stalin: The Man and His Era. New York: Viking, 1973. Rev. by M. Lewin, JIH, 7(Sum 1976):105-17.

Ullendorff, Edward, trans. see Selassie, Haile

Ullmann, Walter. The Church and the Law in the Earlier Ages. London: Variorum, 1975. Rev. by C. Duggan, JEccH, 27 (Jl 1976):312-15.

_____. Law and Politics in the Middle Ages. London: Hodder and Stoughton, 1975. Rev. by H. S. Offler, EHR, 91(Oct 1976):885-7; M. Wilks, History, 61(Je 1976):246-7; T. M. Parker, JEccH, 27(Jl 1976):311-12.

_____. A Short History of the Papacy in the Middle Ages. New York: Harper and Row, 1974. Rev. by W. M. Stevens, CH, 45(Sep 1976):376-8; R. L. Reid, JCS, 18(Win 1976):120-2; R. L. Reid, JCS, 18(Win 1976):120-2.

Ullrich, Hartmut. Le elezioni del 1913 a Roma. Milan: Società Editrice Dante Alighieri, 1972. Rev. by F. J. Coppa, AHR, 81(Apr 1976):416.

Ulmschneider, Helgard. Götz von Berlichingen. Sigmaringen: Jan Thorbecke Verlag, 1974. Rev. by H. J. Cohn, EHR, 91 (Jan 1976):178-9.

Ulunian, A. A. The Bulgarian People and the Russo-Turkish War, 1877-1878. Moscow: Izdatel'stvo "Nauka," 1971. Rev. by M. Pundeff, AHR, 81(Apr 1976):419.

Unger, Aryeh L. The Totalitarian Party: Party and People in Nazi Germany and Soviet Russia. Cambridge: Cam U Press, 1974. Rev. by R. Lenman, EHR, 91(Apr 1976):461-2; S. Andreski, History, 61(Je 1976):324-5.

Unger, Irwin and Debi Unger. The Movement: A History of the American New Left, 1959-1972. New York: Dodd, Mead, 1974. Rev. by B. Sternsher, AHR, 81(Feb 1976):222; J. A. Neuchterlein, CHR, 57(Je 1976):227-8.

United Banks of Colorado. Colorado Headlines. Denver: United Banks of Colorado, 1976. Rev. by D. A. Smith, JOW, 15 (Apr 1976):137.

U.S. Cabinet Committee on Opportunities for Spanish Speaking People, comp. The Spanish Speaking in the United States: A Guide to Materials. Detroit: Blaine Ethridge, 1975. Rev. by A. Gutiérrez, HAHR, 56(Feb 1976):183.

United States Department of State. Foreign Relations of the United States, 1919, Volume IX: The Far East: China. Washington, D.C.: Government Printing Office, 1974. Rev. by R. Dingman, PHR, 45(Feb 1976):153-4.

_____. Foreign Relations of the United States, 1947. Vol. I, General: The United Nations. Washington: Government Printing Office, 1973. Rev. by W. N. Medlicott, EHR, 91(Oct 1976):948.

_____. Foreign Relations of the United States; 1947, Vol. VII, The American Republics. Washington: Government Printing Office, 1972. Rev. by W. N. Medlicott, EHR, 81(Oct 1976):940.

_____. Foreign Relations of the United States, 1948. Vol. I, Part 1, General: The United Nations. Washington: Government Printing Office, 1975. Rev. by T. M. Campbell, AHR, 81(Je 1976):690-1.

_____. Foreign Relations of the United States, 1948. Vol. IV. Washington: Government Printing Office, 1974. Rev. by W. W. Kulski, AHR, 81(Feb 1976):221-2.

_____. Foreign Relations of the United States, 1948. Vol. VI. Washington: Government Printing Office, 1974. Rev. by R. W. Leopold, JAH, 62(Mar 1976):952-3; R. Dingham, PHR, 45(Aug 1976):461-3; K. L. Nelson, PNQ, 67(Apr 1976):93-4.

_____. Foreign Relations of the United States; 1948, no. VI and 1949, no. IX. Washington: Government Printing Office, 1974. Rev. by I. Nish, EHR, 91(Jl 1976):692-3.

_____. Foreign Relations of the United States, 1949. Vol. I: General: The United Nations, Part I: 1949. Vol. II. The United Nations: The Western Hemisphere; 1949, Vol. IV. Western Europe. Washington: Government Printing Office, 1975. Rev. by H.G.N., EHR, 91(Oct 1976):941.

_____. Foreign Relations of the United States; 1949, Vol. II,

The United Nations: The Western Hemisphere. Washington:
Government Printing Office, 1975. Rev. by T. M. Campbell,
AHR, 81(Je 1976):690-1.

_____. Foreign Relations of the United States: 1949. Vol. III:
Council of Foreign Ministers; Germany and Austria. Washington: Government Printing Office, 1974. Rev. by A. Norman,
AHR, 81(Je 1976):691-2; A. K. Henriksen, JAH, 63(Je 1976):
94-5.

Unverhau, Dagmar. Approbatio--Reprobatio. Lübeck: Matthiesen
Verlag, 1973. Rev. by S. Williams, AHR, 81(Feb 1976):
114-15.

Upton, Richard, comp. The Custer Adventure. Fort Collins, Colo.:
Old Army, 1975. Rev. by S. R. Davison, JOW, 15(Apr
1976):132.

Urness, Carol, ed. see Parker, John, ed.

Urofsky, Melvin I., ed. see Brandeis, Louis

Usoro, Eno J. The Nigerian Oil Palm Industry. Ibadan: Ibadan
U Press, 1974. Rev. by M. Johnson, AfAf, 75(Jl 1976):398.

Utley, Francis Lee, ed. see Goff, John H.

Utley, Robert M. Frontier Regulars. New York: Macmillan, 1973.
Rev. by J. W. Bailey, AIQ, 2(Spr 1975):37-9; R. L. Whitner,
PNQ, 67(Apr 1976):89-90.

Uzoigwe, G. N. Britain and the Conquest of Africa. Ann Arbor:
U Mich Press, 1974. Rev. by H. P. Meritt, AHR, 81(Feb
1976):143.

Vacalopoulos, Apostolos E. The Greek Nation, 1453-1669: The
Cultural and Economic Background of Modern Greek Society.
New Brunswick, N.J.: Rutgers U Press, 1976. Rev. by W.
H. McNeill, AHR, 81(Oct 1976):894-5.

Vago, Bela and George L. Mosse, eds. Jews and Non-Jews in
Eastern Europe, 1918-1945. New York: Wiley, 1975. Rev.
by J. F. Zacek, HRNB, 4(Jl 1976):182.

Vaizey, John. The History of British Steel. London: Weidenfeld
and Nicolson, 1974. Rev. by L. Hannah, BHR, 50(Spr 1976):
109.

Vale, M. G. A. Charles VII. Berkeley: U Cal Press, 1974.
Rev. by J. B. Henneman, AHR, 81(Apr 1976):370; R.
Vaughn, EHR, 91(Jan 1976):182-3.

Valjean, Nelson. John Steinbeck. San Francisco: Chronicle

Books, 1975. Rev. by M. H. Cox, CHQ, 55(Spr 1976):91-2;
L. Caughey, PHR, 45(Feb 1976):137-8.

Vallenilla, Luis. Oil: The Making of a New Economic Order.
New York: McGraw-Hill, 1975. Rev. by F. Tugwell, HAHR,
56(Nov 1976):673-5.

Van Allen, Rodger. The Commonweal and American Catholicism.
Philadelphia: Fortress, 1974. Rev. by G. Q. Flynn, CaHR,
62(Jl 1976):517-18.

van Beneden, Pierre. Aux origines d'une terminologie sacramentelle. Louvain: Spicilegium, 1974. Rev. by S. L.
Greenslade, JEccH, 27(Jan 1976):73-4.

Van Buitenen, J. A. B., trans. and ed. The Mahabharata. Books
2 and 3. Chicago: U Chicago Press, 1975. Rev. by B. S.
Miller, JAS, 36(Nov 1976):168-70.

Van Cleve, Thomas Curtis. The Emperor Frederick II of Hohen-
staufen. Oxford: Clarendon Press, 1972. Rev. by B. Mc-
Ginn, CH, 45(Mar 1976):103-4; J. Gillingham, EHR, 91(Apr
1976):358-63.

van den Haag, Ernest. Punishing Criminals. New York: Basic
Books, 1975. Rev. by J. Marsh, Commentary, 62(Sep 1976):
116, 118-20.

van der Meer, Haye. Women Priests in the Catholic Church?
Philadelphia: Temple U Press, 1973. Rev. by M. Fousek,
CH, 45(Mar 1976):124-5.

Vandersleyen, Claude. Les Guerres d'Amosis fondateur de la
XVIIIᵉ Dynastie. Brussels: Foundation Egyptologique Reine
Elisabeth, 1971. Rev. by D. Mueller, JNES, 35(Jan 1976):
53-4.

van der Wal, S. L., ed. Officiële bescheiden betreffende de
Nederlands-Indonesische betrekkingen 1945-1950. Gravenhage:
Martinus Nijhoff, 1974. Rev. by R. T. McVey, 91(Oct 1976):
879-81.

Van de Walle, Etienne. The Female Population of France. Princeton, N.J.: Prin U Press, 1974. Rev. by R. Magraw, History, 61(Feb 1976):136-7; P. V. Adams, JIH, 7(Sum 1976):
79-90; J. W. Scott, JMH, 48(Je 1976):333-4.

Van Dillen, J. G. Sources for the History of the Trade and the
Gilds of Amsterdam. Vol. 3. The Hague: Martinus Nijhoff,
1974. Rev. by E. J. Van Kley, AHR, 81(Apr 1976):401-2.

Vandiver, Frank E. The Southwest: South or West? College Station: Texas A and M U Press, 1975. Rev. by W. H. Split-
ter, JOW, 15(Jan 1976):137-8.

385   VAN DULMEN

van Dülmen, Richard. Der Geheimbund der Illuminaten. Stuttgart:
Frommann-Holzboog, 1975. Rev. by J. M. Roberts, EHR,
91(Oct 1976):919-20.

van Eyll, Klara see Kellenbenz, Hermann

van Heekeren, H. R. The Stone Age of Indonesia. The Hague:
Martinus Nijhoff, 1972. Rev. by J. Stargandt, Antiquity, 50
(Mar 1976):75.

Van Kley, Dale. The Jansenists and the Expulsion of the Jesuits
from France, 1757-1765. New Haven, Conn.: Yale U Press,
1975. Rev. by H. C. Payne, AHR, 81(Oct 1976):867-8; J.
D. Woodbridge, CH, 45(Je 1976):260-1; F. Fox, HRNB, 4
(Mar 1976):110-11.

Van Kooij, K. R., ed. and trans. Worship of the Goddess According to the Kalikapurana. Part I. Leiden: E. J. Brill, 1972.
Rev. by R. W. Nicholas, JAS, 36(Nov 1976):172-4.

Van Rensburg, Patrick. Report from Swaneng Hill. Uppsala:
Almqvist and Wiksell, 1974. Rev. by R. P. Werbner,
Africa, 46(Num 2, 1976):212-13.

Van Schreeven, William J. and Robert L. Scribner, eds. and comps.
Revolutionary Virginia. Vol. II. Charlottesville: U Press
Va, 1974. Rev. by G. M. Curtis, III, FCHQ, 50(Jl 1976):
321-2; H. D. Peters, JSH, 42(Feb 1976):107-8.

Van Seters, John. Abraham in History and Tradition. New Haven,
Conn.: Yale U Press, 1975. Rev. by E. J. Polak, HRNB,
4(Mar 1976):105.

Van Thal, Herbert, ed. The Prime Ministers. Vol. 2. London:
Allen and Unwin, 1975. Rev. by D. Southgate, History, 61
(Oct 1976):488-90.

Van Tine, Warren. The Making of the Labor Bureaucrat. Amherst, Mass.: U Mass Press, 1973. Rev. by J. A. Thompson, HJ, 19(Mar 1976):257-74.

Van Zwanenberg, R. M. A. An Economic History of Kenya and
Uganda, 1800-1970. Atlantic Highlands, N.J.: Humanities,
1975. Rev. by H. G. Soff, HRNB, 4(Jl 1976):170.

Varkey, Ouseph. At the Crossroads. Calcutta: Minerva Associates, 1974. Rev. by G. P. Deshpande, IQ, 32(Jan-Mar
1976):103-4.

Varley, H. P. Japanese Culture. London: Faber, 1973. Rev.
by C. D. Sheldon, MAS, 10(Apr 1976):310-11.

Varona, Alberto J. Francisco Bilbao. Panama: Ediciones Excel-

sior, 1973. **Rev. by J. Fisher, History, 61(Oct 1976):428-9;
H. E. Davis, TAm, 32(Apr 1976):637-8.**

Vashrishta, H. B. Land Revenue and Public Finance in Maratha
Administration. Delhi: Oriental Publishers, 1975. Rev. by
V. D. Divekar, IESHR, 13(Jan-Mar 1976):117-18.

Vasil, R. K. Politics in a Plural Society: A Study of Non-Com-
munal Parties in West Malaysia. Oxford: Oxford U Press,
1971. Rev. by C. H. Enloe, JAAS, 11(Jl-Oct 1976):236-9.

Vass, Henrik, ed. Studies on the History of the Hungarian Working-
Class Movement, 1867-1966. Budapest: Akadémiai Kiadó,
1975. Rev. by N. Masterman, History, 61(Je 1976):325-6.

Vassilevsky, A., et al. Moscow 1941-1942 Stalingrad: Recollections, Stories, Reports. Moscow: Progress Publ'rs., 1970.
Rev. by E. F. Ziemke, AHR, 81(Je 1976):638-9.

Vateishvili, D. L. Russian Social Thought and Publishing in the
Caucasus During the First Third of the 19th Century. Moscow: Izdatel'stvo "Nauka," 1973. Rev. by R. G. Suny, AHR,
81(Apr 1976):424-5.

Vaughan, Michalina and Margaret Scotford Archer. Social Conflict
and Educational Change in England and France, 1789-1848.
Cambridge: Cam U Press, 1971. Rev. by J. K. Burton,
JMH, 48(Sep 1976):555-7.

Vaughan, Richard. Charles the Bold, the last Valois duke of Burgundy. London: Longman, 1973. Rev. by C. A. J. Armstrong, EHR, 91(Apr 1976):374-8; J. B. Henneman, Historian,
38(Feb 1976):325-6.

_____. Valois Burgundy. London: Allen Lane, 1975. Rev.
by D. Nicholas, AHR, 81(Oct 1976):836-7; P. S. Lewis, EHR,
91(Oct 1976):902-3.

Vaughn, William Preston. Schools for All: The Blacks and Public
Education in the South, 1865-1877. Lexington: U Press Ky,
1974. Rev. by R. Welter, AHR, 81(Apr 1976):452-3; H. Shapiro, FCHQ, 50(Jan 1976):76-8.

Vazquez de Prada, Valentin, intro. El Método Histórico. Pamplona: EUNSA, 1974. Rev. by R. A. H. Robinson, History,
61(Feb 1976):74-5.

Veblen, Eric. The Manchester Union Leader in New Hampshire
Elections. Hanover, N.H.: U Press of New England, 1975.
Rev. by E. D. Canham, NEQ, 49(Mar 1976):144-6.

Vedder, Richard K., ed. see Klingaman, David C., ed.

Veenhof, K. R. Aspects of Old Assyrian Trade and Its Terminology. Leiden: E. J. Brill, 1972. Rev. by N. Yoffee, JNES, 35(Jan 1976):62-5.

Vendler, Zeno. Res cogitans: An Essay in Rational Psychology. Ithaca: Cornell U Press, 1972. Rev. by R. A. Watson, JHP, 14(Apr 1976):249-54.

Venkataraman, B. Laddigam. New Delhi: Orient Longmans, 1971. Rev. by M. W. Meister, JAS, 36(Nov 1976):167-8.

Vercoutter, Jean, et al. Mirgissa I. Paris: Ministère des Affaires Etrangères, 1970. Rev. by C. E. De Vries, JNES, 35(Jan 1976):55-7.

Vermaseren, M. J. see Kater-Sibbes, C. J. F.

Vermeule, Emily T. Toumba tou Skourou. Boston: Harvard U, 1971-1974. Rev. by R. S. Merrillees, AJA, 80(Sum 1976): 308-9.

Vernam, Glenn R. see Rice, Lee M.

Versey, G. R. see Darby, H. C.

Ver Steeg, Clarence L. Origins of a Southern Mosaic: Studies of Early Carolina and Georgia. Athens: U Ga Press, 1975. Rev. by C. Eaton, AHR, 81(Oct 1976):957; R. K. Murdoch, FHQ, 55(Jl 1976):86-7; G. C. Rogers, Jr., GHQ, 60(Spr 1976):73-5; J. A. Hodges, HRNB, 4(Feb 1976):77-8; T. W. Tate, JAH, 63(Dec 1976):684-5; L. E. Pennington, JSH, 42 (Aug 1976):415-16; L. C. Steelman, NCHR, 53(Spr 1976):225-7; A. N. Sanders, SCHM, 77(Apr 1976):130.

Vess, David M. Medical Revolution in France 1789-1796. Gainesville: U Presses Fla, 1975. Rev. by D. B. Weiner, AHR, 81(Apr 1976):397.

Vexler, Robert I., ed. and comp. Cincinnati: A Chronological & Documentary History, 1676-1970. Dobbs Ferry, N.Y.: Oceana Publications, Inc., 1975. Rev. by W. D. Aeschbacher, IMH, 72(Je 1976):262-3.

_____. The Vice Presidents and Cabinet Members. Dobbs Ferry, N.Y.: Oceana, 1975. Rev. by P. Riddleberger, JAH, 63(Sep 1976):400.

Vicinus, Martha. The Industrial Muse. New York: Barnes and Noble, 1975. Rev. by F. M. Leventhal, AHR, 81(Je 1976): 589; D. Bythell, EHR, 91(Jl 1976):656-7.

Vickers, Michael see Post, Kenneth

Vilar, Pierre. A History of Gold and Money, 1450-1920. Atlantic Highlands, N.J.: Humanities, 1976. Rev. by J. Boughton, AHR, 81(Oct 1976):815-16.

Vilkov, O. N., ed. The Cities of Siberia (The Economy, Management, and Culture of Siberian Cities in the Pre-Soviet Period). Novosibirsk: Izdatel'stvo "Nauka," 1974. Rev. by S. Watrous, AHR, 81(Oct 1976):905-6.

Viñas, Angel. La Alemania nazi y el 18 de julio. Madrid: Alianza Editorial, 1974. Rev. by E. R. Beck, AHR, 81(Apr 1976):381; G. Jackson, JMH, 48(Mar 1976):135-8.

Vincent, Charles. Black Legislators in Louisiana during Reconstruction. Baton Rouge: LSU Press, 1975. Rev. by A. M. Kraut, HRNB, 4(Sep 1976):218; W. J. Fraser, Jr., THQ, 35(Fall 1976):338-9.

Vincent, John see Cooke, A. B.

Viola, Herman J. Thomas L. McKenney, Architect of America's Early Indian Policy, 1816-1830. Chicago: Swallow, 1974. Rev. by M. Rogin, AHR, 81(Oct 1976):969-70; G. A. Schultz, IMH, 72(Mar 1976):69-71; A. H. DeRosier, Jr., PHR, 45 (Aug 1976):441-2; W. D. Baird, WHQ, 7(Jan 1976):67-8.

Vital, David. The Origins of Zionism. New York: Oxford U Press, 1975. Rev. by A. Elon, Commentary, 61(Je 1976): 68-72; F. Rosenthal, HRNB, 4(Sep 1976):224.

Vitzthum, Richard C. The American Compromise. Norman: U Ok Press, 1974. Rev. by H. Brogan, History, 61(Oct 1976): 423-4; O. A. Pease, JAH, 63(Je 1976):150-2; R. E. Levinson, JOW, 15(Jan 1976):135; C. Singer, PNQ, 67(Apr 1976): 90.

Vivelo, Frank R. and Jacqueline J., ed. see Levitas, Gloria, ed.

Vloyantes, John P. Silk Glove Hegemony: Finnish-Soviet Relations, 1944-1974. Kent, Ohio: Kent St U Press, 1975. Rev. by D. R. Papazian, HRNB, 4(Feb 1976):88.

Voegelin, Eric. From Enlightenment to Revolution. Durham, N.C.: Duke U Press, 1975. Rev. by G. Cavanaugh, AHR, 81(Apr 1976):359; D. Germino, JMH, 48(Sep 1976):533-5.

_____. Order and History. Vol. IV. Baton Rouge: LSU Press, 1975. Rev. by W. C. Havard, AHR, 81(Je 1976): 557-8.

Vogel, Barbara. Deutsche Russlandpolitik: Das Scheitern der deutschen Weltpolitik unter Bülow, 1900-1906. [Gütersloh:] Bertelsmann Universitätsverlag, 1973. Rev. by G. O. Kent, AHR, 81(Oct 1976):883.

Vogel, John J. Indians of Ohio and Wyandot County. New York: Vantage, 1975. Rev. by D. L. Smith, JAH, 63(Dec 1976): 686-7.

Vogelgesang, Sandy. The Long Dark Night of the Soul. New York: Harper and Row, 1974. Rev. by B. J. Bernstein, AHR, 81 (Apr 1976):470.

Vogt, Joseph. Ancient Slavery and the Ideal of Man. Cambridge, Mass.: Harv U Press, 1975. Rev. by L. Pearson, AHR, 81(Oct 1976):825-6.

Vohra, Ranbir. Lao She and the Chinese Revolution. Cambridge, Mass.: Harvard U Press, 1974. Rev. by Tien-Wei Wu, AHR, 81(Apr 1976):432-3.

Volker, Michels, ed. see Carlson, Anni, ed.

Volkmar, Lloyd B. Luther's Response to Violence. New York: Vantage, 1974. Rev. by H. J. Grimm, JCS, 17(Spr 1975): 301-2.

Vollenweider, Marie-Louise. Die Porträtgemmen der Romischen Republik. 2 vols. Mainz: Verlag Philipp von zabern, 1972, 1974. Rev. by U. W. Heisinger, AJA, 80(Spr 1976):216-17.

von Bar, Carl Ludwig. Staat und katholische Kirche in Preussen. Aalen: Scientia Verlag, 1971 (Reprint). Rev. by D. J. Diephouse, JCS, 17(Aut 1975):541-2.

Von Breton, Harriette see Gebhard, David

von Dechen, H. see von Oeynhausen, C.

Von Euw, Eric see Graham, Ian

von Hagen, Victor Wolfgang. The Germanic People in America. Norman: U Ok Press, n.d. Rev. by F. R. DiFederico, Smithsonian, 7(Sep 1976):162, 164, 166.

von Oeynhausen, C. and H. von Dechen. Railways in England, 1826 and 1827. n.p.: Newcomen Society, 1971. Rev. by G. Ottley, JTH, 3(Sep 1976):301.

von Saldern, Axel, et al. Gläser der Antike, Sammlung Erwin Oppenländer. Mainz am Rhein: Verlag Philipp von Zabern, 1974. Rev. by E. B. Dusenberry, AJA, 80(Sum 1976):319-20.

von Sauer, Franz A. The Alienated "Loyal" Opposition. Albuquerque: U NM Press, 1974. Rev. by R. A. Camp, TAm, 32 (Apr 1976):653-4.

Voorhies, Barbara see Martin, M. Kay

Vroomans, A. P. J. see Newell, R. R.

Vucinich, Alexander. Science in Russian Culture 1861-1917. Stanford, Cal.: Stanford U Press, 1971. Rev. by R. A. Lewis, ESR, 6(Apr 1976):266-9.

Vucinich, Wayne S., ed. see Lederer, Ivo J., ed.

Wacher, John. The Towns of Roman Britain. London: Batsford, 1974. Rev. by J. J. Wilkes, History, 61(Oct 1976):433-4.

Wacholder, Ben Zion. Eupolemus: A Study of Judaeo-Greek Literature. Cincinnati: Hebrew Union College Press, 1974. Rev. by J. R. Rosenbloom, AHR, 81(Oct 1976):918-19.

Wacker, Peter O. Land and People: A Cultural Geography of Preindustrial New Jersey. New Brunswick, N.J.: Rutgers U Press, 1975. Rev. by R. V. Wells, JAH, 63(Dec 1976): 682-3.

Wadsworth, Nelson B. Through Camera Eyes. Provo: BYU Press, 1975. Rev. by A. Hinckley, UHQ, 44(Sum 1976): 305-6.

Waeber, Paul. La formation du canton de Genève, 1814-1816. Geneva: Author, 1974. Rev. by M. S. Anderson, EHR, 91 (Jl 1976):659-60.

Wagenblass, Horst. Der Eisen bahnbau und das Wachstum der deutschen Eisen. Stuttgart: Gustav Fischer Verlag, n.d. Rev. by W. O. Henderson, ESR, 6(Jl 1976):385-7.

Wagley, Charles, ed. Man in the Amazon. Gainesville: U Fla Press, 1974. Rev. by C. M. MacLachlan, TAm, 32(Jan 1976):484-6.

Wagner, Ewald, ed. Der Diwan des Abu Nuwas. Vol. 2. Wiesbaden: Franz Steiner Verlag, 1972. Rev. by J. A. Bellamy, JNES, 35(Apr 1976):144-5.

Wagner, Walter. Der Volksgerichtshof im nationalsozialistischen Staat. Stuttgart: Deutsche verlags-Anstalt, 1974. Rev. by W. Sweet, JMH, 48(Je 1976):352-6.

Wagoner, Jay J. Early Arizona. Tucson: U Ariz Press, 1975. Rev. by J. A. Wilson, JAH, 62(Mar 1976):961-2; W. H. Lyon, JOW, 15(Jan 1976):131; A. T. Row, NDH, 43(Win 1976):38-9; L. R. Murphy, NMHR, 51(Jan 1976):80-1; C. S. Peterson, UHQ, 44(Sum 1976):308-9; J. S. Goff, WHQ, 7 (Jl 1976):327-8.

Wai, Dunstan M., ed. The Southern Sudan. London: Frank Cass, 1973. Rev. by D. J. Sconyers, IJMES, 7(Jan 1976):133-4.

Wakefield, Walter L. Heresy, Crusade and Inquisition in Southern France, 1100-1250. Berkeley: U Cal Press, 1974. Rev. by J. N. Hillgarth, AHR, 81(Feb 1976):113-14; J. Mundy, CaHR, 62(Jan 1976):78-9; C. Morris, History, 61(Feb 1976):99; R. M. Golden, JCS, 18(Aut 1976):548-50.

Wakeman, Frederic, Jr. and Carolyn Grant, eds. Conflict and Control in Late Imperial China. Berkeley: U Cal Press, 1976. Rev. by M. Gassler, Historian, 39(Nov 1976):141-2; T. C. Rhee, HRNB, 4(Jl 1976):172.

_____. The Fall of Imperial China. New York: Free Press, 1975. Rev. by T. C. Rhee, HRNB, 4(Sep 1976):221; S. Karnow, Smithsonian, 6(Jan 1976):106-8.

Waldman, Milton. The Lady Mary. New York: Scribner's, 1972. Rev. by J. G. Dwyer, CaHR, 62(Jan 1976):133-4.

Walker, A. Keith. William Law: His Life and Thought. London: Society for Promoting Christian Knowledge, 1973. Rev. by A. C. Outler, CaHR, 62(Apr 1976):296-7.

Walker, Dale L. Death Was the Black Horse: The Story of Rough Rider Buckey O'Neill. Austin: Madrona Press, 1975. Rev. by Andrew Wallace, A & W, 18(Aut 1976):292-3.

Walker, Deward E., Jr., ed. Systems of North American Witchcraft and Sorcery. Moscow, Ida.: U Idaho, 1970. Rev. by A. B. Kehoe, AA, 78(Je 1976):399-400.

Wall, Bennett H. and George S. Gibb. Teagle of Jersey Standard. New Orleans: Tulane U, 1974. Rev. by K. L. Bryant, Jr., SWHQ, 80(Jl 1976):121-2.

Walle, Dennis F. see Brichford, Maynard J.

Waller, Bruce. Bismarck at the Crossroads. London: Athlone, 1974. Rev. by P. W. Becker, AHR, 81(Apr 1976):407; J. A. S. Grenville, History, 61(Oct 1976):1976.

Waller, Charles T. see Killion, Ronald G.

Waller, Derek J. The Kiangsi Soviet Republic: Mao and the National Congresses of 1931 and 1934. Berkeley: U Cal, 1972. Rev. by J. P. Harrison, AHR, 81(Oct 1976):938-9.

Waller, George M. The American Revolution in the West. Chicago: Nelson-Hall, 1976. Rev. by L. H. Harrison, AHI, 11 (Dec 1976):50.

Wallerstein, Immanuel. The Modern World-System: Capitalist
   Agriculture and the Origins of the European World-Economy
   in the Sixteenth Century. London: Academic Press, 1974.
   Rev. by D. S. Kennitzer, AA, 78(Je 1976):392-3; G. Parker,
   History, 61(Je 1976):269-70; R. T. Rapp, JEH, 36(Sep 1976):
   801-3; R. Cameron, JIH, 7(Sum 1976):140-4.

Walls, William J. The African Methodist Episcopal Zion Church.
   Charlotte, N.C.: A. M. E. Zion Publishing House, 1974.
   Rev. by W. H. Daniel, NYHSQ, 60(Jan/Apr 1976):78-9.

Walmsley, Lewis C. Bishop in Honan. Toronto: U Tor Press,
   1974. Rev. by J. G. Endicott, CHR, 57(Je 1976):202-4.

Walpole, Horace. Horace Walpole's Correspondence. Vols. 37-39.
   (W. S. Lewis, et al., eds.) New Haven, Conn.: Yale U
   Press, 1974. Rev. by D. M. Clark, AHR, 81(Feb 1976):133-
   4; P. Langford, EHR, 91(Apr 1976):433.

Walsdorff, Martin. Westorientierung und Ostpolitik. Bremen:
   Schünemann Universitätsverlag, 1971. Rev. by A. E. Corne-
   hise, ESR, 6(Jl 1976):398-400.

Walsh, John Evangelist. One Day at Kitty Hawk: The Untold
   Story of the Wright Brothers and the Airplane. New York:
   Crowell, 1975. Rev. by J. B. Rae, AHR, 81(Oct 1976):990.

Walsh, Katherine. The "De Vita Evangelica" of Geoffrey Hardeby,
   O. E. S. A. (c. 1320-c. 1385). Rome: Institutum Historicum
   Augustianum, 1972. Rev. by J. Smet, CaHR, 62(Jan 1976):
   98-9.

Walsh, Richard and William Lloyd Fox, eds. Maryland: A History,
   1632-1974. Baltimore: Maryland Historical Society, 1974.
   Rev. by W. H. Ridgway, AHR, 81(Oct 1976):959; G. H. Callcott, JAH, 63(Je 1976):103-4.

Walter, Benjamin, ed. see Blumstein, James F., ed.

Walton, Gary M. see Shepherd, James F.

Walton, Hanes, Jr. Black Republicans. Metuchen, N.J.: Scarecrow, 1975. Rev. by R. F. Durden, JAH, 62(Mar 1976):
   1026-7; B. A. Crouch, JSH, 42(Aug 1976):437-8; G. W. Reid,
   NCHR, 53(Win 1976):100-2.

Walzer, Michael and Marion Rothstein, ed. and trans. Regicide
   and Revolution: Speeches at the Trial of Louis XVI. New
   York: Cam U Press, 1974. Rev. by D. P. Jordan, JMH,
   48(Mar 1976):149-52.

Wandycz, Piotr S. The Lands of Partitioned Poland 1795-1918.
   Seattle: U Wash Press, 1974. Rev. by R. F. Leslie, EHR,
   91(Jl 1976):655-6.

Ward, Alan. A Show of Justice. Canberra: Australian National
U Press, 1974. Rev. by C. Newberry, EHR, 91(Jl 1976):
668-9.

Ward, J. R. The Finance of Canal Building in Eighteenth-Century
England. Oxford: Oxford U Press, 1974. Rev. by M. C.
Reed, BH, 17(Jl 1975):212-14; P. S. Bagwell, EHR, 91(Jan
1976):208-9; B. F. Duckham, History, 61(Feb 1976):117-18.

Ward, J. T. Chartism. Toronto: Copp Clark, 1974. Rev. by D.
Bowen, CHR, 57(Mar 1976):74-6.

Ward, James A. That Man Haupt. Baton Rouge: LSU Press,
1973. Rev. by R. M. Sutton, JISHS, 69(May 1976):149-50;
J. R. Killick, JTH, 3(Sep 1976):302-3.

Ward, Stephen R., ed. The War Generation: Veterans of the First
World War. Port Washington, N.Y.: Kennikat, 1975. Rev.
by M. R. Dearing, AHR, 81(Oct 1976):818; M. Berg, Historian, 39(Nov 1976):122-3; R. M. Clutter, IMH, 72(Je 1976):
178-9.

Wardman, Alan. Plutarch's Lives. Berkeley: U Cal Press, 1974.
Rev. by T. W. Africa, AHR, 81(Feb 1976):105-6.

Warne, Arthur. Church and Society in Eighteenth-Century Devon.
Newton Abbot, Devon: David and Charles, 1973. Rev. by G.
L. Vincitorio, CaHR, 62(Apr 1976):297-9.

Warner, Denis and Peggy Warner. The Tide at Sunrise. New
York: Charterhouse, 1974. Rev. by W. L. Mathes, Historian, 39(Nov 1976):139-40.

Warner, Ezra J. and W. Buck Yearns. Biographical Register of
the Confederate Congress. Baton Rouge: LSU Press, 1975.
Rev. by M. L. Ervin, ChOk, 54(Win 1976):535-6; T. B.
Alexander, JAH, 63(Sep 1976):421-2; J. I. Robertson, Jr.,
JMiH, 38(Feb 1976):120-1; R. E. Beringer, JSH, 42(Aug
1976):431-2; M. R. Williams, NCHR, 53(Spr 1976):229-31;
F. N. Boney, VMHB, 84(Apr 1976):212-14.

Warren, David B. see Taylor, Lonn

Warren, Donald R. To Enforce Education. Detroit: Wayne St U
Press, 1974. Rev. by T. R. Sizer, AHR, 81(Feb 1976):211.

Warren, J. Benedict. Hans P. Kraus Collection of Hispanic American Manuscripts, A Guide. Washington: Library of Congress,
1974. Rev. by U. L., HAHR, 56(Feb 1976):174; N. L. Benson,
NMHR, 51(Jl 1976):260-1.

Warren, Peter. The Aegean Civilizations. London: Elsevier-
Phaidon, 1976. Rev. by F. H. Stubbings, Antiquity, 50(Je
1976):172-3.

Warren, W. L. Henry II. Berkeley: U Cal Press, 1973. Rev. by J. W. Alexander, CaHR, 62(Jan 1976):84-6.

Washburn, Wilcomb E. The Assault on Indian Tribalism: The General Allotment Law (Dawes Act) of 1887. Philadelphia: Lippincott, 1975. Rev. by I. Sutton, PHR, 45(May 1976):293-4.

_____. The Indian in America. New York: Harper and Row, 1975. Rev. by W. T. Hagan, AHR, 81(Je 1976):649; T. P. Wilson, AIQ, 2(Spr 1975):23-4; W. R. Jacobs, PHR, 45(Nov 1976):604-5; P. R. Metcalf, WHQ, 7(Jl 1976):317-18.

Waters, Frank. Mexico Mystique. Chicago: Swallow, 1975. Rev. by D. M. Vigness, ETHJ, 14(Spr 1976):56-7.

Watson, Alan D. Society in Colonial North Carolina. Raleigh: Div Archives and History, 1975. Rev. by W. S. Powell, NCHR, 53(Spr 1976):232-3.

Watson, Charles S. Antebellum Charleston Dramatists. University: U Ala Press, 1976. Rev. by P. C. Robinson, SCHM, 77(Jan 1976):268.

Watson, Elizabeth. Fight and Survive! Conway, Ark.: River Road Press, 1974. Rev. by R. D. Hoffsommer, CWTI, 15 (Aug 1976):49.

Watson, James T., ed. see Kimball, Solon T., ed.

Watson, Richard L., Jr. The Development of National Power. Boston: Houghton Mifflin, 1976. Rev. by J. M. Gowaskie, HRNB, 4(Aug 1976):192.

Watt, Donald Cameron. Too Serious a Business: European Armed Forces and the Approach to the Second World War. Berkeley: U Cal Press, 1975. Rev. by D. S. Birn, AHR, 81(Je 1976): 579; B. Bond, History, 61(Je 1976):327-8; S. R. Williamson, Jr., JIH, 7(Aut 1976):370-2.

Watt, W. Montgomery. The Majesty That Was Islam. New York: Praeger, 1974. Rev. by W. B. Bishai, AHR, 81(Feb 1976): 191.

Watts, S. J. From Border to Middle Shire. Atlantic Highlands, N.J.: Humanities, 1975. Rev. by F. F. Foster, AHR, 81 (Oct 1976):854; C. Kitching, Archives, 12(Spr 1976):146-7.

Wauchope, Robert and Howard Cline, et al., eds. Handbook of Middle American Indians: Guide to Ethnohistorical Sources. Vols. 12-15. Austin: U Texas Press, 1975. Rev. by E. M. Brumfiel, AmAn, 41(Jl 1976):398-403; J. K. Chance, HAHR, 56(May 1976):304-7; S. A. Colston, TAm, 32(Apr 1976):638-9.

Waung, W. S. K. Revolution and Liberation. Hong Kong: Heine-
    mann, 1974. Rev. by D. S. G. Goodman, CQ, May 1976, pp.
    403-5.

Wax, Murray L. and Robert W. Buchanan, eds. Solving "The In-
    dian Problem." New York: New York Times Book Co., 1975.
    Rev. by K. R. Philp, AIQ, 2(Sum 1975):155-6.

Wayman, Alex and Hideko Wayman, trans. The Lion's Roar of
    Queen Srimala. New York: Columbia U Press, 1974. Rev.
    by K. R. Norman, MAS, 10(Jl 1976):472-3.

Weatherby, Harold L. Cardinal Newman in His Age. Nashville:
    Vanderbilt U Press, 1973. Rev. by M. R. O'Connell, CaHR,
    ʳ2(Oct 1976):630-1; F. H. Thompsett, HMPEC, 45(Dec 1976):
    459-60.

Weaver, Andrew T., ed. see Byrne, Frank L., ed.

Weaver, Herbert, ed. see Polk, James K.

Weaver, John D. El Pueblo Grande. Los Angeles: Ward Ritchie,
    1973. Rev. by L. Leader, JOW, 15(Jan 1976):132.

Weaver, Thomas, ed. Indians of Arizona. Tucson: U Ariz Press,
    1974. Rev. by L. C. Kelly, AIQ, 2(Sum 1975):156-7.

Webb, Beatrice. Our Partnership. New York: Cam U Press,
    1975. Rev. by W. H. Dunham, Jr., JRNB, 4(Mar 1976):112.

Webb, Todd and Willard B. Robinson. Texas Public Buildings of
    the Nineteenth Century. Austin: U Texas Press, 1974. Rev.
    by F. Tarpley, ETHJ, 14(Spr 1976):66-7.

Webber, Bert. Retaliation: Japanese Attacks and Allied Counter-
    measures on the Pacific Coast in World War II. Corvallis,
    Ore.: Ore St U Press, 1975. Rev. by R. Higham, JAH, 63
    (Je 1976):187-8; P. E. Onstad, OrHQ, 77(Je 1976):194-5.

Weber, Christoph. Aufklärung und Orthodoxie am Mittelrheim,
    1820-1850. Paderborn: Verlag Ferdinand Schöningh, 1973.
    Rev. by S. J. Tonsor, CaHR, 62(Apr 1976):315-16.

Weber, Francis J. California Catholicism: A Holy Year Tribute.
    Los Angeles: Dawson's, 1975. Rev. by F. F. Guest, NMHR,
    51(Jan 1976):85-7; J. A. Schutz, SCQ, 58(Spr 1976):129-31.

_____. Mayor of Indianapolis. Worcester: Dawson's, 1975.
    Rev. by L. L. Sylvester, JAH, 62(Mar 1976):1030-1.

_____, comp. The Mission in the Valley: A Documentary His-
    tory of San Fernando, Rey de Espana. Los Angeles: Arch-
    diocese of Los Angeles, 1975. Rev. by F. F. Guest, NMHR,
    51(Apr 1976):166-7.

Weber, Marianne. Max Weber: A Biography. New York: Wiley, 1975. Rev. by R. L. Hoffman, Historian, 39(Nov 1976):132-3.

Weber, Ronald, ed. America in Change. Notre Dame, Ind.: U Notre Dame Press, 1972. Rev. by G. H. Wamble, JCS, 17 (Spr 1975):346.

Weber, William. Music and the Middle Class: The Social Structure of Concert Life in London, Paris and Vienna. New York: Holmes and Meier, 1976. Rev. by N. Temperley, AHR, 81 (Oct 1976):844-5.

Webster, Bruce. Scotland from the Eleventh Century to 1603. London: Sources of History, 1975. Rev. by M. Lee, Jr., AHR, 81(Apr 1976):392; G. W. S. Barrow, JEccH, 27(Oct 1976):421-2.

Webster, Charles. The Great Instauration. London: Duckworth, 1975. Rev. by A. R. Hall, EHR, 91(Oct 1976):853-9; R. Porter, HJ, 19(Dec 1976):1026-30.

Webster, Graham. Practical Archaeology. London: A & C Black, 1974. Rev. by J. Alexander, Antiquity, 50(Je 1976):170.

Webster, R. A. Industrial Imperialism in Italy, 1908-1915. Berkeley: U Cal Press, 1975. Rev. by H. Cliadakis, HRNB, 4(May/Je 1976):156.

Wechter, Nell Wise. Some Whisper of Our Name. Manteo, N.C.: Times Printing, 1975. Rev. by E. C. Bearss, NCHR, 53 (Win 1976):85-6.

Weddle, Robert S. Plowhorse Cavalry. Austin, Texas: Madrona, 1974. Rev. by R. D. Hoffsommer, CWTI, 15(Je 1976):49-50.

_____ and Robert H. Thonhoff. Drama and Conflict: The Texas Sage of 1776. Austin: Madrona Press, 1976. Rev. by W. Gard, SWHQ, 80(Oct 1976):237-8.

Weems, John Edward. To Conquer a Peace. Garden City, N.Y.: Doubleday, 1974. Rev. by A. P. McDonald, CWH, 22(Mar 1976):81-3; S. V. Connor, WHQ, 7(Apr 1976):199-200.

Wehler, Hans-Ulrich. Der Aufstieg des amerikanischen Imperialismus. Göttingen: Vandenhoeck and Ruprecht, 1974. Rev. by L. E. Ambrosius, AHR, 81(Feb 1976):212; T. Schoonover, JAH, 62(Mar 1976):1011-12.

Weichmann, Louis J. A True History of the Assassination of Abraham Lincoln and of the Conspiracy of 1865. New York: Knopf, 1975. Rev. by L. H. Johnson, III, CWH, 22(Mar 1976):77-81; W. Hanchett, JAH, 63(Je 1976):137; W. C. Temple, JISHS, 69(May 1976):150-1; W. J. Niven, Jr., JSH, 42 (May 1976):288-90.

Weichold, Arthur. Johann Andreas Schubert. Leipzig: Urania
Verlag, 1968. Rev. by W. O. Henderson, ESR, 6(Jl 1976):
385-7.

Weigle, Marta. Brothers of Light, Brothers of Blood. Albuquerque: U NM Press, 1976. Rev. by L. R. Murphy, A & W,
18(Win 1976):385-6; D. M. Vigness, NMHR, 51(Oct 1976):
340-1.

Weinberg, Gerhard L., ed. Transformation of a Continent. Minneapolis: Burgess, 1975. Rev. by R. J. Plowman, HRNB,
4(Jan 1976):64-5.

Weiner, Hanna, ed. see Weizmann, Chaim

Weiner, Myron and John Osgood Field, eds. Electoral Politics in
the Indian States. Delhi: Manohar Book Service, 1975. Rev.
by M. Sirsikar, IQ, 32(Apr.Je 1976):258-9.

Weinrich, A. K. H. African Farmers in Rhodesia. Oxford: Oxford U Press, 1975. Rev. by O. B. Pollack, AfAf, 75(Jl
1976):404-5.

Weinstein, James. Ambiguous Legacy. New York: New Viewpoints,
1975. Rev. by B. K. Johnpoll, Commentary, 61(Apr 1976):
90-4; F. A. Warren, JAH, 63(Dec 1976):750-1; S. Rosswurm,
NDH, 43(Fall 1976):42.

Weinstein, Martin. Uruguay: The Politics of Failure. Westport:
Conn.: Greenwood, 1975. Rev. by C. Little, AHR, 81(Oct
1976):1012-13; M. Alisky, HAHR, 56(Feb 1976):142-3.

Weinstein, Warren, ed. Chinese and Soviet Aid to Africa. New
York: Praeger, 1975. Rev. by M. Bailey, AfAf, 75(Apr
1976):251-2; T. H. Henriksen, JMAS, 14(Je 1976):350-3.

Weisbord, Robert G. Genocide? Birth Control and the Black
American. Westport, Conn.: Greenwood, 1975. Rev. by
T. A. Krueger, JAH, 63(Dec 1976):782-3.

Weisbrod, Bernd, ed. see Mommsen, Hans, ed.

Weisheipl, James A. Friar Thomas d'Aquino. Garden City, N.Y.:
Doubleday, 1974. Rev. by V. J. Bourke, CaHR, 62(Jan
1976):90-2; G. Leff, EHR, 91(Oct 1976):895; D. L. Douie,
JEccH, 27(Apr 1976):195-6.

Weissman, Benjamin M. Herbert Hoover and Famine Relief to
Soviet Russia, 1921-1923. Stanford, Cal.: Hoover Institution
Press, 1974. Rev. by R. H. Zieger, AHR, 81(Oct 1976):
800-10; J. M. Thompson, JAH, 63(Sep 1976):452-3.

Weissman, Stephen R. American Foreign Policy in the Congo,

1960-1964. Ithaca: Cornell U Press, 1974. Rev. by R. Emerson, PHR, 45(May 1976):305-6.

Weizmann, Chaim. The Letters and Papers of Chaim Weizmann, 1907-1913. (Hanna Weiner and Barnett Litvinoff, eds.) London: Oxford U Press, 1974. Rev. by J. Parker, EHR, 91(Jl 1976):679-80.

_____ see also Yogev, G., et al., eds.

Welch, Edwin, ed. Two Calvinistic Methodist Chapels, 1743-1811. London: Record Society, 1975. Rev. by F. Baker, CH, 45 (Je 1976):261.

Welch, Holmes. Buddhism Under Mao. Cambridge, Mass.: Harvard U Press, 1972. Rev. by J. R. Carter, JCS, 18(Aut 1976):545-8; T. Barrett, MAS, 10(Feb 1976):154-6.

Welker, Robert Henry. Natural Man. Bloomington: Ind U Press, n.d. Rev. by J. Hope, Smithsonian, 6(Oct 1976):146-7.

Weller, John, ed. see Ranger, T. O., ed.

Wellhausen, Julius. The Religio-Political Factions in Early Islam. New York: American Elsevier, 1975. Rev. by A. C. Hess, AHR, 81(Oct 1976):788-99; W. M. Watt, History, 61(Oct 1976): 436-7.

Wells, David F. and John D. Woodbridge, eds. The Evangelicals: What They Believe, Who They Are, Where They Are Changing. Nashville, Tenn.: Abingdon, 1975. Rev. by R. E. Wentz, CH, 45(Sep 1976):399-400.

Wells, Elsie C. Bakersfield, Vermont: The Way It Was, the Way It Is. Canaan, N.H.: Phoenix Publishing Co., 1976. Rev. by R. Teagle, VH, 44(Fall 1976):239-42.

Wells, Robert V. The Population of the British Colonies in America Before 1776. Princeton, N.J.: Prin U Press, 1975. Rev. by L. R. Gerlach, HRNB, 4(Apr 1976):119; R. J. Cain, NCHR, 53(Sum 1976):327-8; T. S. Berry, VMHB, 84(Oct 1976):490-1.

Welter, Rush. The Mind of America 1820-1860. New York: Columbia U Press, 1975. Rev. by M. Klein, AHI, 11(May 1976):49-50; D. Grimsted, AHR, 81(Oct 1976):970-1; G. T. Blakey, IMH, 72(Mar 1976):71-2; J. O. Robertson, NEQ, 49 (Mar 1976):148-51.

Wendell, Charles. The Evolution of the Egyptian National Image: From Its Origins to Ahmad Luṭfī al-Sayyid. Berkeley: U Cal Press, 1972. Rev. by J. P. Entelis, AHR, 81(Oct 1976):920; A. L. Marsot, IJMES, 7(Jl 1976):459-60.

Wendt, Bernd Jürgen, ed. see Geiss, Imanuel, ed.

Were, Gideon S. A History of South Africa. London: Evans,
    1974. Rev. by D. Killingray, JAfH, 17(Num 3, 1976):458-9。

Werkmeister, W. H. Historical Spectrum of Value Theories. Vol.
    II. Anglo-American Group. Lincoln, Neb.: Johnsen, 1973.
    Rev. by A. Stern, JHP, 14(Apr 1976):247-9.

Wermelinger, Otto. Rom und Pelagius: die theologische Position
    der romischen Bischofe im Pelagianischen Streit in den Fahren
    411-432. Stuttgart: Hiersemann, 1975. Rev. by R. A.
    Markus, JEccH, 27(Oct 1976):416-7.

Werner, T. G., ed. Scripta Mercaturae. Vol. I. München:
    Scripta Mercaturae Verlag, 1973. Rev. by W. R. Lee, BH,
    17(Jl 1975):214-15.

Wertheim, Arthur Frank. The New York Little Renaissance. New
    York: NYU Press, 1976. Rev. by L. B. Miller, HRNB, 4
    (Sep 1976):213.

Weslager, C. A. The Delaware Indians. New Brunswick, N. J.:
    Rutgers U Press, 1972. Rev. by M. D. Thurman, AA, 78
    (Mar 1976):163.

_____. Magic Medicines of the Indians. Somerset, N. J.:
    Middle Atlantic Press, 1973. Rev. by L. Mason, AIQ, 2
    (Sum 1975):148-9.

Wesson, Robert G. Why Marxism? New York: Basic Books,
    1975. Rev. by Victor Baras, Commentary, 62(Sep 1976):
    123-4.

West, E. G. Education and the Industrial Revolution. London:
    Batsford, 1975. Rev. by N. McCord, EHR, 91(Jl 1976):
    670-2.

West, Elliot see DeBoe, David C.

Westerman, Ekkehard. Das Eislebener und Garkupfer und seine
    Bedeutung für den europäischen Kupfer-Markt, 1460-1560.
    Cologne: Böhlau Verlag, 1971. Rev. by R. Knauerhase, JEH,
    36(Je 1976):472-6.

Westin, Alan F. and Barry Mahoney. The Trial of Martin Luther
    King. New York: Crowell, 1974. Rev。 by D. Lewis, AHR,
    81(Apr 1976):469-70.

Weth, Rudolph, ed. see Feil, Ernst, ed.

Wetmore, Ruth Y. First on the Land. Winston-Salem, N. C.:
    Blair, 1975. Rev. by W. L. Williams, NCHR, 53(Spr 1976):
    219-20.

Whalley, Joyce Irene. Cobwebs to Catch Flies. Berkeley: U Cal
    Press, 1975. Rev. by W. Claire, Smithsonian, 6(Feb 1976):
    127-9.

Wheeler, Keith. The Townsmen. New York: Time-Life Books,
    1975. Rev. by J. White, ChOk, 54(Fall 1976):416-7.

Wheeler-Bennett, John. Knaves, Fools, and Heroes in Europe Be-
    tween the Wars. New York: St. Martin's, 1975. Rev. by E.
    V. Gulick, AHR, 81(Oct 1976):848.

Wherry, Joseph H. Indian Masks and Myths of the West. New
    York: Funk and Wagnalls, 1974. Rev. by C. Vaughn, JOW,
    15(Jl 1976):98.

Whetter, James. Cornwall in the Seventeenth Century: An Eco-
    nomic Survey of Kernow. Padstow: Lodenek, 1974. Rev.
    by J. Youings, History, 61(Je 1976):282-3.

Whisenhunt, Donald W. The Environment and the American Experi-
    ence. Port Washington, N. Y.: Kennikat, 1974. Rev. by E.
    Spring, BHR, 50(Spr 1976):126-7; J. L. Rogers, WHQ, 7(Jan
    1976):79.

Whitaker, James W., ed. Farming in the Midwest, 1840-1900: A
    Symposium. Washington, D. C.: Agricultural History Society,
    1974. Rev. by T. Saloutos, PHR, 45(Feb 1976):124-5.

_____. Feedlot Empire. Ames: Ia St U Press, 1975. Rev.
    by J. O. Steffen, AI, 43(Win 1976):233-4; L. McFarlane, A
    & W, 18(Sum 1976):180-1; R. G. Dunbar, PNQ, 67(Oct 1976):
    175.

White, Dan S. The Splintered Party. Cambridge, Mass.: Har-
    vard U Press, 1976. Rev. by G. O. Kent, HRNB, 4(Sep
    1976):231.

White, John I. Git Along Little Dogies. Urbana: U Ill Press,
    1975. Rev. by K. Lee, JAriH, 17(Sum 1976):236-7; W.
    Rundell, Jr., SWHQ, 80(Jl 1976):118-19; R. L. Welsch,
    WHQ, 7(Oct 1976):431-2.

White, Jon Manchip. A World Elsewhere: One Man's Fascination
    with the American Southwest. New York: Crowell, 1975.
    Rev. by N. S. Furman, JOW, 15(Jl 1976):104-5; R. F.
    Locke, Mankind, 5(Je 1976):59.

White, Lonnie J., ed. Chronicle of a Congressional Journey.
    Boulder, Colo.: Pruett, 1975. Rev. by H. G. Jordan,
    JAriH, 17(Spr 1976):113-14; R. M. Miller, JOW, 15(Apr
    1976):130.

Whitehead, John S. The Separation of College and State. New

Haven, Conn.: Yale U Press, 1973. Rev. by H. Miller, JCS, 17(Spr 1975):308-11.

Whitelaw, R. N. S. Charleston--Come Hell or High Water. Columbia: R. L. Bryan Co., 1975. Rev. by J. I. Waring, SCHM, 77(Jan 1976):55-6.

Whitelock, Dorothy. Some Anglo-Saxon Bishops of London. London: H. K. Lewis, 1975. Rev. by F. Barlow, EHR, 91(Oct 1976):883-4.

Whiteside, Andrew G. The Socialism of Fools. Berkeley: U Cal Press, 1975. Rev. by D. E. Showalter, HRNB, 4(Apr 1976): 132-3.

Whitfield, Stephen J. Scott Nearing. New York: Columbia U Press, 1974. Rev. by D. Miller, AHR, 81(Apr 1976):462-3.

Whitman, George Washington. Civil War Letters of George Washington Whitman. (Jerome M. Loving, ed.) Durham, N.C.: Duke U Press, 1975. Rev. by R. D. Hoffsommer, CWTI, 15(Jl 1976):49-50; L. H. Croce, JSH, 42(May 1976):286-7.

Whitney, Marylou. Cornelia Vanderbilt Whitney's Dollhouse. New York: Farrar, Straus and Giroux, 1975. Rev. by R. L. Hagy, FCHQ, 50(Jan 1976):80-1.

Whittemore, Reed. William Carlos Williams. Boston: Houghton Mifflin, 1975. Rev. by J. Romano, Commentary, 61(May 1976):80-2.

Whitten, Norman E., Jr. Black Frontiersman. New York: Wiley, 1974. Rev. by C. Guillén, Américas, 28(Aug 1976): 22-3.

Whittier, John Greenleaf. The Letters of John Greenleaf Whittier. (John B. Pickard, ed.) Cambridge, Mass.: Harvard U Press, 1975. Rev. by W. J. Gilmore, JAH, 63(Dec 1976): 672-3; L. Leary, NEQ, 49(Mar 1976):119-21.

Whitworth, John McKelvie. God's Blueprints: A Sociological Study of Three Utopian Sects. Boston: Routledge and Kegan Paul, 1975. Rev. by M. S. De Pillis, AHR, 81(Oct 1976):841-2; J. B. Quandt, JIH, 7(Aut 1976):340-1.

Whorton, James. Before Silent Spring. Princeton, N.J.: Prin U Press, 1975. Rev. by C. O. Jackson, AHR, 81(Je 1976): 679-80.

Wicker, Brian. First the Political Kingdom. Notre Dame: U Notre Dame Press, 1967. Rev. by J. W. Vardaman, JCS, 18(Win 1976):144.

Widstrand, C., ed. Multinational Firms in Africa. Uppsala: Scandinavian Institute for African Studies, 1975. Rev. by M. A. Tribe, AfAf, 75(Jl 1976):388-90.

Wiebe, Robert W. The Segmented Society. Oxford: Oxford U Press, 1975. Rev. by J. Zvesper, History, 61(Oct 1976): 422.

Wiegelmann, Gunter see Teuteberg, Hans J.

Wigdor, David. Roscoe Pound. Westport, Conn.: Greenwood, 1974. Rev. by A. H. Kelly, AHR, 81(Apr 1976):460-1.

Wilcox, Francis O., ed. China and the Great Powers. New York: Praeger, 1974. Rev. by O. E. Clubb, CQ, Jan 1976, pp. 147-8.

Wildes, Harry Emerson. William Penn. New York: Macmillan, 1974. Rev. by R. A. Brown, PH, 43(Jl 1976):270-1; H. Alexander, Smithsonian, 6(Mar 1975):108.

Wiley, Bell Irwin. The Common Soldier of the Civil War. New York: Scribner's, 1975. Rev. by J. B. Reaves, ChOk, 54 (Win 1976):539; D. F. Riggs, VMHB, 84(Oct 1976):504-6.

_____. Confederate Women. Westport, Conn.: Greenwood, 1975. Rev. by S. M. Hartmann, AHR, 81(Oct 1976):978; G. Riley, AI, 43(Spr 1976):317-18; H. Hattaway, ETHJ, 14 (Spr 1976):63-4; J. L. Robertson, Jr., FHQ, 55(Jl 1976):94-6; J. D. Hall, JAH, 62(Mar 1976):998-9; C. Capers, JMiH, 38(May 1976):226-8; L. H. Johnson, III, VMHB, 84(Jan 1976): 118-20.

Wilharm, Irmgard. Die Anfange des griechischen Nationalstaates, 1833-1843. Munich: R. Oldenbourg, 1973. Rev. by F. B. Chary, AHR, 81(Feb 1976):180-1.

Wilkie, William E. The Cardinal Protectors of England. New York: Cam U Press, 1974. Rev. by B. P. Flood, Jr., AHR, 81(Feb 1976):122-3; P. Heath, EHR, 91(Jan 1976): 184-5; C. W. Brockwell, Jr., JCS, 17(Aut 1975):507-8.

Wilkins, Mira. The Maturing of Multinational Enterprise. Cambridge, Mass.: Harvard U Press, 1974. Rev. by L. Galambos, AHR, 81(Feb 1976):216-17.

Wilkinson, Charles K. Nishapur. New York: Metro Art Museum, 1973. Rev. by O. Grabar, IJMES, 7(Jl 1976):462-4.

Wilkinson, Ernest L., ed. Brigham Young University: The First One Hundred Years. Provo, Utah: BYU Press, 1975. Rev. by S. F. Kropp, A & W, 18(Win 1976):380-2.

Wilkinson, Paul. Political Terrorism. London: Macmillan, 1974.
Rev. by P. Calvert, History, 61(Feb 1976):93-4.

Wilks, Ivor. Asante in the Nineteenth Century. Cambridge: Cam
U Press, 1975. Rev. by R.C.C.L., JAfH, 17(Num 1, 1976):
137-9.

Willard, Berton C. Russell W. Porter: Arctic Explorer, Artist,
Telescope Maker. Freeport, Me. : Bond Wheelwright Co.,
1976. Rev. by A. M. Wilson, VH, 44(Fall 1976):248-50.

Willcocks, R. M. England's Postal History to 1840 with Notes on
Scotland, Wales and Ireland. Ontario, Can.: S. W. Shelton,
1975. Rev. by B. S. Smith, Archives, 12(Aut 1976):197.

Wille, Wilhelm, ed. see Hoffman, Gerhard, ed.

Willeke, Venâncio. Missoes Franciscanas no Brazil, 1500-1975.
Petropolis: Editora Vozes, 1974. Rev. by M. C. Kiemen,
TAm, 33(Oct 1976):370-1.

Williams, Beryl J., ed. see Abramsky, Chimen, ed.

Williams, Edward G., ed. Bouquet's March to the Ohio. Pittsburgh: Historical Society of Western Pa., 1975. Rev. by J.
Sosin, JAH, 63(Sep 1976):390-1.

Williams, Edward J. Latin American Political Thought. Tucson:
U Ariz Press, 1974. Rev. by J. E. Pluta, HAHR, 56(Feb
1976):167.

Williams, George H., ed. see Hooker, Thomas

Williams, Glanmor, ed. Glamorgan County History. Vol. IV.
Early Modern Glamorgan. Cardiff: U Wales Press, 1974.
Rev. by J. S. Cockburn, AHR, 81(Je 1976):580-1; B. Howells,
History, 61(Je 1976):274-5.

Williams, Glyndwr, ed. Hudson's Bay Miscellany, 1670-1870.
Hudson's Bay: Hudson's Bay Record Society, 1975. Rev. by
B. Gough, OHQ, 77(Mar 1976):83-5.

Williams, Hattie Plum. The Czar's Germans. Lincoln: American
Historical Society of Germans from Russia, 1975. Rev. by
L. J. Rippley, NDH, 43(Sum 1976):43-4.

Williams, Jack F. China in Maps, 1880-1960. East Lansing:
Mich St U Press, 1974. Rev. by R. Murphy, CQ, May 1976,
pp. 399-400.

Williams, John Alexander. West Virginia and the Captains of In-
dustry. Morgantown: W Va U Library, 1976. Rev. by K. A.
Kerr, JAH, 63(Dec 1976):741-2; P. D. Casdorph, WVH, 38
(Oct 1976):60-2.

Williams, Kenny Jackson. In the City of Men. Nashville: Town-
send, 1974. Rev. by C. L. P. Silet, AS, 16(Fall 1975):98.

Williams, L. A. Road Transport in Cumbria in the Nineteenth Century. London: Allen and Unwin, 1975. Rev. by P. L. Payne,
EHR, 91(Oct 1976):923; B. C. Jones, History, 61(Oct 1976):
487; J. K. Walton, JTH, 3(Sep 1976):298-9.

Williams, Lea A. Southeast Asia: A History. New York: Oxford
U Press, 1976. Rev. by J. F. Cady, HRNB, 5(Oct 1976):
13-14.

Williams, Melvin D. Community in a Black Pentecostal Church.
Pittsburgh, Pa.: U Pittsburgh Press, 1974. Rev. by J.
Aschenbrenner, JNH, 61(Jl 1976):322-4.

Williams, Michael. The Making of the South Australian Landscape.
New York: Academic, 1974. Rev. by A. H. Grey, AgH, 50
(Jl 1976):533-4.

Williams, Neville. The Cardinal and the Secretary. New York:
Macmillan, 1976. Rev. by R. Howell, Jr., HRNB, 4(Jl 1976):
176.

Williams, O. B., ed. see Alexander, G., ed.

Williams, R. Hal. The Democratic Party and California Politics,
1880-1896. Stanford, Cal.: Stanford U Press, 1973. Rev.
by G. D. Nash, Historian, 39(Nov 1976):158-60.

Williams, Robert P. By the Bulls That Redamed Me. New York:
Exposition, 1972. Rev. by G. Wright, FCHQ, 50(Jan 1976):
78-9.

Williamson, Audrey. Thomas Paine. New York: St. Martin's,
1973. Rev. by T. Parsons, Jr., NYSHQ, 60(Jan/Apr 1976):
72-4.

Williamson, Harold F., ed. Evolution of International Management
Structures. Philadelphia: Temple U Press, 1975. Rev. by
R. D. Cuff, JEH, 36(Sep 1976):803-4.

Williamson, Jeffrey G. Late Nineteenth-Century American Development: A General Equilibrium History. New York: Cam U
Press, 1975. Rev. by G. C. Fite, AHR, 81(Oct 1976):983.

_____ see Kelley, Allen C.

Williamson, Robert G. Eskimo Underground. Uppsala: Uppsala
Universitet, 1974. Rev. by J. W. Van Stone, AA, 78(Mar
1976):157-8.

Williford, William Bailey. Americus Through the Years. Atlanta:

405   WILLIS

Cherokee, 1975. Rev. by F. M. Chalker, GHQ, 60(Spr 1976):87-8; S. Gurr, JAH, 63(Sep 1976):419; W. W. Rogers, JSH, 52(Aug 1976):452-3; K. Coleman, NCHR, 53(Spr 1976): 226-7.

Willis, Jean L. Historical Dictionary of Uruguay. Metuchen, N.J.: Scarecrow, 1974. Rev. by H. Delpar, HAHR, 56(Feb 1976):182.

Wills, John E., Jr. Pepper, Guns, and Parleys: The Dutch East India Company and China, 1622-1681. Cambridge, Mass.: Har U Press, 1974. Rev. by F. Wakeman, Jr., AHR, 81 (Oct 1976):932.

Wills, Mary Alice. The Confederate Blockade of Washington, D.C.: 1861-1862. Parsons, W.Va.: McClain, 1975. Rev. by C. F. Cooney, CWTI, 15(May 1976):50; H. B. Simpson, Texana, 12(Num 4, 1976):382; E. M. Eller, VMHB, 84(Jan 1976):115-17.

Wilson, A. Jayaratnam. Politics in Sri Lanka, 1947-1973. New Delhi: Macmillan, 1974. Rev. by S. P. Varma, IQ, 32(Jan-Mar 1976):80-2; B. H. Farmer, MAS, 10(Jl 1976):479-80.

Wilson, Carter. Crazy February. Berkeley: U Cal Press, 1974. Rev. by B. Pabst, AIQ, 2(Spr 1975):39-40.

Wilson, David. In Search of Penicillin. New York: Knopf, n.d. Rev. by J. F. Warner, Smithsonian, 7(Sep 1976):158-9.

Wilson, Derek. A History of South and Central Africa. London: Cam U Press, 1975. Rev. by R. L. Smith, HT, 10(Nov 1976):130-1.

Wilson, Don W. Governor Charles Robinson of Kansas. Lawrence: U Kan Press, 1975. Rev. by S. Carroll, A & W, 18(Sum 1976):187-8; M. L. Tate, ChOk, 54(Fall 1976):415-6; B. Procter, HRNB, 4(Jan 1976):60; E. H. Berwanger, JAH, 63 (Je 1976):135-6; J. V. Mering, JSH, 42(Feb 1976):122-3.

Wilson, Dorothy Clarke. Stranger and Traveler. Boston: Little, Brown, 1975. Rev. by R. E. Goerler, OH, 85(Sum 1976): 271-3.

Wilson, E. Raymond. Uphill for Peace. Richmond, Ind.: Friends United Press, 1975. Rev. by L. S. Wittner, JAH, 63(Je 1976):199-200.

Wilson, Edward Thomas. Russia and Black Africa Before World War II. London: Holmes and Meier, 1974. Rev. by J. D. Hargreaves, History, 61(Feb 1976):152.

Wilson, F. and D. Perrot, eds. Outlook on a Century. Love-

dale: Lovedale Press, 1973. Rev. by S. Brock, JAfH, 17
(Num 1, 1976):144-5.

Wilson, Francis. Labour in the South African Gold Mines. Cambridge: Cam U Press, 1972. Rev. by S. E. Katzenellenbogen,
BH, 17(Jan 1975):77-9.

Wilson, James W. People in the Way. Toronto: U Tor Press,
1973. Rev. by L. Higgins, CHR, 57(Mar 1976):67-9.

Wilson, Joan Hoff. Herbert Hoover: Forgotten Progressive. Bos-
ton: Little, Brown, 1975. Rev. by R. H. Zieger, AHR, 81
(Oct 1976):800-10; J. M. Dobson, AI, 43(Win 1976):231-2;
M. I. Fausold, JAH, 62(Mar 1976):1037-8.

Wilson, Keith and Elva Motherall, eds. The Poet's Record. Winnipeg: Peguis, 1975. Rev. by D. Duffy, CHR, 57(Je 1976):
191-3.

Wilson, Larman C., ed. see Davis, Harold Eugene, ed.

Wilson, Major L. Space, Time, and Freedom: The Quest for Na-
tionality and the Irrepressible Conflict, 1815-1861. Westport,
Conn.: Greenwood, 1974. Rev. by G. Sorin, AHR, 81(Oct
1976):969; T. R. Sawers, JISHS, 69(May 1976):155-6; F.
Somkin, PHR, 45(May 1976):283-5; R. L. Hume, PNQ, 67
(Jan 1976):34.

Wilson, Reba Shropshire and Betty Shropshire Glover. The Lees
and Kings of Virginia and North Carolina, 1636-1976. Ridge-
ly, Tenn.: Wilson and Glover Publishing Co., 1975. Rev.
by G. H. S. King, VMHB, 84(Jl 1976):369-71.

Wilson, Steve. Oklahoma Treasures and Treasure Tales. Norman:
U Ok Press, 1976. Rev. by K. A. Franks, A & W, 18(Win
1976):386-7.

Wilson, Woodrow. The Papers of Woodrow Wilson. Volume 21.
1910. (Arthur S. Link, ed.) Princeton: Prin U Press,
1976. Rev. by L. E. Gelfand, WVH, 38(Oct 1976):62-4.

_____. The Papers of Woodrow Wilson. Vols. 18 and 19.
(Arthur S. Link, ed.) Princeton, N.J.: Prin U Press, 1974.
Rev. by D. W. Grantham, JAH, 63(Je 1976):165-7; R. F.
Durden, NCHR, 53(Spr 1976):231-2.

Wilt, Alan F. The Atlantic Wall: Hitler's Defenses in the West,
1941-1944. Ames: Iowa St U Press, 1975. Rev. by H. H.
Herwig, AHR, 81(Oct 1976):884; J. Mendelsohn, HRNB, 4(Feb
1976):89.

Windrich, Elaine. The Rhodesian Problem. London: Routledge
and Kegan Paul, 1975. Rev. by T. I. Matthews, AfAf, 75
(Jan 1976):115-17.

Winegarten, Renee. Writers and Revolution. New York: New Viewpoints, 1974. Rev. by J. Wain, Commentary, 61(Jan 1976):83-6.

Winetrout, Kenneth. Arnold Toynbee: The Ecumenical Vision. Boston: Twayne, 1975. Rev. by C. R. Cole, AHR, 81(Oct 1976):811.

Winfield, Nath, Jr. see Puryear, Pamela Ashworth

Wingert, Norman. No Place to Stop Killing. Chicago: Moody Press, 1974. Rev. by W. Weinstein, JMAS, 14(Mar 1976): 161-3.

Winius, George Davison. The Fatal History of Portuguese Ceylon. Cambridge, Mass.: Harvard U Press, 1971. Rev. by G. V. Scammell, MAS, 10(Jl 1976):475-7.

Winnett, A. R. Peter Browne. London: S. P. C. K., 1974. Rev. by W. R. Ward, EHR, 91(Jan 1976):206.

Winter, Eduard. Russland und das Papsttum. Part 3, Die Sowjetunion und der Vatikan. Berlin: Akademie-Verlag, 1972. Rev. by W. W. Kulski, AHR, 81(Je 1976):636-7.

_____ and Maria Winter. Domprediger Johann Emanuel Veith und Kardinal Friedrich Schwarzenberg. Vienna: Herman Böhlaus Nachf., 1972. Rev. by T. W. Simons, Jr., CaHr, 62(Apr 1976):316-18.

Winter, J. M. Socialism and the Challenge of War. London: Routledge and Kegan Paul, 1974. Rev. by B. Semmel, AHR, 81(Feb 1976):145-6; A. Warwick, EHR, 91(Jan 1976):233-4.

_____, ed. War and Economic Development: Essays in Memory of David Joslin. New York: Cam U Press, 1975. Rev. by G. Best, AHR, 81(Oct 1976):842; R. D. Cuff, BHR, 50(Spr 1976):113-14; V. G. Kiernan, History, 61(Feb 1976):71.

Winter, James. Robert Lowe. Toronto: U Tor Press, 1976. Rev. by B. Hilton, HJ, 19(Dec 1976):1036-7.

Winterbotham, F. W. The Ultra Secret. London: Weidenfeld and Nicolson, 1974. Rev. by J. Gooch, History, 61(Oct 1976): 475-6.

Winters, Stanley B. and Joseph Held, eds. Intellectual and Social Developments in the Habsburg Empire from Maria Theresa to World War I. Boulder, Colo.: East European Quarterly, 1975. Rev. by H. Heilbronner, Historian, 39(Nov 1976):128-9; R. Anchor, HRNB, 4(Jan 1976):69-70.

Wittner, Lawrence S. Cold War America: From Hiroshima to

Watergate. New York: Praeger, 1974. Rev. by G. F. Herken, AHR, 81(Oct 1976):1003-4; T. H. Etzold, Historian, 39(Nov 1976):167.

Wolanin, Thomas R. Presidential Advisory Commissions. Madison: U Wis, 1975. Rev. by C. E. Finn, Jr., Commentary, 61(Feb 1976):87-9.

Wolcott, Harry F. The African Beer Gardens of Bulawayo. New Brunswick, N.J.: Rutgers U Center of Alcohol Studies, 1974. Rev. by S. Von Lutes, JAAS, 11(Jan & Apr 1976):115-16.

Wolf, Arthur P., ed. Religion and Ritual in Chinese Society. Stanford, Cal.: Stanford U Press, 1975. Rev. by J. L. Watson, CQ, Je 1976, pp. 355-64.

Wolf, Edwin, II, comp. The Library of James Logan of Philadelphia, 1674-1751. Philadelphia: Library Company of Philadelphia, 1974. Rev. by G. A. and C. Z. Stiverson, WMQ, 33(Jan 1976):176-7.

Wolf, Susan see Rothchild, John

Wolfe, Willard. From Radicalism to Socialism: Men and Ideas in the Formation of Fabian Socialist Doctrines, 1881-1889. New Haven, Conn.: Yale U Press, 1975. Rev. by P. Stansky, AHR, 81(Je 1976):593-4; H. Pelling, History, 61(Je 1976):309-10; L. E. Grugel, JMH, 48(Sep 1976):545-7.

Wolff, M., ed. see Dyos, H. J., ed.

Wolff, Nelson. Challenge of Change. San Antonio: Naylor, 1975. Rev. by J. E. Ericson, ETHJ, 14(Spr 1976):71.

Wolff, Richard D. The Economics of Colonialism. New Haven, Conn.: Yale U Press, 1974. Rev. by C. Brantley, AgH, 50(Jl 1976):538-40; H. G. Soff, AHR, 81(Feb 1976):141-2.

Wollek, Christoph. Das Domkapitel von Plock, 1524-1564. Cologne: Böhlau Verlag, 1972. Rev. by J. Przygoda, CaHR, 62(Jan 1976):129-30.

Wolny, Reinhold Joseph. Die josephinische Toleranz unter besonderer Berüchsichtigung ihres geistlichen Wegbereiters Johann Leopold Hay. Munich: Verlag Robert Lerche, 1973. Rev. by C. H. O'Brien, CaHR, 62(Apr 1976):304-6.

Wolpe, Howard. Urban Politics in Nigeria: A Study of Port Harcourt. Berkeley: U Cal Press, 1974. Rev. by D. R. Aronson, JAAS, 11(Jl-Oct 1976):249-50.

Wong, John. Land Reform in the People's Republic of China. New York: Praeger, 1973. Rev. by R. Ash, CQ, Jan 1976, pp. 153-5.

Wood, Forrest G. The Era of Reconstruction, 1863-1877. New York: Crowell, 1975. Rev. by J. K. Folmar, HT, 10(Nov 1976):145-6.

Wood, Leyland E. The Vermont Hollows, A History of Gilead and Little Hollows. Vermont: L. E. Wood, 1976. Rev. by R. Teagle, VH, 44(Fall 1976):239-42.

Wood, Peter H. Black Majority. New York: Knopf, 1974. Rev. by R. McColley, AHR, 81(Feb 1976):204; M. Drimmer, HRNB, 4(May/Je 1976):142-3; M. Kilson, MIH, 7(Sum 1976): 169-70.

Woodcock, George. Who Killed the British Empire? London: Jonathan Cape, 1974. Rev. by D. K. Fieldhouse, History, 61(Feb 1976):85-6.

Woodhouse, H. C. see Lee, D. N.

Woodruff, William. America's Impact on the World. New York: Wiley, 1975. Rev. by O. Handlin, BHR, 50(Spr 1976):127-8; R. S. Woodbury, FHQ, 55(Jl 1976):102-4; D. Wightman, History, 61(Oct 1976):425; W. E. Brownlee, JAH, 62(Mar 1976): 967-8; A. J. Morrison, JAmS, 10(Apr 1976):119-20; E. W. Fox, JMH, 48(Je 1976):322-3.

Woodward, John. To Do the Sick No Harm. Boston: Routledge and Kegan Paul, 1974. Rev. by J. L. Brand, AHR, 81(Oct 1976):860.

Woodward, Ralph Lee, Jr. Central America: A Nation Divided. New York: Oxford U Press, 1976. Rev. by D. E. Worcester, HRNB, 4(May/Je 1976):148.

Woodyard, George W., ed. see Lyday, Leon F., ed.

Wooster, Ralph A. Politicians, Planters and Plain Folk. Knoxville: U Tenn Press, 1975. Rev. by J. E. Sefton, HRNB, 4(Feb 1976):79; R. M. Ireland, JAH, 63(Sep 1976):419-20; C. R. Lee, Jr., JSH, 42(Aug 1976):430-1; F. N. Boney, NCHR, 53(Sum 1976):330-1; D. P. Jordan, VMHB, 84(Oct 1976):503-4.

Worcester, Donald E., ed. Forked Tongues and Broken Treaties. Caldwell, Idaho: Caxton, 1975. Rev. by R. M. Miller, JOW, 15(Jl 1976):100.

World Bank, The. Kenya: Into the Second Decade. Baltimore: JHU Press, 1975. Rev. by F. C. Child, AgH, 50(Jl 1976): 540-2.

Worthy, Pauline Marion, ed. see Loy, Ursula F., ed.

Woytanowitz, George M. University Extension. Iowa City: American College Testing Publications, 1974. Rev. by W. L. Fox, AHR, 81(Je 1976):673-4; G. P. Coleman, JAH, 62(Mar 1976): 1025-6.

Wright, Barton. The Unchanging Hope. Flagstaff, Ariz.: Northland, 1975. Rev. by B. L. Fontana, JAriH, 17(Spr 1976): 118-19.

Wright, Basil. The Long View. New York: Knopf, 1974. Rev. by A. Sesonske, Gr, 6(Spr 1976):211-15.

Wright, Conrad, ed. A Stream of Light. Boston: Unitarian Unitarian Universalist Assn, 1975. Rev. by E. S. Gaustad, JAH, 63(Sep 1976):412-13; C. A. Holbrook, NEQ, 49(Je 1976):305-7.

Wright, Esmond, ed. A Tug of Loyalties. London: U London, 1975. Rev. by P. Goodman, JAH, 63(Je 1976):106-7.

Wright, J. R. C. "Above Parties:" The Political Attitudes of the German Protestant Church Leadership, 1918-1933. New York: Oxford U Press, 1974. Rev. by A. Dorpalen, CaHR, 62 (Oct 1976):661; M. Balfour, EHR, 91(Apr 1976):463; J. Stephenson, History, 61(Feb 1976):141-2.

Wright, J. Leitch, Jr. Britain and the American Frontier, 1783- 1815. Athens, Ga.: U Ga Press, 1975. Rev. by J. L. Stokesbury, AHI, 11(Oct 1976):49-50; R. F. Broussard, GHQ, 60(Sum 1976):189-90; L. Williams, HRNB, 4(Jl 1976):166-7; R. Horsman, JAH, 63(Dec 1976):704-5; W. H. Masterson, JSH, 42(Nov 1976):586-7; J. R. Finger, THQ, 35(Win 1976): 430-1; E. Cometti, VMHB, 84(Jl 1976):372-3.

_____. Florida in the American Revolution. Gainesville: U Presses Fla, 1975. Rev. by R. R. Rea, AlaR, 29(Jl 1976): 237-9; D. Higginbotham, FHQ, 55(Jl 1976):79-80; P. D. Chase, JAH, 63(Dec 1976):696-7; G. C. Din, JMiH, 38(Aug 1976):320-1; R. G. Starr, JSH, 42(Nov 1976):585-6; C. H. Bowman, Jr., NCHR, 53(Sum 1976):321; P. E. Hoffman, TAm, 33(Oct 1976):374.

Wright, James Edward. The Politics of Populism. New Haven, Conn.: Yale U Press, 1974. Rev. by G. M. Ostrander, A & W, 18(Spr 1976):96-8; W. T. K. Nugent, AgH, 50(Apr 1976):431-2; L. L. Gould, AHR, 81(Feb 1976):213; J. A. Thompson, HJ, 19(Mar 1976):257-74; G. Clanton, PNQ, 67(Jan 1976):38.

Wright, John, trans. The Life of Cola di Rienzo. Toronto: Pontifical Institute of Mediaeval Studies, 1975. Rev. by J. Kirshner, CH, 45(Je 1976):252-3.

Wright, John D. , Jr. Transylvania: Tutor to the West. Lexing-

411   WRIGHT

ton, Ky.: Transylvania U Press, 1975. Rev. by W. C.
Ringenberg, JAH, 63(Dec 1976):710-11.

Wright, L. R. The Origins of British Borneo. Hong Kong: Hong
Kong U Press, 1970. Rev. by B. Powell, MAS, 10(Feb 1976):
149-54.

Wright, Louis B., et al. The Arts in America: The Colonial
Period. New York: Schocken, 1975. Rev. by R. P. Gildrie,
HRNB, 4(Jan 1976):57.

_____. South Carolina. New York: Norton, 1976. Rev. by H.
C. Ferrell, Jr., HRNB, 4(Sep 1976):211.

_____. Tradition and the Founding Fathers. Charlottesville:
U Press Va, 1975. Rev. by D. A. Bernstein, JSH, 42(Feb
1976):114; R. V. Sparks, NEQ, 49(Mar 1976):140-2.

Wright, William C., ed. Urban New Jersey Since 1870. Trenton:
N.J. Historical Commission, 1975. Rev. by J. D. Buenker,
JAH, 63(Je 1976):149.

Wrigley, E. A., ed. Identifying People in the Past. London:
Arnold, 1973. Rev. by P. Slack, EHR, 91(Jan 1976):171-2.

Wroth, L. Kinvin, et al., eds. Province in Rebellion. Cambridge,
Mass.: Harvard U Press, 1975. Rev. by J. A. Schutz,
JAH, 63(Dec 1976):695-6.

Wurster, Wolfgang W. Alt-Agina I, I. Mainz am Rhein: Philipp
von Zabern, 1974. Rev. by S. G. Miller, AJA, 80(Sum 1976):
310-11.

Wyeth, John A. The Life of Nathan Bedford Forrest. Dayton:
Morningside, 1975. Rev. in CWH, 22(Mar 1976):92.

Wynear, Lubomyr R. Ethnic Groups in Ohio. Cleveland: Cleveland
St U Press, 1975. Rev. by P. L. Simon, OH, 85(Spr 1976):
165-7.

Wynot, Edward D., Jr. Polish Politics in Transition: The Camp
of National Unity and the Sturggle for Power, 1935-1939.
Athens: U Ga Press, 1974. Rev. by A. Bromke, AHR, 81
(Oct 1976):902-3.

_____, ed. see also Cannistraro, Philip V., ed.

Xan, Erna Oleson. Wisconsin, My Home: The Story of Thurine
Oleson as Told to Her Daughter. Madison: U Wis Press,
1975. Rev. by B. Logan, WMH, 60(Aut 1976):56-7.

Xántus, John. Letters from North America. Detroit: Wayne St
U Press, 1976. Rev. by M. L. Spence, A & W, 18(Win 1976):
382-4.

Xydis, Stephen G. Cyprus: Reluctant Republic. Atlantic High-
    lands, N. J.: Humanities, 1973. Rev. by R. Albrecht-Carrie,
    AHR, 81(Feb 1976):126-7.

Yadin, Yigael. Hazor. New York: Random House, 1975. Rev.
    by A. Rosenfeld, Smithsonian, 6(May 1975):100, 102.

Yapp, M. E., ed. see Parry, V. J., ed.

Yarnell, Allen. Democrats and Progressives. Berkeley: U Cal
    Press, 1974. Rev. by W. L. Ziglar, AHR, 81(Apr 1976):
    467.

Yates, Frances A. Astraea: The Imperial Theme in the Sixteenth
    Century. London: Routledge and Kegan Paul, 1975. Rev.
    by M. A. Breslow, AHR, 81(Je 1976):574; R. J. Knecht,
    History, 61(Je 1976):275-6.

Yates, Gale Graham. What Women Want. Cambridge, Mass.:
    Harvard U Press, 1975. Rev. by W. L. O'Neill, JAH, 63
    (Sep 1976):471-2.

Yazawa, Melvin, ed. Representative Government and the Revolu-
    tion. Baltimore: JHU Press, 1975. Rev. by A. F. Perry,
    HRNB, 4(Jan 1976):56; J. C. Van Horne, MHM, 71(Sum
    1976):278-9; R. R. Menard, NCHR, 53(Sum 1976):322; E. L.
    Shepard, VMHB, 84(Jan 1976):111-12.

Yearns, W. Buck see Warner, Ezra J.

Yen, W. W. East-West Kaleidoscope, 1877-1944. Jamaica, N. Y.:
    St. John's, 1974. Rev. by S. I. Levine, CQ, May 1976, pp.
    371-2.

Yesufu, T. M., ed. Creating the African University. Ibadan:
    Oxford U Press, 1973. Rev. by A. H. M. Kirk-Greene,
    Africa, 46(Num 1, 1976):103-4.

Yinger, Winthrop. Cesar Chavez. New York: Exposition, n. d.
    Rev. by A. Cardona-Hine, Mankind, 5(Feb 1976):9, 67.

Yoder, Don, ed. American Folklife. Austin: U Texas Press,
    1975. Rev. by J. Coyne, Smithsonian, 7(Sep 1976):166, 168.

Yogev, G., et al., eds. The Letters and Papers of Chaim Weiz-
    mann. Series A., VI. London: Oxford U Press, 1974.
    Rev. by J. Parker, EHR, 91(Jl 1976):680.

Young, A. Industrial Diversification in Zambia. New York:
    Praeger, 1973. Rev. by P. Mosley, JMAS, 14(Sep 1976):
    543-6.

Young, A. P. The "X" Documents. London: André Deutsch,

1974. Rev. by K. von Klemperer, JMH, 48(Mar 1976):138-40.

Young, Betty Lou and Thomas R. Young. Rustic Canyon and the Story of the Uplifters. Santa Monica: Casa Vieja Press, 1975. Rev. by R. Wentz, SCQ, 58(Win 1976):535-6.

Young, George F. W. The Germans in Chile. New York: Center for Migration Studies, 1974. Rev. by L. L. Baily, AHR, 81(Apr 1976):474.

Young, James Harvey. American Self-Dosage Medicines. Lawrence, Kan.: Coronado, 1974. Rev. by W. L. Fox, JAH, 63(Je 1976):143-4; J. P. Morris, JSH, 42(Feb 1976):150-1.

Young, Otis E., Jr. Black Powder and Hard Steel. Norman: U Ok Press, 1975. Rev. by D. Bufkin, JAriH, 17(Aut 1976):353-5.

Youngdale, James M. Populism: A Psychohistorical Perspective. Port Washington, N.Y.: Kennikat, 1975. Rev. by M. Rogin, AHR, 81(Oct 1976):982-3; R. C. McMath, Jr., HRNB, 4 (May/Je 1976):142; D. P. Thelen, JAH, 63(Dec 1976):746-7; M. Ridge, MinnH, 45(Sum 1976):76; T. D. Isern, NDH, 43 (Fall 1976):38.

Yu, George T. China's Africa Policy. New York: Praeger, 1975. Rev. by M. Bailey, AfAf, 75(Apr 1976):251-2.

Yudkin, Leon I. Escape into Siege. Boston: Routledge and Kegan Paul, 1974. Rev. by W. Bargad, Judaism, 25(Spr 1976): 251-5.

Yui, Tsunehiko see Hirschmeier, Johannes

Yu-Wen, Jen. The Taiping Revolutionary Movement. New Haven, Conn.: Yale U Press, 1973. Rev. by S. W. Barnett, JIH, 7(Sum 1976):136-40.

Yzermans, Vincent A., ed. Days of Hope and Promise. Collegeville, Minn.: Liturgical Press, 1973. Rev. by N. J. Callahan, CaHR, 62(Oct 1976):687-8.

Zablocki, Benjamin D. The Joyful Community: An Account of Bruderhof. Baltimore: Penguin, n.d. Rev. by J. W. Kuyendall, MQR, 50(Jan 1976):78-80.

Zaghi, Carlo. I Russi in Ethiopia. 2 vols. Naples: Guida Editori, 1972. Rev. by H. G. Marcus, JMH, 48(Mar 1976): 171-2.

Zahniser, Marvin R. Uncertain Friendship. New York: Wiley, 1975. Rev. by L. S. Kaplan, JAH, 63(Sep 1976):401-2; H. Blumenthal, OH, 85(Aut 1976):339-40.

Zakharov, M. V., ed. Finale: A Retrospective Review of Im-
perialist Japan's Defeat in 1945. Moscow: Progress Publ'rs.,
1972. Rev. by E. F. Ziemke, AHR, 81(Je 1976):638-9.

Zala, Tamás. The Ordeal of the New World. Budapest: Kossuth,
1975. Rev. by T. L. Sakmyster, JAH, 63(Dec 1976):748-9.

Zamora, Mario D. Studies in Philippine Anthropology. Quezon
City, Philippines: Alemar-Phoenix, 1967. Rev. by H. T.
Lewis, AA, 78(Je 1976):405.

Zanker, Paul. Klassizistiche Statuen. Mainz: Verlag Philipp
von Zabern, 1974. Rev. by D. E. E. Kleiner, AJA, 80(Sum
1976):324-5.

Zaretsky, Irving I. and Mark P. Leone, eds. Religious Movements
in Contemporary America. Princeton, N.J.: Prin U Press,
1974. Rev. by T. Miller, AS, 16(Spr 1975):77-8; L. Billington, JAmS, 10(Apr 1976):125-6.

Zasloff, Joseph J. The Pathet Lao. Lexington, Mass.: Heath,
1973. Rev. by R. T. McVey, MAS, 10(Oct 1976):637-9.

Zehnacker, Hubert. Moneta. Recherches sur L'organisation et
L'art des émissions monétaires de la République Romaine.
2 vols. Rome: Ecoles françaises d'Athènes, 1973. Rev. by
R. E. Mitchell, AJA, 80(Win 1976):106-7.

Zeldin, Theodore. France 1848-1945. Oxford: Clarendon Press,
1973. Rev. by J. Talbott, JIH, 7(Sum 1976):99-104.

Zell, H., ed. see Oluwasanmi, E., ed.

Zetterberg, Kent. Liberalism i kris. Stockholm: Liber Förlag,
1975. Rev. by P. M. Hayes, EHR, 91(Oct 1976):939-40.

Zibart, Carl F. Yesterday's Nashville. Miami: E. A. Seemann,
1976. Rev. by M. Mendelsohn, THQ, 36(Fall 1976):337-8.

Ziegler, Adolf W. Das Verhältnis von Kirche und Staat in Amerika.
München: Manz Verlag, 1974. Rev. by W. A. Mueller, JCS,
18(Win 1976):129-30.

Ziegler, Walter, ed. Die Kirchliche Lage in Bayern nach den
Regierungs präsidentenberichten, 1933-1943. Mainz: Matthias-
Grünewald, 1973. Rev. by H. W. L. Freudenthal, CaHR, 62
(Oct 1976):663-5.

Ziesler, J. A. Christian Asceticism. Grand Rapids, Mich.:
Eerdmans, 1974. Rev. by J. Helgeland, CH, 45(Mar 1976):
97-8.

Ziff, Larzer. Puritanism in America. New York: Viking, 1973.

Rev. by J. W. Raimo, JAmS, 10(Dec 1976):387-8; R. D.
Cohen, JCS, 17(Spr 1975):305-7.

Zimmerman, Harald. Der Canossagang von 1077 Wirkungen und
Wirklichkeit. Weisbaden: Steiner, 1975. Rev. by B. Arnold,
JEccH, 27(Jl 1976):328.

Zoli, Sergio. La Cine e l'età dell'Illuminismo in Italia. Bologna:
Pàtron Editore, 1974. Rev. by E. P. Noether, AHR, 81(Apr
1976):414.

Zophy, Jonathan W., ed. see Buck, Lawrence P., ed.

Zuck, Lowell H. Christianity and Revolution: Radical Christian
Testimonies 1520-1650. Philadelphia: Temple U Press, 1975.
Rev. by A. C. Deeter, CH, 45(Mar 1976):111; W. Klaassen,
MQR, 50(Jan 1976):77-8.

Zucker, Stanley. Ludwig Bamberger. Pittsburgh: U Pittsburgh
Press, 1975. Rev. by P. W. Schroeder, HRNB, 4(Jan 1976):
69.

Zug, Joan Liffring and John Zug. The Amanas Yesterday. n.p.:
The Amana Society, 1975. Rev. by J.G., AI, 43(Win 1976):
236-7.

Alan of Lille. James J. Sheridan. ed. and trans.

The Alaska Purchase and Russian-American Relations. Ronald J. Jensen.

Albert D. Kirwan. Frank Furlong Mathias.

Albert Mathiez. James Friguglietti.

Albion's Fatal Tree: Crime and Society in Eighteenth-Century England. D. Hay, et al., eds.

La Alemania nazi y el 18 de julio. Angel Viñas.

Alex: The Life of Field Marshal Earl Alexander of Tunis. Nigel Nicolson.

Alexander Hamilton. Broadus Mitchell.

Alexander McDougall and the American Revolution in New York. Roger J. Champagne.

Alexander I. Tsar of War and Peace. Alan Palmer.

Alexandre 1er et sa Sainte-Alliance (1811-1825). Francis Ley.

Alfred R. Waud: Civil War Artist. Frederic E. Ray.

Algiers in the Age of the Corsairs. William Spencer.

The Alienated "Loyal" Opposition. Franz A. Von Sauer.

All God's Dangers: The Life of Nate Shaw. Theodore Rosengarten.

All Mankind Is One: A Study of the Disputation Between Bartolomé de Las Casas and Juan Ginés de Sepúlveda in 1550 on the Intellectual and Religious Capacity of the American Indians. Lewis Hanke.

All Things Are Possible. David Edwin Harrell, Jr.

Allah's Commonwealth: A History of Islam in the Near East 600-1100 A.D. F. E. Peters.

Allan Nevins on History. Ray Allen Billington, comp.

Allan Nevins on History. Allan Nevins.

Allan Shivers: The Pied Piper of Texas Politics. Sam Kinch and Stuart Long.

Alle origini dell'Italia industriale. Giuseppe Are.

Les Allemands au Chili, 1816-1945. Jean-Pierre Blancpain.

Allen: The Biography of an Army Officer, 1859-1930. Heath Twichell, Jr.

Allies for Freedom: Blacks and John Brown. Benjamin Quarles.

Alt-Agina I, I. Wolfgang W. Wurster.

Altajische Studien II. Japanisch und Altajisch. Karl H. Menges.

Alteraciones Andaluzas. Antonio Domíngues Ortiz.

Alternative to Extinction: Federal Indian Policy and the Beginnings of the Reservation System, 1846-51. Robert A. Trennert, Jr.

Alto Adige--South Tyrol: Italy's Frontier With the German World. Mario Toscano.

Alton Huston: Reminiscences of a South Plains Youth. William Curry Holden.

L'altro Niccolò di Bernardo Machiavelli. Mario Martelli.

The Amanas Yesterday. Joan L. and John Zug.

Ambiguous Imperialism. Goran Rystad.

Ambiguous Legacy. James Weinstein.

Amel-Marduk 562-560 B.C. Ronald Herbert Sack.

The Amendment That Refused to Die. Howard N. Meyer.

America and the Arab States. Robert W. Stookey.

America in a Divided World 1945-1972. Robert H. Ferrell, ed.

America in Change. Ronald Weber, ed.

America in the Twentieth Century. James T. Patterson.

American and British Writers in Mexico 1556-1973. Drewey Wayne Gunn.

American and French Culture, 1800-1900: Interchanges in Art, Science, Literature and Society. Henry Blumenthal.

American Attitude Towards the Indian Nationalist Movement. Diwaker Prasad Singh.

American Attitudes Toward Japan, 1941-1975. Sheila K. Johnson.

The American Banking Community and New Deal Banking Reforms, 1933-1935. Helen M. Burns.

American Catholicism and European Immigrants (1900-1924). Richard M. Linkh.

The American Civil War. Peter J. Parish.

American Classic. Laurence La
Fore.
The American Compromise.
Richard C. Vitzthum.
American Corporations and Peruvi-
an Politics. Charles T. Good-
sell.
American Defense Policy from
Eisenhower to Kennedy: The
Politics of Changing Military
Requirements, 1957-1961.
Richard A. Aliano.
American Diplomacy and the Nar-
cotics Traffic, 1900-1939.
Arnold H. Taylor.
The American Economy. Stanley
Lebergott.
The American Economy Between
the World Wars. Jim Potter.
An American First: John T. Flynn
and the American First Com-
mittee. Michele Flynn Steneh-
jem.
American Folk Painters. John
Ebert and Katherine Ebert.
American Folklife. Don Yoder,
ed.
American Foreign Policy in the
Congo, 1960-1964. Stephen
R. Weissman.
The American Heritage History of
Railroads in America. Oliver
O. Jensen.
American Imperialism and Anti-
Imperialism. Thomas G.
Paterson, ed.
American Indian Mythology. Alice
Marriott and Carol Rachlin.
American Indian Policy in the
Jacksonian Era. Ronald N.
Satz.
American Indian Prose and Poetry.
Gloria Levitas and Frank P.
and Jacqueline J. Vivelo, eds.
The American Italians. Andrew
F. Rolle.
American Jews and the Zionist
Idea. Naomi W. Cohen.
American Labor Songs of the
Nineteenth Century. Philip
S. Foner.
American Liberalism: Laudable
End, Controversial Means.
William Gerber.
American Military Equipage:
1851-1872. Frederick P.
Todd, et al.
The American Musical Theater.

Lehman Engle.
American Narrative Painting. Nancy
Wall Moure and Donnelson F.
Hoopes.
American Negro Slavery. Michael
Mullin, ed.
The American Non-Policy Towards
Eastern Europe, 1943-1947:
Universalism in an Area Not of
Essential Interest to the United
States. Geir Lundestad.
American Physicians in the Nine-
teenth Century. William G.
Rothstein.
American Policy and the Division of
Germany. Bruce Kuklick.
The American Problem in British
Diplomacy, 1841-1861. Wilbur
Devereux Jones.
The American Radical Press, 1880-
1960. Joseph R. Conlin, ed.
American Religious Groups View
Foreign Policy. Alfred O. Hero,
Jr.
The American Revolution: A Heri-
tage of Change. John Parker and
Carol Urness, eds.
The American Revolution and the
West Indies. Charles W. Toth,
ed.
The American Revolution in the
West. George M. Waller.
The American Revolution of 1800.
Daniel Sisson.
The American Revolution Within
America. Merrill Jensen.
The American Scene: American
Painting of the 1930's. Matthew
Baigell.
American Slavery, American Free-
dom. Edmund S. Morgan.
American Society and Black Revolu-
tion. Frank Hercules.
American Sportsmen and the Origins
of Conservation. John F. Reiger.
American Transcendentalism, 1830-
1860: An Intellectual Inquiry.
Paul F. Boller, Jr.
The American West and the Religious
Experience. William M. Kromer,
ed.
The American Woman: Her Changing
Social, Economic and Political
Role 1920-1970. William H.
Chafe.
Americanization of the Common Law.
William E. Nelson.
The Americanization of the Synagogue

1820-1870. Leon A. Jick.
Americanizing the American In-
dians: Writings by the "Friends
of the Indian," 1880-1900.
Francis Paul Prucha, ed.
Les Americans à Nantes et Saint-
Nazaire, 1917-1919. Yves-
Henri Nouailhat.
Americans and the California
Dream, 1850-1915. Kevin
Starr.
America's Continuing Revolution.
American Enterprise Institute.
America's Impact on the World.
William Woodruff.
America's Sporting Heritage: 1850-
1950. John Rickards Betts.
America's Wooden Age: Aspects
of Its Early Technology. Brooke
Hindle, ed.
Americus Through the Years.
William Bailey Williford.
Die amerikanische Russlandpolitik
in der Zeit des Hitler-Stalin-
Pakts 1939-1941. Franz Knip-
ping.
Amerikanuak: Basques in the New
World. William A. Douglass
and Jon Bilbao.
Among the Mescalero Apaches:
The Story of Father Albert Braun,
OFM. Dorothy Emerson.
Amy. Jean Gould.
An der Schwelle zum gespaltenen
Europa. Eberhard Bethge and
Ronald C. D. Jasper, eds.
Anabaptism and Asceticism. Ken-
neth Ronald Davis.
Anabaptists and the Sword. James
M. Stayer.
Anabaptists Four Centuries Later.
J. Howard Kauffman and Leland
Harder.
Analphabetentum und Lekture: zur
Sozialgeschichte des Lesens in
Deutschland zwischen feudaler
und industrieller Gesellschaft.
Rolf Engelsing.
Ananda K. Coomaraswamy. P. S.
Sastri.
Anarchisten im Freiheitskampf:
Die Geschichte der Machno-
Bewegung 1918-1921. Peter
Arschinow.
The Anatomical Works of George
Stubbs. Terence Doherty.
Anatomy and Destiny. Stephen
Kern.

The Anatomy of Influence: Decision
Making in International Organiza-
tions. Robert W. Cox, et al.
The Anatomy of Poverty. Terry
Copp.
Ancestor Worship in Contemporary
Japan. Robert J. Smith.
L'Ancien Régime. Vol. II. Pierre
Goubert.
Ancient Art: The Norbert Schimmel
Collection. Oscar White Muscarel-
la, ed.
Ancient Civilization and Trade.
Jeremy A. Sabloff and C. C. Lam-
berg-Karlovsky, eds.
Ancient Egyptian Literature. Vol. I.
Miriam Lichtheim.
Ancient Sicily from the First Farm-
ers to the Early Christians.
Paul Ashbee.
Ancient Slavery and the Ideal of Man.
Joseph Vogt.
The Ancient State Authoritie and Pro-
ceedings of the Court of Requests
by Sir Julius Caesar. L. M.
Hill, ed.
... and Bid Him Sing. David
Graham Du Bois.
And They All Sang Hallelujah: Plain-
Folk Camp-Meeting Religion,
1800-1845. Dickson D. Bruce,
Jr.
Andalucía en el siglo XV. M. A.
Ladero Quesada.
The Andean Group. David Morawetz.
Andrea Palladio. Lionello Puppi.
Andreas Bodenstein Von Karlstadt:
The Development of His Thought,
1517-1525. Ronald J. Sider.
Andreas Osiander d. A. Gesam-
tausgabe. Vol. 1. Andreas
Osiander.
Andrew Carnegie and the Rise of
Big Business. Harold C. Live-
say.
Andrew Jackson and the Search for
Vindication. James C. Curtis.
Die Anfange des griechischen Na-
tional staates, 1833-1843. Irm-
gard Wilharm.
Die Anfange einer ständigen Inquisi-
tion in Böhmen. Alexander
Patschovsky.
The Angelo Herndon Case and South-
ern Justice. Charles H. Martin.
L'Angleterre Triomphante, 1832-
1914. François Bédarida.
Anglo-Dutch Wars of the Seventeenth

Century. C. R. Boxer.
Anglo-Saxon England III. P.
Clemoes, ed.
Anglo-Vatican Relations, 1914-
1939: Confidential Annual Re-
ports of the British Ministers
to the Holy See. Thomas E.
Hacney, ed.
Anodoi, Essai sur L'imagerie des
Passages Chthoniens. Claude
Bérard.
Another Place: Photographs of a
Mayan Community. Frank
Cancian.
The Anschluss Movement, 1918-
1919 and the Paris Peace Con-
ference. Alfred D. Low.
Antarctic Adventure. Raymond
E. Priestley.
Antebellum Charleston Dramatists.
Charles S. Watson.
Ante-Bellum Pensacola and the
Military Presence. Ernest F.
Dibble.
Anthropologie du Conscrit français,
d'après le comptes numériques
et sommaires du recrutement de
l'armée (1818-1826): Présenta-
tion Cartographique. Jean-Paul
Aron.
Anthropologie structurale deux.
Claude Levi-Strauss.
Anthropology and the American In-
dian: A Symposium. American
Anthropological Association.
The Anti-Hitler Coalition. Victor
Issraeljan.
Antioch: City and Imperial Ad-
ministration in the Later Roman
Empire. J. H. W. G. Lie-
beschuetz.
Antiqui und Moderni im Mittelalter:
eine geschichtliche Standort
bestimmung. Elisabeth Gössmann.
Antiquities of North Ethiopia: A
Guide. Otto A. Jäger and Ivy
Pearce.
Antologia Poezji Afrykanskiej.
Wanda Leopold and Zbigniew
Stolarek.
Antonio Gallenga: An Italian Writer
in Victorian England. Toni
Cerutti.
The Anzin Coal Company, 1800-
1833: Big Business in the
Early Stages of the French In-
dustrial. Reed G. Geiger.
Apache Lightning. Joseph A.

Stout, Jr.
Apis I. The Monuments of the
Hellenistic-Roman Period from
Egypt. II. G. J. F. Kater-
Sibbes and M. J. Vermaseren.
Apocalypse et Révolution au Mexique.
Jean Meyer.
The Apocalyptic Movement. Walter
Schmithals.
L'apolitisme des idéologies qué-
bécoises: Le grand tournant de
1934-1936. André-J. Bélanger.
The Appian Way. Dora Jane Ham-
blin and Mary Jane Grunsfeld.
Appointments at Armageddon: Muck-
raking and Progressivism in the
American Tradition. Louis Filler.
Approaches to Asia: Australian Post-
war Policies and Attitudes. Gor-
don Greenwood.
Approbatio--Reprobatio. Dagmar
Unverhau.
Arab Guerilla Power, 1967-1972.
Edgar O'Ballance.
The Arab Institute for Research and
Publishing. Elias Shoufani.
Arabs and Israelis: A Dialogue.
Saul Friedlander and Mahmoud
Hussein.
The Arabs and Medieval Europe.
Norman Daniel.
Archaeologia Homerica: Die Denk-
maler und das Fruhgriechische
Epos. Friedrich Matz and Hans-
Gunter Buchholz, eds.
Archaeological Chemistry. Curt W.
Beck, ed.
Archaeological Investigations at
Molpa, San Diego County, Cali-
fornia. C. W. Meighan True and
Harvey Crew.
Archaeology and the Dead Sea
Scrolls. R. De Vaux.
Archaeology by Experiment. John
Coles.
Archaeology in Northern Belize.
Norman Hammond, et al.
The Archaeology of Arizona: A
Study of the Southwest Region.
Paul Martin and Fred Plog.
The Archaeology of Benin. Graham
Connah.
The Archaeology of Missouri, I.
Carl H. Chapman.
The Archaeology of Ships. Paul
Johnstone.
Archaeozoological Studies. Papers
of the Archaeozoological Confer-

ence, Groningen, 1974. A. T. Clason, ed.

Archaic Greece: The City-States c. 700-500 B.C. L. H. Jeffery.

Archaïsme et modernité en Limousin au XIXe siècle, 1845-1880. Alain Corbin.

Architectural Space in Ancient Greece. C. A. Doxiadis.

The Architecture and Art of Early Hispanic Colorado. Robert Adams.

The Architecture of John Wellborn Root. Donald Hoffmann.

The Architecture of Maximilian Godefroy. Robert L. Alexander.

Archives and Manuscript Repositories in the USSR; Moscow and Leningrad. Patricia Kennedy Grimstead.

The Archives of New College, Oxford. Francis Steer, comp.

Arctic Passage: The Turbulent History of the Land and People of the Bering Sea 1697-1975. William R. Hunt.

The Arduous Beginning. A. Eremenko.

Arfive. A. B. Guthrie, Jr.

Argentina and the Failure of Democracy: Conflict Among Political Elites, 1904-1955. Peter H. Smith.

Argentina in the Twentieth Century. David Rock, ed.

Argentina: The Peronist Myth. An Essay on the Cultural Decay in Argentina After the Second World War. Roberto Aizcorbe.

The Argentine Republic 1516-1971. H. S. Ferns.

Århus Domkapitlets Jordebøger II og III. Poul Rasmussen, ed.

Aristocratic Enterprise. Graham Mee.

Aristocratic Government and Society in Eighteenth-Century England: The Foundations of Stability. Daniel A. Baugh, ed.

Aristotele: Trattato sul Cosmo per Alessandro. Giovanni Reale, ed. and trans.

Aristotle's School. John Patrick Lynch.

The Arizona of Joseph Pratt Allyn. John Nicolson, ed.

Arizona Ranch Houses. Janet Ann Stewart.

Arizona Territorial Officials. John S. Goff.

Armand-Jean de Rancé, Abbot of La Trappe. A. J. Krailsheimer.

Armenia and the Armenians in Academic Dissertations. Anne M. Avakian, comp.

Armenia: The Case for a Forgotten Genocide. Dickran H. Boyajian.

Armies of the American Wars, 1753-1815. Philip Katcher.

The Armies of the Streets: The New York City Draft Riots of 1863. Adrian Cook.

Arming the Union: Small Arms in the Civil War. Carl L. Davis.

The Armstrong Empire: A Look at the Worldwide Church of God. Joseph Hopkins.

The Army and the Navajo. Gerald Thompson.

The Army of Flanders and the Spanish Road, 1567-1659: The Logistics of Spanish Victory and Defeat in the Low Countries' Wars. Geoffrey Parker.

The Army of the Caesars. Michael Grant.

An Army Wife on the Frontier. R. C. and E. R. Carriker.

An Army Wife on the Frontier: The Memoirs of Alice Blackwood Baldwin, 1867-1877. Alice Blackwood Baldwin.

Arnauld d'Andilly: Défenseur de Port-Royal (1654-1659). P. Jansen.

Arnold Toynbee: The Ecumenical Vision. Kenneth Winetrout.

Arnold Van Gennup: le créateur de l'ethnographie française. Nicole Belmont.

Art and the Public: The Democratization of the Fine Arts in the United States, 1830-1860. Lucille Wrubel Grindhammer.

The Art of the Migration Period. Gyula László.

The Art of Warfare in the Age of Marlborough. David Chandler.

Art on the Rocks of Southern Africa. D. N. Lee and H. C. Woodhouse.

Arthurian Sites in the West. C. A. Radford and Michael J. Swanton.

Articles and Speeches on the Nationality Question. Mykola Skrypnyk.

The Austrian Mind: An Intellectual
and Social History, 1848-1938.
William M. Johnston.
The Austrian People and the
Anschluss, 1938. M. A. Poltav-
skii.
Austro-German Relations in the
Anschluss Era. Radomir Luza.
Authors, Publishers and Politicians.
James J. Barnes.
L'Autobiographie de Hamed ben
Mohammed el-Murjebi Tippu
Tip (ca 1840-1905). François
Bontinck and Koen Janssen,
eds. and trans.
The Autobiography of Emperor
Haile Selassie. Vol. I.
Haile Selassie.
Autocracy at Work: A Study of
the Yung-cheng Period, 1723-
1735. Pei Huang.
Automatic Artifact Registration
Systems for Archaeological
Analysis With the Phillips
P1100 Computer. R. R.
Newell and A. P. J. Vroo-
mans.
L'Autorità della storia profana.
Albano Biondi.
L'autorité dans le Catholicisme
contemporain, du Syllabus
à Vatican II. Pierre Hégy.
Autour d'Alexandre Herzen. S.
Stelling-Michard, et al., eds.
Aux origines d'une terminologie
sacramentelle. Pierre von
Beneden.
The Awkward Class. Teodor
Shanin.
The Ayia Triadha Sarcophagus.
Charlotte R. Long.
The Aztecs. Nigel Davies.
Aztlan: Historia del Pueblo
Chicano (1848-1910). David
Maciel and Patricia Bueno.

-B-

Backward Toward Revolution:
The Chinese Revolutionary
Party. Edward Friedman.
Backyard Classic: An Adven-
ture in Nostalgia. Lambert
Florin.
Bad Nigger: The National Im-

pact of Jack Johnson. Al-Tony
Gilmore.
Bakersfield, Vermont: The Way It
Was, The Way It Is. Elsie C.
Wells.
Ballots for Freedom. Richard H.
Sewell.
Balzac and the Nineteenth Century.
D. G. Charlton, J. Gaudon, and
A. R. Pugh, eds.
Banca e industria in Italia, 1894-
1906. Vol. I. Antonio Con-
falonieri.
Banks or No Banks: The Money Is-
sue in Western Politics, 1832-
1865. William Gerald Shade.
Banners of the King: The War of
the Vendée, 1793-4. Michael
Ross.
The Bantu Speaking Peoples of
Southern Africa. W. D. Ham-
mond-Tooke, ed.
The Baptist Almanac. Reuben Her-
ring.
Baptist Relations With Other Chris-
tians. James Leo Garrett, Jr.
Baptists in Kentucky, 1776-1976.
Leo Taylor Crimson, ed.
Barns of Chester County, Pennsyl-
vania. Berenice Ball.
Baroque Architecture in Classical
Antiquity. Margaret Lyttelton.
The Barristers of Toulouse in the
Eighteenth Century (1740-1793).
Lenard R. Berlanstein.
Basic Principles of Geopolitics and
History. Debabrata Sen.
Basic Problems of the History of the
USA in American Historiography
from the Colonial Period to the
Civil War, 1861-1865.
Basque Nationalism. Stanley G.
Payne.
Battle for the Bundu: The First
World War in East Africa.
Charles Miller.
Battle for the Caucasus. Andrei
Grechko.
The Battle of Bunker's Hill. John
R. Elting.
The Battle of New Market. William
C. Davis.
The Battle of Sardarabad. Jacques
Kayaloff.
The Battle of Seven Pines. Gustavus
Woodson Smith.
Battles Lost and Won: Essays from
Civil War History. John T.

Hubbell, ed.

Bauern in Peru: Entwicklungsfaktoren in der Wirtschafts- und Sozialgeschichte der Indianischen Landbevölkerung von der Inkazeit bis Heute. Jürgen Golte.

Bauernland Oberösterreich: Entwicklungsgeschichte seiner Land-und Forstwirtschaft. Alfred Hoffmann, et al.

Beauduin: A Prophet Vindicated. Sonya A. Quitslund.

The Beaulieu Cartulary. S. F. Hockey, ed.

The Beauty and the Lore of Coins, Currency, and Medals. Elvira and Vladimir Clain-Stefanelli.

Bebel und die Strategie der Kriegsverhütung 1904-1913. Helmut Bley.

Before Silent Spring. James Whorton.

Before the Blossoms Fall: Life and Death in Japan. Agnes Newton Keith.

Before the Industrial Revolution: European Society and Economy, 1000-1700. Carlo M. Cipolla.

Beginnings of Modern Education in Mithila. Jata Shankar Jha.

Beginnings on Market Street (Nashville and Her Jewry 1861-1901). Fedora Small Frank.

Beiträge zu Italienischen und griechischen Bronzefunde. Hermann Müller-Karpe, ed.

Beitrage zu Wirtschaftswachstum und Wirtschaftsstruktur in 16en und 19en Jahrhundert. Wolfram Fischer, ed.

Beitrage zur ägyptischen Bauforschung und Altertumskunde, zum 70. G. Haeny, ed.

Beleaguered Tower: The Dilemma of Political Catholicism in Wilhelmine Germany. Ronald J. Ross.

Belfast: Approach to Crisis. Ian Budge and Cornelius O'Leary.

Bengal: The Nationalist Movement 1876-1940. Leonard A. Gordon.

Benito Arias Montano (1527-1598). B. Rekers.

Benito Juárez. Ivie E. Cadenhead, Jr.

Benjamin Franklin and the Zealous Presbyterians. Melvin H. Buxbaum.

Benjamin Franklin: His Wit, Wisdom, and Women. Seymour Stanton Block.

Benjamin Rush: Philosopher of the American Revolution. Donald J. D'Elia.

Bergson et le calcul infinitésimal: ou, la raison et le temps. Jean Milet.

The Bergthal Colony. William Schroeder.

Berkeley: The Philosophy of Immaterialism. I. C. Tipton.

Berlin in der Welt politik 1945-1970. Hans Herzeld.

Berner Oberland und Staat Bern. Udo Robé.

Bernhard Dernberg 1865-1937. Werner Schiefel.

The Best Seat in Baseball, But You Have to Stand: The Game as Umpires See It. Lee Gutkind.

Bethany in Kansas. Emory Lindquist.

Bethel, the Early Years: A Collection of Photographs with Text. Irene Cushing and Irene Stafford, eds.

Between Reaction and Revolution. Jan Kozik.

Between Science and Religion. Frank Miller Turner.

Between Two Plenums: China's Intraleadership Conflict, 1959-1962. Ellis Joffe.

Bexley Hall: 150 Years. Richard M. Spielman.

Beyond Dependency: The Developing World Speaks Out. Guy F. Erb and Valeriana Kallab, eds.

Beyond Kissinger. George Liska.

Beyond the Atlantic Roar: A Study of the Nova Scotia Scots. D. Campbell and R. A. MacLean.

Beyond the Cape Frontier. Christopher Saunders and Robin Derricourt, eds.

Beyond the Civil War Synthesis: Political Essays of the Civil War Era. Robert P. Swierenga, ed.

Beyond the Enlightenment. Charles Rearick.

The Bible Belt Mystique. C. Dwight Dorough.

A Bibliography of English History to 1485. Edgar B. Graves, ed.

A Bibliography of Norfolk History. Elizabeth Darroch and Barry

Taylor, eds.
A Bibliography of Printed Battle
Plans of the American Revolu-
tion, 1775-1795. Kenneth
Nebenzahl.
A Bibliography of Studies and
Translations of Modern Chinese
Literature, 1918-1942. Donald
A. Gibbs, et al.
A Bibliography of the Cameroon.
Mark W. and Virginia H.
DeLancey.
The Bibliography of the Reform
1450-1648. Derek Baker, ed.
Bibliography on Labour in Nigeria,
1910-1970. Oluronke O. Orima-
lade, comp.
The Big Bend. Ronnie C. Tyler.
Big Bend: A Homesteader's Story.
J. O. Langford.
The Big Green Book: A Four-
Season Guide to Vermont.
Madeline Kunin.
Big Outfit: Ranching on the Baca
Float. Robert L. Sharp.
The Big Sky. A. B. Guthrie, Jr.
The Big Woods: Logging and Lum-
bering ... in the Pacific North-
west. Ellis Lucia.
Das Bild des Antichrist im Mit-
telalter. Horst Dieter Rauh.
Bill W. Robert Thomsen.
Biographical Dictionary of Ameri-
can Labor Leaders. Gary Fink
and Milton Cantor, eds.
Biographical Register of the Con-
federate Congress. Ezra J.
Warner and W. Buck Yearns.
A Biographical Register of the
University of Oxford, A.D. 1501
to 1540. A. B. Emden.
Biographical Sketches of Those Who
Attended Harvard College in the
Classes 1768-1771. Clifford K.
Shipton.
Biographisches Wörterbuch zur
deutschen Geschichte. Karl
Bosl, et al.
A Biography of Eva Thompson
Clark. Annie C. Tanner.
Biology of Man in History. Robert
Forster and Orest Ranum, eds.
Birmingham 1939-1970. Anthony
Sutcliffe and Roger Smith.
The Birth of Forestry in America:
Biltmore Forest School, 1898-
1915. Carl Alvin Schenck.
The Birth of Missions in America.

Charles L. Chaney.
The Birth of Nations. Philip C.
Jessup.
The Birth of Popular Heresy. R. I.
Moore.
The Birth of the Talkies. Harry M.
Geduld.
Bishop Alexander Macdonell and the
Politics of Upper Canada. J. E.
Rea.
Bishop in Honan. Lewis C. Walms-
ley.
Birmarck. Alan Palmer.
Bismarck at the Crossroads. Bruce
Waller.
Das Bistum Halberstadt im 12.
Jahrhundert. Karlotto Bogumil.
Black Activism: Racial Revolution
in the United States, 1954-1970.
Robert H. Brisbane.
Black Americans and the White
Man's Burden, 1898-1903. Wil-
lard B. Gatewood, Jr.
Black Church in the Sixties. Hart
M. and Anne Kusener Nelsen.
The Black Experience: American
Blacks Since 1865. Mary Ellison.
Black Frontiersman. Norman E.
Whitten, Jr.
The Black Interpreters: Notes on
African Writing. Nadine Gordi-
mer.
Black into White. Thomas E. Skid-
more.
Black Jack Davidson: A Cavalry
Commander on the Western
Frontier. Homer K. Davidson.
Black Legislators in Louisiana
During Reconstruction. Charles
Vincent.
Black Majority. Peter H. Wood.
Black Men and Businessmen: The
Browing Awareness of a Social
Responsibility. Steven M. Gelber.
Black Migration: Movement North,
1900-1920. Florette Henri.
The Black Mind: A History of Afri-
can Literature. O. R. Dathorne.
The Black Oklahomans. Arthur
Tolson.
The Black on New Spain's Northern
Frontier: San José de Parral,
1631-1641. Vincent Mayer, Jr.
Black Pastor and Leaders: The
Memphis Clergy, 1819-1972.
David M. Tucker.
Black Politics in New York City.
Edwin R. Lewinson.

Black Powder and Hard Steel. Otis E. Young, Jr.

Black Power/White Control: The Struggle of the Woodlawn Organization in Chicago. John Hall Fish.

Black Protest: Issues and Tactics. Robert C. Dick.

Black Religion and American Evangelicalism. Milton C. Sernett.

Black Republicans. Hanes Walton, Jr.

Black Slaves in Britain. F. O. Shyllon.

The Black Soldier and Officer in the United States Army, 1891-1917. Marvin E. Fletcher.

Black Students in Protest. Anthony M. Orum.

Blackbeard the Pirate. Robert E. Lee.

Blacking Up: The Minstrel Show in Nineteenth-Century America. Robert C. Toll.

Blacks in Bondage. Robert S. Starobin, ed.

Blacks in Colonial Cuba, 1774-1899. Kenneth F. Kiple.

Blacks in Films. Jim Pines.

Blacks in White Colleges: Oklahoma's Landmark Cases. George L. Cross.

Blacks on John Brown. Benjamin Quarles, ed.

The Blathwayt Atlas. Vols. 1 and 2. Jeannette Black, ed.

Blood Over Texas. Sanford H. Montaigne.

Blood, Toil, Tears and Sweat. Roger Parkinson.

Bloody Knife: Custer's Favorite Scout. Ben Innis.

Blue-Collar Aristocrats. E. E. Lemasters.

Bolingbroke and Harley. Sheila Biddle.

The Bolsheviks and the October Revolution: Minutes of the Central Committee of the Russian Social-Democratic Labour Party (Bolsheviks), August 1917-February 1918. Ann Bone, trans.

Bonanza Victorian. C. Eric Stoehr.

The Bonapartes. Felix Markham.

Bond Men Made Free: Medieval Peasant Movements and the English Rising of 1381. Rodney Hilton.

The Book in Russia in the First Quarter of the 18th Century. S. P. Luppov.

The Book of Abigail and John: Selected Letters of the Adams Family, 1762-1784. L. H. Butterfield, et al., eds.

The Book of Common Prayer 1559. John E. Booty, ed.

The Booker T. Washington Papers. Louis D. Harlan, ed.

The Books of the Pilgrims. Lawrence D. Geller and Peter J. Gomes.

The Border South States: People, Politics, and Power. Neil R. Pierce.

Borderland in Retreat. Abraham P. Nasatir.

The Borgias. Clemente Fusero.

Borodino and the War of 1812. Christopher Duffy.

The Bosnian Church: A New Interpretation. John V. A. Fine, Jr.

Boston Furniture of the Eighteenth Century. Colonial Society of Massachusetts.

Boston Priests, 1848-1910: A Study of Social and Intellectual Change. Donna Merwick.

Boston Red Sox: 75th Anniversary History, 1901-1975. Ellery H. Clark.

Bound with Them in Chains. Jane H. and William H. Pease.

Bouquet's March to the Ohio. Edward G. Williams, ed.

Brahmin Priest of Tamilnadu. K. Subramanian.

Brazil. Stefan H. Robock.

Brazil and the Great Powers, 1930-1939: The Politics of Trade Rivalry. Stanley E. Hilton.

The Brazilian-American Alliance 1937-1945. Frank D. McCann, Jr.

The Brazilian Coffee Valorization of 1906: Regional Politics and Economic Dependence. Thomas H. Holloway.

The Brazilian Peasantry. Shepard Forman.

Brazilian Serial Documents. Mary Lombardi.

Brazilian Society. T. Lynn Smith.

Breckinridge. William C. Davis.
Brecknock and Abergavenny and
Monmouthshire Canals. R. A.
Stevens.
The Brethren in Virginia: The
History of the Church of the
Brethren in Virginia. Roger
E. Sappington.
Brevet's North Dakota Historical
Markers and Sites. Kaye L.
Roehrich, ed.
Bridewealth and Dowry. Jack
Goody and S. J. Tambiah.
Der Brief des Priesters Gerhard
an den Erzbischof Friedrich
von Mainz. Friedrich Lotter.
A Brief History of New Mexico.
Myra Ellen Jenkins and Albert
H. Schroeder.
A Brief History of the United
States Since 1945. Robert D.
Marcus.
Briefe. Constantin Frantz.
Die Briefe des Matthias von
Ephesos im Codex Vindobonen-
sis Theol. gr. 174. D. Reinsch.
Die Briefe Pachoms. Hans
Quecke, ed.
Briefe und Grepräche, 1934-1945.
Heinrich Brüning.
Briefwechsel, 1816-1849. Johann
Jacoby.
Brigham Young University: The
First One Hundred Years.
Ernest L. Wilkinson, ed.
Bringing the War Home: The
American Soldier in Vietnam
and After. John Helmer.
Britain and East Asia 1933-1937.
Ann Trotter.
Britain and Slavery in East Africa.
Moses D. E. Nwulie.
Britain and the American Frontier,
1783-1815. J. Leitch Wright,
Jr.
Britain and the "Casus Belli,"
1822-1902: A Study of Brit-
ain's International Position
from Canning to Salisbury.
Christopher Howard.
Britain and the Conquest of
Africa. G. N. Uzoigwe.
Britain and the Ending of the
Slave Trade. Suzanne Miers.
Britain and the Origins of the
New Europe, 1914-1918.
Kenneth J. Calder.
Britain and the War for the

Union. Brian Jenkins.
Britain Before the Norman Conquest.
Ordnance Survey.
Britain in the Nineteen Twenties.
Noreen Branson.
Britain, India and the Turkish Em-
pire, 1853-1882. Ram L.
Shukla.
Britain's Railways. Harold Pollins.
British and American Abolitionists.
Clare Taylor, ed.
The British at the Gates: The New
Orleans Campaign in the War of
1812. Robin Reilly.
British Drums on the Southern
Frontier. Larry Ivers.
British Economic Policy and the
Empire, 1919-1939. Ian M.
Drummond.
British Economic Thought and India,
1600-1858: A Study in the His-
tory of Development Economics.
William J. Barber.
British Entrepreneurship in the
Nineteenth Century. P. L. Payne.
British Farming in the Great De-
pression, 1870-1914. P. J.
Perry.
British Government and Administra-
tion. H. Hearder and H. R.
Loyn, eds.
British Historical Facts, 1830-1900.
Chris Cook and Brendan Keith.
British Nitrates and Chilean Poli-
tics, 1886-1896: Balmaceda and
North. Harold Blakemore.
British Overseas Investment in the
Nineteenth Century. P. L. Cot-
trell.
British Policy Towards Wartime Re-
sistance in Yugoslavia and Greece.
Phyllis Auty and Richard Clogg,
eds.
British Politics and Government,
1951-1970. Mary Proudfoot.
British Politics and the Stamp Act
Crisis. P. D. G. Thomas.
British Slave Emancipation: The
Sugar Colonies and the Great
Experiment, 1830-1865. William
A. Green.
British Transport Since 1914: An
Economic History. Derek H.
Aldcroft.
Broadcasting in Africa: A Con-
tinental Survey of Radio and
Television. Sydney W. Head,
ed.

California Gold Camps. Erwin G. Gudde.

The California Gold Rush Overland Diary of Byron N. McKinstry, 1850-1852. Bruce L. McKinstry.

California III. W. Michael Mathes, ed.

California--Where the Twain Did Meet. Anne Loftis.

The Cambridge Ancient History. Vol. II, Part 2: History of the Middle East and the Aegean Region, c. 1380-1000 B.C. I. E. S. Edwards, N. G. L. Hammond and E. Sollberger, eds.

The Cambridge History of Africa. Vol. IV. Richard Gray, J. D. Fage and R. Oliver, eds.

The Cambridge History of Iran. Vol. I. W. B. Fisher, ed.

Cambridge South Asian Archive. Mary Hatcher, ed. and comp.

Camden Miscellany. Vol. XXV. Royal Historical Society.

Camillo di Cavour. Frank J. Coppa.

Campaigns of the American Revolution: an Atlas of Manuscript Maps. Douglas W. and Howard H. Marshall.

Los Campesinos de la tierra de Zapata. I. Sinecio López Méndex, et al.

Les camps de concentration dans l'économie du Reich hitlérien. Joseph Billig.

Can America Win the Next War? Drew Middleton.

Canada, 1896-1921: A Nation Transformed. Robert Craig Brown and Ramsay Cook.

Canada in the North Atlantic Triangle: Two Centuries of Social Change. John L. Finlay.

The Canada Land Company: The Early Years. Clarence Karr.

Canada's War: The Politics of the Mackenzie King Government, 1939-1945. J. L. Granatstein.

Canadian-American Relations in Wartime. R. D. Cuff and J. L. Granatstein.

The Canadian General: Sir William Otter. Desmond Morton.

Canadian Public Land Use in Perspective. J. G. Nelson, R. C. Scace, and R. Kouri, eds.

Canadian Watercolours and Drawings in the Royal Ontario Museum. Mary Alladi.

The Canal Boatmen 1760-1914. Harry Hanson.

Canossa als Wende: Ausgewählte Aufsätze zur Neuren Forschung. Helmut Kämpf, ed.

Der Canossagang von 1077 Wirkungen und Wirklichkeit. Harald Zimmerman.

Canterbury Professions. Michael Richter, ed.

Capital Cities of Arab Islam. Philip K. Hitti.

The Captain America Complex: The Dilemma of Zealous Nationalism. Robert Jewett.

Captain Phillip Dimmit's Commandancy of Goliad.... Hobart Huson.

Caput and Colonate: Towards a History of Late Roman Taxation. Walter Goffart.

The Car Culture. James J. Flink.

El Cardenal Lorenzana y la Ilustracion. Luis Sierra Nava-Lasa.

The Cardinal and the Secretary. Neville Williams.

Cardinal Newman in His Age. Harold L. Weatherby.

The Cardinal Protectors of England. William E. Wilkie.

Il Cardinale Gasparri e la Questione Romana. Giovanni Spadolini, ed.

Carlism and Crisis in Spain, 1931-1939. Martin Blinkhorn.

Caroline Courtier: The Life of Lord Cottington. Martin J. Havran.

Carracks, Caravans and Companies. Niels Steensgaard.

Il Carteggio Antonelli-Barli, 1859-1861. Carla Meneguzzi Rostagni, ed.

Carthage Conspiracy. D. H. Oaks and M. S. Hill.

The Cartoon History of the American Revolution. Michael Wynn Jones.

Carvaho: Portrait of a Forgotten American. Joan Sturhahn.

Casas Grandes: A Fallen Trade Center of the Gran Chichimeca. 3 vols. Charles C. Di Peso.

A Case for Due Process in the Church: Father Eugene O'Callaghan, American Pioneer of Dissent. Nelson J. Callahan.

The Case for the Arab Oil Em-
bargo. Ibrahim F. I. Shihata.
Casements and Cannonballs:
Archaeological Investigations at
Fort Stanwix, Rome, New York.
Lee Hanson and Dick Ping Hsu.
Cases of Conscience. Elliot Rose.
Cassius Marcellus Clay. H. Ed-
ward Richardson.
Castlereagh. John W. Derry.
Castro: epistolaria presidencial.
Elías Pino Iturrieta, ed.
Catalan Domination of Athens 1311-
1388. K. M. Setton.
The Catalpa Bow. A Study of
Shamanistic Practices in Japan.
Carmen Blacker.
Catholic Sunday Preaching. Robert
F. McNamara.
Catholics, Peasants and Chews Re-
sistance in Nyasaland 1889-1939.
Ian and Jane Linden.
Causal Explanation and Model
Building in History, Economics,
and the New Economic History.
Peter D. McClelland.
Causal Factors in American
Economic Growth in the Nine-
teenth Century. Peter Temin.
The Cavendish Laboratory 1874-
1974. J. G. Crowther.
Céline. Patrick McCarthy.
Le censier d'Herchies de 1287.
Reine Mantou, ed.
Centennial. James E. Michener.
Centennial History: The Univer-
sity of Wisconsin-River Falls,
1874-1974. James T. King.
A Centennial History of Texas
A & M University, 1876-1976.
2 vols. Henry C. Dethloff.
Central America: A Nation
Divided. Ralph Lee Wood-
ward, Jr.
A Century of Agricultural Growth
in Japan. Yujiro Hayami, et
al.
A Century of Jewish Life in Dixie:
The Birmingham Experience.
Mark H. Elovitz.
A Century of News and People
in the East Oregonian, 1875-
1975. Gordon MacNab.
A Century of Service: A His-
tory of the World Alliance of
Reformed Churches, 1875-
1975. Marcel Pradervand.
Century of Struggle: The

Woman's Rights Movement in the
United States. Eleanor Flexner.
La céramique Chypriote de style
figure. 2 vols. Vassos Kara-
georghis and J. des Gagniers.
A Certain Eventuality. P. M. H.
Bell.
The Certificate of Musters for
Buckinghamshire in 1522. A. C.
Chibnall.
Cesar Chavez. Winthrop Yinger.
Cesare Beccaria and the Origins of
Penal Reform. Marcello Maestro.
Challenge of Change. Nelson Wolff.
Change and Continuity in Seventeenth-
Century England. Christopher
Hill.
Change and Persistence in Thai So-
ciety. G. William Skinner and
A. Thomas Kirsch, eds.
Change in Contemporary Africa.
Leonard Thompson and Jeffrey
Butler, eds.
Un changeur florentin du Trecento:
Lippo di Fede del Sega. Charles
M. de la Roncière.
Changing Perspectives in the History
of Science: Essays in Honour of
Joseph Needham. Mikuláš Teich
and Robert Young, eds.
The Changing Rhythm. Sasson
Somekh.
The Character of John Adams.
Peter Shaw.
The Character of Kinship. Jack
Goody, ed.
Charismatic Bureaucrat: A Political
Biography of Matsudaira Sadanobu,
1758-1829. Herman Ooms.
Charles A. Lindbergh and the Battle
Against American Intervention in
World War II. Wayne S. Cole.
Charles C. Rich: Mormon General
and Western Frontiersman.
Leonard J. Arrington.
Charles E. Merriam and the Study
of Politics. Barry D. Karl.
Charles F. Lummis: The Man and
His West. Turbesé Lummis
Fiske and Keith Lummis.
Charles Ives and His America.
Frank R. Rossiter.
Charles Ives and the American
Mind. Rosalie Sandra Perry.
Charles Redd Monographs in West-
ern History ... 1973-1974.
Thomas G. Alexander, ed.
Charles the Bold. Richard Vaughan.

Charles I's Lord Treasurer: Sir Richard Weston, Earl of Portland (1577-1635). Michael Van Cleave Alexander.

Charles VII. M. G. A. Vale.

Charles W. Chesnutt, America's First Great Black Novelist. J. Noel Heermance.

Charleston--Come Hell or High Water. R. N. S. Whitelaw.

The Charters of Norwich Cathedral Priory, Part One. Barbara Dodwell, ed.

Chartism. J. T. Ward.

Chartism and the Chartists. David Jones.

Chase City and Its Environs, 1765-1975: The Southside Virginia Experience. Douglas Summers Brown.

Chautauqua: A Center for Education, Religion, and the Arts in America. Theodore Morrison.

Chavez and the Farm Workers. Ronald B. Taylor.

Chemical Disarmament. Stockholm International Peace Research Institute.

The Chemists and the Word: The Didactic Origins of Chemistry. Owen Hannaway.

The Cherokee Nation of Indians. Charles C. Royce.

Cheshire 1630-1660. J. S. Morrill.

The Chetnik Movement & the Yugoslav Resistance. Matteo J. Milazzo.

The Chetniks. Jozo Thomasevich.

Chicago's White City of 1893. David F. Burg.

The Chicano. Norris Hundley, Jr., ed.

Chicano Revolt in a Texas Town. John Staples Shockley.

The Chicopee Manufacturing Company, 1823-1915. John Michael Cudd.

A Chief Is a Chief by the People: The Autobiography of Stimela Jason Jingoes. John and Cassandra Perry.

Chief of Staff: The Diaries of Lieutenant General Sir Henry Pownall. Vol. 2. Brian Bond, ed.

Chiefs and Challengers. George Harwood Phillips.

Chiefs and Clerics: Abdul Bokar Kan and Futa Toro, 1853-1891. David Robinson.

The Child Jesus. Adey Horton.

Child of the Hogan. Ray Baldwin Louis.

Childhood in China. William Kessen, ed.

The Children of the Counterculture. John Rothchild and Susan Wolf.

Children of the Raven. H. R. Hays.

Children of the Sun: A Narrative of "Decadence" in England After 1918. Martin Green.

Chile: A Historical Interpretation. Jay Kinsbrunner.

Chilean Rural Society from the Spanish Conquest to 1930. Arnold J. Bauer.

China and the Great Powers. Francis O. Wilcox, ed.

China Handbuch. Wolfgang Franke, ed.

The China Hands: America's Foreign Service Officers and What Befell Them. E. J. Kahn, Jr.

China in Disintegration. James E. Sheridan.

China in Maps, 1880-1960. Jack F. Williams.

China in World Politics. Harish Kapur.

China Now. D. J. Dwyer, ed.

China, Pakistan, and Bangladesh. J. P. Jain.

China: The People's Republic of China and Richard Nixon. Claude A. Buss.

China's Africa Policy. George T. Yu.

China's African Revolution. Alan Hutchison.

China's Civilization: A Survey of Its History, Arts, and Technology. Arthur Cotterell and David Morgan.

China's Economic Aid. Wolfgang Bartke.

China's Foreign Trade Statistics, 1864-1949. Liang-lin Hsiao.

China's Imperial Past: An Introduction to Chinese History and Culture. Charles O. Hucker.

China's Modern Economy in Historical Perspective. Dwight H. Perkins, ed.

China's Policy in Africa, 1958-1971. Alaba Ogunsanwo.

La Chine rurale: des villages aux
Communes populaires. Marthe
Engelborghs-Bertels.

Chinese and Soviet Aid to Africa.
Warren Weinstein, ed.

The Chinese City Between Two
Worlds. Mark Elvin and G.
William Skinner, eds.

Chinese Historiography on the Revolution of 1911: A Critical Survey and a Selected Bibliography.
Winston Hsieh.

The Chinese in America, 1820-1973.
William L. Tung.

Chinese Policy Toward Indonesia.
David Mozingo.

Chinese Ways in Warfare. Frank
A. Kierman, Jr. and John K.
Fairbank, eds.

A Choice of Sundials. Winthrop
W. Dolan.

Christ in Christian Tradition. I.
Aloys Grillmeier.

Christian Asceticism. J. Z.
Ziesler.

Christian Churches of America:
Origins and Beliefs. Milton
V. Beckman, Jr.

The Christian Revolutionary: John
Milton. Hugh M. Richmond.

Christian Socialism and Co-Opera-
tion in Victorian England.
Philip N. Backstrom.

The Christian Tradition. Vol. 2.
Jaroslav Pelikan.

A Christian View of History?
George Marsden and Frank
Roberts, eds.

Christianity and Culture. Georges
Florovsky.

Christianity Through the Thirteenth
Century. Marshall W. Baldwin,
ed.

Christians and Jews in Germany:
1870-1914. Uriel Tal.

Christians and Socialism: Docu-
mentation of the Christians for
Socialism Movement in Latin
America. John Eagleson, ed.

Christians in Secular India.
Abraham Vazhayil Thomas.

Christians Under the Hammer
and Sickle. Winrich Scheffbuch.

Christopher Gist: Colonial Frontiersman, Explorer, and Indian
Agent. Kenneth Bailey.

Christ's Glorious Church: The

Story of Canterbury Cathedral.
Derek Imgram Hill.

Chronicle of a Congressional Journey. Lonnie J. White, ed.

A Chronicle of North Carolina During the American Revolution,
1763-1789. Jeffrey J. Crow.

The Chronicle of the Election of
Hugh, Abbot of Bury St Edmunds
and Later Bishop of Ely. R. M.
Thomson, ed. and trans.

The Chronology of Oral Tradition:
Quest for a Chimera. David P.
Henige.

Church and Society in Eighteenth-
Century Devon. Arthur Warne.

Church and State After the Dreyfus
Affair. Maurice Larkin.

Church and State in France, 1870-
1914. John McManners.

Church and State in Tonga. Sione
Lātūkefu.

The Church and the Law in the
Earlier Ages. Walter Ullmann.

The Church Before the Covenants:
The Church of Scotland 1596-
1638. Walter Roland Foster.

The Church in Victorian Scotland,
1843-1874. Andrew L. Drummond and James Bulloch.

Church, Society and Politics.
Derek Baker, ed.

Church, State, and Nation in Ireland, 1898-1921. David W. Miller.

Church, State and Opposition in the
U.S.S.R. Gerhard Simon.

The Churches and Politics in Germany. Frederic Spotts.

The Churches and the Nations. O.
Frederick Nolde.

The Churches Militant: The War of
1812 and American Religion.
William Gribbin.

Cincinnati: A Chronological and
Documentary History, 1676-1970.
Robert I. Vexler, ed. and comp.

Cinco Haciendas Mexicanas. Tres
siglos de vida rural en San Luis
Potosi (1600-1910). Jan Bazant.

La Cine e l'età dell'Illuminismo in
Italia. Sergio Zoli.

Cities and Schools in the Gilded
Age: The Evolution of an Urban
Institution. William A. Bul-
lough.

The Cities of Siberia (The Economy,
Management and Culture of Si-

berian Cities in the Pre-Soviet
Period). O. N. Vilkov, ed.
The Citizen and the State.
George J. Stigler.
Citta e campagne nella. Puglia
del secolo XIX: L'evoluzione
demografica. Franca Assante.
The City Bountiful: Utah's Second
Settlement from Pioneers to
Present. Leslie T. Foy.
A City in Terror: 1919--The
Boston Police Strike. Francis
Russell.
City Invincible. K. A. Meretskov.
The City of Londin in International
Politics at the Accession of
Elizabeth Tudor. G. D. Ramsay.
The City of the Cosmic Dance:
Chidambaram. B. Natarajan.
Las ciudades latinoamericanas. 2
vols. Richard M. Morse.
Civil Disobedience in Antiquity.
David Daube.
The Civil War: A Narrative.
Vol. 3. Red River to Appomat-
tox. Shelby Foote.
The Civil War Era in Indian Terri-
tory. LeRoy H. Fischer, ed.
The Civil War in Indian Territory.
Donald and Lary Rampp.
The Civil War in Kentucky. Low-
ell H. Harrison.
Civil War in Russia 1917-1920.
J. F. N. Bradley.
Civil War Letters of George Wash-
ington Whitman. George Wash-
ington Whitman.
A Civil War Soldier's Last Letters.
William F. Margraff.
Civilization on Loan. Heinz Edgar
Kiewe.
The Civilized Wilderness: Back-
grounds to American Romantic
Literature, 1817-1860. Edward
Halsey Foster.
Civilizing the Machine: Tech-
nology and Republican Values in
America, 1776-1900. John F.
Kasson.
The Clansman. Thomas Dixon,
Jr.
Clash of Titans: Africa and U.S.
Foreign Policy. Edward W.
Chester.
Class and Religion in the Late
Victorian City. Hugh McLeod.
Class Struggle and the Industrial
Revolution. John Foster.

Classic Maya Pottery at Dumbarton
Oaks. Michael D. Coe.
The Classical Heritage of Islam.
Franz Rosenthal.
The Classical Style: Haydn, Mozart,
Beethoven. Charles Rosen.
The Classical Text. E. J. Kenney.
The Classick Pages: Classical
Reading of Eighteenth-Century
Americans. Meyer Reinhold, ed.
The Classless Profession: American
Schoolmen in the Nineteenth Cen-
tury. Paul H. Mattingly.
The Classroom and the Chancellery.
Allen Sinel.
Clio and the Doctors: Psycho-His-
tory, Quanto-History, and History.
Jacques Barzun.
Clive of India. Mark Bence-Jones.
Coal Age Empire: Pennsylvania Coal
and Its Utilization to 1860.
Frederick Moore Binder.
Coal-Mining Safety in the Progres-
sive Period: The Political Econ-
omy of Reform. William Graeb-
ner.
Cobwebs to Catch Flies. Joyce
Irene Whalley.
Codex diplomaticus Amiatinus, I
(736-951). Wilhelm Kurze.
Código Negro Carolino. Javier
Malagón y Barceló.
Coke of Norfolk. Robert A. C.
Parker.
Cold War America. Lawrence S.
Wittner.
The Cold War Begins: Soviet-
American Conflict Over Eastern
Europe. Lynn Etheridge Davis.
Colette: A Taste for Life. Yvonne
Mitchell.
The Collected Works of Abraham
Lincoln: Supplement 1832-1865.
Roy P. Basler, ed.
Collectors' Illustrated Encyclopedia
of the American Revolution.
George C. Neuman and Frank J.
Kravic.
Colloquia Erasmiana Turonensia.
Jean Claude Margolin, ed.
Colonel Greene and the Copper Sky-
rocket. C. L. Sonnichsen.
Colonial and Historic Homes of
Maryland. Don Swann, Sr. and
Don Swann, Jr.
Colonial and Revolutionary Morris
County. Theodore Thayer.
Colonial Delaware. Gardell Dano

Christensen and Eugenia Burney.
Colonial New York: A History.
Michael Kammen.
The Colonial Origins of the United
States: 1607-1763. W. W.
Abbot.
Colonial Pennsylvania: A History.
Joseph E. Illick.
The Colonial Physician and Other
Essays. Whitfield J. Bell, Jr.
Colonial Rhode Island: A History.
Sydney V. James.
Colonial Rule and the Kamba:
Social Change in the Kenya High-
lands, 1889-1939. J. Forbes
Munro.
The Colonial Transformation of
Kenya: The Kamba, Kikuyu,
and Maasai from 1900 to 1939.
Robert L. Tignor.
Colonialism in Africa, 1870-1960.
Peter Duignan and L. H. Gann,
eds.
Colonizzazione e Decolonizzazione.
Carlo Giglio.
Colorado. Frank Fossett.
Colorado: A History of the Cen-
tennial State. Carl Abbott.
Colorado Headlines. United Banks
of Colorado.
Coming of Age: The United States
1920-1930. Donald R. McCoy.
The Coming of the Friars. Rosa-
lind B. Brooke.
Commitment on Campus: Changes
in Religion and Values Over
Five Decades. Dean R. Hoge.
The Common Soldier of the Civil
War. Bell I. Wiley.
The Commonweal and American
Catholicism. Rodger Van Allen.
Communications and National Inte-
gration in Communist China.
Alan P. L. Liu.
The Communist Party in Canada:
A History. Ivan Avakumovic.
Community and Class in Ameri-
can Education, 1865-1918.
Patricia Albjerg Graham.
Community in a Black Pente-
costal Church. Melvin D. Wil-
liams.
A Community in Conflict: Frank-
furt Society in the Seventeenth
and Early Eighteenth Centuries.
Gerald L. Soliday.
The Community of the Realm.
Michael R. Powicke.

The Comparative Reception of Dar-
winism. Thomas F. Glick, ed.
A Compromise of Principle: Con-
gressional Republicans and Recon-
struction, 1863-1869. Michael
Les Benedict.
The Compromising of the Constitu-
tion. Rexford G. Tugwell.
The Compton Effect. Roger H.
Stuewer.
Compulsory Education and the Amish:
The Right Not to Be Modern. Al-
bert N. Keim.
The Concept of Benevolence: As-
pects of 18th-Century Moral
Philosophy. T. A. Roberts.
Concepts of Judaism. Isaac Breuer.
Condorcet: From Natural Philosophy
to Social Mathematics. Keith
Michael Baker.
The Confederate Blockade of Wash-
ington, D.C.: 1861-1862. Mary
Alice Wills.
Confederate Finance and Purchasing
in Great Britain. Richard I.
Lester.
Confederate Imprints at the Georgia
Historical Society. Richard B.
Harwell.
Confederate Women. Bell Irvin
Wiley.
The Confederates and Federals at
War. H. C. B. Rogers.
Conferencia Internacional: Modelos
de desarrollo en América Latina.
Gerhard Brekonja, ed.
Confieso Que He Vivido, Memorias.
Pablo Neruda.
Conflict and Control in Late Im-
perial China. Frederic Wake-
man, Jr. and Carolyn Grant, eds.
Conflict and Transformation. Wil-
liam R. Brock.
Conflict on the Northwest Coast.
Howard I. Kushner.
Le conflit de chypre, 1946-1959.
2 vols. François Crouzet.
Confrontation and Accommodation in
Southern Africa: The Limits of
Independence. Kenneth W.
Grundy.
Confrontation at Winnipeg: Labour,
Industrial Relations, and the
General Strike. David Jay
Bercuson.
Confrontation at Worms: Martin
Luther and the Diet of Worms.
De Lamar Jensen.

ment and Reform in Ireland, 1649-1660. T. C. Barnard.
Cronaca di Roma, 1844-1870. Vol. I. Maria Luisa Trebiliani, ed.
Cross and Crucible. John Warwick Montgomery.
Crossing Cultural Boundaries. Solon T. Kimball and James T. Watson, eds.
Crossing the Crest. Aubra Dair and Patricia Lee Ciccorello.
Crown and Charter: The Early Years of the British South Africa Company. John S. Galbraith.
The Crucial Years, 1939-1941. Hanson W. Baldwin.
The Crucible of Europe. Geoffrey Barraclough.
The Crucifixion of the Jews. Franklin H. Littell.
Cruel Habitations: A History of Working-Class Housing, 1780-1918. Enid Gauldie.
Cruelty and Civilization: The Roman Games. Roland Auguet.
Crusade Against Radicalism. Julian F. Jaffe.
Crusader Manuscript Illumination at Saint-Jean d'Arc, 1275-1291. Jaroslav Folda.
The Crusaders. R. C. Smail.
Cuatro historiadores de Indias, siglo XVI. Edmundo O'Gorman.
Cuba: Economía y sociedad. 2 vols. Levi Marrero.
Cuba Under Castro: The Limits of Charisma. Edward González.
The Cuban Missile Crisis: International Crises and the Role of Law. Abram Chayes.
The Cult of the Dead in a Chinese Village. Emily M. Ahern.
La Cultura en la época de Rosas: Aportes a la decolonización mental de la Argentina. Fermín Chávez.
The Cultural Contradiction of Capitalism. Daniel Bell.
The Cultural Ecology of Chinese Civilization. Leon E. Stover.
Cultural Revolution and Industrial Organization in China. Chalres Bettelheim.
Culture and Society in the Dutch Republic During the Seventeenth Century. J. L. Price.

Cunard and the North Atlantic 1840-1973. Francis E. Hyde.
Curtain. Agatha Christie.
The Custer Adventure. Richard Upton, comp.
Custer and the Epic of Defeat. Bruce A. Rosenberg.
Custer in '76; Walter Camp's Notes on the Custer Fight. Walter Camp.
Custer in Texas: An Interrupted Narrative. John M. Carroll, comp. and ed.
Custer's Last Stand: The Anatomy of an American Myth. Brian W. Dippie.
Custom and Government in the Lower Congo. Wyatt MacGaffey.
Cyprus and the War of Greek Independence 1821-1829. John T. A. Koumoulides.
Cyprus: Reluctant Republic. Stephen G. Xydis.
Cyrus Clay Carpenter and Iowa Politics, 1854-1898. Mildred Throne.
The Czar's Germans. Hattie Plum Williams.

-D-

The Dacian Stones Speak. Paul MacKendrick.
Dahomey Between Tradition and Modernity. Dov Ronen.
The Dakota Maverick: The Political Life of William Langer. Agnes Geelan.
Dakota Twilight: The Standing Rock Sioux, 1874-1890. Edward A. Milligan.
Dakota Wheat Fields 1880. C. C. Coffin.
The Damndest Yankees: Ethan Allen and His Clan. Edwin P. Hoyt.
The Damned Inheritance: The Soviet Union and the Manchurian Crises, 1924-1935. George Alexander Lensen.
The Dangerous Class. Eric H. Monkkonen.
Daniel Smith, Frontier Statesman. Walter T. Durham.
Dans la Tourmente: Les Relations

Hungaro-Roumaines de 1940 à 1945. Dániel Csatári.

The Dark Ages & the Age of Gold. Russell Fraser.

Darlington Municipal Transport. Ron Howe.

Darwin in America. Cynthia Eagle Russett.

Darwin on Man: A Psychological Study of Scientific Creativity. Howard E. Gruber.

Daughter of a Revolutionary: Natalie Herzen and the Bakunin-Nechayev Circle. Michael Confino, ed.

David Eccles: Pioneer Western Industrialist. Leonard J. Arrington.

David Friedrich Strauss and His Place in Modern Thought. Richard S. Cromwell.

David Jayne Hill and the Problem of World Peace. Aubrey Parkman.

David Livingstone: His Triumph, Decline and Fall. Cecil Northcott.

David Livingstone: South African Papers, 1849-1853. I. Schapera, ed.

Dawsons in the Revolutionary War (and Their Descendants). Carol Ruth (Anderson) Dawson.

Days at the Factories: or, the Manufacturing Industry of Great Britain Described, and Illustrated by Numerous Engravings of Machines and Processes. George Dodd.

The Days of Augusta. Jean E. Speare, ed.

Days of Hope and Promise. Vincent A. Yzermans, ed.

The Days That We Have Seen. George Ewart Evans.

Il "De Officio Collectoris in Regno Angliae" di Pietro Griffi da Pisa (1469-1516). Michele Monaco.

The "De Vita Evangelica" of Geoffrey Hardeby, O.E.S.A. (c. 1320-c. 1385). Katherine Walsh.

The Dean: The Life of Julien C. Monnet. Dave R. McKown.

Death, Disease and Famine in Pre-Industrial England. Leslie Clarkson.

Death in America. David E. Stannard, ed.

The Death of Communal Liberty: A History of Freedom in a Swiss Mountain Canton. Benjamin R. Barber.

Death Was the Black Horse: The Story of Rough Rider Buckey O'Neill. Dale L. Walker.

Debate on Europe, 1815-1850. George Rudé.

Debtors and Creditors in America. Peter J. Coleman.

Les débuts de l'industrie chimique dans les Pays-Bas autrichiens. Annette André-Félix.

Le débuts du régime seigneurial. Marcel Trudel.

Decade of Disillusionment: The Kennedy-Johnson Years. Jim F. Heath.

A Decade of Public Administration in Africa. Anthony H. Rweyemanu and Göran Hydén.

Decentralization and Self-Government in Russia, 1830-1870. S. Frederick Starr.

Decisive Day: The Battle for Bunker Hill. Richard N. Ketchum.

Decline and Fall of Byzantium to the Ottoman Turks. Harry J. Magoulias, trans.

The Decline and Fall of Radical Catholicism. James Hitchcock.

The Decline and Fall of the Neoplatonic Interpretation of Plato. E. N. Tigerstedt.

The Decline of American Gentility. Stow Persons.

Decline or Renewal? France Since the 1930's. Stanley Hoffmann.

De Gaulle. I and II. Brian Crozier.

A Delaware Indian Symposium. Herbert C. Kraft, ed.

The Delaware Indians. C. A. Weslager.

DeLesseps S. Morrison and the Image of Reform: New Orleans Politics, 1946-1961. Edward F. Haas.

The Delights of a Rare Book Librarian. Frederick R. Goff.

Democracy Ancient and Modern. M. I. Finley.

Democracy and Organization in the Chinese Industrial Enterprise. William Brugger.

The Democratic Enlightenment.

Donald H. Meyer.
The Democratic Party and California Politics, 1880-1896.
R. Hal Williams.
The Democratic Party and the Negro: Northern and National Politics, 1868-92. Lawrence Grossman.
The Democratic Party and the Politics of Sectionalism, 1941-1948. Robert A. Garson.
Democrats and Progressives. Allen Yarnell.
The Democrats: The Years after FDR. Herbert S. Parmet.
Denken über Geschichte: Aufsätze zur heutigen Saituation des geschichtlichen Bewusstseins und der Geschichtswissenschaft. Friedrich Engel-Janosi, et al., eds.
Denker gegen den Strom/Schopenhauer. Arthur Hübscher.
Dependence and Opportunity: Political Change in Ahafo. John Dunn and A. F. Robertson.
A Dependent Commonwealth: Utah's Economy from Statehood to the Great Depression. Leonard J. Arrington and Thomas G. Alexander.
A Description of the Country: Virginia's Cartographers and Their Maps, 1607-1881. E. M. Sanchez-Saavedra.
A Descriptive Guide to the Harvard University Archives. Clark A. Elliott.
Deseret, 1776-1976: A Bicentennial History of Utah by the Deseret News. William B. Smart and Henry A. Smith, eds.
Desert River Crossing. W. L. Rusho and C. Gregory Crampton.
Desiderius Erasmus. J. Kelley Sowards.
Designing the Industrial State: The Intellectual Pursuit of Collectivism in America, 1880-1940. James Gilbert.
Desperate Diplomacy: William H. Seward's Foreign Policy, 1861. Norman B. Ferris.
Destination America. Maldwyn A. Jones.
Destruction and Survival. Charles W. Steckel.
Deterrence in American Foreign

Policy: Theory and Practice. Alexander L. George and Richard Smoke.
Deutsche Industrie und Politik: Von Bismarck bis Heute. George W. F. Hallgarten and Joachim Radkau.
Die deutsche Politik im spanischen Bürgerkrieg, 1936-1939. Manfred Merkes.
Deutsche Russlandpolitik. Barbara Vogel.
Das deutsche Wehrmachttransportwesen im Zweiten Weltkrieg: Entstehung--Organisation--Aufgaben. Horst Rohde.
Deutschland in der Weltpolitik des 19. und 20. Jahrhunderts. Imanuel Geiss and Bernd Jürgen Wendt, eds.
Deutschland und der Kalte Krieg. Ernst Nolte.
Deutschland und die Tschechen. Ferdinand Seibt.
Deutschland und die Vereinigten Staaten, 1933-1939: Wirtschaft und Politik in der Entwicklund des deutsch-Amerikanischen Gegensatzes. Hans-Jurgen Schroder.
Development Administration: The Kenya Experience. Göran Hyden, Robert Jackson and John Okumu, eds.
Development and the Debt Trap: Economic Planning and External Borrowing in Ghana. A. Krassowski.
The Development of Education in Ghana. H. O. A. McWilliam and M. A. Kwamena-Poh.
The Development of English Glassmaking 1560-1640. Eleanor S. Godfrey.
The Development of Japanese Business. Johannes Hirschmeier and Tsunehiko Yui.
Development of Marginal Farmers and Agriculture Labourers. S. M. Pandey.
The Development of National Power. Richard L. Watson, Jr.
The Development of the Government of Jersey 1771-1972. R. G. Le Hérissier.
The Development of the West of Scotland. Anthony Slaven.
Development Policy in Small Countries. Percy Selwyn, ed.
Devil on Horseback: A Biography

Galbraith.
Domesday Gazeteer. H. C. Darby and G. R. Versey.
The Domestic Revolution: The Modernization of Household Service in England and France 1820-1920. Theresa M. McBride.
Domestic Slavery in West Africa: With Particular Reference to the Sierra Leone Protectorate, 1896-1927. John Grace.
La dominación haitiana, 1822-1844. Frank Moya Pons.
Dominican Architecture in Sixteenth-Century Oaxaca. Robert James Mullen.
Das Domkapitel von Plock, 1524-1564. Christoph Wollek.
Domprediger Johann Emanuel Veith und Kardinal Friedrich Schwarzenberg. Eduard and Maria Winter.
Don Rodrigo Ximénez de Rada, gran señor y hombre de negocios en la Castilla del siglo XIII. Hilda Grassotti.
Dopoguerra e fascismo in Sardegna. Salvatore Sechi.
La dottrina sansimoniana nel pensiero italiano del Risorgimento. Renato Treves.
Douai College Documents 1639-1794. P. R. Harris, ed.
The Downfall and the Anti-Semitic Political Parties in Imperial Germany. Richard S. Levy.
Downriver: Orrin H. Ingram and the Empire Lumber Company. Charles E. Twining.
The Draft and the Rest of Your Life. Richard L. Killmer and Charles P. Lutz.
Drama and Conflict: The Texas Saga of 1776. Robert S. Weddle and Robert H. Thonhoff.
The Drama of the Martyrs. Jan Luyken.
Drama on the Connecticut. Robert E. Pike.
Dramatists in Revolt: The New Latin American Theatre. Leon F. Lyday and George W. Woodyard, eds.
Dream by the River. William Barnaby Faherty.
Drei Münzhorte des 4. Jahrhunderts aus dem Banat. Eugen Chirilă, Nicolae Gudea, and

Ioan Stratan.
Dualistic Economic Development, Theory and History. Allen C. Kelley, Jeffrey G. Williamson, and Russell J. Cheetham.
Duel Between the First Ironclads. William C. Davis.
The Duke of Newcastle. Reed Browning.
The Dukes. Douglas E. Harker.
The Dukes of Durham, 1865-1929. Robert F. Durden.
Dumbarton Oaks Papers, Number 27. Dumbarton Oaks Center.
The Dunne Family. James T. Farrell.
The Dutch in America, 1609-1974. Gerald F. De Jong.
The Dutch Rural Economy in the Golden Age, 1500-1700. Jan de Vries.
"The Dye Is Now Cast": The Road to American Independence, 1774-1776. Lillian B. Miller.
The Dying Lion. Patrick Gilkes.
Dynamique Sociale et Appréhension due Monde au Sein d'une Société Hausa. Guy Nicolas.
The Dynasty: The Rise and Fall of Social Credit in Alberta. John J. Barr.

-E-

Eadweard Muybridge: The Father of the Motion Picture. Gordon Hendricks.
The Eagle and Brooklyn. Raymond A. Schroth.
Eagle and Sword: The Federalists and the Creation of the Military Establishment in America, 1783-1802. Richard H. Kohn.
The Eagles of Savoy: The House of Savoy in Thirteenth-Century Europe. Eugene L. Cox.
Earldom of Gloucester Charters. R. B. Patterson.
Early Arizona. Jay J. Wagoner.
The Early Bronze-Age Daggers in Great Britain and a Reconsideration of the Wessex Culture. Sabine Gerloff.
Early Celtic Masterpieces from Britain in the British Museum.

John Brailsford.
The Early Charters of Northern
England and the North Midlands.
C. R. Hart.
Early Children's Books and Their
Illustrations. Gerald Gottlieb.
Early Chola Temples: Parantaka I
to Rajaraja I (A. D. 907-985).
S. R. Balasubrahmanyam.
The Early English Lyric and Fran-
ciscan Spirituality. David L.
Jeffrey.
Early Farmers of West Mediter-
ranean Europe. Patricia Phil-
lips.
Early Film Making in Los Angeles.
Charles G. Clarke.
Early Indian Economic History.
R. N. Saletore.
The Early Jews of New Orleans.
Bertram Wallace Korn.
Early National Education: 1776-
1830. David Madsen.
Early Nurserymen. John Harvey.
Early Times in the Cumberland
Valley, From Its Beginnings
Until 1800. James A. Crutch-
field.
Early Vermont Broadsides. John
Duffy, ed.
Early Yuma: A Graphic History
of the American Nile. Rosalie
Crowe and Sydney B. Brincker-
hoff, eds.
East Africa and the Orient: Cul-
tural Syntheses in Pre-Colonial
Times. H. Neville Chittick and
Robert I. Rotberg, eds.
East Central Europe Between the
Two World Wars. Joseph Roth-
schild.
East European Perspectives on
European Security and Coopera-
tion. Robert R. King and Robert
W. Dean, eds.
The East India Company and Army
Reform, 1783-1798. Raymond
Callahan.
East of Malta, West of Suez.
Lawrence R. Pratt.
East-West Kaleidoscope, 1877-
1944. W. W. Yen.
The Eastern Association in the
English Civil War. Clive
Holmes.
Eastern Civilization. G. Robina
Quale.
Eastern Europe: A Geography of

the Common Countries. Roy
E. H. Mellor.
Eastern Europe and the Downfall
of the Golden Horde (at the Turn
of the Fourteenth and Fifteenth
Centuries). I. B. Grekov.
The Eastern Front, 1914-1917.
Norman Stone.
Ebenezer Cooke: The Sot-Weed
Canon. Edward H. Cohen.
The Ecclesiastical History of Orderic
Vitalis. Marjorie Chibnall, ed.
and trans.
Echo of a Distant Drum: Winslow
Homer and the Civil War. Julian
Grossman.
Echoes of Distant Thunder: Life in
the United States, 1914-1918.
Edward Robb Ellis.
The Eclipse of Biblical Narrative:
A Study in 18th- and 19th-Century
Hermeneutics. Hans W. Frei.
Ecology in Ancient Civilisations. J.
Donald Hughes.
Economic Analysis Before Adam
Smith. Barry Gordon.
Economic and Political Peace.
Shirley Telford.
An Economic Background to Munich.
Alice Teichova.
Economic Change in Precolonial
Africa. 2 vols. Philip D. Cur-
tin.
The Economic Development of Revo-
lutionary Cuba. Archibald R. M.
Ritter.
The Economic Development of the
Third World Since 1900. Paul
Bairoch.
An Economic History of Kenya and
Uganda, 1800-1970. R. M. A.
Van Zwanenberg.
An Economic History of Medieval
Europe. N. J. G. Pounds.
Economic History of the Jews. Salo
W. Baron, et al.
Economic Integration and Industrial
Location. F. I. Nixson.
Economic Integration: The East
African Experience. Arthur
Hazlewood.
Economic Maturity and Entrepre-
neurial Decline: British Iron
and Steel, 1870-1913. Donald
M. McCloskey.
The Economic Modernisation of
France, 1730-1880. Roger
Price.

Die Einnahmen der Apostolischen
Kammer unter Innozenz VI.
Hermann Hoberg, ed.

Der Eisen bahnban und das Wachstum der deutschen Eisen.
Horst Wagenblass.

Eisenhower: Portrait of the Hero.
Peter Lyon.

Das Eislebener und Garkupfer und
seine Bedeutung für den
europäischen Kupfel-Markt, 1460-
1560. Ekkehard Westerman.

Eleanor of Aquitaine. William W.
Kibler, ed.

Election Campaign: Anatomy of
Mass Influence. Prayag Mehta.

The Election of 1827 in France.
Sherman Kent.

Electoral Politics in the Indian
States. Myron Weiner and
John Osgood Field, eds.

The Electric Telegraph: A Social
and Economic History. J. L.
Kieve.

The Electronic War in the Middle
East, 1968-70. Edgar O'Ballance.

Elementa ad Fontium Editiones.
Vols. XXIX to XXXV. Carolina
Lanckoronska, ed.

Elementary Structures Reconsidered.
Francis Korn.

The Elephant in the Greek and
Roman World. H. H. Scullard.

Le elezioni del 1913 a Roma.
Hartmut Ullrich.

Der Elitekreislauf in der Unternehmerschaft. Wilhelm Stahl.

Elizabeth: A Study in Power and
Intellect. Paul Johnson.

Elizabeth Bowen. Edwin J. Kenney.

Elizabeth Tudor: Portrait of a
Queen. Lacey Baldwin Smith.

Elizabethan California. Robert F.
Heizer.

Elizabethan Prisons and Prison
Scenes. E. D. Pendry.

The Elusive Peace in the Middle
East. Malcolm H. Kerr, ed.

The Emancipation of Angelina
Grimké. Katharine Du Pre
Lumpkin.

Embassy at War. Harold Joyce
Noble.

The Embattled Mountain. F. W.
D. Deakin.

The Emergence of a UAW Local,
1936-1939: A Study in Class

and Culture. Peter Friedlander.

The Emergence of Agricultural Science. Margaret W. Rossiter.

The Emergence of Christian Science
in American Religious Life.
Stephen Gottschalk.

The Emergence of Probability. Ian
Hacking.

The Emergence of Spanish America.
Jaime E. Rodriguez.

The Emergence of the New French
Eastern European Alliance Policy,
1917-1919. Kalervo Hovi.

Emerson: Prophecy, Metamorphosis,
and Influences. David Levin.

Eminent Women of the West.
Elinor Richey.

Emma Lee. Juanita Brooks.

Un empereur de Byzance à Rome.
Vingt ans de travail pour l'uniôn
des églises et pour la défense de
l'empire d'Orient, 1355-1375.
Oskar Halecki.

The Emperor Frederick II of Hohen-
staufen. Thomas Curtis Van
Cleve.

The Emperor Julian. Robert Browning.

Empire and Liberty: American Resistance to British Authority,
1755-1763. Alan Rogers.

L'Empire du Monomotapa du XVe
au XIXe Siecle. W. G. L.
Randles.

Empire or Independence 1760-1776:
A British-American Dialogue on
the Coming of the American Revolution. Ian R. Christie and
Benjamin W. Labaree.

L'Empire romain et le christianisme.
Claude Lepelley.

Empires to Nations. Max Savelle.

Employment Growth and Basic Needs:
A One-World Problem. Director-
General, ILO.

Las empresas trasnacionales en
Mexico. Bernardo Sepúlveda
Amor, et al.

Encomenderos y estrancieros.
Mario Góngora.

Encomienda y mita en Nueva
Granada. Julian B. Ruíz Rivera.

Encounter with an Angry God.
Carobeth Laird.

Encyclopedia of American Agricultural History. Edward L. and
Frederick H. Schapsmeier.

Encyclopedia of American Biography.

Essai sur l'Architecture Musalmane. Vol. 3. Lucien Golvin.

Essays and Assays: California History Reappraised. George H.
Knoles, ed.

Essays in Anti-Labour History: Re-
sponses to the Rise of Labour in
Britain. Kenneth D. Brown, ed.

Essays in Honour of E. H. Carr.
C. Abramsky and Beryl J. Williams, eds.

Essays in Nineteenth-Century Economic History. David C. Klingaman, and Richard K. Vedder,
eds.

Essays in Population History:
Mexico and the Caribbean. Sher-
burne F. Cook and Woodrow
Borah.

Essays on American Foreign Policy. David C. DeBoe, Van
Mitchell Smith, Elliot West,
and Norman A. Graebner.

Essays on the American West,
1973-1974. Thomas G. Alexander.

Essays on the Armed Struggle of
the Siberian Soviets Against the
Counterrevolution, 1917-1918.
V. S. Poznanskii.

Essays on the Cultural Life of Siberia from the 17th to the Beginning of the 19th Century.
A. N. Kopylov.

Essays on the History of Schools
and Pedagogical Thought of the
Peoples of the USSR. M. F.
Shabaeva, ed.

Essays on the Political Economy of
Africa. G. Arrighi and J. S.
Saul.

Essays on the Reconstruction of
Medieval History. Vaclav Mudroch and G. S. Couse, eds.

Essays on the Semitic Background
of the New Testament. Joseph
A. Fitzmyer.

Essener Gespräche zum Thema
Staat und Kirche. Joseph Krautscheidt and Heiner Marre, eds.

Essential Kanji. P. G. O'Neill.

Essex and the Industrial Revolution.
J. Booker.

Estienne Pasquier. D. Thickett,
ed.

Estudio económica de América
Latina 1973. Comisión
Económica Para América Latina.

Les establissements asto à l'époque
préhispanique. Vol. I. Danielle
Lavallée and Michele Julien.

L'État et la mendicité dans la
première moitié du XVIIIe
siècle: Auvergne, Beaujolais,
Forea, Lyonnais. Jean-Pierre
Gutton.

Ethics in the New Testament. Jack
T. Sanders.

Ethiopia: Anatomy of a Traditional
Polity. John Markakis.

Ethiopia: Political Contradictions in
Agricultural Development.
Michael Stahl.

Ethnic Alienation: The Italian
Americans. Patrick J. Gallo.

Ethnic Americans: A History of Im-
migration and Assimilation.
Leonard Dinnerstein and David
M. Reimers.

Ethnic Groups in Ohio with Special
Emphasis on Cleveland. Lubomyr
R. Wynear.

Ethnic Processes in Russian America. Svetlana G. Fedorova.

Etruscan Dress. Larissa Bonfante.

Etruscan Red-Figured Vase-Painting
at Caere. Mario A. Del Chiaro.

Etudes sur les missionaires bretons
dans le Middle West Américain.
Tome I. Charles Lemarié.

Etudes sur l'histoire de la Pauvreté
(Moyen Age-XVIe siècle). Michel
Mollat, ed.

Eugen Brote (1850-1912). Lucian
Boia.

Eupolemius das Bibelgedicht. Karl
Manitius, ed.

Eupolemus: A Study of Judaeo-
Greek Literature. Ben Zion
Wacholder.

Europe: Hierarchy and Revolt 1320-
1450. George Holmes.

Europe in the Era of Social Transformation: 1700--Present. Vincent J. Knapp.

Europe, Scotland and the United
States from the 16th to the 20th
Century (Vol. II). Lawrence
Stone, ed.

European and Muscovite: Ivan
Kireyevsky and the Origins of
Slavophilism. Abbot Gleason.

The European Discovery of America:
The Northern Voyages, A. D.
500-1600. Samuel Eliot Morison.

The European Discovery of America:

The Southern Voyages, A. D. 1492-1616. Samuel Eliot Morison.

European Historical Statistics 1750-1970. B. R. Mitchell.

European Imperialism and the Partition of Africa. E. F. Penrose, ed.

European Peasants and Their Markets. William N. Parker and Eric L. Jones, eds.

Europe's Crucial Years: The Diplomatic Background of World War I, 1902-1914. Dwight E. Lee.

Europe's Inner Demons. Norman Cohn.

The Evangelicals: What They Believe, Who They Are, Where They Are Changing. David F. Wells and John D. Woodbridge, eds.

Evelyn Underhill (1875-1941): An Introduction to Her Life and Writings. Christopher J. R. Armstrong.

Every Need Supplied. Donald F. Durnbaugh, ed.

Everyone a Witness. A. F. Scott, ed.

Evil in the Morning of the World. John Stephen Lansing.

The Evolution of a Tidewater Settlement System. Carville V. Earle.

The Evolution of American Urban Society. Howard P. Chudacoff.

Evolution of International Management Structures. Harold F. Williamson, ed.

The Evolution of Law in the Barrios of Caracas. Kenneth L. Karst and Murray L. and Audrey J. Schwartz.

The Evolution of the Egyptian National Image: From Its Origins to Ahmad Luftī al-Sayyid. Charles Wendell.

Evolution of the House: An Introduction. Stephen Gardiner.

The Evolution of the Labour Party, 1910-1924. Ross McKibbin.

Evolutionary Studies in World Crops: Diversity and Change in the Indian Subcontinent. Joseph Hutchinson, ed.

The Example of Edward Taylor. Karl Keller.

Excavaciones en al Poblado de la Edad del Bronce "Cerro de la Encina" Monachil. A Arribas Palau, et al.

Excavations in Medieval Southampton, 1953-1969. 2 vols. Colin Platt, et. al.

The Exchange Economy of Pre-Colonial Tropical Africa. Lars Sundström.

The Excise Crisis: Society and Politics in the Age of Walpole. Paul Langford.

The Exploration of North America 1630-1776. W. P. Cumming, et al.

Exploring Historic California. Jack Adler.

The Exploring Spirit: America and the World, Then and Now. Daniel J. Boorstin.

The Expressmen. David Nevin.

Expropriation of U. S. Property in South America: Nationalization of Oil and Copper Companies in Peru, Bolivia, and Chile. George M. Ingram.

La Expulsión de los españoles de Mexico (1821-1828). Harold D. Sims.

Expulsion of a Minority. Michael Twaddle, ed.

Extermination of the Polish Intelligentsia in the Gdańsk-Pomerania Region (September-December 1939). Barbara Bojarska.

-F-

Failure of a Dream? John H. M. Laslett and Seymour Martin Lipset, eds.

The Failure of the NRA. Bernard Bellush.

A Fair and Happy Land. William A. Owens.

The Fairfax Family in Fairfax County: A Brief History. Kenton Kilmer and Donald Sweig.

Faith and Fratricide: The Theological Roots of Anti-Semitism. Rosemary Ruether.

Faith and the World of Politics. Johannes Metz, ed.

The Fall and Rise of Europe. Henry

M. Pachter.
The Fall of Imperial China. Frederic Wakeman, Jr.
The Fall of Saxon England. Richard Humble.
The Fall of the House of Borgia. E. R. Chamberlin.
The Fall of the House of Savoy. Robert Katz.
The Fall of the Roman Empire: A Reappraisal. Michael Grant.
The False Dawn: European Imperialism in the Nineteenth Century. Raymond F. Betts.
Familiar to All: William Lilly and Astrology in the Seventeenth Century. Derek Parker.
Familie et parenté en Acadie. Marc Abelard Tremblay and Marc Laplante.
Families and Communities. David J. Russo.
Families of Fengsheng. Ruth Sidel.
Family and Fortune. Lawrence Stone.
The Family in History. Charles E. Rosenberg.
Family, Lineage, and Civil Society: a Study of Society, Politics and Mentality in the Durham Region, 1500-1640. Mervyn James.
Famine in Russia, 1891-1892: The Imperial Government Responds to a Crisis. Richard G. Robbins, Jr.
The Far Country: A Regional History of Moab and La Sal, Utah. Faun McConkie Tanner.
Faraday as a Natural Philosopher. Joseph Agassi.
Farm and Nation in Modern Japan: Agrarian Nationalism, 1870-1940. Thomas R. H. Havens.
Farming in Prehistory. Barbara Bender.
Farming in the Midwest, 1840-1900: A Symposium. James W. Whitaker, ed.
Farmland, U.S.A. James H. and Harold Hamil.
Faschismus--Nationalsozialismus. Gerhard Schulz.
Fascism and Dictatorship. Nicos Poulantzas.
Fascism in Ferrara, 1915-1925. . Paul Corner.
The Fascist Ego. William R. Tucker.
The Fascist Persuasion in Radical Politics. A. James Gregor.
Fat Mutton and Liberty of Conscience: Society in Rhode Island, 1636-1690. Carl Bridenbaugh.
The Fatal History of Portuguese Ceylon. George Davison Winius.
The Fate of a Nation: The American Revolution Through Contemporary Eyes. William P. Cumming and Hugh F. Rankin.
Father Coughlin. Sheldon Marcus.
Father José Burgos. John N. Schumacher.
Fatherland or Promised Land. Jehuda Reinharz.
Feather Fashions and Bird Preservation: A Study in Nature Protection. Robin W. Doughty.
The Federal Machine: Beginnings of Bureaucracy in Jacksonian America. Matthew A. Crenson.
Feedlot Empire. James W. Whitaker.
Female and Male in Latin America. Ann Pescatello.
Female of the Species. M. Kay Martin and Barbara Voorhies.
The Female Population of France. Etienne Van de Walle.
Fenianism in North America. W. S. Neidhardt.
Ferdinand and Isabella. Felipe Fernández-Armesto.
Fermin Francisco de Lasuén (1736-1803): A Biography. Francis F. Guest.
Ferryboats on the Columbia River. Robert H. Ruby and John A. Brown.
Festivals in Classical China: New Year and Other Annual Observances During the Han Dynasty 206 B.C.-A.D. 220. Derk Bodde.
The Feudal Nobility and the Kingdom of Jerusalem, 1174-1277. Jonathan Riley-Smith.
Feudal Society in the Bailliage of Troyes Under the Counts of Champagne, 1152-1284. Theodore Evergates.
Feudalism, Capitalism and Beyond. Eugene Camenka and R. S. Neale, eds.
Die Feudalmonarchien. Hans Kammler.
Die Fibeln in Süddeutschland, Österreich und der Schweiz I. Paul Betzler.

Seventeenth Centuries. Carlo
M. Cipolla, ed.
Fonti e Documenti I. Centro Studi
per la Storia del Modernismo.
The Foochow Missionaries, 1847-
1880. Ellsworth C. Carlson.
Food on the Frontier. Marjorie
Kreidberg.
Footsteps into the Future. Rajni
Kothari.
For Friends at Home. Richard
Arthur Preston, ed.
For God and Country. Victor
Greene.
For God's Sake, Go! An Auto-
biography. Sir George Catlin.
For the Family's Sake. Olive
Parker.
The Forbidden Game: A Social
History of Drugs. Brian Inglis.
A Ford, Not a Lincoln. Richard
Reeves.
Foreign Policy and Federalism (The
Nigerian Experience). A. B.
Akinyemi.
Foreign Policy and Interdependence
in Gaullist France. Edward L.
Morse.
Foreign Policy and U. S. Presidential
Elections. 2 vols. Robert A.
Divine.
The Foreign Policy of France
From 1914 to 1945. J. Néré.
The Foreign Policy of the Third
Reich. Klaus Hildebrand.
Foreign Relations of the United
States, 1947. Vol. I, General:
The United Nations. United
States Department of State.
Foreign Relations of the United
States; 1947, Vol. VII, The
American Republics. United
States Department of State.
Foreign Relations of the United
States, 1948. Vol. I, Part 1.
General; The United Nations.
United States Department of
State.
Foreign Relations of the United
States, 1948. Vol. IV. United
States Department of State.
Foreign Relations of the United
States, 1948. Vol. VI. United
States Department of State.
Foreign Relations of the United
States; 1948, no. VI and 1949,
no. IX. United States Depart-
ment of State.

Foreign Relations of the United
States, 1949. Vol. I: General,
The United Nationa, Part 1: 1949;
Vol. II: The United Nations: The
Western Hemisphere, 1949; Vol.
IV: Western Europe. United
States Department of State.
Foreign Relations of the United
States, 1949. Vol. II, The
United Nations: The Western
Hemisphere. United States De-
partment of State.
Foreign Relations of the United
States: 1949. Vol. III, Council
of Foreign Ministers: Germany
and Austria. United States De-
partment of State.
Foreign Students: The Indian Ex-
perience. H. C. Ganguly.
The Forest Killers. Jack Shepherd.
The Forest Service. Glen O. Robin-
son.
Forgotten Canadians: The Blacks of
Nova Scotia. Frances Henry.
The Forgotten People. Harry
Forrest Lupold.
The Forgotten Sioux. Ernest L.
Schusky.
Forked Tongues and Broken Treaties.
Donald E. Worcester, ed.
La formación del estado populista
en América Latina. Octávio
Ianni.
La formación del poder politico en
México. Arnaldo Córdova.
Formaciones economicas y politicos
del mundo andino. John V. Mur-
ra.
La formation du canton de Genève,
1814-1816. Paul Waeber.
The Formation of a Modern Labor
Force: Upper Silesia, 1865-1914.
Lawrence Schofer.
The Formation of National States in
Western Europe. Charles Tilly,
ed.
The Formation of the American
Scientific Community. Sally
Gregory Kohlstedt.
Fort Bridger: Island in the Wilder-
ness. Fred R. Gowans and
Eugene E. Campbell.
Fort Jesus: A Portuguese Fortress
on the East African Coast. James
Kirkman.
Fort Laurens, 1778-79. Thomas I.
Pieper and James B. Gidney.
Fort Meigs and the War of 1812:

Orderly Book of Cushing's Company, 2nd U.S. Artillery, April, 1813-February, 1814 and Personal Diary of Daniel Cushing, October, 1812-July, 1813. Harlow Lindley, ed.

Fort Michilimackinac 1715-1781. Lyle M. Stone.

Fort William--India House Correspondence. Raghubir Sinh, ed.

Der Fortschrittsklub im Abgeordnetenhaus des Österreichischen Reichsrats. Diethild Harrington-Müller.

Les Fortunes Françaises au XIXe Siècle. Adeline Daumard.

The Forty-Niners. William Weber Johnson.

Forum for Protest: The Black Press During World War II. Lee Finkle.

Fouilles de Xanthos V: Tombes-Maisons, Tombes Rupestres et Sarcophages. Pierre Demargne.

The Foundation Directory. Marianna O. Lewis, ed.

Foundations of Indo-Soviet Relations. Nirmala Joshi.

Four Centuries of Southern Indians. Charles M. Hudson, ed.

The Four Churches of Pecos. Alden C. Hayes.

Four-Masted Schooners of the East Coast. Paul C. Morris.

The Fourteenth and Fifteenth Centuries. Vol. III. H. W. Hazard, ed.

The Fourth Dimension of Warfare. Vol. II. Revolt to Revolution: Studies in the 19th- and 20th-Century European Experience. Michael Elliott-Bateman, et al.

El fracaso de la revolución industrial en España, 1814-1913. Jordi Nadal.

The Framework of Anglo-Saxon History to A.D. 900. Kenneth Harrison.

France and Belgium 1939-1940 (The Politics and Strategy of the Second World War). Brian Bond.

France and North America: Over Three Hundred Years of Dialogue. Mathé Allain and Glenn R. Conrad, ed.

France and the Chesapeake. Jacob M. Price.

France 1848-1945. Theodore Zeldin.

France in the Age of Louis XIII and Richelieu. Victor-Lucien Tapie.

France Under the Directory. Martyn Lyon.

Frances Warde: American Founder of the Sisters of Mercy. Kathleen Healy.

Francis Bacon: Discovery and the Art of Discourse. Lisa Jardine.

Francis Galton: The Life and Work of a Victorian Genius. D. W. Forrest.

Francis Marion: The Swamp Fox. Hugh F. Rankin.

Francis of Assisi. John Holland Smith.

Francis Place and the Early History of the Greenwich Observatory. Derek Howse.

The Franciscan Concept of Mission in the High Middle Ages. E. Randolph Daniel.

Franciscan Studies. Vol. 33. Franciscan Institute.

Francisco Bilbao. Alberto J. Varona.

François Hotman: A Revolutionary's Ordeal. Donald R. Kelley.

Francois X. Aubry: Trader, Trailmaker and Voyageur in the Southwest, 1846-1854. Donald Chaput.

Frank Murphy: The Detroit Years. Sidney Fine.

Franklin. David Freeman Hawke.

Franklin D. Roosevelt: The Contribution of the New Deal to American Political Thought and Practice. Morton J. Frisch.

Frédéric Romanet du Caillaud, "Comte" de Sudbury (1847-1919). Lorenzo Cadieux.

Frederick Jackson Turner. James D. Bennett.

Frederick the Great: Absolutism and Administration. Walther Hubatsch.

Frederick the Great and His Officials. Hubert C. Johnson.

Free and Independent: The Initiation of a College Professor into State Politics--Candid Look at How Our Laws Begin. Frank Smallwood.

Free Booters Must Die! The Life and Death of William Walker, the Most Notorious Soldier of Fortune of the Nineteenth Century. Fred-

erick Rosengarten, Jr.
Freedom and Development. Julius
K. Nyerere.
Freedom and Order: Collected
Essays. Eugene Forsey.
The French Achievement: Private
School Aid, A Lesson for Amer-
ica. Robert M. Healey.
The French Against the French:
Collaboration and Resistance.
Milton Dank.
The French Colonel. Roy Macnab.
The French Colonial Myth and Con-
stitution-Making in the Fourth
Republic. D. Bruce Marshall.
French Economic Growth. J.-J.
Carré, P. Dubois, and E. Malin-
vaud.
The French Foreign Legion. John
Laffin.
French International Policy Under
De Gaulle and Pompidou. Ed-
ward A. Kolodziej.
French Legislators, 1800-1834:
A Study in Quantitative History.
Thomas D. Beck.
French Legitimists and the Politics
of Moral Order in the Early
Third Republic. Robert R.
Locke.
The French Navy and American
Independence. Jonathan R. Dull.
The French Revolution. Norman
Hampson.
The Freud/Jung Letters. William
McQuire, ed.
Friar Thomas d'Aquino. James A.
Weisheipl.
Friedensinitiativen und Machtpolitik
im zweiten Weltkrieg 1939-1942.
Bernd Martin.
Friedrich Fabri und der Imperialis-
mus in der Bismarckzeit: Rev-
olution--Depression--Expansion.
Klaus J. Bade.
From Adam Smith to Maynard
Keynes: The Heritage of Po-
litical Economy. V. W. Bladen.
From Africa to the United States
and Then ... a Concise Afro-
American History. Kenneth G.
Goode.
From Basserman to Bebel. Bever-
ly Heckart.
From Blowing Rock to Georgetown.
J. K. Rouse.
From Border to Middle Shire. S.
J. Watts.

From Byzantium to Sasanian Iran
and the Islamic World. Richard
Ettinghausen.
From Colony to Country: 1759-1820.
Ralph Ketcham.
From Colony to Nation. A. J. R.
Russell-Wood, ed.
From Community to Metropolis: A
Biography of São Paulo, Brazil.
Richard M. Morse, ed.
From Croesus to Constantine: The
Cities of Western Asia Minor and
Their Arts in Greek and Roman
Times. George M. A. Hanfmann.
From Encroachment to Involvement.
Yaacov Ro'i.
From Enlightenment to Revolution.
Eric Voegelin.
From Glory to Oblivion: The Real
Truth About the Mexican Revolu-
tion. Guy Weddington McCreary.
From Know-How to Nowhere. Elting
E. Morison.
From Medical Police to Social Medi-
cine. George Rosen.
From Paris to Sevres: The Parti-
tion of the Ottoman Empire at the
Peace Conference of 1919-1920.
Paul C. Helmreich.
From Poor Law to Welfare State.
Walter I. Trattner.
From Radicalism to Socialism: Men
and Ideas in the Formation of
Fabian Socialist Doctrines, 1881-
1889. Willard Wolfe.
From Revolution to Rapprochement:
The United States and Great
Britain, 1783-1900. Charles S.
Campbell.
From Sambo to Superspade: The
Black Experience in Motion Pic-
tures. Daniel J. Leab.
From Slave to Priest. Caroline
Hemesath.
From Symbolism to Structuralism:
Levi Strauss in a Literary Tradi-
tion. James A. Boon.
From the Dardanelles to Oran.
Arthur J. Marder.
From the Diaries of Felix Frank-
furter. Joseph P. Lash.
From the Old Diplomacy to the New,
1865-1900. Robert L. Beisner.
From the Volga to the Baltic.
A. M. Samsanov.
From the Wings. Alec Kirkbride.
From Tiberius to the Antonines: A
History of the Roman Empire,

AD 14-192. Albino Garzetti.
Frontier Historian: The Life and
Work of Edward Everett Dale.
Arrell M. Gibson, ed.
The Frontier in Alaska and the
Matanuska Colony. Orlando W.
Miller.
Frontier Kentucky. Otis K. Rice.
Frontier Regulars. Robert M.
Utley.
Fruits of the Shaker Tree of Life:
Memoirs of Fifty Years of
Collecting and Research. Ed-
ward D. and Faith Andrews.
Führer durch die Antikenabteilung
des Martin von Wagner Museums
der Universität Würzburg. Erika
Simon, ed.
The Funnel of Gold. Mendel Peter-
son.
Furia y Muerte: Los Bandidos
Chicanos. Pedro Castillo and
Albert Camarillo, eds.
Furman University. Alfred Sand-
lin Reid.
The Future of Democracy in Latin
America. Frank Tannenbaum.
The Future of Inter-Bloc Relations
in Europe. Louis Mensonides and
James A. Kuhlman, eds.
The Future of the China Market.
Edward Neilan and Charles R.
Smith.

-G-

G. D. H. Cole. L. P. Carpenter.
The G.I. Bill, the Veterans, and
the Colleges. Keith W. Olson.
The G.I.'s: The Americans in
Britain 1942-1945. Norman
Longmate.
G. K. Chesterton. Dudley Barker.
Gambetta and the Making of the
Third Republic. J. P. T. Bury.
A Gardener Touched with Genius:
The Life of Luther Burbank.
Peter Dreyer.
Garibaldi. Jasper Ridley.
Garnier's Becket. Janet Shirley,
trans.
Gascon Register A. 2 vols. G.
P. Cuttino.
Gathering of Animals, an Uncon-
ventional History of the New

York Zoological Society. William
Bridges.
Gaúcho Politics in Brazil: The
Politics of Rio Grande do Sul,
1930-1964. Carlos E. Cortés.
Gedichte und Lieder deutscher
Jakobiner. Hans Werner Engels.
Gefässmarken von Bogazköy, Bogaz-
köy Hattusa, Ergebnisse der Aus-
grabungen des Deutschen Archä-
ologischen Instituts und der
Deutschen Orient--Gesellschaft.
Ursala Seidl.
Der Geheimbund der Illuminaten.
Richard van Dulmen.
Gehlen: Spy of the Century. E. H.
Cookridge.
Gemeinwohlformeln im national-
sozialistischen Recht. Michael
Stolleis.
General Horatio Gates: A Biography.
Paul David Nelson.
General Maurice Sarrail 1856-1929.
Jan Karl Tanenbaum.
General Oglethorpe's Georgia:
Colonial Letters, 1733-1743.
Mills Lane, ed.
The General: Robert L. Bullard and
Officership in the United States
Army, 1881-1925. Allan R. Mil-
lett.
General Sidney Sherman: Texas
Soldier, Statesman, and Builder.
W. N. Bate.
General Stephen D. Lee. Herman
Hattaway.
A General Systems Philosophy for
the Social and Behaviorial Sci-
ences. John Sutherland.
Generale Missiven van Gouverneurs-
General en Raden aan Heren XVII
der Verenigde Oostindische Com-
pagnie, v, 1686-1697. W. Ph.
Coolhaas, ed.
Genesis of Pakistan. V. V. Na-
garkan.
Genocide? Birth Control and the
Black American. Robert G.
Weisbord.
Gentilz: Artist of the Old South-
west. Dorothy Steinbomer
Kendall and Carmen Perry.
Gentleman Boss: The Life of
Chester Alan Arthur. Thomas
C. Reeves.
Gentlemen of Large Property &
Judicious Men: The Kennebeck
Proprietors, 1749-1775. Gordon

E. Kershaw.

Geoffrey of Auxerre: Expositio in Cantica Canticorum. 2 vols. Gerruccio Gasteldelli, ed.

Geographic and Hydrographic Descriptions of Many Northern and Southern Lands and Seas in the Indies. Nicolás de Cardona.

The Geographic Regions of Vermont. Harold A. Meeks.

Géographie de la Fortune et Structures Sociales à Lyon au XIXe Siècle. Pierre Léon.

George Bancroft. Robert H. Canary.

George Canning. Wendy Hinde.

George Catlin: Letters and Notes on the North American Indian. Michael M. Mooney, ed.

George Jacob Holyoake: A Study in the Evolution of a Victorian Radical. Lee E. Grugel.

George Joachim Goschen. Thomas J. Spinner, Jr.

George Mason: Gentleman Revolutionary. Helen Hill Miller.

George Owen of Henllys: A Welsh Elizabethan. B. G. Charles.

George Williams and the YMCA: A Study in Victorian Social Attitudes. Clyde Binfield.

George Wythe of Williamsburg. Joyce Blackburn.

Georgi Vins: Testament from Prison. Michael Bourdeaux, ed.

Georgia and the Revolution. Ronald G. Killion and Charles T. Waller.

A Georgian at Princeton. Robert Manson Myers.

The German Church Struggle and the Holocaust. Franklin H. Littell and Hubert G. Locke, eds.

German Colonists and Their Descendants in Houstin, Including Usener and Allied Families. Dorothy E. Justman.

The German Enlightenment and Rise of Historicism. Peter Hanns Reill.

German Foreign Policies, West and East. Peter H. Merkle.

The German Historians and England. Charles E. McClelland.

The German Nation and Martin Luther. A. G. Dickens.

The German Naval Officer Corps:

A Social and Political History, 1890-1918. Holger H. Herwig.

The German Occupation of the Channel Islands. Charles Chruckshank.

German Politics Under Soviet Occupation. Henry Krisch.

The German Tradition of Self-Cultivation. W. H. Bruford.

Germania Sacra, neue Folge 8. Hans Goetting, ed.

The Germanic People in America. Victor Wolfgang von Hagen.

The Germans. Erich Kahler.

The Germans in Chile. George F. W. Young.

The Germans in Texas: A Study in Immigration. Gilbert Giddings Benjamin.

Die Gesandten der europäischen Mächte, vornehmlich des Kaisers und des Reiches, 1490-1500. Walter Höflechner.

Geschichte der Hethiter. Friedrich Cornelius.

Geschichte der Perser und Araber zur Zeit der Sasaniden. Th. Nöldeke.

Geschichte der Sozialpolitik in Deutschland: Eine Analyse ihrer Bedingungen, Formen, zeilsetzungen und Auswirkungen. Albin Gladen.

Die Geschichte der unternehmerischen Selbstverwaltung in Köln 1797-1914. Hermann Kellenbenz and Klara van Eyll.

Geschichte oder Gegenwart: Reflexionen über das Verhältnis von zeit und Geist. Heinz Angermeier.

Geschichtsschreibung zwischen Alteuropa und moderner Welt: Jacob Burckhardt in seiner Zeit. Wolfgang Hardtwig.

Gesellschaft, Parlament und Regierung: zur Geschichte des Parlamentarismus in Deutschland. Gerhard A. Ritter, ed.

Gesellschaftsstruktur und politisches Bewusstsein in einer katholischen Region, 1928-1933. Günter Plum.

Gesta Henrici Quinti: The Deeds of Henry the Fifth. Frank Taylor and John S. Roskell, eds. and trans.

Getting Around Vermont: A Study of Twenty Years. Benjamin L. Huffman.

and Now. Eugene Hollon.
The Great American Nude: A
History in Art. William H.
Gerdts.
Great Britain and the Caribbean,
1901-1913. Warren G. Kneer.
The Great Chiefs. Benjamin Capps.
A Great Expectation: Eschatological
Thought in English Protestantism
to 1660. Bryan W. Ball.
The Great Instauration. Charles
Webster.
The Great March of Liberation.
I. S. Konev.
Great Plains Command: William
B. Hazen in the Frontier West.
Marvin E. Kroeker.
The Great Reform Act. Michael
Brock.
The Great Rumanian Peasant Re-
volt of 1907: Origins of a
Modern Jacquerie. Philip G.
Eidelberg.
The Great Southwest. Elliot S.
Baker.
Great Times: An Informal Social
History of the United States,
1914-1929. J. C. Furnas.
The Great United States Exploring
Expedition of 1838-1842. Wil-
liam Stanton.
The Great Victorian Boom, 1850-
1873. R. A. Church.
Greater Ethiopia. Donald W. Le-
vine.
Greece and the Eastern Crisis,
1875-1878. Evangelos Kofos.
The Greek Accounts of Eastern
History. Robert Drews.
The Greek Experience: Imperial-
ism and Social Conflict, 800-400
B.C. R. J. Littman.
The Greek Nation, 1453-1669.
Apostolos E. Vacalopoulos.
The Green Flag: A History of
Irish Nationalism. Robert Kee.
The Green Revolution in India.
Bandhudas Sen.
Gregorio di Elvira, La Fede.
Manlio Simonetti, ed.
Griechenland zwischen Revolution
und Kounterrevolution (1936-
1946). Heinz Richter.
Griechische Mythen auf Römischen
Sarkophagen. Hellmut Sichter-
mann and Guntram Koch.
Growing Metropolis: Aspects of
Development in Nashville.

James F. Blumstein and Benjamin
Walter, eds.
Growing Up Female: A Personal
Photojournal. Abigail Heyman.
Growing Up in America. Fred M.
and Grace Hechinger.
The Growth of Education and Political
Development in India, 1898-1920.
Aparna Basu.
Growth of Nationalism in India. 2
vols. Sukhbir Choudhary.
The Growth of Presidential Power:
A Documented History. 3 vols.
William M. Goldsmith.
Growth of the American Revolution,
1766-1775. Bernhard Knollenberg.
Growth of the Modern American
Economy. Stuart Bruchey.
Guerilla Struggle in Africa: An
Analysis and Preview. Kenneth
W. Grundy.
La guerra aerea in Africa Setten-
trionale: Assalto dal cielo 1940-
41; 1942-43. Alberto Borgiotti
and Cesare Gori.
La guerra del 47 y la opinión pública,
1845-1848. Jesús Velasco Már-
quez.
La guerre en Mediterranée 1939-
1945: Actes du Colloque Interna-
tional tenu à Paris du 8 au 11
avril 1969. Comité d'Histoire de
la Deuxième Guerre Mondiale.
Les Guerres d'Amosis fondateur de
la XVIIIe Dynastie. Claude Van-
dersleyen.
Guida delle Fonti per la Storia
dell'Africa a Sud del Sahara
esistenti in Italia. Vol. II.
Carlo Giglio and Elio Lodolini,
eds.
A Guide to America's Indians.
Arnold Marquis.
A Guide to Ancient Maya Ruins. C.
Bruce Hunter.
Guide to Archives in the Connecticut
State Library. Robert Claus,
comp.
Guide to Manuscripts Collections
and Institutional Records in Ohio.
David R. Larson, et al., eds.
Guide to Shaker Manuscripts. Ker-
mit J. Pike.
A Guide to the Archives of Labor
History and Urban Affairs.
Warner W. Pflug, ed.
Guide to the Manuscript Holdings of
the Immigrant Archives. Center

for Immigration Studies.
A Guide to the Missouri State
Archives. Secretary of State
of Missouri.
Guide to the Orin G. Libby
Manuscript Collection at the
University of North Dakota.
John B. Davenport, comp.
Guided Change in an African Com-
munity: Bushi in the Colonial
Period. P. Beghin.
Guides to Materials for African
History in European Archives.
Noel Matthews.
Guillaume Budé and Humanism in
the Reign of Francis I. David
O. McNeil.
The Gulag Archipelago, vol. II.
Alesander I. Solzhenitsyn.
The Gun in America. Lee Kennett
and James La Verne Anderson.
Gunboat Diplomacy: Great Power
Pressure in Venezuela, 1895-
1905. Miriam Hood.
Gunboat Diplomacy in the Wilson
Era: The U.S. Navy in Haiti,
1915-1916. David Healy.
The Gunfighters. Paul Trachtman.
Gunpowder and Galleys: Changing
Technology and Mediterranean
Warfare at Sea in the Sixteenth
Century. J. F. Guilmartin, Jr.
The Gunsmith in Colonial Virginia.
Harold B. Gill, Jr.
Gupta Sculpture. James Harle.

-H-

Habitants et marchands de Montreal
au XVIIe siècle. Louise Dechêne.
The Habsburg-Valois Wars and the
French War of Religion. Blaise
de Monluc.
Haciendas, latifundios, y planta-
ciones en América Latina.
Enrique Florescano, ed.
The Hakluyt Handbook. D. B.
Quinn, ed.
The Hamadsha: A Study in Moroc-
can Ethnopsychiatry. Vincent
Crapanzano.
Hampstead. F. M. L. Thompson.
Han Social Structure. T'ung Tsu
Ch'ü.
Handbook of Latin American Studies.

Donald E. J. Stewart, ed.
Handbook of Middle American In-
dians: Guide to Ethnohistorical
Sources. Vols. 12-15. Robert
Wauchope, et al., eds.
Handbuch der Kirchengeschichte.
Band VI. Hubert Jedin, ed.
Hans Christian Andersen. Elias
Bredsdorff.
Hans P. Kraus Collection of His-
panis American Manuscripts, A
Guide. J. Benedict Warren.
Har Dayal: Hindu Revolutionary
and Rationalist. Emily C. Brown.
The Hard Rock Men. John Rowe.
Hard Trails on My Way. John
Anthony Scott.
The Hardrock Miners. Richard E.
Lingenfelter.
The Harrowing of Eden. J. E.
Chamberlin.
Harry Hopkins and the New Deal.
Paul A. Kurzman.
A Harsh and Dreadful Love. Wil-
liam D. Miller.
Harvard College Records. Robert
W. Lovett, ed.
Harvard Guide to American History.
2 vols. Frank Freidel, ed.
Haskell of Gettysburg: His Life
and Civil War Papers. Frank
L. Byrne and Andrew T. Weaver,
eds.
Havasupai Baskets and Their Makers:
1930-1940. Barbara and Edwin
McKee and Joyce Herold.
Hawaii Under Army Rule: The Real
Story of Three Years of Martial
Law in a Loyal American Terri-
tory. J. Garner Anthony.
Hawker of Morwenstow: Portrait of
a Victorian Eccentric. Piers
Brendon.
Hazard, the Painter. William Mere-
dith.
Hazor. Yigael Yadin.
The Healing Hand: Man and Wound
in the Ancient World. Guido
Majno.
Health, Conflict and the Chinese Po-
litical System. David M. Lamp-
ton.
Heart Mountain. Douglas W. Nelson.
The Heavens Are Opened. Eber-
hard and Emmy and Heini Arnold.
Hebrew Union College-Jewish Insti-
tute of Religion at One Hundred
Years. Samuel E. Karff, ed.

Hegel on Reason and History.
George Dennis O'Brien.
Heinrich Bullinger, 1504-1575:
Gesammelte Aufsätz zum 400.
Todestag. Ulrich Gäbler and
Erland Herkenrath, eds.
Hell and the Victorians. Geoffrey
Rowell.
Hell or Connaught! The Cromwel-
lian Colonisation of Ireland, 1652-
1660. Peter Berresford Ellis.
The Hellenistic Kingdoms: Portrait
Coins and History. Norman Davis
and Colin M. Kraay.
Helvetia Sacra. A. Bruckner and
Brigitte Degler-Spangler, eds.
Henri Pirenne. Bryce Lyon.
Henrik Ibsen, 1828-1888: A Critical
Biography. Henrik Jaeger.
Henry Adams. James G. Murray.
Henry B. Fuller of Chicago: The
Ordeal of a Genteel Realist in
Ungenteel America. Bernard R.
Bowron, Jr.
Henry Burney: A Political Biography.
D. G. E. Hall.
Henry James: The Drama of Ful-
fillment. An Approach to the
Novels. Kenneth Graham.
Henry Sylvester Williams: Imperial
Pan-Africanist. J. R. Hooker.
Henry II. W. L. Warren.
Henry III and the Jesuit Politicians.
A. Lynn Martin.
Herbert H. Lehman and New York's
Little New Deal. Robert P. In-
galls.
Herbert Hoover and Famine Relief
to Soviet Russia, 1921-1923.
Benjamin W. Weissman.
Herbert Hoover and the Crisis of
American Capitalism. J. Joseph
Huthmacher and Warren I. Sus-
man, eds.
Herbert Hoover: Forgotten Progres-
sive. Joan Hoff Wilson.
Herbert Hoover: President of the
United States. Edgar Eugene
Robinson and Vaughn David Bornet.
Herbert Marcuse: From Marx to
Freud and Beyond. Sidney
Lipshires.
Heresy, Crusade and Inquisition in
Southern France, 1100-1250.
Walter L. Wakefield.
The Heritage of Dubuque. Law-
rence J. Sommer.
Heritage of Excellence: The John

Hopkins Medical Institutions,
1914-1947. Thomas B. Turner.
Herlufsholm Frie Skoles Regnskab
1585-86. Merete Dahlerup, ed.
Hermann Rauschnings "Gesprache
mit Hitler" als Geschichtsquelle.
Theodor Schieder.
The Hermeneutics of Peter Riede-
man (1506-1556). Robert Charles
Holand.
The Hesse/Mann Letters. Anni
Carlsson and Wolker Michels, eds.
Hidden from History: Rediscovering
Women in History from the 17th
Century to the Present. Sheila
Rowbotham.
The Hidden History of the Sino-
Indian Frontier. Karunakar Gupta.
Hilary Abner Herbert: A Southerner
Returns to the Union. Hugh B.
Hammett.
Hills of Home: The Rural Ozarks
of Arkansas. Bob Minick.
Hippolyte Fortoul, 1851-1856: Un
ministre de l'instruction publique
sous l'Empire autoritaire. Paul
Raphael and Maurice Gontard.
Hired Hands and Plowboys. David
E. Schob.
His Own Man: Essays in Honour of
Arthur Reginald Marsden Lower.
W. H. Heick and Roger Graham,
eds.
Histoire de la chartreuse de Val-
Royal à Gand et de la chartreuse
du Bois-Saint-Martin à Lierde-
Saint-Martin. Jan de Grauwe.
Histoire de la Louisiane française,
Vol. IV. Marcel Giraud.
Histoire de l'Ile de Grenade en
Amérique, 1649-1659. Jacques
Petitjean Roget, ed.
Histoire de l'impôt. Book 2.
Gabriel Ardant.
Histoire des Croquants: Etude des
soulèvements populaires au XVIIe
siècle dans le sud-ouest de la
France. 2 vols. Yves-Marie
Bercé.
Histoire des emprunts de la ville de
Paris (1814-1875). Genevieve
Massa-Gille.
L'Histoire des rois d'Imerina: In-
terpretation d'une tradition orale.
A. Delivré.
Histoire des Usines Renault. Vol. I.
Patrick Fridensen.
Histoire et psychoanalyse: Essai sur

les possibilités et les limites de
la psychohistoire. Saul Fried-
länder.
Histoire generale de la presse
française. Vol. 4. Claude Bel-
langer, et al.
Histoire générale du Socialisme.
Vol. 2. Jacques Droz, ed.
Histoire memorable de la guerre
faite par le Duc de Savoye,
Emanuel Philebert, contre ses
subjectz des Vallées d'Angrogne,
Perosse, S. Martin, et autres
Vallées circonvoisines, pour
compte de la Religion. Enea
Balmas and Vittorio Diena, eds.
Historia colonial de Santo Domingo.
Frank Moya Pons.
Historia de la Iglesia en America
Latina. Enrique Dussell.
Historia de la Isla de Cuba. Car-
los Márquez and Manuel Mar-
quez Sterling.
Historia del capitalismo en Mexico,
Los Origenes, 1521/1763. En-
rique Semo.
Historia económica y social de
Venezuela: Una estructura para
su estudio. Federico Brito
Figueroa.
História geral de civilização
brasileira. Tomo II. Sérgio
Buarque de Holanda.
The Historian and Film. Paul
Smith, ed.
Historians in the Middle Ages.
Beryl Smalley.
Historic Pottery of the Pueblo
Indians, 1600-1880. Larry
Frank and Francis B. Harlow.
Historical Atlas of California.
Warren A. Beck and Ynez D.
Haase.
A Historical Atlas of Texas.
William C. Pool.
Historical Dictionary of Cameroon.
Victor T. Levine and Roger P.
Nye.
Historical Dictionary of Uruguay.
Jean L. Willis.
The Historical Essays of Otto
Hintze. Otto Hintze.
Historical Knowing. Leon J.
Goldstein.
Historical Perspectives. Neil
McKendrick, ed.
Historical Sketch of the Cherokee.
James Mooney.

Historical Sketches of Colonial
Florida. Richard L. Campbell.
Historical Spectrum of Value The-
ories. Vol. 2. W. H. Werk-
meister.
Historical Studies. Vol. IX. John
G. Barry, ed.
Historical Studies in the Physical
Sciences. Vol. 5. Russell
McCormmach, ed.
The Historical Study of African Re-
ligion. T. O. Ranger and I. N.
Kimambo, eds.
Historical Thought in America: Post-
war Patterns. Timothy Paul
Donovan.
Historical Writing in England c. 550-
1307. Antonia Gransden.
The History and Antiquities of the
City of St. Augustine, Florida.
George R. Fairbanks.
History and Revolution in China.
Owen Lattimore.
History and the Theology of Libera-
tion: A Latin American Per-
spective. Enrique Dussell.
The History of Anti-Semitism. 3
vols. Léon Poliakov.
A History of Baton Rouge, 1699-
1812. Rose Meyers.
History of Black Americans: From
Africa to the Emergence of the
Cotton Kingdom. Philip S. Foner.
The History of Braintree, Vermont.
Volume II, 1883-1975. Katharine
F. DuClos.
The History of British India. James
Mill.
A History of British Pewter. John
Hatcher and T. C. Barker.
The History of British Steel. John
Vaizey.
A History of Christian Thought. Vol.
3. Justo L. González.
A History of Contract at Common
Law. S. J. Stoljar.
History of Darbhanga Raj. Jata
Shankar Jha.
A History of Early Renaissance Italy:
From the Mid-Thirteenth to the
Mid-Fifteenth Century. Brian
Pullan.
A History of Economic Theory and
Method. Robert B. Ekelund, Jr.
and Robert F. Hebert.
A History of Education in McDowell
County, West Virginia, 1858-1876.
Joseph Friedl.

A History of Finland. Ein Jutik-
kala and Kauko Pirinen.
A History of French Louisiana.
Volume I. The Reign of Louis
XIV, 1698-1715. Marcel Giraud.
A History of Gold and Money,
1450-1920. Pierre Vilar.
A History of Greek Art. Vols. 1
and 2. Martin Robertson.
History of Guildhall, Vermont.
Patricia Rogers, ed.
A History of Hungary. Ervin Pam-
lényi, ed.
The History of Ideas. Vol. 1.
Jeremy L. Tobey.
A History of Islamic Study. Aziz
Ahmad.
A History of Israel. John Bright.
The History of Jews in Utah and
Idaho. Juanita Brooks.
A History of Madison County, and
Incidentally of North Alabama.
Thomas Jones Taylor.
History of Medieval Deccan, 1295-
1724. Vol. II. H. K. Sher-
wani and P. M. Joshi, eds.
A History of Medieval Spain.
Joseph F. O'Callaghan.
History of Modern China. R. S.
Gupta.
A History of Modern Norway,
1814-1972. T. K. Derry.
A History of Oxford University.
V. H. H. Green.
The History of Painting in Canada.
Barry Lord.
A History of Public Health in New
York City, 1866-1966. John
Duffy.
A History of Russia: Medieval,
Modern, Contemporary. Paul
Dukes.
History of Samarkand. 2 vols.
I. M. Muminov, et al.
A History of Scandinavian Archae-
ology. Ole Klindt-Jensen.
A History of South Africa. Gideon
S. Were.
A History of South and Central
Africa. Derek Wilson.
History of South Dakota. Herbert
S. Schell.
A History of the Army Medical
Department. 2 vols. Sir
Neil Cantlie.
History of the Art of War within
the Framework of Political
History. Vol. 1. Hans Delbrück.

History of the Atchison, Topeka and
Santa Fe Railway. Keith L.
Bryant, Jr.
A History of the Bemba: Political
Growth and Change in North-
Eastern Zambia Before 1900.
Andrew D. Roberts.
A History of the British Cavalry,
1816-1919. The Marquess of
Anglesey.
A History of the Cameroon. Tambi
Eyongetah and Robert Brain.
A History of the Chilean Boundaries.
Robert D. Talbott.
A History of the Christian Church in
the South. Durward T. Stokes
and William T. Scott.
History of the Cities and Villages
of the Ukrainian SSR. 7 vols.
O. E. Kas'ianenko, et al., eds.
A History of the City of Cairo,
Illinois. John M. Lansden.
A History of the Congregation of
the Mission, 1625-1843. Stafford
Poole.
History of the Congress of the United
States. Alvin M. Josephy, Jr.
A History of the County of Somerset.
Vol. 3. R. W. Dunning, ed.
A History of the County of York.
Vol. II. K. J. Allison, ed.
A History of the Czechs. A. H.
Hermann.
The History of the Dominican Order.
Volume 2: Intellectual and Cul-
tural Life to 1500. William A.
Hinnebusch.
History of the Fourth Regiment of
S. C. Volunteers. J. W. Reid.
History of the Free Presbyterian
Church of Scotland. A. McPher-
son, ed.
A History of the Habsburg Empire,
1526-1918. Robert A. Kann.
A History of the ICC. Art and Olive
Hoogenboom.
A History of the Igbo People.
Elizabeth Isichei.
History of the Illinois Central Rail-
road. John F. Stover.
A History of the Kikuyu, 1500-1900.
Godfrey Muriuki.
History of the Makhnovist Movement.
Peter Arshinov.
A History of the Mennonite Brethren
Church: Pilgrims and Pioneers.
J. A. Toews.
A History of the Old South: The

Development. Ivan T. Berend
and Gregori Ranki.
Hunters in the Barrens. Georg
Henriksen.
Hurrell Froude and the Oxford
Movement. Piers Brendon.
Hutterite Society. John A. Hostet-
ler.
Hydace, Chronique. 2 vols. Alain
Tranoy, ed.

-I-

I Buccheri con Figurazioni Graf-
fite. Marisa Bonamici.
I Combattenti nel primo dopoguerra.
G. Sabbatucci.
I Russi in Ethiopia. 2 vols. Carlo
Zaghi.
Ibn Tufayl's Hayy Ibn Yaqzān.
Lenn Evan Goodman.
The Idea of Fraternity in America.
Wilson Carey McWilliams.
The Ideal of the Practical. Frank
Safford.
Les Idées de Necker. Henri
Grange.
Identifying People in the Past.
E. A. Wrigley, ed.
La ideología de la Revolución
Mexicana: La formación del
nuevo régimen. Arnaldo Cór-
dova.
The Ideological Origins of the
Batavian Revolution. I. Leonard
Leeb.
Ideology and Politics in Uganda.
James H. Mittelman.
Ideology and Reality in Soviet
Policy in Asia: Indo-Soviet
Relations, 1947-60. Zafar
Imam.
Ideology and Social Knowledge.
Harold J. Bershady.
The Ideology of Order: A
Comparative Analysis of Jean
Bodin and Thomas Hobbes.
Preston King.
Ideology, Reason and the Limita-
tion of War: Religious and
Secular Concepts, 1200-1740.
James Turner Johnson.
Idols of the Tribe. Harold R.
Isaacs.
If Beale Street Could Talk.

James Baldwin.
Illegitimacy. Shirley Foster Hartley.
Im Kampf zwischen Epochen.
Friedrich Muckermann.
The Image of the Indian and the
Black Man in American Art,
1590-1900. Ellwood Parry.
The Image of the Jew in American
Literature: From Early Republic
to Mass Immigration. Louis
Harap.
Images of American Society. G. D.
Lillibridge.
Images of Ethnic and Racial Violence
in California Politics, 1917-1930.
Howard A. DeWitt.
The Immigrant Church: New York's
Irish and German Catholics, 1815-
1865. Jay P. Dolan.
Immigrant Pastor: The Life of the
Right Reverend Monsignor Lucyan
Bojnowski of New Britain, Con-
necticut. Daniel S. Buczek.
Immigrants: A Portrait of the Urban
Experience, 1890-1930. Robert
F. Harney and Harold Troper.
An Immigrant's American Odyssey.
Emory Lindquist.
Immigrants and the City: Ethnicity
and Mobility in a Nineteenth-
Century Midwestern Community.
Dean R. Esslinger.
Immigrants, Baptists, and the
Protestant Mind in America.
Lawrence B. Davis.
The Impact of Hitler. Maurice
Cowling.
Impeachment and Parliamentary
Judicature in Early Stuart England.
C. G. C. Tite.
The Impending Crisis, 1848-1861.
David M. Potter.
The Imperial Achievement: The
Rise and Transformation of the
British Empire. John Bowle.
Imperial Chemical Industries. Vol.
2. W. J. Reader.
Imperial Cities and the Reformation.
Bernd Moeller.
Imperial Economic Policy 1917-1939:
Studies in Expansion and Protec-
tion. Ian M. Drummond.
Imperial Germany and a World
Without War: The Peace Move-
ment and German Society, 1892-
1914. Roger Chickering.
The Imperial History of China.
J. MacGowan.

René A. Bravmann.
Islam from the Prophet Muhammad
to the Capture of Constantinople.
2 vols. Bernard Lewis, ed.
and trans.
Islam in Afghanistan Under King
Muhammed Zahir Shah. Jan
Samuelsson.
Islam in Uganda. Arye Oded.
Islamic Civilisation, 950-1150.
D. H. Richards, ed.
Islamic Historiography. Tarif
Khalidi.
Islamic History: Ideas, Men and
Events in the Middle East.
Bernard Lewis.
Islamic Rationalism: The Ethics
of 'Abd al-Jabbar. George F.
Hourani.
Israel Among the Nations. Jacob
L. Talmon.
Israel Divided: Ideological Politics
in the Jewish State. Rael Isaac.
Israel, the Korean War and China:
Images, Decisions and Conse-
quences. Michael Brecher.
Israel Without Zionism: A Plan
for Peace in the Middle East.
Uri Avnery.
Isthmia. Vol. II. Oscar
Broneer.
It Must Be Now the Kingdom
Coming. Perry Lentz.
Italia 1945-48: Le Origini della
Repubblica. Enzo Piscitelli,
et al.
Italian Foreign Policy, 1870-1940.
C. J. Lowe and F. Marzari.
Italian Intervention in the Spanish
Civil War. John F. Coverdale.
Italy in the 1970's. John Earle.
Italy--Republic Without Govern-
ment? P. A. Allum.
Ius Patronatus: Studien zur
Entwicklung des Patronats im
Dekretalenrecht und der Kanon-
istik des 12. und 13. Jahr-
hunderts. Peter Landau.
Ius Sacrum. Audomar Scheuerman
and Georg May, eds.
Ivan Franko--Historian of the
Ukraine. M. M. Kravets'.
Ivories from Nimrod (1949-1963).
Max Mallowan and Georgina Herr-
mann.
Ivory and Slaves: Changing Pat-
terns of International Trade in
East Central Africa to the Later

Nineteenth Century. Edward A.
Alpers.

-J-

J. S. Mill. Alan Ryan.
Jacob A. Riis and the American
City. James B. Lane.
Jacobellus de Střibro (1429), premier
theologien du hussitisme. Paul
De Vooght.
Jacopo Sansovino. Deborah Howard.
Jacques Maritain: Antimodern or
Ultramodern? Brooke Williams
Smith.
Jakobinerschauspiel und Jakobiner-
theater. Hans Werner Engels.
Jalal al-din al Suyūti. 2 vols. E.
M. Sartain.
James and John Stuart Mill. Bruce
Mazlish.
James Baldwin. Keneth Kinnamon,
ed.
James Baldwin: A Critical Study.
Stanley Macebuh.
James Franklin Gilman: Nineteenth
Century Painter. Adele God-
chaux Dawson.
James Madison Alden: Yankee Artist
of the Pacific Coast, 1854-1860.
Franz Stenzel.
James Patton and the Appalachian
Colonists. Patricia Givens John-
son.
James T. Shotwell and the Rise of
Internationalism in America.
Harold Josephson.
James II: Soldier and Sailor. Jock
Haswell.
James W. Wadsworth, Jr.: Gentle-
man from New York. Martin L.
Fausold.
The Jammu Fox. Bawa Satinder
Singh.
Ja-Nein-und Trotzdem. Hans-
Joachim Schoeps.
The Jansenists and the Expulsion of
the Jesuits from France, 1757-
1765. Dale Van Kley.
Japan and China: From War to
Peace, 1894-1972. Marius B.
Jansen.
Japan Faces China. Chae-jin Lee.
Japan in Crisis. Bernard Silberman
and H. D. Harootunian, eds.

Japan: The Fragile Superpower.
Frank Gibney.
Japan: The New Superstate.
Nabutake Ike.
Japan Today: People, Places,
Power. William H. Forbis.
The Japanese and Peru 1873-1973.
C. Harvey Gardiner.
The Japanese Army in North China,
1937-1941. Lincoln Li.
Japanese Culture. H. P. Varley.
The Japanese Economy in Interna-
tional Perspective. Isaiah Frank,
ed.
Japanese Piracy in Ming China
During the 16th Century. Kwan-
Wai So.
Japanese Urbanism: Industry and
Politics in Kariya, 1872-1972.
Gary D. Allinson.
Japan's First Student Radicals.
Henry DeWitt Smith, II.
Jawaharlal Nehru: A Biography.
Vol. I. 1889-1947. Sarvepalli
Gopal.
Jeanne d'Arc. W. S. Scott.
Jeannette Rankin: First Lady in
Congress. Hannah Josephson.
Jefferson the President: Second
Term, 1805-1809. Dumas Ma-
lone.
Jefferson's Louisiana: Politics
and the Clash of Legal Traditions.
George Dargo.
Jennison's Jayhawkers: A Civil War
Cavalry Regiment and Its Com-
mander. Stephen Z. Starr.
Jerome: His Life, Writings and
Controversies. J. N. D. Kelly.
Jessie White Mario: Risorgimento
Revolutionary. Elizabeth Adams
Daniels.
Jewish Resistance in Nazi-Occupied
Eastern Europe. Reuben Ainsz-
tein.
The Jewish Woman in America.
Charlotte Baum, Paula Hyman
and Sonya Michel.
The Jewish Woman in America:
Two Female Immigrant Genera-
tions, 1820-1929. Vol. I.
Rudolph Glanz.
Jews and Non-Jews in Eastern
Europe, 1918-1945. Bela Vago
and George L. Mosse, eds.
The Jews in the World Renais-
sance. Moses A. Shulvass.
The Jews of Medieval York and

the Massacre of March 1190.
R. B. Dobson.
Jews, Wars, and Communism.
Vols. 1 and 2. Zosa Szajkowski.
The Jicarilla Apaches: A Study in
Survival. Dolores A. Gunnerson.
Jogjakarta Under Sultan Magkubumi,
1749-1792: A History of the
Division of Java. M. C. Ricklefs.
Johann Andreas Schubert. Arthur
Weichold.
Johann Martin Lappenberg: Ein
Beitrag zur Geschichte der
Geschichtswissenschaft im 19.
Jahrhundert. Rainer Postel.
Johannes Trithemius: In Praise of
Scribes. Klaus Arnold, ed.
John Aubrey and the Realm of
Learning. Michael Hunter.
John Burgoyne of Saratoga. James
Lunt.
John C. Greenway and the Opening
of the Western Mesabi. Donald
L. Boese.
The John Doe Associates: Backdoor
Diplomacy for Peace, 1941.
R. J. C. Butow.
John Foxe and the Elizabethan
Church. V. Norskon Olsen.
John George Jackson. Dorothy
Davis.
John Hay: The Gentleman as
Diplomat. Kenton J. Clymer.
John James Tigert: American
Educator. George Coleman Os-
born.
John Jones Pettus, Mississippi
Fire-Eater: His Life and Times,
1813-1867. Robert W. Dubay.
John Knox. Duncan Shaw, ed.
John Lydford's Book. Dorothy M.
Owen, ed.
John McLoughlin's Business Cor-
respondence, 1847-48. William
R. Sampson, ed.
John Marshall: A Life in Law.
Leonard Baker.
John Muir's Longest Walk. John
Muir and John Earl.
John Steinbeck. Nelson Valjean.
John Stuart Mill: A Mind at Large.
Eugene August.
John Trumbull: Patriot-Artist of
the American Revolution. Irma
B. Jaffe.
John Winebrenner: Nineteenth-Cen-
tury Reformer. Richard Kern.
John Wycliff as Legal Reformer.

William Farr.

Johnson, Grant, and the Politics of Reconstruction. Martin E. Mantell.

Jonathan Edwards: Theologian of the Heart. Harold P. Simonson.

Jonathan Sewall: Odyssey of an American Loyalist. Carol Berkin.

Joscelyn III and the Fall of the Crusader States. Robert Lawrence Nicholson.

José Carlos Mariategui y su pensamiento revolucionario. Diego Meseguer Illán.

José Martí: Letras y huellas desconocidas. Carlos Ripoll.

Jose Miguel de Tagle. Lilians Betty Romera Cabrera.

Joseph Jones, M. D.: Scientist of the Old South. James O. Breeden.

Joseph M. Dixon of Montana. Jules A. Karlin.

Joseph Stalin: Man and Legend. Ronald Hingley.

Joseph von Sonnenfels und die österreichische Reformbewegung im Zeitalter des aufgeklärten. Karl-Heinz Osterloh.

Josephine: The Empress and Her Children. Nina Epton.

Die josephinische Toleranz unter besonderer Berücksichtigung ihres gestlichen Wegbereiters Johann Leopole Hay. Reinhold Joseph Wolny.

Josiah Quincy, 1772-1864: The Last Federalist. Robert A. McCaughey.

Journal and Letter Book of Nicholas Buckeridge, 1651-1654. John R. Jensen.

Journal d'un voiage fait en Bambouc en 1744. Pierre David.

The Journal of the Commons House of Assembly, 23 April 1750-31 August 1751. R. Nicholas Olsberg, ed.

Journal of the Senate of Virginia: November Session, 1795. Thomas S. Headlee, Jr.

A Journal of Two Visits Made to Some Nations of Indians on the West Side of the River Ohio, in the Years 1772 and 1773. David Jones.

The Journals of Alfred Doten,

1849-1903. Alfred Doten.

The Journals of Jonathan Carver. John Parker, ed.

Journey in Faith. Lester G. McAllister and William E. Tucker.

The Journey of August King. John Ehle.

The Joy of Sports. Michael Novak.

The Joyful Community: An Account of Bruderhof. Benjamin D. Zablocki.

Judaism in America from Curiosity to Third Faith. Joseph L. Blau.

Die Juden in Hamburg. Helga Krohn.

The Just War in the Middle Ages. Frederick H. Russell.

Justice Accused: Antislavery and the Judicial Process. Robert M. Cover.

Justice in Medieval Russia: Muscovite Judgment Charters (Pravye Gramoty) of the Fifteenth and Sixteenth Centuries. Ann M. Kleimola.

Justices and Presidents: A Political History of Appointments to the Supreme Court. Henry J. Abraham.

-K-

K. Marx's "Capital" and Philosophical Thought in Russia. V. F. Pustarnakov.

Die Kaap tydens die Eerste Britse Bewind 1795-1803. Germann Giliomee.

Die Kabinette Marx I und II: 30. November 1923 bis 3. Juni 1924; 3 Juni 1924 bis 15. Januar 1925. Gunter Abramowski, ed.

Die Kabinette Wirth I und II. Ingrid Schulze-Bidlingmaier, ed.

Die Kaiserliche Universität von Konstantinopel. Paul Speck.

Kalambo Falls Prehistoric Site. 2 vols. J. Desmond Clark.

Kansas: A Land of Contrasts. Robert W. Richmond.

Kant and the Problem of History. William A. Galston.

The Kant-Eberhard Controversy. Henry E. Allison.

Kant und das Problem der Dinge an

Mackie.

Konrad Adenauer, Oberbürgermeister von Köln. Hugo Stehkämper, ed.

Konrad Adenauer, Reden 1917-1967: Eine Auswahl. Hans Peter Schwarz, ed.

Die Konstituierung der deutschen Arbeiterbewegung 1862/3 Darstellung und Dokumentation. S. Na'aman.

Das Konzil von Pavia-Siena, 1423-1424. Walter Brandmüller.

Korean Pricing Policies and Economic Development in the 1960's. Gilbert T. Brown.

Koreareport. Harry Sichrovsky.

Kriegsallianz und Wirtschaftsinteressen: Russland in den Wirtschaftsplänen Englands und Frankreichs, 1914-1917. Bernd Bonwetsch.

Kritik und Krise. Reinhart Koselleck.

Les Kroumen de la côte occidentale d'Afrique. Christine Behrens.

"Kubla Khan" and "The Fall of Jerusalem." E. S. Shaffer.

Die Kultur der Bronzezeit im Sudwesten der Iberischen. Hermanfrid Schubart.

The Kuril Islands. J. J. Stephan.

Kurrachee: Past, Present and Future. Alexander F. Baillie.

-L-

L.A. in the Thirties. David Gebhard and Harriette Von Breton.

Labor and Socialism in America. William M. Dick.

Labor and the Ambivalent Revolutionaries: Mexico, 1911-1933. Ramon E. Ruiz.

Labour in the South African Gold Mines, 1911-1969. Francis Wilson.

The Labour Party and the Struggle for Socialism. David Coates.

Labour, Race and Colonial Rule: The Copperbelt from 1924 to Independence. Elena L. Berger.

Laddigam. B. Venkataraman.

The Lady and the President: The Letters of Dorothea Dix and Millard Fillmore. Charles M. Snyder.

The Lady Mary. Milton Waldman.

Lamentations. Delbert R. Hillers.

Lamy of Santa Fe: His Life and Times. Paul Horgan.

Lancashire in Decline. Lars G. Sandberg.

Lancastrian Kings and Lollard Knights. K. B. McFarlane.

Land and People: A Cultural Geography of Preindustrial New Jersey. Peter O. Wacker.

The Land and the People of Nineteenth-Century Cork: The Rural Economy and the Land Question. James S. Donnelly, Jr.

Land from the Sea: The Geologic Story of South Florida. John Edward Hoffmeister.

Land, Man, and the Law: The Disposal of Crown Lands in British Columbia, 1871-1913. Robert E. Cail.

The Land of Little Rain. Mary Austin.

Land, People and Politics: A History of the Land Question in the United Kingdom, 1878-1952. Roy Douglas.

The Land Question and European Society Since 1650. Frank E. Huggett.

Land Reform in the People's Republic of China. John Wong.

Land Revenue and Public Finance in Maratha Administration. H. B. Vashrishta.

Landebischof D. Wurm und der nationalsozialistische Staat, 1940-1945: Eine Dokumentation. Richard Fischer and Gerhard Schäfer, comps.

Landesherrschaft und Bergbauwirtschaft. Ekkehard Hennschke.

Landlords and Tenants on the Prairie Frontier. Studies in American Land Policy. Paul W. Gates.

The Lands of Partitioned Poland 1795-1918. Piotr S. Wandycz.

The Lands of St. Peter. Peter Partner.

Language in Education. The Problem in Commonwealth Africa and the Indo-Pakistan Sub-continent.

475 The Letters

Customs, and Conditions of North American Indians; Written During Eight Years' Travel (1832-1839) Amongst the Wildest Tribes of Indians in North America. 2 vols. George Catlin.

The Letters and Papers of Chaim Weizmann, 1907-1913. Chaim Weizmann.

Letters and People of the Spanish Indies: Sixteenth Century. James Lockhart and Enrique Otte, eds. and trans.

Letters from North America. John Xántus.

Letters from the Promised Land: Swedes in America, 1840-1914. H. Arnold Barton, ed.

The Letters of Bernard De Voto. Wallace Stegner, ed.

Letters of Brigham Young to His Sons. Dean C. Jessee.

Letters of Hart Crane and His Family. Thomas S. W. Lewis, ed.

The Letters of John Greenleaf Whittier. John Greenleaf Whittier.

The Letters of John Hus. Matthew Spinka, trans.

Letters of Louis D. Brandeis. Vol. IV. Louis Brandeis.

Letters of Medieval Jewish Traders. S. D. Goitein.

Letters of Sir George Etherege. Frederick Bracher, ed.

The Letters of Thomas Babington Macaulay: Volume I, 1807-February 1831; Volume II, March 1831-December 1833. Thomas Pinney, ed.

The Letters of William Lloyd Garrison. Vol. IV. Louis Ruchames, ed.

The Levellers in the English Revolution. G. E. Aylmer, ed.

Levi Coffin and the Underground Railroad. Charles Ludwig.

Leviné: The Life of a Revolutionary. Rosa Leviné-Meyer.

Lewis and Clark. Roy E. Appleman.

Lexikon der Ägyptologie. Vol. 1. Wolfgang Helck and Eberhard Otto, eds.

Liable to Floods. J. R. Ravensdale.

Liang Ch'i-ch'ao and Modern Chinese Liberalism. Philip

C. Huang.

Libellus de Diversis Ordinibus et Professionibus qui sunt Aecclesia. G. Constable and B. Smith, eds.

Liberal Europe. W. E. Mosse.

The Liberal Imperialists: The Ideas and Politics of a Post-Gladstonian Elite. H. C. G. Matthew.

Liberaler Staat und Kirche in der Ara von Reichsgrundung und Kulturkampf. Josef Becker.

Liberalism and Tradition. Bernard Reardon.

Liberalism i kris. Kent Zetterberg.

Liberalismus und Revolution. Michael Neumüller.

Liberals Among the Orthodox. Walter Donald Kring.

Liberals in the Russian Revolution. William G. Rosenberg.

Liberals, Radicals and Social Politics, 1892-1914. H. V. Emy.

Liberated Woman: A Life of May Arkwright Hutton. James W. Montgomery.

Liberating Women's History. Berenice A. Carroll.

Liberty, Liberty County, and the Atascosito District. Miriam Partlow.

Library of Congress Symposia on the American Revolution. Alfred H. Kelly, et al.

The Library of James Logan of Philadelphia, 1674-1751. Edwin Wolf, II, comp.

A Licence to Trade: A History of the English Chartered Companies. Sir Percival Griffiths.

The Life and Death of Leon Trotsky. Victor Serge and Natalia Sedova Trotsky.

The Life and Death of St. Kilda. Tom Steel.

The Life and Opinions of Maximilien Robespierre. Norman Hampson.

The Life and Thought of Yeh Shih. Winston Wan Lo.

The Life and Times of Menelik II: Ethiopia 1844-1913. Harold G. Marcus.

Life and Writings of Amelia Bloomer. D. C. Bloomer.

The Life of a Cowboy. George Phippen.

The Life of Bertrand Russell. Ronald W. Clark.

The Life of Captain James Cook.

J. C. Beaglehole.
The Life of Cola di Rienzo. John
Wright, trans.
The Life of Nathan Bedford For-
rest. John A. Wyeth.
The Life of Orator Henley.
Graham Midgley.
The Life of Saladin. Sir Hamilton
Gibb.
Life Studies of the Great Army.
Edwin Forbes.
The Life That Ruth Built. Marshall
Smelser.
The Limits of Foreign Policy.
Christopher Thorne.
The Limits of Reason: The Ger-
man Democratic Press and the
Collapse of the Weimar De-
mocracy. Modris Eksteins.
Lincoln and the War Democrats:
The Grand Erosion of Conser-
vative Tradition. Christopher
Dell.
Lincoln Steffens: A Biography.
Justin Kaplan.
Lineages of the Absolutist State.
Perry Anderson.
Linksliberalismus und Sozial-
demokratie in der Weimarer
Republik 1919-1930. Hartmut
Schustereit.
Linnaeus. Heinz Goerke.
The Lion and the Unicorn in
Africa. F. Pedler.
The Lion of Tashkent: The
Career of General M. G.
Cherniaev. David MacKenzie.
Lion Rampant. D. A. Low.
Lions and Foxes: Men and Ideas
of the Italian Renaissance.
Sidney Alexander.
The Lion's Roar of Queen Srimala.
Alex and Hideko Wayman, trans.
The Lion's Share: A Short History
of British Imperialism, 1850-
1976. Bernard Porter.
The Liquidation of the Anti-Soviet
Kronstadt Revolt of 1921. S.
N. Semanov.
List and Index to the Proceedings
in Star Chamber for the Reign
of James I. Thomas G. Barnes,
ed. and comp.
A List of References for the History
of Agriculture in the Great
Plains. Earl M. Rogers, comp.
A List of References for the History
of Apiculture and Sericulture in

America. William Pickens,
comp.
Literacy in Colonial New England.
Kenneth A. Lockridge.
A Literary History of France. I.
D. McFarlane.
Literary New York. Susan Edmiston
and Linda Cirino.
The Little Darlings: A History of
Child Rearing in America. Mary
Cable.
A Little Group of Willful Men.
Thomas W. Ryley.
The Little Lion of the Southwest.
Marc Simmons.
Liu Shao-ch'i and the Chinese Cul-
tural Revolution: The Politics of
Mass Criticism. Lowell Dittmar.
Lives of Labor: Work in a Maturing
Industrial Society. Peter N.
Stearns.
The Lives of Roger Casement. B.
L. Reid.
Living an Era: India's March to
Freedom. Vol. I. D. P.
Mishra.
A Living Profit: Studies in the So-
cial History of Canadian Business,
1883-1911. Michael Bliss.
Lloyd George Family Letters, 1885-
1936. Kenneth O. Morgan, ed.
Logging the Redwoods. Lynwood
Carranco and John T. Labbe.
Logistics and the Failure of the
British Army in America, 1775-
1783. R. Arthur Bowler.
Lola Shri Ram: A Study in Entre-
preneurship and Industrial Manage-
ment. Arun Joshi.
London 800-1216: The Shaping of
a City. Christopher N. L. Brooke
and Gillian Keir.
The Long Dark Night of the Soul.
Sandy Vogelgesang.
The Long Generation: Germany from
Empire to Ruin, 1913-1945. Hen-
ry Cord Meyer.
The Long Hunter: A New Life of
Daniel Boone. Lawrence Elliott.
The Long Thirst. Thomas M. Cof-
fey.
The Long View. Basil Wright.
Look to the Mountains. Charles S.
Peterson.
Looking at Pictures with Bernard
Berenson. Bernard Berenson.
Lopez of Newport: Colonial Ameri-
can Merchant Prince. Stanley

F. Chyet.
Lord Acton on Papal Power. H.
    A. MacDougall, ed.
Lord Leighton. Leonee and
    Richard Ormond.
Lord Liverpool's Administration.
    J. E. Cookson.
Lord North. P. D. G. Thomas.
Lord Salisbury. Robert Taylor.
Lord Somers: A Political Por-
    trait. William L. Sachse.
Lord William Bentinck. John
    Rosselli.
Lordship and Community: Battle
    Abbey and Its Banlieu, 1066-
    1538. Eleanor Searle.
Los Angeles and Its Environs in
    the Twentieth Century. Doyce
    B. Nunis, Jr., ed.
Los Angeles: Epic of a City.
    Lynn Bowman.
Los Angeles: The Architecture
    of Four Ecologies. Reyner
    Banham.
Lost Chicago. David Lowe.
The Lost War: Letters from
    British Officers During the
    American Revolution. Marion
    Balderston and David Syrett, eds.
Lothar Franz von Schönborn and the
    Diplomacy of the Electroate of
    Mainz from the Treaty of Rys-
    wick to the Outbreak of the War
    of the Spanish Succession.
    Richard H. Thompson.
Louis and Antoinette. Vincent
    Cronin.
Louis Kossuth in America, 1851-
    1852. John H. Komlos.
Louis XIV in Historical Thought.
    William F. Church.
Louisiana: A Pictorial History.
    Leonard V. Huber.
Louisiana Reconstructed, 1863-
    1877. Joe Gray Taylor.
The Loyalist Americans: A Focus
    on Greater New York. Robert
    A. East and Jacob Judd, eds.
The Loyalist Experience in North
    Carolina. Carole Watterson
    Troxler.
The Loyalists in Revolutionary
    America, 1760-1781. Robert
    McCluer Calhoon.
Lucca und das Reich bis zum
    Ende des 11. Jahrhunderts.
    Hansmartin Schwarzmaier.
Lucien Febvre. Hans-Dieter Mann.

Lucy M. Stanton, Artist. Stanton
    M. Forbes.
Ludwig Bamberger. Stanley Zucker.
Luigi Albertini. Ottavio Barié.
Luis María Peralta and His Adobe.
    Francis L. Fox.
Lunda Under Belgian Rule: The
    Politics of Ethnicity. Edouard
    Bustin.
The Lusitania Disaster: An Episode
    in Modern Warfare and Diplomacy.
    Thomas Andrew Bailey and Paul
    B. Ryan.
Luther and the Dawn of the Modern
    Era. Heiko A. Obermann, ed.
Luther and the False Brethren.
    Mark U. Edwards, Jr.
Luther and the Peasants' War:
    Luther's Actions and Reactions.
    Robert N. Crossley.
Luther and the Radicals: Another
    Look at Some Aspects of the
    Struggle Between Luther and the
    Radical Reformers. Harry Loe-
    wen.
Lutheran Historical Conference ...
    19-20 October 1972. Lutheran
    Historical Conference.
Luther's Response to Violence.
    Lloyd B. Volkmar.
Lying, Despair, Jealousy, Envy,
    Sex, Suicide, Drugs, and the
    Good Life. Leslie H. Farber.
Lyndon Johnson and the American
    Dream. Doris Kearns.
The Lyon Uprising of 1834: Social
    and Political Conflict in the Early
    July Monarchy. Robert J.
    Bezucha.

-M-

The Maccabees. Moshe Pearlman.
The McGraw-Hill Encyclopedia of
    World Biography. David I. Eg-
    genberger, ed.
The Machiavellian Moment. J. G.
    A. Pocock.
A Machiavellian Treatise by Stephen
    Gardiner. Peter Donaldson, ed.
    and trans.
Macht durch Organisation: Die
    Grundlegung des Hugenbergschen
    Presseimperiums. Dankwart
    Guratzsch.

Madam Secretary: Frances Perkins. George Martin.

Madame Catherine. Irene Mahoney.

Madeline Island and the Chequamegon Region. John O. Holzhueter.

Madonnas and Magdalens. Eric Trudgill.

Magic Medicines of the Indians. C. A. Weslager.

The Mahabharata. Books 2 and 3. J. A. B. Van Buitenen, trans. and ed.

Maharaja Lakshmiswar Singh of Darbhanga. Jata Shankar Jha.

Main Currents in Cultural Anthropology. Raoul and Frada Naroll, eds.

Mainland Southeast Asia. Ronald Provencher.

Maisons a Mosaiques du quartier contral de Djemila. Michele Blanchard-Lemee.

The Majesty That Was Islam. W. Montgomery Watt.

Major Themes in Northern Black Religious Thought. Monroe Fordham.

Making Democracy Safe for Oil. Christopher T. Rand.

The Making of a Saint. J. H. Huizinga.

The Making of an Arab Nationalist: Ottomanism and Arabism in the Life and Thought of Sâti'al-Husri. William L. Cleveland.

The Making of China: Main Themes in Premodern Chinese History. Chun-shu Chang, ed.

The Making of King Kong. Orville Goldner and George E. Turner.

The Making of Modern English Society from 1850. Janet Roebuck.

The Making of the Diplomatic Mind: The Training, Outlook, and Style of United States Foreign Service Officers, 1908-1931. Robert D. Schulzinger.

The Making of the Labor Bureaucrat. Warren Van Tine.

The Making of the Modern Family. Edward Shorter.

The Making of the Monroe Doctrine. Ernest R. May.

The Making of the South Australian Landscape. Michael Williams.

The Making of the Third Republic. Sanford Elwitt.

The Malagasy and the Europeans. Phares M. Mutibwa.

Mallet Du Pan (1749-1800): A Career in Political Journalism. Frances Acomb.

Mallia, Plan du site, plans du palais, indices. Olivier Pelon, comp.

Man and His Foods. C. Earle Smith, Jr., ed.

Man and Woman Among the Azande. E. E. Evans-Pritchard, ed.

A Man for Now: The Life of Damien de Veuster, Friend of Lepers. John Beevers.

Man in the Amazon. Charles Wagley, ed.

The Man of Only Yesterday: Frederick Lewis Allen. Darwin Payne.

Managers and Workers: Origins of the New Factory System in the United States, 1880-1920. Daniel Nelson.

Manchester Mormons: The Journal of William Clayton, 1840 to 1842. James B. Allen and Thomas G. Alexander, eds.

The Manchester Union Leader in New Hampshire Elections. Eric Veblen.

The Mandarins of Western Europe: The Political Role of Top Civil Servants. Mattei Dogan, ed.

Manohar Malgonkar. James Y. Dayananda.

Manuel d'archéologie médiévale: de la fouille à l'histoire. Michel de Botlard.

Les manuels d'histoire du Canada au Québec et en Ontario (de 1867 à 1914). Genevieve Laloux-Jain.

Manuscript Sources in the Library of Congress for Research on the American Revolution. John R. Sellers, et al., eds.

Many Are the Hearts: The Agony and the Triumph of Ulysses S. Grant. Richard Goldhurst.

Mao Tse Tung and China. C. P. Fitzgerald.

Mao Tse-tung and Education: His Thoughts and Teachings. John N. Hawkins.

Mediaeval Jewry in Northern France: A Political and Social History. Robert Chazan.

The Medical Profession and Social Reform, 1885-1945. Lloyd C. Taylor, Jr.

Medical Revolution in France 1789-1796. David M. Vess.

The Medieval Architect. John Harvey.

Medieval Colonialism: Postcrusade Exploitation of Islamic Valencia. Robert Ignatius Burns.

The Medieval Craftsmen. John Harvey.

Medieval English Medicine. Stanley Rubin.

The Medieval Experience. Francis Oakley.

The Medieval Guildhall of London. Caroline M. Barron.

Medieval Japan: Essays in Institutional History. David L. Davis, et al.

Medieval Learning and Literature: Essays Presented to Richard William Hunt. J. J. G. Alexander and M. T. Gibson, eds.

Medieval Religious Houses: Scotland. Ian B. Cowan and David E. Easson, eds.

Medieval Texts and Studies. C. R. Cheney.

The Medieval Universities: Their Development and Organisation. A. B. Cobban.

Medieval Women. Eileen Power.

Medievalia et Humanistica. Paul Maurice Clogan, ed.

The Mediterranean and the Mediterranean World in the Age of Philip II. Vol II. Fernand Braudel.

The Mediterranean Naval Situation 1908-1914. Paul G. Halpern.

A Mediterranean Society: The Jewish Communities of the Arab World as Portrayed in the Documents of the Cairo Geniza. Vol. II. The Community. S. D. Goitein.

Il Mediterraneo nella seconda metà del 1500 alla luce di Lepanto. Gino Benzoni, ed.

Memo for 1976: Some Political Options. Wesley Pippert.

A Memoir of China in Revolution: From the Boxer Rebellion to the People's Republic. Chester Ronning.

A Memoir of the Peace Conference, 1919. James Headlam-Morley.

Memoirs of a Confederate Veteran, 1861-1865. Isaac Hermann.

The Memoirs of Henry Heth. James L. Morrison, Jr., ed.

Memphis Sketches. Paul R. Coppock.

Men Against McCarthy. Richard M. Fried.

Men and Brothers: Anglo-American Antislavery Cooperation. Betty Fladeland.

Men and Wealth in the United States, 1850-1870. Lee Soltow.

Men in Scarlet. Hugh A. Dempsey.

Mendizabal y la Instauración de la Monarquia Constitucional en españa 1790-1853. Peter Janke.

Mennonites in Canada, 1786-1920. Frank H. Epp.

The Menskeviks: From the Revolution of 1917 to the Second World War. Leopold H. Haimson, ed.

Mental Disorder in Earlier Britain. Basil Clarke.

Merchants and Rulers in Gujarat. M. N. Pearson.

Mesoamerican Archaeology: New Approaches. Norman Hammond.

Metairie: A Tongue of Land to Pasture. Henry C. Bezou.

Metal Weapons, Tools, and Ornaments of the Teton Dakota Indians. James Austin Hanson.

Metamorphosis of a Death Symbol. The Transi Tomb in the Late Middle Ages and the Renaissance. Kathleen Cohen.

Meteora: The Rock Monasteries of Thessaly. Donald M. Nicol.

The Method of Melville's Short Fiction. R. Bruce Bickley, Jr.

The Methodist Revolution. Bernard Semmel.

El Metodo Histórico. Valentin Vázquez de Prada.

Metternich. Alan Palmer.

Mexican Americans. Ellwyn Stoddard.

Mexican-Americans Tomorrow. Gus Taylor, ed.

A Mexican Family Empire: The Latifundio of the Sanchez Navarros, 1765-1867. Charles H. Harris, III.

The Missionary Enterprise in China and America. John K. Fairbank, ed.

The Missions of New Mexico, 1776. Eleanor B. Adams and Fray Angelico Cháves, trans.

Missoes Franciscanas no Brazil, 1500-1975. Venâncio Willeke.

Mr. Polk's War. John H. Schroeder.

Mittelbronzezeitliche Tell-Siedlung bei Békés. János Banner and István Bóna.

Mobility, Support, Endurance: A Story of Naval Operational Logistics in the Vietnam War, 1965-1968. Edwin Bickford Hooper.

Moche Occupation of the Santa Valley, Peru. Christopher B. Donnan.

Moderatismo politico e riforma religioso in Terenzio Mamiani. Marcella Pincherle.

Modern and Traditional Elites in the Politics of Lagos. Patrick Cole.

A Modern China and a New World: K'ang yu-wei, Reformer and Utopian, 1858-1927. Kung-ch'tlan Hsiao.

The Modern History of Israel. Noah Lucas.

Modern Indian Poetry. Pritish Nandy, ed.

Modern Indian Short Stories. Suresh Kohli, ed.

Modern Japan: Aspects of History, Literature and Society. W. G. Beasley, ed.

Modern Jewish Ethics. Marvin Fox, ed.

Modern Manuscripts: A Practical Manual for Their Management, Care, and Use. Kenneth W. Duckett.

Modern Marriage in Sierra Leone: A Study of the Professional Group. R. E. Harrell-Bond.

Modern Migrations in Western Africa. Samir Amin, ed.

Modern Revolutions: An Introduction to the Analysis of a Political Phenomenon. John Dunn.

The Modern World-System: Capitalist Agriculture and the Origins of the European World-Economy in the Sixteenth Century. Immanuel Wallerstein.

The Modernist Impulse in American Protestantism. William R. Hutchison.

The Modernity of the Eighteenth Century. Louis T. Milic, ed.

The Modernization of Japan and Russia: A Comparative Study. Cyril E. Black, et al.

The Mojave Road. Dennis G. Casebier.

The Mojave Road in Newspapers. Dennis G. Casebier, comp.

Moment of Truth for Protestant America. Eldon G. Ernst.

Mona Lisa--The Picture and the Myth. Roy McMullen.

The Monastic World, 1000-1300. Christopher Brooke.

Le Monde Contemporain 1945-1973. Marcel Pacaut and Paul M. Bouju, eds.

Moneta. Recherches. Hubert Zehnacker.

Money and Banking in England: The Development of the Banking System, 1694-1914. B. L. Anderson and P. L. Cottrell.

Money and Credit in Developing Africa. Eric L. Furness.

Money and Empire: The International Gold Standard, 1890-1914. Marcello de Cecco.

Money and Monetary Policy in Communist China. Katharine Huang Hsiao.

Money and Politics in America, 1755-1775. Joseph Albert Ernst.

Money: Whence It Came, Where It Went. John Kenneth Galbraith.

Monks, Bishops and Pagans. Edward Peters, ed.

The Monks of War: The Military Religious Orders. Desmond Seward.

Monks, Priests and Peasants. Hans-Dieter Evers.

Monseigneur Bruté de Rémur. Charles Lemarié.

Les Monuments funéraires de Rhénée. Marie-Thérèse Couilloud.

Moon of Popping Trees. Rex Allan Smith.

Moorfield Storey and the Abolitionist Tradition. William B. Hixson, Jr.

The Moors in Spain and Portugal.
Jan Read.
"Moral Order" and the Criminal
Law: Reform Efforts in the
United States and West Germany.
Orlan Lee and T. A. Robertson.
A Moral Tale. Anne Scott MacLeod.
Moralities on the Gospels: A New
Source of "Ancrene Wisse." E.
J. Dobson.
Morality and Social Class in
Eighteenth-Century French Liter-
ature and Painting. Warren
Roberts.
More Than a Century. Jim W.
Corder.
Mori Arinori. Ivan Parker Hall.
Morocco Under Colonial Rule:
French Administration of Tri-
bal Areas, 1912-1956. Robin
Bidwell.
Morris R. Cohen and the Scientific
Ideal. David A. Hollinger.
Moscow and the West. S. F.
Platonov.
Moscow 1941-1942 Stalingrad:
Recollections, Stories, Re-
ports. A. Vassilevsky, et al.
Moses: The Man and His Vision.
David Daiches.
The Most Dangerous Man in Amer-
ica: Scenes from the Life of
Benjamin Franklin. Catherine
Drinker Bowen.
A Most Unsettling Person: The
Life and Ideas of Patrick Geddes.
Paddy Kitchen.
Mosty und Dirschau 1939: Zwei
Handstreiche der Wehrmacht
vor Beginn des Polenfeldzuges.
Herbert Schindler.
Mother Jones, the Miner's Angel:
A Portrait. Dale Fetherling.
Mother Was a Lady: Self and
Society in Selected American
Children's Periodicals, 1865-
1890. R. Gordon Kelly.
The Mothman Prophecies. John
A. Keel.
Motya, a Phoenician and Cartha-
ginian City in Sicily. Vol. I.
B. S. J. Isserlin and Joan du
Plat Taylor.
Mounier: A Personalist View of
History. Eileen Cantin.
Mounier and Maritain: A French
Catholic Understanding of the
Modern World. Joseph Amato.

Mount Hood. Don and Roberta Lowe.
Mountain Folks. Homer T. Rosen-
berger.
The Mountains and the Sky. Lorne
E. Render.
Mounted Raids of the Civil War.
Edward G. Longacre.
Le Mouvement de réforme de
l'enseignement en France, 1760-
1798. J. Morange and J. F.
Chassaing.
The Movement: A History of the
American New Left, 1959-1972.
Irwin and Debi Unger.
Movie-Made America. Robert Sklar.
Mughal Administration in Golconda.
J. F. Richards.
Multinational Corporations and the
Politics of Dependence: Copper
in Chile. Theodore H. Moran.
Multinational Firms in Africa. C.
Widstrand, ed.
Multinational Oil. Neil H. Jacoby.
Multi-Storey Living. Anthony Sut-
cliffe, ed.
The Municipal Revolution in America.
Jon C. Teaford.
Museum Cataloging in the Computer
Age. Robert G. Chenhall.
Music and the Middle Class. Wil-
liam Weber.
Music of the Americas: An Illus-
trated Music Ethnology of the
Eskimo and American Indian Peo-
ples. Paul Collaer.
The Muslim Dilemma in India.
M. R. A. Baig.
Muslim Merchants. Mattison Mines.
Muslim Spain: Its History and
Culture. Anwar G. Chejne.
Muslims in India. Zafar Imam, ed.
The Muslims of British India.
Peter Hardy.
Mussolini's Roman Empire. Denis
Mack Smith.
Mutual Images: Essays in American-
Japanese Relations. Akira Iriye,
ed.
My Country and the World. Andrei
D. Sakharov.
My Darling Pussy. A. J. P. Tay-
lor, ed.
My Father: A Remembrance.
Hugh Black, Jr.
My Life. Golda Meir.
My Penitente Land: Reflections on
Spanish New Mexico. Angelico
Chavez.

My People the Sioux.   Luther
  Standing Bear.
My South African Years.   W. M.
  Macmillan.
My Years with Bob Wills.   Al
  Stricklin and Joh McConal.
The Mycenaean World.   John Chad-
  wick.
Mykola Skrypnyk.   Iwan Koszeliwec.
Myrtleville: A Canadian Farm and
  Family, 1837-1967.   Beth Good
  Latzer.
The Mystery of Arthur.   Elizabeth
  Jenkins.
The Myth of the Guerrilla: Revo-
  lutionary Theory and Malprac-
  tice.   J. Bowyer Bell.
The Myth of the Lost Cause,
  1865-1900.   Rollin G. Osterweis.
Mythes et croyances dans l'ancienne
  France.   Nicole Belmont.
The Mythical World of Nazi War
  Propaganda, 1949-1945.   Jay W.
  Baird.
The Mythology of the Secret So-
  cieties.   J. M. Roberts.

-N-

N. W. Rowell: Ontario National-
  ist.   Margaret Prang.
N.Y.S.E.:   A History of the New
  York Stock Exchange, 1935-
  1975.   Robert Sobel.
Naissance d'une capitale: Con-
  stantinople et ses institutions de
  330 à 451.   Gilbert Dagron.
Naissance et croissance de la
  Suisse industrielle.   Jean-Fran-
  çoise Bergier.
Napoleon's Death: An Inquest.
  Frank Richardson.
Napoleon's Peninsular Marshals:
  A Reassessment.   Richard
  Humble.
A Narrative History of Brazoria
  County, Texas.   James A.
  Creighton.
Nathan Appleton: Merchant and
  Entrepreneur, 1779-1861.
  Frances W. Gregory.
A Nation Divided: Problems and
  Issues of the Civil War and
  Reconstruction.   George M.
  Fredrickson, ed.

A Nation of Cities: The Federal
  Government and Urban America,
  1933-1965.   Mark I. Gelfand.
A Nation Unaware: The Canadian
  Economic Culture.   Herschel
  Hardin.
A Nation Within a Nation.   Mark E.
  Nackman.
The National Archives and Foreign
  Relations Research.   Milton O.
  Gustafson, ed.
The National Archives and Urban
  Research.   Jerome Finster, ed.
National Consciousness, History, and
  Political Culture in Early-Modern
  Europe.   Orest Ranum, ed.
Nationalism, Communism, and
  Canadian Labour: The CIO, the
  Communist Party, and the Canadi-
  an Congress of Labour, 1935-1956.
  Irving Martin Abella.
The Nationalities Question in the
  USSR: A Collection of Docu-
  ments.   Roman Kupchinsky, comp.
The Nationalization of the Masses.
  George L. Mosse.
The Native American Factor.   Howard
  L. Meredith.
Native Americans of North America.
  David Perkins and Norman Tanis,
  comps.
Natural Man.   Robert Henry Welker.
Natural Philosophy at Dartmouth:
  From Surveyors' Chains to the
  Pressure of Light.   Sanborn C.
  Brown and Leonard M. Rieser.
El Naturalista en Nicaragua.
  Thomas Belt.
The Nature and Dynamics of Fac-
  tional Conflict.   P. N. Rastogi.
Nature and the American Mind:
  Louis Agassiz and the Culture of
  Science.   Edward Lurie.
Nature's Yellowstone.   Richard A.
  Bartlett.
Nauvoo: The City of Joseph.   David
  E. and Della S. Miller.
Navajo Livestock Reduction.   Ruth
  Roessel and B. H. Johnson.
The Navajos and the New Deal.
  Donald L. Parman.
The Navajo's Long Walk for Educa-
  tion.   Hildegard Thompson.
Naval Historical Foundation Manu-
  script Collections: A Catalog.
  The Naval Historical Foundation.
The Naval Side of King William's
  War.   Edward B. Powley.

A Navigator's Universe: The "Libro de Cosmographia" of 1538. Pedro de Medina.

The Nazi Party Courts. Donald M. McKale.

The Nazi Secret Service. André Brissaud.

Nazi Youth in the Weimar Republic. Peter D. Stachura.

Les Négociants Bordelais: L'Europe et les îles au XVIIIe Siècle. Paul Butel.

Negocios coloniais. Luis Lisanti.

Negro Slavery in Latin America. Rolando Mellafe.

Neither Toleration nor Favour: The Australian Chapter of Jewish Emancipation. Israel Getzler.

Nella Valtellina del tardo cinquecento: fede, cultura, società. Alessandro Pastore.

Neo-Colonialism in West Africa. Samir Amin.

The Neolithic of the Near East. James Mellaart.

Le Néolithique de la Provence. Jean Courtin.

The Nepalese Dilemma. Tribhuvan Nath.

Nepali Politics: Retrospect and Prospect. Rishikesh Shaha.

Neues zum Rätsel des Grand Camée de France. Kristian Jeppesen.

Neutrality or Commitment: The Evolution of Dutch Foreign Policy, 1667-1795. Alice Clare Carter.

Never Look Back: The Career and Concerns of John J. Burke. John B. Sheerin.

A New Age Now Begins. Page Smith.

The New American Ideology. George C. Lodge.

New Approaches to Latin American History. Richard Graham and Peter H. Smith, eds.

The New Corporatism. Fredrick B. Pike and Thomas Stritch, eds.

The New Country: A Social History of the American Frontier, 1776-1890. Richard A. Bartlett.

The New Deal. John Braeman, et al., eds.

The New Deal in Georgia: An Administrative History. Michael S. Holmes.

New Directions in European Historiography. Georg G. Iggers.

New Directions in Literary History. Ralph Cohen, ed.

New England Cemeteries. Andrew Kull.

New England in the English Nation, 1689-1713. Philip S. Haffenden.

The New England Mind in Transition: Samuel Johnson of Connecticut, 1696-1772. Joseph J. Ellis.

The New Found Land of Stephen Parmenius. D. B. Quinn and N. M. Cheshire, eds.

The New Guide to the Diplomatic Archives of Western Europe. Daniel H. Thomas and Lynn M. Case, ed.

New Hampshire's University: The Story of a New England Land Grant College. Everett B. Sackett.

A New Historical Geography of England. H. C. Darby, ed.

A New History of Australia. F. K. Crowley, ed.

The New Hungarian Agriculture. Lewis A. Fischer and Philip E. Uren.

The New Jersey Federalists. Rudolph J. Pasler and Margaret C. Pasler.

New Mexico Historic Documents. Richard N. Ellis, ed.

New Mexico Newspapers: A Comprehensive Guide to Bibliographical Entries and Locations. Pearce Grove, Becky J. Barnett and Sandra J. Hanses, ed.

New Mexico Populism. Robert W. Larson.

The New Psychohistory. Lloyd De Mause, ed.

New Religions. Haralds Biezais, ed.

New Spain: The Birth of Modern Mexico. Nicolas Cheetham.

The New Testament and the Roman State. D. R. Griffiths.

The New Urban History. Leo F. Schnore, ed.

New World Utopias. Paul Kagan.

New York City, 1664-1710: Conquest and Change. Thomas F. Archdeacon.

New York in the Revolution: A

The One Best System. David B. Tyack.

One Day at Kitty Hawk: The Untold Story of the Wright Brothers and the Airplane. John Evangelist Walsh.

One Small Candle: The Pilgrims' First Year in America. Thomas J. Fleming.

One Time Harvest. Mike Jacobs.

The Only Land I Know: A History of the Lumbee Indians. Adolph L. Dial and David K. Eliades.

Ontario Towns. Ralph Greenhill, et al.

Open Doors: A History of the General Conference Mennonite Church. S. F. Pannabecker.

The Opening of the Nile Basin. Elias Toniolo and Richard Hill, eds.

Opera Omnia di Sidney Sonnino. Benjamin F. Brown, ed.

Operation "Menace." Arthur Marder.

L'opinione publica inglese e l'avvento del fascismo (1919-1925). Aldo Berselli.

The Opium War 1840-1842. Peter Ward Fay.

Oral History for the Local Historical Society. Willa K. Baum.

Die Oraon. Matthias Hermanns.

The Orators in Cicero's "Brutus." G. V. Sumner.

The Ordeal of Civilty. John Murray Cuddihy.

The Ordeal of the New World. Tamas Zala.

The Ordeal of Thomas Hutchinson. Bernard Bailyn.

Order and History. Vol. IV. Eric Voegelin.

Oregon Biography Index. Patricia Brandt and Nancy Guilford.

Oregon Regional Union List of Serials. William H. Abrams, ed.

The Organization of African Unity After Ten Years: Comparative Perspectives. Yassin El-Ayouty, ed.

Organized Labor and the Black Worker: 1619-1973. Philip S. Foner.

Organizing the Farmers. Björn Beckman.

Origène: Commentaire sur s. Jean, Tome 3 (Livré 13). Cécile Blanc, ed.

The Origin of Partocracy. A. Avtorkhanov.

Le origini dell'imperialismo americano: Da McKinley a Taft (1897-1913). Alberto Aquarone.

Le origini diplomatiche dell'accordo navale anglo-tedesco del giugno 1935. Paola Brundu Olla.

Origins of a Southern Mosaic: Studies of Early Carolina and Georgia. Clarence L. Ver Steeg.

The Origins of British Borneo. L. R. Wright.

The Origins of British Industrial Relations: The Nineteenth-Century Experience. Keith Burgess.

The Origins of Christian Art. Michael Gough.

The Origins of Crowd Psychology. Robert A. Nye.

Origins of English Feudalism. R. Allen Brown.

The Origins of Liberal Welfare Reform. J. R. Hay.

The Origins of the Cultural Revolution. Roderick MacFarquhar.

The Origins of the French Labor Movement, 1830-1914. Bernard H. Moss.

The Origins of the Lloyd George Coalition. Robert J. Scally.

The Origins of the Marshall Plan. John Gimbel.

The Origins of the Modern European State 1450-1725. J. H. Shennan.

Origins of the Modern Japanese State: Selected Writings of E. H. Norman. John W. Dower, ed.

The Origins of the Second World War. Joachim Remak.

The Origins of Zionism. David Vital.

Osiander in Preussen, 1549-1552. Martin Stupperich.

Osmanische Bibliographie mit Besonderer Berucksichtigung der Türkei in Europa. Hans-Jürgen and Miterbeit von Jutta Kornrumpf.

Österreich-Ungarn und der französisch-preussische Krieg, 1870-1871. István Diószegi.

Oswald Mosley. Robert Skidelsky.

The Other Livingstone. Judith Listowel.

De oudst Antwerpse lijsten van
nieuwe poorsters (28 januari
1390-28 december 1414).
Francine de Nave, ed.
Our Ancestors Were Engineers.
Arthur Weir Crouch and Harry
Dixon Claybrook.
Our Common History as Christians.
John Deschner, Leroy T. Howe,
and Klaus Penzel, eds.
Our Partnership. Beatrice Webb.
Our People and Our History.
Rodolphe Lucien Desdunes.
Out of Great Tribulation: Baptists
in the U.S.S.R. Ernest A.
Payne.
Out of Nazareth: A Centenary of
the Sisters of the Holy Family
of Nazareth in the Service of
the Church. M. DeChantal.
Out of This World: Poems from
the Hawkeye State. Gary and
Judith Gildner, eds.
Out Under the Sky of the Great
Smokies. Harvey Broome.
Outlook on a Century. F. Wilson
and D. Perrot, eds.
Les Ouvriers en Grève: France
1871-1890. Michelle Perrot.
Oxford and Cambridge from the
14th to the early 19th Century.
(Vol. I.) Lawrence Stone, ed.

-P-

The Pacific Slope. Earl Pomeroy.
Pages from Hopi History. Harry
C. James.
Paine. David Freeman Hawke.
Painting and Sculpture in Min-
nesota, 1820-1914. Rena Neu-
mann Coen.
Pakistan: A Bibliography 1962-74.
Satyaparkash, comp. and ed.
Palace and Politics in Prewar
Japan. David Anson Titus.
Palaces and Forts of the Hawaiian
Kingdom: From Thatch to
American Florentine. Walter
F. Judd.
The Palestine Liberation Organisa-
tion. Mehmood Hussian.
Palestine Papers, 1917-1922:
Seeds of Conflict. Doreen
Ingrams, ed.

Paley: Evidences for the Man.
M. L. Clarke.
Palmerston, Guizot and the Col-
lapse of the Entente Cordiale.
Roger Bullen.
Palmyre VI. Le Temple Palmyreni-
en. Michal Gawlikowski.
The Pampangans: Colonial Society
in a Philippine Province. John
A. Larkin.
The Pan-African Movement.
Imanuel Geiss.
Pan-Africanism and Nationalism in
West Africa 1900-1945. A Study
in Ideology and Social Classes.
J. Ayodele Langley.
Pan-Africanism from Within.
Ras Makonnen.
Panajachel: A Guatemalan Town in
Thirty-Year Perspective. Robert
E. Hinshaw.
Panama's Economic Development:
The Role of Agriculture. Wil-
liam C. Merrill, et al.
The Papacy and Totalitarianism Be-
tween Two World Wars. Charles
F. Delzell, ed.
Paper Voices. A. C. H. Smith,
et al.
Papers Concerning Robertson's
Colony in Texas. Vols. I & II.
Malcolm D. McLean.
The Papers of Alexander Hamilton.
Alexander Hamilton.
The Papers of Andrew Johnson,
Vol. IV. Andrew Johnson.
The Papers of General Lucius D.
Clay. Lucius D. Clay.
The Papers of George Ekem
Ferguson. George Eken Fergu-
son.
The Papers of James Madison.
James Madison.
The Papers of Jefferson Davis.
Vol. 2. Jefferson Davis.
The Papers of John C. Calhoun.
Vol. III. 1823-1824. John C.
Calhoun.
Papers of John Mackenzie. Anthony
J. Dachs, ed.
The Papers of John Marshall.
Vol. I. Herbert A. Johnson, ed.
The Papers of Robert Morris.
E. James Ferguson, ed.
The Papers of the Order of Indian
Wars. John M. Carroll, ed.
The Papers of the Texas Revolu-
tion, 1835-1836. John H.

The Papers   490

Jenkins, ed.
The Papers of Woodrow Wilson.
Woodrow Wilson.
Papers on the Archaeology of
Black Mesa, Arizona. George
J. Gumerman and Robert C.
Euler, eds.
Paradise Lost: The Decline of the
Auto-Industrial Age. Emma
Rothschild.
Parched Earth: Maharashtra
Drought 1970-73. V. Subramani-
an.
Paris and Its Provinces, 1792-1802.
Richard Cobb.
The Paris Commune, 1871. Stew-
ard Edwards.
The Parish Republic: Hlinka's
Slovak People's Party, 1939-
1945. Yeshayaher Jelinek.
Parker's Virginia Battery, C.S.A.
Robert K. Krick.
Parlament und Aussenpolitik in
England 1911-1914. Karsten
Schröder.
O Parlemento e a evolução nacion-
al. 5 vols. José Honório
Rodrigues.
The Parliament of Bordeaux and
the End of the Old Regime.
William Doyle.
Parliamentary Privileges Under
the Indian Constitution. D. C.
Jain.
Parliamentary Reform 1640-1832.
John Cannon.
The Parliamentary Structuring of
British-Road-Rail Freight Co-
ordination. Jordan Jay Hill-
man.
Parliaments and Estates in Europe
to 1789. A. R. Myers.
Parroci e contadini nel Veneto
alla fine dell'Ottocento. Angelo
Gambasin.
Partial Magic: The Novel as a
Self-Conscious Genre. Robert
Alter.
Parties and Power in Modern
Argentina (1930-1946). Alberto
Ciria.
Partisan Warfare in 19th-Century
Poland. Emanuel Halicz.
Partisans of Freedom. William
O. Reichert.
Partnership and Profit in Medieval
Islam. Abraham L. Udovitch.
Partnership in Excellence: A

Late-Victorian Educational Ven-
ture: The Leys School, Cam-
bridge, 1875-1975. Derek Baker.
Party and Faction in American Poli-
tics. Rudolph M. Bell.
Party and Locality in Northern
Uganda, 1945-1962. Cherry
Gertzel.
Party Politics in the Continental
Congress. H. James Henderson.
Passage Through the Garden. John
L. Allen.
Passages from Antiquity to Feudal-
ism. Perry Anderson.
The Passaic Textile Strike of 1926.
Paul L. Murphy.
The Passenger Pigeon. A. W.
Schorger.
Passing By. Roger Morris, et al.
The Pastoral Industries of Australia:
Practice and Technology of Sheep
and Cattle Production. G. Alex-
ander and O. B. Williams, eds.
Pat Garrett: The Story of a Western
Lawman. Leon C. Metz.
The Pathet Lao. Joseph J. Zasloff.
Pathways to the Present. Eldon
Turner.
Patriarchalism in Political Thought.
Gordon J. Schochet.
Patrician in Politics: Daniel Dewey
Barnard of New York. Sherry
Penny.
Patrick Henry: A Biography.
Richard R. Beeman.
Patriotism with Profit: British Agri-
cultural Societies in the 18th and
19th Centuries. Kenneth Hudson.
The Patriots. Virginius Dabney, ed.
The Patristic Roots of Reformed
Worship. Hughes Oliphant Old.
Patronage & Exploitation. Jan Breman.
Pattern and Process: Research in
Historical Geography. Ralph E.
Ehrenberg, ed.
The Pattern of California History.
Edward Staniford.
The Pattern of Sino-American Crises.
J. H. Kalicki.
The Pattern of the Chinese Past.
Mark Elvin.
Patterns of Development 1950-1970.
Hollis Chenery, Moises Syrquin,
and Hazel Elkington.
Patton: A Study in Command. H.
Essame.
The Patton Papers: 1940-1945.
Martin Blumenson.

Paul Laurence Dunbar. E. W. Metcalf, Jr.

Paupers and Scholars: The Transformation of Student Life in Nineteenth-Century New England. David F. Allmendinger, Jr.

Paysannerie Francaise, Paysannerie Hongroise XVIe-XXe siecles. Bela Köpecki and E. H. Balázs, ed.

Peanuts Jubilee. Charles M. Schulz.

Pearl Harbor as History: Japanese-American Relations, 1931-1941. Dorothy Borg and Shumpei Okamoto, eds.

Peasant Citizens: Politics, Religion, and Modernization in Kelantan, Malaysia. Manning Nash.

The Peasant Marketing System of Oaxaca, Mexico. Ralph L. Beals.

Peasant Revolts in China, 1840-1949. Jean Chesneaux.

Peasants and Strangers: Italians, Rumanians and Slovaks in an American City, 1890-1950. Josef J. Barton.

The Peasants of Languedoc. Emmanuel Le Roy Ladurie.

A Peculiar People. Elmer and Dorothy Schwieder.

Pedro de la Torre: Doctor to Conquerors. John Tate Lanning.

Peel. Norman Gash.

Peirce's Concept of Sign. Douglas Greenlee.

Pektorale nichtköniglicher Personen. Erika Feucht.

Pelts, Plumes and Hides. Harry A. Kersey, Jr.

The Pennsylvania Navy, 1775-1781. John W. Jackson.

Pennsylvania, 1776. Robert Secor, ed.

Pennsylvania Speculator and Patriot: The Entrepreneurial John Nicholson, 1757-1800. Robert D. Arbuckle.

La pensée philosophique et théologique de Gersonide. Charles Touati.

Il pensiero degli Idéologues: scienza e filosofia in Francia, (1780-1815). Sergio Moravia.

The Pentecostals: The Charismatic Movement in the Churches.

Walter J. Hollenweger.

People in the Way. James W. Wilson.

A People Numerous and Armed. John Shy.

The People of Africa. Jean Hiernaux.

The People of Hamilton, Canada West: Family and Class in a Mid-Nineteenth-Century City. Michael B. Katz.

The People of Pylos. Margareta Lindgren.

People of the Valley: Life in an Isolated Afrikaner Community of South Africa. Brian M. Du Toit.

A People of Two Kingdoms: The Political Acculturation of the Kansas Mennonites. James C. Juhnke.

The Peoples and Cultures of Ancient Peru. Luis G. Lumbreras.

The Peoples of Philadelphia: A History of Ethnic Groups and Lower-Class Life, 1790-1940. Allen F. Davis and Mark H. Haller, eds.

Pepper, Guns, and Parleys: The Dutch East India Company and China, 1622-1681. John E. Wills, Jr.

Perfection and Progress. Elisabeth Hansot.

Perfectionist Persuasion. Charles Edwin Jones.

El periodismo tucumano (1817-1900): Ensayo de investigación sobre un aspecto de la cultura de Tucumán durante el siglo XIX. Manuel García Soriano.

Persia: An Archaeological Guide. Sylvia A. Matheson.

The Persistent Tradition in New South Politics. George Brown Tindall.

The Personal Memoirs of Julia Dent Grant. Julia Dent Grant.

Perspectives nouvelles sur le passé de l'Afrique noire et de Madagascar. Charles-Andre Julien, et al.

The Peruvian Experiment: Continuity and Change Under Military Rule. Abraham F. Lowenthal, ed.

Peter Browne. A. R. Winnett.

Peter Dillon on Vanikoro: Chevalier of the South Seas. J. W. Davidson.

Peter Olivi's Rule Commentary.

David Flood.

Peter Richard Kenrick, Bishop and Archbishop of St. Louis 1806-1896. S. J. Miller.

Peter Skene Ogden and the Hudson's Bay Company. Gloria Griffin Cline.

Peter Thompson's Narrative of the Little Bighorn Campaign, 1876: A Critical Analysis of an Eye-witness Account of the Custer Debacle. Daniel O. Magnussen, ed.

Peter Tudebode. John Hugh and Lauritia L. Hill, trans.

Peterborough Abbey, 1086-1310. Edmund King.

Die Petersburger Religiös-Philosophischen Vereinigungen. Jutta Scherrer.

El petroleo en la historiografia venezolana. Tomo II. Irene Rodríguez Gallad.

The Phantom Homestead. Otis Dunbar Richardson.

The Phenomenon of Revolution. Mark N. Hagopian.

The Philadelphia Quakers in the Industrial Age, 1865-1920. Philip S. Benjamin.

The Philadelphia Riots of 1844: A Study in Ethnic Conflict. Michael Feldberg.

Philadelphia: 1776-2076. Dennis Clark, ed.

Philadelphia's Philosopher Mechanics. Bruce Sinclair.

Philip Mazzei: Jefferson's "Zealous Whig." Margherita Marchione, ed.

Philipp Hedderich, 1744-1808: Ein rheinischer Kanonist aus dem Minoritenorden im zeitalter der Aufklärung. Peter Frowein.

The Philippine Claim to Sabah. Michael Leifer.

The Philosophers and the People. Harry C. Payne.

The Phoenicians: The Purple Empire of the Ancient World. Gerhard Herm.

Photius and the Carolingians: The Trinitarian Controversy. R. Haugh.

The Photographic Eye of Ben Shahn. Davis Pratt, ed.

Physics and Archaeology. M. J. Aitken.

A Pictorial History of Texas A & M University, 1876-1976. Henry C. Dethloff.

Pictorial Treasury of U.S. Stamps. Elene Marzulla, ed.

Pietro Taglialatela. Giovanni Iurato.

Piety and Power. Silvano M. Tomasi.

The Pigtail War: American Involvement in the Sino-Japanese War of 1894-1895. Jeffery M. Dorwart.

Pilgrimage: An Image of Mediaeval Religion. Jonathan Sumption.

The Pilgrims. Francis Dillon.

Pillars of Profit. Martin Robin.

The Pima Indians. Frank Russell.

Pioneer Bush Pilot: The Story of Noel Wien. Ira Harkey.

A Pioneer Churchman. E. Clifford Nelson, ed.

Pioneering the Union Pacific: A Reappraisal of the Builders of the Railroad. Charles Edgar Ames.

The Pioneers. Huston Horn.

Placenames of Georgia: Essays of John H. Goff. John H. Goff.

"A Plainer Translation:" Joseph Smith's Translation of the Bible-- A History and Commentary. Robert J. Matthews.

The Plains Apache. John Upton Terrell.

Plains Indian Mythology. Alice Marriott and Carol K. Rachlin.

The Plains Indians. Francis Haines.

The Plans of War: The General Staff and British Military Strategy c. 1900-1916. John Gooch.

Plantation Societies, Race Relations, and the South. Edgar T. Thompson.

Les plats attiques à figures noires. Denise Callipolitis-Feytmans.

Le plébiscite des Cent-jours (avril-mai 1815). Frédéric Bluche.

The Pluralist State. David Nicholls.

Plutarch's Lives. Alan Wardman.

Poder y conflicto social en el valle del Mantaro (1900-1974). Georgio Alberti and Rodrigo Sanchez.

Podestaria e Capitanato di Padova. Amelio Tagliaferri, ed.

The Poet's Record. Keith Wilson and Elva Motherall, eds.

Poverty and Charity in Aix-en-
Provence, 1640-1789. Cissie
C. Fairchilds.
Poverty in New York, 1783-1825.
Raymond A. Mohl.
The Poverty of Power: Energy
and the Economic Crisis.
Barry Commoner.
Power and Independence. P. C.
Lloyd.
Power and the Pulpit in Puritan
New England. Emory Elliott.
The Power Broker: Robert Moses
and the Fall of New York.
Robert A. Caro.
Power, Law, and Society: A
Study of the Will to Power and
the Will to Law. Edgar Boden-
heimer.
Power, Persistence and Change.
Margaret Stacey, et al.
Power Shift. Kirkpatrick Sale.
Power to Dissolve: Lawyers and
Marriages in the Courts of the
Roman Curia. John T. Noonan,
Jr.
The Power to Probe: A Study of
Congressional Investigations.
James Hamilton.
Pradzieje Europy ad XL do IV
tysiaclecia. Janusz Krzystof
and Stefan Karol Kozlowki.
Prairie Oasis. Donovan L. Hop-
sommer.
Prairie Politics: Parties and
Platforms in North Dakota,
1889-1914. Warren A. Henke,
comp.
Prairie School Architecture. H.
Allen Brooks.
The Prairie West to 1905. Lewis
G. Thomas, ed.
Pre-Capitalist Modes of Produc-
tion. Barry Hindess and Paul
Q. Hirst.
Precious Women: A Feminist
Phenomenon in the Age of
Louis XIV. Dorothy Anne
Liot Backer.
Precolonial Africa: An Economic
and Social History. Robert W.
July.
Prefaces. J. Frank Dobie.
Prehistoric Art of Australia.
Dacre Stubbs.
Prehistoric Greece and Cyprus:
An Archaeological Handbook.
Hans-Günter Buchholz and

Vassos Karageorghis.
The Prehistory and Protohistory of
India and Pakistan. H. D. San-
kalia.
The Prehistory of the Tehuacan
Valley. Vol. 5. Richard S.
MacNeish, ed.
A Preliminary Study of the Ruins
of Xcaret, Quintana Roo, Mexico.
E. Wyllys Andrews IV and
Anthony P. Andrews.
Preliminary Survey of Documents
in the Archives of the Russian
Orthodox Church in Alaska.
Barbara Sweetland Smith.
Prelude to Disaster: The American
Role in Vietnam 1940-1963.
Weldon A. Brown.
Prelude to Revolution: Mao, the
Party, and the Peasant Question,
1962-66. Richard Baum.
Les premières années du parle-
mentarisme québécois (1867-1878).
Marcel Hamelin.
The Presidency of George Washing-
ton. Forrest McDonald.
The Presidency of James Buchanan.
Elbert B. Smith.
The Presidency of John Adams.
Ralph Adams Brown.
The Presidency of William Howard
Taft. Paolo E. Coletta.
The President and Protest. Donald
J. Lisio.
The President Is Calling. Milton S.
Eisenhower.
President of the Concil C. Th.
Zahle's Diary 1914-1917. Tage
Kaarsted.
Presidential Advisory Commissions.
Thomas R. Wolanin.
Presidential Spending Power. Louis
Fisher.
The Presidio: Bastion of Spanish
Borderlands. Max L. Moorhead.
Pressure from Without in Early Vic-
torian England. Patricia Hollis,
ed.
The Prestes Column Revolution in
Brazil. Neill Macauley.
Pretty Shield: Medicine Woman in
the Crows. Frank B. Linderman.
Preventive Medicine in the United
States, 1900-1975. George Rosen.
Prezzi e mercedi a Milano dal 1701
al 1860. Vols. 1 and 2. Aldo
de Maddalena.
The Price of Dependency: Civil Lib-

Provincial Magistrates and Revolutionary Politics in France, 1789-1795. Philip Dawson.

Provincial Politics and Indian Nationalism. Gordon Johnson.

The Provincial Towns of Georgian England: A Study of the Building Process, 1740-1820. C. W. Chalklin.

Provision for the Relief of the Poor in Manchester 1754-1826. G. B. Hindle.

The Pseudo-Jonathan Targum and Its Relationship to Targum Onkelos. Gerard J. Kuiper.

The Psychological and Ethical Aspects of Mormon Group Life. E. E. Ericksen.

Psychology of the Mexican: Culture and Personality. R. Díaz-Guerrero.

The Public and the Schools. Selwyn K. Troen.

Public Archaeology. Charles R. McGimsey, III.

The Public Career of Cully A. Cobb. Roy V. Scott and J. G. Shoalmire.

Public Health and the Medical Profession in the Renaissance. Carlo M. Cipolla.

The Public Image of Big Business in America, 1880-1940: A Quantitative Study in Social Change. Louis Galambos.

The Public Life of Eugene Semple: Promoter and Politician of the Pacific Northwest. Alan Hynding.

Public Papers of the Presidents of the United States: Herbert Hoover. National Archives and Records Service.

Public Papers of the Presidents of the United States: Richard Nixon. National Archives and Records Service.

Public Papers of the Secretaries-General of the United Nations. Vols. 4 and 5. Andrew W. Cordier and Wilder Foote, eds.

Published in Paris: American and British Writers, Printers, and Publishers in Paris, 1920-1939. Hugh Ford.

Publishing in Africa in the 70's. E. Oluwasanmi, E. McLean, and H. Zell, eds.

Pueblo Animals and Myths. Hamilton A. Tyler.

Puerto Rico and the Puerto Ricans. Clifford A. Hauberg.

Puerto Rico and the Puerto Ricans. Adalberto Lopez and James Petras, eds.

Puerto Rico y la crisis de la Guerra Hispanoamericana: 1895-1898. Carmelo Rosario Natal.

The Pulse of Freedom: American Liberties, 1920-1970's. Alan D. Reitman.

Punishing Criminals. Ernest van den Haag.

The Punjab Tradition ... in Nineteenth-Century India. P. H. M. VanDen Dungen.

The Purchase of Paradise. Joel T. Rosenthal.

The Puritan Origins of the American Self. Sacvan Bercovitch.

Puritanism in America. Larzer Ziff.

Purity Crusade: Sexual Morality and Social Control, 1868-1900. David J. Pivar.

Pursuing the American Dream. Richard Krickus.

The Pursuit of Knowledge in the Early American Republic. Alexandra Oleson and Sanborn C. Brown, eds.

Pursuit of the Ancient Maya: Some Archaeologists of Yesterday. Robert L. Brunhouse.

-Q-

Quaderni per la storia dell'Università di Padova. 6 vols. Istituto per la Storia dell'Università di Padova.

Quaker Encounters, Vol. I. John Ormerod Greenwood.

The Quaker Family in Colonial America: A Portrait of the Society of Friends. J. William Frost.

La Quantification en Histoire. G. Kurgan and P. Moureaux.

The Queen v. Louis Riel. Desmond Morton.

Quellen zur Geschichte der Taufer in der Schweiz, IV Bd. Martin Haas, ed.

The Quest for Orthodox Church Unity in America. Archimandrite Serafim.

The Quest for Ulysses. W. B. Stanford and J. V. Luce.

The Quiet Warrior: A Biography of Admiral Raymond A. Spruance. Thomas B. Buell.

Quiroga y Rosas. Enrique M. Barba.

Quisling: The Career and Political Ideas of Vidkun Quisling, 1887-1945. Paul M. Hayes.

-R-

R. A. Long's Planned City: The Story of Longview. John M. McClelland, Jr.

Race Against Time. Dom Hélder Cámara.

Race and Economics. Thomas Sowell.

Race and Politics in Urban Malaya. Alvin Rabushka.

Race and Slavery in the Western Hemisphere: Quantitative Studies. Stanley L. Engerman and Eugene D. Genovese, eds.

Race, Class and Politics in Colonial Mexico, 1610-1670. J. I. Israel.

Race, Class, and Power. Leo Kuper.

The Race Concept. Michael Banton and Jonathan Harwood.

Rachel of Old Louisiana. Avery O. Craven.

Racism and Empire: White Settlers and Colored Immigrants in the British Self-Governing Colonies 1830-1910. Robert A. Huttenback.

Radical Artisan: William James Linton 1812-97. F. B. Smith.

Radical Christian Testimonies 1520-1650. Lowell H. Zuck.

Radical Journalist: H. W. Massingham (1860-1924). Alfred F. Havighurst.

Radical Politics in Modern Turkey. Jacob M. Landau.

Radical Politics in West Bengal. Marcus F. Franda.

Radical Reform and Political Persuasion in the Life and Writings of Thomas More. Martin Fleisher.

Radical Republicans in the North. James C. Mohr, ed.

The Radical Republicans: Lincoln's Vanguard for Racial Justice. Hans L. Trefousse.

Radicalism in Mediterranean France. Leo Loubère.

Radicals in Urban Politics: The Alinsky Approach. Robert Bailey, Jr.

Radioactivity and Atomic Theory. Thaddeus J. Trenn, ed.

Railroads and Rifles. Dennis E. Showalter.

Railroads of Arizona. David F. Myrick.

The Railway History of Lincoln. J. G. Ruddock and R. E. Pearson.

Railways and the Copper Mines of Katanga. S. E. Katzenellenbogen.

Railways in England, 1826 and 1827. C. von Oeynhausen and H. Von Dechen.

Rajahs and Rebels: The Ibans of Sarawak under Brooke Rule, 1841-1941. Robert Pringle.

Le ralliement du clergé français à la morale liquorienne. L'abbé Gousset et ses précurseurs (1785-1832). Jean Guerber.

The Ramapo Mountain People. David S. Cohen.

Ramesses II: A Chronological Structure of His Reign. John D. Schmidt.

Ranch Schoolteacher. Eulalia Bourne.

Rancho Cucamonga and Dona Merced. Esther B. Black.

Ravenscrag: The Allan Royal Mail Line. Thomas E. Appleton.

Reactions to the French Revolution. Richard Cobb.

Readings on La Raza. Matt S. Meier and Feliciano Rivera, eds.

The Reaffirmation of Republicanism: Eisenhower and the Eighty-Third Congress. Gary W. Reichard.

Reappraisals in British Imperial History. Ronald Hyam and Ged Martin.

Reason, Experiment, and Mysticism in the Scientific Revolution. M. L. Righini Bonelli and William R. Shea, eds.

The Rebel on the Bridge. Glyn Barratt.

Thessaloniki. Hans Peter
Laubscher.
Religion and Political Culture in
Kano. John N. Paden.
Religion and Ritual in Chinese So-
ciety. Arthur P. Wolf, ed.
Religion and Social Class: The
Disruption Years in Aberdeen.
A. Allen MacLaren.
Religion and Soviet Foreign Policy,
1945-1970. William C. Fletcher.
Religion and State in Iran, 1785-
1906: The Role of the Ulama in
the Qajar Period. Hamid Algar.
Religion and Trade in New Nether-
land. George L. Smith.
Religion and Violence: A Primer
for White Americans. Robert
McAfee Brown.
Religion and World History.
Christopher Dawson.
The Religion of Isaac Newton.
Frank E. Manuel.
Religion versus Revolution: The
Interpretation of the French Rev-
olution by German Protestant
Churchmen, 1789-1799. Edward
Dixon Junkin.
Religión y política en la Cuba del
siglo XIX: El Obispo Espada
visto a la luz de los archivos
romanos, 1802-1832. Miguel
Figueroa y Miranda.
Religions of Ancient India. Louis
Renou.
Religious Liberty in the United
States. Elwyn A. Smith.
Religious Movements in Contem-
porary America. Irving I.
Zaretsky and Mark P. Leone,
eds.
"Remember the Ladies": New
Perspectives on Women in
American History. Essays in
Honor of Nelson Manfred Blake.
Carol V. R. George, ed.
The Reminiscences of Doctor John
Sebastian Helmcken. Dorothy
Blakey Smith.
The Reminiscences of Doctor John
Sebastian Helmcken. John
Sebastian Helmcken.
The Renaissance of Canadian His-
tory. Lewis H. Thomas.
A Repertoire of League of Nations
Serial Documents, 1919-1947.
Victor Yves Ghebali and Catherine
Ghebali.

Report from Swaneng Hill. Patrick
Van Rensburg.
The Report of the Royal Commission
of 1552. W. C. Richardson, ed.
Representative Government and the
Revolution. Melvin Yazawa, ed.
The Representative of the People?
Voters and Voting in England
Under the Early Stuarts. Derek
Hirst.
The Republic of Armenia. Vol. I.
Richard G. Hovannisian.
Republikanische Verfassung und
Bürgerliche Freiheit: Die Verfas-
sungen und politischen Ideen der
amerikanischen Revolution. Willi
Paul Adams.
Research in Mexican History: Topics,
Methodology, Sources, and a
Practical Guide to Field Research.
Richard E. Greenleaf and Michael
C. Meyer.
Research in the Administration of
Public Policy. Frank B. Evans
and Harold T. Pinkett, eds.
Researches in Altaic Languages.
Louis Ligeti, ed.
Researches on the United States.
Philip Mazzei.
Resistance and Revolution in China:
The Communists and the Second
United Front. Tetsuya Kataoka.
Resistance at Christiana: The Fugi-
tive Slave Rebellion, Christiana,
Pennsylvania, September 11, 1851;
A Documentary Account. Jonathan
Katz.
Respect for Life. Sylvester M.
Morey and Olivia L. Gilliam, eds.
Respectable Folly. Clarke Garrett.
Restless River: International Law
and the Behavior of the Rio
Grande. Jerry E. Mueller.
Restoration Historians and the English
Civil War. Royce MacGillivray.
Retaliation: Japanese Attacks and
Allied Countermeasures on the
Pacific Coast in World War II.
Bert Webber.
La Reunión: a Personal Chronicle of
the Municipal Consolidation of Las
Vegas, New Mexico. Lynn I.
Perrigo.
Revelations of New England Archi-
tecture. Jill Grossman.
Revolt in Bussa. Michael Crowder.
Revolution and Cosmopolitanism.
Joseph R. Levenson.

sical Culture and Celtic So-
ciety. Keith Branigan and P.
J. Fowler, eds.
Romanian-Bulgarian Relations in
the Course of the Centuries
(12th-19th Centuries). M.
Berza, et al., eds.
Romantic Revolutionary: A Bi-
ography of John Reed. Robert
A. Rosenstone.
Rome and Canterbury Through
Four Centuries: A Study of the
Relations Between the Church of
Rome and the Anglican Churches,
1530-1973. Bernard and
Margaret Pawley.
Rome Before Avignon: A Social
History of Thirteenth-Century
Rome. Robert Brentano.
Roosevelt and Batista: Good Neigh-
bor Diplomacy in Cuba, 1933-
1945. Irwin F. Gellman.
Roosevelt's Image Brokers: Poets,
Playwrights, and the Use of the
Lincoln Symbol. Alfred Hayworth
Jones.
The Roots of Black Nationalism.
Rodney Carlisle.
Roscoe Pound. David Wigdor.
The Round Table Movement and
Imperial Union. John E. Ken-
dle.
Rousseau: Solitude et com-
munauté. Bronisław Baczko.
Rousseau: Stoic and Romantic.
Kennedy F. Roche.
Rowan County. James S. Brawley.
Royalton, Vermont. Hope Nash.
Rubricae Cartusiae Gosnayensis.
James Hogg, ed.
Rudolf II and His World. J. W.
Evans.
Rudyard Kipling and His World.
Kingsley Amis.
The Ruins of Time. David Adam-
son.
Rules and Precepts of the Jesuit
Missions of Northwestern New
Spain. Charles W. Polzer.
Ruling from Horseback: Manchu
Politics in the Oboi Regency,
1661-1669. Robert B. Oxnam.
Rural Change and Urban Growth
1500-1800. C. W. Chalklin
and M. A. Havinden, eds.
Rural Development and Bureaucra-
cy in Tanzania: The Case of
the Mwanza Region. James R.

Finucane.
Rural Development: World Fron-
tiers. Laurence Hewes.
Rural Discontent in Nineteenth-
Century Britain. J. P. D. Dun-
babin.
Rural Industry in the Port Philip
Region, 1835-1880. Lynnette J.
Peel.
Rural Protest: Peasant Movements
and Social Change. Henry A.
Landsberger, ed.
Rural Settlement and Farming in
Germany. Alan Mayhew.
Russell W. Porter: Arctic Explorer,
Artist, Telescope Maker. Berton
C. Willard.
Russia and Black Africa Before
World War II. Edward Thomas
Wilson.
Russia and Kazan. Jaroslaw Pelen-
ski.
Russia in Asia: A Record and a
Study, 1558-1899. Alexis
Krausse.
Russia, the People and the Power.
Robert G. Kaiser.
Russia Under the Old Regime.
Richard Pipes.
The Russian Autocracy in Crisis,
1905-1907. Ann Erickson Healy.
The Russian Constitutional Experi-
ment: Government and Duma,
1907-1914. Geoffrey A. Hosking.
Russian Imperialism From Ivan the
Great to the Revolution. Taras
Hunczak, ed.
Russian Internationalists in the
Struggle for the Hungarian Soviet
Republic, 1919. A. A. Solov'ev,
et al., eds.
The Russian Library in the 16th and
17th Centuries. M. I. Slukhov-
skii.
Russian Peasants and Soviet Power.
M. Lewin.
Russian Social Thought and Publish-
ing in the Caucasus During the
First Third of the 19th Century.
D. L. Vateishvili.
The Russian State During the 15th-
17th Centuries. M. N. Tik-
homirov.
Russians on the Pacific, 1743-1799.
Raisa V. Makarova.
Russische Orientpolitik und die
Entstehung des deutschen
Kaiserreiches 1866-1870/71.

Dietrich Beyrau.
Russko-amerikanskie otnoshenii,
1815-1832. N. N. Bolkhovitinov.
Russland und das Papsttum. Part
3. Eduard Winter.
Russland und Deutschland. Uwe
Liszkowski, ed.
Rustic Canyon and the Story of the
Uplifters. Betty Lou Young and
Thomas R. Young.

-S-

S. O. S. for Catholic Schools.
C. Albert Koob and Russell
Shaw.
S. Michele in Africisco zu Raven-
na. Peter Grossmann.
Sabbatai Sevi. Gershom Scholem.
Sabers on the Rio Grande. Jerry
Thompson.
Die sächsische Landeskirche im
Kirchenkampf, 1933-1937.
Joachim Fischer.
Sacrae Domus Militiae Templi
Hierosolymitani Magistri. M.
L. Bulst-Thiele.
The Sacred Meadows. Abdul
Hamid M. el-Zein.
The Sacred Scrolls of the Southern
Ojibway. Selwyn Dewdney.
Safeguarding the Public Health:
Newark, 1895-1918. Stuart
Galishoff.
Saint Francis: Nature Mystic.
Edward A. Armstrong.
St. Mary's County, Maryland in
the American Revolution. Ed-
win W. Beitzell.
Saint Paul. Michael Grant.
Le Saint Siège et les victimes de
la guerre, Janvier 1941-Décem-
bre 1942. Pierre Blet, et al.,
eds.
Saint Stanislaus Kostka. Joseph
Majkowski.
Saints and Politicians: Essays
on the Organisation of a
Senegalese Peasant Society.
Donal B. Cruise O'Brien.
Salamis. Vol. 5. Vassos Kara-
georghis.
Salem, Massachusetts, 1626-
1683: A Covenant Community.
Richard P. Gildrie.

Salem Possessed: The Social Ori-
gins of Witchcraft. Paul Boyer
and Stephen Nissenbaum.
Salt Lake Sketchbook: Historic
Buildings from an Artist's View.
J. Hogue Case.
The Saltonstall Papers, 1607-1815.
Robert E. Moody.
"Salutary Neglect": The American
Colonies in the First Half of the
Eighteenth Century. Murray N.
Rothbard.
Salvien de Marseille, Oeuvres Tome
II. Georges Lagarrigue, ed.
Sam Adams' Revolution: 1765-1776.
Cass Canfield.
Sam Rayburn. Alfred Steinberg.
The Samoan Tangle: A Study in
Anglo-German-American Rela-
tions, 1878-1900. Paul M. Ken-
nedy.
Samos XI: Bildwerke der Archaischen
Zeit und des Strengen Stils.
Brigitte Freyer-Schauenburg.
Samuel Adam's Revolution 1765-1776.
Cass Canfield.
Samuel Colt's Submarine Battery.
Philip K. Lundeberg.
Samuel Gompers and the Origins
of the American Federation of
Labor 1848-1896. Stuart Bruce
Kaufman.
Samuel May Williams: Early Texas
Entrepreneur. Margaret Swett
Henson.
Samuel Seabury, 1729-1796. Bruce
E. Steiner.
San Augustin. G. W. Chambers
and C. L. Sonnichsen.
San Francisco, 1846-1856. Roger
W. Lotchin.
The San Xavier Altarpiece. Robert
C. Goss.
Sandbars and Sternwheelers.
Pamela Ashworth Puryear and
Nath Winfield, Jr.
Sangha and State in Burma. E.
Michael Mendelson.
The Santa Fe Trail. R. L. Duffus.
Santeria: African Magic in Latin
America. Migene Gonzalez-
Wippler.
Sarah Winnemucca: A Most Extra-
ordinary Woman of the Paiute Na-
tion. Katherine Gehm.
Sarvodaya and the Problem of
Political Sovereignty. T. S.
Devadoss.

Der Sâsânidische Siegelkanon:
Handbücher der Mittelasiatischen
Numismatik. Vol. 4. Robert
Göbl.
Satan and Mára: Christian and
Buddhist Symbols of Evil.
James W. Boyd.
Savoir et Pouvoir. Pierre Thi-
bault.
Sayyid Jamāl ad-Dīn "al Afghānī:
A Political Biography. Nikki
R. Keddie.
The Scalpel, the Sword: The
Story of Doctor Norman Bethune.
Ted Allan and Sydney Gordon.
Scandinavia. Franklin D. Scott.
Scandinavian England. H. P. R.
Finberg.
La schiavitù nella società Sicilians
dell'età moderna. Giovanni Mar-
rone.
Schiffahrt und Güterverkehr zwischen
Koln und Rotterdam, 1794-1850/
51. J. H. Schachwacht.
Schmuckarbeiten in Edelmetall,
Band II. Adolf Greifenhagen.
Scholars, Saints, and Sufis: Mus-
lim Religious Institutions in the
Middle East since 1500. Nikki
R. Keddie, ed.
Scholastic World History Program.
4 vols. Ira Peck, William
Johnson and Frances Plotkin.
The School of the French Revolu-
tion. R. R. Palmer, ed. and
trans.
The School Upon a Hill: Education
and Society in Colonial New
England. James Axtell.
Schooling in Capitalist America.
Samuel Bowles and Herbert
Gintis.
Schools for All: The Blacks and
Public Education in the South,
1865-1877. William Preston
Vaughn.
Schwerpunkte der Eisengewinnung
und Eisenverarbeitung in
Europa, 1500-1650. Herman
Kellenbenz, ed.
Science and Civilisation in China.
Vol. 5. Joseph Needham.
Science and Controversy. A. J.
Meadows.
Science and Creation in the Mid-
dle Ages. Nicholas H. Steneck.
Science and the Ante-Bellum
American College. Stanley

M. Guralnick.
Science in Russian Culture 1861-
1917. Alexander Vucinich.
Scientia Augustiniana. Cornelius
Petrus Mayer and Willigis
Eckermann.
The Scientific Breakthrough: The
Impact of Modern Invention.
Ronald W. Clark.
The Scientist and Ethical Decision.
Charles Hatfield, ed.
Scotland from the Eleventh Century
to 1603. Bruce Webster.
Scotland: The Later Middle Ages.
Ranald Nicholson.
Scotland: The Making of the King-
dom. Archibald A. M. Duncan.
Scotland: The Shaping of a Nation.
Gordon Donaldson.
The Scots in Franconia: A Century
of Monastic Life. Mark Dil-
worth.
Scott Nearing. Stephen J. Whitfield.
The Scottish Revolution, 1637-1644.
David Stevenson.
The Scottish Tradition: Essays in
Honour of Ronald Gordon Cant.
G. W. S. Barrow, ed.
Scripta Hierosolymitana. Vol.
XXVI. B. Jozef, ed.
Scripta Mercaturae. T. G. Werner,
ed.
Scritti e discorsi extraparlamentari,
1870-1920. 2 vols. Sidney
Sonnino.
Sculpture of a City: Philadelphia's
Treasures in Bronze and Stone.
Fairmont Park Assn.
Sculture del Foro severiano di
Leptis Magna. Maria Floriani
Squarciapino.
The Sea Change: The Migration of
Social Thought, 1930-1965. H.
Stuart Hughes.
The Sea Peoples and Egypt. Ales-
sandra Nibbi.
The Sea Shell Islands: A History
of Sanibel and Captiva. Eli-
nore M. Dormer.
The Search for a Black Nationality:
Black Emigration and Coloniza-
tion, 1787-1863. Floyd J.
Miller.
A Search for Solvency: Bretton
Woods and the International
Monetary System, 1941-1971.
Alfred E. Eckes, Jr.
Seascape and the American Imagina-

tion. Roger B. Stein.
The Second Chinese Revolution.
K. S. Karol.
The Second Empire and the Press:
A Study of Government-Inspired
Brochures on French Foreign
Policy in Their Propaganda
Milieu. Natalie Isser.
A Second Identity. Richard Cobb.
The Second World War: An Il-
lustrated History. A. J. P.
Taylor.
Seconda Mostra della Preistoria
e della Protostoria nel Salerni-
tano. Gianni Bailo Modesti,
Bruno d'Agostino and Patrizia
Gastaldi, eds.
Secrets of the Fascist Era.
Howard McGaw Smyth.
The Secularization of the European
Mind in the Nineteenth Century.
Owen Chadwick.
Seeking for the Kingdom of God.
Eberhard and Emmy Arnold.
The Segmented Society. Robert
W. Wiebe.
The Segregation Struggle in
Louisiana, 1862-77. Roger A.
Fischer.
La seigneurie et le vignoble de
Chateau Latour: Histoire d'un
grand cru du Médoc (XIVe-XXe
siècle). Vols. I and II.
Charles Higounet, et al., eds.
Die Selbstbehauptung einer Nation:
Nationalsozialistische Kultur-
politik und polnische Wider-
standsbewegung im Genaral-
gouvernement, 1939-1945.
Christoph Klessman.
Die "Selbstverwaltungsidee" des
Freiherrn vom Stein und ihre
geistigen Grundlagen: Zugleich
ein Beitrag zur Geschichte der
politischen Ethik im 18. Jahr-
hundert. Dieter Schwab.
Select Papers of the Late R. G.
Goodchild. Joyce Reynolds, ed.
A Selected Bibliography on George
Washington's Interest in Agri-
culture. Alan and Donna Jean
Fusonie, comps.
Selected Works of Jawaharlal Nehru.
S. Gopal, ed.
Selected Writings on Science, In-
dustry and Social Organisation
(1760-1825). Henri Saint-
Simon.

Selective Genocide in Burundi.
René Lemarchand and David
Martin.
The Seleucid Army: Organization
and Tactics in the Great Cam-
paigns. Bezalel Bar-Kochva.
Self-Evident Truths: Being a Dis-
course on the Origins and De-
velopment of the First Principles
of American Government--Popular
Sovereignty, Natural Rights, and
Balance and Separation of Powers.
Paul K. Conkin.
Self-Governing Socialism, a Reader.
2 vols. Branko Horvat, Mihailo
Marković and Rudi Supek, eds.
Sembradores Ricardo Flores Magon
y el Partido Liberal Mexicano:
A Eulogy and Critique. Juan
Gómez-Quiñones.
Senator Joseph McCarthy and the
American Labor Movement.
David M. Oshinsky.
Send These to Me: Jews and Other
Immigrants in Urban America.
John Higham.
Senegal: Tradition, Diversification
and Economic Development; A
Report. International Bank of
Reconstruction and Development.
Senegambia: Proceedings of a Col-
loquium at the University of
Aberdeen, April 1974. R. C.
Bridges, ed.
The Separation of College and State.
John S. Whitehead.
Separatism Among Indian Muslims.
Francis Robinson.
Septimius Severus: The African
Emperor. Anthony Birley.
Sequatchie: A Story of the Southern
Cumberlands. J. Leonard Raul-
ston and James W. Livingood.
Serbia, Nikola Pasic, and Yugo-
slavia. Alex N. Dragnich.
Sergei Zubatov and Revolutionary
Marxism. Jeremiah Scheiderman.
Sermons, 2(18-39). Isaac de
l'Etoile.
Les Sermons de Jean XXII sur la
Vision Béatifique. Marc Dyk-
mans.
Servants of the Sword: French In-
tendants of the Army 1630-1690.
Douglas Clark Baxter.
Serve the People, Observations
on Medicine in the People's Re-
public of China. Victor W. and

Ruth Sidel.
Serving the People. K. A. Meretskov.
Serving the Small Farmer: Policy Choices in Indian Agricultural Development. Guy Hunter and Anthony F. Botterall, eds.
The Setting of Second Clement in Early Christianity. Karl Paul Donfried.
Settlement Houses and the Great Depression. Judith Ann Trolander.
The Seven Sisters. Anthony Sampson.
1776: Year of Illusions. Thomas Fleming.
Seventeenth-Century England. Paul S. Seaver, ed.
The Seventh Hero. Philip Rosenberg.
The Severing Line. Sara Cardiff.
Sex and Marriage in Utopian Communities. Raymond Lee Muncy.
Sex and Society in Shakespeare's Age. A. L. Rowse.
Shadow of a Continent. Larry L. Meyer.
The Shadow War: European Resistance 1939-1945. Henri Michel.
Shadows of Old Saddleback. Terry E. Stephenson.
Shaftesbury: A Biography of the Seventh Earl, 1801-1885. Georgina Battiscombe.
The Shambaa Kingdom: A History. S. Feierman.
The Shape of European History. William H. McNeill.
The Shape of the Puritan Mind. Ernest Benson Lowrie.
The Shaping of Southern Politics. J. Morgan Kousser.
Sharlot Hall on the Arizona Strip: A Diary of a Journey Through Northern Arizona in 1911. Sharlott M. Hall.
The Shattered Synthesis: New England Puritanism Before the Great Awakening. James W. Jones.
Shen Pu-hai: A Chinese Political Philosopher of the Fourth Century B.C. Herrlee G. Creel.
Shiloh: Bloody April. Wiley Sword.
Shipbuilding in Colonial America.

Joseph A. Goldenberg.
Shipping, Maritime Trade and the Economic Development of Colonial North America. James F. Shepherd and Gary M. Walton.
Ships Beneath the Sea. Robert F. Burgess.
Ships, Seas, and Scientists: U.S. Naval Exploration in the Nineteenth Century. Vincent Ponko, Jr.
The Shires of Bennington: A Sampler of Green Mountain Heritage. Tyler Resch.
Shirley Jackson. Lenemaja Friedman.
Shōgun: A Novel of Japan. James Clavell.
Shoot Me a Biscuit. Daniel G. Moore.
Shop Talk. James Lawton, ed.
A Short History of Guerrilla Warfare. John Ellis.
A Short History of the Papacy in the Middle Ages. Walter Ullmann.
A Show of Justice. Alan Ward.
Showdown: Western Gunfighters in Moments of Truth. Herman Toepperwein.
La Sicilia nella Politica mediterranea delle grandi potenze. Gaetano Falzone.
The "Sick Heart" of Modern Europe: The Problem of the Danubian Lands. Hugh Seton-Watson.
Sierra Leone. A. P. Kup.
Silas Deane--Patriot or Traitor? Coy Hilton James.
Silas Downer: Forgotten Patriot: His Life and Writings. Carl Bridenbaugh.
Silchester: The Roman Town of Calleva. George C. Boon.
Silent Sisterhood: Middle Class Women in the Victorian Home. Patricia Branca.
Silk Glove Hegemony: Finnish-Soviet Relations, 1944-1974. John P. Vloyantes.
Silver Saga. Duane A. Smith.
Simple Justice. Richard Kluger.
Since Columbus: Poverty and Pluralism in the History of the Americas. Peter d'A Jones.
Since 1945: Politics and Diplomacy in Recent American History. Robert A. Divine.
The Sinews of Independence. Charles

The Social History of the Reformation. Lawrence P. Buck and Jonathan W. Zophy, eds.

The Social Origins of the French Revolution: The Debate on the Role of the Middle Classes. Ralph W. Greenlaw.

The Social Passion: Religion and Social Reform in Canada, 1914-1928. Richard Allen.

The Social Philosophers. Robert Nisbet.

The Social Prelude to Stalinism. Roger Pethybridge.

The Social Problem in the Philosophy of Rousseau. John Charvet.

Social Science and the Ignoble Savage. Ronald L. Meek.

Social Security in Africa. Pierre Mouton.

The Social Sources of Division in the Disciples of Christ, 1865-1900. David Elwin Harrell.

The Social Thought of Rousseau and Burke. David Cameron.

Socialism and the Challenge of War. J. M. Winter.

Socialism and the Cities. Bruce M. Stave, ed.

Socialism and the Great War: The Collapse of the Second International. Georges Haupt.

Socialism in India. B. R. Nanda, ed.

The Socialism of Fools. Andrew G. Whiteside.

Il socialismo: Da Moses Hess alla Prima Internazionale nella recente storiografia. Gian Mario Bravo.

The Socialist Left and the German Revolution. David W. Morgan.

Socialist Ownership and Political Systems. Wlodzimierz Brus.

Las Sociedades Patrioticas 1820-1823. 2 vols. Alberto Gil Novales.

La société et les pauvres en Europe (XVIe-XVIIIe siècles). Jean-Pierre Gutton.

Society and Culture in Early Modern France. Natalie Zemon Davis.

Society and Politics in Germany 1500-1750. G. Benecke.

Society and Politics in Medieval Italy: The Evolution of the Civil Life, 1000-1350. J. K. Hyde.

Society and Politics in Revolutionary Bordeaux. Alan Forrest.

Society in Colonial North Carolina. Alan D. Watson.

Society in Crisis: France in the Sixteenth Century. J. H. M. Salmon.

The Socioeconomic Development of Bulgar and Gaguzi Villages in Southern Bessarabia (1808-1856). I. I. Meshcheriuk.

Sociology as Social Criticism. T. B. Bottomore.

The Soil Soldiers: The Civilian Conservation Corps in the Great Depression. Leslie Alexander Lacy.

Soldiers and Kinsmen in Uganda. Ali A. Mazrui.

A Soldier's Duty. K. Rokossovsky.

Soldiers, Indians and Silver: North America's First Frontier War. Philip Wayne Powell.

Soleb. Vol. 2. Michela Schiff Giorgini, et al.

Solving "The Indian Problem." Murray L. Wax and Robert W. Buchanan, eds.

Some Anglo-Saxon Bishops of London. Dorothy Whitelock.

Some Men and Some Controversies. Richard Ruggle, ed.

Some Questions on the Historiography of Siberia's Entry into the Russian State. G. P. Basharin.

Some Still Do. Francis E. Abernethy.

Some Whisper of Our Name. Nell Wise Wechter.

Somos Chicanos: Strangers in Our Own Land. David F. Gómez.

Song Branch Settlers. Leonard Roberts.

The Sonoma Mission: San Francisco de Sonoma. Robert S. Smilie.

Soul Force: African Heritage in Afro-American Religion. Leonard E. Barrett.

Sources for English Local History. W. B. Stephens.

Sources for the History of Science, 1660-1914. David Knight.

Sources for the History of the Trade and the Gilds of Amsterdam. Vol. 3. J. G. Van Dillen.

Sources in British Political History 1900-1951. Vol. I: A Guide to

and Barbara Bradshaw, eds.
The Spearheads of the Anglo-Saxon
Settlements. M. J. Swanton.
Special Envoy to Churchill and
Stalin, 1941-1946. W. Averell
Harriman and Elie Abel.
The Spirit of '76: The Growth of
American Patriotism Before In-
dependence, 1607-1776. Carl
Bridenbaugh.
The Spirit of 'Seventy-Six: The
Story of the American Revolution
as Told by Participants. Henry
Steele Commager and Richard B.
Morris, eds.
Spirit Up the People. Taylor Lewis,
Jr.
The Spiritual Power. Richard C.
Trexler.
The Spiritual Regulation of Peter the
Great. Alexander V. Muller, ed.
and trans.
La Spiritualité de Bossuet. Jacques
Le Brun.
The Spirituality of John Calvin.
Lucien Joseph Richard.
The Splintered Party. Dan S.
White.
The Spoiled Child of the Western
World: The Miscarriage of the
American Idea of Our Time.
Henry Fairlie.
Spotted Tail's Folk: A History of
the Brulé Sioux. George E.
Hyde.
Spuddin' In: Recollections of Pi-
oneer Days in the California
Oil Fields. William Rintoul.
Staat und katholische Kirche in
Preussen. Carl Ludwig von
Bar.
Staatliche Sammlung ägyptischer
Kunst in der Müncher Residenz
am Hofgarten. Hans Wolfgang
Müller.
Stability and Change in an English
County Town: A Social Study
of York 1801-1851. Alan
Armstrong.
Staffordshire and Worcestershire
Canal. J. I. Langford.
Stagecoaching on El Camino Real.
Charles F. Outland.
Stalin as Revolutionary, 1879-1929:
A Study in History and Person-
ality. Robert C. Tucker.
Stalin: The Man and His Era.
Adam B. Ulam.

Stalin und Hitler: Die Sowjetrus-
sische Aussenpolitik 1930-1941.
Sven Allard.
Stalingrad, Analyse und Dokumenta-
tion einer Schlacht. Manfred
Kehrig.
Stalingrad Risse im Bündnis, 1942-
43. Jürgen Förster.
A Standard of Excellence: Andrew W.
Mellon Founds the National Gal-
lery of Art at Washington. David
Edward Finley.
The Standard of Living in Britain in
the Industrial Revolution. Arthur
J. Taylor, ed.
The Standard-Vacuum Oil Company
and United States East Asian
Policy 1933-1941. Irvine H.
Anderson.
Stanley: An Adventurer Explored.
Richard Hall.
Stanovlenie russko-amerikanskikh
otnoshenii, 1775-1815. N. N.
Bolkhovitinov.
Stark Young. John Pilkington, ed.
Star-Spangled Kitsch. Curtis F.
Brown.
State and Regional Patterns in
American Manufacturing, 1860-
1900. Albert W. Niemi, Jr.
State and Society in Seventeenth-
Century France. Raymond F.
Kierstead, ed.
State and Society in the Politics of
Turkey's Development. Ilkay
Sunar.
Statesmen at War. Piers Mackesy.
The Statistical Movement in Early
Victorian Britain. M. J. Cullen.
Steel Titan: The Life of Charles M.
Schwab. Robert Hessen.
Stellite: A History of the Haynes
Stellite Company, 1912-1972.
Ralph D. Gray.
Stettinius, Sr.: Portrait of a Mor-
gan Business Partner. John
Douglas Forbes.
The Stone Age of Indonesia. H. R.
van Heekeren.
Stone Circles--Standing Stones.
Evan Hadingham.
Storbritannien og Danmark, 1914-
1920. Tage Kaarsted.
Storia di Torino Operaia e So-
cialista. Paolo Spriano.
Storms Brewed in Other Men's
Worlds: The Confrontation of
Indians, Spanish, and French in

the Southwest, 1540-1795.
Elizabeth A. H. John.

Stormy Petrel: N. G. Gonzales
and His State. Lewis Pinckney
Jones.

The Story of American Methodism.
Frederick A. Norwood.

The Story of Mining in New Mexico.
Paige Christiansen.

The Story of the Jewish Community
of Burlington Vermont. Myron
Samuelson.

The Story of the Pony Express:
An Account of the Most Remarkable Mail Service Ever in
Existence and Its Place in History. Glenn D. Bradley.

Strain of Violence: Historical
Studies of American Violence
and Vigilantism. Richard Maxwell Brown.

The Strained Alliance. Robert R.
Simmons.

Strange Contrarieties: Pascal in
England During the Age of
Reason. John Barker.

Stranger and Traveler. Dorothy
Clarke Wilson.

Strangers Devour the Land: A
Chronicle of the Assault Upon
the Last Coherent Hunting Cul-
ture in North America, the Cree
Indians of Northern Quebec, and
Their Vast Primeval Homelands.
Boyce Richardson.

Strategies for Change in the South.
Thomas H. Naylor and James
Clotfelter.

Straw Sandals: Chinese Short
Stories 1918-1933. Harold R.
Isaacs, ed.

A Stream of Light. Conrad
Wright, ed.

Street Life in Medieval England.
G. T. Salusbury-Jones.

The Street Where You Live: A
Guide to the Street Names of
St. Paul. Donald Empson.

Strife on the Waterfront. Vernon
H. Jensen.

Strikes in France: 1830-1968.
Edward Shorter and Charles
Tilly.

Structuralist Poetics. Jonathan
Culler.

Structure and Conflict in Nigeria
1960-1966. Kenneth Post and
Michael Vickers.

The Structure of Jewish History.
Heinrich Graetz.

Les structures du Latium medieval.
Pierre Toubert.

The Struggle for Neutrality: Franco-
American Diplomacy During the
Federalist Era. Albert Hall
Bowman.

Struggle for Synthesis: The Seven-
teenth-Century Background of
Leibniz's Synthesis of Order and
Freedom. Leroy E. Loemker.

Struggle for the American Mediterranean. Lester D. Langley.

Struggle in the Andes: Peasant
Political Mobilization in Peru.
Howard Handelman.

Stuart Royal Proclamations. Vol. I.
James F. Larkin and Paul L.
Hughes, eds.

Stubble and Slough in Dakota.
Frederic Remington.

The Student Political Movement in
Poland. Andrzej Pilch.

Students and Society in Early
Modern Spain. Richard L. Kagan.

Studi e richerche di storia ereticale
italiana del Cinquecento. Antonio Rotondò.

Studi sulla Legazia Apostolica di
Sicilia. Gaetano Catalano.

Studien zur Frühgeschichte des
Deutschen Ordens. Marie-Luise
Favreau.

Studier i Landnámabók. S. Rafnsson.

Studies in African Social Anthropology. Meyer Fortes and Sheila
Patterson, eds.

Studies in British Transport History, 1870-1970. Derek H. Aldcroft.

Studies in Family Planning: India.
Kamala Gopal Rao.

Studies in Joseph ibn Caspi. Barry
Mesch.

Studies in Old Ottoman Criminal
Law. Uriel Heyd.

Studies in Philippine Anthropology.
Mario D. Zamora.

Studies in Richard Hooker: Essays
Preliminary to an Edition of His
Works. W. Speed Hill, ed.

Studies in Southeastern Indian
Languages. James Crawford, ed.

Studies in the Colonial History of
Spanish America. Mario Góngora.

Studies in the History of Dalriada.
J. Bannerman.
Studies in the History of the Near
East. P. M. Holt.
Studies in Tudor and Stuart Poli-
tics and Government: Papers
and Reviews, 1946-1972. 2 vols.
G. R. Elton.
Studies of Field Systems in the
British Isles. A. R. H. Baker
and R. A. Butlin, eds.
Studies on the History of the Hun-
garian Working-Class Movement,
1867-1966. Henrik Vass, ed.
Studies over Jodenvervolging. B.
A. Sijes.
A Study of Future Worlds. Richard
A. Falk.
A Study of Naima. Lewis V.
Thomas.
Style in History. Peter Gay.
Subah of Allahabad Under the
Mughals (1580-1707). S. N.
Sinha.
Successful Negotiation: Trieste
1954. John C. Campbell, ed.
Succession in International Law.
T. T. Poulose.
Succession in the Muslim Family.
Noel J. Coulson.
Sucre, soldado y revolucionario.
John P. Hoover.
The Sudeten Problem 1933-1938:
"Volkstumspolitik" and the
Formulation of Nazi Foreign
Policy. Ronald M. Smelser.
Suffering to Silence: 29th Texas
Cavalry, CSA Regimental His-
tory. John C. Grady and Brad-
ford K. Felmly.
Suffragists and Liberals. David
Morgan.
The Sugar Industry in Pernambuco:
Modernization Without Change,
1840-1910. Peter Eisenberg.
Sukarno: A Political Biography.
J. D. Legge.
Sūkās III. The Neolithic Periods.
P. J. Riis and Hendrik Thrane.
Sumerian Economic Texts from
the Umma Archive. Shin T.
Kang.
The Super Sixth: History of the
6th Armored Division in World
War II and Its Post-War Associ-
ation. George F. Hofmann.
Superculture: American Popular
Culture and Europe. C. W. E.

Bigsby.
The Supreme Court and Religion.
Richard E. Morgan.
The Supreme Court Review: 1973.
Philip B. Kurland, ed.
The Surrogate Proletariat. Gregory
J. Massell.
A Survey of Research in Geography.
The Indian Council of Social
Science Research.
Survival in Two Worlds. Leonard
Thompson.
The Sutton-Taylor Feud. Robert C.
Sutton, Jr.
The Swadeshi Movement in Bengal,
1903-1908. Sumit Sarkar.
Sweden's Development from Poverty
to Affluence, 1750-1970. Steven
Koblick, ed.
The Swedish Heritage in America.
Allan Kastrup.
The Sword and the Flute. David R.
Kinsley.
The Sword of Truth: The Life and
Times of the Shehu Usuman Dan
Fodio. Mervyn Hiskett.
The Swordbearers: Supreme Com-
mand in the First World War.
Correlli Barnett.
Symbol, Sword, and Shield: De-
fending Washington During the
Civil War. Benjamin Franklin
Cooling.
Symbola: Les étrangers et la justice
dans les cités grecques. Philippe
Gauthier.
Symposia on the American Revolu-
tion. (1973 and 1974). Library
of Congress.
Symposium L'Epoque Phanariote.
Institute for Balkan Studies.
Syrian Christians in Muslim Society:
An Interpretation. Robert M.
Haddad.
Systems of North American Witch-
craft and Sorcery. Deward E.
Walker, Jr., ed.
Szechwan and the Chinese Republic:
Provincial Militarism and Central
Power, 1911-1938. Robert A.
Kapp.

-T-

The Taching Oilfield: A Maoist

1945-1953. A. Ross Johnson.
Transformations of the American
Party System: Political Coali-
tions from the New Deal to the
1970s. Everett Carll Ladd, Jr.
The Transition from Feudalism to
Capitalism. Paul Sweezy, et
al.
The Transport Revolution from
1770. Philip S. Bagwell.
Transylvania: Tutor to the West.
John D. Wright, Jr.
Les Travailleurs du Coton au
Quebec 1900-1915. Jacques
Rouillard.
Travel on Southern Antebellum
Railroads, 1828-1860. Eugene
Alvarez.
Travels in the Old South. Eugene
L. Schwaab.
Treasures Among Men: The Fudai
Daimyo in Tokugawa Japan.
Harold Bolitho.
The Treasury of Loyal Retainers.
Takeda Izumo, Miyoshi Shoraku
and Namiki Senryn.
Treaty-Breakers or 'Realpolitiker'?
The Anglo-German Naval Agree-
ment of June 1935. E. H.
Haraszti.
Trek of the Oil Finders. Edgar
Wesley Owen.
Trekking in South Central Africa.
Clement M. Doke.
Trent's Impact on the Portuguese
Patronage Mission. A. da Silva.
Le Trésor des Chartes d'Albret, I.
J.-B. Marquette.
Trial of Faith: Religion and Poli-
tics in Tocqueville's Thought.
Doris S. Goldstein.
The Trial of Martin Luther King.
Alan F. Westin and Barry Ma-
honey.
The Trials of Counsel: Francis
Bacon in 1621. Jonathan Marwil.
Triumph of the Nomads: A History
of Aboriginal Australia. Geoffrey
Blainey.
Tro och Makt i Sovjet. Alex
Milits.
Le Troisième Reich et la Suisse,
1933-1941. Daniel Bourgeois.
Trotsky: An Appreciation of His
Life. Joel Carmichael.
The Trouble They Seen. Dorothy
Sterling.
Truman, the Jewish Vote, and the

Creation of Israel. John
Snetsinger.
Tsarism and the Labor Question in
Russia (1861-1917). V. Ia.
Laverychev.
Tseng Kuo-fan's Private Bureaucracy.
Jonathan Porter.
Tuckahoe Plantation. Jessie Ball
Thompson Krusen.
A Tug of Loyalties. Esmond Wright,
ed.
Turgot on Progress, Sociology and
Economics. R. L. Meek, ed.
Turkey: Geographic and Social Per-
spectives. Peter Benedict, et
al., eds.
Turkey, the Straits and U.S. Policy.
Harry N. Howard.
The Turks of Central Asia. M. A.
Czaplicka.
The Tweedmakers: A History of the
Scottish Fancy Woollen Industry
1600-1914. Clifford Gulvin.
The Twelve Caesars. Michael Grant.
Twelve Mormon Homes Visited in
Succession on a Journey Through
Utah to Arizona. Elizabeth Wood
Kane.
Twentieth-Century Businessmen.
Elwood R. Maunder.
Twentieth-Century Germany: From
Bismarck to Brandt. A. J.
Ryder.
Twentieth-Century Yugoslavia. Fred
Singleton.
Twenty Alabama Books. Rucker Agee.
The Twenty-First Missouri: From
Home Guard to Union Regiment.
Leslie Anders.
Twenty-five Years of Arnhem Trol-
leybuses. G. Aberson.
Twenty-Four Architectural Plans of
Chan Chan, Peru. Michael Ed-
ward Moseley and Carol J.
Mackey.
Twilight of Authority. Robert Nisbet.
Two Calvinistic Methodist Chapels,
1743-1811. Edwin Welch, ed.
Two Classes of Men: Platonism and
English Romantic Thought. David
Newsome.
Two Earths, Two Heavens. Burr
Cartwright Brundage.
200 Trails to Gold: A Guide to
Promising Old Mines and Hidden
Lodes Throughout the West.
Samuel B. Jackson.
Two Hundred Years of Pharmacy in

The U.S. and the Developing World: Agenda for Action 1974. James W. Howe, et al.

The United States and the Development of the Puerto Rican Status Question, 1936-1968. Surendra Bhana.

The United States and the Second Hague Peace Conference: American Diplomacy and International Organization 1899-1914. Calvin DeArmond Davis.

The United States and West Germany, 1945-1973. Roger Morgan.

The U.S. Camel Corps: An Army Experiment. Odie B. Faulk.

U.S. Foreign Policy and the Third World Peasant. Gary L. Olson.

The U.S.A.: A History of Its People and Society. Peter d'A Jones.

Die USA in den berichten italienischer Reisender. Heinz Reiske.

The United States: 1789-1890. William R. Brock.

The United States Since 1945: The Ordeal of Power. Dewey W. Grantham.

Unity and Diversity: Essays in the History, Literature, and Religion of the Ancient Near East. Hans Goedicke and J. J. M. Roberts, eds.

Universal Fascism: The Theory and Practice of the Fascist International, 1928-1936. Michael Arthur Ledeen.

Universalism in America: A Documentary History. Ernest Cassara, ed.

Universities in Politics: Case Studies from the Late Middle Ages and Early Modern Period. J. W. Baldwin and R. A. Goldthwaite, eds.

University Extension. George M. Woytanowitz.

The University in Society. 2 vols. Lawrence Stone, ed.

The University of Ibadan 1948-73. J. F. Ade Ajayi and Tekena N. Tamuno, eds.

The University of South Dakota, 1862-1966. Cedric Cummins.

The University of Wisconsin: One Hundred and Twenty-Five Years. Allan G. Bogue and Robert

Taylor, eds.

Unknown Mexico. Carl Lumholtz.

The Unknown Revolution. V. M. Eichenbaum.

Unrecognized Patriots: The Jews in the American Revolution. Samuel Reznek.

Unternehmen Sonnenblume: Der Entschluss zum Afrika-Feldzug. Charles B. Burdick.

Untersuchungen zu den Klosterreformen Wilhelms von Dijon (962-1031). Neithard Bulst.

Untersuchungen zu einigen Wichtigen Bodenrechtlichen Konsequenzen der Islamischen Eroberungsbewegung. Werner Schmucker.

Unvanquished Puritan: A Portrait of Lyman Beecher. Stuart C. Henry.

Up from Communism: Conservative Odysseys in American Intellectual History. John P. Diggins.

Up to the Front of the Line. Robert P. Turner.

Uphill for Peace. E. Raymond Wilson.

Upton Sinclair: American Rebel. Leon Harris.

The Urban Catholic University. Paul C. Reinert.

The Urban Elite. Sheo Kumar Lal.

Urban Growth and the Circulation of Information. Allan R. Pred.

Urban Networks in Russia, 1750-1800. Gilbert Rozman.

Urban New Jersey Since 1870. William C. Wright, ed.

Urban Politics in Nigeria: A Study of Port Harcourt. Howard Wolpe.

Urbanization and the Government of Migration: The Inter-relation of Urban and Rural Life in Zambia. Helmuth Heisler.

Urbanization as a Social Process. Kenneth Little.

Urbanization at Teotihuacán, Mexico. Vol. I. René Millon, ed.

Urbanization in Latin America. Jorge E. Hardoy, ed.

Uruguay: The Politics of Failure. Martin Weinstein.

The Uses of Media by the Chicano Movement. Francisco J. Lewels, Jr.

Utah: A Hispanic History. Vicente V. Mayer, Jr.

Utbildning till statens tjänst.
David Gaunt.
Utopian Communism in France:
Cabet and the Icarians, 1839-
1851. Christopher H. Johnson.
Utopias on Puget Sound, 1885-1915.
Charles Pierce Lewarne.
L'Utopie ou la Mort. René
Dumont.

-V-

V. D. Nabokov and the Russian
Provisional Government, 1917.
Virgil D. Medlin and Stephen
L. Parsons, eds.
V. Leben und Werker norddeutscher
Jakobiner. Walter Grab.
Valley Forge Rebel. Reinhold
W. Goll.
Valley of Discord. Paul R. Lucas.
Valley of the Spirits: The Upper
Skagit Indians of Western Wash-
ington. June McCormick Col-
lins.
Valois Burgundy. Richard Vaughan.
Vancouver's Past. Raymond Hull,
and Gordon and Christine Soules.
Vanha maataloutemme. Arvo M.
Soininen.
The Vatican and the Americanist
Crisis: Denis J. O'Connell,
American Agent in Rome, 1885-
1903. Gerald P. Fogarty.
The Vatican in the Age of the
Dictators. Anthony Rhodes.
Vatican, U. S. A. Nino Lo Bello.
Les Vaudois au Moyen Age. Jean
Gonnet and Amedeo Molnar.
The Vegetable Passion: A History
of the Vegetarian State of Mind.
Janet Barkas.
A Venetian Family and Its For-
tune, 1500-1900: The Donà and
the Conservation of Their
Wealth. James C. Davis.
Venetian Phoenix. John Leon
Lievsay.
Venice: A Maritime Republic.
Frederic C. Lane.
Venice and Amsterdam: A Study
of Seventeenth-Century Elites.
Peter Burke.
Venice: The Hinge of Europe,
1081-1797. William H.

McNeill.
The Venture of Islam: Conscience
and History in a World Civilization.
3 vols. Marshall G. S. Hodgson.
Verfassungsrecht in Fällen. Chris-
tian Starck.
Das Verhältnis von Kirche und Staat
in Amerika. Adolf W. Ziegler.
Veritas Sacramenti: A Study of
Vermigli's Doctrine of the Lord's
Supper. Salvatore Corda.
The Vermont Hollows, a History of
Gilead and Little Hollows. Ley-
land E. Wood.
Vermont Under Four Flags, a His-
tory of the Green Mountain State,
1635-1975. Perry H. Merrill.
Versions of the Past: The His-
torical Imagination in American
Fiction. Harry B. Henderson,
III.
Un vescovo umanista alla Corte Pon-
tificia: Giannantonio Campano
(1429-1477). Flavio di Bernardo.
The Vice-Presidents and Cabinet
Members. Robert I. Vexler.
Vico. Leon Pompa.
Vico and Herder: Two Studies in the
History of Ideas. Isaiah Berlin.
Victoria County History of Essex.
Vol. VI. W. R. Powell, ed.
Victoria County History of Oxford.
Vol. X. Alan Crossley, ed.
Victoria County History of Shrop-
shire. Vol. II. A. T. Gaydon,
ed.
The Victorian City: Images and
Realities. H. J. Dyos and M.
Wolff, eds.
Victorian Engineering. L. T. C.
Rolt.
Victorian Infidels. Edward Royle.
Victorian Ladies at Work: Middle-
Class Working Women in England
and Wales, 1850-1914. Lee
Holcombe.
Victorian Lincoln. Sir Francis
Hill.
Victorian People and Ideas.
Richard D. Altick.
The Victorian Public School. Brian
Simon and Ian Bradley, eds.
The Victorian School Manager.
Peter Gordon.
Victorio and the Mimbres Apaches.
Dan L. Thrapp.
Victors Divided: America and the
Allies in Germany, 1918-1923.

Keith L. Nelson.
Vidyasagar: The Traditional
Modernizer. Amales Tripathi.
La vie musicale à Genève au
dixneuvième siècle (1814-1918).
Claude Tappolet.
Vietnamese Communism: A Re-
search Bibliography. Phan Thien
Chau.
Vietnamese Communism: Its Ori-
gins and Development. Robert
F. Turner.
Village Life and Labour. Raphael
Samuel, ed.
Vilyatpur, 1848-1968: Social and
Economic Change in a North
Indian Village. Tom G. Kes-
singer.
Violence and Repression in Latin
America: A Quantitative and His-
torical Analysis. Ernest A. Duff,
et al.
Virginia: A Pictorial History.
Parke Rouse, Jr.
The Virginia Manufactory of Arms.
Giles Cromwell.
Virginiana in the Printed Book Col-
lections of the Virginia State
Library. 2 vols. Donald
Haynes, ed.
The Vision of Politics on the Eve
of the Reformation. J. H.
Hexter.
Visionary Vine: Psychedelic Heal-
ing in the Peruvian Amazon.
Marlene Dobkin de Rios.
A Visit to Texas in 1831. Robert
S. Gray.
¡Viva Cristo Rey! The Cristero
Rebellion and the Church-State
Conflict in Mexico. David C.
Bailey.
Vladivostok Under Red and White
Rule. Canfield F. Smith.
The Voice of the People: John
Doherty, Trade Unionist, Radi-
cal and Factory Reformer. R.
G. Kirby and A. E. Musson.
Voices Against War. Keith L.
Sprunger, et al., eds.
Voices from the Hills. Robert
J. Higgs and Ambrose N.
Manning, eds.
Der Volksgerichtshof im national-
sozialistischen Staat. Walter
Wagner.
The Volunteer Force: A Social
and Political History. Hugh

Cunningham.
Vom Chaos zur Katastrophe:
Vatikanische Gespräche, 1918-
1938. Vornehmlich auf Grund
der Berichte der österreichischen
Gesandten beim Heiligen Stuhl.
Friedrich Engel-Janosi.
Von Georg Simmel zu Franz
Rosenzweig. Hans Liebeschütz.
Vor- und Frühformen der euro-
päischen Stadt im Mittelalter:
Bericht über ein Symposium in
Reinhausen bei Göttingen in der
Zeit vom 18. bis 24. April 1972.
Vol. 2. Herbert Jankuhn, et al.,
eds.
A Voyage on the Indus. Alexander
Burnes.
The Voyages of Mohamed Ibrahim
Munshi. Amin Sweeney and Nigel
Phillips, eds. and trans.

-W-

W. D. and H. O. Wills and the De-
velopment of the U. K. Tobacco
Industry. B. W. E. Alford.
The Wahhabiyya: Islamic Reform
and Politics in French West
Africa. Lansiné Kaba.
Walker River Paiutes: A Tribal
History. Edward C. Johnson.
The Wall of Separation. Frank J.
Sorauf.
Walter Prescott Webb: His Life
and Impact. Necah Stewart Fur-
man.
Der Wandel der Nahrungsgewohn-
heiten unter dem Einfluss der In-
dustrialisierung. Hans J. Teute-
berg and Günter Wiegelmann.
The War Against the Jews. Lucy
Davidwicz.
War and Economic Development.
J. M. Winter, ed.
War and Politics. Bernard Brodie.
War and Revolution in Yugoslavia,
1941-1945: The Chetniks. Jozo
Tomasevich.
War and Social Change in the Twen-
tieth Century. Arthur Marwick.
The War Generation. Stephen R.
Ward, ed.
War Is Hell! William T. Sherman.
The War of Atonement. Chaim

"The Western States in the Civil
War. " The Journal of the
West, 14(January 1975). LeRoy
H. Fischer, ed.
Westorientierung und Ostpolitik.
Martin Walsdorff.
What Women Want. Gayle Graham
Yates.
The Wheat Album. Kirby Brumfield.
Where I'm Bound. Sidonie Smith.
Where Judaism Differed. Abba
Hillel Silver.
Where the Law Ends. Christopher
D. Stone.
Whereby We Thrive. John T.
Schlebecker.
Whig Principles and Party Politics.
E. A. Smith.
Whigs and Hunters. E. P. Thomp-
son.
White Already to Harvest. Mar-
garet Simms McDonald.
Whitelaw Reid: Journalist, Poli-
tician, Diplomat. Bingham Dun-
can.
Who Defends Rome: The Forty-
Five Days, July 25-September 8,
1943. Melton S. Davis.
Who Killed the British Empire?
George Woodcock.
Who the Hell Is William Loeb?
Kevin Cash.
Why Is the Third World Poor?
Piero Gheddo.
Why Marxism? Robert G. Wesson.
Die Wiener Jakobiner: Schriften
und Dokumente. Alfred Körner.
The Wild Man from Sugar Creek:
The Political Career of Eugene
Talmadge. William Anderson.
The Wild Man Within. An Image
in Western Thought from the
Renaissance to Romanticism.
Edward Dudley and Maximillian
E. Novak, eds.
William Allen White: Maverick on
Main Street. John De Witt
McKee.
William Beckford. James Lees-
Milne.
William Billings of Boston. David
P. McKay and Richard Crawford.
William Carlos Williams. Robert
Coles.
William Carlos Williams. Reed
Whittemore.
William Ellery: A Rhode Island
Politico and Lord of Admirality.

William M. Fowler, Jr.
William Gibbs McAdoo: A Passion
for Change, 1863-1917. John J.
Broesamle.
William Howard Taft and the United
States Foreign Policy. Ralph
Eldin Minger.
William Law: His Life and
Thought. A. Keith Walker.
William Melrose in China 1845-1855.
Hoh-Cheung and Lorna H. Mui,
eds.
William O'Brien and the Course of
Irish Politics, 1881-1918. Joseph
V. O'Brien.
William Penn. Harry Emerson
Wildes.
William Penn and Early Quakerism.
Melvin B. Endy, Jr.
William Penn: Apostle of Dissent.
Hans Fantel.
Wilson's Diplomacy. Arthur S.
Link, et al.
The Windows to His World: The
Story of Trevor Kincaid. Muriel
L. Guberlet.
The Winds of Tomorrow. Richard
A. Thompson.
Windsor Heritage: Birthplace of
Vermont's Constitution and In-
dustry. Katherine E. Conlin.
The Wine Trade. A. D. Francis.
Wings Over Hellas. Raymond V.
Schoder.
The Winnipeg Strike: 1919. Kenneth
McNaught and David J. Bercuson.
Winston S. Churchill. Vol. IV.
Martin Gilbert.
Winter Quarters: George Washing-
ton and the Continental Army at
Valley Forge. Noel F. Busch.
The Winter War: The Russo-Fin-
nish Conflict, 1939-40. Eloise
Engle and Lauri Paananen.
Wirtschaftliche und soziale Struk-
turen im saekularen Wandel:
Festschrift fur Wilhelm Abel zum
70. Geburtstag. Ingomar Bog,
et al.
Die Wirtschaftlichen Auswirkungen
der Türken Kriege. Othmar
Pickl, ed.
Wisconsin, My Home: The Story of
Thurine Oleson as Told to Her
Daughter. Erna Oleson Xan.
Witchcraft and Sorcery. John A.
Rush.
Witchcraft in the Southwest: Spanish

and Indian Supernaturalism on the Rio Grande. Marc Simmons.

With Santa Anna in Texas. José Enrique de la Peña.

With Sovereign Reverence: The First Twenty-Five Years of Americans United. Harold E. Fey.

Without Noise of Arms. Walter Briggs.

Without Parallel: The American-Korean Relationship Since 1945. Frank Baldwin, ed.

Witness to Power. Marquis Childs.

Wittgenstein's Vienna. Allan Janik and Stephen Toulmin.

Wole Soyinka. Modern African Writers. Gerald Moore.

Wolfgang Capito. James M. Kittelson.

Womanhood in America. Mary P. Ryan.

Woman's Work: The Housewife, Past and Present. Ann Oakley.

Women at Work. Janice Acton, et al., eds.

Women in Early Texas. Evelyn M. Carrington, ed.

Women in Iberian Expansion Overseas, 1415-1815: Some Facts, Fancies and Personalities. C. R. Boxer.

Women in Stuart England and America. Roger Thompson.

Women Priests in the Catholic Church? Haye van der Meer.

Women Together. Judith Papachristou.

Women Who Spied for the Blue and the Gray. Oscar A. Kinchen.

The Women's Movement in China: A Selection of Readings, 1949-1973. Elisabeth Croll.

Wool, Cloth, and Gold. John H. A. Munro.

WOP! A Documentary History of Anti-Italian Discrimination in the United States. Salvatore J. La Gumina, ed.

The Word in Stone. Robert R. Taylor.

The Work of Sahagún. Munro S. Edmondson, ed.

Workingmen of Waltham: Mobility in American Urban Industrial Development, 1850-1890. Howard M. Gitelman.

The World Between the Wars, 1919-1939. Joseph S. Davis.

World Capitals: Toward Guided Urbanization. H. Wentworth Eldredge, ed.

World Culture and the Black Experience. Ali A. Mazrui.

A World Destroyed. Martin J. Sherwin.

A World Elsewhere: One Man's Fascination with the American Southwest. Jon Manchip White.

World Employment Programme. Director-General, ILO.

World Mission and World Communism. Gerhard Hoffman and Wilhelm Wille, eds.

The World of George Washington. Richard M. Ketchum.

World of Our Fathers. Irving Howe.

The World of the Reformation. Hans J. Hillerbrand.

World Power or Decline: The Controversy Over "Germany's Aims in the First World War." Fritz Fischer.

The World Turned Upside Down: Prose and Poetry of the American Revolution. James H. Pickering, ed.

World War I: A Compact History. Grace P. Hayes.

Worship and Theology in England: From Andrews to Baxter to Fox, 1603-1690. Horton Davies.

Worship of the Goddess According to the Kalikapurana. Part I. K. R. Van Kooij, ed. and trans.

The Wound Within: America in the Vietnam Years, 1945-1974. Alexander Kendrick.

Writers and Revolution. Renee Winegarten.

The Writings of Stephen B. Luce. John D. Hayes and John B. Hattendorf, eds.

Writings on American History: A Subject Bibliography of Articles. James Dougherty, ed. and comp.

Wyoming Homestead Heritage. Charles Floyd Spencer.

-X-

The "X" Documents. A. P.
Young.
Xantus Janos. István Sándor.

-Y-

Yad Vashem Studies on the
European Jewish Catastrophe
and Resistance. Livia Roth-
kirchen, ed.
Yankee Artillerymen. John W.
Rowell.
A Yankee Guerrillero. Thomas
W. Crouch.
The Yaos: Chiikala Cha Wayao.
Yohanna B. Abdallah and
Meredith Sanderson, comp.
and ed.
Year 1920 and Its Climax. Jozef
Pilsudski.
The Year of the Four Emperors.
P. A. L. Greenhalgh.
Yearbook on International Com-
munist Affairs, 1975. Richard
F. Starr, ed.
The Years of MacArthur. Vol. II,
1941-1945. D. Clayton James.
Years of Struggle: The Farm Di-
ary of Elmer G. Powers, 1931-
1936. H. Roger Grant and L.
Edward Purcell, eds.
Yeats: Golden Dawn. George
Mills Harper.
Yenan in June 1937: Talks With
the Communist Leaders. T.
A. Bisson.
Yesterday's Akron. Kenneth
Nichols.
Yesterday's Asheville. Joan and
Wright Langley.
Yesterday's Birmingham. Mal-
colm C. McMillan.
Yesterday's California. Russ
Leadbrand, Shelly Lowenkopf,
and Bryce Patterson.
Yesterday's Memphis. Charles W.
Crawford.
Yesterday's Nashville. Carl F.
Zibart.
Yohannes IV of Ethiopia: A Po-
litical Biography. Zewde
Gabre-Selassie.

The Young Douglas Hyde: The
Dawn of the Irish Revolution and
Renaissance, 1874-1893.
Dominic Daly.
Young John Dewey: An Essay in
American Intellectual History.
Neil Coughlan.
The Young Voter's Manual: A
Topical Dictionary of American
Government and Politics. Leon
W. Blevins.
Youth and History: Tradition and
Change in European Age Rela-
tions 1770-Present. John R.
Gillis.
Youth and Politics in Japan. Joseph
A. Massey.
Yvon Delbos at the Quai d'Orsay:
French Foreign Policy During the
Popular Front, 1936-1938. John
E. Dreifort.

-Z-

Zaklady petroarcheologie. Jinurich
Stelcl and Jaroslav Malina.
Zambia Before 1890. H. W. Lang-
worthy.
Zapata. Roger Parkinson.
Zapata: Fantasía y realidad. Al-
fonso Taracena.
Zion in America: The Jewish Ex-
perience from Colonial Times to
the Present. Henry L. Feingold.
Zionism: The Dream and the Re-
ality. Gary V. Smith.
The Zirids of Granada. Andrew
Handler.
Zoo Animals, People, Places.
Bernard Livingston.
The Zulu Kings. Brian Roberts.
Zum Begriff der Negativität bei
Schelling und Hegel. Fredrich
W. Schmidt.
Zur Ikonographie von Raffaels Dis-
puta. Heinrich Pfeiffer.
Zur Vorgeschichte des Preussisch-
Sachsischen Eisenbahnkrieges.
Hans-Friedrich Gisevius.